URBAN DEVELOPMENT IN EAST-CENTRAL EUROPE: POLAND, CZECHOSLOVAKIA, AND HUNGARY

INTERNATIONAL HISTORY OF CITY DEVELOPMENT

VOLUME   I: *Urban Development in Central Europe*

VOLUME   II: *Urban Development in the Alpine and Scandinavian Countries*

VOLUME III: *Urban Development in Southern Europe: Spain and Portugal*

VOLUME IV: *Urban Development in Southern Europe: Italy and Greece*

VOLUME   V: *Urban Development in Western Europe: France and Belgium*

VOLUME VI: *Urban Development in Western Europe: The Netherlands and Great Britain*

VOLUME VII: *Urban Development in East-Central Europe: Poland, Czechoslovakia, and Hungary*

VOLUME VII

URBAN DEVELOPMENT IN EAST-CENTRAL EUROPE: POLAND, CZECHOSLOVAKIA, AND HUNGARY

E. A. GUTKIND

with contributions by
Dr. Wojciech Kalinowski, *on Poland*
Members of the Union of Architects
    of the Czechoslovak Socialist Republic
Prof. Imre Perényi, *on Hungary*
Edited by Gabriele Gutkind

The Free Press, New York
Collier–Macmillan Limited, London

Copyright © 1972 by The Free Press

A Division of The Macmillan Company

Printed in the United States of America

All rights reserved. No part of this book may be reproduced or transmitted in any form or by any means, electronic or mechanical, including photocopying, recording, or by any information storage and retrieval system, without permission in writing from the Publisher.

The Free Press
A Division of The Macmillan Company
866 Third Avenue, New York, New York 10022

Collier-Macmillan Canada Ltd., Toronto, Ontario

Library of Congress Catalog Card Number: 64–13231

printing number
1 2 3 4 5 6 7 8 9 10

Preface

WHEN ERWIN A. GUTKIND died on August 7, 1968, he had completed the writing of eight volumes of the *International History of City Development*. The preparation of the Asian and African material was far advanced, and a manuscript on China half finished. He left the following incomplete preface to introduce Vol. VII: *Urban Development in East-Central Europe*, intending to conclude it at a later date. As editor, I feel justified in retaining this preface since it expresses the author's intentions more clearly than a mere summary of his notes.

As the series title implies, the *International History of City Development* is an attempt to present a worldwide survey of the origin and growth of urban civilization. Throughout history, cities have been the power stations of new ideas and the seismographs on which the impact and transformation of these ideas can be read.

The *International History of City Development* endeavors to describe and analyze this continually renewed interplay of adaptation and readaptation, of challenge and response, which has made cities in all parts of the world the most significant agents of renewal and decline, of expansion and contraction.

The present volume, comprising the three East-Central European countries of Poland, Czechoslovakia, and Hungary, represents a cooperative undertaking. Although each section was written independently, reflecting some basic philosophic differences, their general arrangement is designed to secure the continuity of the format established in previous volumes. My own contribution is therefore intended to complement the work of Dr. Kalinowski, the members of the Union of Architects of the Czechoslovak Socialist Republic, and Professor Perényi, and to serve as a connecting link in order to maintain the general trend of the *History* as a whole, its thesis, and approach.

Poland, Czechoslovakia, and Hungary are historically part of the Eastern Marchlands. The term "Eastern Europe," as applied to these countries, has been conveniently justified by political events of the more recent past. Linguistically, Poland and Czechoslovakia are Slavic countries, but the urban and architectural development of these countries and Hungary owes much to Central European concepts and traditions. It seemed therefore appropriate to replace the designation of "Eastern Europe" with the more accurate one of East-Central Europe.

The role of Germany, the dominant central power, as the principal agent in the great West-East movement of colonization, and her influence on the urban and architectural evolution of her neighbors, made it advisable to enlist the cooperation of Polish, Czech, and Hungarian experts to redress the balance of some of the more widely held assumptions, according to which an inordinately large number of towns and villages in the eastern regions of Europe had been established by German settlers. Recent independent research and archeological investigations undertaken in the East-Central European countries are beginning to undermine some of these nationalistic theories which are reflected in many German writings, especially those of the period between 1933 and 1945.

This volume, the first to appear in English on urban development in Poland, Czechoslovakia, and Hungary, is intended as an introduction to the subject and makes no claim to be exhaustive. So far there are few comprehensive works on the general evolution of settlement in the East, and fewer still in West European languages. Archeological investigations of certain periods—for example, the early and prehistoric periods in Hungary—are still sporadic rather than comprehensive. Lack of data and inequalities in the available material impede the work of urban historians. These facts explain, at least partly, the absence of "City Survey" sections for Poland and Hungary on the level of previous volumes. Moreover, the necessary procurement of plans, photographs, old drawings and engravings from the respective municipalities proved insuperable. It is hoped, therefore, that readers will regard this volume as the body around which others will plan more detailed investigations to fill the gaps in our knowledge of the process of urbanization in the East-Central European countries. Such work should not mean a mere proliferation of disconnected local studies, but rather a combination of research into small-scale areas with investigations of the broader historical trends that transcend the limited range of particular places, thus furnishing a meaningful framework into which individual studies based on empirical evidence can be fitted.

Certain basic problems, such as the changing ideas of space and scale, have been discussed in Volume I. This discussion should be consulted, if possible, whenever relevant questions are mentioned.

The number of footnotes has been kept to a minimum. Complete acknowledgement of references to sources is, in any case, impossible in a work of this kind, nor am I convinced that innumerable footnotes are a proof of scholarly competence.

The bibliography for each country is fairly comprehensive, although by no means complete. Completeness would have been not only unattainable but also unnecessary, as many of the books mentioned in the bibliographies contain full lists of works on the general history of the respective countries and on the local histories of individual cities.

In a history of city planning, old plans, maps, drawings, and engravings of general and detailed aspects of cities are one of the most valuable types of primary sources. The documentation therefore includes a considerable number of reproductions of this type of material, apart from ground and aerial photographs of historically important views. While the urban historian can draw on a wealth of plans and views of West European cities by the great Dutch, German, Italian, and French cartographers and engravers of the 16th, 17th, and 18th centuries, the same is not true for the countries of Eastern Europe. Nevertheless, a considerable number of old plans and views of Polish, Czech, and Hungarian towns has been assembled which forms an integral part of the text.

I cannot emphasize too strongly that the scholarly value of a work of this kind does not exclusively depend on recorded historical evidence. In dealing with the historical development of city planning, especially with the physical growth of cities, one is in the fortunate position of having available a sufficient quantity of visual documentation, very often of outstanding quality. I maintain that this visual documentation is more important for scholarly research in this field than most of the available written evidence and that its wise interpretation is more enlightening than the usual old records and other similar sources. This is not to say that written evidence should not be used, but merely to stress the point that in many cases it tells us only something about so-called facts, about symptoms, and rarely anything about causes. Moreover, the value of this evidence is often dubious, since it was frequently written by people who lacked objectivity and for opportunist reasons glossed over or tampered with the "how it really was." But even if we accept the recorded evidence at its face value, a definite interpretation is more often than not difficult, as the squabbles of learned men prove only too well. This overestimation of written evidence has led to a "scholarly" distrust of visual documentation. But these doubters should be reminded, for instance, that air photography has produced results, in many cases, that written records could never have revealed. It is the same with old maps, drawings, and other contemporary representations. Consequently, ample use has been made of this sort of material *in addition* to old written records in those cases that could furnish incontestable interpretation.

Readers should keep these considerations in mind and should regard this volume, and the other volumes of the *International History of City Development*, not as "picture" books, but as works diagnosing the intricate problems of urban development by what we can still see *and* by what we can still read about them.

Moreover, it is essential to remember that this work is a history of city development, not of architecture or of the general unfolding of historical evolution. This explains why some cities famous for individual architectural achievements may not have been mentioned, while others without claim to architectural excellence have been included in the text, their layout, growth, and origin being of particular interest as characteristic stages of urban development.

Here the Preface breaks off, to be concluded by the editor.

It had been the author's intention to discuss the modern phase of urbanization in the countries represented in the *International History of City Development*—namely, the period from about the middle of the 19th century to the present time, when clearly defined national characteristics began to dissolve into a general uniformity that coincided with the nadir in city planning—in a final and concluding volume. In addition to dealing with the impact of the Industrial Revolution and modern technology on rural and urban settlement, Dr. Gutkind wanted to review the lessons of the past in relation to present problems. This part, fundamentally different from preceding periods and essential to the understanding of the world-wide urban crisis, will of necessity be missing from the series.

Equally regrettable is the fact that Yugoslavia had to be deleted from the *History* for lack of cooperation, despite repeated approaches to local governments, research institutes, and the Head of State.

The preparation of this volume was dependent, directly and indirectly, on the work of many scholars and writers, in particular on the cooperation of Polish, Czech, and Hungarian urbanists. Our work could not have proceeded with the same degree of success but for the dedication and willingness of the East European authors to give so freely of their time. For this we are deeply indebted to Dr. Wojciech Kalinowski, Associate Professor, Institute of Town Planning and Architecture in Warsaw; Drs. J. Hrůza, D. Líbal, T. Zalčík, O. Dostál, O. Nový, O. Kuča, S. Voděra, D. Riedl, B. Fuchs, K. Kňava, and V. Richter, Members of the Union of Architects of the Czechoslovak Socialist Republic; and to Professor I. Perényi, Department of City Planning, Technical University of Budapest. I am particularly glad to acknowledge their contributions and extend my sincere thanks for their ever-ready and generous assistance.

As far as East European names, terms, and place names are concerned, the local spelling has been retained, except for towns like Warsaw, Budapest, and Prague, where the familiar Anglicized version has been preferred. In some cases, the German or Anglicized names of rivers, towns, mountains, and regions have been added to avoid confusion and facilitate understanding.

After my father's death, an advisory committee was set up to pilot the *History* to its conclusion. This Committee is made up of Lewis Mumford, Professor G. Holmes Perkins, Dean of the Graduate School of Fine Arts of the University of Pennsylvania, and Professor Ann L. Strong, Director of the Institute for Environmental Studies of the University of Pennsylvania. I am deeply indebted to each member of the Committee for assistance at a time of great distress. Their determination to see through publication that portion of the *History* which Dr. Gutkind had completed was a source of great encouragement to me. In particular, I would like to express my gratitude to Professor Strong, whose understanding and experience helped steer the *History* through innumerable difficulties arising from the author's death.

Without the generous financial support of several foundations the work could not have been undertaken. We owe a special debt, which I am particularly glad to acknowledge, to Mr. Edward F. D'Arms of the Rockefeller Foundation (now at the Ford Foundation), and Dr. A. Hollis Edens, then Executive Director of the Mary Reynolds Babcock Foundation. Their discernment and repeated assistance not only launched the *History* but helped accelerate research and publication.

I take great pleasure in extending my deep appreciation to the National Foundation on the Arts and the Humanities for the grants placed at my disposal which have enabled me to proceed with the publication of the *History* as originally planned. My special thanks go to Dr. Saunders Redding, then Director, Division of Research and Publication of the National Endowment for the Humanities, and to Mr. Paul D. Spreiregen, Program Director for Architecture, Planning and Design of the National Endowment for the Arts, for their interest, insight, and unfailing support.

Gabriele Gutkind

March, 1970
University of Pennsylvania

Contents

Preface   v

List of Illustrations   xv

POLAND

Introduction by E. A. Gutkind   1

Chapter 1. Settlement and Colonization   3

Chapter 2. Origins of Urban Civilization   8

City Development in Poland by Dr. Wojciech Kalinowski. Translated by Agnieszka Glinka   11

Chapter 3. Introduction   13

Chapter 4. Polish Urban Settlement Before the 13th Century   17

Chapter 5. Evolution of Cities in the High and Late Middle Ages   26

Chapter 6. Evolution of Cities in the Period of the Renaissance   52

Chapter 7. Evolution of Cities from the Middle of the 17th Century to the Fall of the Polish Commonwealth in 1793   70

Chapter 8. Evolution of Cities in the First Half of the 19th Century   88

CZECHOSLOVAKIA

Introduction by E. A. Gutkind   109

Chapter 9. Evolution of Early Settlement   111

Development of the Historical Towns of Czechoslovakia by Jiří Hrůza, Dobroslav Líbal, Tibor Zalčík, Oldřich Dostál, Otakar Nový, and Otakar Kuča. Translated by Z. Jeníková and J. Kadečková   119

Chapter 10. Pre-Slavonic Period by H. Hrůza   121

Chapter 11. Slavonic Tribes and the Great Moravian Empire by J. Hrůza   125

Chapter 12. The Origin of Towns by D. Líbal and T. Zalčík   129

Chapter 13. The Golden Age of the Founding of New Towns by D. Líbal   136

Chapter 14. Urban Development in the High Middle Ages by D. Líbal   145

Chapter 15. Medieval Towns of Slovakia by T. Zalčík   154

Chapter 16. The Hussite Movement and the Close of the Middle Ages by J. Hrůza   158

Chapter 17. The Impact of the Renaissance by J. Hrůza and T. Zalčík   162

Chapter 18. The Impact of the Baroque Period by O. Dostál   171

Chapter 19. The Transformation of Town and Country in the
Baroque Period by O. Dostál   177

Chapter 20. Rural Settlement by O. Dostál   187

Chapter 21. On the Eve of the Industrial Revolution by
O. Nový and T. Zalčík   190

Chapter 22. The Historic Towns in Modern Times by J. Hrůza   196

Chapter 23. City Survey/Czechoslovakia by O. Dostál, J. Hrůza,
D. Líbal, O. Nový, S. Voděra, T. Zalčík,
and collaborators   199

   Prague by J. Hrůza and D. Líbal   200
   Banská Štiavnica, Central Slovakia, by T. Zalčík   208
   Bardejov, Eastern Slovakia, by T. Zalčík   210
   Boskovice, Northern Moravia, by D. Riedl   212
   Bratislava, Western Slovakia, by T. Zalčík   213
   Brno, Southern Moravia, by B. Fuchs   216
   Cheb, Western Bohemia, by D. Líbal   220
   Chomutov, Northern Bohemia, by D. Líbal   224
   Čáslav, Eastern Bohemia, by J. Hrůza   225
   České Budějovice, Southern Bohemia, by D. Líbal   227
   Český Krumlov, Southern Bohemia, by D. Líbal   229
   Dolní Bojanovice, Southern Moravia, by O. Dostál   231
   Domažlice, Western Bohemia, by J. Hrůza   232
   Františkovy Lázně, Western Bohemia, by O. Nový   233
   Frýdlant, Northern Bohemia, by S. Voděra   235
   Fulnek, Northern Moravia, by O. Dostál   236
   Hradec Králové, Eastern Bohemia, by D. Líbal   237
   Hruštín, Central Slovakia, by K. Kňava   240
   Jaroměř and Josefov, Eastern Bohemia, by D. Líbal   241
   Jaroměřice nad Rokytnou, Southern Moravia, by O. Kuča   243
   Jičín, Eastern Bohemia, by D. Líbal   245
   Jihlava, Southern Bohemia, by D. Líbal   247
   Jindřichův Hradec, Southern Bohemia, by J. Hrůza   249
   Karlovy Vary, Western Bohemia, by O. Nový   251
   Kežmarok, Northern Slovakia, by T. Zalčík   253
   Klatovy, Western Bohemia, by J. Hrůza   254
   Kolín, Central Bohemia, by D. Líbal   256
   Košice, Eastern Slovakia, by T. Zalčík   257
   Kouřim, Central Bohemia, by D. Líbal   259
   Kremnica, Central Slovakia, by T. Zalčík   260
   Kroměříž, Southern Moravia, by O. Kuča   262
   Kuks, Eastern Bohemia, by O. Dostál   264
   Kutná Hora, Central Bohemia, by D. Líbal   265
   Kyjov, Southern Moravia, by D. Riedl   269
   Leopoldov, Western Slovakia, by T. Zalčík   270
   Levoča, Eastern Slovakia, by T. Zalčík   271
   Liptovská Teplička, Central Slovakia, by K. Kňava   273
   Litava, Central Slovakia, by K. Kňava   274
   Litoměřice, Northern Bohemia, by D. Líbal   276

Litomyšl, Eastern Bohemia, by J. Hrůza	*278*
Manětín, Western Bohemia, by O. Dostál	*280*
Mariánské Lázně, Western Bohemia, by O. Nový	*282*
Mikulov, Southern Moravia, by J. Hrůza	*284*
Mladá Boleslav, Central Bohemia, by J. Hrůza	*286*
Moravská Třebová, Western Moravia, by D. Líbal	*287*
Moravský Krumlov, Southern Moravia, by D. Riedl	*288*
Most, Northern Bohemia, by J. Hrůza	*288*
Netolice and Kratochvíle, Southern Bohemia, by S. Voděra	*290*
Nové Město nad Metují, Eastern Bohemia, by D. Líbal	*293*
Nové Zámky, Southern Slovakia, by T. Zalčík	*295*
Nový Bydžov, Eastern Bohemia, by D. Líbal	*296*
Nový Jičín, Northern Moravia, by D. Líbal	*297*
Nymburk, Central Bohemia, by D. Líbal	*298*
Olomouc, Northern Moravia, by V. Richter	*299*
Ostrov near Karlovy Vary, Western Bohemia, by O. Kuča	*301*
Pardubice, Eastern Bohemia, by D. Líbal	*302*
Pelhřimov, Southern Bohemia, by D. Líbal	*305*
Písek, Southern Bohemia, by D. Líbal	*306*
Plástovice, Southern Bohemia, by S. Voděra	*308*
Prachatice, Southern Bohemia, by D. Líbal	*310*
Prešov, Eastern Slovakia, by T. Zalčík	*312*
Ružindol, Western Slovakia, by K. Kňava	*313*
Sobotka, Eastern Bohemia, by O. Dostál	*314*
Stará Boleslav—Brandýs nad Labem, Central Bohemia, by D. Líbal	*315*
Tábor, Southern Bohemia, by J. Hrůza	*317*
Terezín, Northern Bohemia, by O. Dostál	*320*
Trnava, Western Slovakia, by T. Zalčík	*321*
Třeboň, Southern Bohemia, by D. Líbal	*323*
Uherské Hradiště, Southern Moravia, by D. Riedl	*324*
Uničov, Northern Moravia, by D. Riedl	*326*
Žatec, Northern Bohemia, by D. Líbal	*327*
Znojmo, Southern Moravia, by D. Líbal	*329*
Zvolen, Central Slovakia, by T. Zalčík	*333*

HUNGARY

Introduction by E. A. Gutkind	337
Chapter 24. The Land, History, and Settlement	**339**
Historical Development of Hungarian Cities by Professor Imre Perényi	361
Chapter 25. Urban Development in Hungary	**363**
Urban Development to the Time of the Turkish Occupation	363
The Towns of Hungary under Turkish Rule	372
Urban Development in the 18th Century	384
Urban Development in the First Half of the 19th Century	389
Urban Development and the Growth of Capitalism	395

Chapter 26. Appendix by E. A. Gutkind   **401**

    Győr (Raab), Győr-Sopron   *402*
    Pápa, Veszprém   *407*
    Szombathely (Steinamanger), Vas   *409*
    Esztergom (Gran), Komárom   *411*
    Vác (Waitzen), Pest   *415*
    Székesfehérvár (Stuhlweissenburg), Fejér   *418*
    Veszprém, Veszprém   *421*
    Debrecen, Hajdú-Bihar   *422*
    Nagykőrös, Pest   *426*

Acknowledgments for Illustrations   *429*

Bibliography   *431*

Index   *465*

List of Illustrations

1. Poland in the 10th and 11th centuries — 14
2. Poland under the reign of Casimir the Great — 15
3. Poland and Lithuania after the Peace of Toruń — 15
4. Remains of Biskupin, sixth to fifth century B.C. — 17
5. Early medieval settlement of Opole — 19
6. Settlement of Opole in relation to the city founded in the early 14th century — 20
7. Szczecin in the early Middle Ages — 22
8. Poznań in the early Middle Ages — 23
9. Radom in the early Middle Ages — 24
10. Collegiate church of St. Andrew, Cracow — 25
11. Plan of the reconstructed city of Trzebnica — 27
12. Medieval layout of Środa Śląska — 27
13. Reconstruction of original plots at Paczków — 29
14. Airview of Paczków — 29
15. Reconstruction of the medieval layout of Wrocław — 31
16. View of Poznań by Braun and Hogenberg — 32
17. Plan of medieval Cracow — 34
18. Reconstructed plan of Warsaw, 1600 — 35
19. Plan of Chełmno with original plots — 36
20. View of Toruń by Matthaeus Merian — 37
21. Plan of medieval Nidzica — 38
22. View of the city and castle of Nidzica — 38
23. Plan of medieval Nowe Miasto Lubawskie — 39
24. Plan of Gdańsk, about 1370 — 40
25. Reconstructed plan of Elbląg, 15th century — 41
26. Plan of Pyrzyce, 1723 — 41
27. Plan of Wieluń, 1799 — 43
28. Plan of Kalisz, 1785 — 44
29. Plan of Cracow, 1702 — 46
30. Medieval settlements of Gdańsk, 15th century — 46
31. Plan of Wrocław, 1562 — 47
32. Center of Gdańsk, before 1939 — 49
33. Main market square at Cracow, late 18th century — 50
34. Market square at Poznań, late 18th century — 50
35. Barbican and St. Florian's Gate, Cracow, 1809 — 51
36. Plan of Stanisławów — 52
37. Cadastral plan of Głogów Małopolski — 53
38. Reconstruction of the "ideal" plan of Głogów Małopolski — 53
39. Reconstruction of the layout of Głogów Małopolski with adjoining fields — 54
40. Plan of Wasilków — 55
41. Plan of Zamość, second half of the 17th century — 57
42. Ormiańska Street, Zamość — 58
43. Plan of Janów Lubelski, about 1850 — 59
44. Plan of Brody, 1844 — 60
45. "Ideal" plan of Brody — 60
46. Plan of Rawicz, late 18th century — 61
47. Plan of Grodzisk Wielkopolski, early 20th century — 62
48. New Town marketplace at Łowicz, late 16th century — 63
49. Town Hall at Poznań — 64
50. Rondelle fortifications at Wrocław — 65
51. Fortifications of Warsaw, 1621 — 66
52. Fortifications of Gdańsk, about 1660 — 67
53. Plan of Łańcut, middle of the 18th century — 68
54. Plan of Warsaw, 1705 — 70
55. Plan for the expansion of Szczecin, 1630 — 71
56. Plan for the expansion of Elbląg, 1630 — 72
57. Plan of a Swedish camp, 1657 — 72
58. Plan of Rakoniewice — 73
59. Reconstruction of the marketplace at Rakoniewice — 74
60. Reconstructed layout of Góra Kalwaria and Calvary Way — 75
61. Plan of Stanisławów, 1792 — 76
62. Plan of Frampol today — 77
63. Original layout of Frampol — 77
64. Site of the Saxon Axis, Warsaw — 78
65. Design for the residence of Augustus II, Warsaw — 79
66. Plan of Warsaw, 1733 — 80
67. Plan of the residence and town of Rydzyna, 1784 — 82
68. Reconstructed plan of Białystok, late 18th century — 83
69. Market square at Biała Podlaska, 1777 — 84
70. Redevelopment plan for Kozienice, 1782 — 85
71. Plan of the center of the village of Kunsztów, 1780 — 87
72. Wilhelm Avenue, Poznań, first half of the 19th century — 88
73. Plan of Ludwinów — 90
74. Redevelopment plan for Stryków, 1809 — 91
75. Plan of Ryczwół, 1811 — 92
76. Plan for the improvement of Radom, 1824 — 95
77. Plan for the artisans' village of Zgierz, 1821 — 97
78. Plans for the artisans' villages at Łódź, 1824–28 — 98
79. Protestant church and Town Hall in the clothiers' village of Łódź — 99
80. Plan for the artisans' village of Częstochowa, 1823 — 99
81. Plan of Aleksandrów, 1821 — 100
82. Plan of Warsaw, 1831 — 102
83. Plan for the improvement of Praga (Warsaw), 1817 — 102
84. Redevelopment plan for Bankowy Square, Warsaw, 1825 — 103
85. View of Bankowy Square, Warsaw, 1833 — 104
86. View of Teatralny Square, Warsaw, 1829 — 104
87. View of Trzy Krzyże Square, Warsaw, 1829 — 105
88. Plan of the village of Barca — 112
89. The walled-in settlement on the Závist Hill — 123
90. The *limes Romanus* — 124
91. Extent of the Great Moravian Empire — 126
92. Model of the Castle of Prague, 12th century — 131
93. View of Znojmo, middle of the 18th century — 137
94. Airview of the main square in Jihlava — 138
95. Airview of the nucleus of Český Krumlov — 141
96. Airview of the nucleus of Domažlice — 142
97. Airview of the nucleus of České Budějovice — 143
98. View of Slaný, beginning of the 17th century — 147
99. Airview of the nucleus of Prachatice — 147
100. Airview of the village of Lipnice — 148

#	Title	Page
101.	View of the center of the Old Town of Prague	150
102.	Section of a view of Prague by J. Sadeler (1606)	153
103.	Airview of the center of Levoča	154
104.	View of Bratislava, 1735	156
105.	Airview of the nucleus of Bardejov	157
106.	View of the center of Tábor	159
107.	Bohemia on Claudian's map, 1518	162
108.	Airview of Nové Město nad Metují	163
109.	Painting of Netolice, near Kratochvíle, 1686	164
110.	Fortifications of Bratislava, 1663	169
111.	Engraving of Nové Zámky, 1595	170
112.	Plan for Jičín by Niccolo Sebregondi, 1633	173
113.	Airview of the center of Klatovy	174
114.	Baroque reconstruction of Slavkov	178
115.	Drawing of the New Town of Prague and its main centers, 1769	179
116.	Square at Polička, 1825	180
117.	The village of Byšičky	183
118.	Baroque farm in Prague-Bohnice	188
119.	View of Karlín, 1870	193
120.	Airview of Františkovy Lázně	194
121.	View of Prague, 1563	201
122.	View of the Small Town of Prague and the Hradčany	201
123.	The Small Town Square in Prague	204
124.	View toward the Old Town Hall in Prague	205
125.	View toward the Small Town of Prague	205
126.	Plan of Prague, 1848	206
127.	Panoramic view of Prague	207
128.	Plan of the center of Banská Štiavnica, middle of the 19th century	208
129.	Square at Banská Štiavnica	209
130.	Plan of the historical center of Bardejov, middle of the 19th century	210
131.	Reconstruction of the Gothic town of Bardejov	211
132.	View of Boskovice, 1723–28	212
133.	Plan of the center of Bratislava	213
134.	Main square in Bratislava	214
135.	View of Bratislava, 18th century	215
136.	Plan of Brno, middle of the 18th century	217
137.	Drawing of Brno, middle of the 18th century	218
138.	Tower of the town hall at Brno	219
139.	Plan of the historic nucleus of Cheb, 1841	220
140.	Plan and view of Cheb, middle of the 18th century	221
141.	Burgher's house at Cheb	221
142.	View of Cheb from the northwest	222
143.	Square at Chomutov	224
144.	Plan of Čáslav, middle of the 19th century	225
145.	Drawing of Čáslav, 1602	226
146.	Plan of the historic core of České Budějovice, 1827	227
147.	View of České Budějovice, 1666	228
148.	Square at České Budějovice	228
149.	Plan of the historical core of Český Krumlov, 1826	229
150.	Drawing of Český Krumlov, middle of the 18th century	229
151.	Partial view of Český Krumlov	230
152.	Plan of the village of Dolní Bojanovice, 1827	231
153.	Plan of the historic core of Domažlice	232
154.	"Lower" Gate at Domažlice	232
155.	Cadastral map of Františkovy Lázně, 1841	233
156.	Plan of Frýdlant, 1841	235
157.	Old view of Fulnek	236
158.	Plan of Hradec Králové by Matthaeus Merian, 1650	238
159.	View of the western part of Hradec Králové, c. 1600	239
160.	Plan of the citadel of Hradec Králové	239
161.	Plan of Hruštín, 1874	240
162.	Farm houses at Hruštín	240
163.	Plan of Jaroměř, 1840	241
164.	Plan of the citadel of Josefov	242
165.	View of the town and castle of Jaroměřice nad Rokytnou	243
166.	Plan for the reconstruction of the castle complex at Jaroměřice nad Rokytnou, beginning of the 18th century	244
167.	Sebregondi's plan for the reconstruction of Jičín, 1633	245
168.	Plan of Jičín, 1842	245
169.	Square at Jičín	246
170.	Plan of the historic nucleus of Jihlava, 1835	247
171.	Model of Jihlava, beginning of the 15th century	248
172.	Painting of Jihlava, 18th century	248
173.	Plan of Jindřichův Hradec, 1828	249
174.	Drawing of Jindřichův Hradec, middle of the 18th century	250
175.	Square at Jindřichův Hradec	250
176.	View of Karlovy Vary by Matthaeus Merian, 1650	251
177.	Center of Karlovy Vary	252
178.	Plan of Kežmarok, 1870	253
179.	Plan of the historic nucleus of Klatovy, 1837	254
180.	Drawing of Klatovy, 17th century	255
181.	Square at Klatovy	255
182.	Plan of Kolín, 1842	256
183.	Plan of Košice and the fortress, 18th century	257
184.	View of Košice, 1617	258
185.	Development of Kouřim	259
186.	Historic center of Kremnica	260
187.	View of the center of Kremnica	260
188.	Plan of Kroměříž, 1830	262
189.	View of the Pleasure Garden at Kroměříž, 1691	263
190.	View of Kuks, 1723	264
191.	Plan of the historic nucleus of Kutná Hora, 1839	265
192.	The Italian Court at Kutná Hora	266
193.	The historic center of Kutná Hora	267
194.	View of Kutná Hora	268
195.	View of Kyjov, 1723–1728	269
196.	Plan of Leopoldov, 17th century	270
197.	Plan of the historic center of Levoča, 19th century	271
198.	Town Hall and church at Levoča	272
199.	Plan of the village of Liptovská Teplička, 1866	273
200.	General view of Liptovská Teplička	273
201.	Plan of the village of Litava, 1935	274
202.	Farmstead in Litava	275
203.	Plan of the historic center of Litoměřice	276
204.	View of Litoměřice, middle of the 18th century	277
205.	Square at Litoměřice	277
206.	Plan of Litomyšl, 1839	278
207.	Square at Litomyšl	279

208. Square at Manětín	281	263. Square of Žatec	328
209. Cadastral plan of Mariánské Lázně	283	264. Plan of the historic nucleus of Znojmo	329
210. Colonnade and Kříž Spring at Mariánské Lázně	283	265. View of Znojmo, 1523	330
211. Plan of Mikulov, 1826	285	266. Old view of Znojmo	331
212. Drawing of Mikulov, 1723–1728	285	267. Plan of Znojmo, 1815	332
213. Plan of Mladá Boleslav, 1842	286	268. Plan of the historic core of Zvolen	333
214. Plan of the historic nucleus of Moravská Třebová, 1835	287	269. View of Zvolen, 1599	334
215. Airview of the historic nucleus of Moravská Třebová	287	270. Airview of the *tanya* of Csorvás, near Orosháza	349
216. Old view of Moravský Krumlov	288	271. Airview of farms near Nyíregyháza	349
217. Plan of Most, 1842	289	272. Plan of the village of Jászapáti	353
218. Historic center of Most	289	273. Plan of Hajdúböszörmény	353
219. Plan of Netolice, 1837	290	274. Plan of Attila's camp	354
220. View of Netolice, 1686	291	275. Plan of Zenta	356
221. Plan of Nové Město nad Metují, 1840	292	276. Plan of Békéscsaba	356
222. Square at Nové Město nad Metují	293	277. Plan of the village of Magyarszákos	357
223. Northern section of the square at Nové Město nad Metují	294	278. Plans of the villages of Kurtakér and Tornova	358
224. View through the arcades of the square at Nové Město nad Metují	294	279. Plan of the medieval settlement of Esztergom	364
225. Plan of Nové Zámky, 18th century	295	280. Plan of Sopron	367
226. Plan of the citadel of Nové Zámky, 17th century	295	281. Plan of Szeged, 1713	368
227. Plan of Nový Bydžov, 1841	296	282. View of Pest, 1728	369
228. Plan of Nový Jičín, 1833	297	283. Plan of Pest, 18th century	369
229. Square at Nový Jičín	297	284. View of Buda, 1493	370
230. Plan of Nymburk, 1842	298	285. Plan of Buda, 17th century	371
231. Airview of the nucleus of Olomouc	299	286. Siege of Buda, 1684	371
232. Fortifications of Olomouc	300	287. Plan of Kecskemét, early 19th century	373
233. View of Ostrov and castle garden by Matthaeus Merian, 1650	301	288. View of Kecskemét, 19th century	374
234. Plan of the historic nucleus of Pardubice, 1839	302	289. Plan of Pécs, 12th century	375
235. View of Pardubice from the southwest, 1602	303	290. Plan of Pécs, 15th century	375
236. Square at Pardubice	304	291. Plan of Pécs, 17th century	376
237. Plan of Pelhřimov, 1829	305	292. View of Pécs, 1686	377
238. Square at Pelhřimov	305	293. Airview of the inner area of Pécs	378
239. Plan of the historic nucleus of Písek, 1837	306	294. Airview of Hajdúböszörmény	379
240. Historic nucleus of Písek	307	295. Airview of Sopron	381
241. Plan of the village of Plástovice, 1827	308	296. Előkapu, Sopron	382
242. Farmstead at Plástovice	309	297. Airview of a *Ringstrasse*, Sopron	382
243. Plan of the historic nucleus of Prachatice	311	298. Houses of the Two Moors, Sopron	383
244. Drawing of Prachatice, early 17th century	311	299. Plan of Debrecen in the 14th and 15th centuries	385
245. Plan of the historic center of Prešov, 19th century	312	300. Plan of the citadel of Eger	387
246. Plan of the village of Ružindol, 1895	313	301. View of Eger, 1687	388
247. Square at Sobotka	314	302. View of Eger from the castle hill	388
248. Timbered town house at Sobotka	314	303. János Hild's plan of Pest, 1805	389
249. Plan of Stará Boleslav and Brandýs nad Labem, 1640	315	304. Theater Square in Pest, 1838	391
250. Plan of Stará Boleslav and Brandýs nad Labem	316	305. Plan of Pest, 1838	391
		306. Plan of Pest, 1839	392
251. Plan of the historic nucleus of Tábor, 1830	317	307. Airview of Budapest	393
252. View of Tábor by Matthaeus Merian, 1650	318	308. Váci utca, Pest, 1845	393
253. Square at Tábor	318	309. Lower Danube Quay at Pest, 1856	394
254. Medieval fortifications of Tábor	319	310. View of Debrecen, 1860	395
255. Plan of Terezín	320	311. Airview of the Buildings of Parliament, Budapest	397
256. Plan of the historic center of Trnava	321	312. View of Szeged, 1686	398
257. View toward the church of St. Nicholas at Trnava	322	313. The "ideal level" plan of Szeged	399
258. View of Třeboň and suburbs, 1693	323	314. Plan of Szeged after the great flood	399
259. Plan of the historic nucleus of Uherské Hradiště, 1827	324	315. Plan of the rebuilt center of Szeged	399
260. Old view of Uherské Hradiště	325	316. Recapture of Győr, 1598	403
261. Plan of Uničov, 1833	326	317. Map of Győr, 1740	404
262. Plan of the historic nucleus of Žatec, 1843	327	318. Baroque houses, Győr	405
		319. Old street in Győr	405
		320. Széchenyi Square, Győr, 1845	406
		321. Pápa, end of the 15th century	407
		322. View of Pápa, beginning of the 17th century	408
		323. Painting of the Main Square at Pápa, end of the 18th century	408
		324. View of Szombathely, about 1791	409

xvii

325. Airview of Szombathely	410	333. View of Székesfehérvár, about 1830	419
326. Plan of Esztergom	411	334. Airview of the center of Székesfehérvár	420
327. View of Esztergom, 1595	413	335. Airview of the center of Veszprém	421
328. The Cathedral of Esztergom	414	336. Plan of Debrecen	422
329. Plan of Vác, beginning of the 18th century	415	337. Airview of Debrecen	424
330. Vác, 18th century	416	338. Piac utca and the Great Calvinist Church, Debrecen	424
331. Airview of Vác	417		
332. View of Székesfehérvár, 1601	418	339. View of Nagykőrös, about 1800	427

URBAN DEVELOPMENT IN EAST-CENTRAL EUROPE: POLAND, CZECHOSLOVAKIA, AND HUNGARY

POLAND

Introduction
by E. A. Gutkind

CHAPTER 1

Settlement and Colonization

IN A.D. 966, the tribes living in the lands between the Odra and the Bug rivers and the Baltic Sea and the Carpathians were converted to Christianity and united by Mieszko I, the founder of the Piast dynasty, in the nucleus of the Polish State. At that time, the population living in this territory of about 250,000 square kilometers may have numbered approximately 1,125,000. This figure, admittedly somewhat vague, has been arrived at by postulating an average population density at the turn of the first millennium of 4 to 5 inhabitants per square kilometer. The country was very unevenly settled. Large, uninhabited parts covered by dense forests extended as the outer boundaries of the state, where no clearings were allowed, or separated the territories of the different tribes. In contrast, the density of population was relatively high in Pomerania, at the mouth of the Odra; around Kołobrzeg (Kolberg), in the center of the country; in Silesia; and in the districts of Cracow and Sandomierz, where it reached 16 to 18 inhabitants per square kilometer.[1]

In general, with the exception of the woodlands and the marshes, almost the whole area of the Polish territory was more or less favorable for settlement, especially the large open regions. The term Polanians (*polana* = clearing, open country), the earliest name of the inhabitants of the oldest part of Poland, refers to the existence of large open spaces, free of forests and inviting settlement and cultivation. From these fertile soils, through the clearings of the woodlands, settlements gradually spread outward until, in the 13th and 14th centuries, the inhabited and cultivated districts formed a continuous area, slowly ascending the hilly and mountainous regions and reducing the forested tracts that separated the tribal territories.

As part of this development, the princes began to divide the land into administrative units focused on and dominated by fortified camps laid out in the manner of a town, with lanes and numerous timber buildings. These strongholds were the seats of the ruler, the administration, the Church, and the garrison. However, these early castellanies were not manors as we know them from Western Europe, from which the feudal lords organized the agricultural economy of their domain, but merely centers "into which flowed the renders from many individual peasant holdings."[2] Here, all the tributes were collected and administered, forming the material basis of the state at a time when cultivation was still a relatively minor part of the primitive economy. Since this system was not directed toward "a maximum production of cereals . . . the Slavonic economy was not stimulated to conquer fresh soil in order to extend arable farming. . . . The sole question [for the Slavonic peasant] was how to make both ends meet, and how much land he must till in order . . . to guarantee his living and enable him to perform his obligations as a subject." The fields were laid out unsystematically in irregular plots, and the hook-shaped plow was the common tool of a shifting agriculture based on clearing the soil by burning and moving on to another site. The settlements were mostly small, their

---

1. Stanisława Zajchowska. "Die Entwicklung der Besiedlung in Polen," *Geografiska Annaler*, Vol. XLII, No. 4, 1960, pp. 339–44 *passim*.
2. R. Koebner. "The Settlement and Colonisation of Europe." In: *The Cambridge Economic History of Europe*. Vol. I. 1942. Pp. 58 ff.

3

huts often extending along a watercourse or grouped as a ring-fence village around an interior green. Villages were only rarely extended. When the number of families grew, a new village was laid out near the old one. Thus it was not the individual village that formed "the legal unit of those who had joint interests in the fields of the district," but a larger group of several settlements.

However, the native peasantry was neither numerous enough nor sufficiently experienced to cope successfully with the great task of clearing the vast woodlands and handling the intricate problems of a more systematic procedure of settlement. Consequently, the owners of land were eager to attract colonists from the West and to employ *locatores* to organize the work. The following excerpt from a record of 1262 may serve as an example of many similar enterprises. It concerns the transfer of a forest near Szczecin (Stettin) by a knight, the owner, to a *locator*.

We, the Knight Gerbord von Köthen, make known that on the advice of our lords and friends we have ceded to Johannes Calbe . . . a forest called Halteshagen as property for a settlement. We make it a condition that all who settle there and reclaim arable land and cultivate it pay one shilling for every hide and tithe in corn of the fields situated in this forest, in addition to the so-called little tithe. Of the income in kind and cash one half falls to me and the other half to the three owners of the forest. . . . As special privilege we guarantee further: Everyone who wants to settle in the forest may do this freely and is allowed to brew and retail beer for a licensed time and also bake bread for sale and sell meat. From Martinmas onward we grant to the settlers ten free years during which they remain exempted from service, rent and tithe.[3]

The influx of German colonists was not welcomed by the native population. Tensions rose, and influential persons felt obliged to draw attention to the dangers of the ever-increasing immigration of foreigners. The warnings of Archbishop Jacob of Gniezno (Gnesen), addressed to the Pope in 1285, may be cited in this connection.

Because the Germans infiltrate and have already acquired property in Poland, it is not only your Holiness who suffers damage; no, we, too, are restricted in our rights. . . . The German princes belong to the Empire and thus the marginal territories [of Poland] occupied by them are drawn into the Empire and the direct rule of the Roman Church is therewith made ineffective. German knights and German settlers have entered Poland and have established themselves in villages which belonged to Poles and pay Peter's pence to the Church. Now, Germans, lords and settlers, raised objections when this tax was to be levied. In this way the Church will lose first one and gradually all her privileges, if no end is put to this state of affairs. . . . Other hardships have also increased since the arrival of these people: The Poles are oppressed, looked down upon, and strife is rampant. Our rights are encroached upon; in deepest silence our property is seized. . . . The sanctity of the Church is violated. . . . The German Minorites have removed all Polish friars and separated, not without strong opposition from

---

3. *Pommersches Urkundenbuch.* Vol. II. No. 720. Ed. by R. Klempin and R. Prümers. 1868.

the population, the Polish province by decreeing that these people be called "Saxons." Right in the center of Poland they erect new houses in spite of our opposition, and in the convents they hardly tolerate one single Polish brother in their midst.

We implore your Holiness to help us that after these abuses the Province of Poland shall be thoroughly reformed and Poles, as earlier, shall not be called by a foreign name.[4]

Gradually, German agrarian methods were adopted in many parts of Poland and, in the 13th and 14th centuries, colonization "under German law" spread over ever-widening areas of the country. Villages or towns laid out under this system by the most influential landowners and the Church were exempt from the jurisdiction of the officials of the princes and from the duties under ducal law.[5] The foundation of a colony was entrusted to a *locator*, who was either the leader of a group of settlers or the agent of the lord. The settlers were townsmen, servants from manors, or peasants, and their headman was the *locator*. Sometimes it was a noble, preferring to give up his own estate in favor of a larger property he would receive in his capacity as *locator*. In any case, apart from land, the headmen were granted extensive and lucrative privileges which enhanced their status and economic position. Almost all villages were laid out as compact settlements. Individual farmsteads belonged to a later period of colonization. As far as possible, villages were associated with a town as their legal center. A Great Polish charter of the early 14th century stated: *"Ville supranominate ad forum et ad judicium debeant pertinere."*[6] This inclusion in the *Weichbild* of a town, that is, the area of the urban jurisdiction, was economically advantageous for the peasants and exempted the German immigrants from Polish law. Moreover, it enlarged the scale of settlement, amounting to what would be called today a primitive sort of regional planning. For example, in 1253 the *locator* of the town of Poznań (Posen) received seventeen neighboring Polish places which, by order of the Grand Duke of Great Poland, were to be colonized by Germans. On the other hand, in contrast to the earlier economic distinction of town and village, the introduction of the *Bannmeile*—the protective zone of the urban handicrafts—made the villages more and more dependent on the urban economy. Only a small number of rural craftsmen indispensable for the villagers were permitted to continue, for example, the smiths, wheelwrights, bakers, and butchers. This procedure was not uncommon but can be found all over Europe. The goal was to strengthen the economic monopoly of the towns and reduce the villages to independent annexes of the urban economy and jurisdiction.

The origin of landownership dates back to a time when land was the property of the ruling prince, the Church, or the indigenous rural population. In the 13th century, the monarch laid claim to all unoccu-

---

4. *Codex diplomaticus maioris Poloniae.* Vol. I, No. 616. 1877.
5. J. Rutkowski. "Medieval Agrarian Society in its Prime. Poland, Lithuania and Hungary." In: *The Cambridge Economic History of Europe.* Vol. I. 1942. Pp. 411 ff.
6. H. Aubin. "The Lands east of the Elbe and German Colonisation eastwards." In: *The Cambridge Economic History of Europe.* Vol. I. 1942. Pp. 385 ff.

pied land and, gradually, to all land worked by the peasants.[7] In the course of time, more and more grants of land from the ruler and private nobles were made to the Church, but toward the end of the Middle Ages, the land in possession of the nobility exceeded the combined total owned by the monarch and the Church. In conjunction with this development, the large estates of the nobles were gradually transformed into manors, an evolution grown complex and widespread by the 12th and 13th centuries.[8] As everywhere else in Europe, the result was an increasing oppression of the peasants, who had to work for the lord as servants or agricultural laborers, paying imposts and duties to their master. The nature of this system is too well known to need further elaboration.[9]

During the Middle Ages a considerable number of villages were founded in all parts of the country. Not all of these were successful. Many were deserted after a short time, either because geographical conditions turned out to be less favorable than expected or because economic and administrative difficulties arose which had not been foreseen. However, in general, the structure of settlement developed evenly until the first half of the 17th century, though the acreage of cultivated fields diminished. This development did not involve a thinning out of the network of settlement as such but merely a reduction of the population in some villages. By the beginning of the 16th century the area of these *Wüstungen* was relatively large. The *Liber beneficiorum* of the Poznań Diocese, of the year 1510, states that of 8,735 hides in 811 villages 2,794 were deserted, representing about one third of the total acreage of peasant holdings, but not including those of village leaders. These fields were abandoned because of epidemics, unrest, or economic misfortunes. In the beginning of the 16th century, the total area of *Wüstungen* for the whole country has been estimated as 30 percent of the cultivable land. In general, most of the deserted fields were situated in densely settled districts which had been inhabited since earliest times. Here, feudal oppression was strongest and therefore most resented by the peasants. However, deserted fields near the towns were rare, owing to the greater security and better economic conditions of the rural population. The same was to be observed in the frontier districts, where the peasants enjoyed considerable independence.[10]

Another factor influencing the structure of settlement was the growing demand for iron, needed for tools and arms. This development began as early as the 13th and 14th centuries and continued to grow during the following centuries. Water power was used, and the forests supplied the fuel. The number of forges increased rapidly, and small settlements in the forests, often grouped in larger mining communities, multiplied. The centers of such activities were situated around Częstochowa (Kielce Department) and in the Góry Swiętokrzyskie (near Kielce). However, by the 17th century a decline set in. The peasants, the principal consumers, were more and more impoverished by feudal exploita-

---

7. J. Rutkowski, *op. cit.*, p. 398.
8. *Ibid.*, p. 402.
9. See Vol. I, pp. 94–97.
10. Stanisława Zajchowska, *op. cit.*, p. 340.

tion, their diminishing purchasing power detrimentally affecting the urban economy. On the other hand, the importation of iron tools increased. The feudal lords who favored this trend tried to suppress the activities of the small and independent smiths, under the pretext of preventing more encroachments on the forests. Only the armament industry developed: As usual, the demand for weapons increased, though it proved a short-lived economic stimulus, ending at the turn of the 18th century, when the military strength of Poland declined. The forges and the settlements that had grown around them were deserted.[11]

The historical sequence of types of villages is still a controversial subject and may remain so for a long time to come, because reliable evidence is lacking and suggestions are more or less based on speculation. However, it would not appear too wide of the mark to assume that the earlier types of villages were connected with the irregular field system of *Gemengelage* and community-regulated cultivation. To this group belong the ring-fence villages, the more or less compact villages arranged around a central green, and the compact nucleated villages. The later group, that is, the type of village founded under the influence of German colonization after the 13th century, consists of the more systematically laid-out line and street villages, *Reihendörfer;* the forest-line villages, *Waldhufendörfer;* and marsh-line villages, *Marschhufendörfer.* In these cases the fields extended in long strips behind the homesteads, which were lined up along a street. This distinction is admittedly vague, and historically the types overlap. But in a broad sense, they follow the principal stages of development of the agricultural landscape of almost all countries of Europe. However, no hard and fast rules can be established. What is of interest in this particular connection is the overriding fact that agriculture had to reach a certain level of efficiency before towns and settlements whose inhabitants were not engaged or only partly engaged in cultivation could come into existence. In other words, agriculture had to pass beyond the stage of a self-supporting rural economy and had to be able not only to feed the tillers of the soil but also to produce a food surplus for those engaged in other activities such as handicrafts, administration, religious pursuits, and war.

11. *Ibid.,* p. 341.

CHAPTER 2

Origins of Urban Civilization

THE THESIS OF earlier German scholars that no towns existed in Poland before the German colonization is no longer tenable. It was dictated mainly by national arrogance, not by results of objective research. Archeological investigations and detailed studies based on written and topographical sources have produced irrefutable evidence of the existence of nonagricultural settlements prior to the period when the waves of the great West-East colonial movement reached the Slavonic sphere of influence. The first fortified castles, *grody*, with *suburbia* inhabited by traders and craftsmen, such as Gniezno (Gnesen), Poznań (Posen), Kalisz (Kalisch), Lednica (?), and Łęczyca (Lentschiza), date back to the eighth and ninth centuries. Both castle and *suburbium* were protected by palisades and moats. During this time, a certain social differentiation of the population had taken place, due to a general improvement of the economy and a slowly developing specialization of production. The combination of castle with trading and handicraft-settlements was not unusual. Similar arrangements are known from many other countries where a settlement of traders and craftsmen grew up around a stronghold, for instance, in Central and Southern Europe, in Japan around the castles of the *daimyos*, or, to mention an even earlier example, the Roman camps with extramural *vici*. These military-economic units in Poland were sited as political-administrative district centers at particularly favorable points, where they developed into market centers and sometimes into towns. It is quite possible that the population of the *suburbia* consisted not only of bondsmen and unfree craftsmen but also of privileged persons who enjoyed a certain liberty in their economic activities. We know, for instance, of Wrocław (Breslau) that at the beginning of the 12th century a distinction was made between the *majores et seniores civitatis* and the *totus populus*. Szczecin (Stettin) and other similar settlements had, at this time, a population of 2,500 to 3,000 inhabitants, a number indicating an urban character.[1]

The situation of Poland as a transit country between the West and the East, the South and the North of Europe, gave rise to a number of important overland routes which remained more or less unchanged in the centuries following the early Middle Ages. These routes are older than has been commonly assumed. To satisfy the growing needs of the Polish population of the 12th century and the first half of the 13th century, export and import began to play a considerable role in the economy of the country. It was therefore a natural evolution that out of the pre-colonial elements—the castle, the *suburbium*, and trading and handicraft-settlements—market centers grew up which had become a characteristic part of the settlement structure by the 13th century. Such a market place was called, in medieval Polish documents, *forum* or, more rarely, *villa forensis* or *locus forensis*, but apparently never *portus, mer-*

---

1. K. Dziewoński. "L'évolution des plans et de l'ordonnance des villes du Haute Moyen Age en Pologne." In: P. Francastel (ed.). *Les Origines des Villes Polonaises*. 1960. Pp. 27–51.
W. Hensel. "Les origines des villes slaves occidentales et orientales," *Atti del VI Congresso Internazionale delle Scienze Preistoriche e Protostoriche*. Vol. I, 1963.
H. Ludat. "Frühformen des Städtewesens in Osteuropa." In: *Studien zu den Anfängen des Europäischen Städtewesens*. Reichenau-Vorträge 1955–1956. 1958. Pp. 541–53.
Vorstufen und Entstehung des Städtewesens in Osteuropa. 1955.
K. Maleczyński. *Die ältesten Märkte Polens*. 1930.
Most of these books contain comprehensive bibliographies of Polish literature.

catorium, or *mercatus* as in the West. The fact that available records do not mention the foundation of new markets during the whole of the 12th century may be taken as proof of the early origin of these markets. What has been recorded in relevant documents is merely the existence of such places, not their nature. It was not until the 13th century that the founding of new markets, under German law, was mentioned by the feudal lords. These small places were the equivalent of the *civitates* of the West, and their function was the promotion and maintenance of commercial activities between the centers of the administration of the State and the Church and more distant regions. The great majority of these Polish markets were situated near the great transit routes where they could easily be visited by foreign merchants.[2] In time, retail traders settled permanently in these places. Thus temporary markets, held only once a year in the early Middle Ages, became permanent institutions, that is, weekly markets. As a result, the urban character of these centers was guaranteed.

Whereas in the 12th and 13th centuries most towns were founded by the princes, the situation changed in the 14th century. Then the feudal lords assumed the leading role in the founding of new towns, an indication of the growing importance of the landed gentry, their increasing influence as territorial magnates, and their strengthened position in relation to the ruling sovereigns.[3] In general, the new towns were regularly laid out, with a large central market square. Some of these squares, even in small places, were disproportionately large, sometimes more than 220 by 220 yards. It was not unusual that around the regular nucleus the later quarters grew up quite unsystematically, resembling irregularly laid-out villages more than systematically planned towns.

---

2. K. Małeczyński, *op. cit.*, pp. 29, 33, 35, 37.
3. W. Kuhn. *Geschichte der Deutschen Ostsiedlung in der Neuzeit.* Vol. II. 1957. Pp. 134, 136.

City Development in Poland
by Dr. Wojciech Kalinowski

ASSOCIATE PROFESSOR, INSTITUTE OF TOWN
PLANNING AND ARCHITECTURE, WARSAW

      Pracę tę poświęcam pamięci wielkiego znawcy i miłośnika dziejów miast—Profesorowi E. A. Gutkind.
                                      Dr Wojciech Kalinowski

      I dedicate this work to the memory of a cognoscente and ardent student of urban history—Professor E. A. Gutkind.
                                      Dr. Wojciech Kalinowski

CHAPTER 3

Introduction

THE FOLLOWING BRIEF outline covers the history of almost a thousand years of city development and city planning in Poland. The physical evolution of cities, the main subject of this essay, was influenced by a great variety of social, economic, political, military, and other factors. The author has tried to present these complicated processes as concisely as possible and in a manner easily undertandable for readers perhaps not too familiar with the history and civilization of the Polish nation, whose native elements evolved under the impact of cultural infiltrations from Eastern, Southern, and Western Europe. In order to achieve this goal it was necessary to introduce simplifications and omit less essential details, although the latter undoubtedly influenced the evolution of urban culture in Poland. The task was particularly difficult since no comprehensive work exists in this country on the history of city development, nor are all the particular periods and regions adequately covered by monographic studies. Finally, the author wishes to justify the brief treatment of such problems as the development of urban self-government, the evolution of the culture of the burghers, and the architectural forms of urban buildings, by the fact that these matters have been dealt with in detail in books listed in the bibliography.

The present essay follows a chronological sequence complying with the accepted division of Polish history into certain periods. It comprises the history of Polish towns from the emergence of the Polish State, toward the end of the first millennium, to the liquidation of Poland's independence as a state resulting from the partitions in the 18th century. Within that period the political boundaries of the Polish State underwent many shifts, reaching the Odra River in the west and, for a time, the Dnieper in the east and encompassing vast areas which ethnically were not Polish. This raised difficulties in establishing the territorial scope of this study. When dealing with particular periods the author deemed it best to introduce different territorial ranges corresponding to the political boundaries of the time. Thus, some of the western areas have been discussed more extensively in the medieval period only, while the colonizing activity of the State and the magnates in the east, in more recent times, has received greater attention since it reflects characteristic Polish ideas of city planning.

The State of the first historic prince of the Piast dynasty, Mieszko I —a domain which was one of several political organisms taking shape in the west and south of Slav territories—came into existence in Wielkopolska (Great Poland) and the adjoining areas of Central Poland. Toward the end of Mieszko's reign (A.D. 992) it reached west to the Odra, east beyond the Vistula, south to the Carpathian and Sudeten Mountains, and north to the Baltic Sea, between the Odra and Vistula rivers. Bolesław the Brave (992–1025) extended the boundaries of his State eastward to the river Bug (Fig. 1) and for a time also controlled Slovakia, Moravia, Bohemia, and Lusatia. After the loss of Western Pomerania, which became a separate state ruled by princes of the Piast dynasty, Poland had access to the Baltic Sea only between Kołobrzeg and the Vistula, while in the south it stretched to the Carpathian Mountains, in

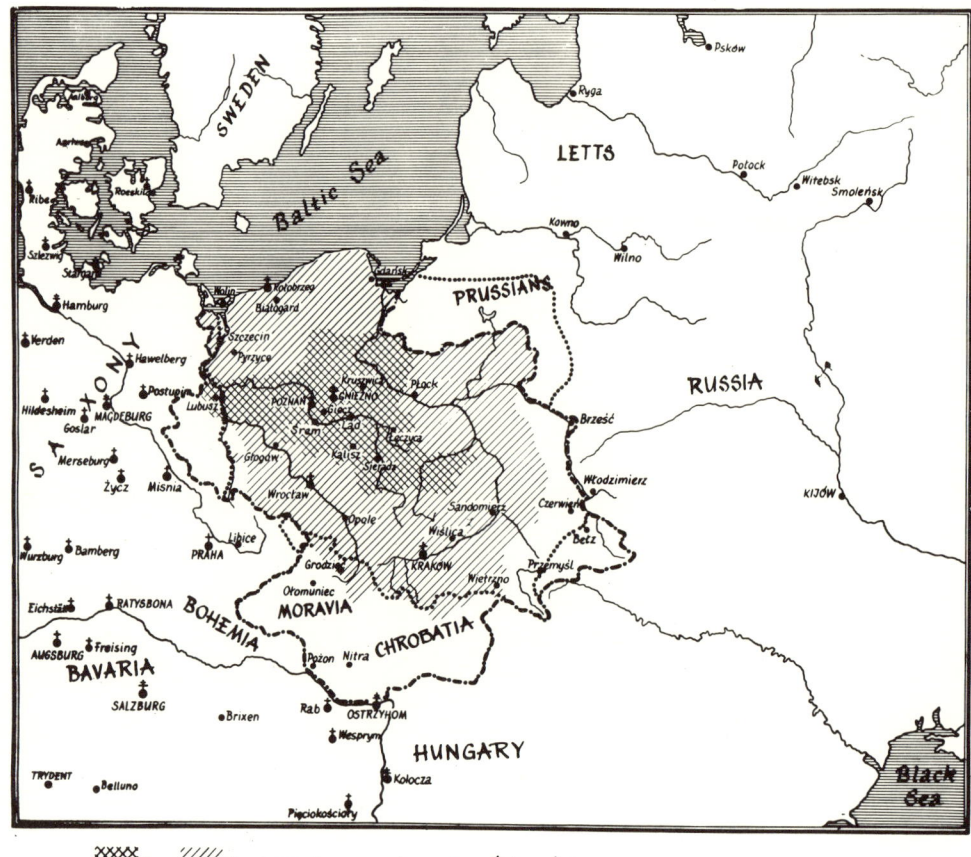

1. Poland in the 10th and 11th centuries. 1. Territory of the Polish State, about 960; 2. Territory of the Polish State toward the end of the reign of Mieszko I (992); 3. Farthest extension of the conquests of Bolesław I the Brave (992–1025); 4. Boundaries of the People's Republic of Poland since 1945; 5. The more important *grody* and settlements; 6. Archbishoprics; 7. Bishoprics.

the west to the Odra, and in the east almost to the Bug. In spite of the feudal division into more than ten petty principalities, this territory maintained itself through the 12th and 13th centuries with but insignificant changes. The restoration of a centralized Polish monarchy took place in 1314 under Władysław Łokietek (the Short), but even before 1314 he exercised control over Great Poland, Little Poland, and the lands of Sieradz and Łęczyca. Since 1308 Gdańsk (Pomerania) had been in the hands of the Teutonic Order which had occupied the land of Chełmno, while the Silesian principalities became feudatory to Bohemia. The State was finally reunited under Kazimierz (Casimir) the Great, who after the conquest of Ruthenia (1366) ruled over a vast territory (Fig. 2) extending eastward as far as Podolia, but no longer reaching the Odra in the west, due to the loss of Silesia. Nor did this State have access to the Baltic Sea, for Gdańsk, together with Prussia, was controlled by the Teutonic Knights. Subsequently, Poland's union with the Grand Duchy of Lithuania under the Treaty of Krewo (1385), a victorious war with the Teutonic Order (1466), and territorial conquests in the east, early in the 16th century, resulted in the formation of a great kingdom, comprising Poland, Lithuania, and Ruthenia (Fig. 3), stretching from the

2. Poland under the reign of Casimir the Great (1333–1370). 1. Lands controlled by the king in 1333; 2. Areas incorporated by 1370; 3. Vassal territories; 4. Boundaries of the State in 1370; 5. Boundaries of the People's Republic of Poland since 1945; 6. Cities founded before 1333; 7. Cities founded between 1333 and 1370; 8. Cities fortified between 1333 and 1370.

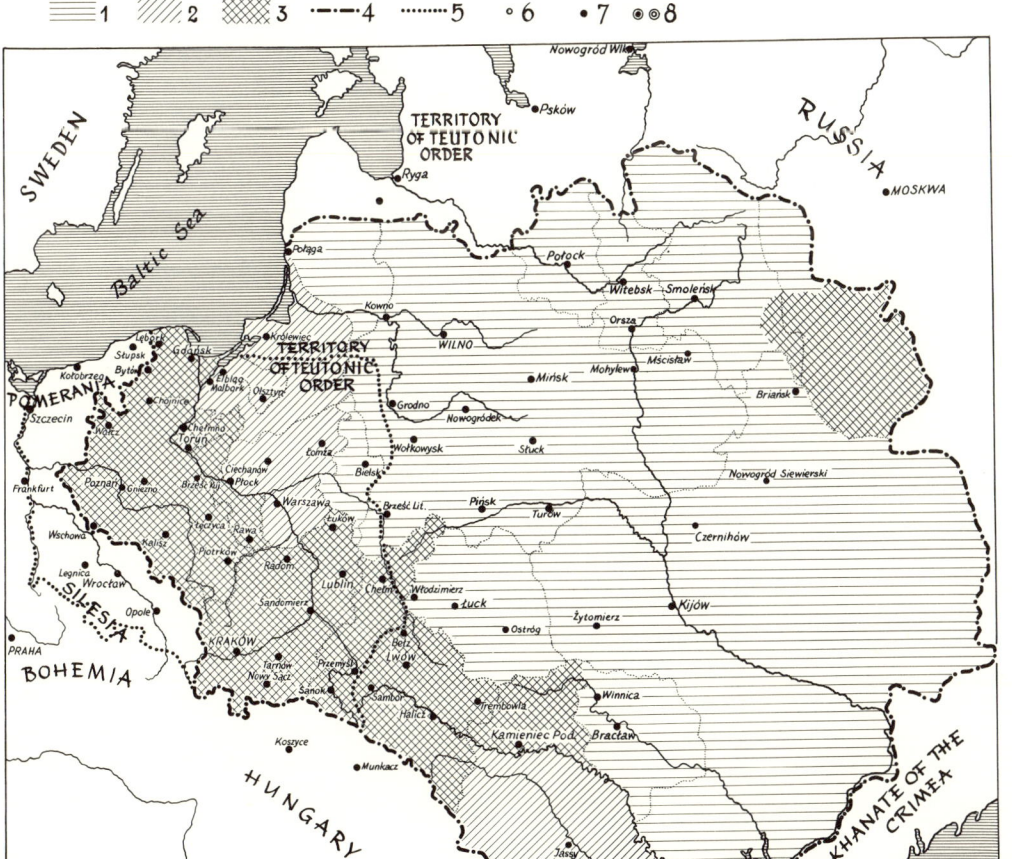

3. Poland and Lithuania after the Peace of Toruń, 1466. 1. Kingdom of Poland; 2. Territories of vassals of the Kingdom of Poland; 3. Grand Duchy of Lithuania; 4. Territories of vassals of the Grand Duchy of Lithuania; 5. Boundaries of the State in 1466; 6. Boundaries of the People's Republic of Poland since 1945; 7. Boundaries of lands and voivodships; 8. The more important cities.

Baltic to the Black Sea. The 17th century was a period of exhausting wars with Sweden and Turkey, with territorial losses both in the east and north (for instance, the loss of the vassal Prussian principality in 1657). In the 18th century, in spite of political and economic difficulties, the multinational "Nobles' Commonwealth" still included a vast territory extending eastward as far as the Dnieper. However, in the course of three successive partitions (1772, 1793, and 1795) the lands of the Polish Commonwealth were incorporated into the respective states of Prussia, Austria, and Russia. In 1807 Napoleon's victorious wars led to the setting up of a short-lived autonomous state called the Duchy of Warsaw, composed of Great Poland and the central areas of Poland up to the river Bug. After Napoleon's defeat in Russia, the Duchy ceased to exist. The Congress of Vienna (1815) resulted in the creation of a Polish Kingdom, the so-called "Congress Kingdom," which included the Polish territory between the river Prosna in the west, the Bug in the east, the Vistula in the south, and the former Prussian frontier in the north. Its king was the Russian Tzar, and it was, in fact, dependent on Russia. Cracow, with a small surrounding area, was declared a Free City, but after 1848 it became part of Austria. The autonomy of the Polish Kingdom was finally abolished after the insurrection in 1863.

The bibliography is a list of the most important writings dealing with the history of Polish cities. Here, the reader may find more detailed information on the development of any particular city or on their condition at a given period. The text contains the names of cities in their original Polish form, with the exception of cities with accepted English names, like Warsaw and Cracow. This may cause some difficulty in reconciling the present study with the German literature concerning Western Pomerania and Silesia. Readers interested in more detailed information are referred to the exhaustive Polish-German vocabulary of toponyms: Stanisław Rospond's *Słownik nazw geograficznych Polski zachodniej i północnej* (Wrocław-Warsaw. 1951).

4. *Opposite page:* View of the remains of Biskupin, a settlement of the Lusatian culture (sixth to fifth century B.C.).

CHAPTER 4

THE REMAINS OF settlements dating from the late Paleolithic and Neolithic Ages discovered on Polish territory in the course of archeological investigations do not provide an adequate basis for a detailed analysis of the development of settlement in those periods. It is certain, however, that a considerable number of settlements came into existence in the Neolithic Age, with a high level of material culture. This is demonstrated by the large settlement linked with the flint mine at Krzemionki Opatowskie, County of Opatów, dating from 2000 B.C., that is considered one of the most interesting relics of ancient mining. Objects made of flint from the mine and discovered in various parts of Europe testify to an extensive trade.

In the Middle Bronze Age (1300–1100 B.C.) there appeared in the area that is now Poland the cultural group of the Lusatians, so called from the earliest burial grounds found in the Lausitz Region (Lusetia), which emerged from the Balto-Slavonic community. Lusatian culture is now recognized as that of the Old Slavonic peoples, evidenced by an undisturbed continuity of settlement and civilization in their territories up to the early Middle Ages.

Archeological finds have made it possible to ascertain that Lusatian culture on Polish soil lasted approximately from 1300 to 400 B.C. and that its peak period of development belonged to the seventh and fifth centuries B.C. One of the most renowned archeological discoveries in Poland before World War II, the marsh settlement at Biskupin, is closely connected with the Lusatian culture. This settlement was thor-

Polish Urban Settlement Before the 13th Century

oughly investigated in the years 1934–1939 and 1946–1957. It was built toward the middle of the first millennium B.C. and functioned for some 100 to 150 years, from about 550 to 400 B.C. It was one of three defensive settlements grouped around a chain of lakes that extended along the little river Gąsawka, a tributary of the Noteć; the other two settlements were Sobiejuchy (650–550 B.C.) and Izdebno (550–400 B.C.).

The Biskupin settlement occupied the whole area, about 4.9 acres of a flat island, now a peninsula, lying close to the lakeshore. It was protected by a breakwater-palisade built of some 15,000 tree trunks (Fig. 4) driven aslant into the bottom of the lake and by a defensive bulwark, 19.7 feet high and 9.8 feet wide, made of wooden cases filled with earth. Within the bulwark a road encircled the settlement and, in the southwest, a gate led to the bridge linking the village with the shore. The village was composed of more than a hundred identical houses (26.2 by 29.5 feet) aligned in rows along parallel streets. This remarkably regular settlement was built all at once; within a short period of time some 280,000 cubic feet of timber were used for its construction! Its population of approximately 1,200 to 1,500 lived as a consanguineous community, mainly on animal husbandry and agriculture. Crafts (bronzes and pottery) were practised primarily to meet the community's own needs. Biskupin, along with other settlements of the Lusatian culture, was not a city but a fortified, agricultural village.

The successive invasions of Scythians in the fifth century B.C., of Celts in the fourth and third century, and of Goths and Gepidae in the first and second centuries A.D. impeded the development of settlement on Polish territory. On the other hand, the first written information on Slavonic tribes (by Herodotus and Ptolemy) dates from this period, and numerous finds of Roman relics and amber from the Baltic shores testify to extensive trade relations. A toponym related to Polish territory was first recorded in the middle of the second century: Calissia, identified as present-day Kalisz, a city on the river Prosna, lying on the so-called Amber Route.

The fall of the Roman Empire in the fifth century, the spontaneous expansion of the Slavs toward the west and the south in the fifth and sixth centuries, and the repeated passage of Huns and Teutonic tribes marked a new stage in the development of the Slavonic peoples living between the Odra and Bug rivers. From various Byzantine, Ruthenian, Bavarian and English records, written between the fifth and tenth centuries, it may be gathered that a number of tribal communities gradually emerged in that area. Subsequently they developed into political units whose existence is confirmed by ninth-century sources: the Polanians in Wielkopolska (Great or Western Poland), the Vistulans in Małopolska (Little or Southern Poland), and the Silesians and Opolanians in Silesia. The setting up of territorial tribal communities was accompanied by the formation of a new settlement structure between the Odra and the Bug rivers, whose centers were the *grody*.[1] These centers

---

1. *Gród*, pl. *grody*—a small fortified settlement, usually with a circular or oval plan, surrounded by earth-and-timber bulwarks and a moat. It was either the seat of the state or local authority or a strategic stronghold manned by a military garrison. The buildings within the fortifications were of wood. Only after the adoption of Christianity (966) were stone churches and *palatia* erected in the *grody*.

either were seats of tribal authorities or defended the boundaries of territorial units. This system of *grody,* as will be shown, formed the basis of the modern settlement structure of Poland.

Large-scale archeological investigations begun after World War II in connection with the celebrations of the Millennium of the Polish State yielded extremely interesting results. They revealed an unexpectedly high level of fully developed settlement forms and of the material culture and handicrafts of the Slav population living between the Bug and the Odra in the period from the 8th to the 13th centuries. Owing to these investigations, it was possible to explain the origin of many cities before they were granted urban rights under the so-called German law and to explode the nationalistic theories of German scholars who claimed that the areas, now Polish, were colonized by Germans in the 13th and 14th centuries.

Excavations in Szczecin, Wolin, Gdańsk, Poznań, Gniezno, Wrocław, Opole, Cracow, Sandomierz, and other cities revealed considerable settlements already existing in the eighth and ninth centuries, that is, long before the Polish State appeared on the stage of History. The centers of these settlements were defensive *grody* close to river crossings or important crossroads, sites chosen for strategic reasons. In Central and Northern Poland they were situated mostly on low-lying land which made it possible to surround the bulwarks with ditches filled with water. In Southern Poland, on the other hand—possibly under the influence of the Southern Slavs and Great Moravia—the *grody* were built on hills,

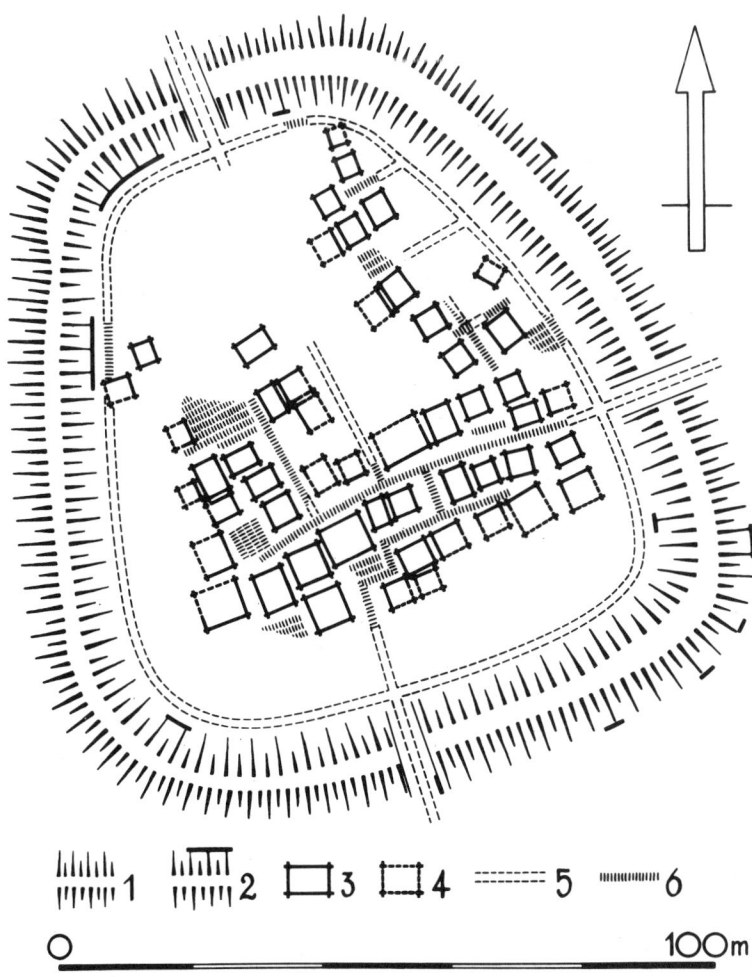

5. The early medieval settlement of Opole, showing the reconstructed bulwarks and excavated remains of buildings. 1. Possible outline of the bulwark; 2. Excavated parts of the bulwark; 3. Excavated buildings or parts of buildings; 4. Reconstructed buildings or parts of buildings; 5. Possible course of roads; 6. Excavated roads paved with wood.

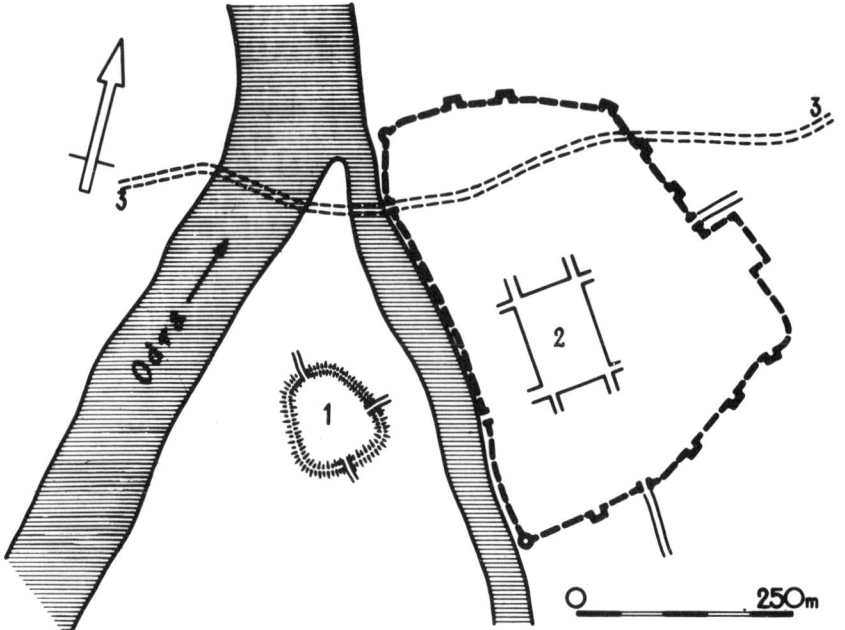

6. The early medieval fortified settlement of Opole in relation to the city founded in the early 14th century. Reconstruction by the author based on the findings of new investigations and a plan of 1787. 1. Early medieval fortified settlement (10th to 13th century); 2. Medieval city founded in the early 14th century; 3. Probable course of the crossing over the Odra in the early Middle Ages.

for instance, the Wawel in Cracow or the *grody* of Sandomierz and Przemyśl. They were protected by bulwarks made up of layers of wooden planks laid crosswise one over the other, covered with stones and earth and coated with clay. These bulwarks were often more than 32.8 feet high, encircled by a moat filled with water and sometimes by palisades driven vertically or diagonally into the ground. The area within the fortifications was densely built up with timber dwellings, usually one-room, and structures serving agricultural purposes (Figs. 5, 6).

The economic need of the *gród* and an increasing exchange of goods led to the formation of a new settlement called *suburbium,* with a servile population working for the *gród* (its main occupations being stockbreeding, fishing, and the practice of various handicrafts). Historical sources—for instance, the accounts of the travels of Ibrahim Ibn Jacob, a Jewish merchant from Córdoba—testify to the considerable importance of these settlements, while archeological finds confirm the high standard of craftsmanship and the existence of trade relations with European countries. The *suburbia* were usually surrounded by ramparts, occasionally connected with those of the *gród,* as in Poznań, Szczecin, Gniezno, and other places; their timber buildings stood close together, along narrow streets 6.6 to 13 feet wide and paved with wood.

The growing hegemony of the state of the Polanians and the territorial conquests under the reigns of Prince Mieszko I and his son, Bolesław I, the Brave (992–1025), resulted in the formation of the Polish State, extending from the river Odra in the west to the rivers Wieprz and San in the east and to the Carpathian Mountains in the south. It also temporarily included Lusatia, Bohemia, Moravia, and Slovakia. The adoption of Christianity by Mieszko I (966) opened the new state to cultural influences from Western and Southern Europe. The former centers of tribal territorial units were incorporated into the organic settlement structure of the Polish state. Existing *grody* were expanded, and new ones were built for state authorities (Kruszwica, Włocławek, Kalisz, Sieradz, Gdańsk, and others). Gradually, three types of settlement were evolved: royal residences, *sedes regni principales;* administrative centers of provinces; and seats of castellanies as local centers of administration. Simultaneously, changes took place within the *grody* and *suburbia:* Stone churches and *palatia* were erected in the *grody* of the main centers of authority, as in Cracow, Legnica, Ostrów Lednicki, Giecz, and Przemyśl, while in the *suburbia* the first Romanesque cathedrals were built near the seats of bishoprics, as in Cracow, Wrocław, Poznań, Gniezno, Kamień Pomorski, Płock, and Włocławek. In addition, the defense system was improved by the introduction of a more effective construction of the fortifications.

The second half of the 11th century witnessed a marked development of settlements which, in view of the increasing social division of labor, deserved the name "city." In the *suburbia,* the crafts thrived, making not only objects of daily use but some luxury items, such as goldware. This production not only catered to the needs of the prince's court but also served for exchange with the agricultural hinterland. Around the *grody* dependent settlements came into existence; their population either attended to the prince's farms as swineherds, shepherds, stablemen, and falconers or were engaged in handicrafts as blacksmiths, arrow-makers, goldsmiths, wheelwrights, and the like. The names of these settlements, most of which have survived to this day, were usually linked with the trades that were plied there, for instance, Świniary (swineherds), Grotniki (arrow-makers), Złotniki (goldsmiths), and so on.

Regular weekly markets, usually attached to already existing settlements, were established probably as early as the 11th century. The most important markets were those adjoining the seats of castellanies. At first the sites for markets were presumably selected outside the *suburbia;* sometimes, as may be inferred from Bishop Thietmar's description, they may have been provided with wooden platforms or benches on which the traders displayed their goods. In the course of time the people whose livelihood depended on the markets settled nearby; later they were followed by colonies of merchants coming to Poland from abroad. The earliest of such merchant colonies confirmed by written sources was in Przemyśl, where a Jewish commune is known to have existed in the 11th century. According to recent research, Poland (without Western Pomerania) had some 200 market centers in the late 12th and early 13th centuries. The function of these localities was reflected in their names, denoting the days of the week on which the markets were held: Środa (Wednesday), Czwartek (Thursday), Piątek (Friday), and so on. A toponym of this kind, *forum in Soboth,* was first recorded in Silesia in the late 12th century.

The formation of markets near the *grody,* which were seats of castellanies, was probably connected with the setting up of customhouses. Markets were the property of the ruler; and special taxes, duties, and other imposts were levied for his benefit. The revenues obtained from the markets gave a new stimulus to the development of settlements, an economic factor that was to play an important role in the shaping of the settlement structure throughout the Middle Ages and the following periods.

In order to create favorable conditions for the development of markets, the ruler granted immunities in the form of partial exemption from taxes and duties, the *libertas fori,* and, later, certain forensic privileges, the *ius fori,* which, however, concerned only the markets as such, not the settlements adjoining them.

The settlements that grew up in the proximity of the markets in the 12th and 13th centuries—*villae forenses* and *civitates forenses*—were inhabited by a free population, often composed of merchants coming from abroad (Fig. 7). This new form of settlement might be called a "protocity." The central feature of its layout was an elongated square accommodating the market facilities and a church, the *ecclesia forensis.* Traces of such layouts may still be discerned in the spatial pattern of some present-day cities, particularly in those cases where the early market settlement did not develop into a medieval city or where the settlement subsequently shifted to another site.

The spatial pattern of the major early urban centers toward the end of the 12th and the beginning of the 13th century generally took the form of a cluster of several units of different types which today we would call an agglomeration. This term applies in particular to the leading political centers of the country such as Cracow, Wrocław, and Poznań, a fact confirmed by historical research and archeological investigations. Poznań represents a good example of an agglomeration of this kind. In the early 13th century it consisted of a number of settlements (Fig. 8). First, there were the *gród* and the *suburbium,* situated near a

7. Plan of Szczecin in the early Middle Ages, based on a reconstruction of a 17th-century plan by T. Wieczorkowski. 1. Probable former course of the Odra; 2. *Gród* (10th to 13th century), later the site of the ducal castle; 3. Slav *suburbium,* surrounded by a bulwark; 4. German *suburbium;* 5. Walls of the medieval city.

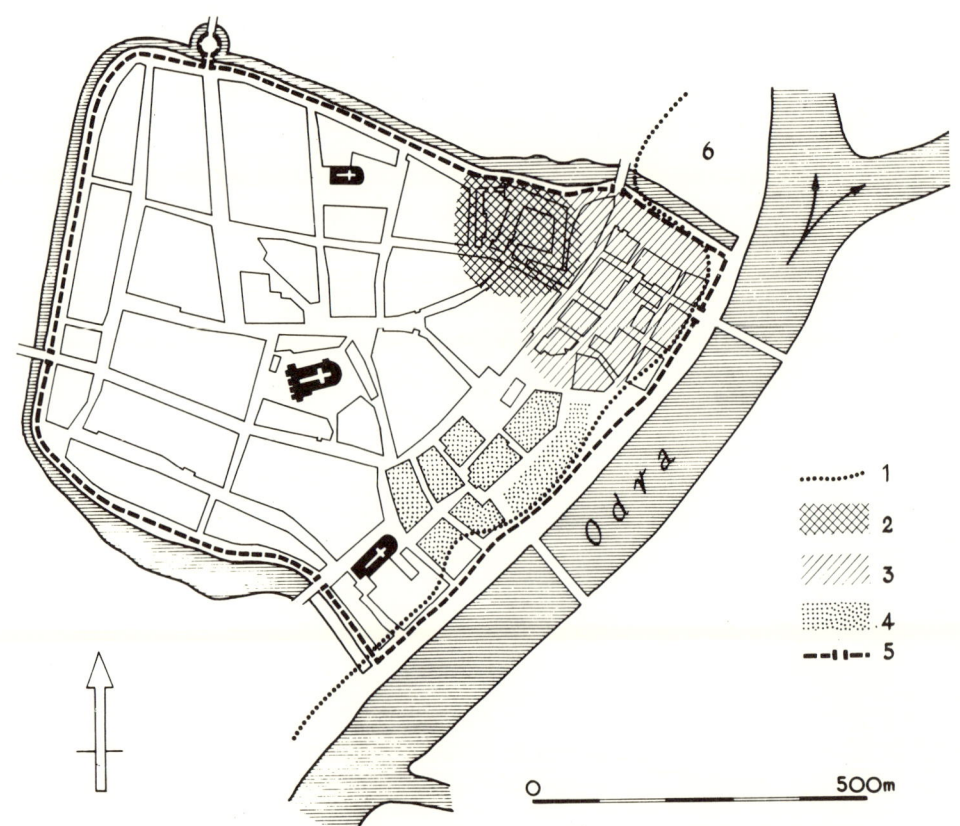

ford, on an island surrounded by the waters of the river Warta and its tributary Cybina. The *gród* probably came into existence as early as the ninth century, and the *suburbium* in the tenth century. After the adoption of Christianity a cathedral was built in the *suburbium,* and a church was dedicated to the Virgin Mary in the *gród*. In the 12th century the *suburbium* was enlarged, covering the whole of the island when St. Nicholas' Church was erected. On the right bank of the Cybina were two settlements: One was called *Śródka,* alluded to as *antiqua civitas* in the 13th century; it performed market functions and included St. Margaret's Church. The other, called *Komandoria,* included St. John's Church and a monastery of the Knights Hospitalers of St. John of Jerusalem. On the left bank of the Warta, near the ford, stood St. Gothard's settlement, *locus S. Gothardi,* with a church dedicated to the same saint, to which Dominican Friars are known to have moved from Śródka in 1244; a settlement attached to St. Martin's Church belonging to the Chapter of the Cathedral; and, finally, a settlement attached to the churches of St. Adalbert (built in 1222) and St. George. The whole cluster was surrounded by a dozen or so dependent settlements. Both Cracow and Wrocław had similar patterns.

8. The structure of Poznań in the early Middle Ages. 1. *Gród* with the Church of the Virgin Mary; 2. *Suburbium* with SS. Peter and Paul's Cathedral; 3. Zagórze with St. Nicholas' Church included within the fortifications of the 12th century; 4. Śródka with St. Margaret's Church (market?); 5. Commandery of the Knights Hospitalers of St. John of Jerusalem; 6. St. George's Hill with the churches of St. George and St. Adalbert; 7. *Locus S. Gothardi*, with the Church of St. Gothard, the parish church for the left-bank city up to 1262; 8. St. Martin's Church; 9. Marketplace, laid out in 1253.

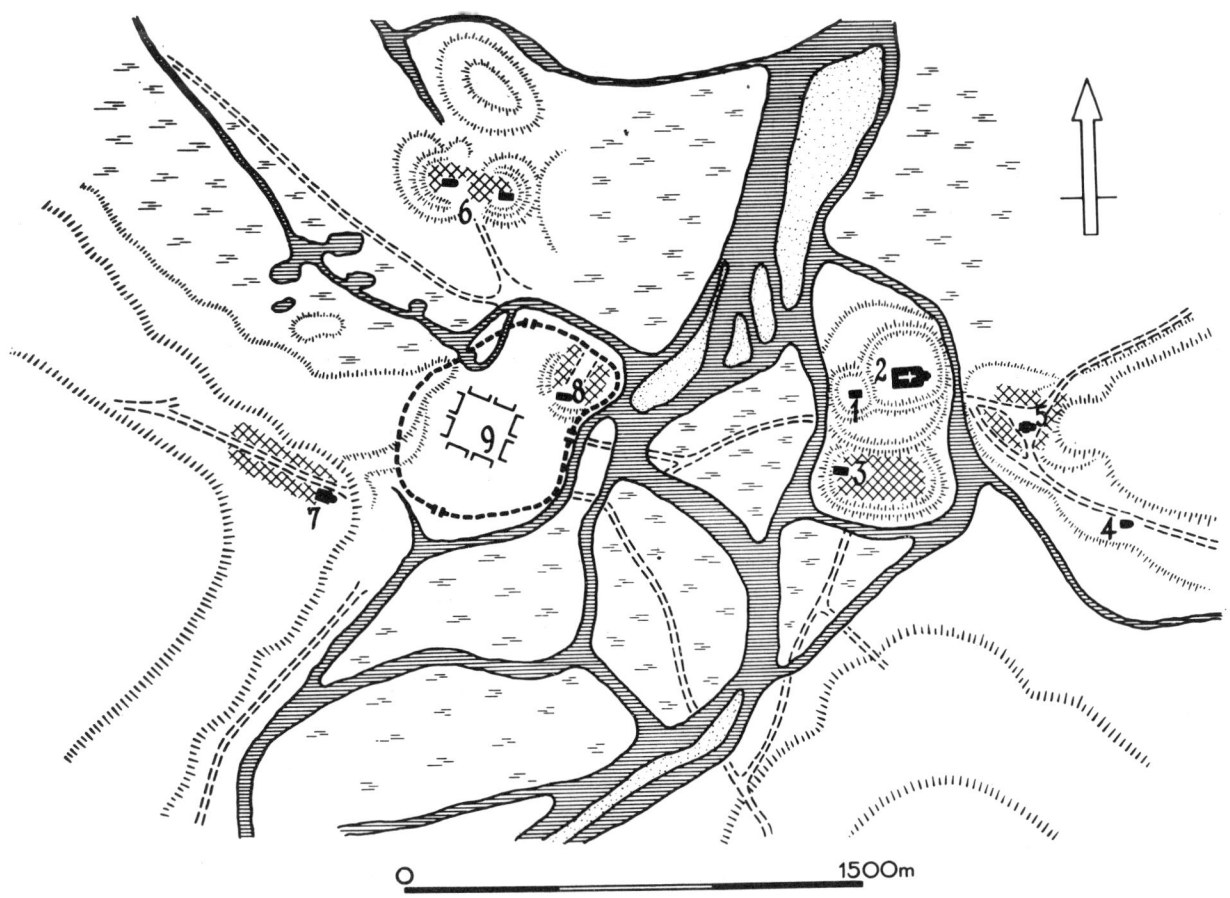

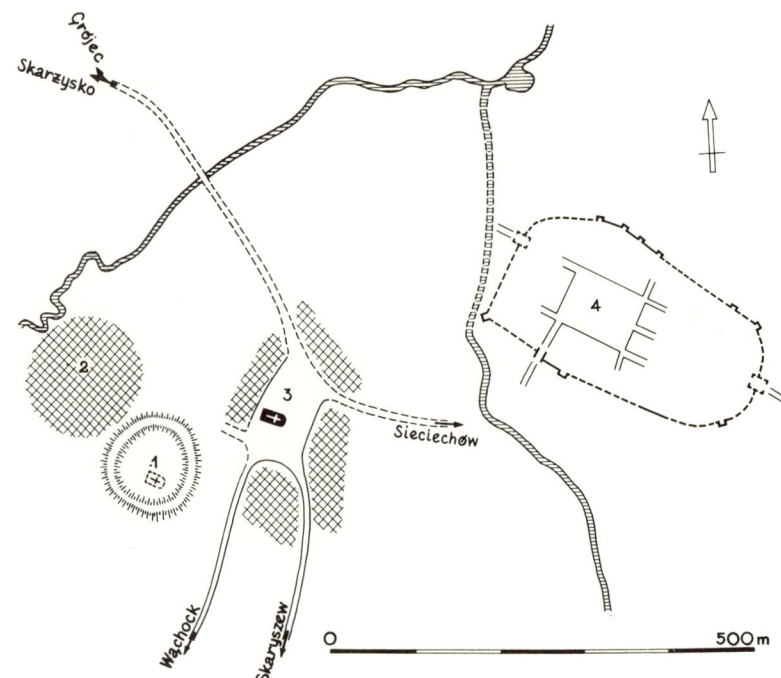

9. Plan of the city of Radom in the early Middle Ages. Reconstruction by the author after a plan of 1821. 1. *Gród* with St. Peter's Church; 2. *Suburbium*; 3. Market settlement with St. Wenceslas' Church (1214); 4. City founded by Casimir the Great (c. 1360).

Smaller settlements showed a remarkable regularity of layout. They were mostly made up of three component parts: the *gród,* the *suburbium,* and the market, all evolving between the 10th and 13th centuries. Radom (Fig. 9), Sieradz, Łęczyca, Sochaczew, and Sandomierz are but a few of the numerous examples of this type of settlement. Up to the beginning of the 13th century, buildings within these early urban settlements were constructed exclusively of wood, although there is reason to suppose that in the main centers in the south, in places like Cracow and Wrocław, there may have been some stone houses similar to those discovered in Prague. In the *grody,* the royal residences, there existed in that period stone Romanesque *palatia,* usually connected with the *gród* churches. The Romanesque cathedrals erected in the 11th and 12th centuries at Poznań, Gniezno, Cracow, and Płock were remarkable for their size and fine architectural forms. The same may be said of monasteries, particularly those of the Cistercians, Dominicans, and Premonstratensians (Fig. 10). By this time, numerous Romanesque churches existed in the seats of castellanies and in the market settlements. Their architecture shows a strong cultural link with Western Europe. Relics of sculpture and applied arts—for example, the bronze door of Gniezno Cathedral—testify to a high standard of artistic craftsmanship, while the coins found in the course of archeological excavations point to the existence of trade relations with the rest of Europe and the Near East.

10. The Benedictine collegiate church of St. Andrew at Cracow (built after 1086).

CHAPTER 5

*Evolution
of Cities
in the High
and Late
Middle Ages*

THE MIDDLE AGES were a period of fundamental importance not only for the development of urban settlements on Polish territory but also for the shaping of their spatial structure. The layout of medieval cities served for a long time—almost to the end of the 18th century—as a model for the foundation of new cities, subject only to certain modifications resulting from new social and economic conditions and changing aesthetic standards. The medieval core, created as a new foundation or resulting from a redevelopment of already existing settlements, may be detected, even today, in the physical structure of the central districts of most Polish cities.

The second half of the 12th and the first half of the 13th century was for Poland an important period of social and economic changes, influenced, no doubt, by similar developments in Western Europe. Technological progress in agriculture and the handicrafts, population growth and migrations, and the emergence of an economy based on the exchange of money and commodities contributed to an increase of the economic importance of the markets, which underwent a gradual social and physical evolution. During the feudal division of Poland into a number of petty principalities these phenomena could be observed especially in Silesia, which at the time played a leading role both economically and politically.

Sources dating from the second half of the 12th century mention that "guests," *hospites,* came to reside in the market settlements of Silesia. Recruited from among the merchants coming from the West and the autochtonic population, these people obtained certain privileges from the Silesian princes, including perhaps the allocation of definite areas in which to settle. Two documents relating to the town of Trzebnica refer to such a process: the first (1203) concerns the re-establishment of a market at Trzebnica by Prince Henry the Bearded; the second (1204) mentions 17 *hospites* by name as having settled in this locality. A recent metrological investigation of the plan of Trzebnica (Fig. 11) suggests that they obtained 17 plots, grouped around a square marketplace. The derivation of this layout would be the earliest instance of surveying connected with the foundation of a city.

In the light of recent research it may be assumed that an intermediate form between the early medieval market settlement and the medieval city was represented by the so-called new markets, *novum forum,* founded in Silesia in the first half of the 13th century. Charters establishing the "new markets" simultaneously transferred existing market settlements to new sites and granted their inhabitants city rights, modeled on those of Magdeburg. The *Nowy Targ* (New Market) in Wrocław, transferred before 1214 from near St. Vincent's Monastery at Ołbin, and the *novum forum* at Środa Śląska (1211?) were presumably settlements (Fig. 12) of this new type. The foundation of "new markets" was the beginning of a large-scale reorganization of the economic and physical structure of the country and was referred to as *melioratio terrae nostrae.* This great campaign of internal colonization, which gradually extended over all the provinces of Poland, involved the local population and foreigners of various origin such as Flemings and Germans.

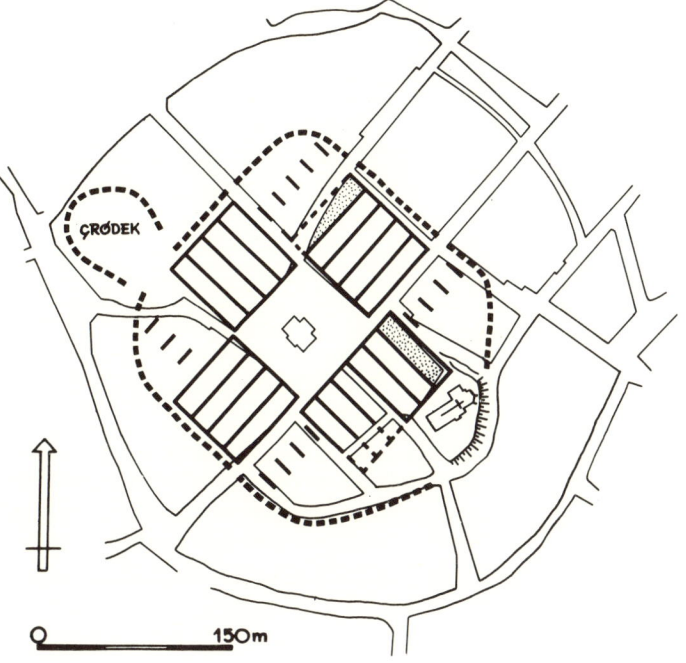

11. Plan of the reconstructed city of Trzebnica with 60-foot-wide plots. The 17 plots fronting the marketplace (not counting the dotted plots) correspond to the number of *hospites* mentioned by name as settlers in a document dating from 1204.

12. Layout of the medieval city of Środa Śląska (founded in 1211?), based on a plan of 1860. 1. Castle; 2. Parish church of St. Andrew; 3. Town hall; 4. Franciscan church and monastery.

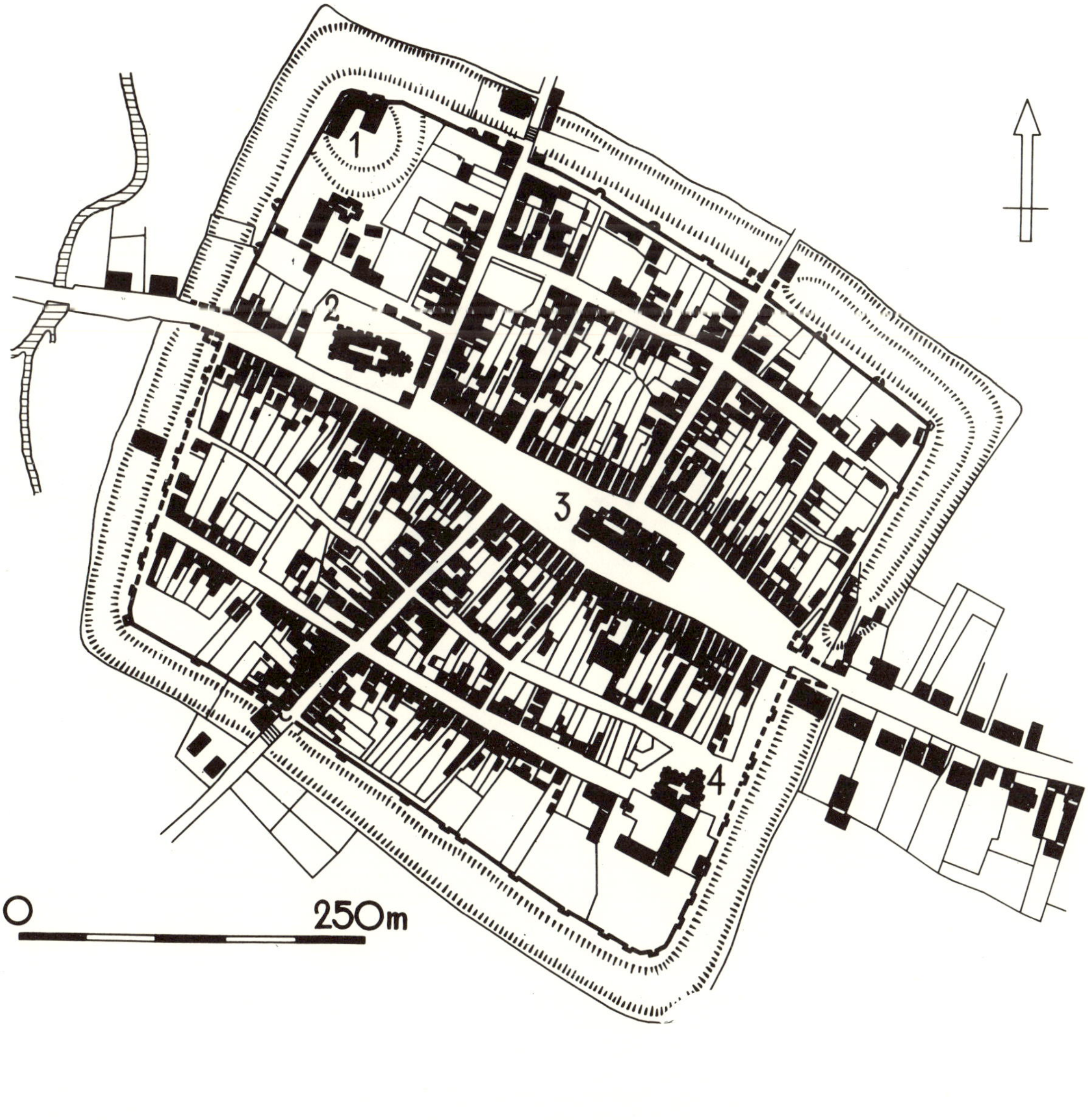

The Tartar invasion which devastated Silesia and Little Poland in 1241 gave an immediate impulse to the intensification of settlement, including the reshaping of the economic structure of the countryside and the foundation of cities according to the new economic and social principles developed in Western Europe. The foundation of cities involved the granting of rights similar to those enjoyed by Magdeburg, the *ius municipale magdeburgense,* later called German law, *ius teutonicum.* However, the granting of city rights was but one element in the foundation charters of new cities. City rights determined the legal status of the city, partly exempted its population from the power and jurisdiction of the king's or prince's magistrates, and established a self-governing administrative and juridical unit headed by a bailiff. A number of West-European historians maintain that the internal colonization of Poland in the 13th and 14th centuries was carried out by Germans and that no settlements of an urban character had existed there before. This theory is untenable in the light of recent research into the origins of cities which demonstrated that the development of cities in Poland involved primarily the native population and followed a course analogous to the somewhat earlier processes of city formation in Western Europe.

The foundation charter regulated, in the first place, all economic matters involved in the founding and functioning of the city. As a rule it determined, among other things, the areas allotted to the city, comprising, in addition to building plots and fields, several villages. (For instance, Poznań had as many as 17 villages.) Further, it defined commercial privileges, that is, exemption from tariffs and the right to establish market facilities such as butchers' and other stalls, as well as the city's obligation to its feudal lord. An essential part of the charter, constituting, in a way, a contract between the monarch or private landowner and the "developer" who actually laid out the city, was the endowment of the bailiff, an office generally held by the original "developer" and his descendants. This endowment comprised land—in Cracow it was 30 łan[1] of rent-free farmland—the right to fell timber and build mills free of charge, a share in the revenue coming from rents or taxes levied on traders' stalls, fines, and sometimes even total exemptions from tariffs. The judicature within the city also was the privilege of the bailiff. Finally, the foundation charter determined revenues to the king or prince from the lease of plots, stalls, and markets. These revenues gave an important stimulus to the foundation of cities.

Some foundation charters mention rents paid by burghers for plots allotted to them, as in Cracow, Rypin, and Tuchola; sometimes they even determine the size of the building plots, gardens, and fields. Such detailed records prove that colonization was accompanied by a delimitation and survey of urban areas. There are grounds to suppose that the notion of "plot" was unknown in the early pre-13th century period

---

1. łan—a land measure used in Poland up to the beginning of the 19th century. 1 łan equals 30 morgas; 1 morga equals 30 square rods; 1 rod equals 15 feet. As the size of the foot varied in different regions and at different periods from 0.295 to 0.314 meters, the size of the łan ranged accordingly from 17.64 hectares or 43.6 acres, to 19.89 hectares, or 49.1 acres.

and that plots first appeared in the "new markets." Under the foundation charter every settler in the medieval city obtained a certain amount of land in emphyteutic tenure on which he paid an annual rent. It is known from documents that in the first years all rents were equal, the social status of all settlers probably being the same. It may therefore be assumed that the plots, as originally delimited, were all of similar size. Metrological analysis of numerous plans of Silesian towns of the 13th century made it possible to establish that the plots were at first rather large, measuring 60 by 120 feet (Ujazd, Brzeg) or 60 by 240 feet (Nysa, Wrocław, Legnica), and somewhat later, 50 by 150 feet (Jawor, Świdnica, Kluczbork). When the city grew and the population increased, the plots were subdivided into halves and quarters (Figs. 13, 14). Judging from the remains of Gothic buildings, erected on already narrow plots, these subdivisions may often have been made soon after the foundation.

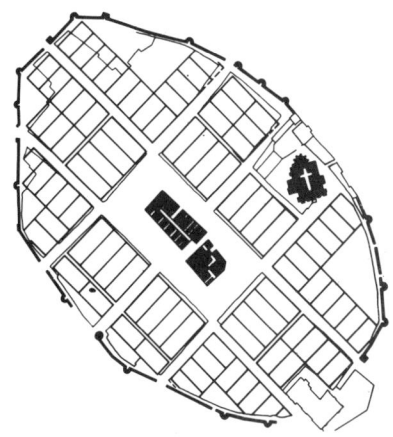

13. Reconstruction of the original plots at Paczków. They probably measured 60 by 130 feet, in the blocks adjoining the marketplace, and 60 by 120 feet in the blocks along the streets.

14. Airview of Paczków, with the Church of St. John (second half of the 14th century) and the town hall in the center of the square.

Before 1250 a type of city layout evolved in Silesia and Bohemia that was to be common to the whole area between the Odra River and the eastern boundary, reaching southward as far as the Danube. Credit for this should be largely given to the Silesian Prince, Henry the Bearded (1201–1238), whose power extended after 1231 over Silesia, Great Poland, and Little Poland. He was the founder of the first Silesian cities—of which Wrocław was probably one—and promoted the internal colonization of the country.

The cities founded in the 13th and 14th centuries had a characteristic spatial pattern and a uniform functional structure. The number of settlers was determined by the number of plots which were grouped in regular, rectangular blocks, each composed of four, six, eight, or more plots, surrounding a square or rectangular marketplace situated more or less in the center of the city. The number of plots varied considerably, ranging from forty to sixty to over one hundred in the largest cities. The central marketplace also covered the area of a building block originally reserved for commercial buildings like the cloth hall and stalls. Later it was also used for buildings connected with the municipal administration, that is, for the town hall, the weigh-house, the pillory, and other structures. The site chosen for the parish church and graveyard was usually not far from the market square, sometimes occupying one of the corner blocks adjoining it. As a rule, sites for a hospital and baths, usually on the fringe of the city, were chosen when the urban area was first delimited and surveyed. Ideal city patterns at that time were rectangular or square. Occasionally, especially during later periods, the street pattern assumed the form of a cross inscribed in a square, the building blocks allotted to settlers constituting the arms of the cross, while the areas between them and the periphery of the city may have originally served as gardens. Soon, however, monasteries, castles, or Jewish quarters, as in Kalisz and Łęczyca, were established in these outlying districts. The city had clearly defined boundaries, surrounded at first presumably by palisades, later by brick or stone walls. Gates in the walls were usually placed on the axis of the streets whose course was a prolongation of the sides of the market square. The regularity of the city layout depended largely on the topography of the site and, what is particularly important, on the property structure and emerging development. Many deformations of "ideal" town patterns resulted from unavoidable adaptations to existing buildings, roads, or property divisions. Documentary evidence exists that land was sometimes pooled or exchanged, as in Poznań, in order to secure areas necessary to found a city. In this connection it should be noted that it was relatively easy to shift a city to a new, undeveloped site, sometimes several miles from the original settlement, as buildings in most of the "proto-urban" settlements in Poland were timber structures, except the churches and a few *palatia*. This was the case in Rawa Mazowiecka and Łęczyca. In view of this fact, the layout of medieval cities in Poland showed a high degree of regularity seldom observed in those countries where development of a more durable nature existed prior to medieval city foundations.

As early as the first half of the 13th century, Henry the Bearded founded numerous cities, including Złotoryja (1211), Wrocław—the "New Market" in 1211 and the city adjacent to the present-day Market

Square in 1232—Środa Śląska (1211?), Lwówek (1217), Nysa (before 1223?), Ujazd (1223), Legnica (1241?), Strzegom (1242), Świdnica (1241 to 1249), and Brzeg (1250).

The largest of the new cities were those performing the function of capitals, for instance, Legnica and Wrocław. For many years the founding of Wrocław has been the subject of discussion among historians. It is now supposed to have been founded in two phases. The settlement around the square still bears the name of "New Market" and was probably founded and laid out about 1211, on the left bank of the Odra, presumably near a ford and a stronghold on the same side of the river. The *gród*, the *suburbium*, and the cathedral were situated opposite, on the islands of Ostrów Tumski and Piasek. Somewhat later, though perhaps still in the lifetime of Henry the Bearded, another part of the city adjoining the Great Market Square of today was founded (1232?). The city was destroyed during the Tartar invasion of 1241 and founded anew in 1261. This second foundation was accompanied by a final improvement of the layout and the boundaries of the entire city. Subsequently it was surrounded by walls and a moat. The layout of Wrocław, completed by the end of the 13th century, differed from that of smaller Silesian towns. The city, of considerable size, including some 40 building blocks whose dimensions were multiples of squares measuring 60 by 60 ells, each block comprising 4 to 10 plots, had two large marketplaces: the Great Market Square and the New Market. The layout of Wrocław proves that its founders were experienced in the art of surveying (Fig. 15).

15. Attempted reconstruction of the medieval layout of Wrocław. On the islands in the Odra, the oldest part of the city with the cathedral and *gród* (the latter not indicated on the plan). Within the inner walls, the medieval city, its layout based on an 8-rod module, and the so-called New Market with a smaller module. The inner line of the walls dates from 1260–1263. After an extension of the urban area, the city was surrounded by new fortifications in the 14th century and, later, by a rampart with rondelles (early 16th century). 1. St. John's Cathedral; 2–5, 7, 9–12, 14, 16. Churches; 6. Ducal castle; 8, 15. Arsenals; 17. Built-up areas after B. Weyner's plan of 1562; 18. Original pattern of plots; 19. Walls in 1562 (no longer existing); 20. Walls and ramparts indicated on the plan of 1562.

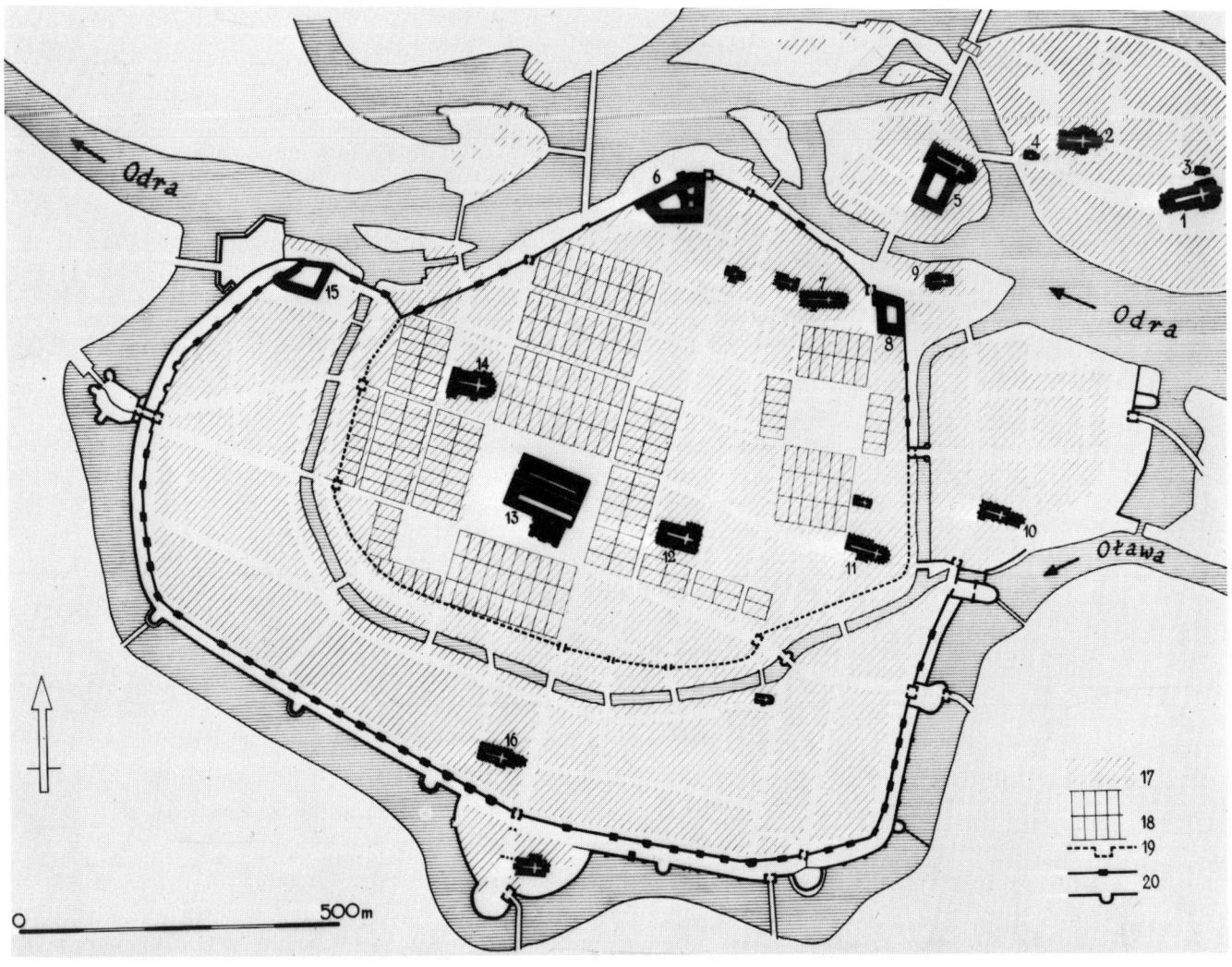

16. View of the city of Poznań, founded in 1253. The town has a regular street pattern and is surrounded by walls. On the left, the Ostrów Tumski Island with the cathedral, site of the early medieval *gród*. Engraving from Braun and Hogenberg. *Civitates Orbis Terrarum*, Cologne, 1618.

In Great and Little Poland the process of founding cities began later than in Silesia. The capitals of both provinces date from the middle of the 13th century (Poznań founded in 1253 and Cracow in 1257). Their plans testify to a final consolidation of the physical structure of medieval cities. They are remarkable for their regularity, and the layouts show a close affinity with those of Silesia. Both cities have regular, square building blocks, although they are based on slightly different modules, resulting perhaps from the fact that their respective marketplaces differed in size. In Poznań the market square was 459.2 feet by 459.2 feet, and in Cracow 656 by 656 feet. As a result of this difference, the blocks adjoining the market squares were also of different sizes. In each city twelve streets issued from the market square, two from each corner and one from the center of each side. Along these streets square blocks, similar to those adjacent to the market, were laid out. Some minor irregularities in the layout of Poznań were due to the settlement of St. Gothard, near the Dominican monastery, which existed before the foundation of the city (Fig. 16).

The 13th-century redevelopment of Cracow was carried out along lines similar to those followed in Poznań and Wrocław. Before its foundation in 1257 more than 10 different settlements existed on the site. The largest was a market settlement called Okół, situated on the road which today connects Wawel with the Main Market Square, and the *gród* with the *suburbium* on Wawel Hill. Many churches existed in these settlements, whose population probably reached several thousand. Romanesque churches or their remains are proof that other settlements were situated on Skałka Hill, near the present Main Market Square, and in Zwierzyniec near the church of the Holy Ghost. Recent investigations established that the present Church of the Virgin Mary in the Main Market Square had been under construction long before the actual founding of the city. The inclusion of some of the settlements within the boundaries of the new city, as fixed in 1257, caused some irregularities in the otherwise regular pattern, for example, Grodzka Street, a road connecting the Wawel with Okół and the settlements lying farther north, Gródek in the western part of the city, and the Hospital of the

Holy Ghost in its northeastern angle (Fig. 17). Immediately after the granting of the foundation charter, or possibly before then, the Main Market Square was laid out along with some twenty-five building blocks measuring 281.4 by 281.4 feet each. Every block was composed of eight plots measuring 36 by 72 ells. These "whole" plots, called *curia* or *gantcze Hof* in documents, were divided into halves in the 13th century. The huge market square and the large number of blocks prove how much importance was attached to the site at the time of the founding of the city.

In the 13th century many cities were founded: 31 in Silesia and 38 in Great Poland. In Little Poland this process was somewhat slower: here Bochnia was founded in 1253, Stary Sącz after 1270, Sandomierz in 1286, and Nowy Sącz in 1292.

In Mazovia, constituting in the 13th century a separate principality often antagonistic toward the rest of Poland, the foundation of cities

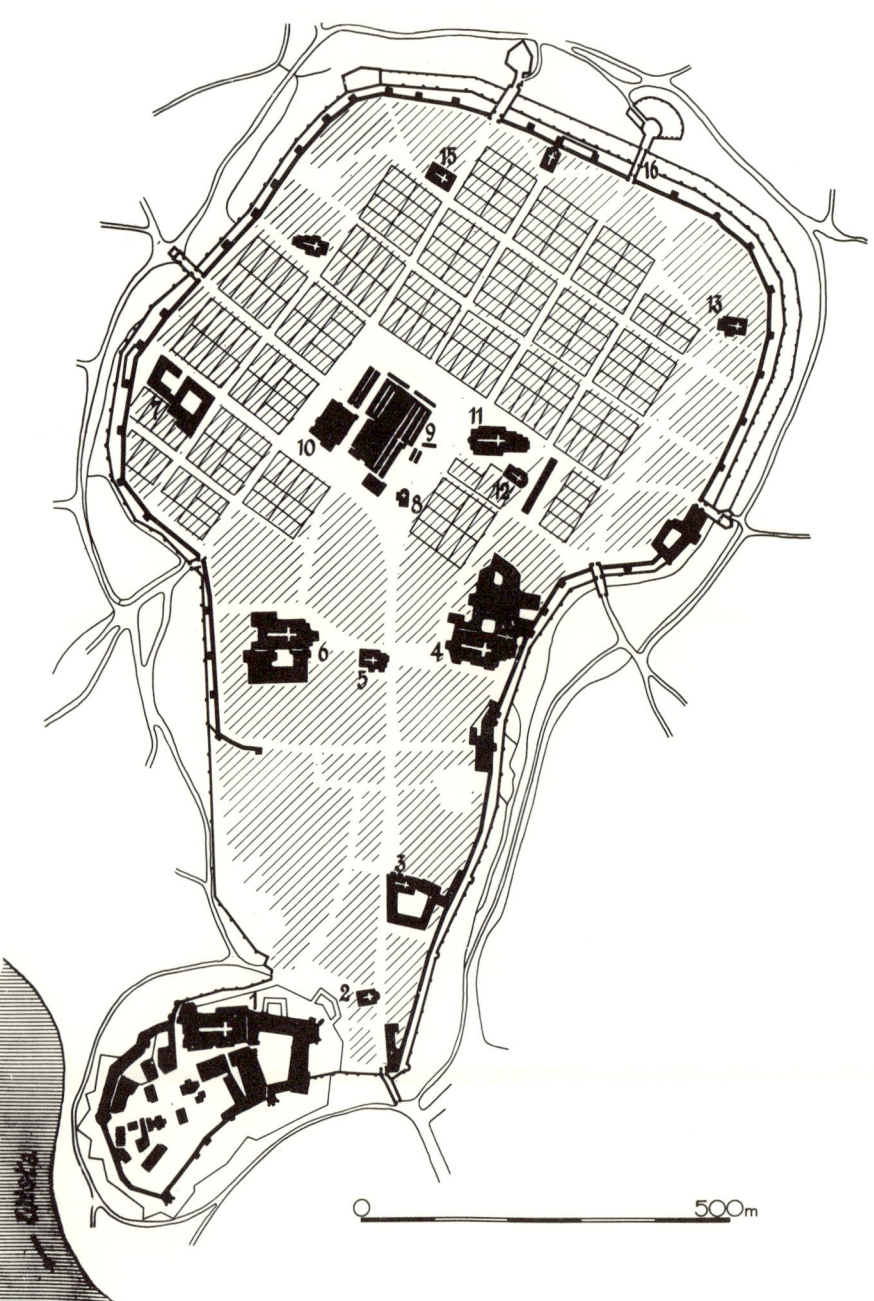

17. Plan of the medieval city of Cracow (founded in 1257) surrounded by walls, with the reconstructed original subdivision of blocks into plots, *curiae*, 36 by 76 ells. An early medieval market and the "Okół" settlement were located between the market square and the castle. 1. Wavel Hill with castle and cathedral; 2–6, 8, 11–15. Churches; 7. Collegium Maius (late 15th century); 9. Drapers' Hall and stalls (14th century, rebuilt in the 16th century); 10. Town Hall (14th century); 16. St. Florian's Gate (about 1300) and barbican (1498–1500).

advanced at a much slower pace. In that period only four cities are known to have been granted urban charters: Płock in 1257, Pułtusk in 1257, Łowicz about 1298, and Warsaw before 1300. These four were relatively small and had regular plans, with rectangular or square marketplaces. Of these cities, Warsaw soon grew in importance, outdistancing the older centers of Płock and Pułtusk, probably on account of its central position in relation to the country as a whole. Its plan is, in a sense, typical of early Mazovian city foundations (Fig. 18).

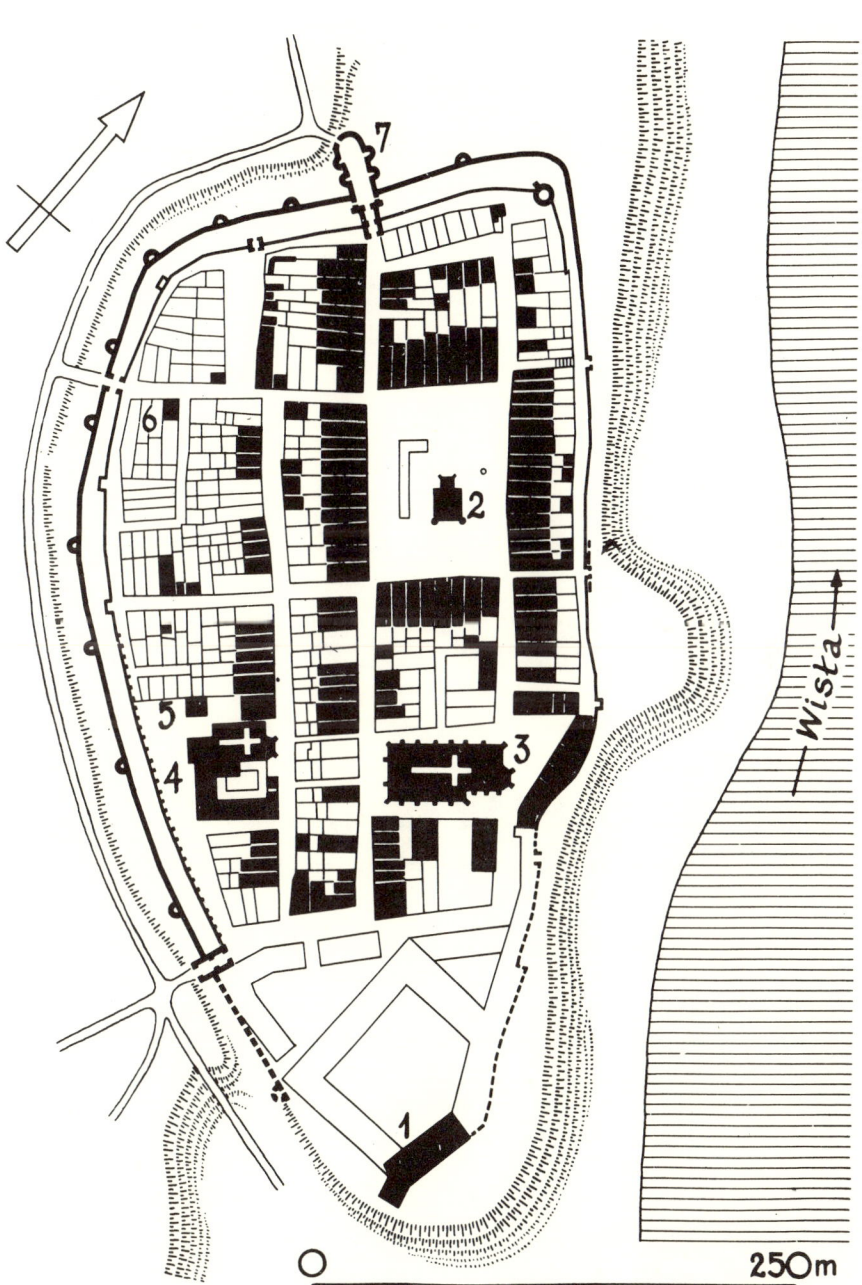

18. Reconstruction of a plan of Warsaw, about 1600. 1. Residential part of the Gothic castle; 2. Town Hall; 3. Collegiate Church of St. John; 4. Augustinian Church and Monastery; 5. Hospital of the Holy Ghost; 6. Synagogue; 7. Barbican leading into the New Town. Remains of Gothic buildings are marked in black.

An event exercising a decisive influence on the development of cities in Northern Poland occurred when, in 1226, Prince Konrad of Mazovia decided to call in the Teutonic Knights, offering them the Land of Chełmno as fief. This Order had been founded in Jerusalem in 1190 when a fraternity of Hospitalers was reorganized by the burghers of Lübeck and Bremen and assumed the name of Order of the Brethren of the German Hospital of St. Mary. The first "Commandery" of the Order in Europe was established in Halle in 1200. In the years 1211 to 1224 the Teutonic Knights fought pagan Mongol tribes in Hungary where, however, their services were soon dispensed with. In 1230 they came to the Land of Chełmno, with the purpose of conquering and converting the heathen Prussians and Lithuanians. They gained control over the whole of old Prussia in fifty years and, after merging with the Brethren of the Sword, created a powerful military and monastic state that extended from the Vistula to Memel in the northeast and unlawfully included in it the Polish territories lying between the Vistula and Prussia. They also seized Gdańsk in Pomerania (1308 to 1309), over which they ruled until 1466, and proceeded to colonize the conquered Prussian and Slav lands with settlers from Germany and Mazovia.

19. Plan of the city of Chełmno with the original plots. 1. Parish church of the Assumption; 2. Town Hall; 3. Franciscan church and monastery; 4. Dominican church and monastery; 5. Benedictine church and convent; 6. Hospital church of the Holy Ghost.

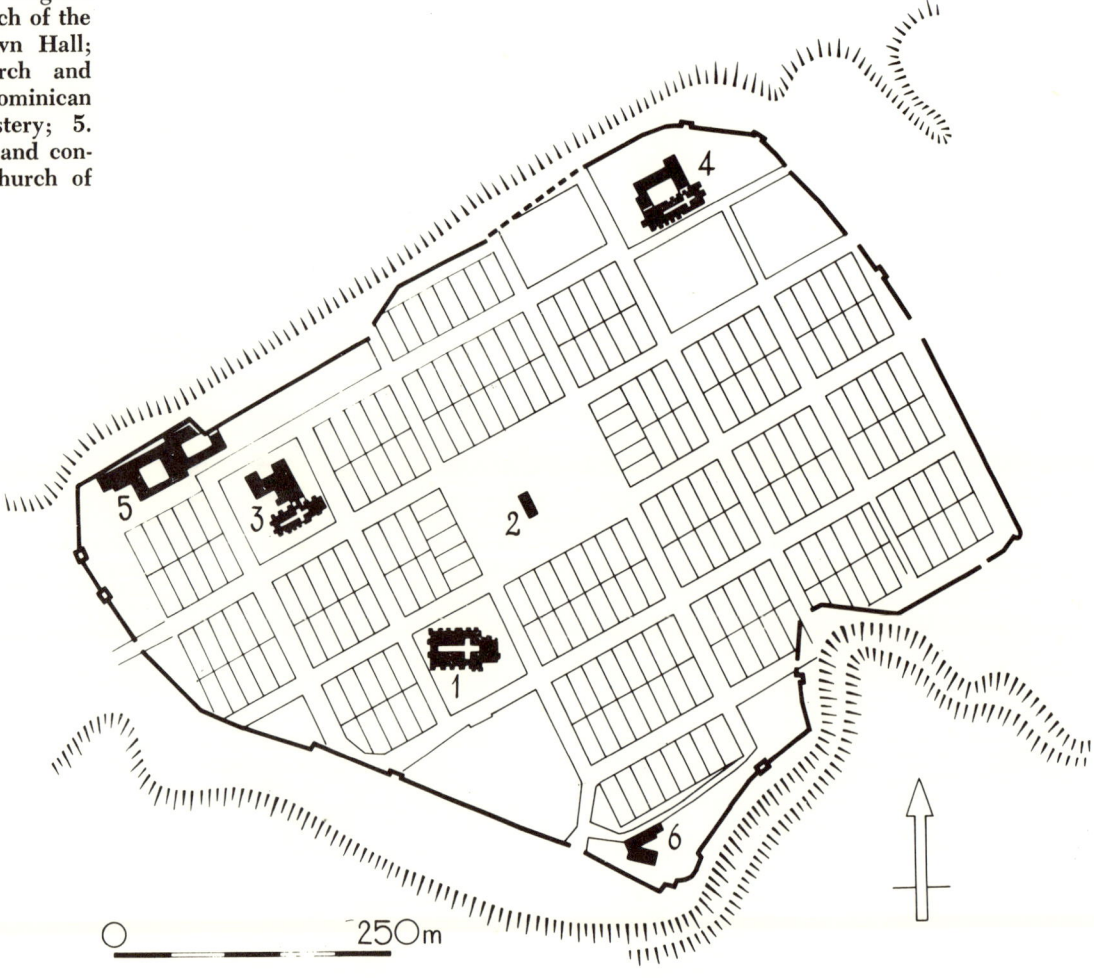

In 1233 the Teutonic Knights founded their first two cities, Chełmno (Fig. 19) and Toruń (Fig. 20), granting them charters according to the Magdeburg Law. Chełmno, intended originally as capital of the State of the Teutonic Order, is of particular interest to historians. A specific variety of the Magdeburg Law, the "Chełmno Law," *ius culmense*, evolved there and was later granted to many of the cities founded in Prussia and Mazovia in the 13th and 14th centuries. Its importance was similar to that of the Środa Law in Silesia and Great Poland.

20. View of the Old Town (1233) and the New Town (1264) of Toruń. Engraving by Matthaeus Merian from the *Topographia Electorat Brandenburgici et Ducatus Pomeraniae*, published in 1652.

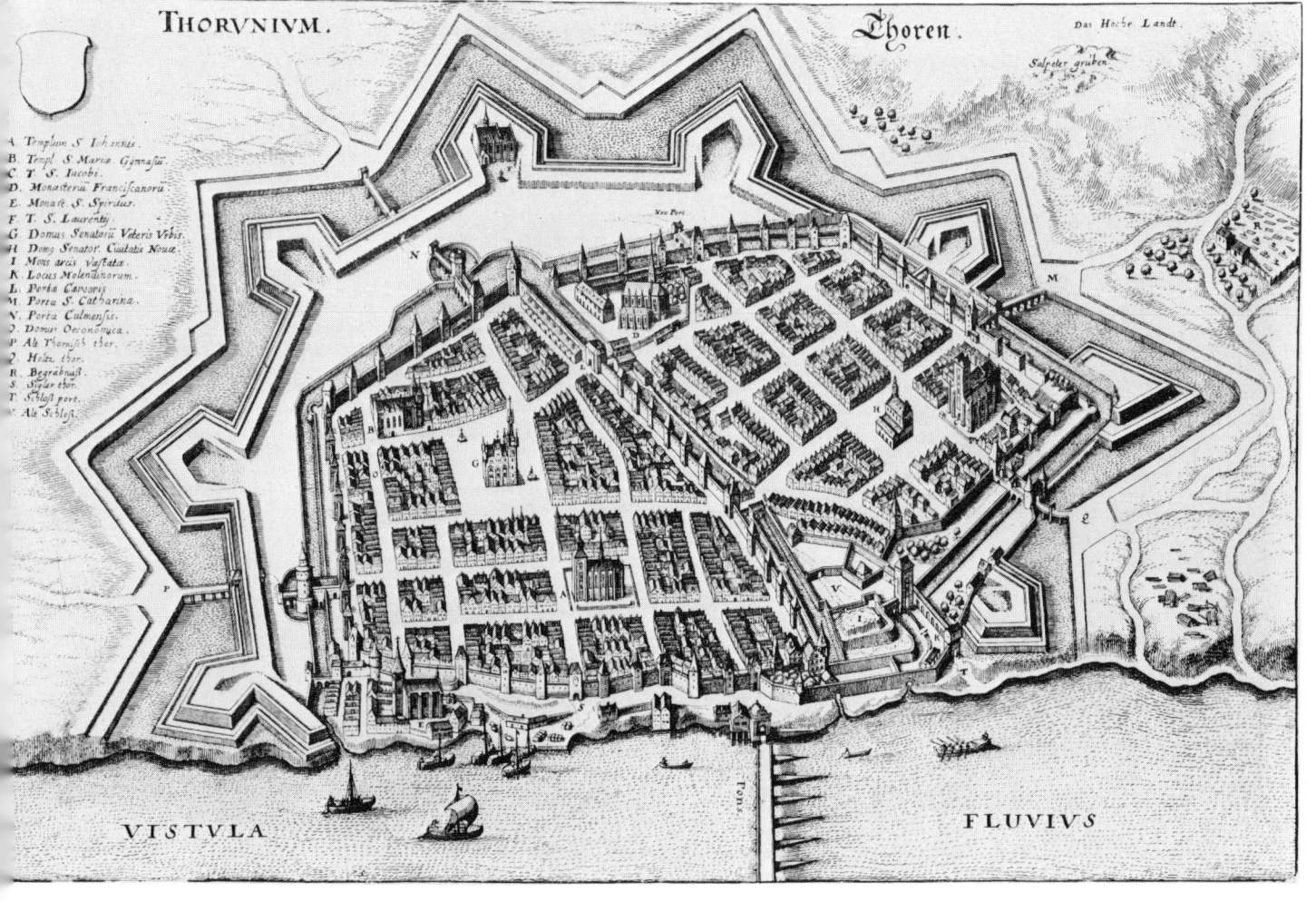

21. Plan of medieval Nidzica. Reconstruction by the author. 1. Castle of the Teutonic Knights; 2. Parish church of St. Adalbert; 3. The "Little Monastery" (late 14th century); 4. The "Little Castle"; 5. Brewery; 6. School; 7. Stalls; 8. Town Hall (built before the 16th century); 9. Bath; 10. Polish Gate; 11. German Gate; 12. Hospital.

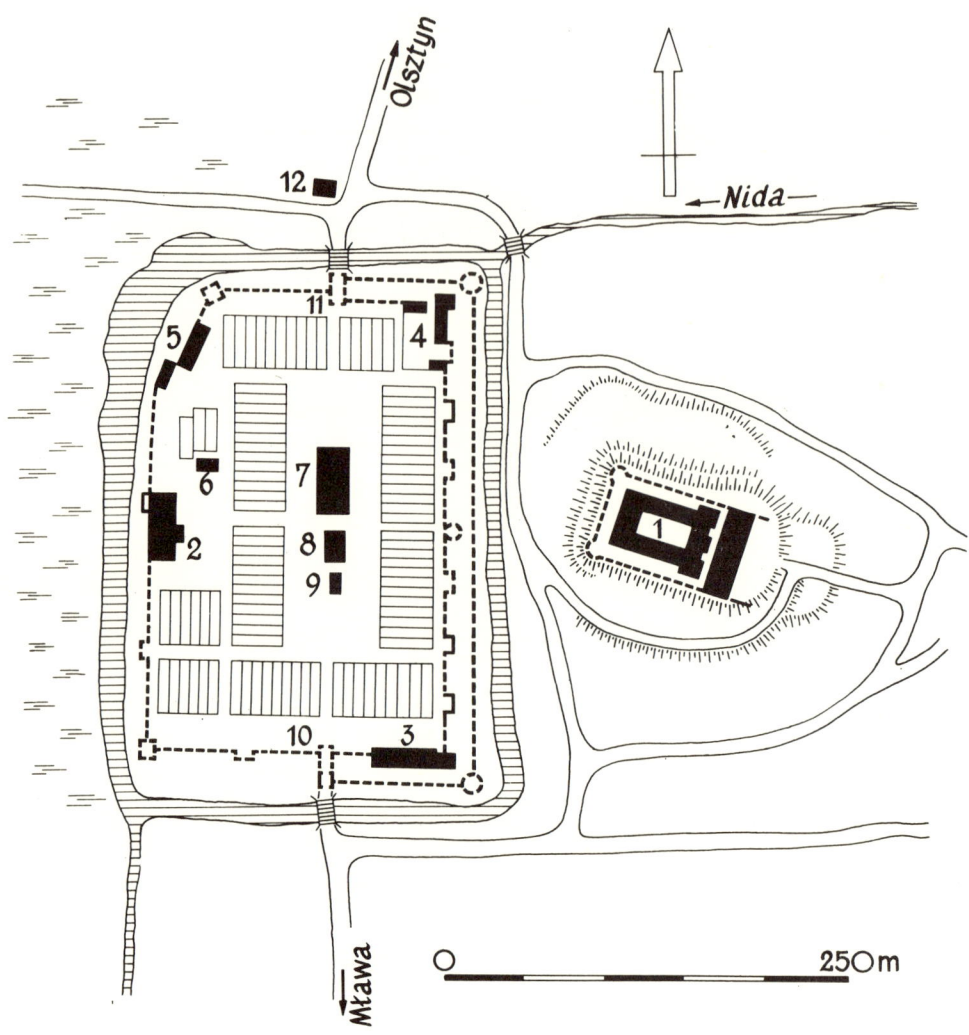

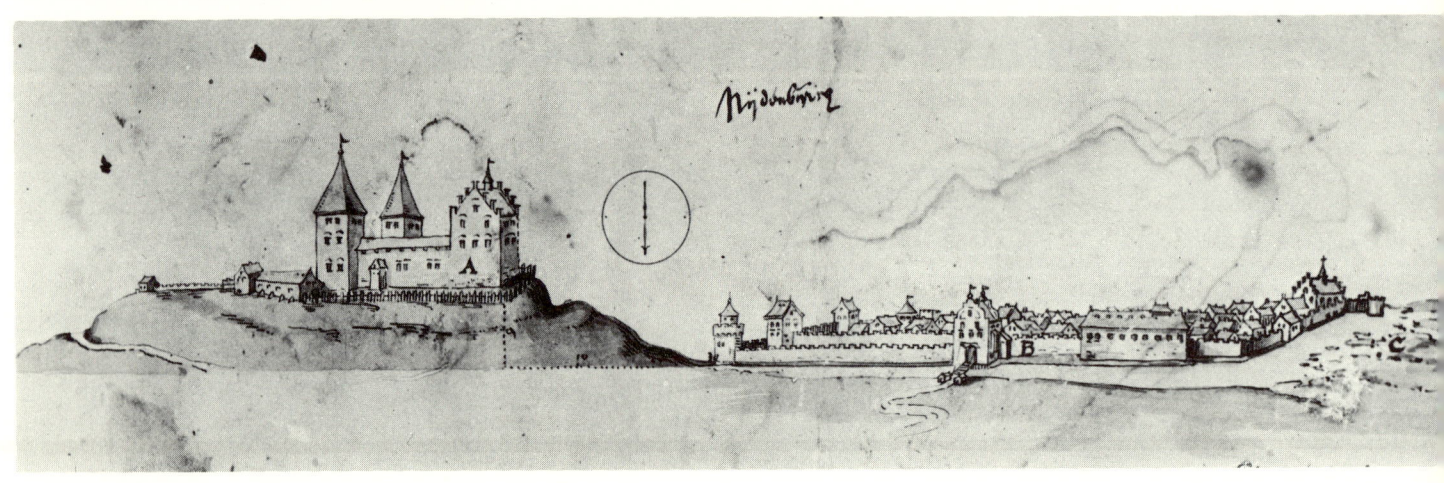

22. View of the city and castle of Nidzica from the northwest. Copy of a drawing of 1602.

Cities founded in the 13th and 14th centuries by the Teutonic Knights were remarkable for their extreme regularity, which may be explained by the fact that the conquered lands were scantily settled and the few previously existing settlements had been largely destroyed in battles. The principles governing the foundation of cities by the Teutonic Knights were much the same as those applied in Silesia and Central Poland, the only difference being that the role of the secular feudal lord in drawing profits from the new cities was here played by the Order. Powerful castles, usually erected in the immediate proximity of these cities, testified to their colonial character. The castles, besides being residences of the Commanders, were intended not only to defend the conquered lands but also to threaten the cities should they attempt to break free of the domination of the Order. That such fears were not groundless was proven by the destruction of the castle of the Teutonic Knights in Gdańsk by the burghers in 1454. The area occupied by a castle was often almost equal to that of the city, as in Gniew and Nidzica (Figs. 21, 22). In Malbork, however, which was the capital of the State of the Teutonic Order, the castle site was actually larger than that of the city!

Three basic types may be distinguished among the cities founded by the Teutonic Knights. First, there were layouts featuring a large, square marketplace, with a system of streets intersecting at right angles, as in Chełmno (1233), Gniew (1297), Nowe Miasto Lubawskie (1325) (Fig. 23), Świecie (1338), Grudziądz (1291), and Lębork (1341). These layouts resembled those of the cities of Silesia or Great and Little Poland. The second type, sometimes referred to as the "comb pattern," was characterized by a rather dense network of parallel streets perpendicular to the harbor, as in Elbląg (1237) and Gdańsk (before 1330). This pattern may have been modeled on Lübeck, which at that time kept up lively relations with the cities of Pomerania. Lübeck burghers are known to have participated actively in the foundation of Elbląg, and many Pomeranian towns obtained charters according to

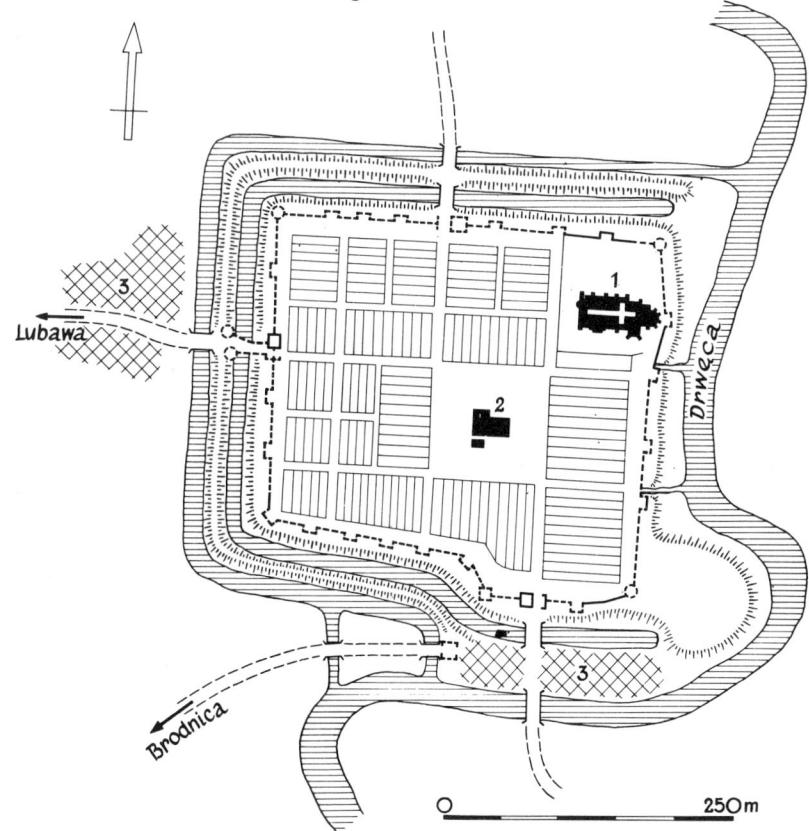

23. Plan of the medieval city of Nowe Miasto Lubawskie. Reconstruction by the author. 1. Parish church of St. Thomas; 2. Town Hall; 3. Suburbs.

Lübeck Law. Finally, the third type of layout had an elongated marketplace, sometimes resembling a wide street, as in Malbork (1276), Puck (1348), and possibly Hel (1378). This typological division is, of course, a purely formal one. Each of the newly founded cities had an individual pattern, corresponding only partly to one of the types described above. In some cases, the ideal pattern was subject to irregularities caused by the configuration of the site, as in Chełmno and Gniew, or by the need to take into account the remains of an earlier settlement, as in Gdańsk (Fig. 24) and Lębork.

The cities of the Teutonic Order, their harbor cities in particular, developed very fast and had to be expanded in the 13th century. Classic examples of such expansions are Elbląg (Fig. 25) and Toruń, where "new towns," each with a parish church, market facilities, and walls, were founded adjoining the "old towns." The buildings in the cities of the Teutonic Order were influenced by the architecture of Northwestern Europe, with its characteristic brick Gothic forms.

Western Pomeranian urbanization processes followed a course similar to that of Silesia and other Polish territories, although its princes, who belonged to the Piast dynasty, had been obliged to acknowledge German and Danish sovereignty as early as the end of the 12th century. The principles of transforming the old *grody* into medieval cities, as in Szczecin, Kamień or Wolin, were almost identical to those applied in Gdańsk, Poznań or Wrocław. Close relations with Northwestern Europe, particularly with Lübeck, were soon established, a fact that was reflected in the layout of cities as well as in the buildings erected in these towns. Many of them, developed from earlier settlements, lack the regularity of the patterns characteristic of cities in the provinces lying farther east. A good example of the layout of a medium-sized town is provided by Pyrzyce (Fig. 26), founded in 1265, its outline being almost that of a triangle, while the pattern of its blocks and plots shows many irregularities.

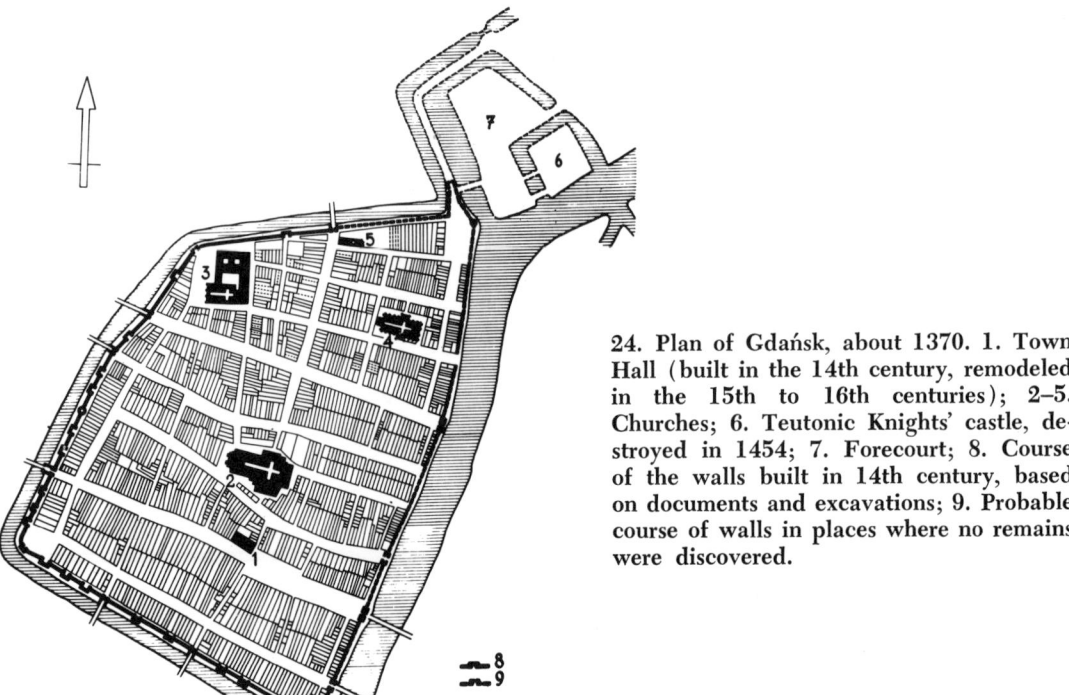

24. Plan of Gdańsk, about 1370. 1. Town Hall (built in the 14th century, remodeled in the 15th to 16th centuries); 2–5. Churches; 6. Teutonic Knights' castle, destroyed in 1454; 7. Forecourt; 8. Course of the walls built in 14th century, based on documents and excavations; 9. Probable course of walls in places where no remains were discovered.

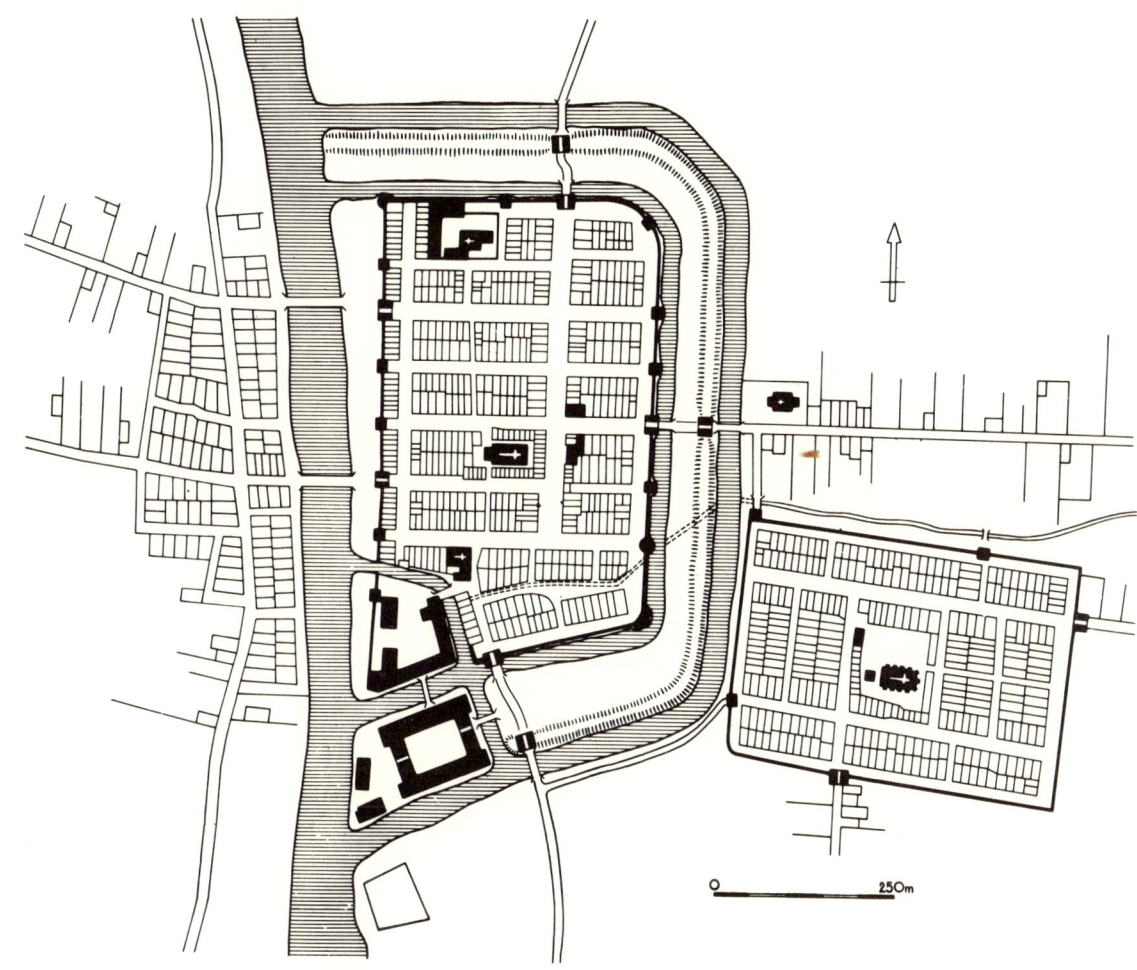

25. Reconstruction of a plan of Elbląg in the 15th century. On the river bank (left) the Old Town, founded in 1237; on the right, the New Town which obtained its first charter in 1347.

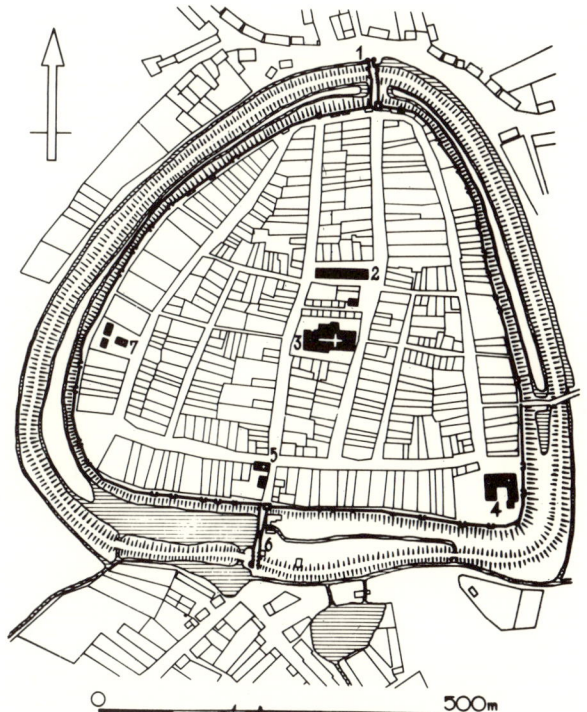

26. Plan of the city of Pyrzyce, 1723. 1. Szczecin Gate; 2. Town Hall; 3. Parish church of St. Maurice; 4. Monastery and school; 5. Church and hospital of the Holy Ghost; 6. Banie Gate; 7. Church and hospital of St. Nicholas.

The city layouts in the Land of Lubusz, which separated from Silesia in the middle of the 13th century, also differ from those in Central Poland.

Urbanization in the 13th century proceeded gradually. Only some of the existing urban settlements were redeveloped under new foundation charters. In the second half of the century, numerous old-type market settlements existed throughout Poland alongside the cities founded under German Law. Earlier settlements which adjoined the new cities gradually disappeared, although in some cases they continued for a long time, their memory surviving today in the form of toponyms, such as the frequent name of *stare miasto,* "Old Town." In general, cities were small, with one thousand or fewer inhabitants. Later, however, in the 13th century there existed a few large urban centers, such as Cracow with approximately 14,000 inhabitants or Wrocław with approximately 17,000. Other large cities of that period were Chełmno, Gdańsk, Głogów, Nysa, Szczecin, and Toruń, with populations ranging from 4,000 to 10,000.

The reunification of the Polish State and its economic and cultural prosperity under the reign of Kazimierz (Casimir) the Great (1333–1370) were accompanied by a new wave of internal colonization. At this period the wealthier knights began to found villages and towns, hoping thereby to increase their incomes. In the 13th century this activity had been the sole domain of princely rulers and ecclesiastical feudal lords, that is, of bishops and monastic orders. In the 14th century, the largest number of cities—fifty-five altogether—were founded in Great Poland, and thirty-six in Mazovia. The southern parts of Little Poland and Ruthenia, conquered by Casimir the Great, were likewise colonized. Urbanization in Silesia, which at that time passed from Poland to Bohemia and whose basic urban structure had evolved in the 13th century, was less intense.

The activity of King Casimir the Great, of whom his contemporaries wrote, with some exaggeration, that he had "found a country of wood and left a country of stone," was of particular importance for the cities of Poland. Not only did he found forty-five cities, but his policy was to encourage the development of the cities that supported him by granting them various privileges and exemptions from tariffs. Among the towns founded in this period were Kazimierz, near Cracow (1335), Nowy Targ (1336), Bydgoszcz (1346), Rzeszów (1354), Lvov (1356), Będzin (1358), Radom (1360), and Koło (1362). Casimir the Great also organized a countrywide system of defense, surrounding nearly thirty cities with walls, including Kalisz, Łęczyca, Piotrków, Płock, Sandomierz, Szydłów, and Wieluń, and erecting more than fifty fortified castles.

With the exception of Lvov and Przemyśl, most of the cities founded at that time were of medium size, usually comprising from 40 to 60 plots for settlers. Their layout was modeled on that of Silesian cities, though the town-planning experience and building activity of the Teutonic Knights may also have played a certain part, particularly as far as the castles and city fortifications were concerned. The outer line of their walls generally had the form of an elongated oval, with two or more gates. In the center was the marketplace, square or rectangular, its proportions frequently being 2:3 or 3:5, with eight streets issuing at right angles from the corners. The streets, running from the market toward the gates situated at opposite ends of the city, often met at these gates, thus giving the city core the shape of a funnel (Fig. 27). The building programs of the new cities, to a certain degree standardized, were applied not only to the size of the city but also to the public buildings. City halls, hospitals, brick parish churches, and other structures showed a pronounced similarity of form and function. Castles serving as residences for city prefects were built in many existing and new cities. They were situated either in the immediate vicinity of the city and incorporated in its defense system as in Będzin and Inowłódz,

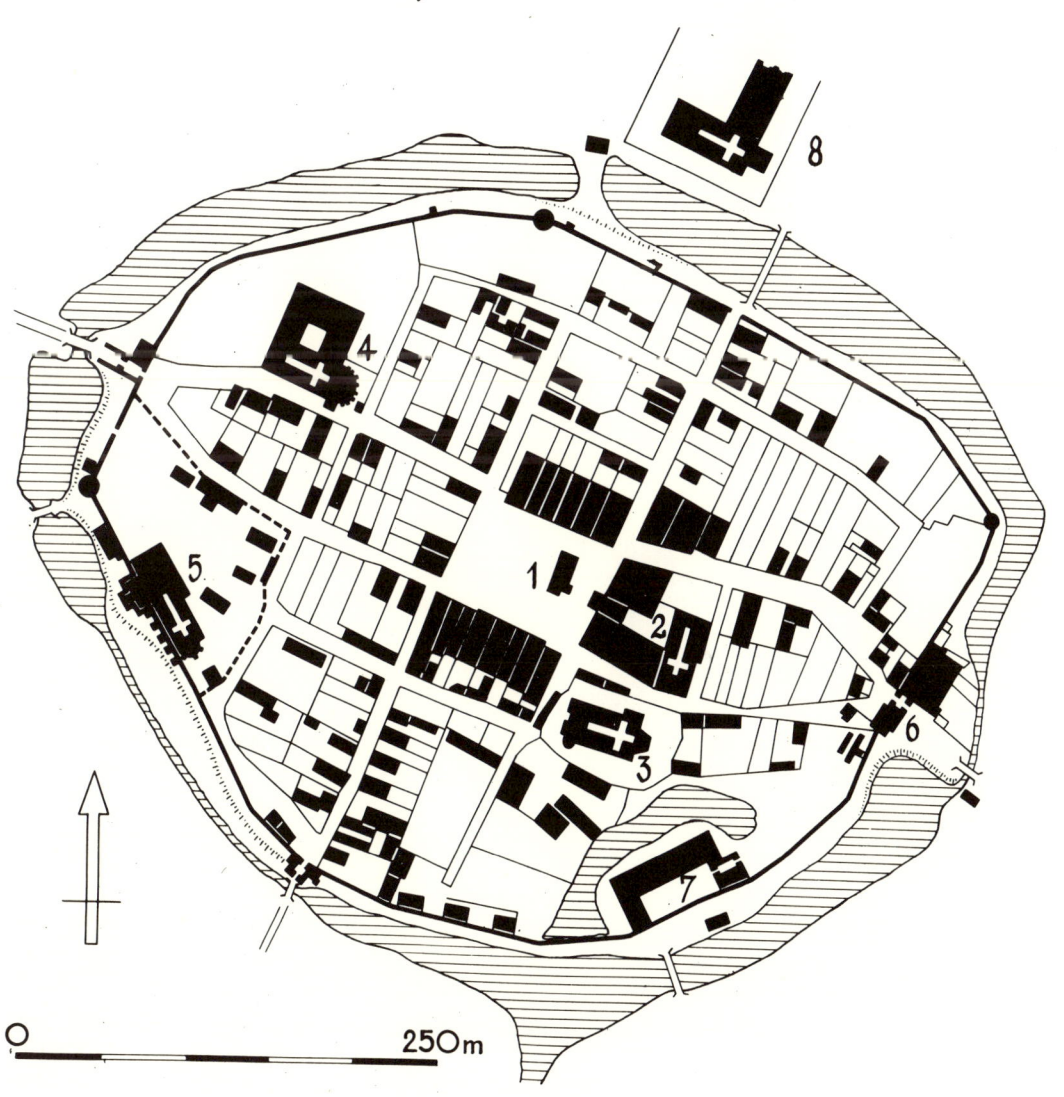

27. Plan of the city of Wieluń, 1799. 1. Town Hall; 2. St. Joseph's Church and Piarist college; 3. Parish church of the Virgin Mary; 4. Church of Corpus Christi and Augustinian Monastery; 5. St. Nicholas' Church and Bernardine (Franciscan-Observant) Convent; 6. Cracow Gate; 7. Castle; 8. Church of the Annunciation and Reformed Franciscans' Monastery.

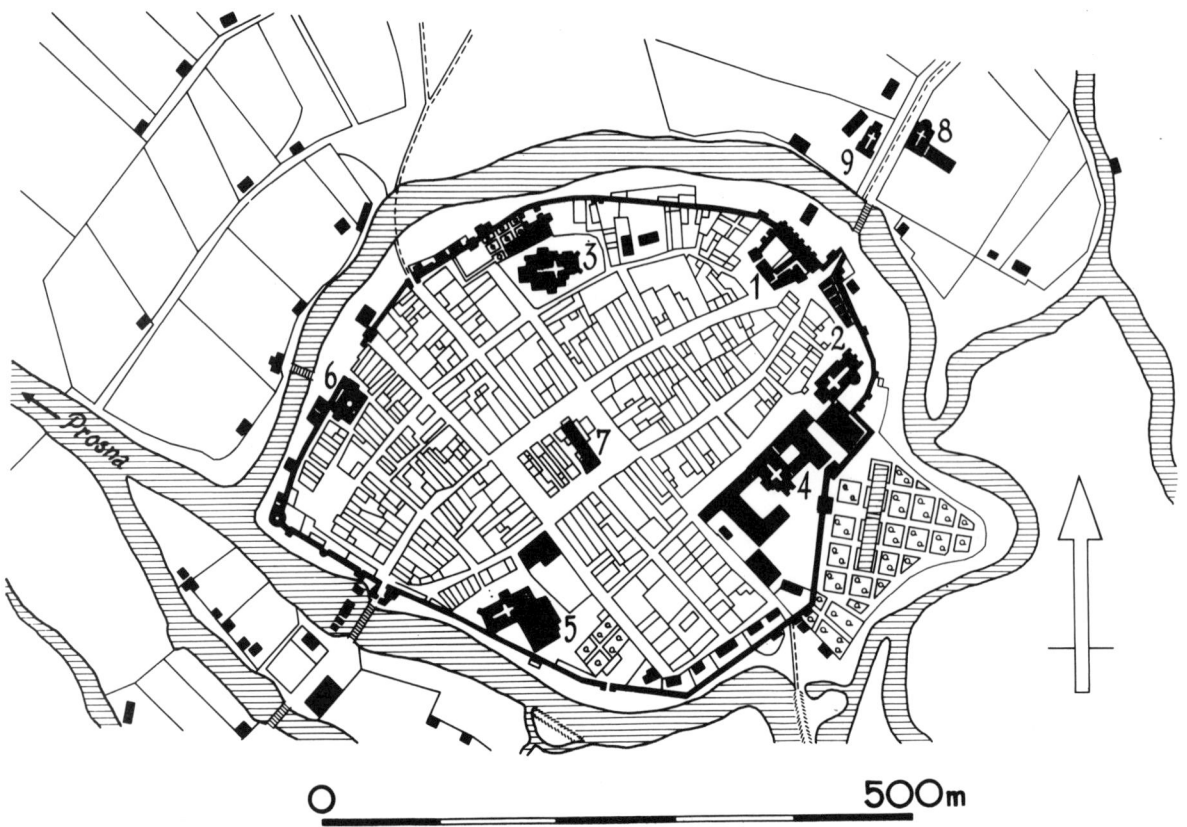

28. Plan of Kalisz in 1785. The medieval layout is almost wholly preserved. The building blocks stretching away from the marketplace were subdivided into plots for the burghers. The ecclesiastic and monastic buildings as well as the castle and the Jewish quarter are located near the periphery. 1. Castle; 2–5, 8–9. Churches; 6. Synagogue in the Jewish quarter; 7. Town Hall and stalls.

or—a particularly characteristic solution—they were built into the city walls, in one of the corners of the walled-in urban area, as in Kalisz (Fig. 28), Wieluń, Radom, and many other places. As may be seen from the detailed dimensions specified in a charter granted to Płock by Casimir the Great for the privilege of building walls, well-defined principles of defense existed at this time.

The consolidation of the power of the State and the stabilization of political conditions favored the rapid development of trade and handicrafts in cities. Artisans began to organize themselves into guilds. The number of guilds testifies to a considerable specialization: in Wrocław, for instance, as many as twenty-nine guilds existed in the early 14th century. In the same century merchant's guilds were also set up and, together with the guilds of the craftsmen, began to compete with the rich patricians for participation in the government of the city. This manifestation of growing class division among the townspeople resulted in an increasing antagonism between the lower class and the ruling patriciate.

By the end of the 13th century elective city councils, composed of six to twelve councillors headed by a burgomaster, existed in the larger cities. These councils gradually tried to restrict the power of the bailiff, and as they grew in wealth they bought out the bailiff's prerogatives, thereby strengthening urban self-government—as in Brzeg (1322), Wrocław (1326–1345), and in Kłodzko (1344)—until the bailiff became a city magistrate appointed by the council, which eventually came to be controlled by the patricians.

A considerable portion of the urban population was of Polish origin, as may be concluded from numerous names and nicknames figuring in city records. However, among the artisans and in particular among the wealthy merchants were many Germans who, in the 13th and 14th centuries, flowed in large numbers into the Polish cities. This immigration ceased toward the end of that period, giving place to a growing influx of Italians, Armenians, and Jews. The latter obtained numerous privileges to settle in cities and formed large religious communities with fine Gothic synagogues, as in Kazimierz, now forming part of Cracow.

The cities of the 14th and 15th centuries enjoyed a high standard of material and artistic culture. Handicrafts flourished, and numerous artistic monuments testify to a well-developed building industry and to the thriving condition of guild painting and sculpture. The activities of Casimir the Great must again be mentioned in this connection. He expanded relations with other European countries, promoted culture and the arts, and originated many monumental works of architecture, such as churches and monastic buildings. In 1364 he founded the first Polish university in Cracow which, after Prague, was the second university to be established in Central Europe.

The population of the old urban centers grew steadily, notwithstanding a very high mortality rate due to unsanitary conditions, epidemic diseases, fires, and other disasters. Late in the 14th and early in the 15th century, Wrocław was leading with a population of approximately 20,000; Gdańsk and Cracow presumably numbered over 15,000 each, and Poznań had about 4,000. This population growth necessitated the expansion of existing cities. New cities were built in the vicinity of old ones—for instance, Kazimierz, built close to Cracow (1335) (Fig. 29), and the New Town in Warsaw (1408). Whole urban clusters came into existence, made up of several cities, each surrounded with walls and its own municipal government and market facilities. Gdańsk is an example of such a composite settlement, which from the 14th to the 16th century was formed of the following components: the Old Town, developed before 1330 on the site of the early medieval settlement; the Main Town (Rechtstadt), founded before 1330; the New Town (Jungstadt), founded in 1380 and destroyed in 1455; the Old Suburb, fortified in the second half of the 15th century; the port, with a group of granaries on islands in the Motława River; and the castle (Fig. 30). All these component parts adjoined one another, forming a large, fortified urban complex. The expansion of Wrocław followed a different course. About 1330 a new ring of walls was built, enclosing a strip of land in the urban area between the old and the new fortifications in the west and the south. The New Town, founded in 1263 east of the New Market, was included within the new walls (Fig. 31).

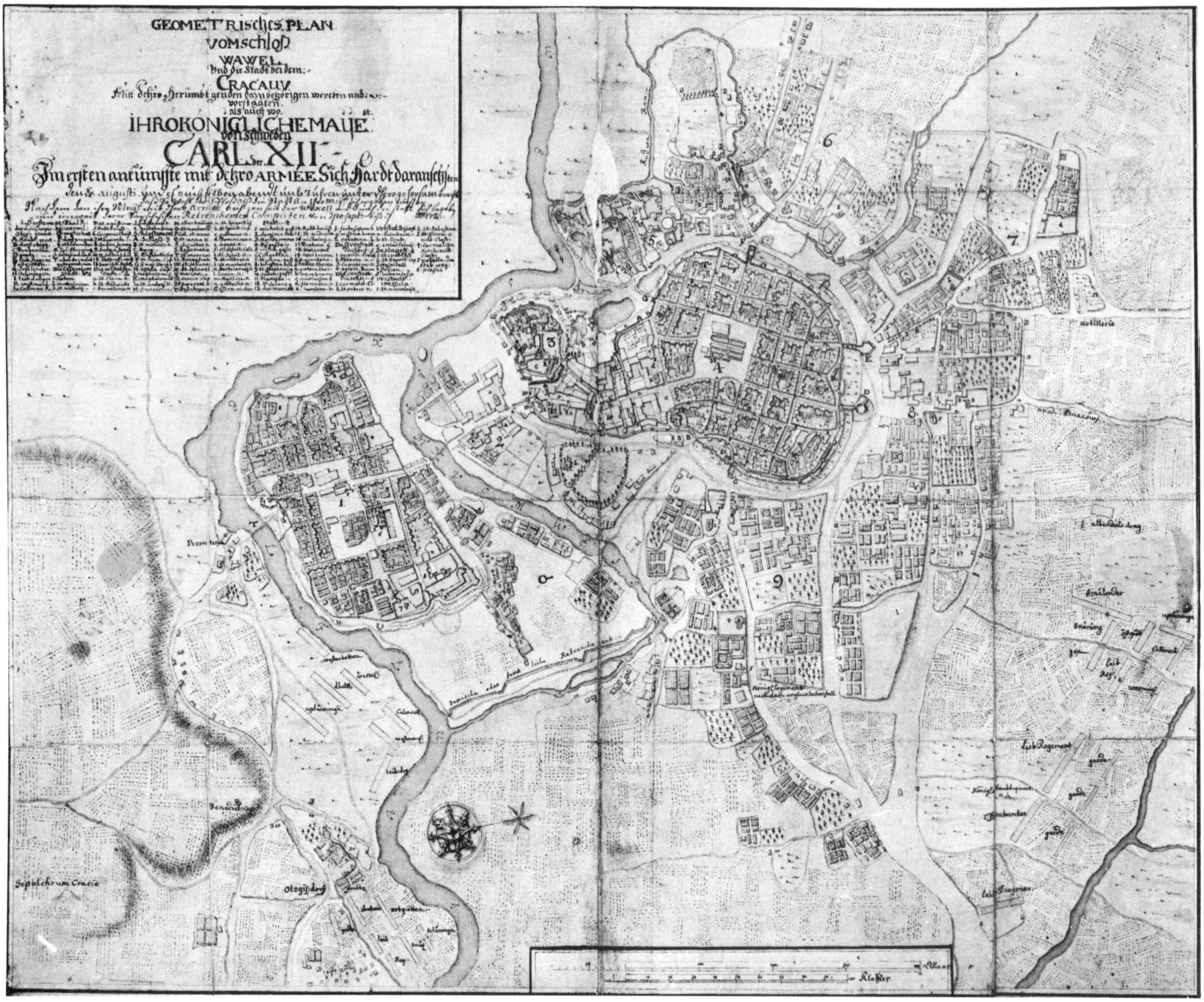

29. Plan of the city of Cracow, 1702. The clearly discernible medieval complex consists of the Royal Castle, the city of the mid-13th century, and the new town of Kazimierz founded by Casimir the Great in 1335. Original in the Kungl. Krigsarkivet, Stockholm.

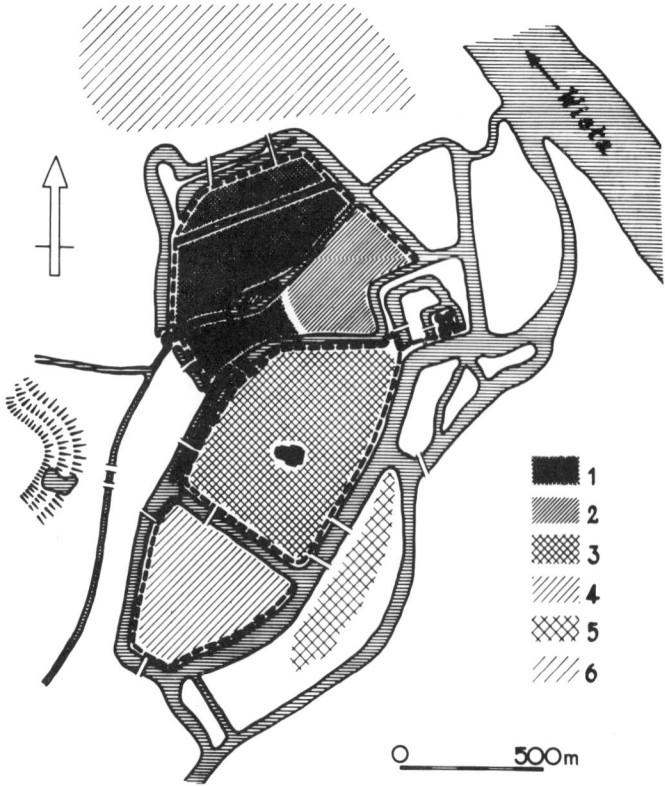

30. Cluster of medieval settlements of Gdańsk in the 15th century. Reconstruction by the author. 1. Old Town about 1330 (the early medieval *suburbium* was situated in its southern part); the Teutonic Knights' castle was subsequently built on the site of the *gród*; 2. Osiek; 3. Main Town (Rechtstadt), founded before 1330; 4. Old Suburb, fortified in the second half of the 15th century; 5. Granary Island; 6. New Town, founded in 1380 and destroyed in 1455.

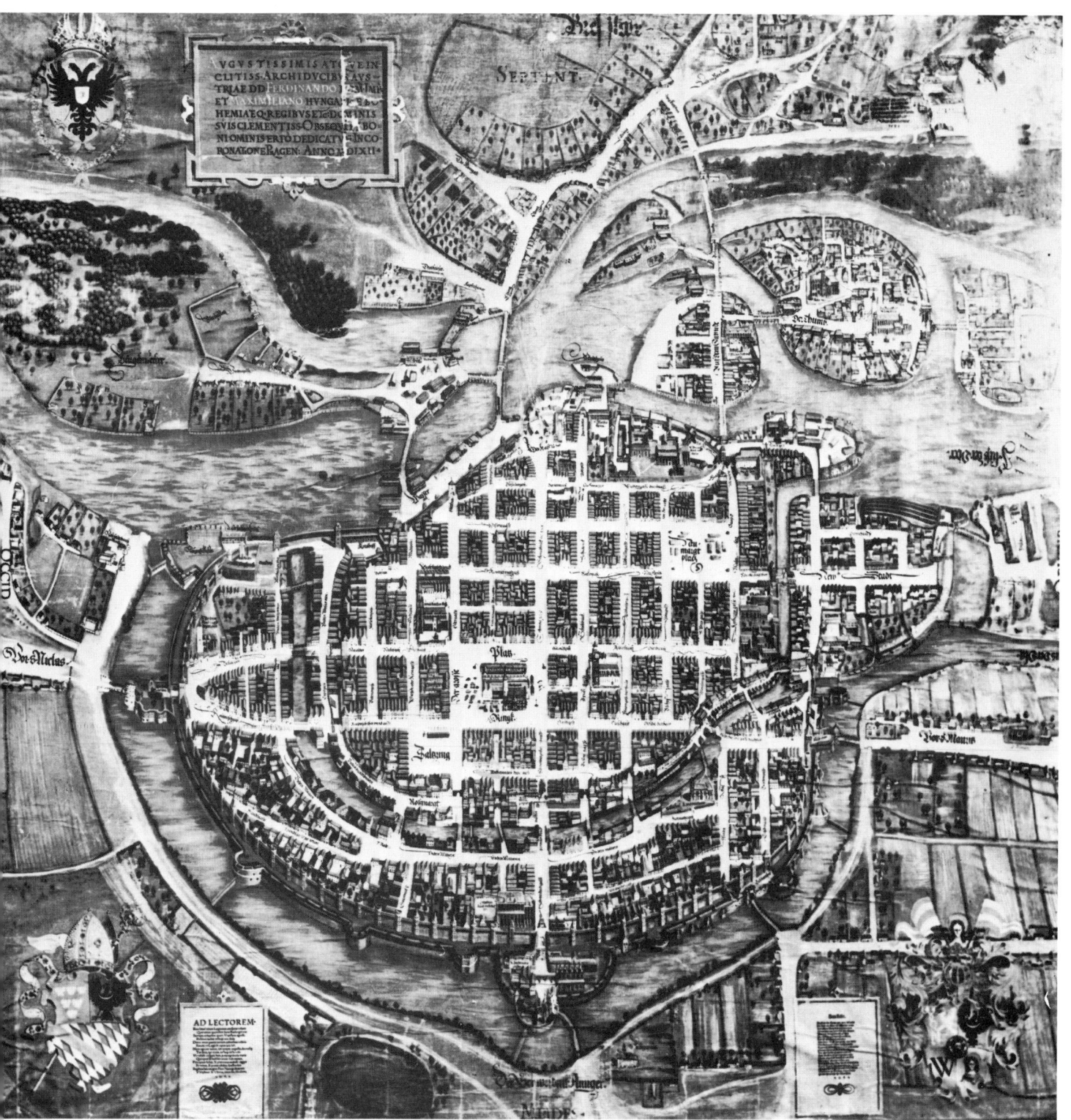

31. Plan of Wrocław in 1562, by B. Weyner. The three lines of the fortifications are clearly distinguishable: the walls surrounding the oldest part of the city, built after 1241; the second circumvallation, enclosing the city and its extension, built about 1350; and the ramparts with rondelles, built in the early 16th century. Copy of the original plan preserved in Prague.

The urban patterns evolved in the 13th and 14th centuries remained valid throughout the 15th century. The founding of new cities continued, particularly in Great Poland (with 60 cities), Mazovia (with 43), and in the colonized eastern territories. More and more "private" towns were founded in this period, especially in Great Poland, by the great landowners whose estates at this time were already vast. Some cities, particularly those in the eastern territories, were founded on the initiative of the kings, such as Bielsk Podlaski (1430), Czerwonogród (1448), Drohiczyn (1498), Kolno (1425), Łomża (1428), Nowogród on the Narew (1428), Suraż (1440), Wąsosz (1436), and Zambrów (1430). In many cases these foundations consisted of granting the Magdeburg Law to already existing settlements, which were then sometimes redeveloped. The layout of the new cities was similar to those dating from the 14th century, their characteristic feature being a rather large marketplace, usually square or approximating a square. Most of the cities founded in this period were not fortified; neither did they have the same opportunities for development as the older commercial centers. Indeed, many of them never grew to any great importance, surviving only as local market towns which served their immediate rural hinterland.

Around the older 13th and 14th-century cities, suburbs gradually grew up, reaching in some cases considerable dimensions in the 15th century. They developed as unfortified settlements outside the city walls, usually along the main overland roads, and were hardly ever subject to planned subdivisions. Their property patterns were accidental, often following the earlier boundaries of the fields. In general, suburbs were laid out along a street with buildings on both sides, which sometimes widened into a square as it reached the gate in the city walls. The population of the suburbs usually lacked the freedoms enjoyed by the burghers.

The second half of the 15th century witnessed an intense building activity by the Franciscan Observants, known in Poland under the name of Bernardine Friars. They built their monasteries close to the larger cities of the country and, as a rule, in the suburbs outside the city walls. This was the case, for instance, with the Bernardine monasteries in the Stradom suburb of Cracow (about 1450), in Warsaw (1454), Koło (1456), Poznań (1456), Radom (1468–1490), Kalisz (1489), Bydgoszcz (1480), and Lvov (1460). These monastic buildings, at first often of wood but executed in masonry toward the end of the century, became new architectural landmarks outside the city walls, causing a break, so to speak, in the hermetic seclusion of the cities within the ring of their fortifications.

In spite of the praise of the building activities of Casimir the Great, most medieval cities in Poland had timber houses. In the 14th and 15th centuries only the largest and richest cities had stone buildings. They were mainly built around the market square and along the main streets. A type of burgher's house emerged in this period, influenced in the

32. The center of the city of Gdańsk before 1939. On the right, the Church of the Virgin Mary, a late Gothic structure, towering like a fortress over the gabled houses of the 16th, 17th, and 18th centuries. On the left, the Town Hall (14th century), whose tower is crowned by a Renaissance spire.

northern provinces by the architecture of the Hanseatic cities and in the south by that prevalent in Lower Saxony. Amidst the more or less standardized burghers' houses, rhythmically flanking the streets with their narrow brick gables, rose monumental Gothic churches and monasteries which, together with the city hall, dominated the skyline of medieval cities (Fig. 32).

The main center of commercial activity was the market square where all buildings connected with the economic and administrative functions of the city were concentrated. These buildings were often grouped in a block which occupied almost the whole market square (Figs. 33, 34). The area not built up was limited to a street encircling the central block of buildings; hence the German name *Ring* and its Polish counterpart, *rynek*. With the emergence of urban self-government the city hall, as the seat of administrative, juridical, and economic authority, became the main feature of the central building block. Adjoining it were the commercial buildings, the cloth hall, merchants' stalls and the like, the weigh house, and the pillory. In the larger cities these structures assumed interesting architectural forms, while in the smaller towns, with the exception of the town hall, they were mostly constructed of wood.

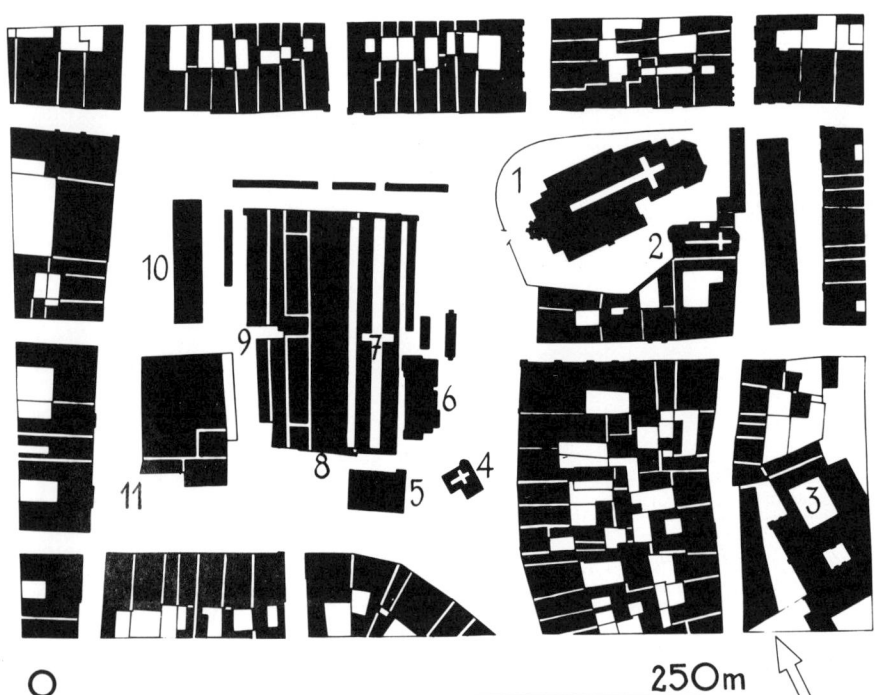

33. Plan of the main market square at Cracow in the late 18th century. Reconstruction by the author. 1. Parish church of the Virgin Mary; 2. St. Barbara's Church; 3. Dominican Monastery; 4. Romanesque church of St. Adalbert (built before the market square was laid out); 5. Big weighing house; 6. Small weighing house (*smatruz*); 7. Rich merchants' stalls; 8. Drapers' hall; 9. Stalls of the tanners, cobblers, potters, and fishmongers; 10. Furriers' house; 11. Town Hall.

34. Plan of the market square at Poznań in the late 18th century. 1. Town Hall (14th century, rebuilt in the 16th to 18th centuries); 2. Weighing house; 3. Guardhouse (late 18th century); 4. Butchers' stalls; 5. Arsenal; 6. Rich merchants' stalls; 7. Drapers' Hall; 8. Cobblers' stalls; 9. Arcaded stalls converted into dwelling houses; 10. Bakers' stalls; 11. Pillory.

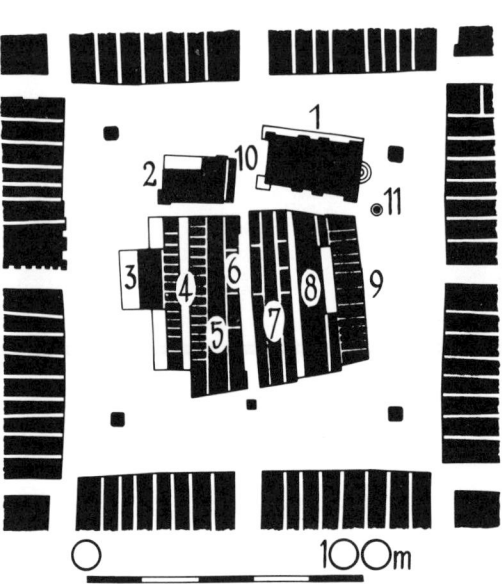

A feature inseparable from medieval cities were the fortifications, with their battlemented walls and towers built of brick (or of stone as in some West Pomeranian cities) and surrounded by a moat filled with water. Entrance into the city was through drawbridges and gates, often with powerful gate towers. A tendency to standardize dimensions and forms of fortifications developed in the 14th century (cf. the charter granted by Casimir the Great to Płock). Towns of lesser strategic and economic importance were sometimes surrounded by earthen ramparts with brick gates or merely by timber palisades. The introduction of firearms in the 15th century made it necessary to expand and improve the fortifications. Some cities, like Warsaw, had a second ring of walls built around them. City gates were also strengthened, either by the construction of barbicans as in Cracow, Warsaw, Chojna, and Toruń, or by outer gates as in Szydłów, Cracow (Fig. 35), Gdańsk, and other places.

35. View of the barbican and St. Florian's Gate at Cracow. Drawing by J. Kurowski, 1809.

CHAPTER 6

Evolution of Cities in the Period of the Renaissance

THE IDEAS OF the Italian Renaissance penetrated Poland in the first years of the 16th century when, as in the rebuilding of the Wawel Castle in Cracow (1502 to 1536), the new esthetic trends were first applied to architecture. Hence, the beginning of the 16th century is recognized as the inauguration of a new era in Polish art, accompanied by important social and economic changes. The year 1655 is the date generally accepted as the close of the Renaissance period in Poland when, as a result of the Swedish invasion and the damages it wrought in cities already suffering from an economic crisis, the physical and economic development of urban communities was checked for many years.

Toward the middle of the 15th century some 650 cities existed in the areas between the Odra and Bug rivers. A century later their number had risen to 1,000 within the boundaries of the Polish Kingdom as it then was—that is, without Silesia and Western Pomerania and their additional 250 cities. By the middle of the 17th century their number had risen to 1,050. Many new cities were founded during the 16th and the first half of the 17th century, especially in Eastern Mazovia, in the Grand Duchy of Lithuania, and in the Ukraine. Quite a number of towns were founded in Great Poland in connection with the intense development of textile industries at that time. These places, however, were often foundations of so-called "new towns" adjoining existing cities.

The layout of cities founded up to about 1575 was still rooted in medieval tradition. They were either replicas of the regular, well-known patterns of the 14th and 15th centuries or reduced versions of these patterns resulting from the abolition of outdated medieval fortifications and the limitation of economic functions. It is difficult to say exactly when elements of Renaissance compositions first made their appearance in the 16th century. As in architecture, it may be assumed that the change was gradual: Medieval plans were combined with a tendency toward axiality, enhancing the importance of buildings of particular architectural interest (Fig. 36). Certain elements of Renais-

36. Plan of the present city of Stanisławów, with the reconstructed old street pattern adjoining the marketplace.

sance compositions may be traced in some cities founded in the first half of the 16th century, for example, at Stanisławów (1523) and Sandomierz (1549), although it is hard to ascertain whether they were not introduced in the course of later redevelopments.

The first city whose layout was inspired by the "ideal" designs of Italian theoreticians was Głogów Małopolski (formerly Głowów), founded in 1570. The town was laid out in the form of an equal-armed cross, with axial streets intersecting in the center of a large marketplace (Figs. 37, 38). Four plots adjoining the corners of the marketplace

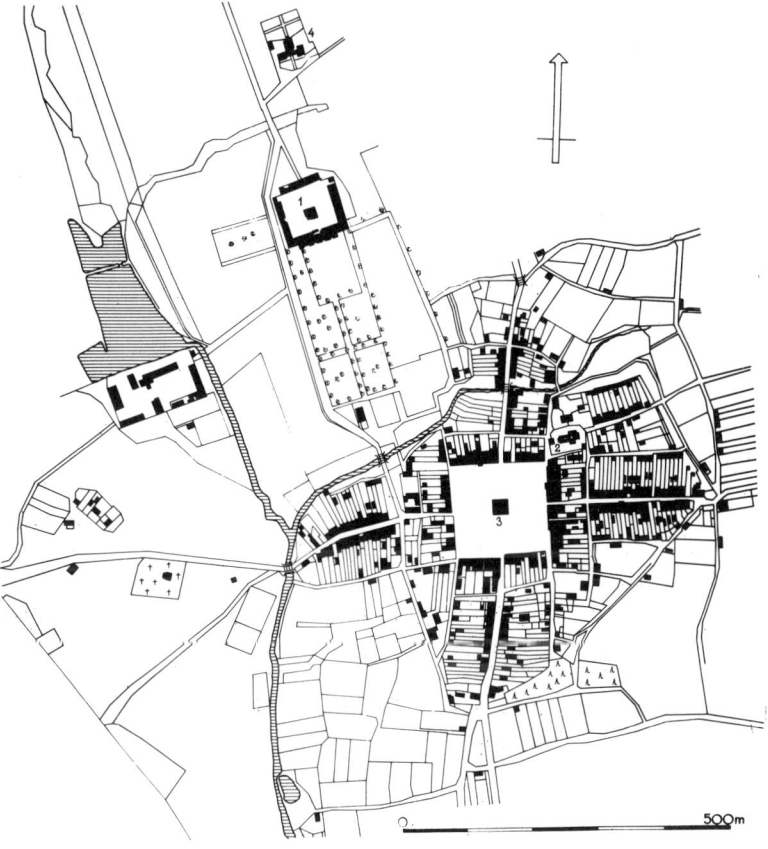

37. Cadastral plan of the city of Głogów Małopolski (formerly Głowów) in the mid-19th century. 1. Palace; 2. Parish church; 3. Town Hall.

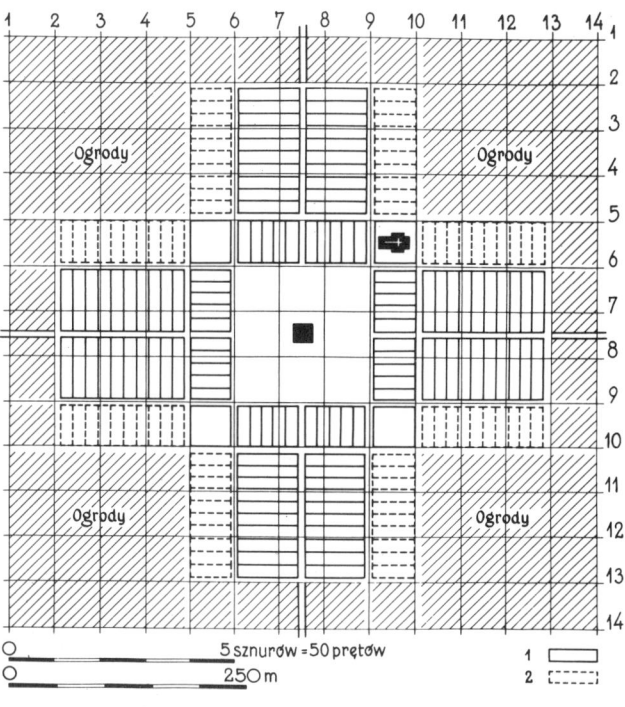

38. Attempted reconstruction of the "ideal" plan of Głogów Małopolski (formerly Głowów) by the author. The city was laid out within a regular square of 14 x 14 ropes. 1. Plots delimited at the founding of the city. Traces of this subdivision are still visible in a mid-19th century plan of the town (see Fig. 37); 2. Plots not delimited, but indicated on the original plan (their number is mentioned in charters).

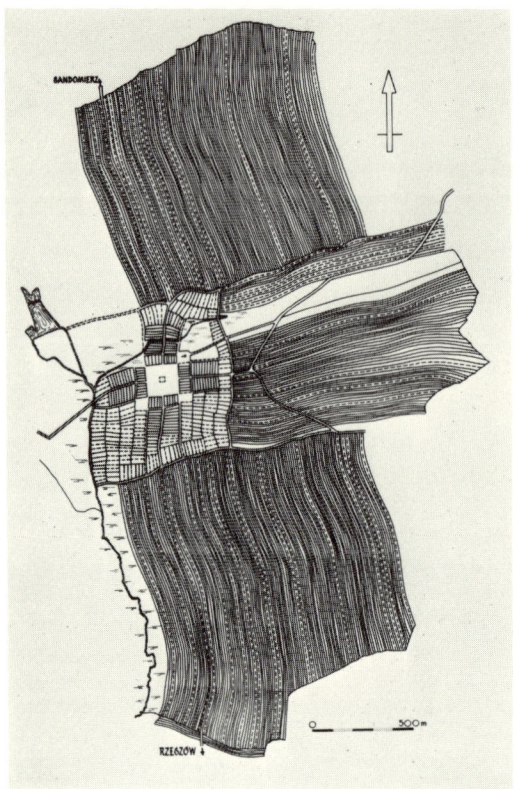

39. Reconstruction of the layout of the city of Głogów Małopolski (formerly Głowów) and the fields of the burghers.

were reserved for public buildings: a church, a bath-house, a hospital, and a brewery. A road, following the outline of a square, constituted the boundary of the city; and the cross formed by the building blocks and marketplace was contained within that square. The corner spaces of the square were intended for the gardens of the burghers, while adjacent to the city were regular field strips (Fig. 39) grouped according to the needs of the three-field system. The pattern of this city is a combination of medieval traditions (the method of subdivision) with new Renaissance principles of design (the axes of the streets converge on the city hall which is placed in the center of the market square). Like other cities founded in that period in Little Poland and Great Poland, Głogów was not fortified.

The new cities founded by Polish magnates in the eastern borderlands presented a different picture. They often had the character of residences and centers of vast landed estates. Their spatial patterns resembled medieval schemes but were enriched by grand stately seats surrounded by powerful, bastioned fortifications. The fortifications not only defended the residence itself but were also designed to keep the ethnically diverse population of the town in check. In contrast to other parts of the country, cities in the eastern borderlands were generally fortified because of the permanent threat of Turkish and Tartar invasions. Among the numerous cities founded at that time in Podolia and the Ukraine were Załoźce (1520), Czortków (1522), Złoczów (1523), Brzeżany (1530), Podhajce (1539), Tarnopol (1540), Budzanów (1549), Husiatyn (1559), and Sokul (1564). All these places were the property of powerful magnates (the Buczacki, Sieniawski, Koniecpolski, Kalinowski, Potocki, Zamoyski, and other families) who owned vast estates in this area. Many of these cities achieved considerable importance as commercial centers, keeping up extensive trade relations between East and West.

In the Grand Duchy of Lithuania the 16th century witnessed a planned campaign for transforming the socage economy, based on the payment of rent, into a farm economy based on serfdom. This involved the redevelopment of existing villages and the construction of new ones. They were laid out in the form of regular ribbon villages, with farmstead plots marked out on both sides of the street and a three-field system. Redevelopment also took place in a number of cities where improvements were sometimes accompanied by territorial expansion. In order to fill the gaps in the network of local markets in the colonized areas, many new towns were founded on royal and private estates, for example, Augustów (1557), Wasilków (1566), Krynki (1569), and Filipów (1570). These new towns were richly endowed with land, their inhabitants being engaged primarily in agriculture and handicrafts. Building blocks of extreme length—sometimes reaching 1,640 feet and more—and composed of two strips were characteristic of the spatial pattern (Fig. 40) in these places, which was analogous to that of villages founded

40. Plan of Wasilków today. 1–4. Former sites of churches, the synagogue, and an old mansion.

at the time. The buildings in these cities did not differ much from those in the villages. Indeed, one might say that these towns consisted of several ribbon villages put together, with a market square added to them.

In the last quarter of the 16th century, the new cities founded on Polish territory began to show the growing influence of theoretical designs, mainly Italian. These influences penetrated the country together with the architects, master masons, and military engineers called in by the kings and the powerful magnates. However, the number of new cities actually modeled on theoretical schemes was relatively small. It may be more appropriate to speak of the introduction of Renaissance features into traditional medieval layouts. In the dozens of cities founded at that time only a few show clear traces of Renaissance design. More cities may have been planned according to Renaissance principles, especially in the eastern borderlands; but because their predominantly wooden buildings were repeatedly destroyed by wars, their original structure was greatly deformed or totally obliterated.

Two trends may be observed in the planning of Polish cities in the 16th and 17th centuries. The first is connected with the activity of Italian (less frequently Dutch or German) and later also Polish architects and military engineers, who endeavored to adapt to local needs and conditions spatial solutions they had seen designed or carried out in the countries of Southern and Central Europe. Their work was indissolubly linked with the architectural and city-planning ideas of their powerful patrons. No wonder, then, that newly founded cities remarkable for their interesting plans are usually associated with the names of the families of powerful magnates.

The other trend arose from the activities of local architects and surveyors who were still firmly rooted in the medieval tradition but who, under the influence of the new artistic concepts, introduced certain elements of Renaissance design and created patterns which were basically an evolution of traditional planning. Renaissance influences found expression in a tendency toward symmetry and axiality; in the spatial connection of the city with the seigniorial residence; and in the development around the marketplace which often assumed the character of a grand *piazza,* with an axially sited town hall as its dominant architectural feature, placed in the middle of the *piazza* or as the central building on one of its sides.

The largest number of cities during this time was founded in the eastern territories. Particularly worthy of notice in this connection are the city-planning activities of Jan Zamoyski, Chancellor and *Hetman* (Commander-in-chief of the Polish Army), and his son Tomasz. Standing high in the favor of the King, Jan Zamoyski came into possession of a huge complex of hereditary estates, called Zamość Fee Tail, in the southern part of what is now the Voivodship of Lublin. Toward the end of his life these estates covered several thousand square miles. In addition, he owned vast tracts of land in the Ukraine. Altogether, Jan Zamoyski was the owner of 23 cities and over 800 villages! The Zamoyskis founded many new cities on their estates. The more important in the Lublin area were Zamość (1580), Jelitkowo, now Tomaszów Lubelski (1590), Janów Lubelski (1640), and, in the Ukraine, Szarogród (1585) and Tomaszpol (early 17th century). Similar activity was developed by other borderland magnates who founded, *inter alia*, in the Lublin area: Biłgoraj (1578), Narol (1585), Annopol and Ulanów (1616), and in the Ukraine, Brody (1586), Żółkiew (1597), Kitajgród (1607), Janów (in the early 17th century), and Nowy Koniecpol (1634).

A city of particular importance in the history of Polish town planning is Zamość, whose layout comes nearest to the theoretical schemes of Francesco di Giorgio Martini and Pietro di Giacomo Cataneo. The city was founded as the center of the Zamość Fee Tail and the seat of the powerful Chancellor, but in addition it performed the role of an important trading community on the route connecting the eastern borderlands with the West. The author of its plan was Bernardo Morando of Padua, an Italian architect who worked there from 1579 until his death in 1600, erecting fortifications, a palace, a collegiate church, a synagogue, a city hall, and other buildings.

The plan of Zamość was originally designed as a square, approximately 1,213 by 1,164 feet, with 272 plots, not counting those for public buildings. The relief of the site as well as the construction of the palace and fortifications was probably the reason for departing from this originally intended theoretical scheme. The 17th-century layout (Fig. 41) of Zamość, which field investigations and cartographic material have reconstructed with considerable precision, consisted of an irregular polygon surrounded by bastioned fortifications (traced about 1588) encompassing

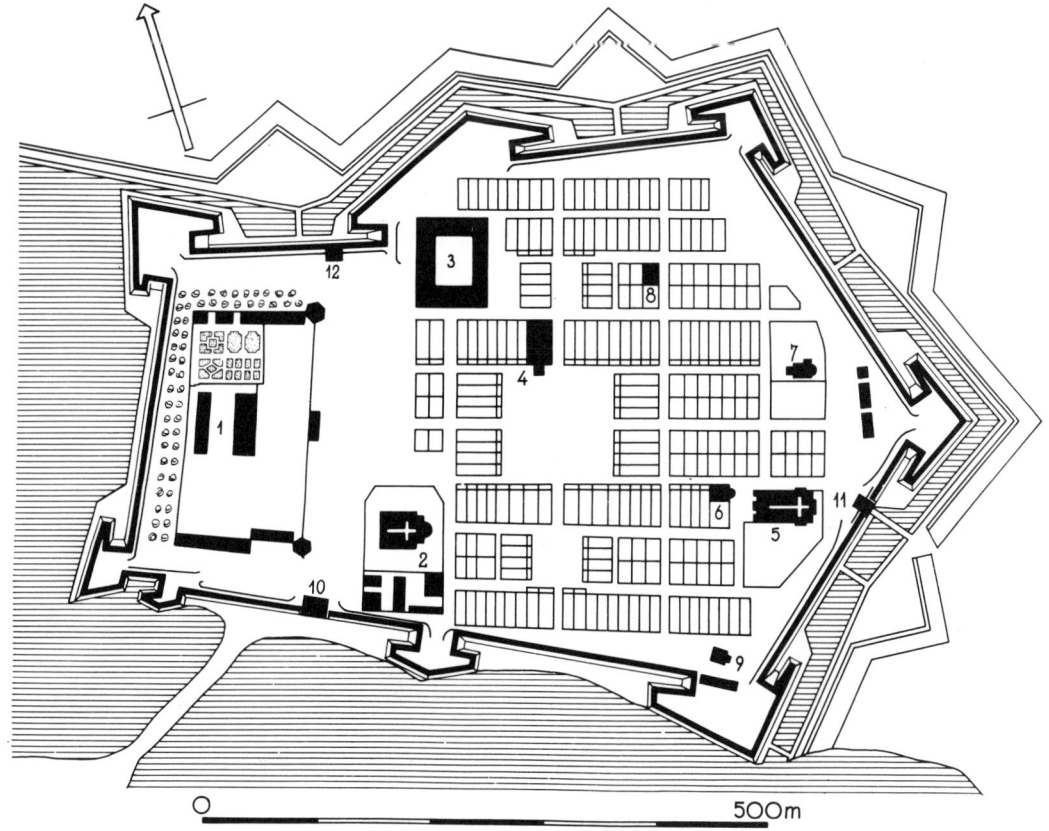

41. Plan of Zamość in the second half of the 17th century. Reconstruction by the author. 1. Jan Zamoyski's palace; 2. Collegiate church of the Assumption; 3. Zamość Academy; 4. Town Hall; 5. Franciscan church; 6. Franciscan convent-church; 7. Armenian church; 8. Synagogue; 9. Greek Catholic church; 10. Szczebrzeszyn Gate; 11. Lvov Gate; 12. Lublin Gate.

42. View of Ormiańska Street at Zamość.

the city and the palace of Jan Zamoyski, built in the years 1581 to 1586. The layout of the city was symmetrical in relation to two axes intersecting each other in the center of a square marketplace. Two smaller marketplaces, situated on the north-south axis, relieved the main square of its market functions, giving it the character of a grand *piazza,* with the city hall on its northern side. The four corners of the city, as in most theoretical schemes, were reserved for public buildings: the collegiate church, the Academy founded by Zamoyski, a Franciscan monastery, and an Armenian church. The palace was placed at the end of the east-west axis which also was the city's main traffic artery. The siting of the public buildings is marked by a tendency to create axial vistas from the streets.

The city developed rapidly, and as early as the beginning of the 17th century had grown into an important commercial center. The squares and main streets were flanked by arcaded houses whose uniform character, on account of the arcades, gives reason to suppose that they were built after a model design, possibly that of Morando's house in the Main Market Square. The fact that the city was built in less than half a century resulted in a uniform and deliberately intended Renaissance character, fully reflecting the concepts of Bernardo Morando and Jan Zamoyski and only insignificantly disfigured by 19th-century redevelopments. This makes Zamość (Fig. 42) a unique city not only in Poland but throughout Europe.

Other towns in the Zamość Fee Tail, for instance, Tomaszów Lubelski, also had regular layouts, sometimes modeled on that of Zamość. An interesting example is that of Janów Lubelski, which, like Zamość, had two symmetrical axes intersecting in the center of a square marketplace. The city was surrounded by concentric belts of gardens (Fig. 43) belong-

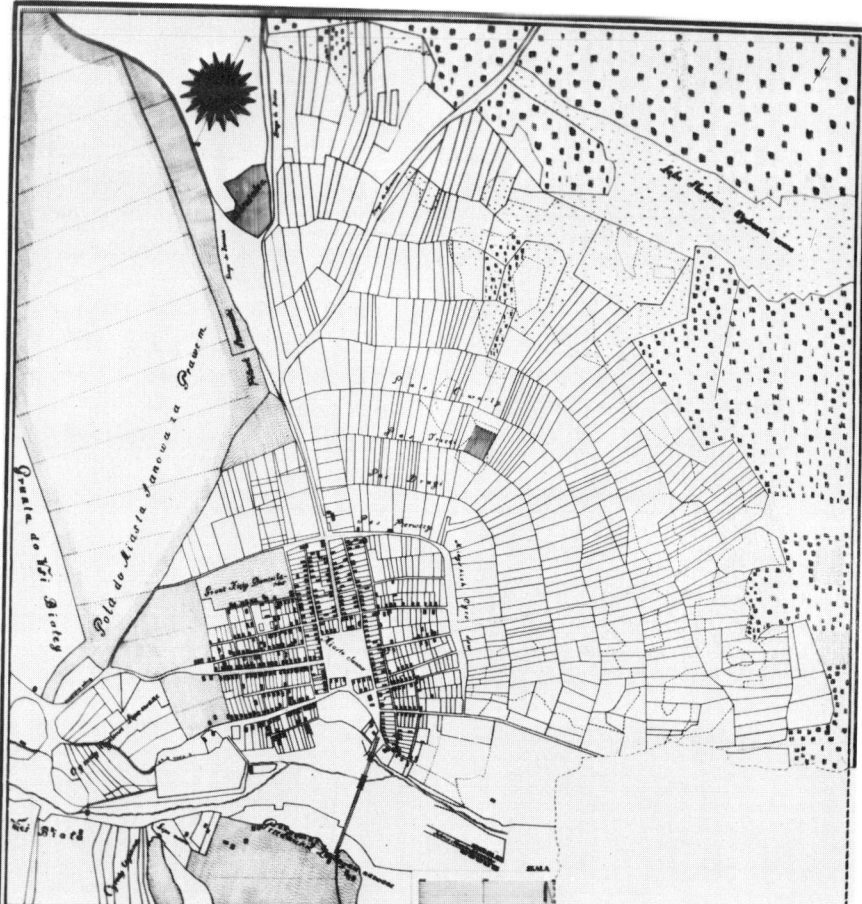

43. Plan of the city of Janów Lubelski and the adjoining land, about 1850.

44. Plan of Brody in 1844, with the superimposed reconstructed outline of the fortifications of city and castle.

45. *Below:* Simplified "ideal" plan of the city of Brody and later fortifications.

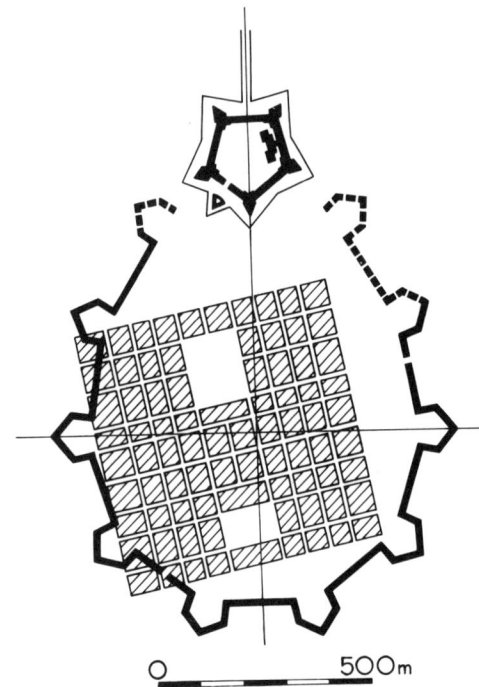

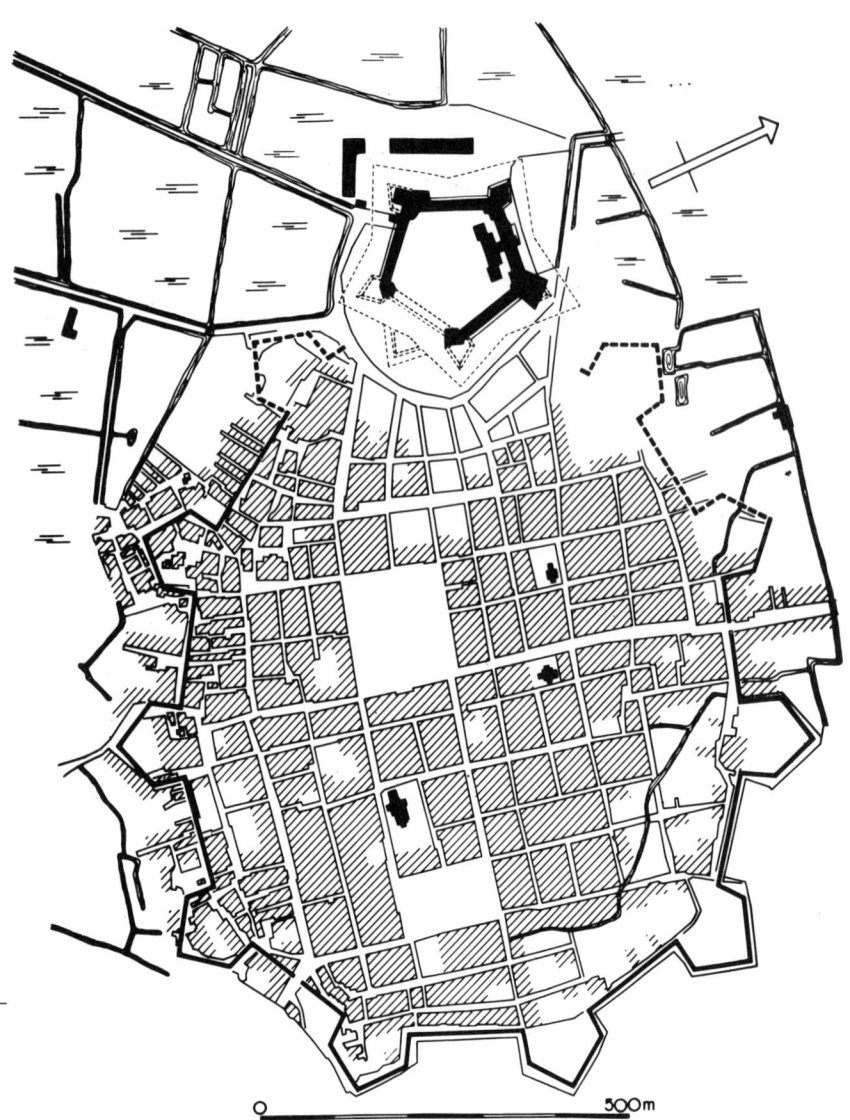

ing to the burghers. It should be noted that in most cities founded in the 16th and 17th centuries the settlers obtained, in addition to a building plot in the city proper, a garden and fields lying immediately outside the walls.

Brody is another interesting example. Founded in 1586 in the eastern borderland by Stanisław Żółkiewski, *Hetman* and Voivode of Ruthenia, it had a regular gridiron pattern, deformed by the construction of fortifications in the years 1630 to 1635. Its two market squares may have resulted from the different nationalities—Poles, Armenians, and Ruthenians—who made up the urban population. A powerful castle, seat of a later owner of the city, *Hetman* Stanisław Koniecpolski, was built on the axis of the fortification system (Figs. 44, 45).

The plans of cities founded at this time in Great Poland were still modeled on medieval prototypes. One of the reasons for adherence to tradition was the restricted financial means of the landowners in this region, compared to the huge fortunes of the borderland magnates. The

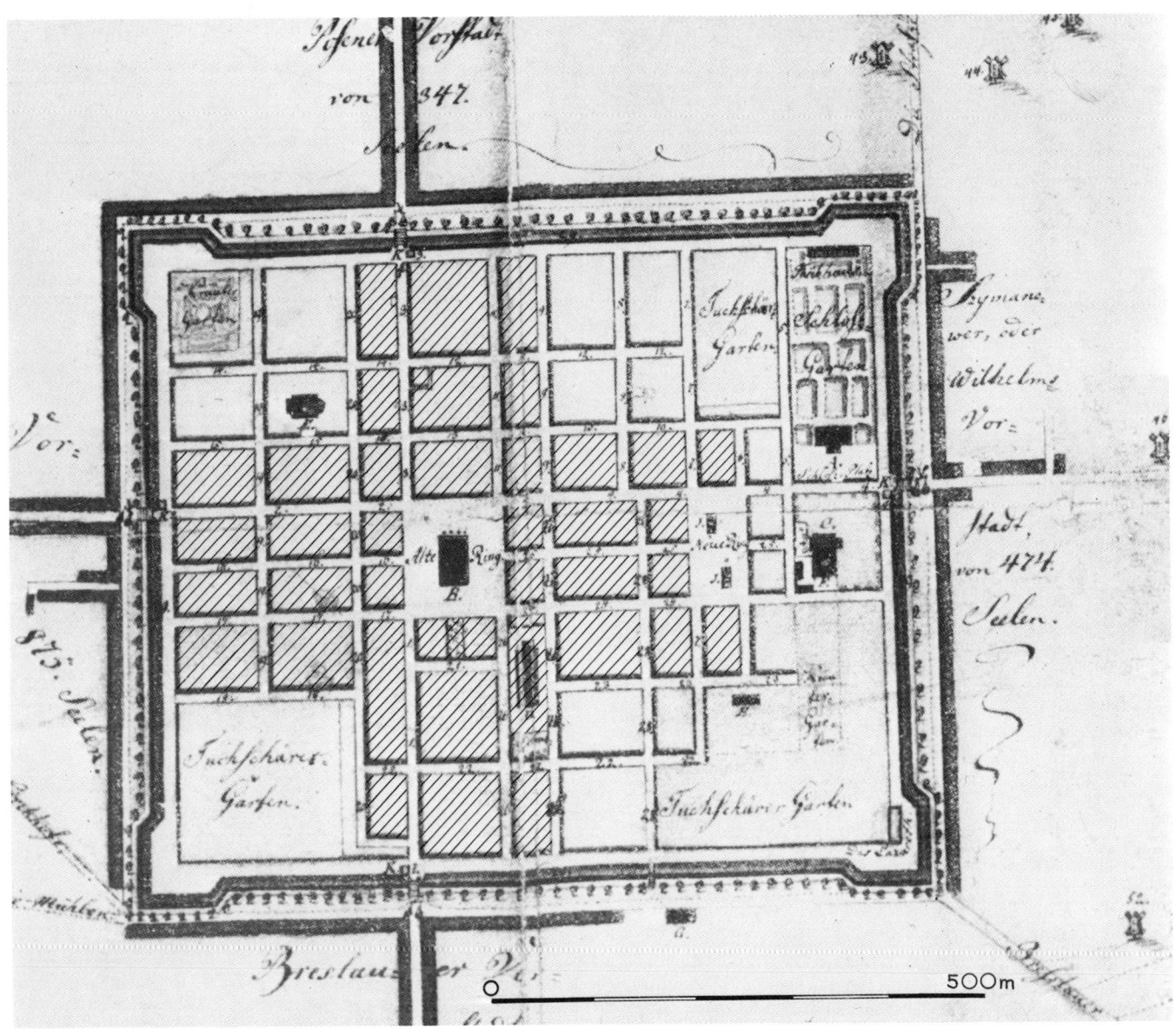

majority of the new towns were centers of handicrafts, primarily concerned with the manufacture of cloth. An interesting example is Rawicz, founded in 1639, which became a model for a number of other towns in the area. Its layout is remarkable for its regularity. Four rows of building blocks extended from the rectangular marketplace, forming a cross within the rectangular outline of the city. Here, too, the corners of the city were probably, at first, left free of buildings. Rawicz, settled mainly by immigrants from Bohemia and Silesia, developed quickly, and in 1663 it had already expanded eastward by the addition of several building blocks and by a small square, the "New Town" Market (Fig. 46). After this expansion the city consisted of some 600 to 700 plots, a relatively large number for that period. The roads running from the city gates along the sides of the marketplace, were still strongly reminiscent of the Middle Ages; but the central position of the siting of the city hall in the marketplace, on the axis of the streets bisecting its longer sides, was in keeping with the principles of Renaissance design.

46. Plan of Rawicz in the late 18th century. Hatching indicates the blocks delimited at the time of the foundation in 1639. The city was extended in 1663 and surrounded with bulwarks in the early 18th century.

47. Simplified plan of the city of Grodzisk Wielkopolski in the early 20th century. 1. Medieval city founded in the 14th century; 2. "New Town" for artisans founded in 1593; 3. Protestant church; 4. Roman Catholic parish church.

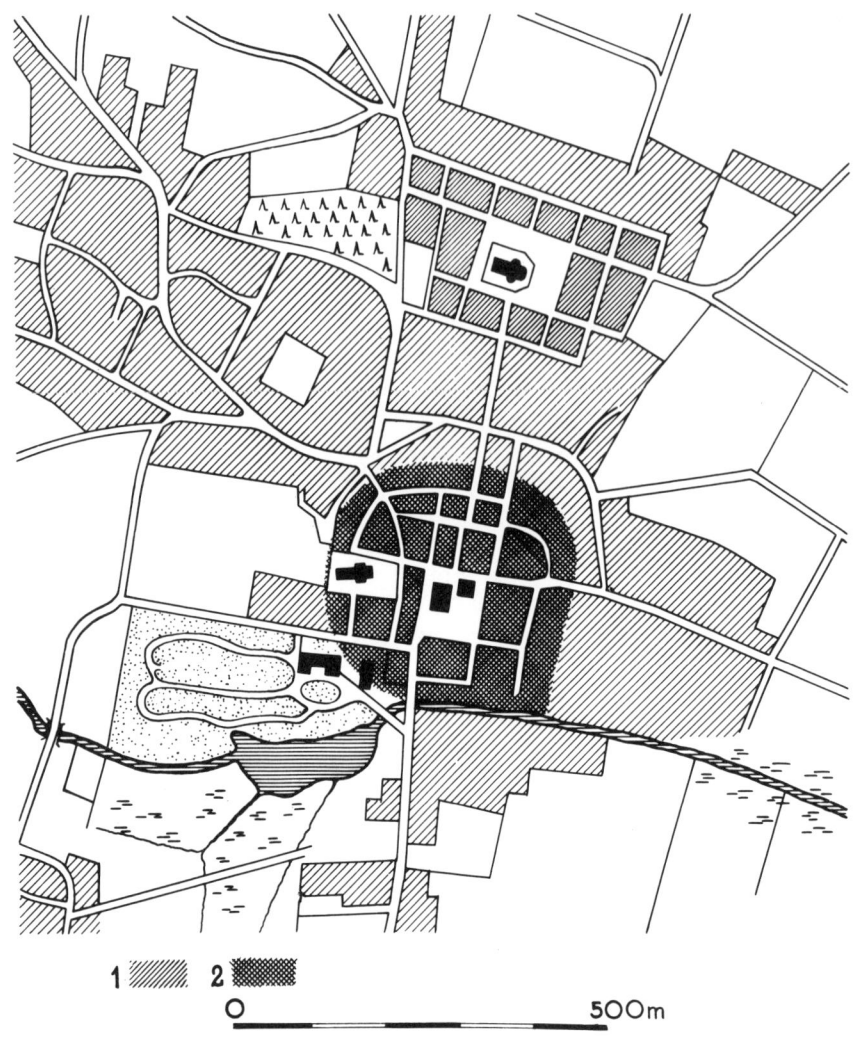

A layout similar to that of Rawicz was applied to Bojanowo (1638). Other towns founded at this time in Great Poland were Brudzew (1579), Jastrów (1602), Obrzycko (1638), Swarzędz (1638), Szlichtyngowa (1644), and Zaborowo (1644). They were designed on a much more modest scale, and their layouts were not particularly interesting.

From the middle of the 16th century to the middle of the 17th century, Great Poland received numerous immigrants of the Bohemian Brethren from Bohemia and Silesia who were fleeing religious persecution. This influx stimulated the development of cities in Great Poland, since most of the newcomers were skilled artisans. "New towns" were founded for them around existing medieval cities by the owners of the latter. From 1593 to 1652 as many as sixteen such "new towns" were built in Great Poland. They were granted foundation charters and enjoyed a certain autonomy. The plans of these settlements varied, ranging from simple ribbon developments to regular schemes resembling those of the cities founded at the same time. The new town founded in 1593 adjoining Grodzisk Wielkopolski may serve as an example of this type of settlement (Fig. 47).

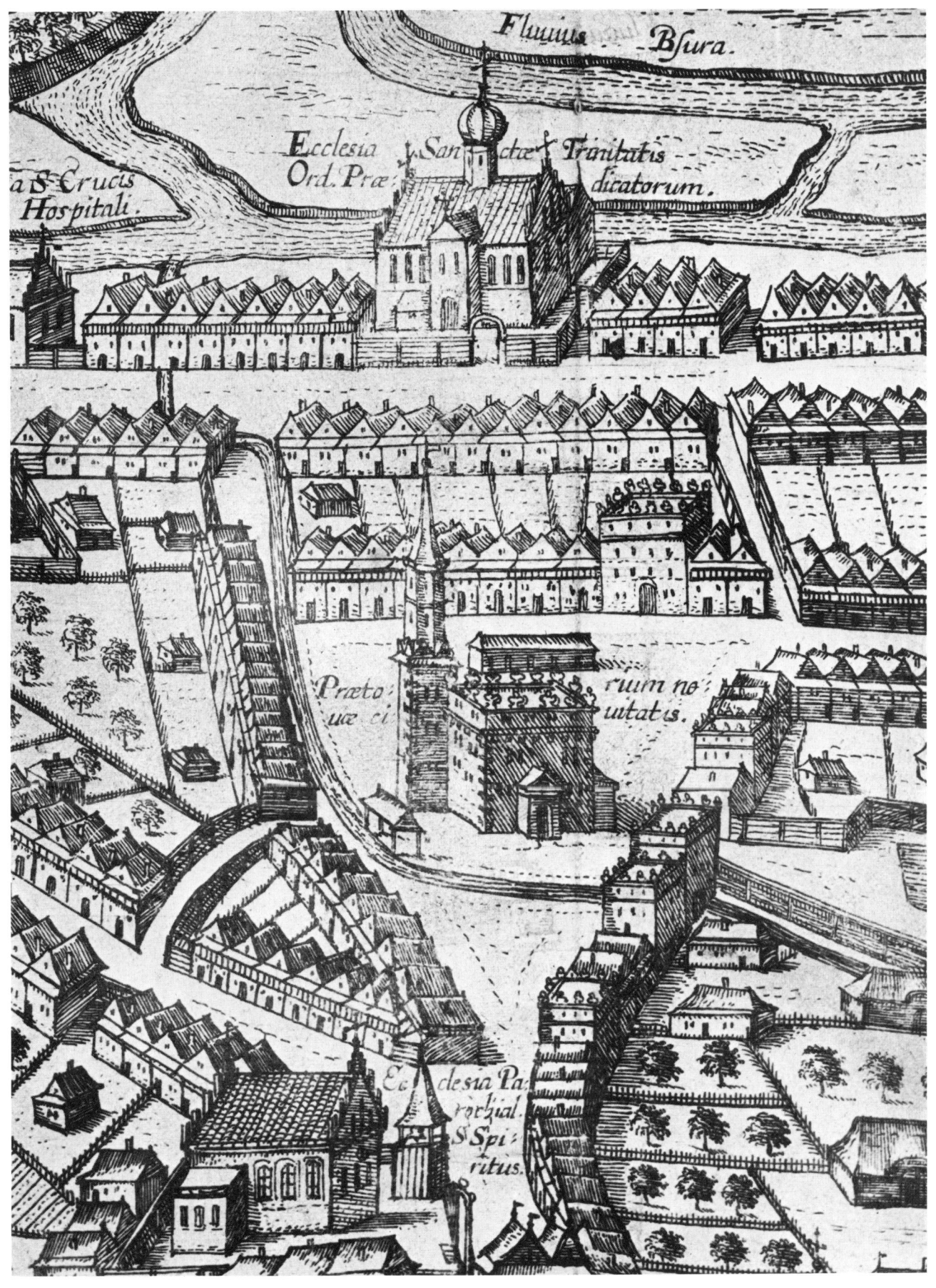

48. Buildings in and around the New Town marketplace at Łowicz, late 16th century. Detail of an engraving from G. Braun and F. Hogenberg's *Theatri praecipuarum totius mundi urbium liber sextus*, Nürnberg, 1617.

49. The town hall, on the Old Market, in Poznań. After a fire in 1535, it was rebuilt by Giovanni Battista di Quadro (1550–1560) with loggias and an attic.

The population in the larger cities increased considerably. Wrocław in the 16th century counted some 30,000 to 40,000 inhabitants; Gdańsk and Cracow had close to 20,000; Poznań had over 15,000; and a number of other cities such as Warsaw, Lublin, Toruń, Elbląg or Bydgoszcz had over 10,000. However, the population of the majority of cities did not exceed 1,000 to 2,000 people. Some large cities, particularly the great seashore emporia, had revenues and financial means which, in those days, were very great indeed. For instance, the revenues of Gdańsk, at the peak of its development in the first half of the 17th century, equalled that of the Treasury of the entire Polish Commonwealth! Consequently, these cities could afford to carry out a vast amount of new construction such as the remodeling of existing public buildings and private mansions, the erection of new, grand edifices, and the expansion of their defenses. The architectural character of cities underwent a far-reaching change (Fig. 48). The Gothic façades of houses disappeared and were replaced by new sumptuous Renaissance designs. Public buildings which have been preserved, such as the City Hall in Poznań (Fig. 49), the Drapers' Hall in Cracow, the Arsenal in Gdańsk, and many others, testify to the large scale and the high architectural standard of the building activities then carried out.

The redevelopment of cities was by no means confined to changes in architectural forms. Another of its important aspects was the reconstruction of fortifications in the 16th and 17th centuries. With the development of firearms, medieval fortifications consisting of stone or brick walls and moats lost much of their usefulness. Now it became necessary to expand the ring of defenses encircling the city and withdraw the defenders behind a complicated system of ramparts and ditches, strengthened by defense works capable of holding back the invaders by flanking fire. Toward the middle of the 16th century some Silesian cities such as Wrocław and Legnica built earthen bulwarks with projecting rondelles, that is, semicircular or polygonal defense works (Fig. 50). The same system was applied in Gdańsk (1534 to 1563). Soon, however, further improvements were to take place: in the 1560s fortifications with bastions, as designed in Italy late in the 15th century, were introduced into Poland. The bastion of Rożnów Castle (1560) and the fortifications of Ołyka Castle (1558 to 1567) were the first defenses of this type in Poland. Late in the 16th century bastions were also constructed in other cities: at Zamość, Legnica, Nysa, Wrocław, and Gdańsk. The 1630s marked the introduction of the Dutch system of fortifications, in which bastions and curtains were added to earthworks, as in Gdańsk, Elbląg, Brody, Toruń, and Wrocław.

The rebuilding of fortifications was a factor of fundamental importance for the physical layout of cities. The wide ring of defenses and their glacis, kept free of buildings, separated the city from the suburbs, which had to be shifted farther outward. At the same time, the new fortifications made it necessary to enclose the city within a regular polygon. Hence it became inevitable either to tear down some of the building blocks, as in Brody and Toruń, or to include large open spaces in the urban area, as in Gdańsk, Warsaw, or Słuck, later to be subdivided into building plots. Traces of these wide belts of fortifications

50. Rondelle fortifications at Wrocław, built outside the medieval walls in the first half of the 16th century. Detail of a plan of 1562 (see Fig. 31).

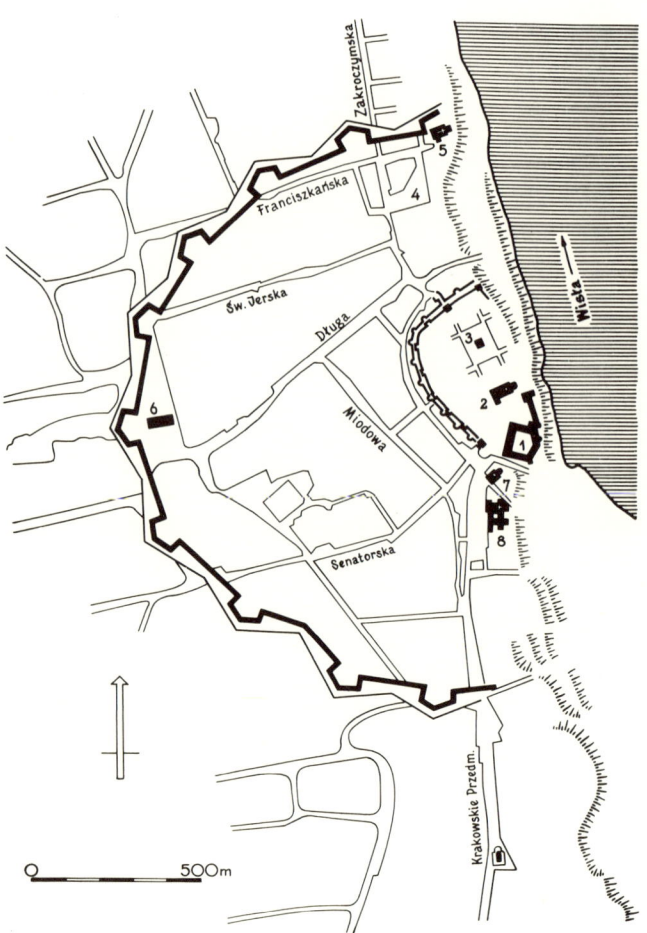

51. The fortifications of Warsaw with bastions built in 1621. Reconstruction by the author. 1. Royal Castle; 2. Parish church of St. John; 3. Old Town market square; 4. New Town market square; 5. Church of the Virgin Mary; 6. Almshouse for old soldiers (later arsenal); 7. St. Clare's Church (torn down in the first half of the 19th century); 8. St. Anne's Church.

are visible today in many cities as remnants of bulwarks and ditches, or in the street pattern which follows the lines of former fortifications (Fig. 51).

The change in the system of fortifications was an extremely costly undertaking. The digging of wide ditches, the building of huge ramparts and defense works called not only for the employment of a labor force running into hundreds or even thousands of people but also for the participation of skilled specialists capable of drawing, measuring, and actually marking out complicated "geometrical designs" in the field. At first these men were exclusively foreigners—mostly Italians, but also Dutchmen and Germans—called in by particular cities or influential magnates. Because of the high cost of these modern fortifications, not all cities could afford to have them built. Bastioned fortifications were constructed, in the first place, by wealthy trading centers such as Gdańsk, Wrocław, and Elbląg, which had large financial means at their disposal. Some royal cities like Warsaw, Lvov, Kamieniec Podolski, and those belonging to wealthy borderland magnates, like Zamość, Brody, and Szarogród, were also fortified. Small wonder that the richest of Polish cities, Gdańsk, erected the most powerful system of defenses in Poland, extending along the Vistula from the city right up to the sea (Fig. 52). The construction of fortifications depended, above all, on the degree of danger to which the cities were exposed. Hence, the largest number of fortifications were built in the eastern borderlands, the scene of incessant wars with the Turks and Tartars; in the northern areas

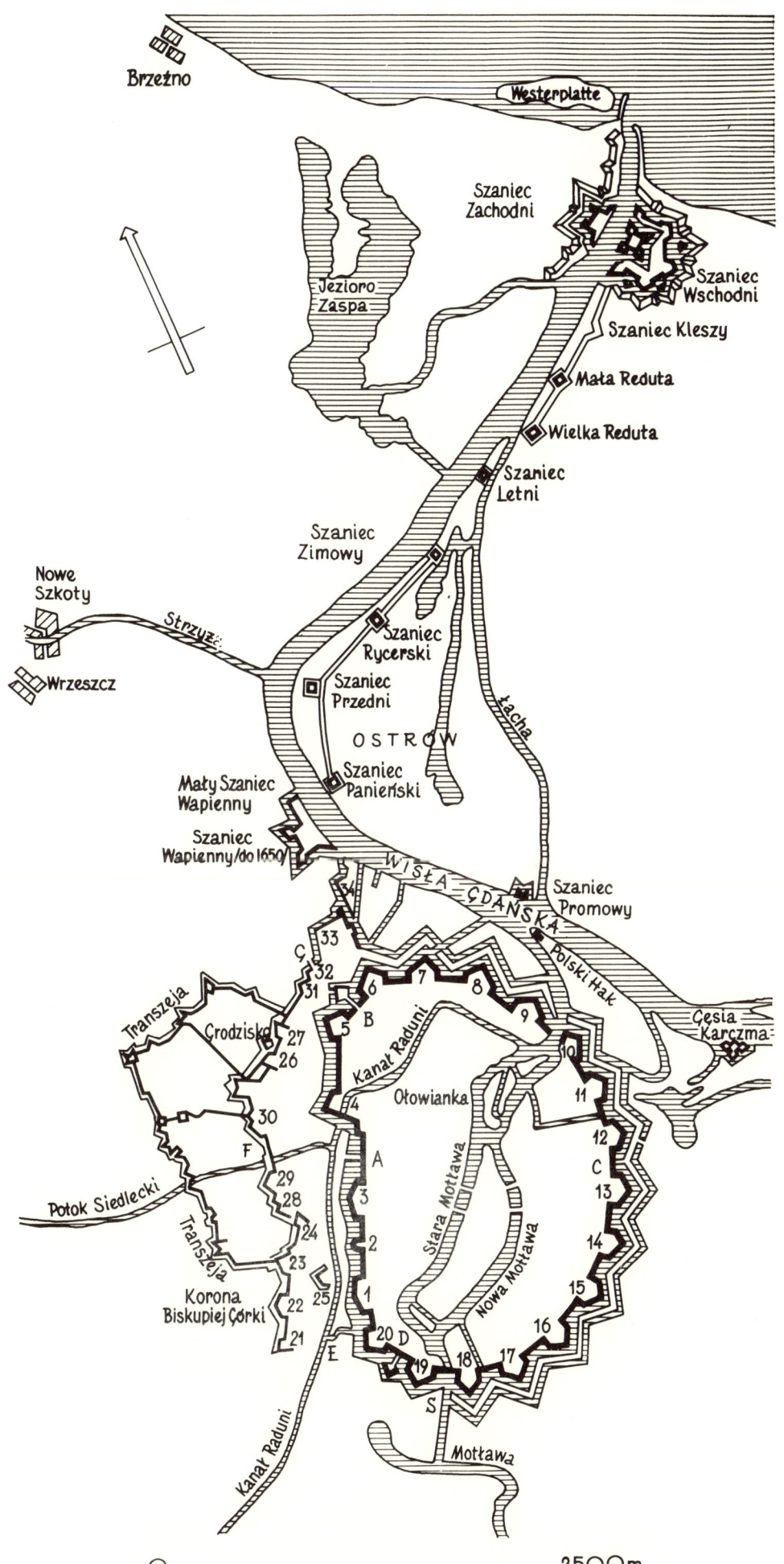

52. Fortifications of the city of Gdańsk and the estuary of the Vistula, about 1660. A. High Gate; B. St. James' Gate; C. Żuławy Gate; D. Low Gate; E. Orunia Gate; F. Siedlce Gate; G. Oliwa Gate; S. Stone Sluice; 1–24. Bastions; 25. Rampart of Biskupia Górka Hill; 26–30. Bastions; 31. Barn zigzag (zigzag = advanced fortifications of a serrated appearance); 32. Oliwa zigzag; 33. Widow's zigzag; 34. Lumber yards.

53. Plan of Łancut in the middle of the 18th century. 1. Lubomirski Castle, erected in 1691; 2. Town Hall of the medieval city.

threatened by the Swedes; and in Silesia during the Thirty Years' War. In Central Poland few existing cities were fortified; and the new cities, mostly rather poor, had no defense systems at all.

The 16th and 17th centuries witnessed a further development of suburbs outside the city walls. Their population was poor and included many Jews who sought refuge in Poland from the religious persecutions to which they were subjected in other countries. Suburban Jewish quarters often grew up on Crown lands controlled by royal prefects and thus did not come under the jurisdiction of the city. Most suburbs were centers of handicrafts which soon began to compete with the trade guilds in the cities. Various monastic orders, thriving on the upsurge of the Counter Reformation in Poland, also settled in the suburbs which often grew into vast, chaotic tracts of wooden houses interspersed here and there with monumental churches and monasteries. Many of these suburbs, particularly when built on land belonging to the Crown or to religious orders, freed themselves from the jurisdiction of the city and became independent settlements called *jurydyka* in Polish. Some of these "judicial" islands developed on lands belonging to lay magnates who had built their town mansions on the outskirts of the larger cities.

Adjoining the places owned by lay or ecclesiastic lords, grand residences surrounded by modern fortifications were often erected (Fig. 53).

These great strongholds were a new feature in the design of cities such as Łańcut, Rzeszów, Biała Podlaska, Nieśwież, Baranów, and Łowicz. Yet another innovation of the 16th century was the patrician's suburban summer residence modeled on Italian prototypes, for instance, the palace of J. L. Decjusz at Wola Justowska, near Cracow (1530).

Redevelopment within the city itself was relatively rare. The principle of subdivision into small plots with gabled houses was still most frequent, though town palaces, occupying several contiguous plots, were built here and there, by both magnates and wealthy burghers. An entirely new phenomenon and, simultaneously, a first manifestation of Baroque composition was the building of Jesuit churches and colleges within the city proper. The Jesuits were called in by Bishop Hozjusz in 1564, primarily with a view to checking the spread of the Reformation in Poland. It is interesting to note that the new monastic complexes were erected almost exclusively in the densely built-up central districts. The Jesuits purchased and demolished existing property to provide sites for their own buildings, whose design was subject to approval by the Order's headquarters in Rome. Most of these Baroque structures were sited on the axes of streets leading away from the market square, as in Poznań (1572), Pułtusk (1566–1606), Kalisz (1583–1595), and Rawa Mazowiecka (after 1613). In Warsaw (1609–1626) and Cracow (1596–1619) the Jesuits built their churches and colleges in the street connecting the market square with the royal castle.

CHAPTER 7

Evolution of Cities from the Middle of the 17th Century to the Fall of the Polish Commonwealth in 1793

TOWARD THE END of the 16th century Polish cities began to show symptoms of an economic retrogression which resulted, *inter alia*, from a reduction in the importance of local markets due to the impoverishment of the countryside, badly exploited as it was by a farm economy based on serfdom. The policy of the nobles and the ecclesiastical lords who aimed at controlling certain branches of trade was another important factor. Wars, continually fought on Polish soil throughout the 17th and early 18th century, with Turkey and Russia in the east (1648–1655, 1654–1667, 1672–1676) and with Sweden in the north (1618–1648, 1655–1660, 1702–1709), further aggravated the retrogression. Particularly heavy damage was wrought by the Swedish invasions of 1655–1656. Many cities ceased to exist, and the population of the country was reduced by 60 to 70 percent. In Warsaw alone (Fig. 54) only 342 out of 1,000 buildings were left standing. The tremendous devastations, coming at a time when the cities were suffering from an economic crisis, explain why the urbanization of the country made little progress during the 18th century. Many small, economically weak towns never recovered from this decline. Nevertheless, from the middle of the 17th to the end of the 18th century some attempts to found new cities, particularly in Great Poland and in the eastern borderlands, and to expand existing ones did take place.

A review of urban communities on Polish soil would be incomplete without mentioning the activity of the Swedes who, after their occupation of Pomerania in the first half of the 17th century, proceeded to redevelop and fortify a number of towns. Szczecin, which together with

54. Plan of Warsaw, drawn in 1705 by C. Albrecht. Original in the Kungl. Krigsarkivet, Stockholm.

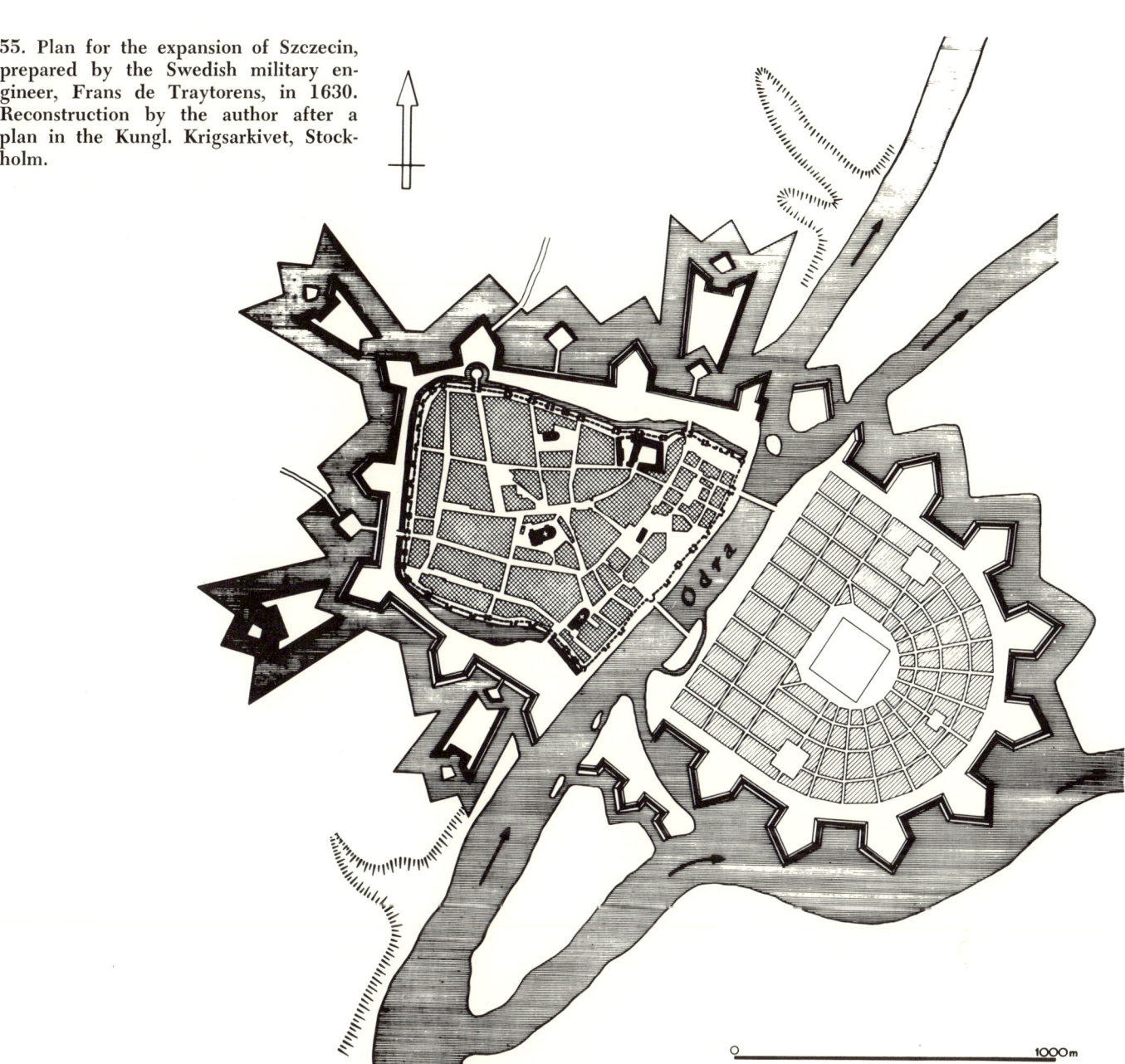

55. Plan for the expansion of Szczecin, prepared by the Swedish military engineer, Frans de Traytorens, in 1630. Reconstruction by the author after a plan in the Kungl. Krigsarkivet, Stockholm.

the rest of Western Pomerania was entirely under Swedish control on the death in 1637 of the last Prince of Pomerania, Bogusław XIV, obtained a new, powerful system of fortifications. There were some interesting plans for expanding Szczecin, in particular a scheme worked out in 1630 by Frans de Traytorens for the construction of a new town, with a radial system of roads, on the opposite bank of the Odra (Fig. 55). These plans, however, were never carried out. New fortifications were also built in Elbląg (after 1626) and Dąbie (1630–1646), and in a number of other places. In Elbląg the building of new fortifications involved the incorporation into the urban area of the lands lying between the

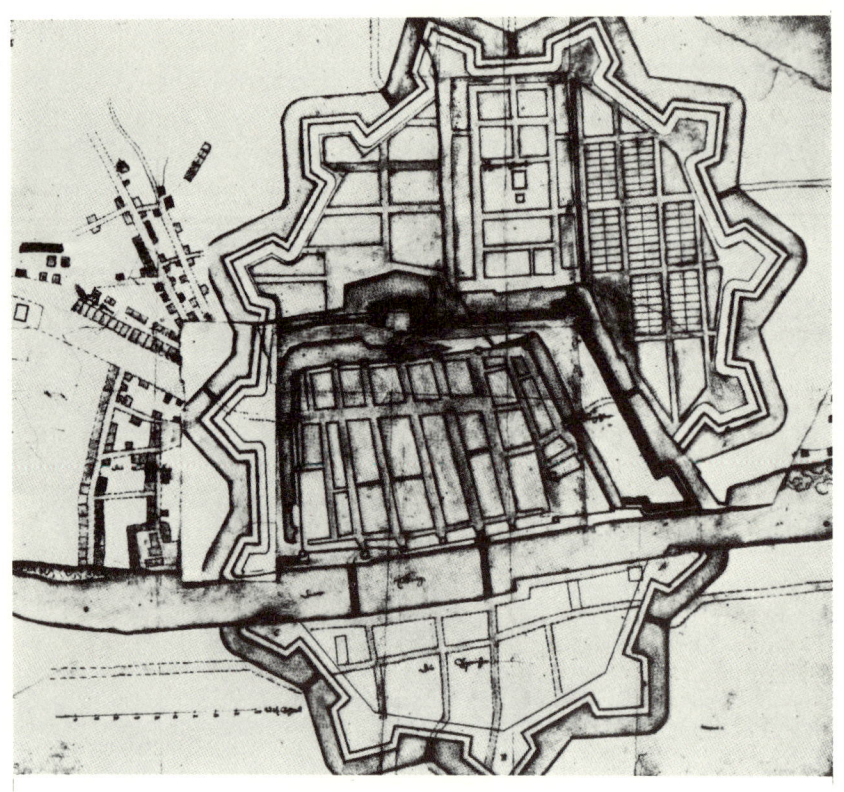

56. Plan for the expansion of the city of Elbląg, prepared in 1630 by Heinrich Thomé. Original in the Kungl. Krigsarkivet, Stockholm.

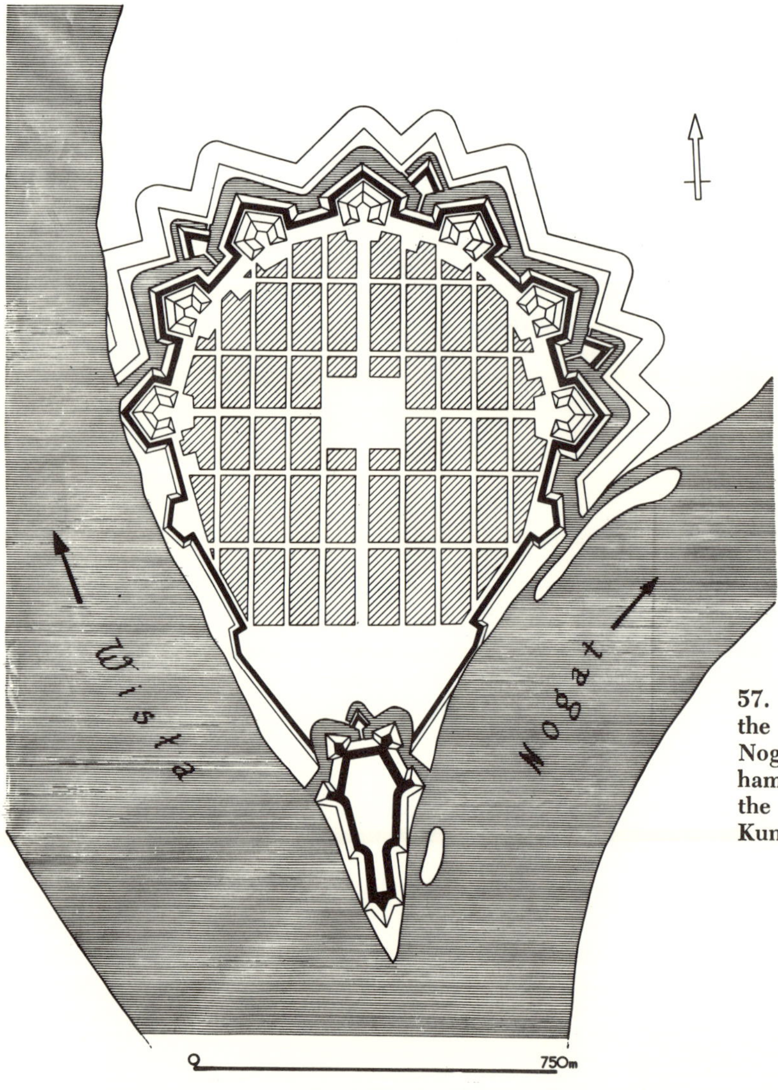

57. Plan of a Swedish camp in the fork of the Vistula and the Nogat, prepared in 1657 by Abraham Loffman. Reconstruction by the author after a plan in the Kungl. Krigsarkivet, Stockholm.

Old and the New Town (Fig. 56), after a plan drawn up by Heinrich Thomé in 1630. The military camps built by the Swedes were interesting because their layout was modeled on theoretical designs of the 16th and 17th centuries (Fig. 57). During the wars fought in Poland the Swedes developed an intense cartographic activity, drawing hundreds of city maps and plans of proposed fortifications. Many fine views of cities were drawn by E. Dahlberg, who had accompanied Charles X during his campaigns in Poland. The plans and drawings, preserved in Swedish archives, constitute one of the richest sources for the history of Polish cities.

Great Poland was economically the most developed part of Poland. It was here that the earliest attempts were made at rehabilitation after the damage wrought by the wars. A factor of great importance for the improvement of the economic situation of the countryside and, consequently, of local markets was the so-called "Dutch colonization" which consisted of establishing villages based on the principle of tenancy on waste lands and in devastated areas. The settlers—Poles and Germans alike—were granted personal freedom and the right to hold their lands in perpetuity, as well as certain commercial privileges. The manufacture of textiles continued to develop in the privately owned cities of Great Poland.

Soon after the end of the war with Sweden, two cities were founded as centers of handicrafts. They were Kargowa, formerly Unruhstatt, founded in 1661 by the Unruh family, and Rakoniewice, formerly Polski Freystad, founded in 1662 by Krzysztof Grzymułtowski, Castellan of Poznań. The plan of Rakoniewice (Fig. 58) was composed of three regular lines of building blocks. A square marketplace, with a wooden town

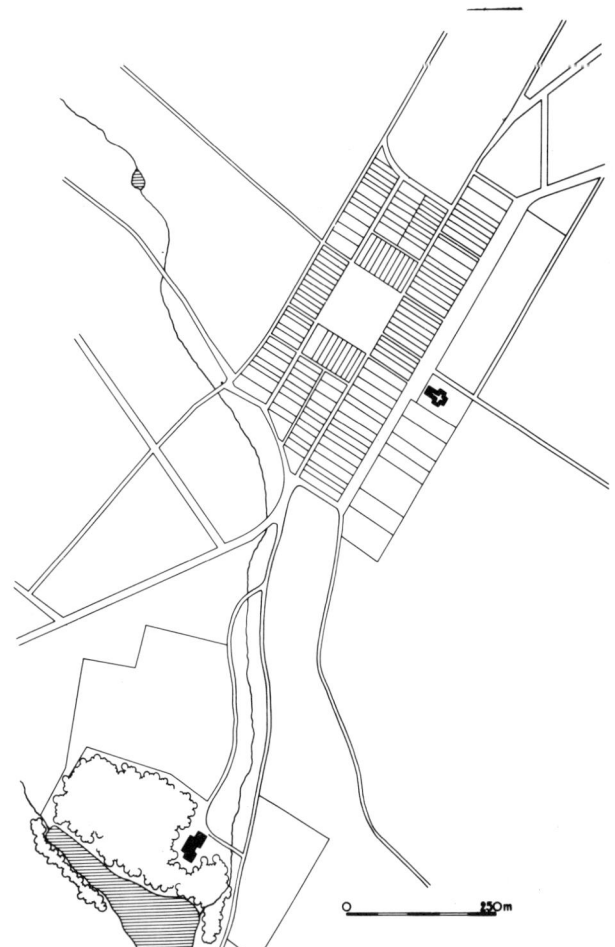

58. Plan of the present town of Rakoniewice.

59. Reconstruction of the development on the northwestern side of the marketplace at Rakoniewice. The buildings date from the second half of the 18th century. The original 17th-century development consisted of wooden gabled houses with porches.

hall, was situated in the center. Some 18th-century artisans' houses have survived to the present; their 17th-century predecessors may have looked much the same. They were uniform timber houses with porches, their gables facing the market square and the streets. It is probable that they were erected after a prescribed model (Fig. 59). The layout of Kargowa presented a similar picture. Adjoining both cities were the residences of their owners. Kargowa and Rakoniewice are typical examples of artisans' towns built in the late 17th and early 18th centuries.

Among other cities founded in Great Poland in that period, Witkowo (1680), Margonin (1696), Ostrów Wielkopolski (1713), Władysławów (1731), Szamocin (1748), and Zaniemyśl (1742) should be mentioned. Not all of them, however, originated in conditions favorable for further development. The founding of "new towns" close to existing centers also continued, for instance, at Nowe Miasto Wielkopolski (1664), Wieleń (1673), Międzychód (1671), Lubniewice (1708), Trzciel and Chodzież (in the 18th century), and Rogoźno (1750). Most of these places were centers of handicrafts.

New features were introduced in the 17th century in connection with the growth of the Counter Reformation in Poland. One phenomenon, discussed earlier in this chapter, was the setting up of monasteries in the suburbs and of Jesuit colleges within the cities. Another manifestation of religious zeal consisted in the laying out of so-called "Calvaries," that is, processional routes with chapels along them, conceived as a reproduction of the Stations of the Cross. Solemn religious services were held at each Station of the Cross.

Such large-scale Calvary schemes were created at Kalwaria Zebrzydowska (1602), Pakość on the Noteć (1628), Wejherowo (1649), Pacław (1668), Góra Kalwaria (1670), Vilna (1670), and Ujazdów near Warsaw (1731). Most of these still survive unchanged or were incorporated in the cities as part of their street systems, as in Góra Kalwaria and Warsaw.

The most interesting example is Góra Kalwaria, where the Calvary was laid out simultaneously with the foundation of the city and where religious functions were closely woven into the city's physical appearance. New Jerusalem, for such was the original name of this town situated near the village of Góra, was founded by the Bishop of Poznań, Stefan Wierzbołowski, under a privilege granted him by King Michał (Michael) Korybut Wiśniowiecki in 1670. A charter issued by Wierzbołowski on January 1st, 1672, established the economic and building program of the city. Emphasis was laid on the development of handicrafts and services catering to the pilgrims participating in the annual religious processions. Even the dates on which markets were held corresponded to those of the Calvary festivities. The city was given the symbolic shape of a cross, the longer arm constituting the principal axis of

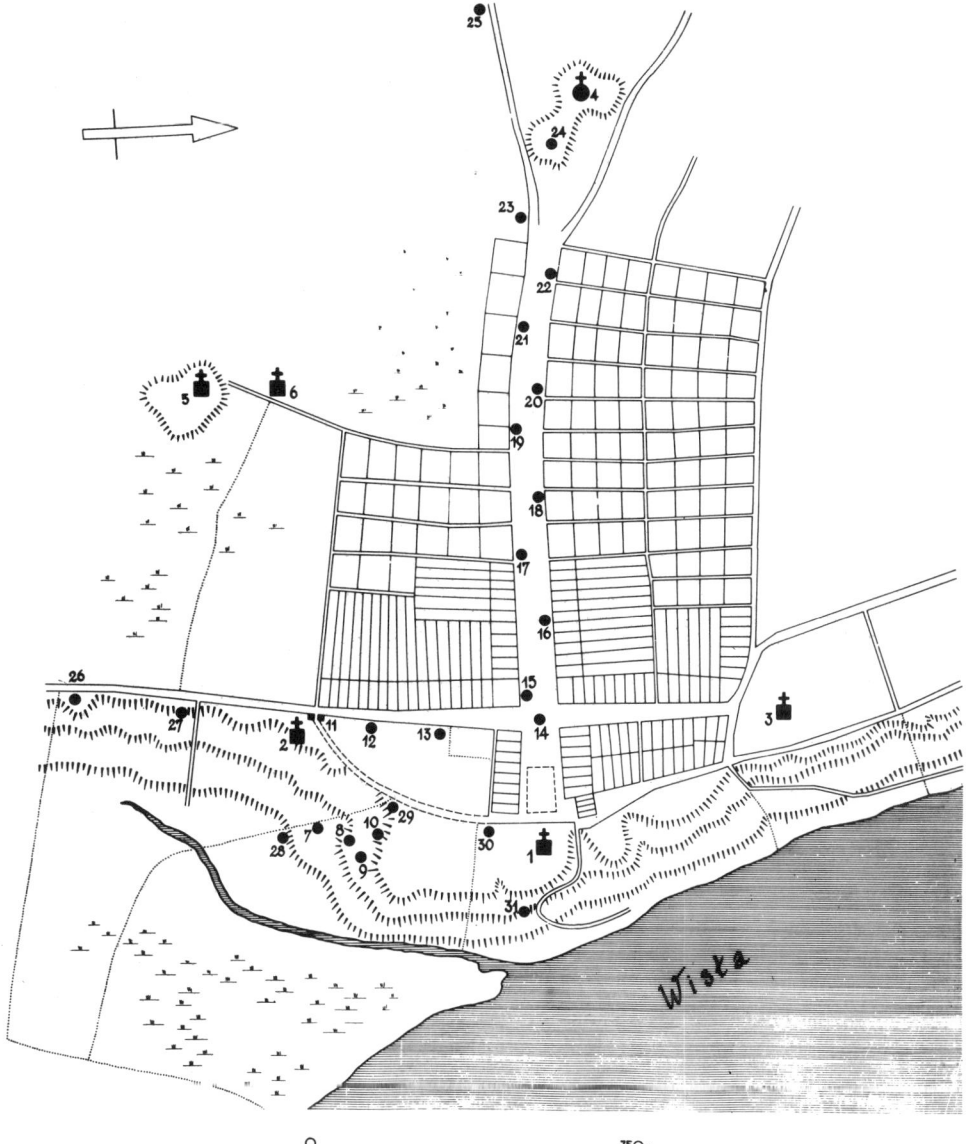

60. Reconstructed layout of Góra Kalwaria and the Calvary Way. 1. Bernardine church and monastery; 2. Dominican church and monastery; 3. Piarist church and monastery; 4. Church of the Holy Cross; 5. Dominican nuns' church and convent; 6. Marist church and monastery (the Cenacle); 7–10. Chapels; 11. Eastern Gate; 12. Caiaphas' House; 13. Prison in the Cellar; 14. Pilate's Town Hall; 15. Herod's House; 16–24. Stations of the Cross; 25–31. Chapels. The dotted lines mark the monastic property boundaries.

the city and, at the same time, forming the main route for the Calvary processions (Fig. 60). Ten chapels lined the route on both sides. This axis was closed at one end by the church of the Holy Cross, built on a low hillock in the western part of the city and, at the other, by Pilate's Town Hall situated where the two arms of the cross intersected and a monastery of Franciscan Observants built on the high bank of the Vistula, east of the city. At the ends of the shorter, transverse arm of the cross were two monasteries, one of the Dominicans and the other of the Piarists. Around the intersection of the arms about a hundred identical building plots (100 by 40 ells) were arranged; and along the longer arm, gardens for the burghers were laid out in the shape of regular squares (100 by 100 ells). The wide road between the intersection and the high bank of the Vistula served as marketplace and commercial center. In this small town, originally intended for 100 settler families, as many as 35 chapels, 6 churches, and 5 monasteries were erected. Due to the situation of the city on the high bank, close to a slight bend of the river, a wide view opened from the main axis on the valley of the Vistula.

The activities furthering the urbanization of Podolia and the Ukraine were of a different nature. As in earlier periods, the founding of cities in these areas aimed at the colonization of conquered territories and consolidation of the rule of the magnates. At the same time, these new cities were strategically important in view of the almost incessant wars with the Turks and Tartars. Consequently, some of these new foundations had the character of strongholds rather than cities. Stanisławów, founded in 1662 by Andrzej Potocki, may serve as an example. It was composed of only a few building blocks around the market square, a castle, and numerous churches and was surrounded by a powerful defense system (Fig. 61). Fortifications were continuously being constructed in the eastern borderlands. Because of the almost uninterrupted wars, the fortress Okopy Świętej Trójcy was strengthened in 1692, and a town was founded near it in 1700. The tremendous devastation in these

61. Plan of the city of Stanisławów (U.S.S.R.), 1792, redrawn after a plan in the Warsaw Polytechnic. 1. Castle; 2. Trinitarian church and monastery; 3. Town Hall; 4. Collegiate church; 5. Armory; 6. Jesuit church and monastery; 7. Synagogue; 8. Greek Catholic church; 9. Armenian church; 10. Tyśmienica Gate; 11. Halicz Gate; 12. Gate for pedestrians.

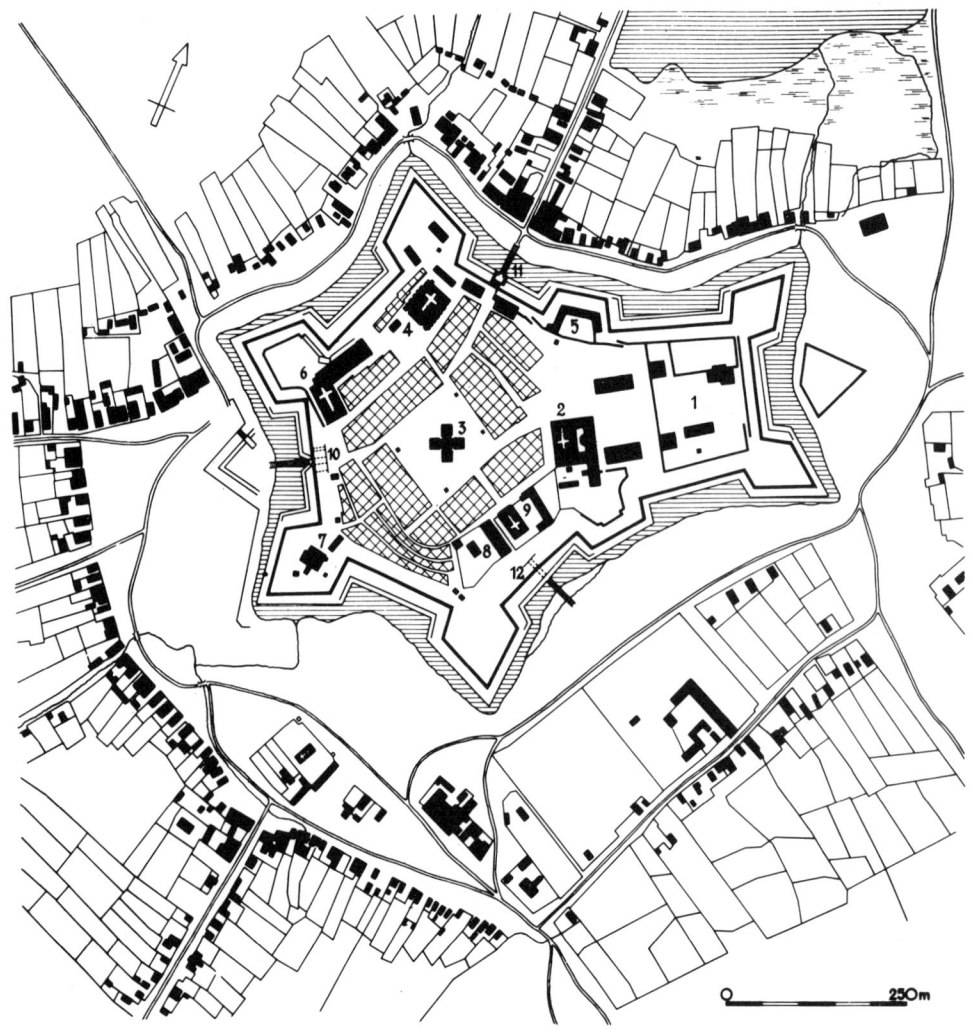

areas impeded their subsequent development. Many cities that had flourished in the 16th and early 17th centuries suffered complete breakdowns, while others were rebuilt in a haphazard manner, obliterating their original regular layouts.

The wars, sweeping over almost all of Poland in the 17th century, caused a considerable depopulation of villages and cities. This slowed down the process of urbanization not only in the eastern borderlands but also in other parts of the country, except in Great Poland. A few cities were still founded along the borderline between Mazovia and the Grand Duchy of Lithuania, such as Białystok (1665–1668), Korycin (1671), Szczuczyn (1690), Raczki (1703), and Suwałki (1715). Several private cities also came into existence in the Lublin area, among them Józefów, founded in 1687 by Andrzej Potocki, and Józefów Ordynacki, founded in 1725 by Tomasz Zamoyski. Frampol, a settlement founded about 1736 in the same region, deserves attention for its layout. It was contained within a regular square of approximately 1,640 by 1,640 feet, with a very large marketplace of 738 by 738 feet in the center, and eight streets, four beginning at the middle of the sides of the square while the other four issued diagonally from it (Figs. 62, 63). A church constituted the terminal feature of one of the axes. This layout proves that 16th and 17th-century theoretical city plans were still used as models in the 18th century. Frampol, however, was an agricultural settlement; compact

62. Plan of the town of Frampol today.

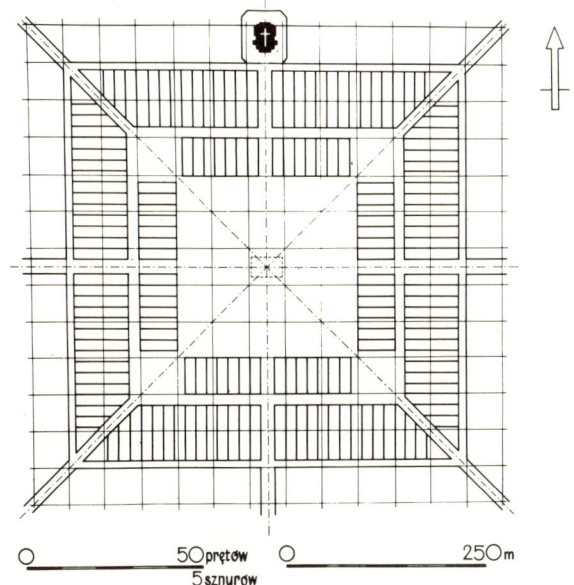

63. Reconstruction of the original layout of Frampol.

rows of barns stand even today along its boundaries. It should be noted that many towns of the time were semi-agricultural in character and that the 17th-century devastations entailed the agrarization of many centers of handicrafts.

In 1697, thanks to the support of the Austrian Habsburgs, Augustus II, the Strong, Elector of Saxony, ascended the Polish throne. This date marks the beginning of a long period of Saxon cultural influences in Poland, especially in city planning. The first years of Augustus' reign, when wars with Turkey and Sweden were in full swing and many foreign troops kept marching through the country, was hardly favorable for building and city-planning activities. The first half of the 18th century, however, in spite of territorial losses and the decline of Poland's political importance, was a period of relative stability that made it possible for the king and the magnates to undertake the construction of great Baroque residences as new elements in the structure of cities.

Having consolidated his power in Poland, Augustus II resolved to build a grand royal residence in Warsaw, in accordance with the practical needs of the Court and in harmony with the prevailing Baroque tastes. Thus, on his initiative, the largest scheme of its kind was carried out in Warsaw. Even today it remains an important component element of the city center. For his royal seat Augustus chose a site lying south of the city, adjoining the fortifications built in 1626. During the years 1713 to 1728, Matthäus Daniel Pöppelmann and Johann Christoph Naumann worked on plans and designs, of which many alternative versions are preserved in the Saxon archives.

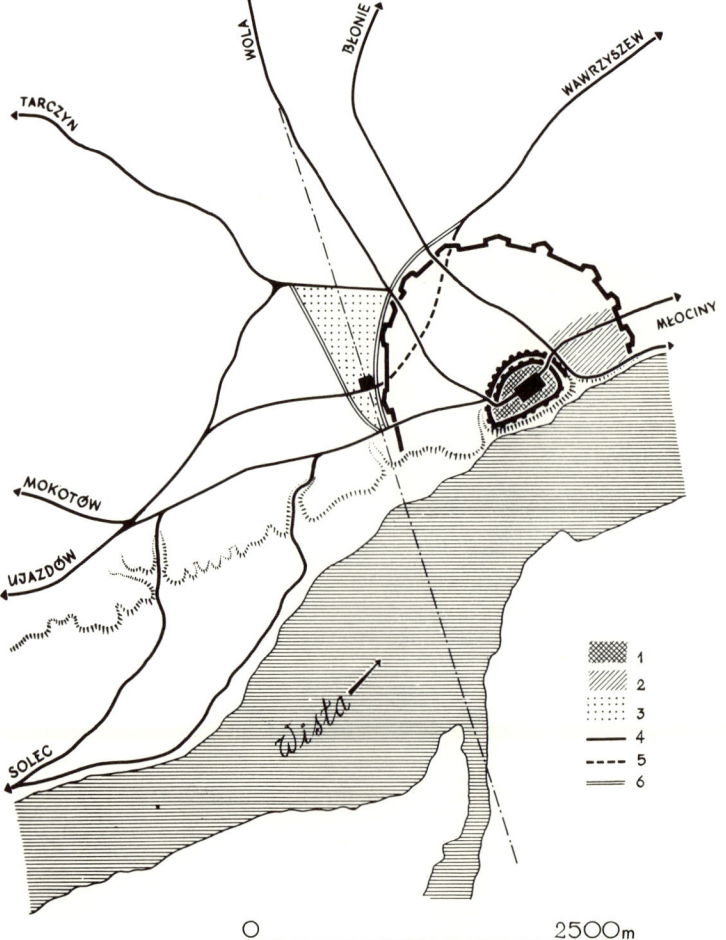

64. The site of the Saxon Axis of Warsaw. 1. Old Town, founded about 1300; 2. New Town founded in 1408; 3. King Augustus II's scheme; 4. Roads before the construction of the Saxon Axis; 5. Roads closed by the ring of fortifications built in 1621; 6. Roads built in connection with the construction of the fortifications.

The basic feature of the entire scheme was a grand axis perpendicular to Krakowskie Przedmieście Street and to the Vistula (Fig. 64). The focus of the composition was the Morstin Palace, expanded into a grand royal residence in the Baroque style. In front of the palace was a vast *cour d'honneur* reaching up to Krakowskie Przedmieście, with a monumental gate, and some ancillary buildings screening it from the street. West of the palace, a large park was laid out in the form of an elongated pentagon (Fig. 65). The park was designed in the Baroque style, with many parterres, "green interiors" and facilities for entertainments, a shooting range, an amphitheater, and other structures. In the western section of the park was a building called *Grand Salon*, from which radial avenues led to the western boundaries of the park. From the splendid gate closing the park, the axis continued westward in the form of a wide parkway, flanked on both sides by barracks.

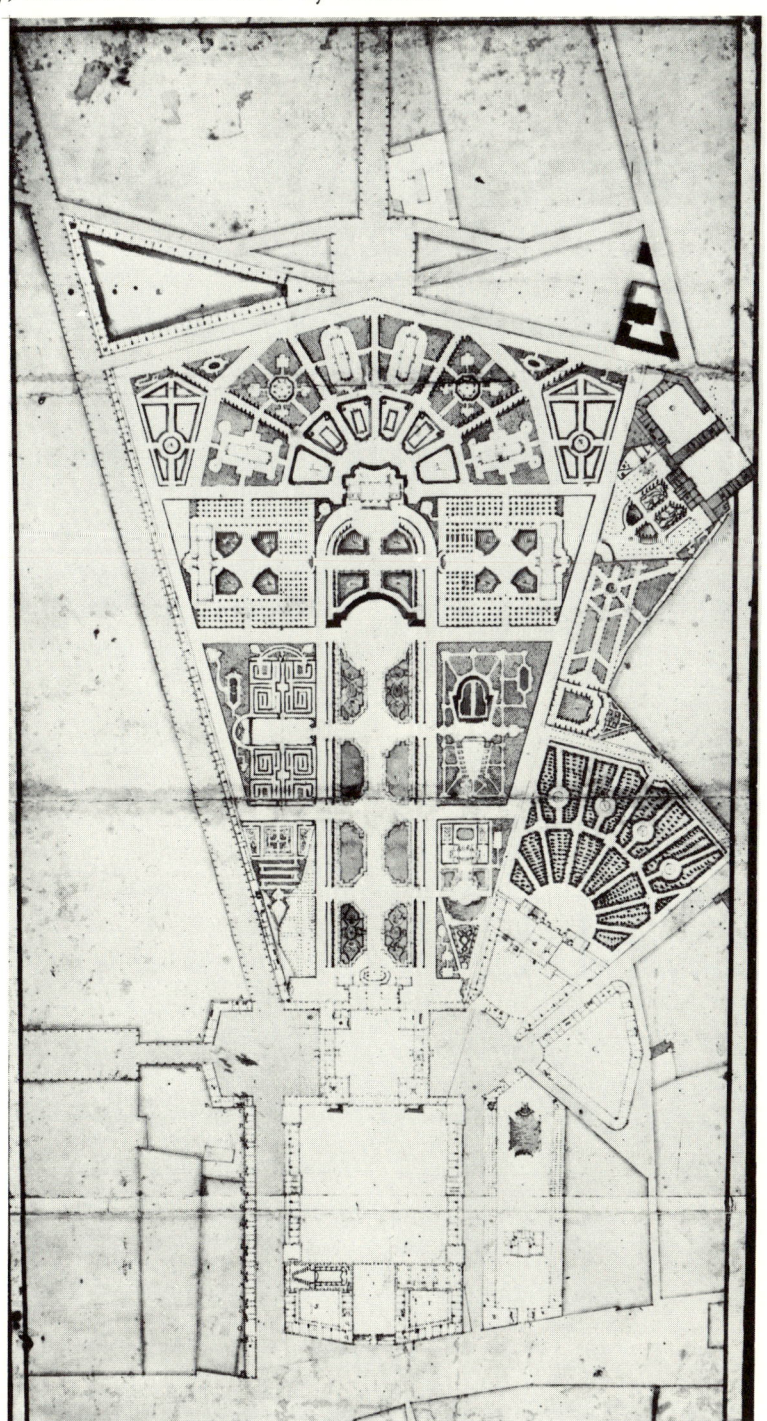

65. Design for the residence of Augustus II at Warsaw. Original in the Sächsische Landeshauptarchiv, Dresden.

The scheme took more than 40 years to carry out. After the death of Augustus the Strong, in 1731, work on the scheme was continued by his son Augustus III. Although Pőppelmann was responsible for the design of the scheme, there is no doubt that it was strongly influenced by August II in person, a great patron of architecture and art and sponsor of many similar schemes in Saxony and Poland. Many Saxon architects participated in the realization of the Warsaw scheme, but Karl Friedrich Pőppelmann, Johann Siegmund Deybel, and Joachim Daniel Jauch should be mentioned among the most renowned. This great Baroque composition, whose importance as royal residence ended with the dethronement of Augustus III in 1763, played an essential role in the shaping of the future center of Warsaw. Although, strictly speaking, it was not a city-planning scheme but rather a grand palace-and-garden composition, it influenced considerably the formation of the central road pattern and was entirely incorporated in it, the park being left as open space. Today, although cut across by three north-south traffic arteries and deformed by subsequent buildings and demolitions, including

66. Plan of Warsaw, 1733. In the center the Saxon Axis; south of the city (left) the residence at Ujazdów, with game park and calvary. Original in the Sächsische Landeshauptarchiv.

the destruction of the palace during World War II, it still constitutes an important feature of that part of the city center.

The Saxon scheme was not the only park to be laid out in the central area of present-day Warsaw. As early as the 17th century, many magnates' residences were built along the high bank of the Vistula and west of the Old Town, for instance, the Krasiński, Przebendowski, Ossoliński, Wiśniowiecki, and other palaces. Under the reign of the Saxon kings still more of them came into existence, such as the residence of the King's Minister, H. Brühl, the "Blue Palace" belonging to the Czartoryski family, and others. Nor was the King's initiative confined to the construction of his palace. Designs for a thorough remodeling of the Royal Castle, built in the 16th to 17th centuries adjoining the Old Town, and of the Ujazdów Castle, a 17th-century suburban royal seat, were prepared. A large game park was laid out close to Ujazdów Castle, with a long axial canal called the Piaseczyński Canal leading away from the high bank below the castle and with a radial system of avenues (Fig. 66). Augustus II was also the initiator of a Calvary scheme in Warsaw,

laid out south of the forking of the roads toward Mokotów and Ujazdów, the present Ujazdowska Avenue. This Calvary led straight south from the fork to the bend of the high bank of the Vistula, where a wooden church of the Holy Cross was erected (later replaced by the Belvedere Palace), and then turned back along the bank to the castle. Trees were planted on both sides of the processional route, and 29 chapels were built along its course, similar to that of the Calvary scheme at Góra Kalwaria described earlier in this chapter.

During the reign of Augustus II, marked by a strong tendency toward absolutism, as many as three groups of military barracks were built in the capital city: one of these west of the palace axis, another adjoining the Casimir Palace in Krakowskie Przedmieście Street, and the third on the road leading to Bielany, north of the city on a site where, in the 19th century, the Russians were to build a citadel.

Large Baroque residences were built not only in Warsaw. Monumental palace and garden schemes, usually axial, were carried out near many cities, private ones in particular. Sometimes they were situated far from the city, as in Wolbórz or at Wilanów near Warsaw, and entirely independent of it. However, in many cases the new residence was architecturally linked with the city, even integrated with it to form a single composition. A good example of such integration is Krystynopol (redeveloped in the years 1756 to 1761), where the *cour d'honneur* of the palace communicated directly with the urban market square. A similar connection of palace and town took place in Worniany about 1769. Elsewhere such an integration was sometimes achieved by means of a new axis, transverse to that of the park scheme, as in Radzyń Podlaski in 1758 to 1766.

One of the grandest residences of that period was the palace at Rydzyna, erected in the years 1693 to 1703 for Rafał Leszczyński, after a design by Pompeo Ferrari. Built on the foundations of a medieval castle,

67. Plan of the residence and the town of Rydzyna, prepared by I. Graff in 1784.

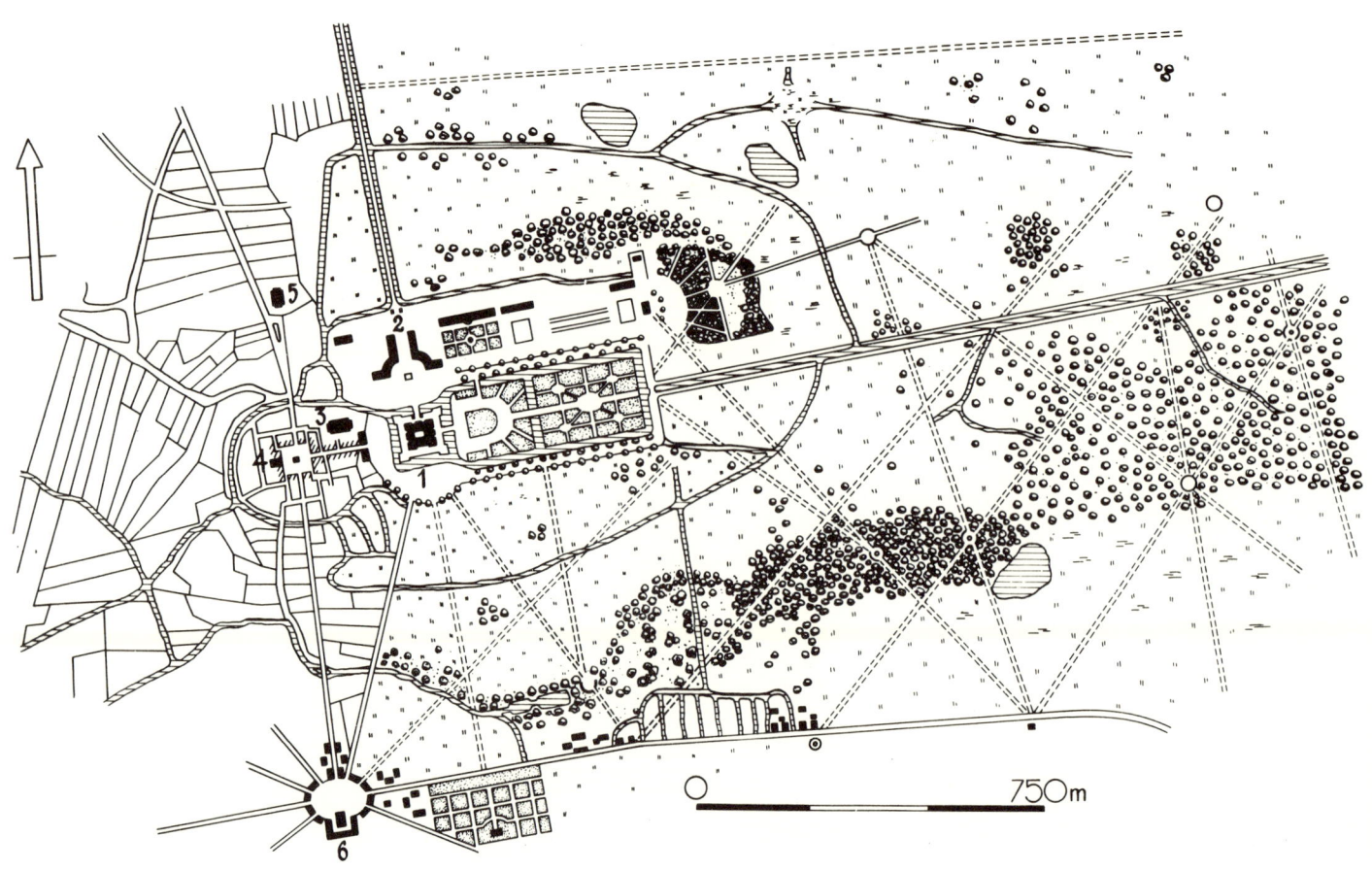

it had a rectangular plan and was surrounded by a moat. It stood facing the city, which had been founded in 1409, redeveloped in the years 1742–1750 by the architect K. M. Frantz (?), and integrated into a single composition with the palace. A new axial street, issuing from the market square, opened a vista on the palace. Its other terminal feature was the city hall, which stood in the center of one of the sides of the market square. The axiality of the entire scheme was further emphasized by a statue of the Holy Trinity erected in the middle of the square (Fig. 67). New improvements were introduced in 1766–1777 by the architect I. Graff. A monumental forecourt was then laid out in front of the northern façade of the palace and, in the southern suburb, an oval circus with radial streets was created. Spatial interaction between the particular component parts of the whole complex was achieved by means of vistas.

Another scheme, remarkable for its large scale, was the residence of Jan Klemens Branicki in Białystok, a city founded in the 17th century on the site of a former village. The palace, situated south of the city, was built in the years 1728–1758 under the direction of the Saxon architect, Johann Siegmund Deybel. A "new town," consisting of two streets intersecting at right angles, was founded on the prolongation of the axis of the palace and the park. Improvements were also carried out in the existing city, including the erection of a monumental city hall in the marketplace (1745–1761). Its tower closed the perspective view of the roads leading into the city (Figs. 68, 69).

68. Reconstructed plan of the city of Białystok in the late 18th century. 1. Branicki Palace; 2. Orangeries; 3. Theater; 4. Farm; 5. Manorial brewery; 6. Parish church; 7. Hospital; 8. Convent of the Sisters of Charity; 9. Town Hall; 10. Weighing house; 11. Synagogue; 12. Uniat church.

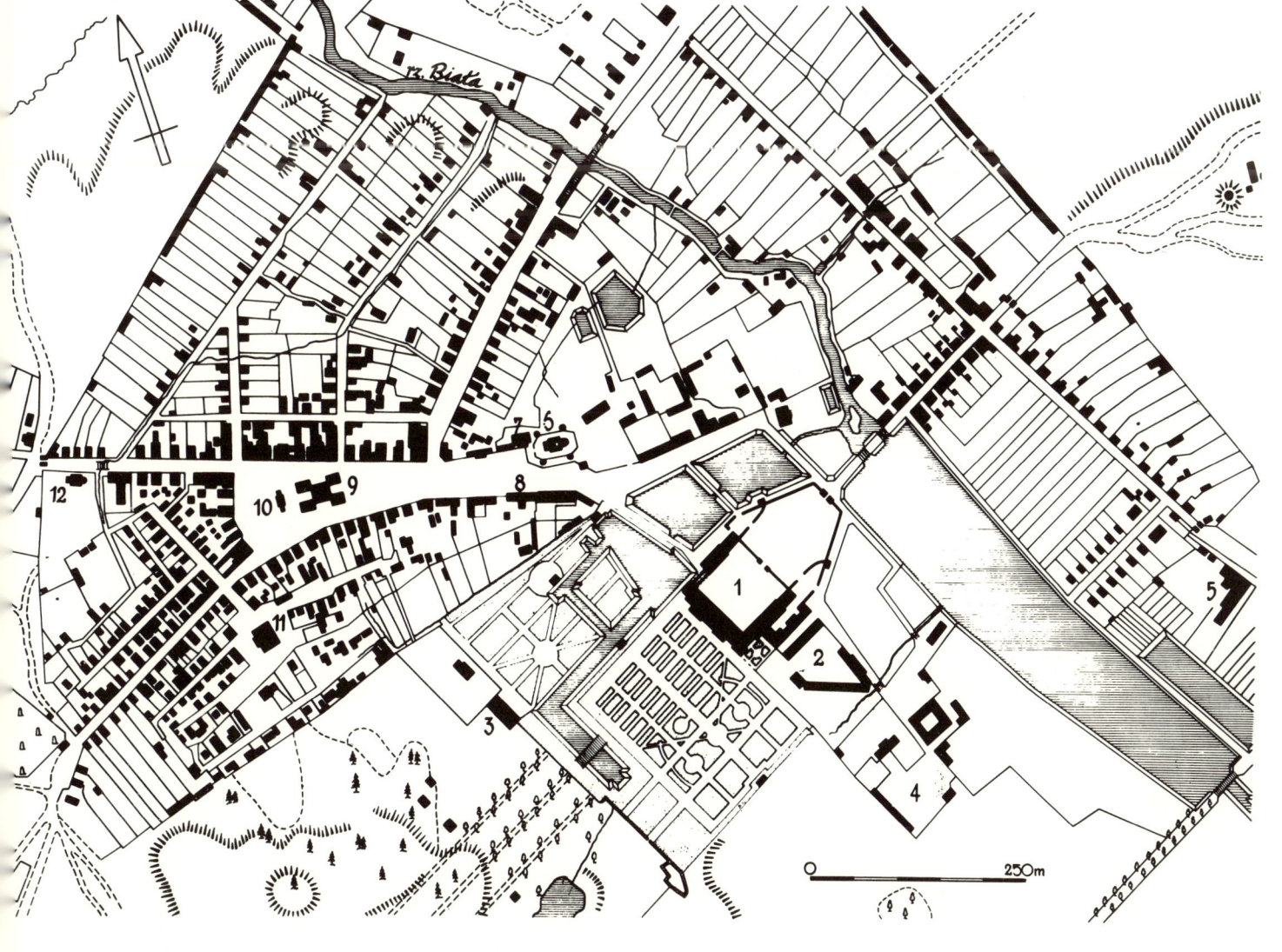

69. Design for one side of the market square at Biała Podlaska by Maciej Jakimowicz (1777). The corner buildings were intended for inns; between them were four residential buildings with shops. Original in the Library of the University of Warsaw.

Among other similar schemes of the time, some of the most noteworthy are the Siedlce Palace, which was built in the years 1755–1766 along with the redevelopment of the city; Terespol, to which urban rights were granted in 1753; Tykocin, where the church was built and the market square redeveloped between 1742–1771; and Biała Podlaska, where the market square was redeveloped in 1777. In the period from 1710–1766 more than 40 cities—only two of them Royal cities—were founded in Western and Central Poland. Almost all of them were small local centers of handicrafts, semi-agricultural in character. A few "new towns" were also built adjoining existing centers, as in Trzciel, Przysucha, and Lublin.

Attempts to improve and rebuild some of the destroyed cities were also made, but the results of these efforts were rather limited. One interesting instance may be noted in Warsaw where, in 1743, Franciszek Bieliński, Grand Marshall of the Crown, created the "Paving Commission" which remained active for over twenty years, the peak years being 1750–1752. Financial means acquired from taxes levied on owners of real estate and from State subsidies were used for the paving of streets, drainage, and refuse disposal. The Commission also initiated the surveying of the city carried out by Jakub Fontana in the years 1744–1752. Bieliński was also the founder of a small town, Bielino (1757), situated in what is today the central area of Warsaw. It had a regular layout and a square marketplace, now known as Dąbrowski Square.

A flourishing development of the arts in Poland took place during the reign of the last of the Polish kings, Stanisław August (Stanislaus Augustus) Poniatowski (1764–1795). His economic, social, and artistic initiatives involved a number of city planning schemes and stimulated many magnates to similar activities.

Soon after ascending the throne, Stanislaus Augustus embarked upon a project connected with the rebuilding of Ujazdów Castle as a royal residence, the creation of the so-called "Stanislaus Axis" which gave shape to the southern part of what is now the center of Warsaw. In the years 1766–1768 a new road system was traced west of Ujazdowskie

Avenue (the former Saxon Calvary Way). A series of star-shaped traffic nodal points linked the new road system with the axis of the castle, which was a prolongation of the Piaseczyński Canal toward the west. Like the Saxon Axis discussed earlier in this chapter, this scheme by Stanislaus Augustus cannot be strictly termed city planning. It was rather a system of traffic arteries and vistas lined by rows of trees. An experimental village was to be founded on the main axis; its trace still survives in the name of the street, Nowowiejska (New Village Street). In the second half of the 19th century the area was subdivided and built up. Thus a new urban complex developed around a system of rural roads.

A few years later Stanislaus Augustus started the construction of a summer residence situated below the high bank of the Vistula, south of Ujazdów Castle. This residence, called Łazienka Królewska (Royal Bath), was surrounded by a vast romantic park which today constitutes the largest and most beautiful open space in the central part of Warsaw. A number of private palace-and-garden schemes were also carried out in what were then the surroundings of Warsaw; for instance, Mokotów for Princess Lubomirska and Królikarnia for K. Thomasis in the south; Powązki for Princess I. Czartoryska in the northwest; and Solec for K. Poniatowski, on the high bank of the Vistula. At the same time there was a revival of building activities in the capital itself, resulting in the construction of many monumental ecclesiastical and secular structures.

Another project due to the initiative of King Stanislaus Augustus was the reconstruction of the small town of Kozienice, where one of the royal residences was situated. The plan (Fig. 70), prepared by J. K. Fontana in 1782, provided for the integration of the residence and the town into a single complex, of which the main landmarks—the palace, the town hall, and the church—were strung on one axis. This plan was partly carried out.

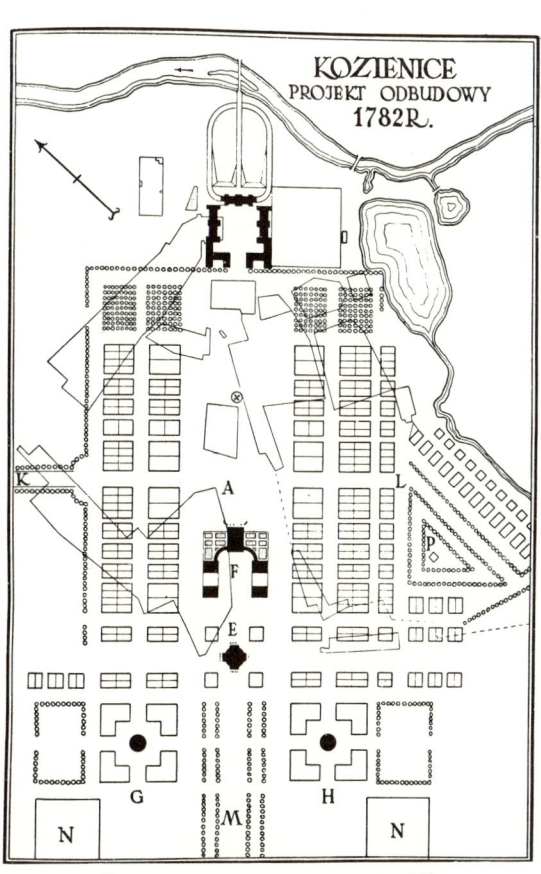

70. Plan for the redevelopment of Kozienice after the fire in 1782. A. Market square; E. Roman Catholic church; F. The ensemble of the town hall, school, priest's house, and hospital; G. Protestant church; H. Synagogue; K. Warsaw Road; L. Ruthenian Road; M. Avenue leading toward the fields; N. Barns belonging to the townspeople; P. Site with steep gradient unfit for building. The thin line indicates the outlines of the building blocks before the fire.

In the later decades of the 18th century attempts were made to industrialize the country. On the initiative of the king and the magnates, a number of manufactories were put into operation with a view to reducing the importation of luxury items such as glassware, faïence, playing-cards, and silk girdles. A number of textile manufactories, mechanical forges, blast furnaces, and gunsmithies were also built. The king's manufactories were set up in his Lithuanian estates; the man responsible for their organization was Antoni Tyzenhaus, Royal Treasurer for Lithuania. In connection with the newly organized manufactories, Tyzenhaus founded several new towns in the area: Suchowola (1766), Szczebra (1768), Jeleniowo (1770), Krasnopol (1770), and Dąbrowa (1765–1775). All of them featured rather regular layouts and standardized houses for the artisans. An interesting example is the settlement attached to the Kunsztów manufactory near the village of Łososna. It was composed of numerous industrial buildings housing extremely varied lines of production—ironware, textiles, fancy goods, gold objects—as well as dwelling houses for the workers. In spite of its utilitarian function, the whole scheme was clearly in keeping with the Baroque trends of spatial composition (Fig. 71). Kunsztów was only partly carried out, for the year of its foundation (1780) coincided with the collapse of Tyzenhaus' entire economic campaign.

The city planning activities of private landowners were greatly stimulated during the reign of Stanislaus Augustus. They established a number of new towns such as Magnuszew (1776), Alwernia (1778), Nowy Dwór (1780), Nowy Tomyśl (1786), and Białaczów (1787). Some of these new towns had regular layouts still rooted in the Baroque tradition, for example, Nowy Dwór. But their subdivisions and development were strictly utilitarian, most of them having been built as centers of handicrafts.

Considerable progress was achieved in the reconstruction and improvement of the Royal Cities, thanks to the so-called *Boni Ordinis* Commissions which were set up in the 1780s in almost all larger cities. Their activity was primarily of an economic nature. They brought order to the cities' finances and property relations, organized the municipal administration, and were the first to encourage the influx of manufacturers into the cities. However, they also directed some efforts at improving the existing development, the repair of pavements, and refuse disposal. The plans of cities prepared by these Commissions were essentially site plans which registered property boundaries rather than plans for improvement and expansion. Nevertheless, in a number of cities like Warsaw and Lublin some minor improvements were carried out, and new streets were cut through. Likewise, in the private cities, attempts were made to bring order into existing developments and to initiate new building projects. For example, a large axis connecting the residence with the market square at Siemiatycze and a new plan for Kock date from that period. Both towns were the property of Princess Anna Jabłonowska, who carried out a whole series of economic and social reforms on her estates. New important public buildings like city halls and churches were erected in the two towns. The layout of Kock, where the city hall and the church were designed as integral parts of a uniform complex of buildings around the marketplace, deserves particular attention.

Thus, the second half of the 18th century brought a distinct improvement in the condition of Polish cities, a gradual reconstruction and expansion. It also witnessed a strengthening of the position of the townspeople who, under the Constitution of 1791, came to be represented in the Diet. However, the first two partitions in 1772 and 1793, in which vast territories in the east were annexed by Russia and considerable areas in the north, south, and west by Prussia and Austria, also took place in that period. The final partition in 1795 and the abdication of Stanislaus Augustus put an end to all the initiatives which had been aimed at the economic and social reorganization of the country.

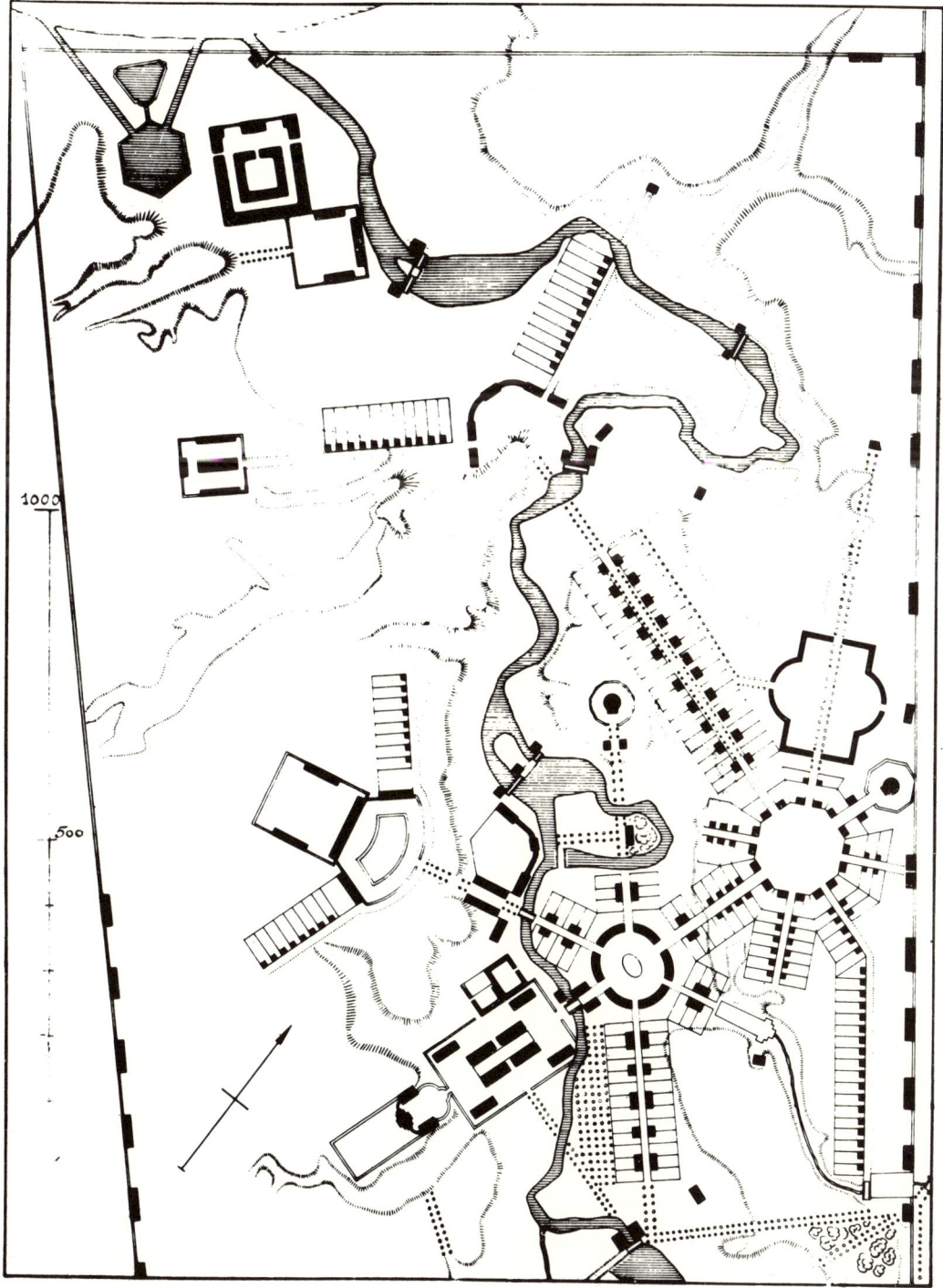

71. Plan of the central part of the industrial village of Kunsztów (Łosośna near Grodno), 1780. Copy of the original plan of 1780. The village consisted of a number of manufactories producing textiles (wool, linen, silks), metalware, paper, and fancy goods. Power was provided by the waters of the little river Łosośna. In the center of the village was a "circus" with streets flanked by artisans' houses issuing radially from it. A large market was situated nearby.

CHAPTER 8

Evolution of Cities in the First Half of the 19th Century

THE DIVISION OF the country into three parts, ruled by three different powers, placed each of those areas in a different sphere of cultural and economic influences. This fact resulted, among other things, in a differentiation of city-planning activities in the particular provinces. Each of the partitioning powers organized a building service of its own in the area under its domination, to which were sent numerous civil servants and builders who, having been trained in Prussia, Austria, or Russia, acted in keeping with city planning and architectural trends prevailing in their respective countries.

The liveliest activity on Polish soil was displayed by the Prussian authorities, who issued a series of regulations dealing with the economy and administration of cities. The colonization launched by Frederick II of Prussia was intended primarily for rural areas where numerous new settlements, with regular layouts and standardized development, came into existence. However, in the years 1772 to 1808 the Prussian authorities embarked upon improvements of a number of cities, together with the laying out of new districts for settlers, as in Lipno (1799), Wizna (1799), and Pułtusk (1803). Particularly noteworthy is the plan of Dąbie, on the Ner, where a new clothiers' village was established in 1799. This plan was to become something of a model for later settlements.

City-planning activities were concentrated mostly in the larger administrative centers such as Poznań, Kalisz, and Płock. In all three cities new residential districts were built for the Prussian civil servants (Fig. 72). In Poznań and Kalisz, wide avenues lined with poplars were laid out as the central features of these new districts. The buildings were erected after standard designs. The extreme austerity of their Neo-Classical architectural forms emphasized their purely utilitarian

72. View of Wilhelm Avenue in Poznań, first half of the 19th century. At the corner of avenue and square the Raczyński Library, built in 1829. Lithograph by L. Sachse, 1833.

character. This type of development was evolved under the influence of David Gilly, the government's official architect and the founder of the Royal Academy of Building in Berlin. In subsequent years this style became common in the Polish Kingdom.

The Prussian authorities also carried out some fortification work in Grudziądz, Warsaw, and Łęczyca. They efficiently controlled all town planning and building activities in the territories under their rule and set up a State building service similar to that existing in Prussia proper, entrusting it with the preparation of the plans for urban improvements and new building projects. These developments of the Prussian period cannot be included in the history of Polish city planning and architecture.

In the area occupied by Austria, comprising Little Poland and the Voivodship of Lublin, the scope of town planning was much smaller. As in the territory under Prussian rule, the successive colonization campaigns launched by Maria Theresa and her son Joseph II were restricted to rural areas. Building activities were mostly concentrated in Cracow and Lvov, the main administrative centers. Here, the old walls were torn down and attempts were made to improve the existing development. Plans for "beautifying" the two cities were worked out, their main purpose being to bring order to the outlying suburbs. In Cracow the first proposal put forward was to lay out a ring of promenades replacing the old medieval walls. This idea was later carried into effect so that today the historic core is encircled by a wide green belt. In 1794 a plan existed to build a frontier fortress in Cracow, but with the annexation of further territories in 1795 the idea was abandoned.

An interesting plan (Fig. 73) was devised in 1779 for the construction of a new town, Ludwinów, near Cracow, on the opposite side of the Vistula, which was to be a borderland center of trade and handicrafts. At that time Cracow still belonged to Poland.

The town planning activities displayed in the years 1772–1808 in the area occupied by Russia dealt with territories which were ethnically not Polish and will therefore not be discussed here at any great length. Suffice it to say that it involved the planned redevelopment of the cities of White Russia. The scale of this activity may be illustrated by the fact that between 1762 and 1796 redevelopment plans, remarkable for their extreme regularity, were prepared for more than 400 cities throughout the Russian Empire.

The Napoleonic Wars brought a brief change in Poland's political situation. The Duchy of Warsaw, comprising the central territories of the former Polish Commonwealth, was set up in 1807, and a Polish State Administration functioned there until 1813. The short existence of the Duchy of Warsaw and the continuous fighting going on throughout these years precluded significant town planning activities. However, some administrative decisions concerning the organization of municipal authorities, the establishment of a building service, and the settling of artisans were later partly taken up and adopted by the government of the so-called Congress Kingdom.

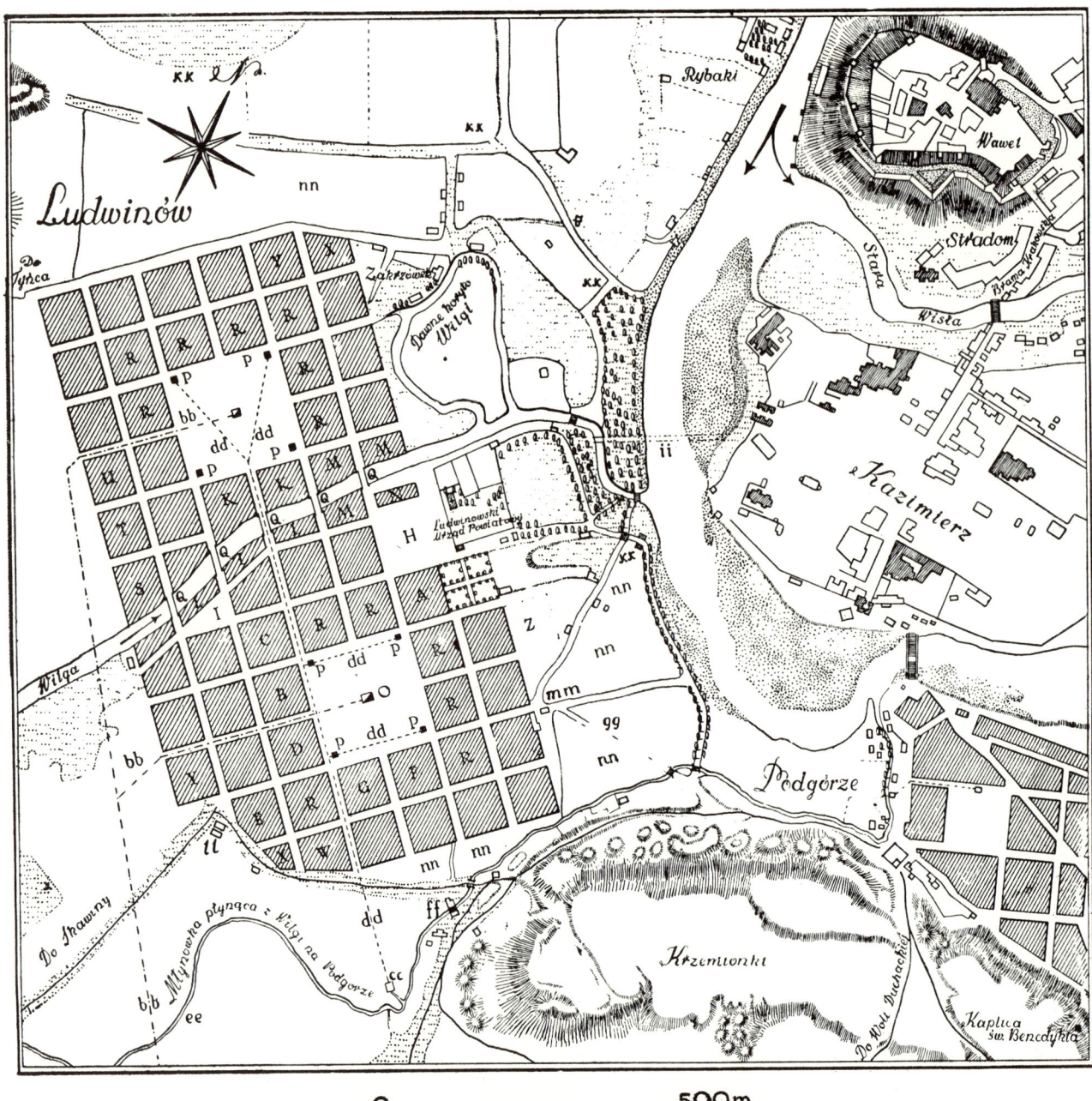

73. Plan for the new town of Ludwinów, on the right bank of the Vistula near Cracow. A. Church of Corpus Christi and monastery; B. Town Hall; C. School; D. Post office; E. Customhouse; F. Town major and guardhouse; G. Seat of the local authority; H. Vegetable market; I. Cattle market; K. Tanners' streets; L. Tawers' streets; M. Slaughterhouses; N. Butchers' stalls; O. Fountain with drinking-water; P. Cisterns with water for cooking and laundering; Q. Proposed bridges on the Wilga; R. Tradesmen; S. Barracks; T. Warehouse; U. Bakery; W. Brewery; X. Smith and cartwright; Y. Wheelwright and saddler; Z. Cemetery; bb. Conduit with spring water; cc. Source of water for cooking and laundering; ee. Millrace supplying water for cooking; ff. Subprefect's mill; gg. New road from Podgórze to the new town; ii. Proposed bridge linking Skawina Gate in Kazimierz with Ludwinów; kk, ll, mm, nn. Pastures, fields, and farms.

Two plans of urban reconstruction, worked out in that period by the builder J. Sadkowski, deserve attention. One was prepared in 1809 for the town of Stryków, which had been destroyed by fire. The central feature of the proposed new development was a triangular market-place (Fig. 74). The second plan was for the town of Ryczywół, which had been flooded in 1811 and was to be rebuilt on another site. The plan was extremely regular, with symmetrically disposed architectural landmarks (Fig. 75). Both designs were carried out only in part.

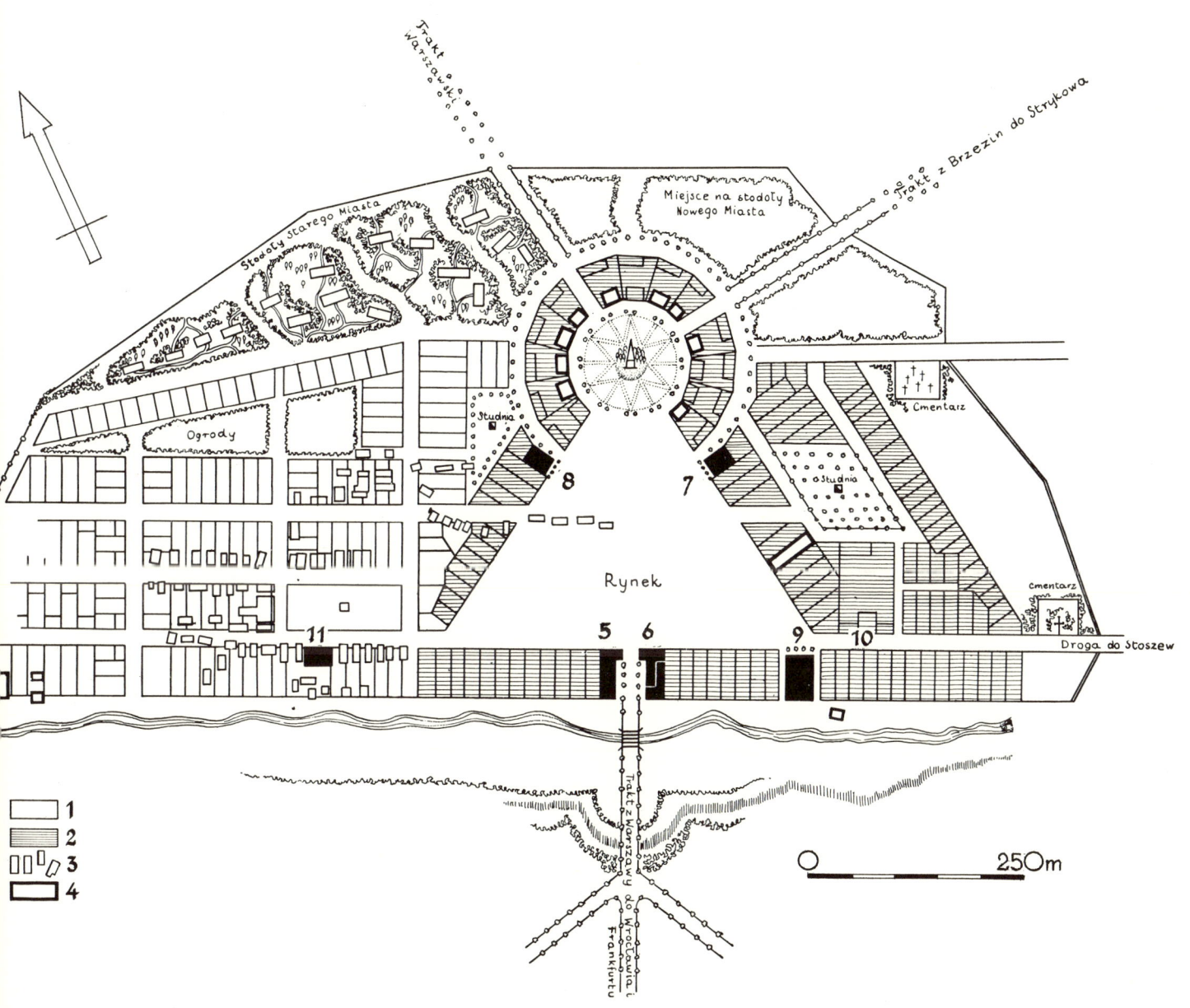

74. Plan for the rebuilding of Stryków after a fire, prepared by J. Sadkowski in 1809. 1. Plots for houses in the Old Town; 2. Plots in the New Town; 3. Old houses spared by the fire; 4. New houses; 5. Public house; 6. Inn; 7. Protestant church; 8. Town Hall; 9. Roman Catholic church; 10. Market; 11. Synagogue.

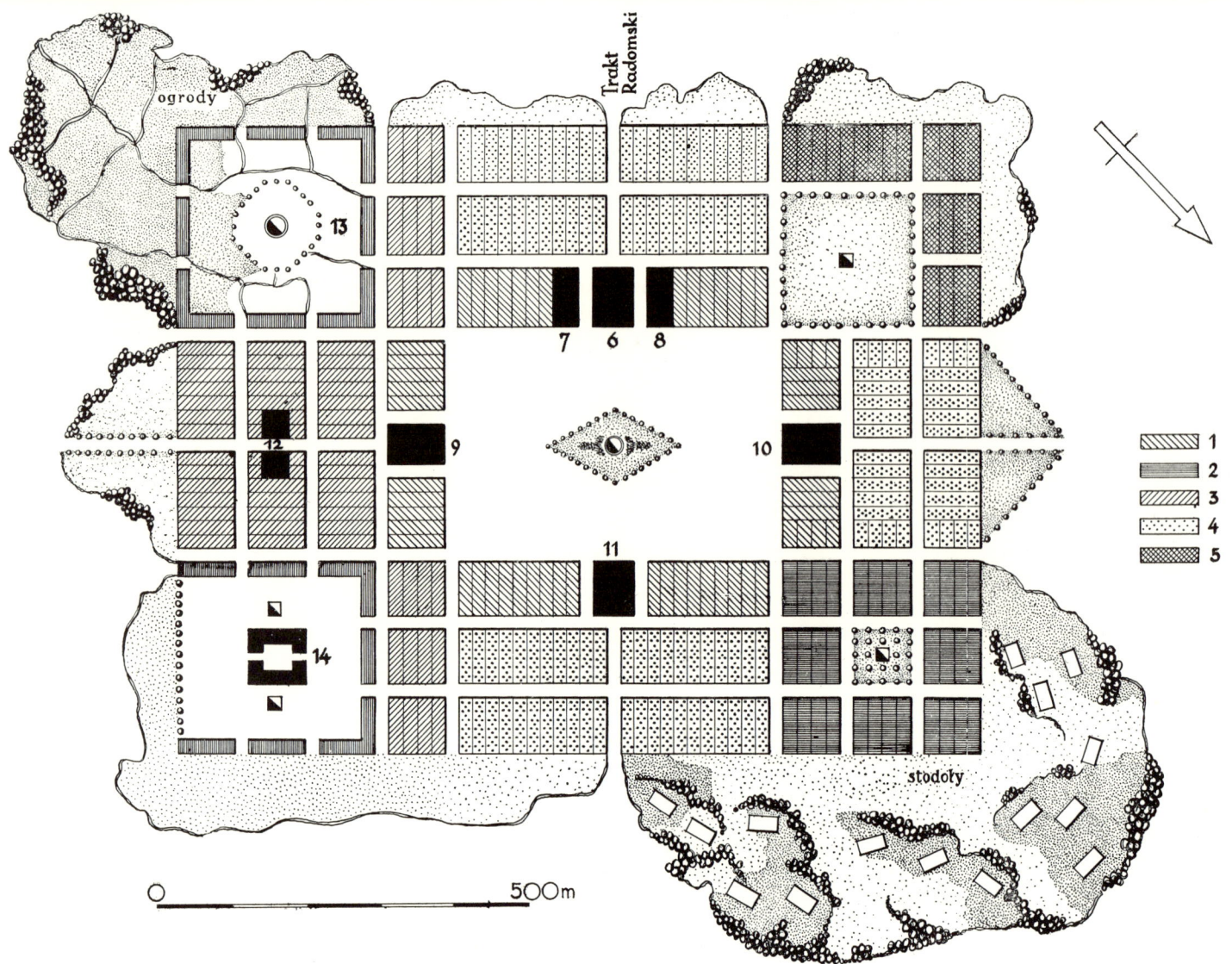

75. Plan of the town of Ryczywół, on a new site after a flood, by J. Sadkowski (1811). 1. Tradesmen's houses; 2. Farmers' houses; 3. Jewish houses; 4. Artisans' houses; 5. Brewers' houses; 6. Church; 7. School; 8. Priest's house; 9. Post office; 10. Town Hall; 11. Inn; 12. Jewish school; 13. Customhouse and warehouses; 14. Barracks. Barns were situated in the northern part of the town (bottom right), outside the built-up area.

The Congress of Vienna (1815) resulted in the creation of a Polish Kingdom, the so-called Congress Kingdom, with the Tsar of Russia as king, which in the years 1815–1832 enjoyed a certain degree of home rule. This enabled the government of the Congress Kingdom to undertake economic improvements aimed at the development of industry and conditions in general. These activities were partly a continuation of trends initiated in the Period of the Enlightenment that had preceded the fall of the Polish Commonwealth. Many architects trained in the time of Stanislaus Augustus, like S. Zawadski and P. C. Aigner, resumed work in the service of the State, along with Prussian builders like A. Groffe, F. J. Trausolt, and F. Bergemann who, after the shift in the frontiers of the areas under Prussian control, remained in the territory now forming part of the Congress Kingdom. Simplifying matters a little, one might say this was the reason why the specific architectural and town planning forms evolved in the Congress Kingdom represented a blending of the classical tradition of the time of Stanislaus Augustus with the rationalist forms of Prussian architecture of the late 18th and early 19th centuries.

After a short period in which the new State took shape, the government of the Congress Kingdom embarked, in the years 1818–1819, on a large-scale campaign aimed at putting the economy and city finances (property relations, municipal revenues, and the like) in order and at improving the existing state of development. Modeled on the Prussian survey carried out in 1793–1794, a comprehensive questionnaire made it possible to obtain detailed information on the financial situation of cities, the number of their inhabitants, and the types and condition of their buildings. Thanks to the wide range of the questions it was also possible to assess the needs of particular cities as well as their opportunities for further development.

A "Municipal Commission," attached to a special commission of the Ministry of Home Affairs and Police, was created to assist in improving the economy of cities and to implement governmental policies with respect to their administration, finances, and building activities.

The General Council for Buildings, Surveying, Roads and Navigation, set up in 1817 and headed by Aleksander Groffe, was the central building authority. This Council organized, in all voivodships and districts, a government building service responsible for carrying into effect the Council's building policy in cities. The State authorities exercised strong control over the planning of cities through the approval of plans and the details of their suggestions. All designs for the more important public buildings in towns were subject to approval by the General Building Council, which not only had a say on the location and cost of building projects but also frequently introduced changes particularly requested by A. Groffe with respect to the architectural treatment of buildings. Since the Council also approved designs for private buildings, whenever government loans were solicited for construction, the result was a growing uniformity of building types and town planning trends throughout the country.

Most cities in the Congress Kingdom were small, with 500 to 3,000 inhabitants. Nearly all the larger cities with populations exceeding 10,000, such as Gdańsk, Cracow, Lvov, Wrocław, and Toruń, were in the areas under Prussian and Austrian rule. In the Kingdom, only Warsaw, the capital, had a population of over 100,000. The population table gives an idea of the size of cities in the Congress Kingdom.

Population	Number of Cities	
	1818	1827
Under 500	95	38
500–1,000	196	135
1,000–3,000	158	210
3,000–5,000	5	49
5,000–10,000	3	6
10,000–15,000	0	2*
50,000–100,000	1**	0
Over 100,000	0	1**
Total	458	441

* Kalisz 12,107 and Lublin 13,475.
** Warsaw, which in 1810 had a population of 77,727 and in 1827 of 131,465. Both figures relate to permanent residents only, without military garrisons.

As may be seen from this table the changes in the structure of urban settlement characteristic of the 19th and 20th centuries, that is, the elimination of small towns and the growth of larger cities, were already beginning to take place in the first half of the 19th century. Twenty-seven towns, mostly very small ones, some with less than 350 inhabitants, lost their urban status between 1810 and 1827, while the number of towns with populations ranging from 3,000 to 5,000 grew from 5 to 49. The majority of these were either seats of voivodship and district authorities or industrialized towns. Ten new towns, almost all industrial, were founded in the same period, and most of them developed very quickly.

The financial means of cities in the first years of the Congress Kingdom were extremely limited. Their revenues in 1819–1820 are shown in the accompanying table.

Revenue in Polish zlotys*	Number of Cities
Over 100,000	2
20,000–10,000	6
10,000–1,000	252
Under 1,000	73
No revenue	121
Total	454

* To give an idea of the value of zloty: the cost of building a one-family brick house (4 rooms) amounted to approximately 4,000 zlotys.

Clearly, most of the cities were incapable of undertaking any new construction out of their own funds. However, thanks to the activities of the various Municipal Commissions which subsidized building projects out of State funds or budget surpluses of other cities, it was possible to execute certain improvements in the poorer towns, erecting buildings for administrative purposes (like town halls) and commercial facilities (like stalls) and to raise the general standard of their development.

Governmental activities in cities included many attempts at improvement and expansion. In the first half of the 19th century, mostly in the years 1820–1830, plans were drawn up for 156 cities (of the 441 which existed in 1827). However, the November Insurrection of 1830–1831 caused a serious setback in this activity.

All plans of this period were drawn to the same scale, so that their graphic presentation was uniform, according to appropriate regulations issued by the government. Two kinds of plans were prepared: cadastral plans (1:5,000) and plans of existing development (1:1,500). The former covered the whole area belonging to a city, including arable lands, forests, and meadows, thus serving as a basis for establishing property boundaries on the fringe of the city. The latter covered built-up areas only and were, in fact, survey maps; only on this basis were projects of improvements and redevelopments planned. All existing buildings were carefully mapped, with indications as to the material used (brick or timber) and whether they were government, municipal, Church, or private property. Detailed property registers were added to these sur-

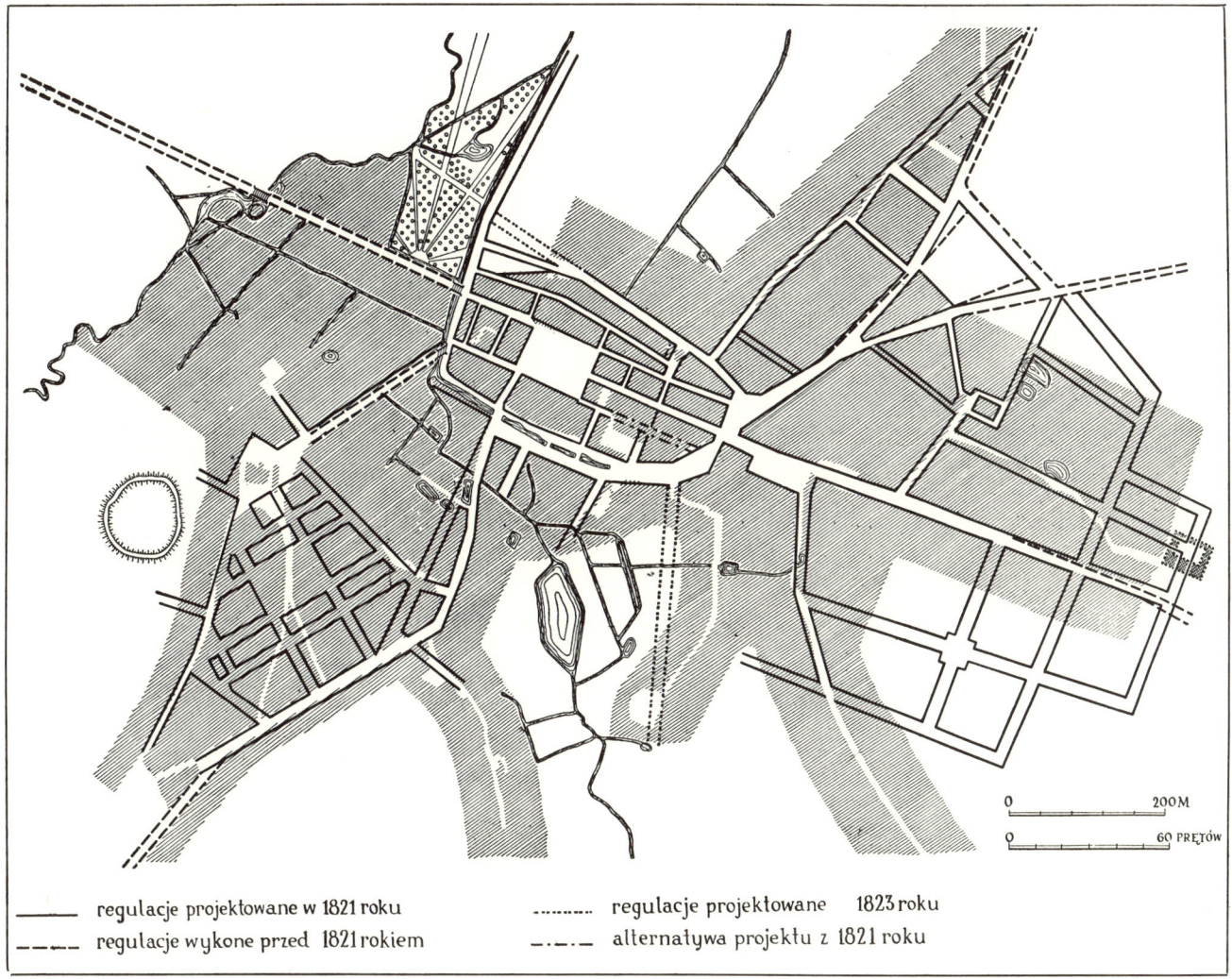

─── regulacje projektowane w 1821 roku   .... regulacje projektowane 1823 roku
---- regulacje wykone przed 1821 rokiem   —·—·— alternatywa projektu z 1821 roku

veys, while redevelopment plans were accompanied by descriptions of the works to be carried out. Most of the plans and records of the Municipal Commission of that time have been preserved and constitute an extremely valuable source of information on Polish cities as they were in the first half of the 19th century, as well as material for retrospective research into earlier periods of their history.

The plan prepared in 1821 for Radom (Fig. 76) is an example of a redevelopment plan for a city of medium size. At that time Radom, as seat of the Sandomierz Voivodship authorities, had some 3,000 inhabitants and consisted of a rather densely built-up oval-shaped medieval core with small suburbs to the east and west, along the road to Lublin, on the site of a former early medieval settlement. Two voivodship officials, engineer Ignacy Ebertowski and builder Józef Sadkowski (author of the plans for Stryków and Ryczywół mentioned earlier), prepared the plan. Approved by the Municipal Commission and the General Building Council in 1822, the plan provided for the construction of two new districts east and southwest of the city, the straightening and widening of streets, the laying out of a public garden and promenade around the demolished walls of the medieval core, and the erection of numerous public buildings such as the offices of the Sandomierz Voivodship Commission, a city hall, a theater (converted

70. Plan for the improvement of Radom, 1824. Hatching indicates the built-up areas before the improvements; continuous and broken lines mark the proposed new streets and the widening and straightening of old ones; the site for the Voivodship Commission is marked in black.

from a hospital church), tollgates, and some butchers' stalls. Much attention was given to the draining of the city's lands. The plan materialized largely in the years 1820–1830; only the proposed construction of the new eastern district had to be abandoned because of difficulties encountered in the expropriation of land. An interesting provision of the plan was the siting of the building of the Voivodship Commission on undeveloped land, at a distance west of the city, with a view to stimulating private building activity in that area and to moving the civic center from within the former medieval core. These hopes proved correct, as the main center did indeed shift from the old marketplace to Lubelska Street.

Similar measures were taken in other places, though the scale of the projects depended, of course, on the size of the cities concerned. Considerable importance was attached to the moving of buildings from the old medieval marketplaces in order to change them into public squares, a step which necessitated the demolition of town halls, stalls, and other structures. The new town halls, of which more than 30 were erected, were usually placed in line with the buildings surrounding the squares. Efforts to eliminate timber buildings from the centers of cities were also made by granting financial aid for the construction of brick buildings. Approaches to cities were put in order, and ditches were dug around the towns to limit the number of roads entering the urban areas. Poplar trees were planted along these roads, and tollgates, in the form of small Neo-Classical pavilions, were built at the city boundaries. Streets and building lines were straightened. In redeveloped cities, street systems assumed the form of rectangular grids, often obliterating the old medieval patterns. Radial systems were introduced in a few cases, as at Kielce.

It should be emphasized that the government's activities were not confined to wishful thinking. Numerous public buildings such as town halls, seats of local authorities, post offices, inns, and stalls were erected; streets were tidied up and paved; and financial aid was granted to townspeople wishing to build new houses. The redevelopment schemes carried out in the period of the Congress Kingdom left a strong imprint on the cities and are still clearly discernible, not only in Warsaw but also in provincial towns.

Cities in the western part of the Congress Kingdom were strongly influenced by the development of the textile industry as directed by the government. The Kingdom had been cut off from the old Polish textile centers in Great Poland and Silesia. The demands from the home market and the possibility of exporting textiles to Russia caused the government to encourage artisans and textile manufacturers from the Poznań area and Silesia to settle in the Kingdom, mainly in the voivodships of Kalisz and Mazovia, within the triangle formed by Kalisz, Płock, and Częstochowa. Settlers were given financial aid for the construction of houses and manufactories; they were exempted from taxes, military service, and billeting. In the industrialized area more than 20 settlements for artisans were laid out as new districts adjoining existing cities. Each settler obtained a perpetual lease, a building plot, usually half a *morga* or .699 acres, and a garden plot of one and a half *morgas* or 2.07 acres. When necessary, he was granted a loan to help him build a house for himself and establish a workshop. Houses in these artisans' villages were erected according to standard designs, usually as a condition for obtaining a loan. They were mostly single-storied, of timber or brick, containing four rooms and a passage in the middle, similar in form to the houses built during the Prussian colonization in the late 18th and early 19th centuries.

The layouts for the artisans' villages were always regular and inspired by the traditions of the 17th and 18th-century artisans' towns of Great Poland, such as Rawicz and Rakoniewice, and by the late 18th-century Prussian colonization in the Brandenburg Mark, as at Zinna and Rathenow. Their size varied considerably, from 40 to 60 plots at Rawa Mazowiecka, Grocholice, and Gąbin to 200 to 400 plots at Łódź, Pabianice, and Zgierz. As a rule, the development was grouped around the central square and main streets where the building plots had been laid out, and gardens were situated separately at some distance from the dwellings. Thanks to the uniformity of the houses and the standardized width of the plots—house frontage plus service road giving access to the rear—these settlements were rather compact.

The first of these artisans' villages was established by the government at Zgierz in 1820. The contract with its settlers served as a model for subsequent villages. The village (Fig. 77) was built on a site forming part of a government-owned estate east of the city. Its central feature was a square with four streets issuing from it, one from the middle of each side. Modeled on 17th-century French solutions, this pattern was used in Polish schemes dating from the early years of the 19th century, as in Konstantynów, Łódź, and Radom. Along the four streets issuing from the square and a network of transverse streets, 230 building plots were arranged, while the garden plots lay east of the village. The settlement developed very quickly, as can be deduced from the fact that seven years later, in 1828, only 29 plots were still unoccupied. A layout similar to Zgierz was offered to the somewhat smaller artisans' villages at Gostynin (1821) and Gąbin (1822–1823).

77. Plan for the artisans' village of Zgierz, 1821. Reconstruction by the author. Hatching indicates the existing town (founded in the 14th century); the proposed sites for the artisans' houses are marked in the new settlement; the plots without houses were intended for gardens.

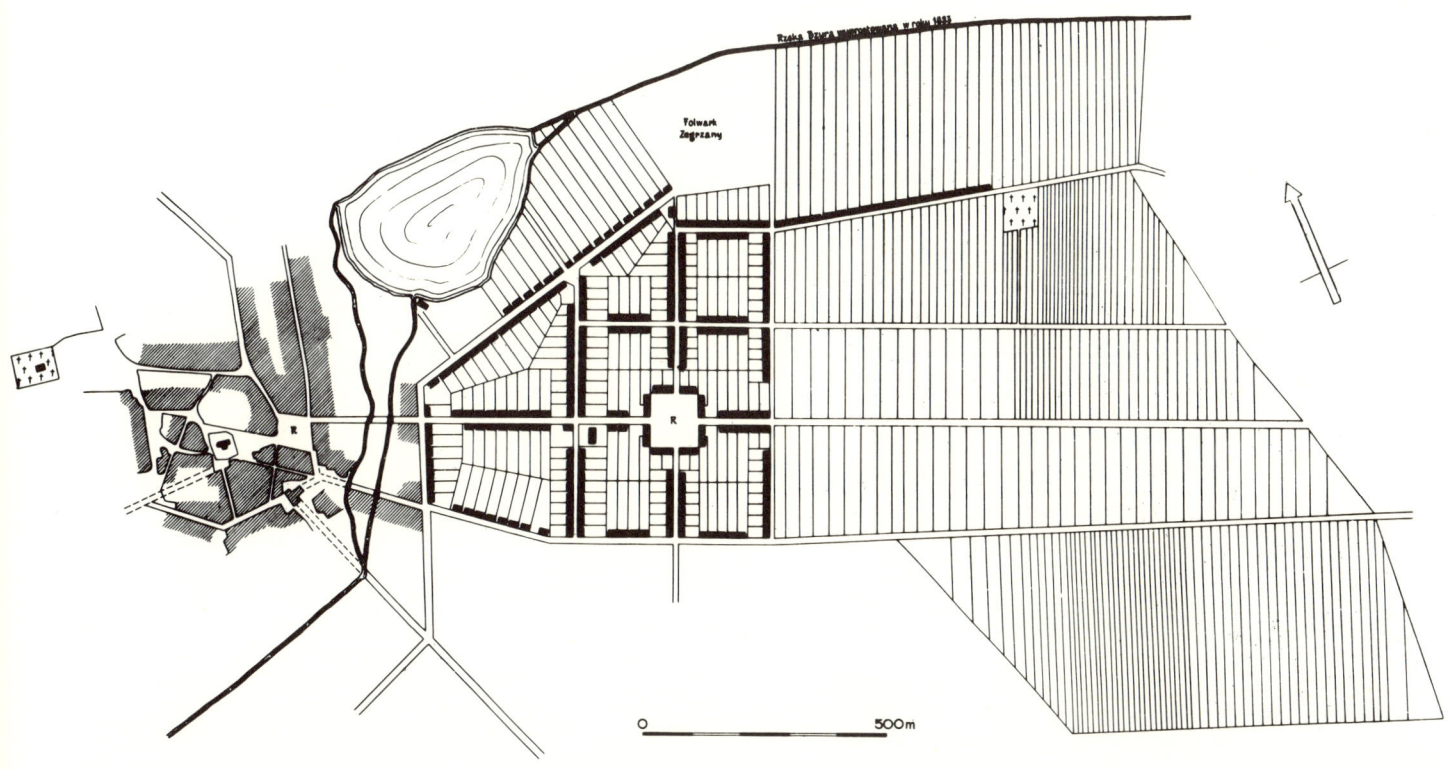

Among the newly founded settlements Łódź grew most rapidly. Today it is the second largest city in Poland, with a population of approximately 700,000. This artisans' village was founded in stages: in 1821–1823 the New Town for clothiers with 202 plots; in 1824 "Łódka," a weavers' village with 307 plots; in 1825 a spinners' village with 167 plots; and in 1827 the "Ślązaki" village with 42 plots—718 plots altogether. Soon all of them were occupied by settlers (Fig. 78). The whole settlement was laid out along Piotrkowska Street (2.17 miles long), which issued from the market square of the medieval town and abutted the buildings of L. Geyer's large textile manufactory. Transverse to this axis several industrial plants were established along the little river Jasień, in order to use its waters for driving power. A town hall and a Protestant church were built in the octagonal marketplace of the New Town (Fig. 79). These two buildings of somewhat similar shape marked the entrance into Piotrkowska Street.

An equally interesting pattern characterized the artisans' village in Częstochowa, founded in 1823 (Fig. 80). Its main street with 150 plots connected the medieval city with the famous monastery on Jasna Góra Hill. Even today, this wide avenue, closed by the commanding silhouette of the fortified monastery, is impressive in its scale. On a similar pattern, the artisans' village at Turek was laid out (1823), as were several smaller settlements of this type.

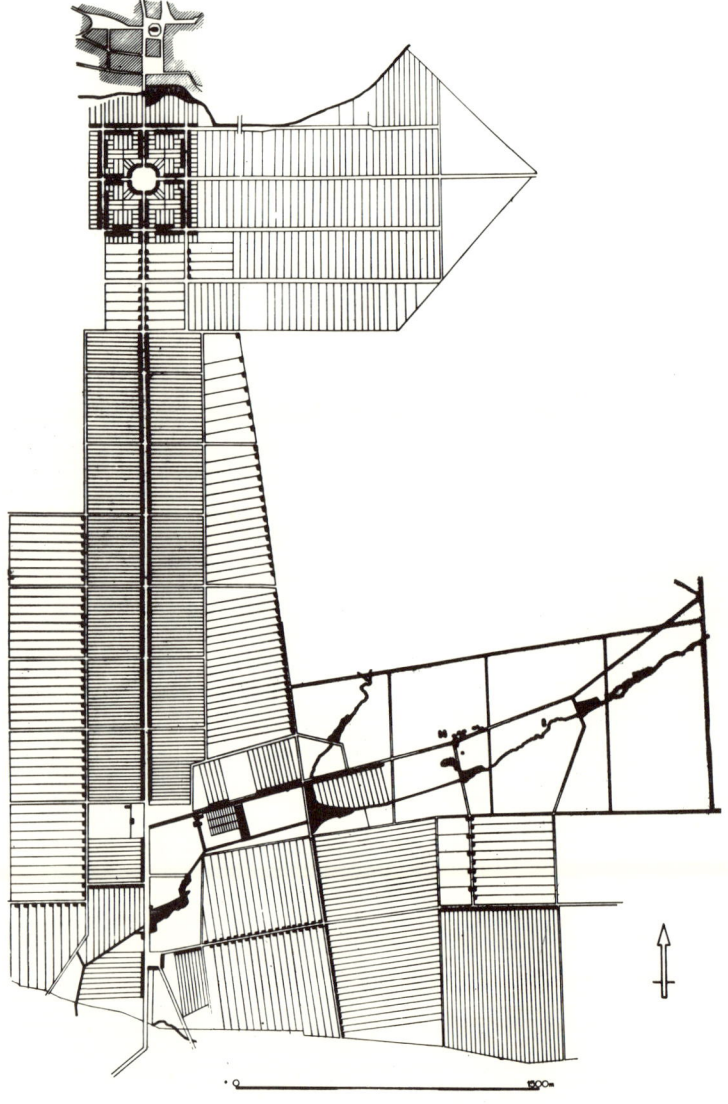

78. Plans for the artisans' villages at Łódź, 1824–28. Reconstruction by the author. The hatched area is the medieval city, founded in the first half of the 15th century (?); the proposed sites for artisans' buildings have been indicated in the new settlements. The plots without houses were intended for gardens. At the top (adjoining the medieval city), the clothiers' village, with an octagonal marketplace laid out in 1823. Along Piotrkowska Street, the weavers' village laid out in 1824. At bottom right, the spinners' village (1825) and the weavers' village "Ślązaki" (1826). The areas along the little river Jasień were reserved for fulling rooms and cotton mills.

79. The Protestant church and the Town Hall at the market square of the clothiers' village of Łódź. Lithograph from a drawing by W. Walkiewicz.

80. Plan for the artisans' village of Częstochowa, 1823. Reconstruction by the author. 1. City founded in the second half of the 14th century; 2. Paulite monastery, founded in 1382 and expanded in the 16th and 17th centuries; 3. New Town, founded in the 18th century; 4. St. Barbara's Church; 5. St. Rochus Church; 6. New town hall.

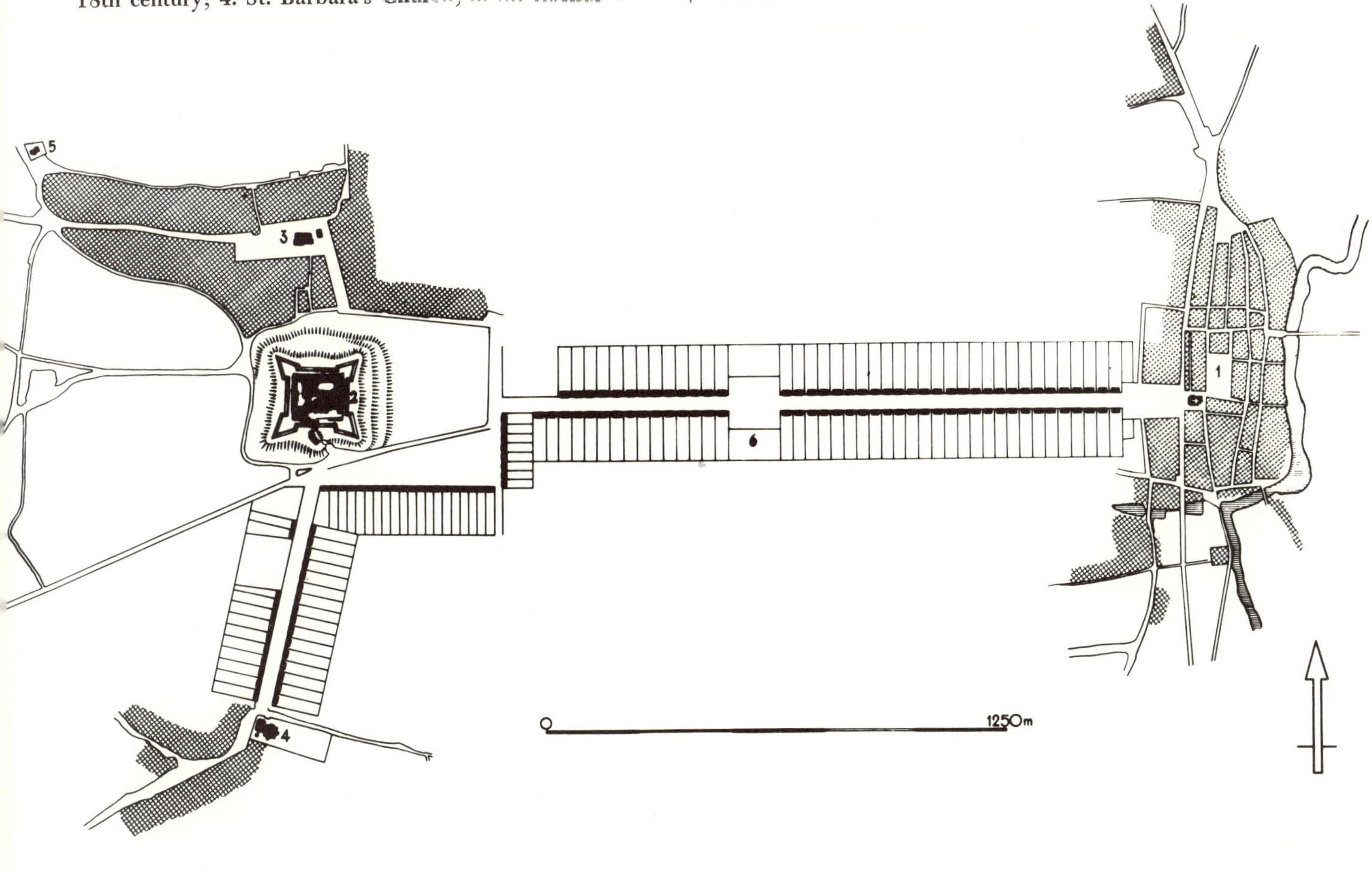

In addition to the villages for the artisans, eight new towns were established as centers of the textile industry. They were Babiak (1815–1816), Ozorków (1816), Aleksandrów (1822) (Fig. 81), Krasnosielsk (1822), Poddębice (1822), Zduńska Wola (1825), Konstantynów (1830), and Tomaszów Mazowiecki (1830). All of them were founded by private landowners who either expected profits from subdivisions, leases, taxes levied on inns, and other municipal charges, or were interested in the setting up of textile manufactories. The latter were established close to industrial villages or new towns and were housed in large, often four or five-storied buildings modeled on late 18th-century English manufactories. Sites were usually chosen on the banks of little rivers for a

81. Plan of the newly founded town of Aleksandrów, 1821. Original in the Archiwum Główne Akt Dawnych, Warsaw.

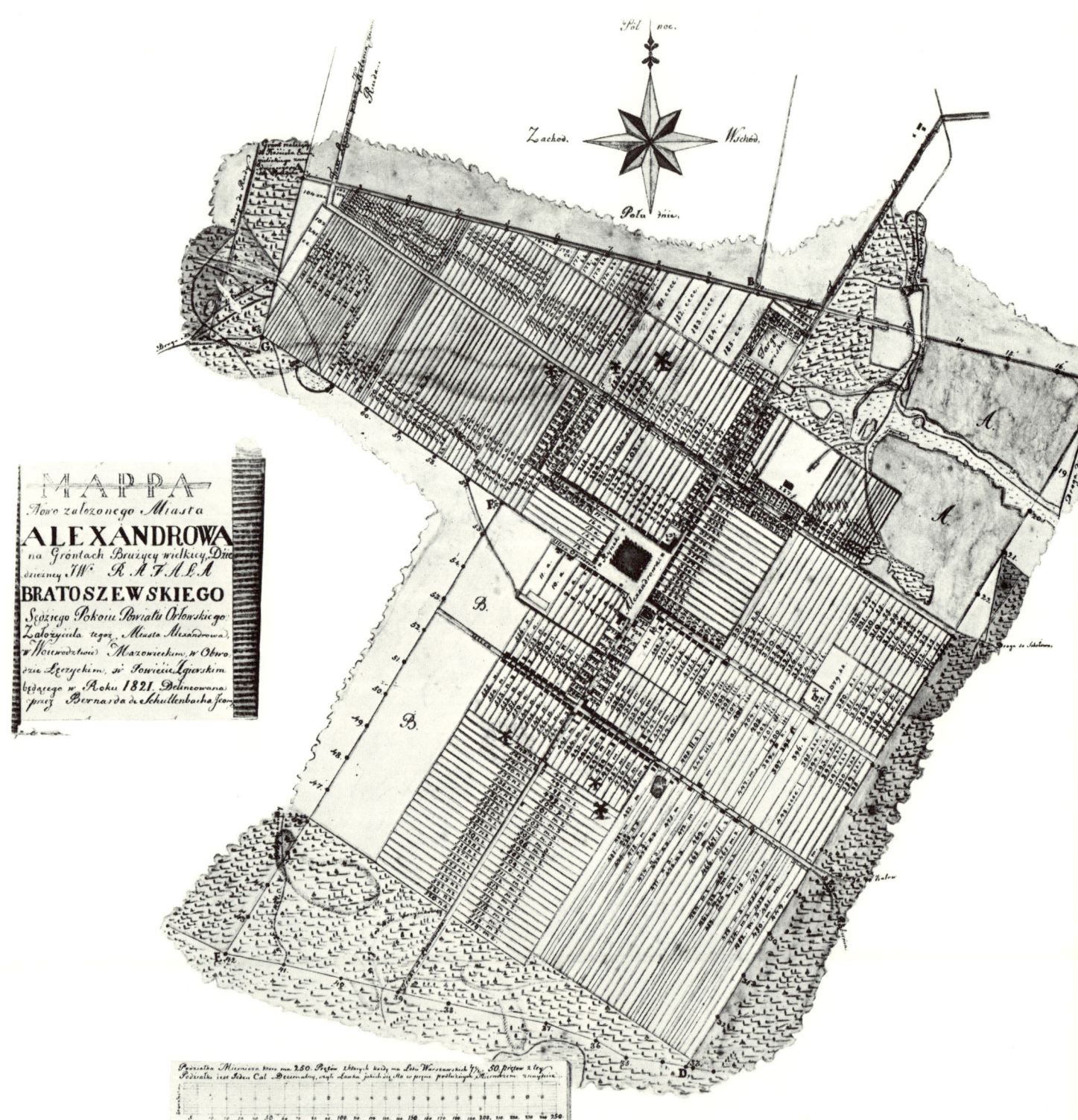

water supply and for the construction of dams for the propulsion of water wheels, as in Kalisz, Sieradz, Opatówek, and Łódź.

Another large industrial center of a different kind came into existence in the Kielce region, along the river Kamienna. In this area—the Old Polish Basin—the production of iron developed from local ore deposits and forests which supplied the charcoal. In the years 1820–1830 several large state-owned ironworks (Bobrza, Sielpia, Nietulisko, and Samsonów) were put into operation. This industry, however, did not lead to the formation of cities, and the workers' villages retained the character of rural settlements. One other large industrial project carried out at the time was the saltern and salt graduation works in Ciechocinek, north of Włocławek, on the Vistula. The salt graduation works, a huge engineering structure over 5,576 feet long and built completely of wood, remains impressive even today. Ciechocinek later developed into a spa, according to the plan of H. Marconi prepared in 1845. Another spa was established in 1836 near the town of Busko, in Southern Poland. These two localities were the first examples of a new form of settlement in the Congress Kingdom, namely, health and summer resorts for seasonal visitors.

Apart from the towns linked to the developing textile industry, new construction was mainly concentrated in the larger cities, particularly in those which were seats of central and voivodship administrations. Warsaw, the capital, enjoyed a most intense building activity in the years 1817–1819 when over 400 new brick dwelling-houses, mostly two-storied, and numerous public buildings were erected (Fig. 82).

Although no master plan was prepared for Warsaw under the Congress Kingdom, many streets were improved, widened, or straightened, and a considerable number of public squares came into existence in that period. On the other hand, two redevelopment plans were worked out in 1817 and 1828 for the Praga district on the right bank of the Vistula, both with a radial pattern of streets converging on the Royal Castle, situated close to the Old Town on the left bank of the river (Fig. 83). A Committee, created in 1856 and entrusted with the drawing up of a plan for improvements in Warsaw, redeveloped some other parts of the city. However, toward 1870, this Committee and the General Building Council were inactivated by the Tsarist authorities.

One of the largest schemes executed in Warsaw before 1830 was the redevelopment of Bankowy Square, now known as Dzierżyński Square. Antoni Corazzi, one of the most active Warsaw architects of the time, prepared two alternative designs for it in 1825. These designs were carried out only insofar as they met the needs of the government. The western side of the square was entirely redeveloped; former private palaces were replaced by the monumental buildings of the Revenue and Treasury Commission, the Director's Palace, and the Bank of Poland. Together, these buildings formed an important Neo-Classical ensemble of high artistic value. The schemes which were abandoned included the enlarging of the square from a triangular to a rectangular shape and the axial linking of the Revenue and Treasury Commission with the State Mint in Miodowa Street, an alternative version proposed in one of Corazzi's plans (Figs. 84, 85).

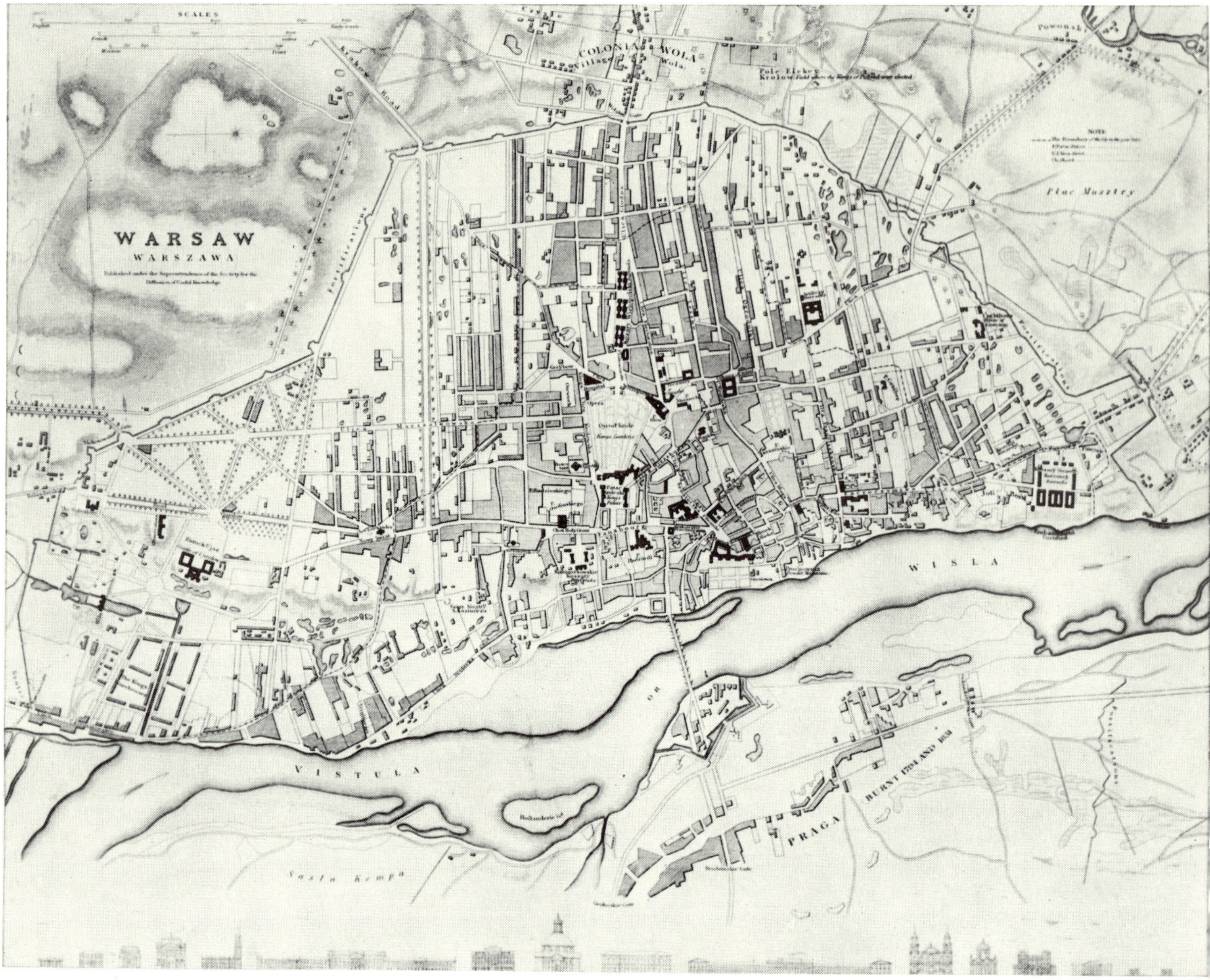
SCALES
WARSAW
WARSZAWA
COLONIA WOLA
Plac Musztry
WISLA
VISTULA
PRAGA

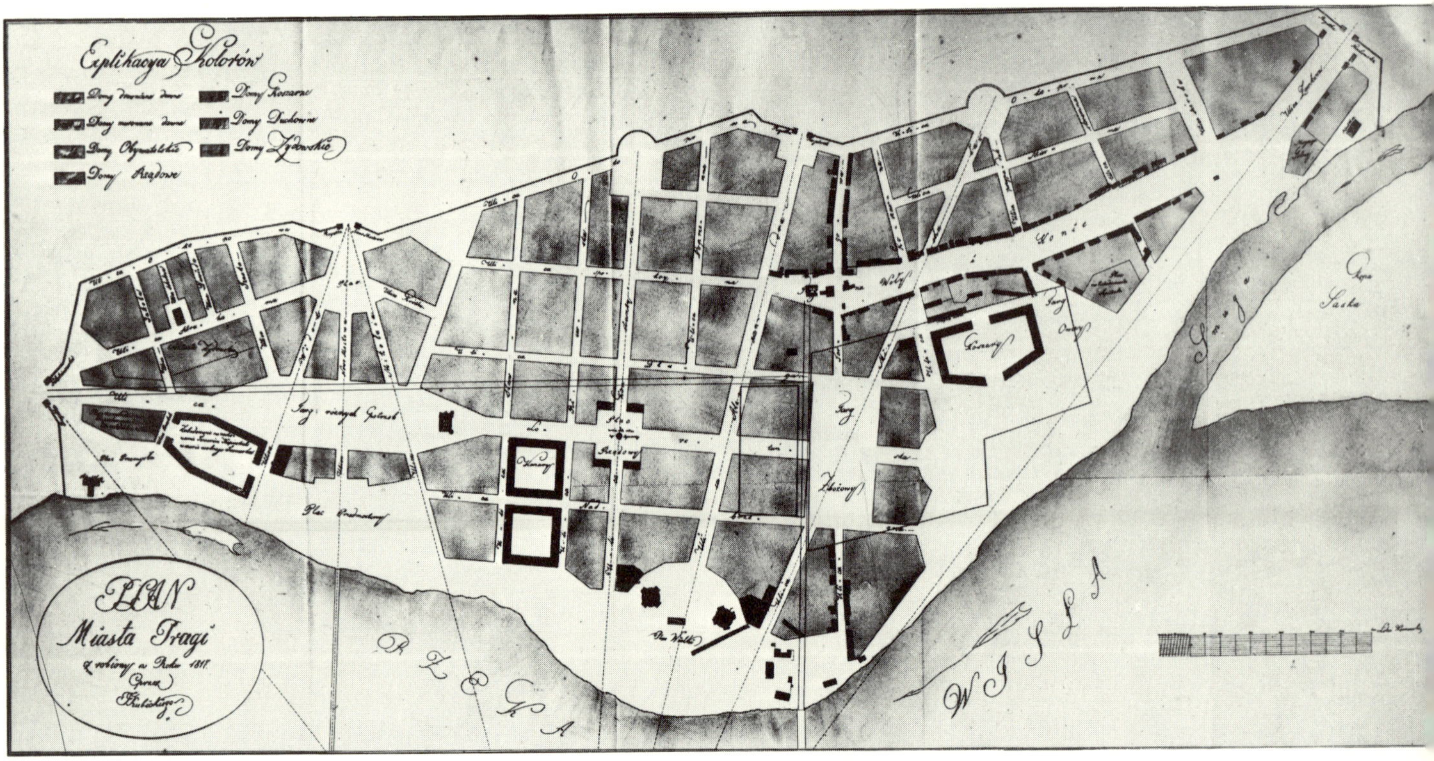
Explikacya Kolorów
PLAN
Miasta Pragi
R Z E K A
W I S L A

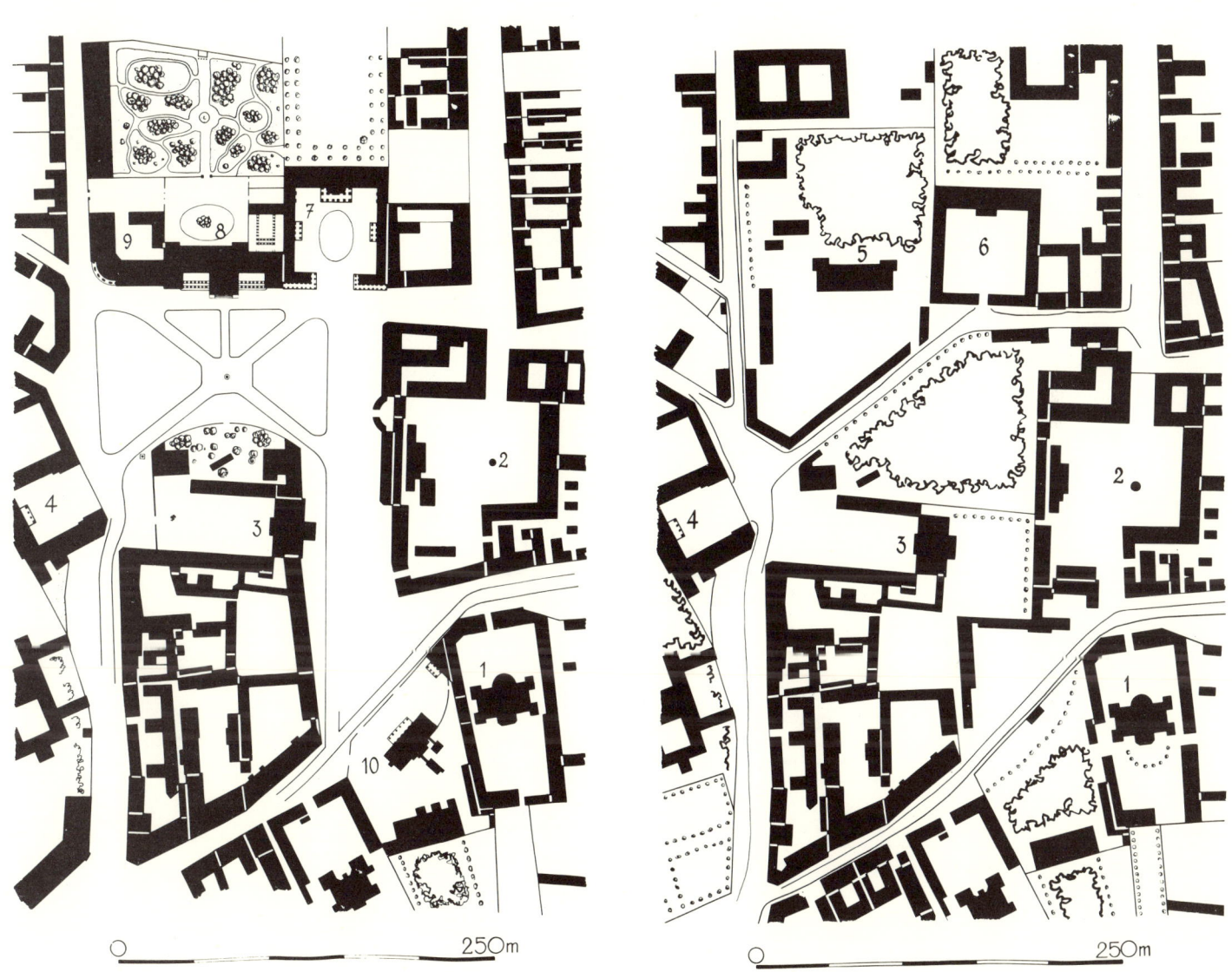

84. Plan for the redevelopment of Bankowy Square at Warsaw, prepared by A. Corazzi in 1825. Left, the square as it was prior to its redevelopment; right, Corazzi's plan. Drawn by the author. 1. Radziwiłł Palace; 2. Mint; 3. Mniszech Palace; 4. Zamoyski Palace; 5. Ogiński (formerly Wiśniowiecki) Palace; 6. Leszczyński Palace; 7. Revenues and Treasury Commission; 8. Directors' Palace; 9. Bank of Poland.

83. *Opposite page:* Plan for the improvement of Praga (the right-bank district of Warsaw), prepared in 1817 by J. Kubicki.

85. View of Bankowy Square at Warsaw. Painting by W. Kasprzycki, 1833. Original in the Muzeum Historyczne m. st. Warszawy, Warsaw.

86. View of Teatralny Square at Warsaw. Drawing by Dietrich, 1829.

Teatralny Square, another square designed by A. Corazzi, was laid out at the intersection of Senatorska and Wierzbowa Streets. In the years 1685–1696, on the initiative of Queen Maria Kazimiera, wife of John III Sobieski, a large building called Marywil, accommodating shops, inns, and a hotel, was erected after the design of Tilman van Gameren. By the 19th century it had fallen into decay and, after an attempt at reconstruction, was finally torn down in 1825, together with other neighboring buildings. In the first phase an annex called "Colonnade Building," designed by C. P. Aigner in 1819 and intended to accommodate shops, with a small square in front of it, was added to Marywil. In 1825, after a competition for the National Theater (known today as the Grand Theater) work was started on the construction of the theater and a second symmetrical colonnaded wing (Fig. 86). Both were completed in 1833. This monumental edifice occupied one whole side of the newly created square, as the central piece of the entire composition. On the opposite side was Blank's Palace, the Jabłonowski Palace (converted into a City Hall), and the Canoness's Convent and Church. The two shorter sides of the square were occupied by Neo-Classical burghers' houses.

Among other squares laid out in Warsaw at that time, mention should be made of Trzy Krzyże (Three Crosses) Square, at the meeting point of Ujazdowska Avenue (former Calvary Way) and Wiejska, Mokotowska, Bracka, and Nowy Świat Streets. The Neo-Classical church of St. Alexander's was erected in the center of this square, after a design by C. P. Aigner (Fig. 87). Next, there was Warecki Square, now known

87. View of the Trzy Krzyże (Three Crosses) Square at Warsaw. Drawing by Dietrich, 1829.

as Powstańców Warszawy Square. One whole side of this square was occupied by the Holy Ghost Hospital, a huge building designed by A. Groffe. Zamkowy (Castle) Square was laid out in front of the Royal Castle after the demolition of the Krakowska Gate; and, finally, came Pole Marsowe *(Champ de Mars)*, the largest square in Warsaw at the time (1,443 by 1,443 feet), used for military drill and parades.

In addition to the Bankowy Square ensemble and the National Theater, many other monumental buildings were erected in Warsaw in the 1820s, such as the Government Commission (Ministry) of Home Affairs and Police, the so-called Mostowski Palace; the Society of the Friends of Learning (the Staszic Palace); the Namiestnikowski (Governor's) Palace, today the seat of the Council of Ministers; the Belvedere, a palace built for Grand Duke Constantine; and the guardhouses in Saski Square adjoining the Bernardine Church in Krakowskie Przedmieście Street. All these buildings, monuments of the era of Classic Revival, were restored after World War II and today constitute important architectural landmarks in the central district of Warsaw.

Simultaneously with the construction of new public buildings much was done to improve the road system in the capital city: the tracing of Jerozolimska Avenue, the demolition of some buildings along Krakowskie Przedmieście Street, the opening of Miodowa Street, and the widening of Marszałkowska Street. These works continued even after the November Insurrection (1830–1831). A fact of considerable importance for the development of Warsaw was the construction in 1844–1845 of the first railway connecting Warsaw and Vienna. The terminal station was built near the intersection of Marszałkowska Street and Jerozolimska Avenue, after a design by H. Marconi. The population of the city grew steadily and by 1870 had risen to 266,000. The civic center shifted from the Market Square of the Old Town to the area between the Old Town and the Saxon Axis (Teatralny Square, Krakowskie Przedmieście Street). The large public park adjacent to the Saxon Axis separated the center from the districts developing in the south. Another feature limiting the expansion of the center was a large citadel built by the Russians, after the November Insurrection, on the bank of the Vistula north of the New Town.

A considerable amount of new construction also took place in Kalisz and Lublin, after Warsaw the two largest cities in the Congress Kingdom. In addition to the improvement and development of existing roads, new streets, squares, and public gardens were laid out in both cities, resulting in the expansion of their centers beyond the confines of the medieval fortifications. In both cities many old buildings were remodeled to serve various public purposes, and new buildings were erected for the administration and the army. In Kalisz these buildings included a new Court of Justice (1820–1824), a Voivodship school (about 1819) designed by S. Szpilowski, and four barracks and a prison designed by H. Marconi and F. Tournelle (1844). The old archiepiscopal palace was rebuilt as the seat of the Voivodship Commission, after a design by S. Szpilowski and F. Reinstein (1824–1825). In Lublin new buildings were constructed for the District Commission and the Customs; the Radziwiłł Palace was rebuilt as the seat of the Voivodship Commission in 1829; a former Carmelite church as a city hall, after a design by A. Groffe (1827–1828); and the castle as a prison, after a design by J. Stompf (1824–1826). All these works, coupled with an intense building activity in the field of residential development, thoroughly changed the aspect of both cities.

Similar activities took place in other towns which were seats of voivodship authorities, such as Płock, Kielce, and Suwałki, or seats of district authorities, such as Rawa Mazowiecka, Łęczyca, and Augustów. Although smaller in scale these new works exercised considerable influence on the building forms and general appearance of the cities concerned.

In earlier periods town planning and architectural activities aimed at the improvement of the urban development were limited to the city in which they took place. However, after the beginning of the 19th century the influence of State authorities extended over the country as a whole, leading to a certain architectural uniformity on a national scale. This consistency was due not only to the issuing of building regulations by the State but, first and foremost, to the fact that a building service subordinate to the General Building Council had been organized throughout the Kingdom. State building authorities not only had their say on all new projects sponsored by the State and municipalities but also saw to it that private construction was in keeping with approved city plans. A factor of vital importance in this connection was the building loans granted to numerous private developers out of a State building fund especially created for this purpose. Since the design of all buildings for which State loans were solicited had to be approved by the building authorities, the latter could, and did in fact, influence the architectural forms of new constructions. This control of design and the bylaws regulating the height of buildings (three stories in the center of Warsaw, two stories in the centers of other cities, and one story in suburbs and artisians' villages) led to a pronounced uniformity of urban development.

The intense building activity in the Congress Kingdom was interrupted by the November Insurrection in 1830. After the failure of the insurrection and the ensuing restriction of the Kingdom's autonomy, neither State nor private building was resumed on the same scale as before. Moreover, the principles of city planning changed. In 1848, by decree of Nicolas I, the regulations valid in the Russian Empire were made obligatory in the Kingdom as well. Copies of a plan drawn up for the city of Krasne were circulated to the provincial authorities, to be adopted as a model for all new plans of city improvement. A certain revival of building and town-planning activities occurred in the middle of the century, but its effects belong to a later period in the development of Polish cities. The complete liquidation of home rule and the final incorporation of the Congress Kingdom into the Russian Empire soon after the suppression of the 1863 Insurrection put a stop to the activities of Polish State authorities in the field of city planning for many years.

In 1815 the Congress of Vienna created another quasi-autonomous unit on Polish territory, the so-called Cracow Republic, wedged in between the Congress Kingdom and the area under Austrian rule. The Republic comprised the Free City of Cracow and a few adjoining small towns such as Chrzanów, Trzebinia, and Nowa Góra. Until 1848, when it was annexed to Austria, this territory was governed by a theoretically autonomous local authority (the Senate of the Free City of Cracow) which, like the government of the Congress Kingdom, devoted much effort to the improvement of the city. A plan to "beautify" Cracow was worked out, based, in part, on earlier Austrian plans, and primarily providing for an improved road system in the suburbs. The creation of a park belt and ring road around the medieval core ranked among the finest achievements of the period. The approaches to the city were likewise improved, assuming the form of long straight suburban roads with regularly shaped squares at the points of entrance into the city. A large amount of new construction brought about considerable changes for the better in the built-up areas, especially in Kazimierz and around the medieval core.

City-planning and building activities in the remaining Polish territories—those directly incorporated into the partitioned States—were guided by foreign building authorities and alien architects. They can hardly be considered to have any connection with Polish creative thinking and will not, therefore, be discussed in this connection.

The second half of the 19th century witnessed an extremely intense development of industry and transport, resulting in an accelerated progress of urbanization and a great deal of new construction in cities. However, as this period is closely bound up with the problems of the contemporary city, it can be discussed only in conjunction with the emergence of modern concepts of physical planning.

CZECHOSLOVAKIA

Introduction

by E. A. Gutkind

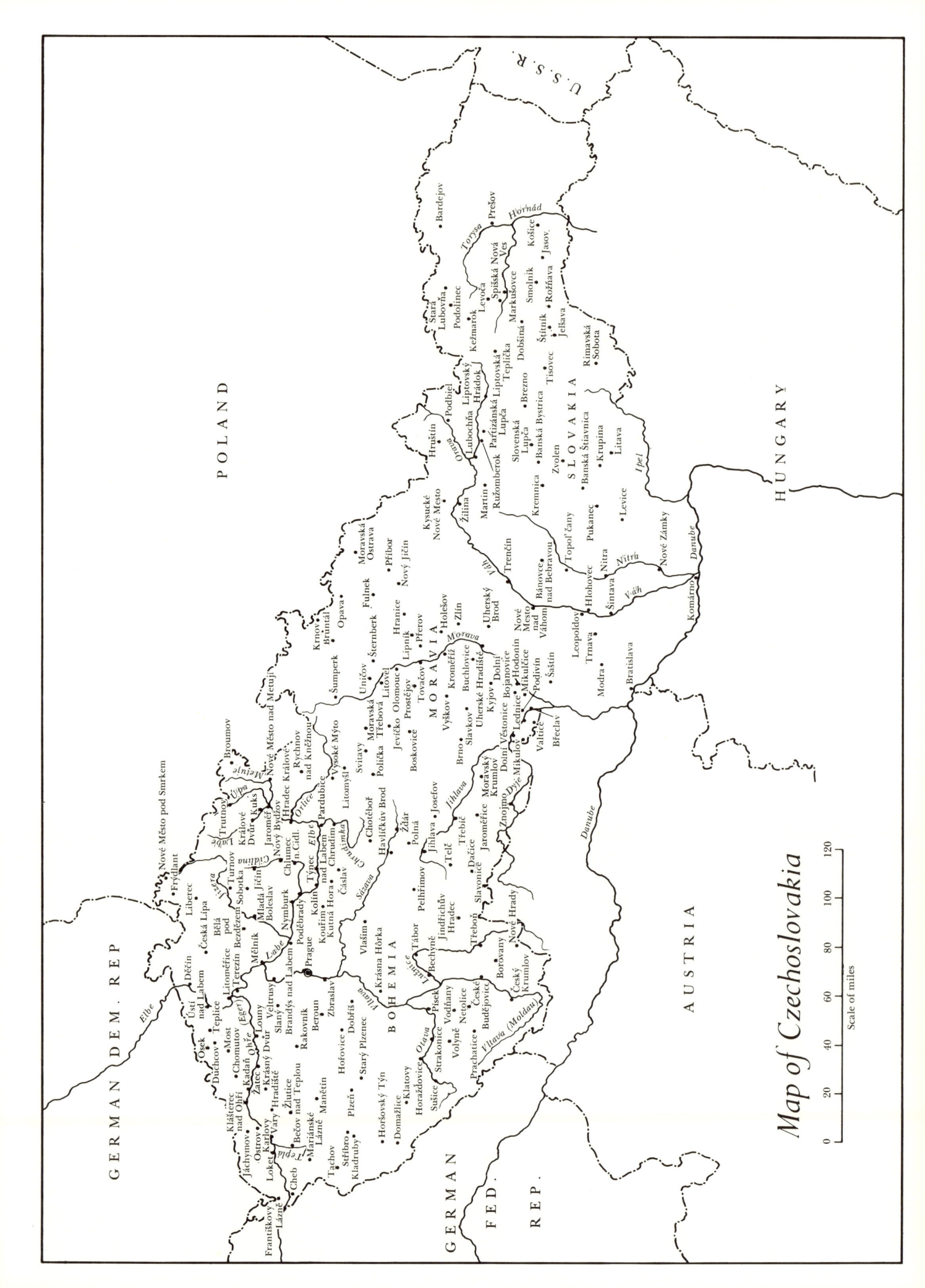
Map of Czechoslovakia

CHAPTER 9

Evolution of Early Settlement

THE REGION CONSTITUTING present-day Czechoslovakia, with its three political units of Bohemia, Moravia, and Slovakia, has been exposed from prehistoric times to influences from the East and West, shaping and reshaping her history and settlement over thousands of years. Landlocked, and situated at the crossroads of greatly different cultures, she extends from Central Europe to the Carpathian Basin, acting as a barrier as well as an intermediary between peoples, absorbing their movements and transforming or rejecting their impact upon the slowly developing national character of her own civilization.

The earliest inhabitants preferred climatically favorable parts of the country and, from the Neolithic Age onward, also those regions where fertile soils made food production, plant cultivation, and stock-breeding possible. In general, their settlements were situated on low-lying lands or on moderate elevations. Mountainous regions were not settled until the Middle Ages. The earliest inhabitants lived in caves, pit-dwellings, or above-ground settlements. They were hunters and food gatherers, and they developed embryonic forms of a division of labor and a social organizatiton. The Neolithic Revolution of the fifth and fourth millennium B.C. initiated a new age, a new attitude of man toward his environment. It was the watershed between "Savagery and Barbarism," as Gordon Childe has called it.[1] It marked the end of man's parasitic dependence on nature and the beginning of a creative response of man to the challenge of nature. Man began to act as an empirical agent, adjusting his environment to his need for protection, food, and shelter. Social organization and spiritual aspirations intensified the complexities of life. Nomadism changed to sedentary existence, and the number of people drawing their food supply from a more permanently settled area increased, although agriculture was still practiced on the slash-and-burn system and settlements remained more or less mobile. However, the inhabited area was restricted to loess regions which could be worked more easily with the primitive implements available and was only rarely extended to loam soils. In general, Neolithic settlements occupied sites on the slopes of loess elevations near a water supply. One large settlement has been identified at Bylany, near Kutná Hora (Kuttenberg) in Bohemia, where more than fifty large timber huts have been excavated, and another at Hluboké Mašůvky, in the south of Moravia, where the settlement was enclosed by a ditch with a number of gates and causeways. Society was organized on a matriarchal and clan basis in which women, as the main producers of food, were the heads of the families.[2]

In the following Eneolithic Age, elements of a patriarchal society were developed which, in the Middle Eneolithic period, caused a far-reaching change in social organization. The division of labor between the sexes shifted the work of women as agricultural producers to the men, and women became domestic workers, preparing the food and producing textiles and pottery. Plowing increased the productivity of the soil, resulting in a surplus of food and, in its wake, a certain stratification of society. No one person could use—or misuse—the work of

1. V. G. Childe. *The Prehistory of European Society.* 1958. P. 34.
2. E. and J. Neustupný. *Czechoslovakia Before the Slavs.* 1961. *Passim.*

111

another and retain the surplus for himself. The patriarchal family—that is, the extended biological family—was the economic entity on which the developing society rested. The large villages of the preceding period, mostly situated in open country, were more and more replaced by smaller fortified hilltop settlements. This change may have been caused by the emergence of a new social class or petty rulers, or simply by the growing need for protection from hostile attacks. The settlement on the Homolka Hill near Kladno in Central Bohemia, for instance, was surrounded by two lines of palisades, with two gates apparently dating from two successive phases of settlement, the earlier consisting of six houses and the later of about ten. The number of inhabitants was therefore very moderate, possibly no more than one to three extended patriarchal families.

In the Early Bronze Age the settled fertile regions continued to be inhabited. New, less fertile districts in the south of Bohemia were opened up, possibly in connection with the transition of several tribes to pastoralism. The settlements often occupied strategically important sites, on elevations or at the confluences of rivers. In many cases they were fortified with ditches and palisades, and sometimes even with stone walls, as at Ivanovce, near Trenčín (Trentschin) in West Slovakia. At Barca, near Košice (Kaschan) in East Slovakia, the rectangular detached houses were arranged in rows, separated by streets about seven feet wide.

The rudimentary beginnings of a stratification of society became more distinct in the Early Iron Age that reached Czechoslovakia in the seventh century B.C. As far as can be concluded from later periods, land was still commonly owned, a phase of development frequently connected with the ample availability of virgin land. Land ownership did not yet play any role in the differentiation of social standing or the appropriation of the means of production, although cultivation with the plow accorded a certain privileged position to the owners of cattle. However, a much more significant trend began to emerge with the appearance of the so-called princely class, to which numerous rich tombs of chieftains, with their funerary gifts of ornaments, vessels, and weapons, testify. The weapons and chariots left by these men—as well as the hilltop strongholds—may be taken as an indication of the martial nature of the period and the social superiority of this minority. However,

Czechoslovakia

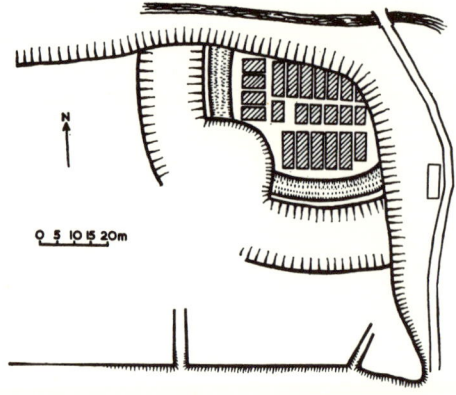

88. Plan of the village of Barca, near Košice, in eastern Slovakia.

the social and political units were still small, not going beyond class or tribal entities.

The Middle and Late La Tène culture, penetrating Bohemia, Moravia, and South-West Slovakia from the third to the first century B.C., may be connected with the influx of the first Celtic population. It was characterized by a general improvement of productivity and, especially, by the exclusive use of iron for implements, ornaments, and weapons. Agricultural activities increased, making considerable progress through ample use of the new technical possibilities which, in turn, resulted in a substantial increase of agricultural production and prosperity. Excavations of fortified *oppida* have revealed that settlements consisted of individual homesteads. The *oppida* were situated in strong positions, often above rivers, sometimes laid out in terraces, and were protected by ditches and stone walls strengthened by timber. The number of people living in the *oppida* must have been relatively great, judging from the often very large area enclosed by the walls, though we may assume that only a part of it was inhabited. The increase and advance of agriculture created, for the first time, a surplus of food sufficient to support a section of the population not directly engaged in agricultural pursuits but working as artisans and craftsmen. Jewelers, potters, and smiths were living in the *oppida,* and, in all probability, other craftsmen catering to the needs of the community. The division of labor—previously based on differentiations of sex and age but now on skill and the exercise of the intellect—continued to increase and to promote the extension of trade, superseding the barter economy of preceding periods.

It is probable that by the end of this era most of the land had been occupied, with the exception of regions particularly unfavorable for agriculture, and that a ruling class had established a firm economic and political hold over the population. As always in times of a growing concentration of people and a division of labor coupled with an increasing variety and size of production, the early consanguineous ties began to dissolve, to be replaced by elective affinities within the gradually forming class society of the *oppida*—however rudimentary their urban character may have been.

At the end of the second century B.C., the Celtic Boii were one of the tribes who arrived in Bohemia and Moravia before the Slavs and gave their name to Bohemia (*Boiohaemum* in Latin). The Boii settled in the northern districts of Bohemia and probably also in Central Silesia. The extent of their territory cannot be clearly defined. They were checked by the Dacians and the Domans. Teutonic and Slavonic tribes followed in the course of the next Christian centuries, initiating a new cultural era.

Agriculture remained the main activity of the population in the Roman period and during the time of the Great Migrations, although a certain recession in its technical equipment set in. In general, the economic standards of the Teutonic tribes were inferior to those of the immediately preceding era and were more akin to those of the Early and Middle La Tène cultures.

"*Iuxta Hermunduros Naristi ac deinde Marcomani et Quadi agunt. Praecipua Marcomanorum gloria viresque, atque ipsa etiam sedes pulsis olim Boiis virtute parta. . . . Sed vis et potentia regibus ex auctoritate*

Romana. Raro armis nostris, saepius pecunia iuvantur, nec minus valent."[3] As Tacitus describes it, Roman aid to these kings was obviously an early example of Foreign Economic and Military Assistance which Rome used with the same determination and skill as practiced today. For the Romans, the territories north of the Danube were a sort of advanced shield to ward off the barbarians. Their main fortifications were on the south bank of the river. Beyond this fortified frontier they merely established outposts with less elaborate defenses.

The attack on the Roman Frontier in A.D. 165 by the Marcomanni led to the Marcomannian Wars, lasting from A.D. 166 to 180. Their tribal center, serving as a fortified station and market center, was at Stradonice near the present town of Beroun (Beraun). It was not until the end of these wars that a more peaceful period began, ending again in the second half of the fourth century when Valentinian's legions penetrated deep into Teutonic territory. The last of the Teutonic tribes entering Czechoslovakia were the Langobardi, concluding the less than six centuries of Teutonic presence in the country.

The penetration of the Western Slavs into Czechoslovakia proceeded not in large compact groups but through isolated small units gradually infiltrating into Bohemia and Moravia. The Czech tribes were first mentioned in historical records about the middle of the fifth century. They tended to occupy the fertile valley of the Elbe River where they engaged in cultivation, while pastoral activities could be carried on in the highlands. In the lowlands they built their settlements, mostly in the form of ring-fence villages, the so-called *okolnice,* whose closed circular layout afforded a primitive, though not inefficient, defense. After the short-lived rule of the Avars in the sixth century, the first Czech political unit emerged in the form of the empire of the mysterious King Samo, that lasted from A.D. 625 to 658. The *Chronicle of Fredegarius Scholasticus* (IV. 48) reports: *"Anno 40 regni Chlotariae homo nomen Samo natione Francos de pago Senonago plures secum negutiantes adsciuit, exercendum negucium in Sclauos coinomento Winedos perrexit."*[4] It appears, therefore, judging from this text and other references in Fredegar's *Chronicle,* that Samo traveled as a private or possibly semi-official merchant-adventurer to Bohemia, where he helped the native tribes to repulse the Avars and, in recognition of his support and advice, was elected by them to be their ruler.[5] How this amazing "conquest" was consummated has provoked a lively controversy of experts. Suffice it to say that this legendary Samo must have been an extraordinary person, a predecessor of Cecil Rhodes who, singlehanded, conquered an African empire for Britain. Samo's realm included the open

---

3. Tacitus. *Germania.* 42. "Next to the Hermunduri are the Naristi and then the Marcomani and the Quadi. The fame and strength of the Marcomani are outstanding: their very home was won by prowess, through the expulsion in ancient times of the Boii. The force and power of their kings rest on the influence of Rome. Occasionally they are assisted by our armed intervention: more often by subsidies, out of which they get as much help."

4. "In the fortieth year of Chlotar's reign, a certain Frank named Samo, from the district of Soignies, joined with other merchants in order to go and do business with those Slavs who are known as Wends."

5. H. Preidel. *Die Anfänge der Slawischen Besiedlung Böhmens und Mährens.* Vol. I. 1954. Pp. 82–106.

landscapes of Bohemia as its core and, however ephemeral and nebulous his actual achievements may have been, he advanced the natural trends of the time toward the formation of a nation and the consolidation of its social and economic evolution.

Early in the ninth century, the second Czech political entity developed in Moravia, known as the Great Moravian Empire, extending to the Oder and the Vistula. It lasted from A.D. 830 to 894, when its last ruler was killed. Magyar invasions following his death disrupted the unity of the Empire. The Magyars settled as farmers in the country and kept it occupied until the Ottoman armies conquered it in the 16th century.

During the time of the Great Moravian Empire, social differentiation increased, metal working reached a high perfection, and considerable cultural progress was made. This trend toward a developed feudal structure of society furthered the construction of numerous fortified hill-forts, which may have been the seats of members of the ruling minority who gradually emerged as a class of feudal lords. These hilltop strongpoints should be clearly distinguished from the small residences of nobles, only lightly protected with palisades, which were situated off the beaten track, on hills or in marshy areas or other terrain not easily accessible. It was only later, in the ninth and tenth centuries, that strongpoints at strategically favorable places were erected and fortified with walls and moats, an unmistakable sign that the aristocratic elite was dissociating itself more and more from the common people. The higher standard of living of this proto-feudal group created demands for new and more sophisticated goods and an increased food supply from the neighborhood. How far the residences acted as economic centers, especially in the early period, is still not clear, but we may assume that in a number of cases these fortified castles became the nucleus of settlements growing up around them, a development to be found in almost all countries.

Beginning in the ninth century, the clearing of deciduous woodlands proceeded in the wake of the great colonial movement toward the East. It was a rather unsystematic enterprise, based mainly on the work of individual pioneer settlers, but it extended to a very considerable degree the area for cultivation and agricultural settlements. Thus, certain groupings of people developed within a clearly defined district. As J. Lippert remarked:

The more agriculture came to the fore, and the more the permanent seat of a family or a group of families as an open district [a Gau] was to be distinguished ... from its surroundings, the mark or the mark-forest, the more heterogeneous grew their reciprocal value and the character and rigidity of the idea of ownership in one or the other. Then the principal function of the mark, the protection it affords for the peace of the district, stands out. It is its enclosure and fence, and the district needs its unimpaired preservation as long as its protection is regarded as essential. When a permanent and peaceful coexistence of several neighboring districts has been established ... the mark ceases to be a prerequisite of security; it becomes, in parts, a field for interior colonization and the extension of cultivation.[6]

6. J. Lippert. *Socialgeschichte Böhmens in Vorhussitischer Zeit.* Vol. I. 1896. P. 7.

That the uncleared belts of forests formed boundaries between tribal units was only natural in the course of the great West-East colonial movement of the early Middle Ages, because the migrations penetrated the new lands not as a mighty stream but as small individual groups whose main concern was to be "left alone" and be protected from unfriendly competitors. Their colonizing expansion proceeded therefore from a nucleus outward within a given district, gradually reducing the wooded area and turning it over to cultivation.

Around the turn of the first Christian millennium, the development of agriculture, the extension of the settled area, the economic and social advance—the preconditions for political unification—and the growing crystallization of the agglomerations of people, however incomplete and unrelated these trends may have been, had laid the foundations on which an urban society could grow. In this respect, the next centuries were a period of creative germination and decisive influence for Czechoslovakia. As for many other countries, the early Middle Ages were the prelude to the mature urban civilization of the later part of this period, to the unfolding of the flourishing and revolutionary role of the urban communities in the life of the nation.

The following contribution by members of the Union of Architects of the Czechoslovak Socialist Republic demands a certain comment. It was unavoidable that the superabundant documentary material and some of the descriptions of individual cities had to be adapted to the scope and character of the *International History of City Development*. The publication of the entire documentation and text would have required a special volume devoted exclusively to the urban development of Czechoslovakia. This possibility had to be ruled out because it would have been incompatible with the general organization of the History and would have taxed the generosity of the publishers beyond the most far-reaching concessions. The author was, therefore, faced with an inevitable and almost painful task of reducing the enormous quantity of first-rate documentation to manageable proportions. This work was undertaken most reluctantly, since it involved difficult and intricate selections and decisions which, very likely, are open to critical assessments.

Consequently, text and captions had to be edited, and the number of cities contained in the City Survey had to be reduced to fit the material into the general framework of the History and the space available. The author wishes to emphasize, however, that this in no way diminishes the value of the work of the Union of Architects of the Czechoslovak Socialist Republic. Their contribution on city development in Czechoslovakia is a unique and precious tribute to international cooperation that will help draw attention to the great achievements of Czechoslovakia in the field of city planning and architecture.

Readers of the *International History of City Development* may observe that the essay by the Czech and Slovak authors is different in emphasis from the character of preceding volumes, though complementary to their general principles. The approach applied to the work as a whole is above all and basically concerned with the development of the physical structure of cities shaped by political, social, economic, and demographic forces—that is, by the evolution of city planning problems—whereas architectural achievements have been given only minor attention. This was, in the opinion of the author, unavoidable, since the work as a whole was conceived as a history of *city planning*, not of architecture. The contribution by members of the Union of Architects of the Czechoslovak Socialist Republic lays great stress on architectural achievements and their detailed description, thus differing in many respects from the author's approach and expressing ideas not necessarily identical with those presented elsewhere in the History. This means not that they are less valuable but merely that they represent other aspects of the same problem which so far have been outside the scope and character of this work.

Although the cities represented in the City Surveys of preceding volumes have been arranged geographically, the author did not feel justified to interfere with the alphabetical sequence of the Czech City Survey. It is hoped, however, that the accompanying maps will help in identifying the geographical location of individual cities.[7]

---

7. As in all other volumes, the urban development of Czechoslovakia has been surveyed to about the middle of the 19th century. It had been the author's intention to discuss the modern phase of urbanization in a final and concluding volume. Ed.

Development of the Historical Towns of Czechoslovakia

by
Jiří Hrůza, Dobroslav Líbal, Tibor Zalčík,
Oldřich Dostál, Otakar Nový, and Otakar Kuča.

CHAPTER 10

THE TERRITORY OF Czechoslovakia, in the heart of Central Europe, is geographically determined by the Bohemian basin, with the river valleys of the Vltava (Moldau) and the Labe (Elbe), the extensive river basin of the Morava, and a section of the Carpathian mountain chain which forms the northern boundary of the Pannonian lowland. During the time of the Great Migrations in the fourth to sixth centuries, the whole territory was inhabited by Slavonic people. The Slavonic tribes, coming from the northeast, arrived in several waves, settling first in Slovakia, then in Moravia, and, finally, during the sixth century A.D., in Bohemia, thus giving rise to the future closely-related nations of the Czechs and the Slovaks.

The new home of the Slavs was a fertile country covered with deciduous forests. From the time of their arrival, when the ethnic pattern of Europe began to be stabilized after the Great Migrations, the history of their settlements may be traced as a continuous development. However, the territory where they settled permanently had passed through a varied and complex transformation, witnessing a succession of different cultures with their corresponding forms of habitation.

The historical sequence of the different cultures has evoked numerous interpretations. More exact data have come to light only gradually, as a result of archeological investigations and scientific discussions. Some scientists consider the individual cultural layers as isolated and self-contained, while others are inclined to postulate their interdependence and gradual stratification, their mutual assimilation as well as their parallel existence on a single territory.

The settlements of that time cannot be regarded as towns, but merely as individual villages and groups of dwellings built in a rather primitive manner. The archeological discoveries consist mostly of small objects and ancient burial places which indicate that individual cultural layers differed primarily in the way in which the dead were buried.

The first finds of traces of settlement within the present territory of Czechoslovakia date approximately from the Stone Age, from about 3000 B.C. The best known is a place called Předmostí, near the town of Přerov in Moravia, where remains of an extensive settlement of hunters were found, with thousands of implements made of stone and bone as well as traces of the first religious and artistic manifestations. Similar settlements existed also in other localities, for instance, the somewhat later settlement of Dolní Věstonice, near the city of Brno, famous for the so-called Venus of Věstonice, a figure testifying to the cult of women as preservers of the human race.

During the Bronze Age, in the second millennium, the agricultural civilization of Únětice developed in Central Europe. It is represented by a number of finds on Bohemian territory, particularly at Bylany, near the town of Kutná Hora. Later, a part of Bohemia was settled by people belonging to the so-called Grave-Mound culture, who are regarded by some archeologists as predecessors of the Celts. At that time, smaller cultural regions with their own specific characteristics were formed which were named after the individual places of discovery. To these belong the various modifications of the culture of the people of Urn Burial Grounds, traces of which have been found all over Europe.

Pre-Slavonic Period

During the same period a significant social differentiation took place, as indicated by ornate chamber-tombs of ruling families from a later era.

In the fifth and third centuries B.C. the predominant area of the present territory of Czechoslovakia was part of an extensive European region settled by Celtic tribes. This era is mentioned in written documents, particularly those of Roman origin. The best known of the Celtic tribes inhabiting Bohemia mainly in the second century B.C. was the tribe of the Boii, after whom the country was called *Boiohaemum.* The names of some rivers and mountain chains are of Celtic origin.

The basic element of Celtic settlements was the agricultural village whose houses, with deep foundations in the ground, were built of wood and covered with straw roofs. In some places, particularly in the south of Bohemia, the houses had walls and foundations of stone. These buildings, however, are difficult to distinguish from the dwellings of the local people who had settled there at an earlier date.

The most characteristic Celtic settlement forms are the walled-in localities and the *oppida,* sometimes referred to as towns. In a number of places remains of fortified settlements with protecting walls have been preserved, built on the summits of hills and often at considerable altitudes. In Bohemia, for instance, the walled-in settlement of *Sedlo* was situated 2,952 feet above sea level. It was enclosed by a stone wall in addition to the natural protection of the steep slopes of the hill.

Oppida, extensive communities of a townlike character, appeared about the second century B.C. They served not only as bastions of defense, but also as centers of production. The best known among them is Hradiště, near Stradonice, in the neighborhood of Beroun, about 18 miles to the southwest of Prague. This settlement covered an area of 202.54 acres on a peninsula about 1,246 feet above sea level. As finds show, it was at one time the center of blacksmith crafts, metalworking, pottery making, and other handicrafts, and was probably also the seat of a mint.

To the south of Prague, near Zbraslav, another *oppidum* covering an area of about 419 acres was located on the summit of a hill called Závist. It consisted of the settlement proper, occupying an area of 66.69 acres and overlooked by an elevated *acropolis,* and of an extensive outer precinct and fortifications. Within the premises of the walled settlement several terraces have been preserved where dwellings were probably situated.

Apart from these two settlements there were a number of Celtic *oppida* in Bohemia, Moravia, and Slovakia. According to finds, it is assumed that Celtic settlements had been located on the sites of the present towns of Bratislava and Nitra and of other modern towns. It may be worth mentioning one of the rare examples of Celtic sculpture found on Czechoslovakian territory, namely, the head of a hero cut in limestone which, so far, remains the only one of its kind east of the Rhine. However, the history of Celtic civilization of the pre-historic period has not yet been fully investigated. It is hoped that further archeological research may add to the accuracy of contemporary opinions and suggestions.

At the beginning of the Christian era, Celtic rule over Central Europe was overthrown by the Roman legions from the South and by

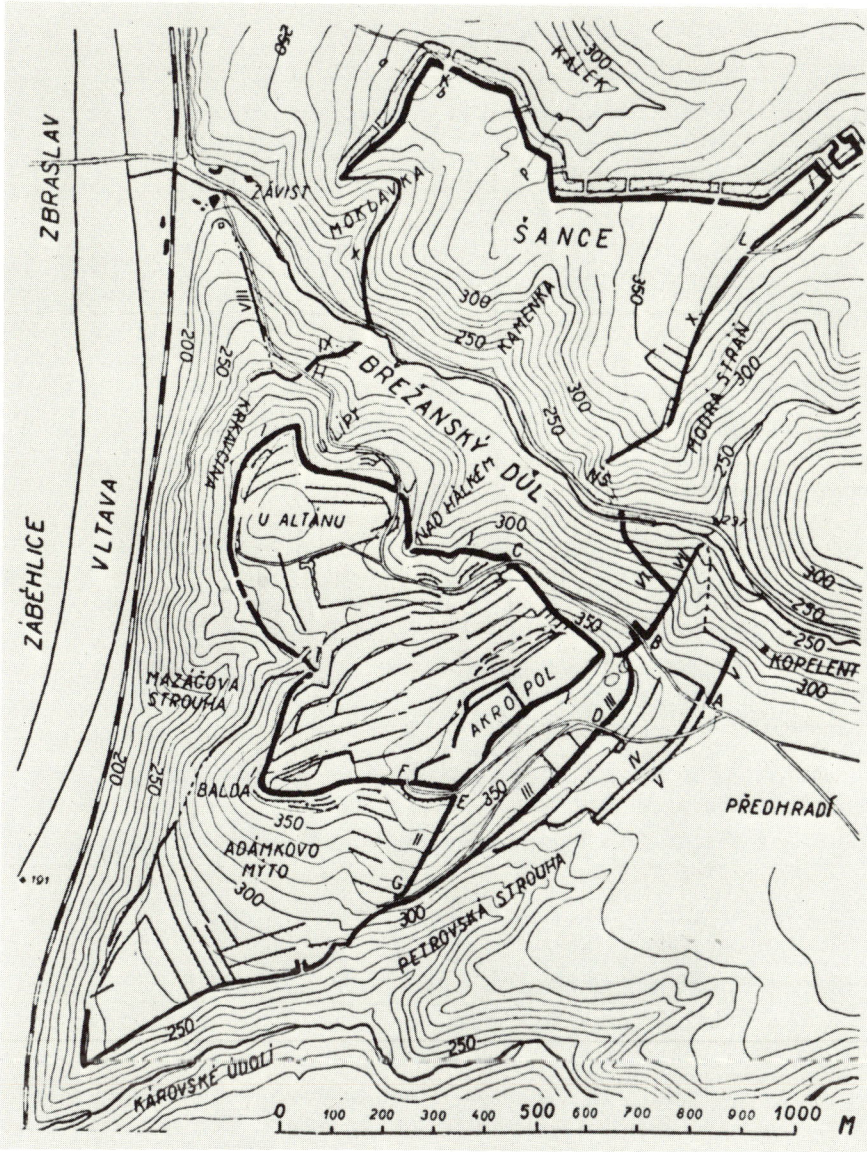

89. The walled-in settlement on the Závist Hill, one of the largest *oppida*, near Zbraslav. The fortifications, 5.58 miles in length, are located on a steep peninsula above the Vltava River. The site was settled as early as the middle of the last millennium B.C., during the Hallstatt Period.

the warlike Germanic tribes of the Marcomanni and Quades who attacked the Celts from the North. The territory of present Czechoslovakia was gradually occupied by different Germanic tribes who, however, did not quite supplant the original population and were, in turn, influenced by Celtic culture. According to Ptolemy, there existed a number of towns on Czechoslovak territory in the second century A.D. whose names may suggest their Celtic origin: *Eburodunon, Meliodunon, Redintuion, Kasurgis, Budorgis, Furgisatis,* and *Koridorgis*. Unfortunately, Ptolemy's inaccurate data make it impossible to identify the location of these towns. It may be assumed that some of the late Celtic *oppida* were hurriedly erected in defense against advancing Germanic tribes. It is also possible that the well-known Germanic center *Marobuduum* may have been a continuation of an earlier Celtic *oppidum*.

In the south, the course of the river Danube marked the frontier of the adjoining Roman Empire. The existence of Roman military camps

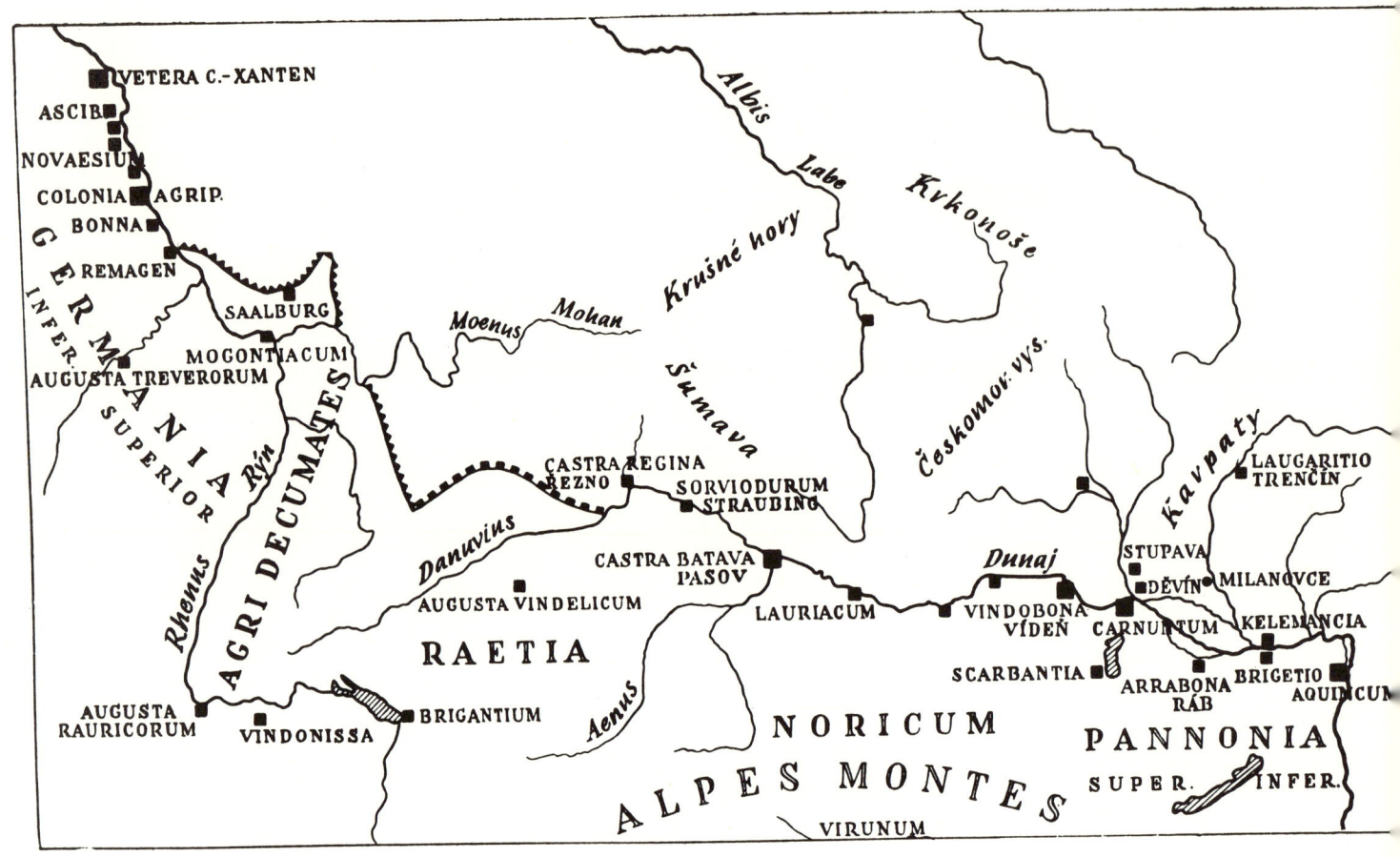

90. The *limes Romanus*, the fortified Roman frontier on the Rhine and the Danube, was settled in the fourth to the sixth centuries by Czech and Slovak tribes.

and Roman country estates in Slovakia has been proved by documentary material. A well-preserved Latin inscription, dating from the year 179 A.D. and cut in rock in Trenčín (identified most probably as the Roman *castellum Langaricium*), testifies to the fact that Roman legions, proceeding from the Danube, advanced far into the valleys of the Slovak mountain chains. Archeological finds in Moravia are of a similar nature. Near a place called Mušov, remains of another Roman *castellum*, founded by the Tenth Legion in a strategic position at the confluence of the rivers Dyje, Jihlava, and Svratka, were discovered. The finds just mentioned represent isolated data on the territory situated at the *limes Romanum*, while the significant Roman centers of the time were situated in close proximity on the southern banks of the Danube held by the Roman fleet.

CHAPTER 11

Slavonic Tribes and the Great Moravian Empire

DURING THE TURBULENT times of the Great Migrations, in the fourth century of our era, the Slavs appeared on the scene, passing through the territories of Slovakia, Moravia, and Bohemia. According to some scholars, the indigenous population was assimilated by the newcomers who, at the time, advanced as far as the Elbe and the Balkan Peninsula. It is known that the city of Berlin and a number of other German towns occupy sites of early Slavonic settlements of the so-called Elbe-Slavs, of which only the ethnic islet of the Lusatian Sorbs or Wends has survived to the present.

The Slavonic settlements were small communities of farmers, living in simply furnished cottages of timber framework, with foundations dug in the ground. They tilled their fields, storing the grain in pits, and engaged in cattle breeding, cloth weaving, pottery making, and the production of iron implements. These people encountered the last of the Roman occupation in the Danube Valley and, in the second half of the sixth century, the nomadic Avars in the south of Moravia and Slovakia.

For a brief period, in the seventh century, these tribes who had settled in the territory of Czechoslovakia were united in the first big state, under the leadership of a Frankish merchant named Samo, and fought the Avars in a series of successful battles. At that time, numerous walled-in fortified settlements were founded, testifying to a rapid economic development of the Slavonic tribes. Their fortified settlements successfully withstood the attacks of the Frankish tribes advancing from the West. As seats of the ruling class they became the centers of handicrafts, in particular of iron smelting and working. The existence of groups of iron workshops and furnaces, dating from the end of the eighth century, has been confirmed by archeological finds near the town of Uničov in Moravia. Contents of the tumulus burial grounds testify to the rising level of culture, to the wealth and the differentiation of a society gradually moving toward a feudal social structure. While the mountains of the Bohemian borderland were a welcome protection against the Frankish Empire, some of the West-Slavonic tribes who had crossed this boundary amalgamated with their new neighbors.

In the eighth and ninth centuries Slavonic tribes settled on the territory of Bohemia, Moravia, and Slovakia, uniting in larger groups referred to as principalities and ruled by hereditary princes. During this time of cultural and economic development the pagan religion was superseded by Christianity.

Recent large-scale archeological investigations in the south of Moravia and Slovakia, particularly in the vicinity of the present towns of Břeclav, Hodonín, Nitra, Uherské Hradiště, and the city of Brno, have thrown light on this interesting and significant period of Slavonic development. Since 1948 earlier archeological finds, discovered by chance in different localities, have been followed up by systematic and extensive investigations carried out under the auspices of the Archaeological Institute of the Czechoslovak Academy of Sciences. These surprising and valuable discoveries met with great interest and helped to modify existing theories on the development of Central Europe during this period.

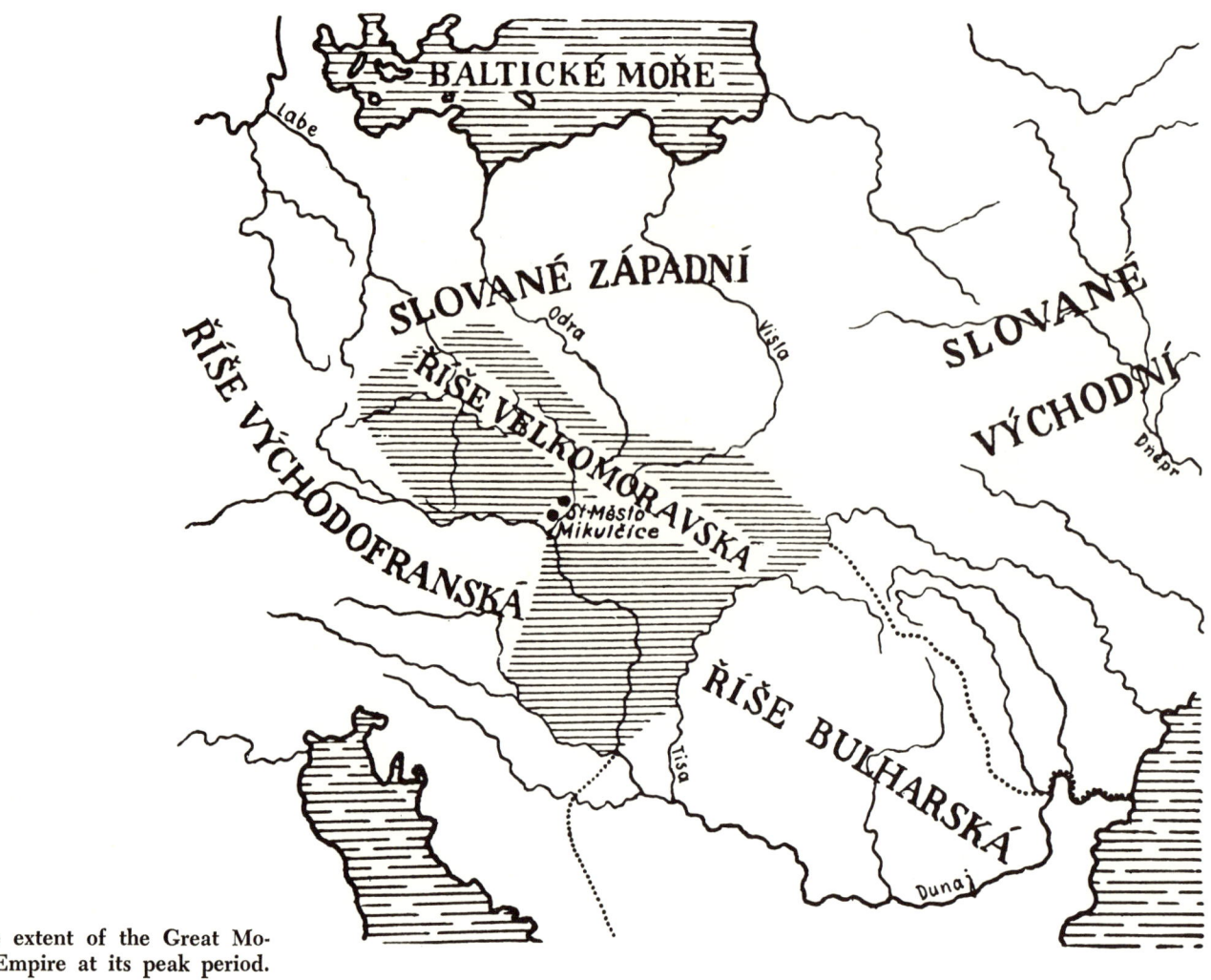

91. The extent of the Great Moravian Empire at its peak period.

The findings date from the time of the Great Moravian Empire which, according to contemporary written documents, flourished in the ninth century. The Great Moravian Empire was the first national organization of some stability, uniting the ancestors of the present Czech and Slovak nations. In this connection mention should be made of the arrival in 863 of the learned Byzantine brothers, Constantine (later called Cyril) and Methodius, natives of Salonica, who were well acquainted with the Slav dialects. They had been sent to Moravia by the Byzantine Emperor Michael, at the request of the Moravian ruler Prince Rastislav, to interpret to the people the teachings of Christ in the vernacular. They laid the foundation of the Slavonic script, and thus of Slavonic literature.

This early period is represented in the archeological discoveries of several strong, fortified Slavonic settlements. Judging from their function and extensive area, they should be regarded as direct predecessors of later towns. It is impossible to describe in detail the different localities of ancient burial places, fortifications, settlements, and remains of stone churches and other buildings. However, one settlement may be mentioned, located near the township of *Mikulčice* in the neighborhood of Hodonín in Southern Moravia, where extensive archeological investigations were started in the year 1954. It seems that the area called *Na Valech* (On the Ramparts) was a walled-in settlement, with an extensive outer precinct. The settlement itself covered an area of 14.82 acres and was enclosed with well-preserved ramparts. On its territory, the foundations of six churches were discovered, among them the foundations of a three-aisled basilica. Besides the remains of the churches, ancient fortifications were found, and a rectangular building whose subdivision of the interior suggests that it may have been either a princely palace or a dwelling of the followers of a prince. The interior of the building was decorated with murals.

In 1960 investigations were carried out in the outer precinct of this settlement whose overall area covered, according to a preliminary estimate, about 247 acres. It is intended to investigate a total area of 2,470 acres. Up to now the foundations of four churches have been discovered in this territory, including one two-apse rotunda, another with four apses, and fragments of block-houses built close to each other. It is possible that the outer precinct of the walled-in settlement was either a compact, fortified town surrounding the princely castle or a group of individual agricultural settlements, each with its own fortifications. The population might have amounted to two thousand people.

Archeological evidence seems to point to the beginning of the ninth century as the approximate time of origin of these buildings. However, it cannot be assumed that all of them were built at the same time, in the course of a few years. During investigations in a lower layer, a Slavonic settlement, fortified with wooden palisades and dating from the seventh to eighth centuries, has been discovered.

In the beginning of the 10th century the important settlement of Mikulčice began to decline. By the 11th century only a small part remained on the ruins of the original great metropolis. The center of political and economic life shifted elsewhere, preserving the original structure of the early settlement for archeological research.

Not only numerous agricultural communities existed on the territory of Bohemia, Moravia, and Slovakia at this time, but also dozens of walled-in settlements situated along rivers, valleys, and on peninsulas. Originally, these walled-in places were tribal centers, changing gradually into seats of the local administration of the united land. It may be assumed that at least the most significant among them had communities of tradesmen outside their walls and were surrounded by villages whose function differed from that of the remaining agricultural communities.

During this period, a net of inland trade routes developed as a continuation of international trade communications. At the same time, a differentiated settlement system grew up, comprising agricultural villages, walled-in settlements with communities outside their walls, castles guarding the overland roads and frontiers, and walled market villages, the latter representing a new form of community. The originally dispersed Slavonic tribes, particularly those settled on Bohemian and Moravian territory, were united in a consolidated and firmly organized state needing more active centers. The population increased, the density of settlement grew, and new places were founded on sites once occupied by extensive forests.

In *Kouřim,* in Central Bohemia, well-preserved fragments of an extensive settlement with strong fortifications, dating from the ninth and tenth centuries, were discovered during recent archeological excavations. In close proximity to the still existing town, dating from the 13th century, ruins of a tribal castle with a little Romanesque church and a community outside the castle walls dating from the 11th century were discovered adjoining the site of the walled-in settlement. In the majority of cases, development took place vertically, in layers deposited one on top of another. Archeological investigations have been impeded by still existing and inhabited historical towns of medieval origin whose ground plans reveal traces of older settlements.

In this period, the origins of the present settlement pattern can be found, characteristic of the change and development of settlement forms and elements from the earliest feudal epoch to modern times.

CHAPTER 12

The Origin of Towns

THE SUCCESSOR AND immediate follower of the Great Moravian Empire was the Bohemian State. The geographical configuration of the country, enclosed by mountain chains and primeval forests, determined the course of the frontiers and the existence of the State. Since the ninth century Bohemia had undergone a development similar to that of the Great Moravian Empire several decades earlier. Individual tribal territories gradually merged into a larger whole. In Bohemia the process of consolidation had not been completed at the time of the decline of the Great Moravian Empire; there were still two integral parts, one ruled by the Přemyslide dynasty from their Prague center and the other by the powerful feudal family of the Slavníks who resided in Libice, near Poděbrady, on the middle course of the Elbe.

However, the political independence of the Slavník family was not of long standing, as the center of political power shifted to Prague. During the reign of Prince Boleslav I (929–967) Moravia, formerly part of the Hungarian State, was joined to Bohemia. The newly founded Central European empire spread to the territory of Slovakia and the Cracow region, bordering in the east on Russia. The walled settlement of Přemysl was founded in the eastern borderland, as a strategic stronghold of the Bohemian power. It was named after Přemysl the Ploughman, the legendary founder of the Přemyslide dynasty. The discovery of a typical Czech rotunda on the *acropolis* of the walled settlement threw light on the origin of Přemysl.

During the 10th century conditions favored the development of large settlements of a townlike character. This fact is mentioned in a report of the year 965 by the Jewish-Arabian traveler Ibrahim Ibn Jacob. He had come to Prague by a long-distance trade route, built at considerable cost, and found the Bohemian capital a significant center of international trade, with well advanced handicrafts and a great number of stone buildings which, at that time, were rare in the territory north of the Danube and east of the Rhine.

Prague's position in the third quarter of the 10th century was neither novel nor singular, its long development being similar to a number of other centers of production and trade.

The origins of the Bohemian townlike settlements, the so-called "proto-towns," go back, no doubt, to the time before the completed tribal centralization. During this period the settlement structure of individual tribal centers and the system of communications was established, a process strongly influenced by the distribution of strategic points in the borderlands and by river crossings. The short period of Hungarian rule over Moravia did not affect the settlement structure of the Great Moravian Empire. By the end of the 10th century the position of the Bohemian State as a great power drew to a close. However, the nucleus of the State withstood the attacks of enemies who surrounded it on all sides. This achievement was due not only to the advantageous geographical position, the energy of the rulers, and the sturdiness and fighting spirit of the people, but also to the system of fortifications, hardly paralleled in ingenuity.

The development of the national state was not completed until the 12th century, when Bohemia and Moravia were joined in a permanent union. Of exceptional significance was the period of King Vladislav II (1140–1172). From its former marginal position in culture and politics, the Bohemian State proceeded rapidly toward joining the ranks of leading European countries. International, cultural, and trade relations were strengthened; and the cultivation of the soil improved together with an extensive colonization of the wooded regions. The entire territory of Bohemia and Moravia was gradually settled, with the sole exception of the borderland forests. The net of long-distance roads grew; and feudal centers, no longer represented merely by royal castles and estates, Benedictine monasteries, and collegiate chapters, increased in number. During the 12th century, new monasteries were founded by the reformed orders of the Premonstratensians and Cistercians, who regarded the cultivation of the soil as one of their primary activities. Simultaneously, the number of minor feudal seats grew, and the first market villages appeared probably as early as the 10th century.

The complex political and economic development of the 11th and 12th centuries had a direct influence on the differentiation of the settlements and on the multiplication of the feudal seats with urban characteristics. The identification of their ground plans involves problems which are difficult to overcome. However, more helpful than written documents are the layouts of castles, the location of churches or monasteries, and the long distance roads, as well as the topography of the country. After eliminating changes which took place during the following centuries, it may be possible to arrive, by way of scientific analysis, at the essential character of the ground plans of early feudal settlements. They are fundamentally different from the urban plans of the Gothic period. The original street pattern of towns laid out on definite plans —the so-called *location towns*[1]—can be reconstructed from still-existing historical buildings, frequently arranged in a continuous building line. For settlements belonging to the Romanesque period this situation is typical only of Prague.

The best example of a large early feudal town is *Prague*. The original stimulus for its intensive development was its favorable position at a ford of the Vltava River and the protection of two royal castles surrounded by communities of craftsmen and tradesmen. The ground plan of early feudal Prague has been partly preserved to this day. It is characterized by a radial arrangement of streets, not only in the central part of the Old Town of Prague—with the roads converging toward the main marketplace, the Old Town Square—but also in other sections of the town. Several of the former wide market streets had the same origin. Numerous Romanesque churches, still existing or at least identifiable by reliable documentary material, monasteries, and, above all, dozens of stone-built town houses enable us to recall the early feudal appearance and structure of Prague. Toward the close of this period Prague was one of the leading cities on the European continent.

1. *Location* and *pre-location* towns are terms used in connection with Czech medieval urban development, *location* meaning a tract of land specifically designated for the purpose of founding a town. In general, the term *location town* refers to towns founded on preconceived regular plans, especially in the 13th century. *Pre-location* towns, on the other hand, are towns originating in the 9th to 12th centuries on previously settled sites, often in the vicinity of monasteries, castles, and old Slavonic settlements. Their original layout is irregular due to the configuration of the terrain and the ground plans of older settlements.

92. Model of the Castle of Prague during the second half of the 12th century. Seen from the southwest, the White Tower is at the western entrance to the castle, and the episcopal residence is next to St. Vitus' Cathedral. The southern entrance gate and tower are located in the center of the southern wall. The old palace with the Chapel of All Saints adjoins the wall farther to the east. The Benedictine Monastery with St. George's Church occupies a site at the northern section of the castle walls. The eastern entrance to the castle is guarded by the Black Tower. Model by Václav and Dobroslava Mencl, 1946.

Another major settlement was *Olomouc,* occupying, during early feudal times, the greater part of the area of the later medieval town. Due to its importance and extent it ranked second only to Prague.

Brno, the second Moravian town of importance, underwent a different development. During the 11th century the settlement center shifted from the area of the so-called Old Brno to the present historical nucleus, thus giving rise to a complex urban agglomeration. The traces of this agglomeration did not entirely disappear in the later regular layout of the town or during the rebuilding in the 13th and following centuries.

The growth of *Znojmo,* another large medieval Moravian town, resembled the development of Brno in many respects. The founding of a new castle in the second quarter of the 11th century was followed by the growth of an extensive agglomeration featuring, in parts, a strongly marked radial layout. The plan of the town of *Opava,* formerly in Silesia, also passed through a complex development, comprising a roadside settlement along an important trade route connecting Silesia with Poland.

The north-Bohemian town of *Litoměřice* grew up from an early feudal settlement. The original walled-in place was gradually surrounded by a number of scattered communities along the main road to Prague, and the widening of this road gave rise to a large, elongated marketplace.

The original design of the town of *Žatec,* in the north of Bohemia, can be reconstructed from the historical nucleus of the medieval suburbs, with small churches of early feudal parishes. During the 11th century a regular, oblong marketplace, with a church in its center, was laid out in front of the main entrance to the royal castle. The layout of the marketplace at Žatec is the oldest example of early feudal town planning in the Bohemian lands.

The town of *Hradec Králové* also occupied an important position during these times. Its center developed within the area of a walled Slavonic settlement around which a number of communities grew up.

All these towns represent important settlements of the early feudal period which maintained their status during the following centuries. It was only in the 19th century that individual differences distinguished one town from the other. Old Slavonic walled-in settlements determined the extent of the urban nuclei of the towns of *Mělník, Jaroměř, Chrudim, Nymburk,* and others.

The basic types of early feudal plans can also be observed in numerous settlements of minor significance. A radial layout was doubtless an exception and occurred only in a limited number of towns, such as Starý Plzenec and Starý Bydžov. Other plans were more prevalent till recent times, so that a reliable reconstruction of their early feudal origin involves considerable difficulties. However, our knowledge of the street pattern in the so-called *pre-location* towns,[2] preserved in the towns of the 14th and 15th centuries, helps to solve this problem. The most representative example of an early feudal street pattern is that of the south-Bohemian town of *Vodňany*.

Domažlice, situated in the western region of Bohemia, is of special interest as a *pre-location town*. During the sixties of the 13th century, only the eastern three fifths of the early feudal marketplace were included within the town walls. The original design is still clearly visible in the plan of the town.

The usual type of street pattern differs from the type of settlement grouped around a common. In the latter, the central area of an early feudal community has a lenticular shape, for example, in the towns of *Litomyšl* and *Bechyně*. A basic feature in the layout of several minor towns of early feudal origin is a bifurcation of diverging roads which determines the shape of the square as at *Týnec nad Labem*. Early feudal villages had many different plans, the result, in part, of the complex development of villages after the decline of the tribal organization. Among the village patterns, compact forms with a central village green predominate. Street villages existed as early as prehistoric times, with the buildings grouped along the road. A particularly interesting type of early village planning in the feudal period is the ring-fence village, with a circular village green and, originally, a single exit only. Villages of this type were relatively frequent during the time of the so-called inner colonization in the course of the 12th century.

The early feudal period also knew villages grouped around lenticular or elliptoidal commons, a pattern similar to that of the original designs of several towns.

The plans of early feudal towns and villages in Bohemia varied greatly. Though they lacked the geometrical order of later medieval towns, it would be wrong to consider them entirely spontaneous foundations. On the contrary, the majority of towns and villages were laid out systematically and, in some cases, according to regular plans. Proof of a certain systematization is also offered by the location of secular and ecclesiastical centers, for instance, the location of parish churches either

2. See p. 130, footnote 1.

on the highest point of the settlement or in the middle of the marketplace.

Important feudal buildings like royal castles or monasteries—with the exception of the buildings of the Cistercian Order—were often situated on elevated positions, a symbolic expression of their dominant function. Some of the early feudal "proto-towns" had splendid architectural ensembles and lively skylines, the finest example being the silhouette of the Prague Castle (Hradčany).

In the 10th century monumental architecture began to appear in the Bohemian lands, in part a continuation of the building tradition of the Great Moravian Empire. Recent archeological investigations have revealed the existence of a magnificent Bohemian Romanesque art. Remarkable buildings, the so-called rotundas, are particularly characteristic examples of Bohemian Romanesque architecture of the 10th to the 13th centuries.

In the 10th century, however, building in stone was limited to the most important centers. An essential stimulus to its further development was the founding of the bishopric of Prague in the year 973 and the rise of the first Benedictine monasteries.

In the course of the 11th century, building activities gained momentum. The Prague cathedral and the churches of several monasteries date from this time, as well as Romanesque chapels scattered throughout Bohemia and Moravia. During the 12th century Romanesque art was fully established in the lands of the Bohemian Crown. Since the beginning of the 12th century architecture had attained a high level of design and form, reaching its culmination in the third quarter of the century, during the reign of King Vladislav II. The first stone houses of Prague most probably date from this era.

The second half of the 12th century above all, the time of Vladislav II—represents the most interesting period of Romanesque architecture, no longer derived from neighboring Saxony or the Danube region but inspired by Italy, the Rhineland, Burgundy, and even southwestern France. Bohemian art at that time ranked with the leading achievements of European culture.

At the close of the early feudal period, the Bohemian settlements were differentiated by their respective layouts, their architectural appearance, and their economic function and importance. By that time, all necessary prerequisites for the *location* movement of the 13th century had emerged.

The early feudal period, in particular its last stage, the 12th century, played a very important role in the formation of the settlement structure of the country. Hundreds of settlements came into being, of which a considerable number have survived to the present.

After the destruction of the territorial and administrative unity of the Great Moravian Empire, the territory of present-day Slovakia was occupied by the descendants of the Avars and Huns, the Hungarians. Toward the end of the ninth century these tribes settled in the southern and eastern parts of the country, gradually spreading to the mountainous districts during the following two centuries. This event contributed to the peculiar character of the settlement structure of Czechoslovakia, that is, to its differentiation between Bohemia and Moravia, on the one hand, and the Slovak regions on the other. While Bohemia and Moravia passed through a period of economic and political stabilization and prosperity, resulting in the foundation and consolidation of the Bohemian State, the Slovak regions, forming part of feudal Hungary, remained dependent for centuries on the economic conditions and opportunities of the Hungarian State.

The feudal order, from the reign of Stephen onward, led to an administrative organization based on the division of the territory into areas owned by ecclesiastical and military dignitaries. Economically viable units were created which rested on the subject-landlord relationship of this period. This, together with the economic utilization of the land, increased the differentiation of settlement, giving rise to agricultural settlements, settlements of craftsmen below castles, and settlements affiliated to monasteries.

During the first two centuries of the Hungarian State, its populated area was bordered by a zone of forests in Central Slovakia, which was gradually pushed back to the mountainous regions of Northern Slovakia. On the edge of these forests the first monasteries were founded, Svätý Beňadik (1075), Bzovík and Zobor, and others, which soon became the owners of vast estates, with a great number of villages.

At that time building activities were concentrated in the hands of the barons, as the castle owners and the military commanders, on the one hand, and the Church on the other. The barons exerted all their efforts to strengthen the defenses of their castles, while the Church devoted its energies to constructing churches and monasteries as centers of its secular power and to propagating religious teaching and education. The beginnings of these building activities date back to the middle of the 13th century. Our knowledge of the nature of these buildings is still vague; their light construction and perishable timber did not resist the impact of time. The latest research of the so-called obsolete settlements of the Middle Ages (Šolda, Zalužany, Milanovce, and others) has revealed highly developed forms of design of the individual residential buildings, reflecting the close connection of the residential and economic functions of a home.

In the course of the 11th century the Hungarian State strengthened its organization by creating a system of regional castles. In general, these strongholds continued the tradition of the former tribal castles of the Slavs, such as Bratislava, Hont, Nitra, and Tekov. The early castles, built of timber and surrounded by a complicated system of ramparts, were rebuilt as stone forts strong enough to withstand invasions and protect the territory of the State, as at Trenčín, Beckov, Šintava, and Hlohovec. This was also their function after the Tartar invasion, which revealed the insufficiency of the original defenses, for example, in the Váh River Valley, Spiš Castle, the castle of Stará Lubovňa, Orava, and numerous other castles of Eastern Slovakia. The siting of these strongholds depended on the relief of the terrain to enhance their dominant position and strategic importance.

Ecclesiastical building activities continued those of the Great Moravian Empire. According to recent research 11th-century builders used stone to construct churches. Although no ecclesiastical buildings from that period have been preserved, new buildings in the Romanesque style were subsequently erected on the original sites.

Ecclesiastical building activities reached their peak at the end of the 11th and the beginning of the 12th century. The Koloman reform (1100) enabled the Church, or individual feudal lords, to build churches without asking the sovereign's consent. In the course of the 12th century this privilege was also granted the immigrants into Hungary who had been called in from other countries to colonize the territory and who contributed to the building of towns in Slovakia.

Of particular interest is the great number of parish and monastery churches built outside the towns. All these buildings, characterized by their monumental design, usually with three aisles and two towers, testify to a highly developed building technique. Examples of these buildings are the church of Diakovce, built prior to 1228 on the site of a church of earlier origin; the churches of Janovce and Bzovík; and the parish church at Krušovce.

The large number of Romanesque buildings testify to the intensity as well as the continuity of the settlement process at this time, on both new and old sites. The transition from extensive to more intensive methods of cultivation stabilized the structure of settlement, increased production and trade, and led to the differentiation of settlement forms.

The beginning of town building in Slovakia corresponded to developments in Hungary. As in Bohemia and Moravia it was based on a system of market settlements situated outside the walls of feudal castles, as at Bratislava, Nitra, Plavecký Štvrtok, and Starý Tekov, or on important trade routes. The most important were the so-called Bohemian Route, connecting Hungary with Bohemia, and the trade route leading along the valleys of the rivers Hornád and Torysa to Poland.

CHAPTER 13

The Golden Age of the Founding of New Towns

THE CLIMAX OF FEUDALISM was characterized by a revolutionary growth of cultural, economic, and social changes. Education became more widespread and common; and the transition to a money economy, resulting in cash payment of ground-rents, mobilized formerly unexploited economic forces. New classes emerged, forming a society which resembled the contemporary sociological structure far more closely than the stratification of antiquity or the early feudal age.

High feudalism coincided not only with the Gothic period but also with extensive transformations of the settlement structure, the rise of new castles, towns, and villages. These changes began in the 12th century and became more intense on the territory of present Czechoslovakia at the beginning of the 13th century, when Přemysl Otakar I (1197–1230) consolidated the position of the Bohemian State as a kingdom. Under an autocratic ruler, a class of feudal lords developed whose political position was strengthened by the economic advancement of the nobility and the erection of strongly fortified castles.

The increasing importance of a money economy and the growing requirements of a more civilized life and a more sophisticated culture led to a higher productivity and specialization of handicrafts and an intensified demand for agricultural products. The forms of colonization of the early feudal period no longer satisfied the changed conditions.

Rulers took an active interest in the founding of towns. The new Royal Towns strengthened their political power and were a source of great economic profit. The most active agent in the process was the *locator,* who received the land from the founder and divided it into lots. For reasons of policy and defense, the king was greatly interested in the layout of the new towns. We may assume that decisions affecting the plans of new towns were not left entirely to the planners. In any case, the building of fortifications was a royal privilege.

The principal source of income of the urban population was handicrafts, trade being limited to a small circle of patricians. In the majority of towns the burghers were also part-time farmers.

Our knowledge of the earliest chartered towns is very obscure. It is probable that the first Czech or Moravian town was established not later than 1221, when *Krnov,* situated on the border between Moravia and Silesia, was mentioned in historical records. It was followed, in 1223, by the town of *Bruntál* in the same region and the Royal Town of *Uničov* in North Moravia. One year later, the important town of *Opava* was founded. In this early group of towns the important township of *Hlubčice,* now on Polish territory, may be included. Apart from these North Moravian towns, the early feudal community of *Podivín* was mentioned in 1222 as a border town in the southern part of the country. In Bohemia only *Hradec* (Králové), apparently raised to the status of a Royal Town in 1225, and perhaps *Kladsko,* situated on the Silesian border, now in Poland, could compete with the towns previously mentioned.

The North Moravian towns suffered greatly in the raids of the Tartars in 1241; despite the resultant devastation we may assume that the present plans of their old centers are the original ones. The layout of *Krnov,* strongly influenced by the crossing of long-distance trade routes, shows a tendency toward a rectangular formation of building blocks. *Bruntál* features regular, oval-shaped fortifications and a gridiron plan, with an oblong square in the center. At present, it represents the oldest known Czechoslovakian example of a town designed according to a systematic plan.

Even now the circular layout of nearby *Uničov* presents certain difficulties, as far as the incorporation of the radial elements of the former street system is concerned. The plan of *Opava* combines elements of the former early feudal structure with modern town planning principles. Traces of a similar process can also be found at *Hradec Králové*, an important center of the early feudal period.

The Moravian town of *Znojmo*, probably founded in 1226, has a complex plan, with early feudal buildings extending along the southeastern side and a large, slightly trapezoidal Lower Square in a part of the town where a regular layout could be applied. Znojmo, measuring approximately 2,130 feet x 3,110 feet, ranks among the foremost historical towns of Czechoslovakia.

93. View of the town of Znojmo from the south. Drawing by Friedrich Bernhard Werner, middle of the 18th century.

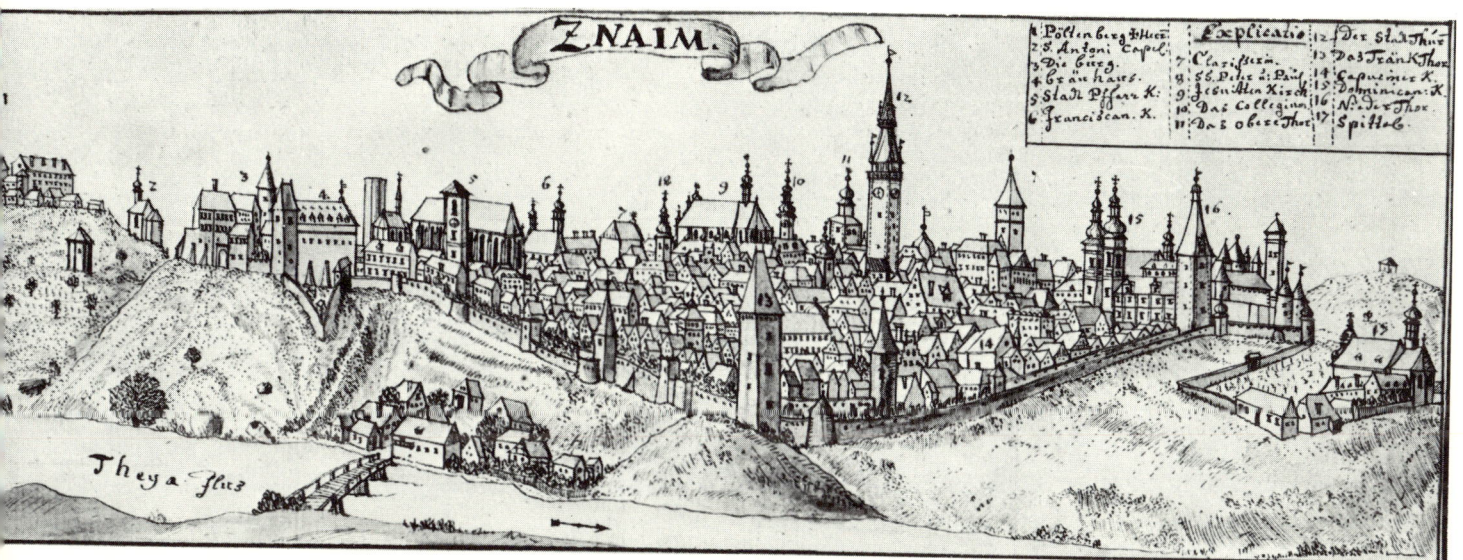

The gradual development of *Prague* began on the right bank of the river Vltava, in the so-called Old Town, the main trade and handicraft center in the early feudal period. Its large number of Romanesque stone houses may have prevented the application of a regular checkerboard street system, thus preserving the older radial plan. The replanning of Prague began at the southeast border of the Old Town, which had the smallest number of inhabitants and buildings. Here, the so-called Havelské Město originated after 1230, with its new central, lens-shaped marketplace.

Prague held a leading position in the town planning activities of the country. In the forties of the 13th century it was followed by the three Moravian towns of Brno, Olomouc, and Jihlava. As in Prague, the complex and densely built-up area of the early feudal settlement of *Brno* prevented a regular layout. *Olomouc*, a rival of Brno, had a layout originating in the merging of the castle with its *suburbium* and the communities extending to the west. Both units were joined by a narrow isthmus. The historical core of Olomouc, situated within the walls, covered an area of about 3,930 x 2,950 feet. After Prague, it was the largest town in the Bohemian state. While the ground plans of the previously mentioned towns are frequently characterized by a combination of town planning principles of the early feudal and the medieval periods, the mining town of *Jihlava*, dating from the beginning of the forties of the 13 century, shows a mature plan, modified perhaps under the reign of Přemysl II. The focal point of the plan is a large oblong square, 328 x 1,148 feet.

The mining town of Stříbro in West Bohemia was founded at about the same time as Jihlava. Its plan, with five parallel streets running east-west and an oblong square, was not repeated anywhere else in Bohemia and Moravia.

The founder of these towns was the king, while earlier feudal towns had been established by lay or ecclesiastical lords, as were *Jablonné* below Mount Ještěd and *Kladruby*.

The four decades of the first half of the 13th century, under the reigns of Přemysl I (1197–1230) and Wenceslas I (1230–1253), were of outstanding importance in the history of urban development in Bohemia and Moravia. The towns of the first half of the 13th century are in many ways more attractive and more interesting than those built in

94. Airview from the southeast of the large square in the center of Jihlava, with the twin-towered parish church in the foreground (right). In the background, at the northeastern corner of the square, the Jesuit church and the roof of the town hall.

the second half of that century. Their layouts reflect the difficult problems of adapting them to the legacy of early feudalism. The majority of these towns stand on areas partially settled in the preceding period. Only a minority were founded on newly cleared land. Within the inherent limits considerable efforts were made to organize the plan of new towns on a regular system. Most of them had one oblong and fairly large square, in some cases two.

The walls, built simultaneously with the town and frequently as oval circumvallations, followed the configuration of the terrain. The site of the parish church varied, while the monasteries of mendicant orders were always situated near the town walls.

By the middle of the 13th century the largest medieval towns in the country, with the exception of Kutná Hora and Žitava, had been built. The founding of new towns naturally resulted in extensive building activities such as improved fortifications with bastions and strong gates, churches and monasteries, and houses for the municipal officers and burghers.

The Přemyslide kings of the first half of the 13th century did not devote the same efforts to the systematic fortification of towns as had Přemysl Otakar II (1253–1278). Town planning was an important instrument in the development of the Bohemian State built up by Přemysl II as a firmly organized Central European political system, whose focal point lay in the Czech lands, gradually incorporating Austria, Styria, Carinthia, and part of Carniola. As in the time of the Boleslavs, in the 10th century, Prague became again the center of a national state that expanded as far as the Adriatic Sea.

The political influence of the Bohemian State was based on sound economic foundations. The economic revolution, reaching its peak during the reign of King Přemysl, seems miraculous after the lapse of so many centuries. Hundreds of new towns and villages grew up on the initiative of the king and the lords temporal and spiritual. The Bohemian nobility, combining their strength with the power of the king, greatly assisted in strengthening the position of the Bohemian State. After the death of the king on the battlefield, the great power of Bohemia in Central Europe declined for a short time. However, the founding of towns in Bohemia continued as a monument to the great period of the reign of King Přemysl II.

Perhaps the earliest town planning activity of King Přemysl II was the transformation of the *suburbium* of Prague Castle into the so-called Small or Lesser Town of Prague, Menší Město Pražské, in 1257. At the same time, he carried out a great building program, mainly along the so-called Trstenice Path, which was then the chief communication between Prague and the Moravian towns of Olomouc and Brno. In the fifties of the 13th century the Royal Towns of Kouřim, Kolín, Čáslav, Chrudim, Vysoké Mýto, and Polička were built along this route or in its vicinity.

Planned development is also characteristic of the Royal Towns founded, for strategic reasons, as a continuous system at some distance from the Bohemian-German border and partly near the Hungarian frontier, thus reviving the ideas of the early feudal system of frontier defense.

The main pillar of the royal power in South Bohemia was the town of *České Budějovice,* followed in the northwest by the towns of *Písek, Sušice, Klatovy, Domažlice,* and *Tachov.* Royal towns also grew up along the northwestern border of Bohemia up to the river Elbe. Situated in the west is *Loket,* with *Ostrov, Kadaň, Most,* and *Ústí nad Labem* to the east. Further inland, the towns of *Žatec* and *Louny* rose on the river Ohře as a second line of defense.

Přemysl's efforts were less apparent along the valley of the Elbe. The town of *Žitava,* on the northern border, originated about 1265. No Royal Town grew up either below the Jizera or the Giant Mountains. The only towns founded at fairly close distances to each other, to the southwest of the upper course of the Elbe, were Hostinné, Dvůr (later Králové Dvůr), and Jaroměř.

In general, Přemysl's building activity in the inner regions of Bohemia was of minor importance. Only the towns of Mělník and Nymburk, situated at crossings of the central course of the Elbe, may be mentioned.

The strategic interests of the king were also directed toward Moravia whose southeastern border was exposed to the danger of attacks from Hungary. Here the dense network of castles, mostly of early feudal origin, was supplemented by two new Royal Towns, *Uherské Hradiště* and *Uherský Brod.* In central Moravia the Royal Towns of *Přerov, Litovel, Jevíčko,* and perhaps *Lipník,* were laid out.

At the same time a large number of towns were founded by secular and ecclesiastical feudal lords. With some exceptions they were smaller than the Royal Towns, and their plans were designed with less care and regularity. Among the most remarkable towns dating from the reign of King Přemysl II were the South Bohemian towns of *Jindřichův Hradec* and *Český Krumlov; Česká Lípa* in North Bohemia; *Trutnov* and *Broumov* in Northeast Bohemia; *Havlíčkův Brod, Chotěboř* and *Litomyšl* in East Bohemia; and, on Moravian territory, the towns of *Svitavy* and *Moravská Třebová.*

An interesting group of smaller towns existed in North Moravia, among them *Šternberk* and *Šumperk.* In the southeast region of the country lay *Hranice, Nový Jičín, Fulnek* and *Příbor;* and *Třebíč* was located in the southwest of Moravia.

A comparison of town planning in the first half of the 13th century with that of Přemysl II shows an extraordinary progress in town building in Bohemia and Moravia in the third quarter of the 13th century. With few exceptions, remains of early feudal plans can be found only in the more important towns such as *Kouřim* and *Přerov.* A perfectly regular ground plan with rectangular blocks laid out on a checkerboard systém and a central square was only rarely applied. This kind of systematic planning was realized most successfully in the towns of *Vysoké Mýto, Litovel, Žlutice, Moravská Třebová,* and *Nový Jičín.*

The circular plan of Šumperk was unique. More widely applied was the oval plan, which encountered great difficulties when combined with a regular layout, resulting in a none too satisfactory compromise. The most successful combination of an oval outline and a regular plan exists at *České Budějovice, Klatovy, Kolín, Hostinné* in Bohemia, and

95. Airview from the northwest of the historic nucleus of Český Krumlov. The pear-shaped core, surrounded by the river, is clearly visible. The skyline is dominated by the parish church, rising above houses of mainly Gothic and Renaissance origin.

96. Airview from the northwest of the historic nucleus of Domažlice. In the foreground, the former Augustinian monastery, situated at the western boundary of the urban center. The parish church with its cylindrical tower, the dominant feature of the town silhouette, is located in the center of the northern side of the rectangular town square.

at *Jevíčko* in Moravia. In general, the regular pattern was preferred regardless of the gradient of the terrain.

An independent group is represented by towns with elongated squares, resembling the widening of a street, as at *Domažlice, Ostrov, Litomyšl, Svitavy,* and *Třebíč.* In most cases, the site and shape of the square were based on the plan of an earlier settlement, particularly of the early feudal period.

In a number of towns the principal roads were wider than streets inhabited by artisans and craftsmen. There was, however, a tendency to give the same width to all streets, for example, at *Klatovy.* On the average, the streets of the new towns were 32.8 feet wide, and were lined

97. Airview from the southeast of the historic nucleus of České Budějovice. The square in the center is surrounded by arcades. On the right, the Black Tower of the parish church; on the left, to the west, the former Dominican monastery and church and, fronting the square, the Renaissance-Baroque town hall.

by single or sometimes two-storied houses. The main streets were up to 49.2 feet wide.

Perhaps the most remarkable feature of Czechoslovak medieval towns were the big squares from the early period of town building during the reigns of Přemysl I and Wenceslas I. In a number of cases these squares were disproportionate to the core areas which, in the majority of Royal Towns, measured 1,312 to 1,804 by 984 to 1,312 feet. Only a few in large towns exceeded this size, as at *České Budějovice* and *Uherský Brod*. In general the dimensions quoted above do not apply to feudal towns, which were sometimes quite small, comprising merely the buildings situated around the square.

143

In many respects the period of Přemysl II was unique. However, it did resemble the peak of contemporary town building in Southern France—the building of the so-called *bastides* during the second third of the 13th century and later—or the East German towns built more-or-less simultaneously.

The strategic purpose of the towns founded by King Přemysl II aroused an extraordinary interest by the ruler in their fortifications. Several regulations issued by the king for the construction of fortifications have been preserved. The most interesting and most detailed are the undated instructions for the fortifications of the towns of *Kolín* and *Čáslav*, whose defense systems have been partly preserved to the present day. The fortifications of *Čáslav*, dating from the third quarter of the 13th century, offer perhaps the best example of such a system in the Přemysl period, consisting of the main walls, the space between the main walls and the moat, the outer walls, another moat, and an embankment formed by the material excavated during the construction of the moat. It can be assumed the bastions were semicircular. An important part of the fortifications were the gates. Relatively complicated in design was the partly preserved Brod Gate at Čáslav, with a massive cylindrical tower on its outer side. However, gates built in the form of prismatic towers protected by portcullises predominated.

The location and number of gates influenced the plan of towns. With the sole exception of *Loket*, all towns had at least two gates, mostly situated on the main roads. However, three or four gates were not unusual. In some cases a street led from the town gates to the square, passing the center of the square or leading to its corners and continuing along its sides. More frequently it crossed the square diagonally.

An important element of the fortifications was the castle, always situated within the walls. A most magnificent example is the castle at *Písek*.

Building activities increased within the town walls, particularly of churches and monasteries. In the first half of Přemysl's reign the influence of the Cistercian-Burgundian early Gothic style continued. The best preserved example from that period is the parish church at Písek. Its architecture was similar to other buildings in the town (the Dominican church and the royal castle) as well as to the nearby royal castle of Zvíkov, built about the same time. A royal workshop schooled in the Cistercian-Burgundian style was responsible for the construction of these buildings.

The application of the checkerboard system was an essential part of the development of the layout and the siting of buildings. The dimensions of building plots differed, depending on their situation in the urban territory and the economic strength of the community. The average width of the sites was 19.68 to 32.8 feet, of the larger ones 49.2 feet or more.

CHAPTER 14

Urban Development in the High Middle Ages

THE BATTLE OF the Moravian Field (1278) and the ensuing decline of the power of the Bohemian State represent the main turning points in the urban evolution of Czechoslovakia. They closed the great epoch of the founding and rebuilding of towns initiated by King Přemysl Otakar II, leaving the work unfinished. His son, Wenceslas II (1283–1305), taking up the reins of government after years of financial difficulties and recession, seems to have considered the achievements of his predecessor completed, at least in their main outline. His attention was principally concentrated on the rapid development of the silver mines at Kutná Hora as the basis of the currency reform of 1300. He introduced the Prague silver groschen, which soon became one of the valuable media of exchange in Central Europe, and disposed of the scars left by the horrors of the interregnum, restoring the Bohemian State to its former powerful position. At the beginning of the 14th century, the Bohemian king was the richest ruler in Christendom. In 1300 King Wenceslas II was crowned King of Poland, and one year later he was offered the Hungarian crown. This he accepted for his son, the later King Wenceslas III, whose murder in 1306 ended the Přemyslide dynasty.

Kutná Hora, the cradle of the Bohemian economic miracle, soon became the most important town after Prague. Intensified mining activities within its territory had a profound effect upon the growth of the town, which combined a radial layout with attempts at more regular planning in the center.

In 1295, during the reign of King Wenceslas II, the West-Bohemian town of *Plzeň* was founded on a gridiron plan, with a large oblong square dominated by a massive church. Plzeň, however, was surpassed by an East-Bohemian town of minor significance, *Nový Bydžov*, built about the year 1290. The importance of Nový Bydžov does not lie merely in its regularly planned core, with its square and its intersecting streets. Its innovative plan extended to the suburbs, linking them directly with the center of the urban area.

Beroun and *Slaný,* in Central Bohemia, were Royal Towns that developed from market villages. In general, however, feudal towns prevailed, such as *Bělá pod Bezdězem,* with an extraordinarily large square; *Horšovský Týn, Chomutov, Jičín* with a regular ground plan, *Pelhřimov* and *Rakovník,* all situated in Bohemia. The leading town in Moravia was *Kroměříž*.

The period of economic prosperity and political ascendancy in the reign of King Wenceslas II did not last long. The extinction of the Přemyslide dynasty in 1306 resulted in new disorders which had a disturbing effect on the Bohemian State. However, the power of the Royal Towns increased under the leadership of a small circle of merchant patricians. For the first time, the merchants became an important political factor in this country, challenging the feudal class whose power had grown considerably.

King John (1310–1346), the founder of the new Luxemburg dynasty, was forced to accede to a number of demands by the Bohemian and Moravian feudal lords. The new king, of a restless and chivalrous nature, conducted a successful foreign policy which, though more limited in extent than that of his predecessors, led to more lasting results. He

incorporated into the Bohemian State the former Bohemian territory of the Budyšín and Zhořelec regions (north of the Bohemian border) and the region of Cheb. Considerable progress was also made in Silesia. For a short time the royal aspirations extended even to Northern Italy.

In 1346 King John, who lived mostly abroad, was succeeded by his son, later known as King Charles IV. In 1344 he managed to have the Prague bishopric raised to an archbishopric. In the same year, the foundations were laid at Prague Castle for the Cathedral of St. Vitus (St. Guy), one of the most remarkable works of Gothic architecture.

The only Royal Town dating from the early 14th century was *Vodňany* in Southern Bohemia, successor of an early feudal village. In Prague itself, to the west of the castle, the small town of *Hradčany*, with a large square, grew up in the year 1320. The new feudal towns *Bechyně, Mladá Boleslav,* and *Prachatice*, all with early feudal nuclei, may be mentioned.

The layout of the towns of the first half of the 14th century had no particularly significant features. However, the founding of towns increased considerably, and their artistic individuality became more pronounced.

The restlessness of this era, together with the growing self-assurance and economic power of the town's patricians, made the construction of fortifications imperative, as at Beroun, Nymburk, Sušice, and Tachov. Probably as early as the first half of the 14th century an important innovation was introduced, the wall towers being fully or partly open on the side facing the town.

In the first half of the 14th century, towns assumed an even more important role in the life of the Bohemian State as political and economic units and centers of individual regions. In the 14th and 15th centuries, castles were founded in increasing numbers, mostly in strategic positions.

All of these changes left their mark on the villages, which were laid out more systematically, with large, regular, oblong, or circular village

98. View of Slaný from the northeast. Drawing by Johann Willenberg, beginning of the 17th century.

99. Airview from the southwest of the nucleus of Prachatice, showing the elliptical shape of the core area. The size of the central square was reduced by a later addition of a block of houses. The church, situated at the periphery of the old urban center, dominates the town. Among the town houses, Gothic and Renaissance buildings predominate.

greens, sometimes surpassing in size Charles Square in Prague. In 1303 the village of *Přehýšov* in Western Bohemia was founded with a large, elongated, slightly trapezoidal green. An interesting example of a village with a circular green is *Lipnice* in Western Bohemia, founded about the middle of the 14th century. The Central-Bohemian villages of *Hudlice* and *Chýňava,* built by King John of Luxemburg in 1341, had large oblong greens; others had square commons. Both features could be found in villages with similar ground plans.

John of Luxemburg was succeeded by his son Charles IV, Roman emperor (1346–1378) who, a few months earlier, had been elected King of Bohemia. From the very beginning of his reign he concentrated his energies on the creation of a powerful Bohemian State, with emphasis on its Slavonic character. As early as 1348 he founded Prague University, the oldest university in Central Europe. At the same time, the capital of the kingdom was extended by building the New Town of Prague, a project grand in conception and dimensions.

Prague became the center of the Bohemian State which, during the reign of King Charles, spread to Upper Lusatia, the remaining territory of Silesia and, for a time, even to the Brandenburg Region. The state system set up by King Charles, the *Corona regni Bohemiae,* lasted until the 18th century.

The quiet years of Charles' rule, undisturbed by domestic or foreign wars, witnessed a great development of towns which played a decisive role in the King's commercial policy and consistent tendency to support the urban patricians against the large number of craftsmen, among whom the weavers were the most advanced.

100. Airview of the village of Lipnice. Founded about the middle of the 14th century, it is an example of a settlement grouped around a circular center. The houses on the village common are of later origin.

148

After the death of King Charles, his son, Wenceslas IV (1378–1419), succeeded to the Bohemian and German throne. However, his power was inadequate to cope with the enormous burden of international politics and the complex situation at home. His authority gradually declined and feudal uprisings, which had ceased under the reign of King Charles, occurred again. On the other hand, the political and ideological importance of Royal Towns, of which there were 35 in Bohemia alone, increased. Ideological and social disintegration grew, a process originating in earlier periods. The crisis was felt most in the culturally rich atmosphere of the Czech lands, especially in Bohemia. The advent of John Huss represented the voice of the conscience of the whole of Europe. The Hussite Revolution broke out after dramatic preparations in 1419, the last year of the reign of King Wenceslas.

Apart from *Telč* and *Prostějov*, practically no important towns originated during the reigns of King Charles IV and King Wenceslas IV. Town planning activities in the 14th century culminated, however, in the New Town of Prague just mentioned. The unison of large, early medieval buildings with a new plan, articulated by a system of three extensive squares the size of building blocks and, for the Middle Ages, the amazing width of some of the streets, bear witness to the grand concept and creative audacity of King Charles' anonymous town planners.

A development similar to that of Prague took place in the North-Bohemian town of *Litoměřice* much later, in the third quarter of the 14th century.

The second half of the 14th century can be regarded as a period of widespread building of large towns. It differed not only quantitatively but qualitatively from preceding epochs.

Individual buildings of this period were more monumental. They included schools, hospitals, market squares, and the symbols of municipal autonomy—the town halls. In Bohemian towns the town halls are usually situated at the corner of one of the sides of the main square. Their location in a street, as at Brno and Znojmo, dates back to an earlier period preceding the erection of town halls. But even in the pre-Hussite period, the custom of building town halls and various kinds of shops in the town square had begun. The booths of the butchers were usually situated in one of the blocks directly adjoining the square or in its immediate neighborhood.

In spite of the peace enjoyed by the country in the second half of the 14th century, the towns paid considerable attention to the construction and improvement of their fortifications. In the forefront of these activities were the fortifications and bastions of the New Town of Prague, built in the amazingly short time of two years. The uniformly designed gates of the New Town were strengthened by two bastions, with a passage between them. The towers of the fortifications were mostly open on the side facing the town.

In the decades preceding the Hussite Revolution, the towns contributed greatly to the architectural development of Bohemia. In the reigns of King Charles IV and King Wenceslas IV, activities were mainly concentrated on residential buildings. Prague, at this time, can be pictured as one huge building site. It was during the construction of

101. View of the central part of the Old Town of Prague, taken from the tower of St. Nicholas' Church in the Small Town. In the foreground, on the right, the Bridge Towers of the Small Town: the Romanesque tower of the 12th century and the Gothic tower of the third quarter of the 15th century. A number of Gothic buildings, and a few from the Baroque period, dominate the skyline of the Old Town.

the New Town that the wooden buildings of the Old Town and the Small Town were replaced with stone or brick houses. The same procedure was undoubtedly followed in several other Royal Towns.

The buildings were either two-storied, mostly around the town square and along the main roads, or single-storied in the peripheral district; in large towns they were three-storied in the more prominent parts of the urban areas. Equally important was the form of the allotments. Wherever the site permitted, the plots were occupied by two-storied buildings turning their gutters to the street and sometimes having several wings at the back.

In the second half of the 14th century, arcades added to already ex-

isting buildings or constructed together with the houses found more widespread application.

The variety of Gothic buildings in Bohemian and Moravian towns is inexhaustible. The exterior of the pre-Hussite houses was plain, with simple door and window frames of stone, whereas the gables, usually built of brick, had more sophisticated designs. The Gothic buildings in Bohemian and Moravian towns of the Luxemburg period represent one of the greatest architectural treasures of Czechoslovakia. They show, far more convincingly than any historical records, that her domestic and public architecture was clearly distinguished from that of the neighboring countries.

102. Section of a view of Prague by J. Sadeler (1606), engraved by J. Wechter after an etching by F. van den Bossche. The prosperity of Renaissance Prague is reflected in Sadeler's prospect.

CHAPTER 15

Medieval Towns of Slovakia

A SIGNIFICANT DEVELOPMENT of urban communities in Slovakia did not take place until the reign of Béla IV, at the beginning of the 13th century (1235–1270). In 1238 a charter was granted to *Trnava,* a market settlement on the Bohemian Route, and in 1244 to *Zvolen* in Central Slovakia. The importance of towns was recognized by the reaffirmation of these charters after the Tartar invasion. Many towns had to be rebuilt in the process of colonization of the devastated territories. Shortly after the departure of the Tartars, a charter was granted to *Košice,* resulting in a fundamental change of the layout along a large spindle-shaped square. At about the same time (1248), city privileges were granted to *Nitra,* situated at the foot of the castle of the same name, the early political center of the principality of the Great Moravian Empire. In the middle of the century *Nové Mesto nad Váhom,* whose buildings were arranged around a rectangular square, received its charter (1248); and the old port of *Komárno* was chartered in 1265. Komárno, known since Roman times, has retained a system of roads converging on the local castle. The town of *Jasov,* developing in the vicinity of a Premonstratensian monastery, has also kept its original layout.

Somewhat different was the development of the territory of the Spiš Region, on the northern border of Slovakia. After the Tartar invasion, a number of settlements were elevated to towns by charters obtained for the whole region. Later, the growth of these small towns slowed down. Among the larger places *Podolinec,* with a semi-lensshaped square and a simple street network, may be mentioned. The same period also gave rise to *Levoča,* one of the biggest towns in Slovakia, with a rectangular square and a rectilinear street pattern with clearly defined rectangular

103. Airview from the southwest of the center of Levoča, with the town square. The area of the square is partly occupied by buildings. The parish church, the belfry, and the town hall occupy the center of the square.

blocks. Levoča gained in importance in the following period of reconstruction of Slovak towns, especially through the architectural quality of its ecclesiastical buildings. Similar was the origin of the town of *Kežmarok;* however, the stages of its development and layout have not yet been clearly ascertained. It is probable that shortly after the colonization of the territory the population abandoned the habit of erecting houses around a central square with the parish church and began to concentrate their buildings along roads passing through the settlement, one of which widened and led to the local castle.

Among the trading towns of East Slovakia was *Prešov* (1247), which developed similarly to Košice from an earlier settlement around a spindle-shaped square, parallel with the streets of the original plan. Toward the end of the century the nearby *Sabinov* was laid out on a plan similar to that of Prešov.

Apart from the group of trading towns which originated in the middle of the 13th century, town building was concentrated on mining towns stimulated by the development of mineral resources. Two of the oldest towns of this type were *Krupina* (1328), still showing traces of its original layout, and *Banská Štiavnica* (prior to 1244) on the site of an earlier walled-in settlement. The layout of the town followed the irregularities of the terrain, the square being somewhat isolated from the main direction of the actual expansion of the town. Rich copper deposits stimulated the development of *Banská Bystrica* (1255) on a road leading to the Central Slovakian Mountains. The widening of the road gave rise to an oblong square dominated by a church which was subsequently rebuilt as the municipal castle. The towns of *Partizánská Lupča* and *Hyby* (1265) grew up at the foot of the northern part of the Low Tatra Mountains, around rectangular squares.

Uncertain conditions after the death of King Béla IV retarded the further development of Slovak towns in the second half of the 13th century. However, building activities flourished in the existing towns where, in addition to new dwelling houses, churches and monasteries were erected. In the last few years of the 13th century, King Ondřej (Andrew) III granted a charter to the town of *Bratislava* (1291), which originated at the foot of an important castle, not far from a village of fishermen and traders. The new town incorporated the nearby villages which had developed independent of the castle and its settlement. The center of the new town was occupied by a small regular square from which roads ran to a ford in the Danube. The town's independence was demonstrated by the early erection of fortifications.

It was not until the reign of Charles Robert, a sovereign of Franco-Italian origin of the Anjou dynasty (1308–1342), that a turn for the better set in. In the period of Anjou rule in Hungary the economic importance of mining and commercial cities increased. Numerous Slovak urban communities participated in foreign trade with towns in Bohemia, Poland, and Russia, furthering the economic consolidation of the country and the development of crafts and mining. This, in turn, led to a considerable increase in the number of towns, despite the fact that the first years of the reign of Charles Robert were marked by wars with his powerful vassal, Matúš Čák, who controlled a considerable part of the Slovak territory from his castle of Trenčín.

104. View of the city of Bratislava across the Danube River. Engraving after a drawing by Friedrich Bernhard Werner, 1735.

The origin of other urban communities can be traced back to the first years of the reign of Charles Robert, that is, no new towns were founded but charters were granted to existing settlements. The most important town in Slovakia was *Žilina* (1310–1312), with a circular layout, a regular street pattern, and a rectangular square in the center. A similar layout, but one lacking the regular street system, can be found in the nearby town of *Kysucké Nové Mesto* (1325).

An interesting town in East Slovakia is *Bardejov* (1320), with a spindle-shaped square dominated by the church. The shape of the square is repeated by the almost rectangular blocks covering the whole urban area.

The original layout of the settlement of *Trenčín* (1324) has been preserved. Its square shows the simplicity of the additions made to the old original plan. Examples of minor importance were *Nitranské Pravno* (1337) and *Martin* (1340), where the square developed from a simple change in the road passing through the settlement.

Similar in design are the towns of *Topoľčany* (1342) and *Rimavská Sobota* (1334), where a regular square forms the center of a checkerboard plan, and the town of *Stará Lubovňa*, of more recent origin and a less systematic street pattern.

The increase in the number of mining towns under Charles Robert was particularly evident in Central Slovakia. The most important among these towns was *Kremnica* (1328), whose beginnings date back to the 13th century, to the period of the first mining towns in this area.

105. Airview from the southeast of the historic nucleus of Bardejov. The town is dominated by the parish church (14th century). The town hall, built in 1505–1518, occupies the center of the rectangular square. The houses date back to the Gothic period.

Its layout around a regular square, in spite of a considerably sloping site, was dominated by the castle. Similar plans existed at *Smolník* (1327) and *Rožňava* (1340), whose sites were more advantageous for the siting of squares.

Other towns from this period have a more spontaneous arrangement of buildings and an irregular street system, such as *Nová Baňa, Slovenská Lupča, Dobšiná,* and *Štítnik*. The squares in these towns were adapted to the sites in a rather haphazard way, without any major trends toward a unified composition.

An interesting example is that of *Ružomberok* (1340), utilizing a terrace. Although of a later date, the mining town of *Brezno*, with its well-proportioned square, should also be mentioned in this connection. *Spišská Nová Ves,* outside the territory of Central Slovakia, had a lens-shaped square, a layout similar to the towns of Eastern Slovakia.

To the early years of the reign of Charles Robert's successor belong the towns of *Bánovce nad Bebravou* (1376) and *Prievidza* (1382), with regular plans, *Skalice*, with a triangular square, and *Modra*.

The towns mentioned represent a small fraction of the general urban system. Other groups of towns also contributed to the development of medieval town building and architecture and to the foundations of the present settlement structure in Slovakia.

CHAPTER 16

The Hussite Movement and the Close of the Middle Ages

BY THE END OF the 14th century a dense net of towns and settlements covered the Bohemian and Moravian and, to a high degree, the Slovakian territory. By then the plans and the silhouettes of the towns, the location of their main squares, and the orientation of their churches had been established. Many of these towns were of considerable political and economic importance, and their appearance was enriched by outstanding works of architecture.

At the turn of the 14th century the inner contradictions of feudal society and the decline of ideological and social unity gave rise to the revolutionary Hussite Movement in Bohemia, which found firm support in the towns, particularly among the poor classes. It was one of the most significant revolutionary movements of the time, generating new ideological and social views and anticipating later social theories. Conflicts between the patrician families and the tradesmen in the towns sharpened; opposition to the ever-increasing wealth of the Church and growing social tensions between the different layers of society resulted in demands for a reformation of the Church and the establishment of a new and more just social order based on the equality of all men.

The immediate cause for the outbreak of the revolutionary movement was the death of the most outstanding herald of the new doctrine, John Huss, Master of Arts and Professor at Prague University. He was condemned by the Church Council of Constance and suffered death at the stake in the year 1415. Open revolt broke out in 1419. During the following decade the Hussite armed forces withstood the attacks of the combined European armies of the Crusaders and, under the leadership of Jan Žižka and other military leaders, penetrated into the neighboring lands.

An important role in the Hussite Movement was played by the towns which became, particularly during the first stage of the movement, its leading centers. They were described as "the towns of the sun" which, according to contemporary chiliastic beliefs, were to survive Doomsday. Hosts of people began to gather in these towns and in their immediate surroundings. From the very beginning of the movement an interesting phenomenon could be observed, namely, the gathering of people in temporary camps, mostly located on the summits of hills, which received biblical names preserved to this day as Sion, Oreb, and Tábor.

In the sphere of town planning, the Hussite revolution is marked by the founding of the town of *Tábor*, called after a mountain in the Bible. It is interesting to note that in the Czech language the word *tábor* came to denote a gathering of people. In 1420 Tábor was founded as a town where, according to a contemporary text, "all people shall be brothers and shall not be subjugated by any lord, not one by another." Especially during the early days of Tábor, the principles of equality and common property formed the basis of its social organization.

The town was located on a steep slope above the river Lužnice, in the south of Bohemia, a region which, at this time, was one of the main centers of the revolutionary movement. The site had been occupied before by a settlement and a baronial castle. The revolutionary masses left their former dwellings in the nearby towns and villages and followed their preachers to the new "settlement of the Tábor hill." In the center of the town was an extensive square used as a meeting place for

106. View of the center of Tábor, situated on a steep headland.

the people, thus differing in its function from other medieval squares which served primarily as market places. Streets radiated from the square in all directions. Some elements of this pattern may have been taken over from an earlier settlement. Nevertheless, taken as a whole, the plan of the town is proof of a functional arrangement with the aim of producing an easily accessible central gathering place and conditions best suited for defense purposes. The street system and the irregular building blocks were, no doubt, influenced by the original pattern of the encampment. It may also be assumed that the meandering streets and, above all, the complex layout of the roads connecting the town gates with the center resulted from the attempt to create the best possible defensive conditions for the town.

According to contemporary reports, part of the defensive system inside the town consisted of extensive cellars interconnecting the individual houses by underground passages and emerging above ground under the castle walls. The significance of the Hussite stronghold was stressed by the choice of the site, accessible only with difficulty, and by the speedy erection of fortifications, which rank as one of the most remarkable examples of medieval military engineering.

The leading role of the towns in the Hussite Movement is confirmed by the creation of so-called "town leagues" which kept their own armies. Tábor was the center of a union of South and West Bohemian towns, of Písek, Prachatice, Horažďovice, Sušice, Klatovy, and Domažlice. Even more powerful was the Prague League which, in 1421, united more than twenty-one Royal Towns, occupying with its revolutionary armies the whole of Eastern Bohemia.

At that time the towns played an ever-increasing role in the administration of the country. Their influence was obvious during the session of the Land Diet in the town of Čáslav, in 1421, where King Sigismund was dethroned and declared an enemy of the country. An interim government was elected by the Diet, composed of twenty members, eight of whom were representatives of the towns, that is, four represented the capital of Prague and four the remaining towns. The Church and the nobility were represented by the other twelve members. However, the actual government of the country during these turbulent times lay mostly in the hands of the Hussite military officers, the majority of whom came from the class of the burghers and yeomen.

The repeated attacks of the armies of the Crusaders failed to subdue the revolutionary state in the heart of Europe. Finally, in 1434, it disintegrated because of inner contradictions and the struggle between the revolutionary and conservative wings of the Hussite Movement. In spite of the brief period of its existence, the Hussite revolution was of the greatest significance to the future of the country. It stimulated culture and education, which gradually spread to all layers of society. The Hussite Movement also promoted a closer relationship between the Czechs and the Slovaks who at this time were included in the Hungarian State.

After a brief interlude of feudal disorders in the wake of the Hussite revolution, the situation in Bohemia and Moravia was consolidated when George of Poděbrad became king of Bohemia, about the middle of the 15th century. The "Hussite King" was to be well known on the international scene by his proposal of a Peace Covenant of European princes which, as early as 1464, called for the formation of an international organization for maintaining the peace of the world.

This period was filled with political struggles between the towns and the nobility, with numerous uprisings of the poor and revolts by the miners against the wealthy patrician families in the mining towns. The economic prosperity of the towns was the basis of municipal power. Some towns owned extensive rural property, including numerous villages and even other urban communities. These towns became feudal landlords and lost their revolutionary spirit. However, in most cases, the political strife between the towns and the nobles ended with victory for the nobility, in spite of a temporary period of successful actions by the towns.

After the death of King George of Poděbrad in 1471, the Land Diet, meeting at Kutná Hora, elected the Polish prince Vladislav of the Jagellon dynasty as king of the Bohemian State. When Vladislav became King of Hungary also, in the year 1490, the two kingdoms formed a political union which joined the Czechs and Slovaks for several centuries. The rule of the Jagellonian kings, which lasted until the year

1526, coincided with the development of architecture, culminating in works of outstanding artistic merit in the Late Gothic style. Hence this period is sometimes referred to as the "Jagellonian" Gothic. Under the rule of the Jagellon kings the political influence of the towns steadily decreased. However, their economic prosperity was not impaired, as the erection of numerous imposing buildings confirms.

During the Jagellonian rule the House of Habsburg tried to secure the right of succession to the Bohemian throne. In 1526, Ferdinand of Habsburg was elected King of Bohemia. Thus lands of the Bohemian Crown became part of the Habsburg monarchy, which included the Austrian and Hungarian countries. With the help of the Fugger family, the Augsburg financial magnates, Ferdinand succeeded in bribing the Bohemian feudal lords, whose sympathies he had won by policies directed against the towns.

The centralization of the Habsburg monarchy could only be accomplished gradually. It was a process accompanied by revolts and local uprisings in which nobles opposing the Habsburg policy participated. The first extensive uprising took place in 1546, headed by the City of Prague and numerous other Bohemian towns of importance. The failure of the revolt was followed by repressive measures which strengthened the power of the monarch at the expense of the towns and the estates.

CHAPTER 17

The Impact of the Renaissance

THE RENAISSANCE STYLE in architecture ran parallel with economic and political changes in Europe. In the Bohemian lands the impact of the Renaissance was first felt in the economic activities of the wealthiest noble families, the owners of extensive estates, breweries, fishponds, textile mills, ironworks, and other lucrative enterprises. The limitations of the trade guilds were swept away, thus making the aristocracy the main representatives of new and more progressive trends, in opposition to the towns where old laws and regulations enforced by the guilds proved a retarding factor.

Toward the end of the 15th century wealthy aristocrats began to call in artists from Italy to rebuild and redecorate their residences, in accordance with the tenets of contemporary art. The work of these artists was at first confined to architectural details and individual buildings and was sponsored almost exclusively by the royal court and the leading noble families. It was not until the middle of the 16th century that the new style made itself felt in the erection of town houses and in town planning.

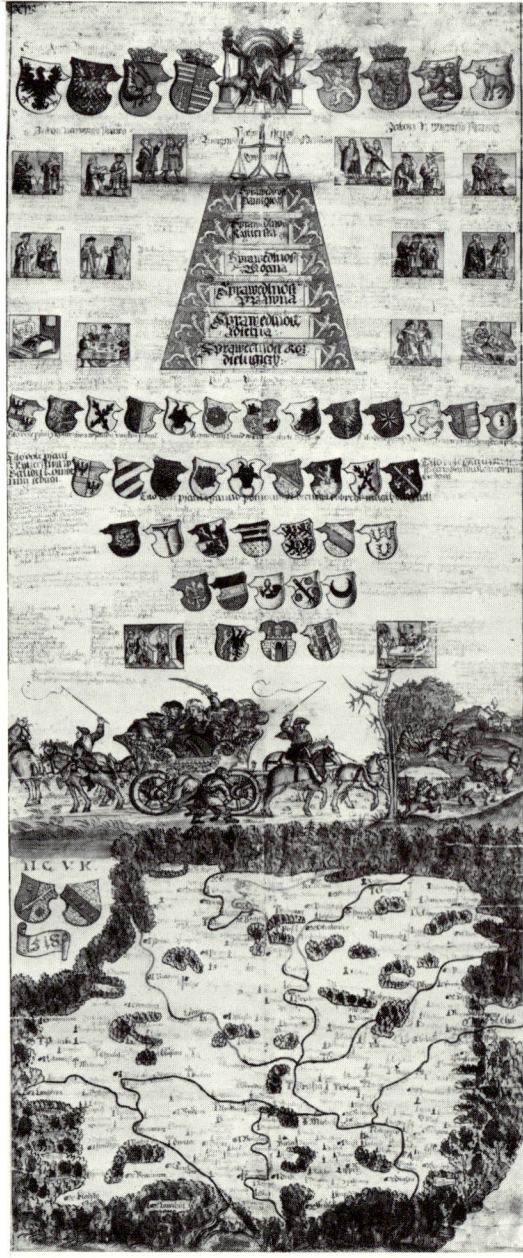

107. First cartographic representation of Bohemia on Claudian's map (1518). It is richly decorated with allegoric pictures and coats of arms of noble families. The map, at the lower section, is oriented toward the north, showing a system of contemporary towns and castles, classified as royal, subject, Catholic, and Utraquist.

108. Airview of Nové Město nad Metují, founded at the beginning of the 16th century. The situation of the castle and the generally regular layout testify to the application of new Renaissance town-planning principles.

The strongly fortified medieval castles of the nobility gave way to Renaissance palaces with arcades, courtyards and extensive parks, as at *Český Krumlov, Jindřichův Hradec,* and *Pardubice,* and even earlier in Moravia, at *Tovačov, Moravská Třebová* and *Boskovice.* The old castles, particularly those located on almost inaccessible hills, were deserted; and new stately mansions were erected on the estates of the nobility and in the towns, sometimes changing the character of older existing places to such a degree that they were transformed into Residence Towns of the family owning them. The result was a more regular plan, a uniformity in height and façades and details of whole groups of houses. The squares, whose shapes in the preceding periods had been determined mainly by their function, assumed the role of ostentatious showpieces, surrounded by elaborate façades and enlivened by fountains. In short, regimentation and standardization began to be the order of the day.

The best examples of Residence Towns of noble families were *Pardubice, Nové Město nad Metují* and *Moravská Třebová*. The enterprising Lords of Pernštejn rebuilt the old town of Pardubice, hitherto only of local importance as an imposing appendage to their palace. It was fortified after the new Renaissance fashion with ramparts and a moat, to defend it—in case of need—against the burghers. After the fires in 1507 and 1538 the town was reconstructed in accordance with the concepts of the period.

The town of *Nové Město nad Metují,* founded at the beginning of the 16th century, passed through a similar development. In recent times, the whole row of town houses facing the square was renewed with façades of a uniform design, and attics and arcades dating from the

163

Renaissance. After a fire at the beginning of the 16th century, the Moravian Lords of Boskovice rebuilt their Residence Town, *Moravská Třebová,* in accordance with the new principles. This included altering the original form of the Gothic square to an almost regular rectangle.

The new element in town planning which began to assert itself in the plans of Central European towns and their surroundings after the end of the 15th century was the Renaissance garden. In the northern countries the palace gardens were a continuation of the older local tradition of town and monastery gardens. In Moravia, traces of the new art date from a somewhat earlier period than in Bohemia. At this time, Moravia was strongly influenced by the neighboring Hungarian state, where the Renaissance royal gardens of King Matthias Corvinus were laid out as early as the second half of the 15th century. Documents mention the gardens of the humanist, Bishop Thurzo, at Vyškov and Kroměříž, dating from the second half of the 15th century, which were laid out as a combination of kitchen and flower gardens.

The layout of the Royal Gardens adjoining the Prague Castle was the first example of a genuine Renaissance design. The Royal Summer Palace, begun in 1535, and the Ball House, dating from the years 1563–1568, belong to the most outstanding works of Renaissance architecture north of the Alps. The pleasure gardens themselves were located near the city walls in the open landscape. Here the garden pavilion was replaced by the more elaborate buildings of a casino or a little *chateau,* as at *Kratochvíle* and *Krásný Dvůr.* At new palaces the gardens were developed on rigid axial principles connecting them organically with the buildings. *Bučovice,* built by the architect Ferrabosco in the third quar-

109. Netolice, near Kratochvíle, in the south of Bohemia: the town on the right; the Renaissance chateau with a triple wall and gardens, dating from 1583–1589, on the left. Painting by Jean de Verle, 1686.

ter of the 16th century, may be the most representative example. Powerful fortifications, reinforced with four corner bastions, separated the *chateau* and the gardens from the town and the surrounding countryside.

In the economic field, the enterprising spirit of the nobility manifested itself in the building of mills, fulling mills, breweries, sawmills, iron mills, and foundries located mostly along canals on the outskirts of towns. In the neighborhood of towns, numerous ponds were newly laid out, a custom dating back to the pre-Hussite era but reaching its culmination in the second half of the 15th and the beginning of the 16th century. The fishponds, sometimes interconnected by ingenious systems of canals, not only served practical economic purposes but also were part of the advanced urban fortifications guarding the approach to the town walls. The pond near Tábor, called by the biblical name of Jordan, or the system of three ponds surrounding the town of *Telč* in the south of Moravia may serve as examples of water reservoirs incorporated in the defenses of towns. The system of ponds on the Pardubice estate belonging to the Lords of Pernštejn was exceptionally complex. It was fed by irrigation canals (the Opatovice Canal) connecting it with the river Elbe. The largest existing pond dating from this time is the Rožmberk Pond, in the south of Bohemia, covering an area of more than two square miles and belonging to an extensive group of water reservoirs preserved in this region. By means of artificial canals called *Zlatá stoka*, the Golden Canal, and *Nová řeka*, the New River, passing between the rivers Lužnice and Nežárka, the builders Jakub Krčín and Štěpánek z Netolic created a perfect irrigation and regulation system which belonged to the greatest technical achievements of Europe in the 16th century.

The new economic enterprises, mainly of the families of Pernštejn, Rožmberk, and Smiřický, had a marked influence on the landscape and the structure of rural settlement. In addition to ponds, many farm buildings, granaries, and sheepfolds were constructed. A number of older hamlets disappeared, and new villages were founded with a novel arrangement of homesteads answering the changing needs of village life. The transformation of the countryside was the result of the consolidation of cultivable land and the layout of large ponds lined by trees. During this period, new hunting grounds were laid out and old ones improved. The erection of the Star Pavilion in the preserve of Liboc, near Prague, the modification of the Royal Preserve in the Prague suburb of Bubeneč and of the old hunting grounds near Brandýs nad Labem may serve as examples.

In the towns Gothic architecture, mostly for churches, continued to be preferred until the first half of the 16th century, for instance, at Jindřichův Hradec, Bechyně, and even Prague. In due course, the well-to-do burghers joined the nobility, rebuilding their old Gothic houses in the Renaissance style or replacing the original timber buildings with stone dwellings. Their houses were adorned with colored façades and gables, frescoes, and arcades lining both the street and courtyard fronts. The inner structure of the burghers' houses also changed, particular care being devoted to the arrangement of the important living rooms and to the rich decoration of the spacious vaulted entrance halls. Often several houses on narrow plots were combined by complete rebuilding or at least by new façades with decorative attics. These changes also influenced the town silhouette and the roofline and, together with the newly erected fortifications, transformed the whole appearance of the town.

With their imposing buildings quite a few towns now surpassed the Royal Towns whose Golden Age belonged to the preceding period. In some of the Royal Towns the town halls had already been built or rebuilt from structures existing during the Gothic era, but the overwhelming majority of town halls were erected during the Renaissance as at *Olomouc, Plzeň, Prachatice, Volyně,* and a number of other towns. Schools, market halls, hospitals, waterworks, and fountains were built in innumerable towns in the new style.

It is characteristic of this period that, in contrast to preceding centuries, only a relatively small number of ecclesiastical buildings were erected in Bohemia and Moravia. Following frequent fires, reconstruction of the churches was mostly limited to the vaults or church towers, the completion of chapels, or the adornment of the church exterior, as at Tábor. One of the most remarkable examples of the few church buildings erected at this time was the church of the religious community of the Moravian Brethren in the town of *Mladá Boleslav* (1544–1554). It became one of the most significant centers of this humanitarian religious movement which continued the Hussite tradition.

Towns and suburbs grew in size and, in many cases, suburbs and monasteries were included within the fortifications. Cemeteries were laid out outside the walls, being transferred from their original sites at the main churches in the town centers.

Renaissance town-planning theories were concerned, above all, with the principles of layout and the building of new towns. Nevertheless, the number of newly laid out towns in Bohemia, Moravia, and Slovakia during the Renaissance remained small. However, some of the earlier communities were granted charters which were a welcome source of profit for feudal lords and the king. The raising of a town to the status of a Royal Town and the grant of rights and privileges entailed in this act required a high indemnity to be paid to the former owner of the town, and an equally high payment to the king.

New mining towns rose in Bohemia and Moravia as a result of the growing production of silver and other metals. Although the older mining towns retained a certain significance, renowned old mining centers like Jihlava or Kutná Hora gradually declined because of new developments in the mining technique. They were superseded by new places, mainly during the first half of the 16th century when mining reached its high point.

In the north of Bohemia and in northern Moravia some of the former mining villages grew in importance. New mining towns were laid out on gridiron plans in accordance with contemporary principles of town planning aiming at regular and systematic layouts, such as that of *Výsluní* in the northwest of Bohemia, founded in 1562, or of *Nové Město pod Smrkem* in northern Bohemia, dating from 1584.

The rapid development of mining is best reflected in the development of the old community of *Jáchymov.* As a result of the growing number of miners, it changed into a large and wealthy town with several hundred new houses built in less than ten years. In the years 1526—1535 the annual mining output amounted to more than 15,000 kilograms of silver, or approximately one quarter of the total mining output of Europe. The word *tolar,* denoting at that time money coined in Jáchymov, became a term generally known and is preserved today in the name of the American *dollar.* The rich output of the silver mines in South America and Mexico, which since the middle of the 16th century had a marked influence on the economy of the whole of Europe, finally terminated the brief flourishing period of these towns, most of which have been preserved as minor centers of purely local importance.

This outline of Renaissance town planning has been limited, so far, to Bohemia and Moravia. Yet, in Slovakia, the Renaissance exerted an even greater influence, endowing the design of Slovak towns with especially characteristic features. Numerous architectural monuments of artistic value have been preserved. The Renaissance came to Slovakia earlier than to Bohemia, emanating from the Hungary of Matthias Hunyady-Corvinus, whose court had close relations with Italy.

It is known, for instance, that Filarete's treatise on the building of towns was translated from the Italian original into Latin, at the direct order of Matthias Hunyady-Corvinus, who called in numerous architects to live and work at his court. As early as the end of the 15th century, examples of the new style could be found on Slovak territory, which was at that time economically the most advanced part of the Hungarian State, with rich silver mines and other production ancillary to mining.

The court of the Hungarian king, Matthias Hunyady-Corvinus, in Buda was the center from which Renaissance art spread throughout the whole of Hungary. The construction of Bratislava Cathedral (1461–1498) or the construction of the chapel of the Zápolský family in the Spiš Chapter were the first representative examples of a combination of Gothic architecture with Renaissance elements.

The basic structure of settlements, particularly the location of the individual towns, was completed by the end of the 15th century. It was during this period that a marked economic development of urban communities took place, which strengthened their economic and political position.

Subsequent changes in the economic and political life of Hungary and the gradual application of new ideas to the administrative organization of the towns were based on the internal economy and international status of the Hungarian State. This was due in no small measure to the expeditions of the Hussites to Spiš and the Váh Valley and, later, to the presence of the armies of Jan Jiskra of Brandýs in the territory of Central and Southeastern Slovakia. The Hussite Movement found a ready response, particularly among the population of the towns who adopted the ideas of this religious movement. At the end of the 15th and the beginning of the 16th century, the development of Hungary was influenced by the change of the sovereign and by the danger of the Turkish raids that threatened all her neighbors. This situation was reflected in the towns, that is, in the growing influence of the feudal class, which disturbed the continuity of urban progress and affected their evolution until the middle of the 19th century. The majority of towns in the territory of Slovakia succumbed to the feudalizing tendencies. Only a few towns retained their economic and political independence. These included the Royal Free Towns of *Bratislava, Košice, Levoča, Bardejov, Trnava, Kremnica, Banská Štiavnica, Banská Bystrica, Lubietová,* and *Kežmarok*. In the course of the 16th century the number of Slovak towns dependent on feudal lords was about 140.

The urban economy was strongly influenced by the development of mining towns, among which Banská Bystrica was the biggest producer of copper. One reason for this development was the emerging capitalist economy as represented by the Fugger and Thurzo families. These two merchant families were not only the main exporters but also the bankers for the majority of copper mines in Hungary. The Fugger family exported copper ore chiefly to the Polish regions, to Thuringia and Austria, whence the ore was forwarded to Venice, Trieste, and other places. Although, at that time, the production of gold and silver was partly reduced, the quantity of silver extracted in Slovakia still represented almost 15 percent of the contemporary world production. At the beginning of the second half of the 16th century, some 8,000 kilograms of silver were produced annually. However, toward the end of the century, production declined to approximately one-quarter of the aforementioned quantity, partially as the result of obsolete extraction methods. Other causes were the disruption of trade routes between Europe and the East and, last but not least, the discovery of new metal deposits on the American continent.

In the course of the 16th century, Hungary was exposed to the Turkish invasion. Although her territory was not permanently occupied, Turkish rule changed the basic condition of the Hungarian economy, as well as the economic and architectural development of the towns. When the territory of present-day Slovakia was invaded by the Turks as early as the first half of the 16th century, after the conquest of Esztergom (1543–1544), their interest centered on the region of the mining towns of Central Slovakia.

As in Bohemia and Moravia, the founding of new towns came to a standstill. The acquisition of city rights by the population of *Skalice* (1577) and *Modra* (1569) and a few other minor settlements in the valleys of the rivers Orava, Váh, and Nitra, and in East Slovakia was of more or less formal significance. Many of these places became administrative centers or seats of feudal lords rather than actual towns, and their development stagnated at the level of former agricultural settlements.

The Renaissance period retained the medieval plans of the towns, with their streets and squares, but changed the architectural appearance of individual buildings. The houses of the burghers which replaced the former Gothic timber structures were often enriched with Renaissance attics, oriels, new façades, and innumerable variants of Renaissance decorative patterns and ornaments.

In addition to the Renaissance town halls which still used Gothic elements in their architecture and layout during the first few years of the 16th century, as in *Bardejov, Banská Bystrica, Levoča,* and *Bratis-*

lava, the municipal belfry became a characteristic landmark of Slovak towns.

Extensive building activities were carried out by the Slovakian aristocracy, who were, however, chiefly concerned with the construction of castles. Surrounded by parks and gardens, these castles were mostly situated in smaller settlements where their dominance was enhanced by their defensive character, as at *Markušovce, Veľké Uherce,* and *Diviaky.* The most monumental among them was the castle of *Bytča* (1571–1605), built on a square ground plan, with powerful circular corner bastions.

Contemporary military engineering methods were introduced after the conquest of Esztergom and Nový Hrad by the Turks in 1543–1544, in a period of defensive construction work lasting until the second half of the 17th century. During this time, frontier forts were constructed and fortifications of existing towns were improved. Municipal castles were erected in mining towns, and churches were fortified. Since the construction of fortifications often went on for decades, features of Baroque military engineering, such as the Vauban system, were applied.

The construction of fortifications and defense systems was directly connected with the extensive design and building activities of Italian experts who, in the course of the 15th century, found sufficient opportunities to apply the knowledge they had acquired in Italy. Thus, it was possible to follow the work of Francesco de Spazio in Bratislava and Komárno; Pietro de Spazio in Trnava; Martin Spozzo in Bratislava; Francesco da Pozzo in Trnava and Zvolen; Pietro Ferrabosco in Bratislava and Komárno; Alessandro da Vedano at Krásna Hôrka; Testo in Komárno; Herculeso at Levice; and Giulio Ferrari in Banská Bystrica and Pukanec.

Of particular interest are the fortifications at Košice, Komárno, Pukanec, Krupina, Levice, Nitra, and Bratislava. At *Košice* a citadel (1671–1677) was constructed, and the old castle at *Komárno* was con-

110. The fortifications of Bratislava in 1663, an example of the application of the new principles of military engineering to older medieval towns.

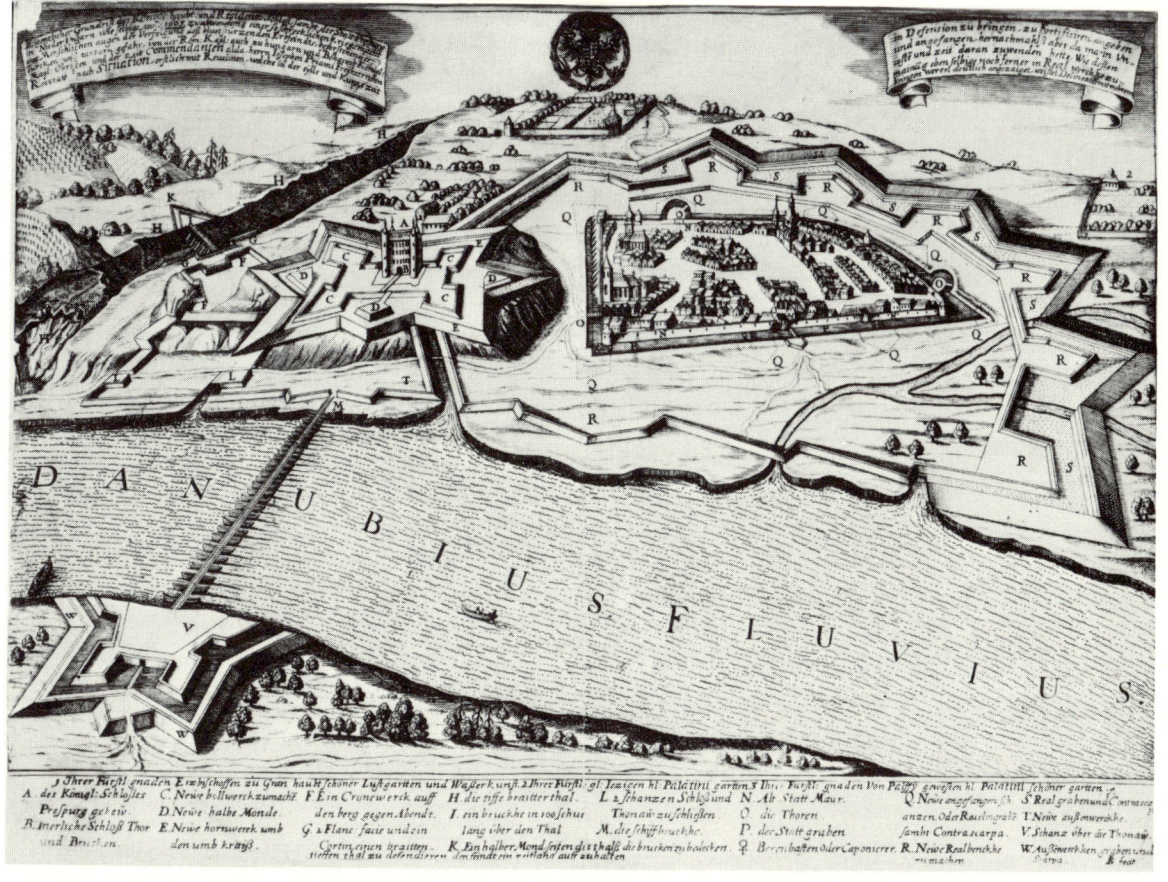

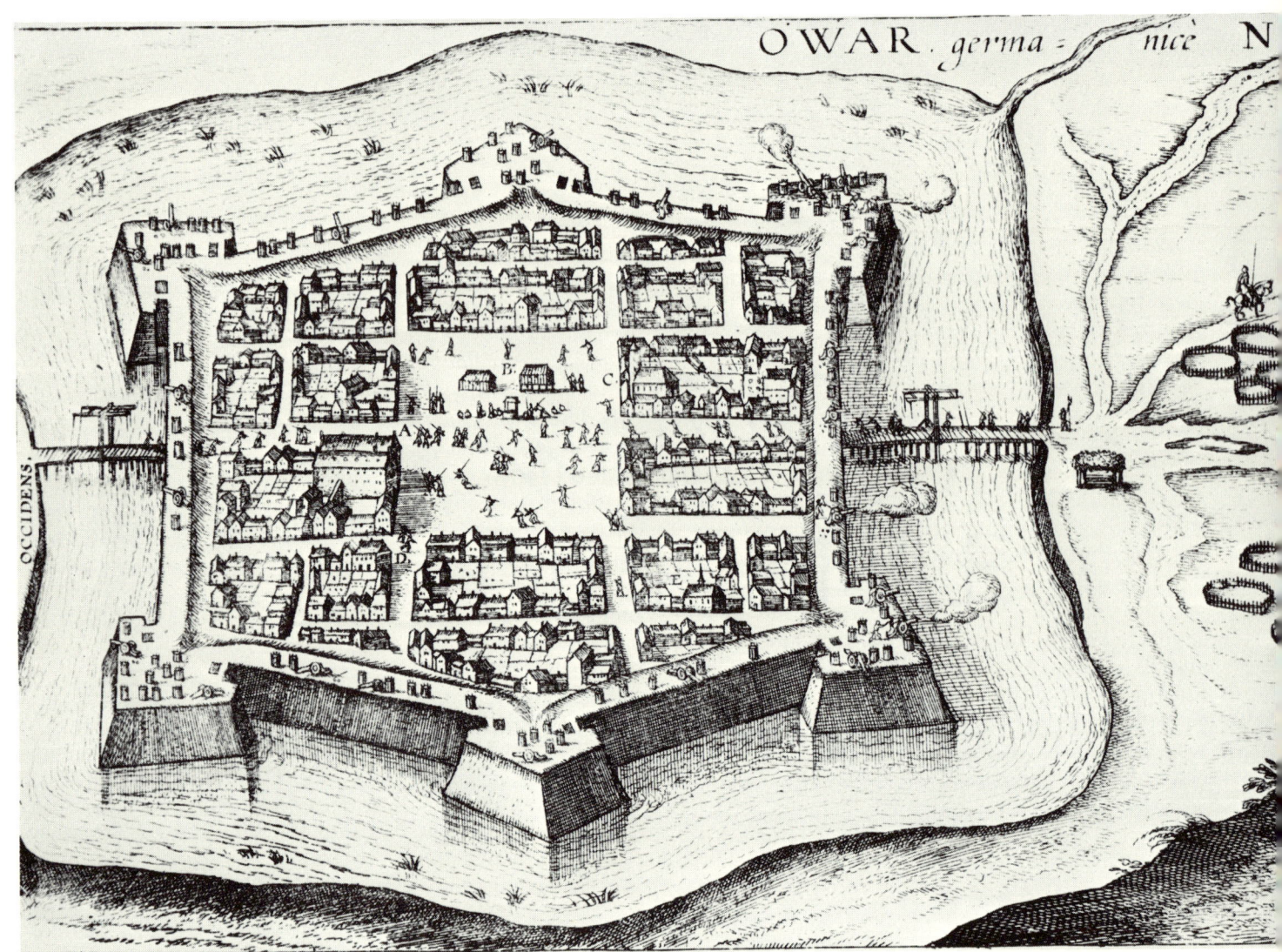

111. The fortress town of Nové Zámky. Built in 1580–1588, after a design of O. Baldigara, it is one of the few contemporary realizations of a Renaissance Ideal City. Engraving by Joris Hoefnagel, 1595.

verted into a fort. In 1663, a new star-shaped citadel was built in Komárno and connected to the old castle. In the second half of the 16th and the first half of the 17th century, the fortifications of *Pukanec* and *Krupina* were stregthened with bastions after the designs of the Italian engineer, Ferrari.

A particularly interesting example of Renaissance fortifications in the second half of the 16th century was the residence and fortress town of *Nové Zámky* (1573), after the design of O. Baldigara. The layout of the town was based on a regular hexagon, surrounded by a star-shaped ring of walls with bastions. The interior was divided into regular square blocks, surrounding a rectangular square. Nové Zámky was built earlier than Palma Nova in Italy.

After the conquest of Nové Zámky by the Turks in 1633, a new fort, *Leopoldov*, was built. Although the builders used the basic scheme of Nové Zámky, on a reduced scale, the later date of construction enabled the builders to apply the knowledge acquired in the construction of fortified towns in Italy and France. Leopoldov was, therefore, laid out on a new division of the inner space into a diagonal system, in contrast to Nové Zámky, where the checkerboard pattern prevailed. The diagonal system was focused on a hexagonal square, from which all diagonal streets radiated to the individual bastions.

CHAPTER 18

The Impact of the Baroque Period

AT THE BEGINNING of the 17th century symptoms of a deep and general change emerged in Bohemia and Moravia, heralding a new artistic feeling and the arrival of the Baroque style, a style that was to be of paramount importance for the transformation of Czech towns and Czech art in the following centuries.

The long-lasting tensions governing the relations of the Bohemian Estates and the Imperial Court of the Hapsburgs culminated in 1618 in an open rebellion of the Bohemian aristocracy and the towns. This rebellion was stimulated by the ever-increasing efforts of the Habsburgs to reduce the privileges and rights of the Bohemian Estates and to convert the country to Catholicism. The struggle of the Bohemian Estates for political and cultural independence of the country, in the course of which the Bohemian aristocracy and bourgeoisie endeavored to ward off the adverse development by electing another king, gave rise to open military conflict. In the Battle of the White Mountain, in 1620, the rebellion of the Bohemian Estates was suppressed, and its representatives were punished in the following year. On the historical Old Town Square in Prague, twenty-seven leaders of the rebellion were executed. Their number included seventeen representatives of the bourgeoisie and one professor of the Charles University, Jan Jessenius. The Bohemian Kingdom, known in Europe for its economic, political, and spiritual strength, stood on the threshold of a three-hundred-year period of subordination to the Austrian House of Habsburg residing in Vienna.

Soon after the defeat of the rebellion, the economic and political importance of Bohemian towns was drastically reduced. Their economic state was rendered worse by numerous confiscations, contributions, and changes in the ownership of their properties. A chronic economic crisis arose which did not end until the late 17th century. Simultaneously, the towns lost all their political rights during the reorganization of the Congress of Estates in 1627. These misfortunes were closely connected with an energetic Counter Reformation suppressing, particularly in the towns, the strong survival of religious freedom, the Hussite tradition, and the humanistic-cultural influence of the Bohemian Brethren. In a country where only one tenth of the population had been Catholic, the Habsburg emperor ordered all those to leave the country who refused to accept the Roman Catholic confession. From one fifth to one quarter of the urban population emigrated, their number including such outstanding learned men as Jan Amos Comenius. Mass emigration temporarily weakened the Czech character of the towns through the systematically applied official policy of Germanization.

Simultaneously with these restrictions, the towns suffered to an ever-increasing extent from the disastrous consequences of the Thirty Years' War, which affected Bohemian towns and villages with particular gravity in the period between 1618 and 1648. Several times the war tempest moved backward and forward over the Czech territory. Many towns were devastated by the disasters of war, by fires, plundering, and epidemics that frequently turned them into depopulated ruins. In the rich and beautiful city of Hradec Králové almost three quarters of its 700 houses were left uninhabited. The lot of the town of Litoměřice was similar. In Tábor almost half of the total number of houses stood unoccupied. However, some towns were unaffected by the war, for example, the South Bohemian town of Český Krumlov. On the other hand, numerous agricultural villages and thousands of individual farms were gravely damaged or totally destroyed. The Bohemian population was reduced to almost one half of its former number, and the Moravian population to one third.

The building activities in the towns, particularly in the Royal Towns, were greatly reduced after 1620, being limited to the barest requirements of reconstruction. More systematic efforts were directed to the strengthening of the fortifications. Besides the usual repairs or increase in height of the city walls, bastioned fortifications were erected at České Budějovice after 1639, and new fortification systems were built, with ravelins and redoubts, at Uničov in 1643. Reconstruction also included the town gates, for instance, at Telč in 1629.

In marked contrast to the stagnation of reconstruction in heavily damaged towns were the building activities of the aristocracy and the Church, although they, too, were reduced during the Thirty Years' War. New churches heralded the arrival of the Baroque. The most energetic builders came from the ranks of the *nouveaux riches,* the gentry and *condottieri,* who arrived on the crest of the wave of the struggle for power and property. Their political ruthlessness was reflected in their town planning ambitions. Their desire for ostentation, competing with the Imperial Court, culminated in monumental aristocratic residences.

The first great project of this type was the palace of the Imperial Generalissimo, Albrecht von Wallenstein. It was built in the Lesser Town of Prague, between 1624 and 1630, by the Italian architects, O. Spezza and N. Sebregondi, under the supervision of G. Pierroni. The vast early Baroque residence, with an extensive garden and rich architectural decoration, swallowed the lots of 26 medieval houses and other buildings.

At the same time, Wallenstein was interested in the development of the towns in his duchy. In *Liberec,* an important center of production on his estate, he enlarged the medieval town center by adding the so-called New Town, in 1630, with uniform buildings. However, particular attention was devoted by Wallenstein to *Jičín,* his Residence Town since 1622. Here, he initiated feverish building activities, resulting in the erection of numerous houses and a church, the organization of residential quarters, and grandiose planning schemes in the countryside. Finally, he entrusted his architect, the military engineer N. Sebregondi, with the preparation of a plan for the reconstruction and development of the whole town. The plan, completed in 1633, remained on paper; nevertheless, it became an important document, a first attempt at a planned concept of reconstruction and expansion of a town in Bohemia and Moravia. Its extraordinary significance lies in the functional division of the whole town, a concept which reoccured at a much later phase of city planning.

Building projects of the Catholic Church were greatly influenced by the Counter Reformation. The Jesuits and other Catholic Orders eagerly took hold of confiscated properties, sometimes of complete blocks, adapting them to their own purpose and erecting the first simple early Baroque buildings.

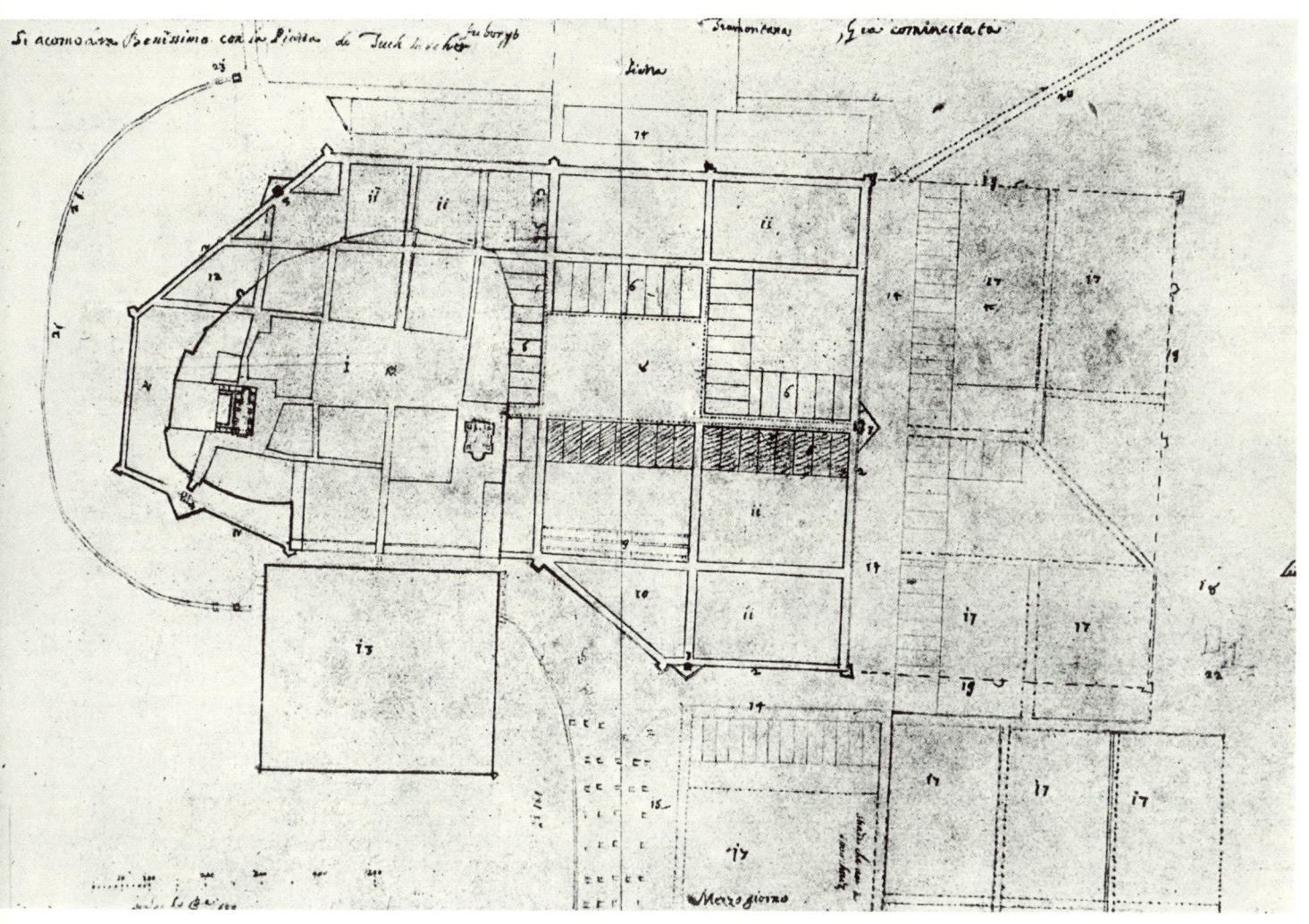

The situation changed after the middle of the 17th century. The new aristocracy succeeded in organizing new domains and revitalizing the economic life. The estate of the nobles was the economic unit that prospered at the cost of the common people who, as subjects of the aristocracy, had to work hard on the nobles' farms and pay heavy taxes.

In the second half of the 17th century, the building activities of the aristocracy and the Church developed steadily, manifesting themselves in the great diversity and individuality of Bohemian towns which, up to this time, were only rarely and slowly reconstructed. The dominant position of monumental early Baroque buildings, contrasting with the stagnating quarters surrounding them, was a typical feature of Bohemian and Moravian towns of this time. These new buildings transformed the character of the squares and the periphery of the towns. When built on unoccupied sites they maintained a severe symmetry, but in the cramped conditions inside the towns they developed asymmetrically, influenced by the historic centers and the surrounding landscape.

The interests of wealthy prospective builders concentrated on Prague which, in spite of the unfortunate events of this time, could boast of some splendid early Baroque architecture. The great ensemble

112. Plan for the reconstruction and expansion of the town of Jičín by Niccolo Sebregondi, 1633. Apart from an extension and the fortification of the Old Town (left), the construction of a vast new part, with its own square, was suggested.

of the central seat of the Jesuit Order, the Clementinum, built from 1653 onward, occupied the sites of several dozen houses, a monastery, several gardens, and three churches in the Old Town of Prague. Another Baroque ensemble was that of the monumental aristocratic residence in the area of the Prague Castle, the Czernin Palace, begun in 1669. Both complexes considerably influenced the structure of the town and determined the scale of its further development. Following the tradition begun in the Renaissance, the area of the Prague Castle and the Small Town of Prague was transformed into palace quarters. Large aristocratic residences situated at important points of the town increased in number, lending a new appearance to many parts of the city with their sumptuous Baroque gardens and imposing façades.

Churches and cathedrals, colleges, monasteries, and other ecclesiastical buildings rose at *Klatovy, Olomouc, Chomutov, Telč,* and *Uherské Hradiště* on sites of devastated houses and other buildings surrounding

113. Airview of the center of Klatovy, with the regularly shaped Gothic square. On the right, an early Baroque Jesuit church, with a college, founded in 1655 on the site of a whole block of burghers' houses.

the squares. Their position within the continuous rows of houses in the immediate vicinity of the square was one of the most important characteristics of the early Baroque transformation of Bohemian towns.

Pleasure gardens and country villas could not be incorporated in the cramped sites of the fortified towns. Thus, gardens and parks as well as aristocratic residences moved ever more frequently into the open spaces beyond the city walls. At first they were provided with their own fortifications, which were reduced, in the course of the 17th century, to decorative moats, with bridges bordered by ballustrades and statues. From the reign of the Emperor Rudolph, at whose court Vredeman de Vries, the famous Dutch theoretician of garden architecture, lived and worked, the influence of Dutch garden design prevailed in Bohemia and Moravia. Later it combined with Italian elements to form a specific kind of mannerism. The standard of the garden decor and sculptural decorations grew with the scale of the gardens. The park of *Kroměříž*, dating from the sixties of the 17th century, covered more than the total area of a medieval town. Similar grandiose dimensions can be seen in the drawings for the gardens surrounding the residence of Julius Heinrich, Duke of Saxony, at *Ostrov nad Ohří*, dating from the forties of the 17th century.

With the resurgence of aristocratic and ecclesiastic power, the interests of the aristocracy and the Church concentrated mainly on the Renaissance towns as centers of the secular and spiritual administration. These towns exemplify best the town planning principles of the Baroque, which considered the whole town an integral organism with a unified architecture. Of particular interest, in this respect, is the development of the town of *Kroměříž*. After the Thirty Years' War it had only 69 inhabited, though gravely damaged, houses. The new bishop, the ruthless Charles Count Lichtenštejn-Kastelkorn, who had been installed in 1664, systematically began the reconstruction of the devastated town, gradually turning it into the dignified center of his diocese. He set up a Building Commission, invited the architects F. Luchese and G. Tencalla from Vienna, and fostered building activities by the Church, the aristocracy, and the municipality. Of interest, too, is Lichtenstejn's decree ordering all citizens to increase the height of their houses in the town by building gables with blind windows.

The building activities financed by the cities, particularly the Royal Cities, were rather modest. In numerous towns and cities ghettos originated outside the walls, continuing the tradition of the 16th century. They consisted usually of groups of modest houses concentrated about a new synagogue or strictly separated from the rest of the town as at Bečov and Teplou, Jičín, Česká Lípa, and the ghetto at Polná dating from 1668. Their layout was irregular or was centered on the streets allotted to the Jews or formed a square with the synagogue in its center.

Only towns like Prague, Cheb, Brno, Olomouc, and Uherské Hradiště which, by decree of the Emperor, were supposed to be imperial forts were allowed to improve their fortifications. At the same time, castles like Rábí and others, representing fortified centers of aristocratic power, were demolished by imperial decree.

In the course of the second half of the 17th century, the hierarchy of towns changed considerably in regard to both their importance and the prerequisites for their further development.

Towns like Nové Město and Slavonice, which had flourished in the Renaissance period, did not recover from the damages caused by the Thirty Years' War. The economic stagnation and the almost complete standstill of building activities in the Royal Towns were far more chronic than in the towns of the aristocracy. Even the Habsburgs began to realize that the consequences of the economic crisis in the towns were more serious than expected.

In general, the towns remained small. Reports of the seventies and eighties of the 17th century stated that no town in Bohemia retained its previous importance and that they were inhabited by a surprisingly small number of citizens. In other words, the towns recovered only very slowly from the disaster of the first half of the 17th century.

CHAPTER 19

The Transformation of Town and Country in the Baroque Period

WHILE THE SECOND half of the 17th century tried to overcome the effects of the disorders caused in the Bohemian lands by the Thirty Years' War, the close of the 17th and the beginning of the 18th century were periods of consolidation and vigorous building activities by the nobility, the Church, and the towns, the last stimulated by the revival of commerce and manufacture and the rise of new branches of production. Although the development of handicrafts was still hampered by the old guild system, which was reformed only in 1739 by decree of the government, the first manufactory, founded by the Abbot of the monastery at Osek, was built in the Bohemian lands as early as 1697. It was soon followed by a number of similar enterprises among which the manufactory of Count V. V. Wallenstein, in the town of Horní Litvínov, occupied a foremost position, employing about 400 workers soon after its foundation and the erection of an extensive building complex in 1715.

The consolidation of the domestic situation of the country was reflected in the architecture of the High Baroque, which derived its strength and grand style from the wealth and ostentatious disposition of the aristocracy and the fanaticism of the Counter Reformation.

Among numerous architects of importance the best known were Christopher and Kilian Dientzenhofer and Giovanni Santini with his followers Octavio Broggio and František Maxmilián Kaňka. The development of architecture was paralleled in painting and sculpture and their symbiosis with architecture and the decorative arts.

A number of towns passed through a new and fundamental phase of their architectural development since the Middle Ages. The town-planning principles of this period met in dramatic conflict with the medieval structure of the towns, particularly if the town was the seat of a wealthy noble family or of leading dignitaries of the Catholic church.

An interesting example of this clash of two cultures was the small town of *Slavkov*, near Brno. In connection with the building of a new mansion by the leading politician of the Habsburg State, the Moravian Count D. C. Kounic, a plan for the entire reconstruction of the town was prepared by V. Petruzzi, influenced by the design of the architect Domenico Martinelli of Lucca. According to the plan, the original medieval town was reduced to a mere appendage of the palace and adapted, in its cruciform plan, to the layout of the residence.

The period of the High Baroque tried to overcome the random placing, side by side, of architectural components more or less isolated in their functions and design, and to transfer their organization to the higher level of the art of town planning. New buildings or building complexes were harmonized with their neighborhood; and the concept of the town as a whole, in its natural setting, reached its most concentrated and integrated form in Prague, Olomouc, Kroměříž, Litoměřice, Hradec Králové, and Brno.

In the Small Town of Prague and in the quarter of the Hradčany, numerous palaces were built, transforming the architectural appearance of the city with Baroque or Baroque-restyled churches and convents: St. Nicholas' Church in the Small Town of Prague, the work of

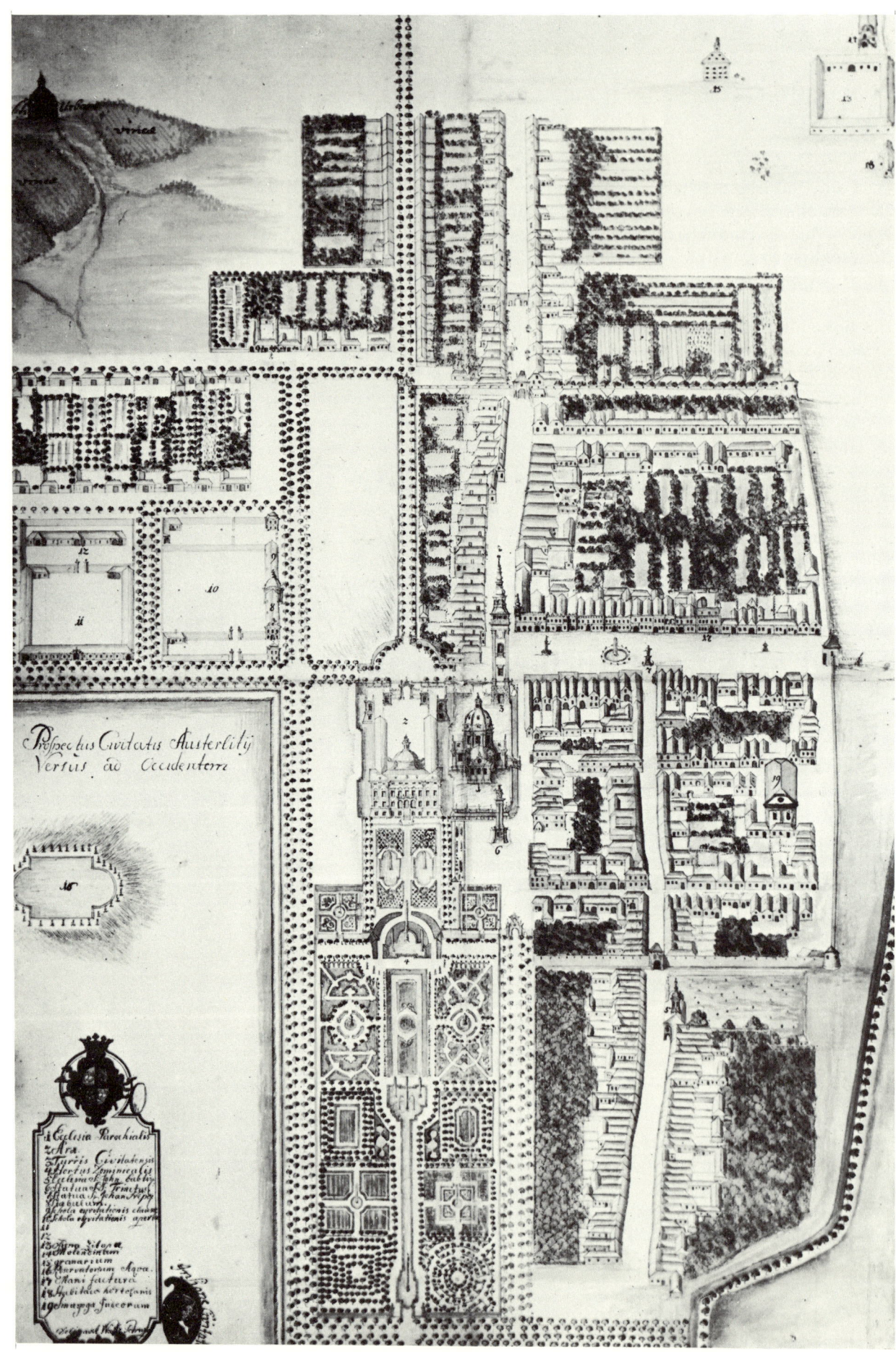

114. Plan of a Baroque reconstruction of Slavkov (Austerlitz), including the project for a new aristocratic residence drawn by V. Petruzzi, after a design by Domenico Martinelli. The construction of the castle was begun in 1700.

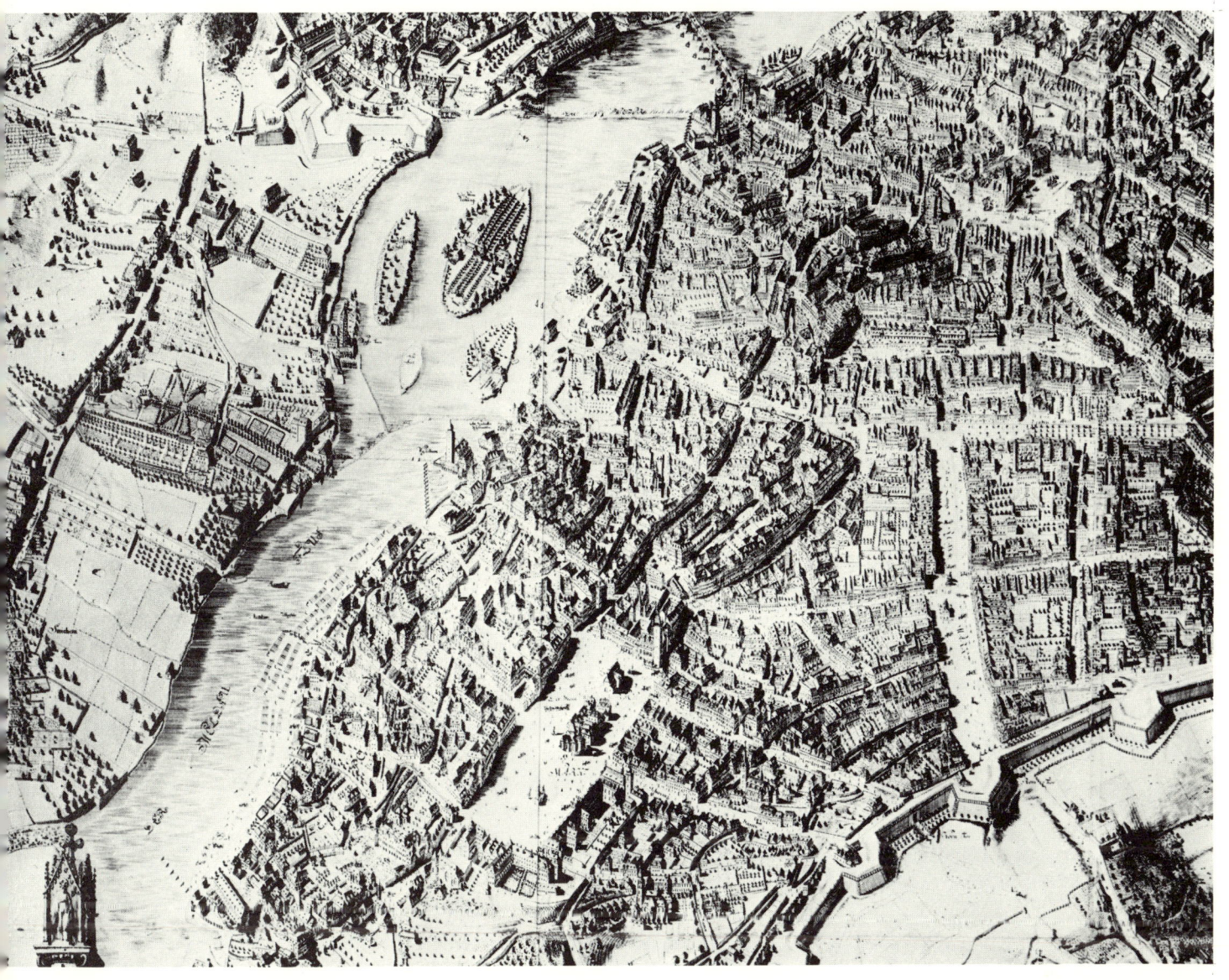

115. The New Town of Prague and its main centers: the present Charles Square (front left), Wenceslas Square (front right), and the Old Town with the Old Town Square (top right), toward the close of the Baroque period. Detail of a large drawing of Prague by Joseph Daniel Huber, 1769.

Christopher and Kilian Dientzenhofer, and numerous other buildings of the first half of the 18th century; the garden complex beneath the Prague Castle, built from the first to the third quarter of the 18th century; and the Vrtba Garden, a work of the architect František Maxmilián Kaňka and the sculptor Matthias Braun, dating from the 1820s. Everywhere in Prague, in the Old and the New Town and in the suburbs, numerous buildings were erected in conformity with contemporary town planning principles. While the appearance of the city was thus transformed, the original layout was retained. The vigorous building activities of the Baroque changed Prague into an architectural ensemble of great unity. In comparison to other towns of Europe it is remarkable for its artistic charm, the picturesqueness and plasticity of its architecture and natural setting, and the beauty of the composition as a whole.

In some towns a single work of architecture dominated, visually and ideologically, the entire urban organism. In this connection the rebuilding of the castle complex at *Rychnov nad Kněžnou*, and par-

179

ticularly of its church, by the architect Giovanni Santini, or the construction of the new convent church at *Jablonné* beneath the Ještěd Mountains, after the design of Johann Lucas von Hildebrandt, may be mentioned. These newly erected or rebuilt Baroque edifices made excellent use of the relief of the terrain, enhancing their effect as dominant features of the town, as at Klášterec nad Ohří, Dačice, Valtice, and Mikulov.

Important changes took place in both the layout and the appearance of squares and the adjoining houses. In the town of *Jaroměřice* on the Rokytná, an entire side of the rectangular square was occupied by the main front of the palace and its *cours d'honneur*.

At *Duchcov*, and a number of smaller towns, a pattern similar to that at Borovany was applied. One of the most interesting examples was the rebuilding of the town square in *Manětín*, after the great fire in 1712, by Giovanni Santini. The palace grounds were extended along the whole southern side of the square, and the church, the town hall, and the burghers' houses adjoining the square were rebuilt in the Baroque style. In the square, terraces were laid out on the sloping ground and adorned with rich sculptural decorations.

In the first half of the 18th century the town squares were often enriched with splendid, almost monumental, town halls, such as the town hall at Loket, built by Abraham Leuthner in 1682–1687. Other outstanding examples by well known architects were the town halls at *České Budějovice* by Anton E. Martinelli (1730), *Písek* (1737–1764), *Cheb,* most probably by Giovanni Battista Alliprandi (1722–1728), and at *Jihlava, Hradec Králové,* and *Chrudim.* These town halls either were situated within the row of houses lining the square, or they were free-standing buildings in the center of the square, as at *Polička*, rebuilt in 1739–1740.

116. Square at Polička in its Baroque form, with the Virgin Mary Column of 1727–1731. The two fountains and the new town hall, probably built after designs by P. M. Kaňka in 1739–1740, replace their Gothic predecessors. Most houses surrounding the square have Baroque gables. Lithograph after a drawing by J. Šembera, 1825.

The houses adjoining the squares grew more numerous and elaborate and were adorned with decorative mouldings. The characteristic motif of arcades was preserved, though sometimes on a different scale, with pillars spaced at greater intervals, the low elliptical arches sometimes extending over the entire width of the main house front. The gables became more articulate and varied, adding a richly curved skyline to the architecture of the squares.

Reconstruction of the houses of the burghers took place all over the country, changing the appearance of whole streets. Originally narrow building plots were united. New houses, turning their gutters toward the street—a development foreshadowed by the interesting earlier example of canons' houses at *Kroměříž* and *Hradec Králové*—were designed according to a uniform conception, forming compact building units.

The majority of new or rebuilt houses did not modify the basic pattern of the medieval plan of the town. Gradually, however, the early Baroque conception was superseded by more pretentious artistic demands. Contrasts of design increased in significance and affected not only the façades of the houses of the burghers and buildings of importance, but also the composition and siting of whole complexes. This dynamism of the Baroque, counterbalancing Gothic functionalism and the Renaissance static character of plane surfaces, contributed toward the architectural wealth of the historical towns of Bohemia.

Numerous fountains, columns, and groups of statues were set up in architecturally advantageous positions. The location of these monuments reveals a great understanding of scale and proportion, and the unity of the town and its components. Series and groups of statues were placed at important points in many Bohemian towns, for example, the statues on Charles Bridge in Prague, the work of outstanding sculptors of the Bohemian Baroque. More modest examples can be found in numerous places outside Prague, in the towns of *Náměšť* on the Oslava, and *Žďár* on the Sázava. Statues were often placed near churches as at *Žatec,* or in front of ecclesiastical buildings as on the terrace of the Jesuit College in *Kutná Hora.* Rows of statues were also set up along roads connecting the town with ecclesiastical buildings in its vicinity, as at *Manětín.*

While the ancient town centers usually remained unaffected by the vigorous building activities, the layouts of towns, particularly of towns without fortifications, were more liable to changes, especially along the town boundaries. This development led, in many cases, to the merging of the urban area and the castle complex situated at some distance from it through the laying out of new residential districts, usually called New Towns as in *Rychnov* on the Kněžná.

In other cases, particularly in smaller towns like *Chlumec* on the Cidlina and *Náměšť na Hané,* residences of the aristocracy were enlarged, sometimes to such an extent that their vast parks and gardens surpassed the size of the urban area, resulting in a fundamental change of the structure of the town and its relation to the surrounding country.

Large terraced gardens were laid out, following the Baroque tradition of Italian garden architecture. The most interesting examples are those at Smilkov, Děčín, Buchlovice, Lysice, and Veselíčko. In the

18th century a new type of garden—occasionally including canals—appeared, whose design was based on the work of Le Nôtre, as at Jaroměřice on the Rokytná, Milotice, Holešov, Dobříš, Hořovice, Hořín, and Chroustovice.

All these artistic efforts culminated in the 18th century, when building activities increased greatly, sponsored by the wealthy aristocracy and the Church. At that time, the last upsurge of feudalism in the Bohemian lands reached its climax, surpassing in significance the physical development of the towns and spreading over a steadily expanding territory. Works of great architectural interest arose, both within and outside the towns, in villages, and in the countryside. Convents were rebuilt and extended (in Kladruby, Želiv, and Sedlec) in the "Baroque-Gothic" style, as developed by Giovanni Santini, a style having hardly a parallel in the rest of Europe.

Owing to vigorous Catholic propaganda, the cult of St. John of Nepomuk resulted in the setting up of statues of the Czech saint in almost every village, in the open country, at crossroads, on bridges, and at roadsides. Innumerable chapels, passion crosses, crucifixes, statues, and groups of statues, often framed by newly planted trees, were dispersed over the whole country.

Reflecting a grand spatial conception, vast tracts of nature and architectural features interconnected by a net of avenues of trees and glades were part of the new landscape, as well as extensive parterres, elaborate bosquets, and canals. One of the best examples of Baroque landscape architecture was the large tract of land between the towns of Lednice and Valtice, in the south of Moravia, which made the towns mere links in the general pattern. Other Baroque designs in the south of Bohemia have survived to the present in the region of Hluboká on the Vltava, and in the neighborhood of Jindřichův Hradec. Works of architecture and sculpture—hunting lodges, pavilions, groups of statues—were components of the designs of these attractive and charming surroundings, often as *point de vue* of valleys and glades.

A deep understanding of the harmony of architecture and nature, characteristic of the Bohemian Baroque, was demonstrated in the layout of *Kuks*, a social center and spa founded by the Bohemian noble, Count F. A. Špork, in northeastern Bohemia. The settlement, dating back to 1694, spread over the hillsides on both banks of the Elbe and was adjoined by the remarkable "Bethlehem," allegorical groups of statues situated in the woods, a work of the distinguished Baroque sculptor, Matthias Braun.

For the first time, new mansions of the aristocracy, as well as dependent villages, were laid out according to preconceived plans, as at Měšice, near Prague, and Náměšť na Hané. Purely agricultural settlements were founded only in exceptional cases. They had the usual double row of houses or an oblong layout. However, *Vápensko* and *Byšičky* in Central Bohemia, founded by Count F. A. Špork in 1713 and 1717, represented a new type of village built on strictly centralized plans.

Half-timbered buildings, mostly covered with thatched roofs, still predominated, although the number of elaborate manorial stone farmsteads increased, especially in Central Bohemia, in the neighborhood of

117. The village of Byšičky, near Lysá nad Labem, founded by Count F. A. Špork in 1717. It has a circular layout and was originally intended for only eight settlers.

Prague, Kutná Hora, and Kolín. Leading architects of the period participated in the original design of these purely utilitarian buildings.

Agriculture, employing a subject peasant population, recovered only slowly and with difficulty from the stagnation and effects of the Thirty Years' War. As a result hardly any changes took place in the architectural appearance of villages. The straitened circumstances of the village population during the whole of the Baroque era were a serious obstacle to any greater building activity. Villages which had fallen into decay or had disappeared during the Thirty Years' War were only slowly replanned or remained deserted. A considerable part of the arable land formerly tilled by the peasants was transferred to the ownership of the landlords. The claims and demands of the nobility led to a far-reaching occupation of peasant lands, sometimes by violent means, and to the colonization of the last, not yet settled territories in the mountainous and submountainous regions of the country, in which the impoverished population of the lowland and the valleys took part. Mountain slopes and plateaus were settled with individual farmsteads located approximately in the center of the holdings. Dispersed villages came into existence, especially in the mountainous districts of the Moravian-Slovakian border and in Northern Slovakia. It was this last process of settlement, the so-called modern colonization, foreshadowed as early as the 16th century, that completed the structure of settlement in present-day Czechoslovakia.

In Slovakia, the Baroque style developed on entirely different lines from those prevailing in Bohemia and Moravia. Apart from its connection with the Counter Reformation, it expressed the increasing power of the Habsburg family, particularly after its victory over the last rebellion of the aristocracy. The first elements of Baroque architecture emerged in Hungary in the first half of the 17th century, when the majority of its territory was still occupied by the Turks. This explains why the early examples were concentrated in the western and northern parts of Hungary, that is, on the territory of present-day Slovakia.

The principal buildings of the Baroque period were ecclesiastical foundations. The number of aristocratic palaces represented an infinitesimal fraction of the building activity, in comparison to the numerous churches and monasteries.

In Slovakia Baroque architecture was centralized in the towns of Trnava and Bratislava. While in *Trnava* Baroque construction was promoted chiefly by the Jesuit Order and by the fact that the town was, for a time, the seat of the Archbishop of Esztergom, building activities in *Bratislava* were due to the concentration of the state administration in the town as the temporary capital of Hungary. In Trnava, Baroque architecture was especially well represented by the complex of buildings surrounding the so-called Academic Square, the *Forum Academicum,* whereas in Bratislava it was shown in the coordination of individual buildings grouped around a newly laid-out square on the eastern outskirts of the old town. While the model for the University Church built in Trnava by Antonio Spazzo was the Roman church Il Gesù, the church of the Holy Trinity in Bratislava rose on a centralized plan and excelled in the systematic use of convex and concave surfaces of the main façade and its two towers.

In the course of the 18th century, the construction of churches continued not only in towns but also in villages. Similarly, the number of new monasteries increased, as at *Ružomberok, Prievidza,* and *Jasov,* which served not only the Jesuits but also other Orders concerned with education. Many towns, palaces, and houses of a more modest architecture were erected. Among the palaces built at this time were the Grassalkovich and the Aspremont palaces in Bratislava, with extensive gardens designed in the manner of English parks. The Baroque reconstruction of Bratislava Castle included the Theresianeum, designed by Franz Anton Hillebrandt (1768), with terraced gardens and symmetrically laid-out flower beds.

The squares of towns were enriched with a new artistic element, the so-called Trinity or Virgin Mary columns. In some places these columns were set up with the purpose of completing the composition of the whole square, as at *Banská Štiavnica,* designed by Dionysius Stanetti (1775–1764), and the Rybne and Októbrové námestie (the Fish and October squares) in *Bratislava*. In other towns, these columns were placed against a background of buildings, as at *Košice*, by Simon Griming (1723), *Nitra, Trenčín, Banská Štiavnica, Prešov,* and *Žilina*. An original conception was the design of a group of statues in *Kremnica* by Stanetti (1765) as a continuation of the architecture of a church.

The Baroque period did not produce major town-planning schemes. It is therefore appropriate to mention Hillebrandt's design for the reconstruction of Bratislava, which differed considerably from all other projects. However, a wider application of the Baroque style was impeded by the decreasing importance of handicrafts. Although at the beginning of the 18th century almost 60 percent of the craftsmen of the whole of Hungary lived in Slovakia, the crafts suffered from a lack of consumers and from their failure to establish themselves in the countryside. The only industry to maintain a certain standard was mining, due to a growing interest in the extraction of rare metals and an increase in the production of copper and iron. In the last years of the century some 9,000 to 10,000 kilograms of silver were mined in Slovakia alone, while the extraction of copper ore represented one tenth of world production. The growing interest in the mining industry resulted in the construction of foundries at Lubietová and iron ore mills at Liptovský Hrádok, Lubochňa, Podbiel, Tisovec, and Spišská Nová Ves. At the same time numerous glassworks, paper mills, and other plants came into being as the basis of industrial development.

However, the changing production and occupations of the population did not result in new settlements, so that the relatively dense network of existing communities—approximately 3,800 towns and villages with some 500,000 to 700,000 inhabitants—can be considered definite.

In the second half of the 18th century large-scale building enterprises of the nobility became less frequent. In the case of ecclesiastical structures, emphasis shifted to the erection of less significant village churches and chapels, built in the simple late Baroque provincial forms. This rustic, unsophisticated phase of the Baroque continued in the country for a long time. Due to the economic situation and the living standard of the population, villages were not prepared for major building activities. It was only after 1781, when serfdom was abolished in Bohemia and Moravia, that villages launched more energetic building programs.

On the other hand, towns progressed favorably after their emancipation from allegiance to the feudal lords. They made full use of the developing trade, the increasing production, and the introduction of new types of working techniques. The development of manufactories, as at Strakonice and Turnov, promoted the transition toward an economic autarchy of the towns, where the enterprising spirit of the burghers manifested itself in a marked way.

In time, the towns were more and more influenced by the centralized power of the State, directed over a long period by the energetic rule of the Empress Maria Theresa (1740–1780). The supremacy of the aristocratic influence was restrained by the imperial administration. Local governments were improved as a means for the State to assert its own interest in the economic prosperity of the towns, which could help to cover the ever-increasing need of money used, above all, for military purposes.

During the second half of the 18th century, the military demands of an absolute state made itself felt in the Bohemian lands in the creation of fortress towns such as *Olomouc* (1742–1757). After the defeat in the Seven Years' War (1756–1763), the town of *Hradec Králové* underwent a similar reconstruction, started in 1766, whereby it was turned into a fortress. Extensive engineering works were begun in the neighborhood of the two streams surrounding the town. These activities culminated in the founding of the new fortress towns of *Josefov* and *Terezín,* in 1780 and 1781 respectively. Their fortification systems were of the late Baroque type, but their ground plans and architecture belonged to the following period of Classical Revival.

Soon after the middle of the 18th century, after a long period of stagnation, the Prague Castle was reconstructed according to plans by the Viennese architect Nikolaus Paccassi, with the cooperation of other experts. The Habsburg rulers, however, continued to reside in Vienna. Through the rebuilding of the older parts and the erection of new tracts and wings, the whole complex of the Prague Castle was united and developed on a grand scale.

In conclusion it can be said that no new towns were laid out in Bohemia or Slovakia in the 17th or during the greater part of the 18th century. A number of 17th and 18th-century towns stagnated, and some of the original settlements did not even attain the character of towns, although their foundation charters had elevated them to urban communities.

CHAPTER 20

Rural Settlement

THE BASIC STRUCTURE of agricultural settlements was formed from the sixth century onward, with the advent of the Slavs. The process of colonization in the Bohemian lands and Slovakia gained momentum in the 13th and 14th centuries, increasing the population of old settlements most favorable for agriculture and populating new extensive areas formerly uncultivated. It was only in isolated cases that new villages founded in the Renaissance and Baroque periods, except for those in the mountain regions, gained any importance in the general rural structure.

In the course of the 18th century, the so-called modern period of colonization came to an end. During this period, which began in the 16th century, the last and, so far as agriculture was concerned, the least favorable regions of the country were gradually settled.

This centuries-long development of settlement resulted in an extraordinarily rich variety of villages, ranging from irregular types of clustered villages to single or two-row communities, built around a village green. The layout of these village greens ranged from a slightly widening lensshape to oval and almost circular forms, probably typical of the early feudal period. More regular oblong village greens and, in exceptional cases, square or round ones represented, in most cases, the more advanced types used during the great period of colonization in the Middle Ages.

The last decade of the 18th century, linked with the new period of rationalism and Classicism, saw the last and more important founding-phase of villages and the last changes in village layouts. At the turn of the 18th and 19th centuries, several hundred villages originated in the Bohemian lands and in Slovakia, scattered in different ways over the area of older settlements. The new villages grew up as a result of the division of cameral and church estates (the so-called "Raabization process" of 1776) carried out by the absolutist state and through the extension of the estates of the nobles.

The layout of the new villages was in no way dependent on arable land or the structural features of the countryside. In most cases it corresponded to the theoretical patterns in architectural works which began to appear in Europe at the end of the 18th century and later in the outstanding volume of model projects by the Czechoslovak architect, J. F. Joendl. The basic layout of these villages consisted of two parallel rows of farmsteads built along a wide, oblong green and interrupted, at regular intervals, by narrower transverse open spaces. Exact land-surveying principles were applied in a number of villages founded in Bohemia—for instance, in Nové Kopisy and Trávčice near Terezín, and in Jáchymov near Třebíč, in Moravia, in 1785.

However, apart from the frequent single rows of farmsteads or the oblong sites of large farms whose yards became village greens after the Raabization process, a number of regular layouts originated, completing the great variety of Czech villages. Especially interesting in this respect were the village of *Nové Kestřany* in Southern Bohemia, founded in 1800 on a polygonal plan, and the attempts to introduce a more varied spatial relation in Nová Ves, Southern Bohemia, in 1804 and in Lesná, Southwest Moravia, in 1794.

While the development of the village layout followed the general

118. Baroque farm, dating from 1777, in Prague-Bohnice, an example of the high standard of architecture for farm buildings in the last quarter of the 18th century, when stone houses began to appear more generally in Bohemian villages.

trends of the time in Central Europe—particularly those of the colonization of the Theresian period in the Central Danubian Basin and, after the division of Poland, in Galicia and Silesia—the actual construction of these villages belonged to a completely different world. All local features of the regional types of village architecture were applied.

Thus, the process of colonization on the territory of Czechoslovakia more or less came to an end, and the structure of villages acquired its final appearance. Between the two extremes, the large towns on the one hand and small agricultural settlements on the other, there existed a whole number of links and transitional types. Many of the small towns were of an agrarian character, while some villages developed into large communities and were supported by other than agricultural production. The towns had no definitely established laws, but many villages enjoyed market and other rights usually pertaining to towns. Some villages changed into towns, while others, enjoying the status of a township, never acquired urban architectural features. The living conditions of the populations of towns and villages were similar, as were their forms of administration.

Rural building activities recommenced with extraordinary intensity toward the end of the 18th and the beginning of the 19th century. It was at this time, too, that the signs of disintegration of feudalism became more obvious as the new social system of capitalism took over. In the preceding period under the reigns of Maria Theresa and Joseph II, the role of the state administration, that is, of the Court in Vienna, had been of utmost importance though, due to the resistance of the nobility, its recommendations sometimes included "the common application" of enlightened laws and reforms. Many of these endeavors, though instigated by blatantly absolutist political, military, and economic interests and not meant primarily for the benefit of the subjects, proved favorable for the rural population. It is undeniable that, after the long period of peasant revolts and rebellions by feudal subjects oppressed by the despotism of the nobility and the required statute labor, a period of calm set in, accompanied by improved conditions in general and an increased building activity in the countryside.

A symbolic landmark of a new beginning for the villages was the year 1781, when serfdom was abolished in Bohemia and Moravia. The changed position of the country population was also influenced by other important circumstances, particularly in the field of production. The increasing population of the country and the newly emerging industries set great demands for agriculture. Simultaneously with the introduction of new crops, an important transition from the ancient system of extensive cultivation to intensive farming was effected at the turn of the 18th century.

Because of the comparatively high density of the structure of settlement, the villages of Bohemia remained generally small. However, larger villages grew up in the most fertile regions, in the Elbe Valley of Bohemia and particularly in Central Moravia. Toward the east of the country, where the density of settlement is lower, long extensive villages can be found, for instance, in eastern Slovakia.

CHAPTER 21

On the Eve of the Industrial Revolution

AT THE TIME when the development of feudal towns seemed to be proceeding steadily, elements of new economic and social forces were beginning to stir and create undreamed-of revolutionary conscquences for towns and whole regions. As early as the end of the 18th century, the first manufactories were built, whose mode of operation was based on that of their predecessors, the big workshops organized by the nobility. The textile works built at Osek, Bohemia, in 1697 and the first big textile factory in Šaštín, Slovakia, built in 1703 may serve as examples. This development began outside the towns. For a long time, production was restricted by outdated medieval guild regulations.

The establishment of the first factories led to a certain redistribution of the population and to the origin of new settlements. Even within the urban area the population density increased, and the owners of the new factories soon found suitable sites for their works in the suburbs, at the periphery of the still-fortified towns. During the whole of the 19th century, we can trace, on the territory of present-day Czechoslovakia, changes in the structure of settlement similar to those caused by capitalist industrialization in the other European countries. These changes were most evident in Bohemia, which soon ranked among the industrially most-developed parts of the Austro-Hungarian monarchy, while Slovakia experienced a state of stagnation after periods of great economic expansion in connection with mining.

The process of industrialization, with few exceptions, did not have any important influence on the structure of towns until the middle of the 19th century. A study of the first accurate cadastral maps from the twenties and thirties of the 19th century still shows towns of an essentially feudal character. One can also trace in detail the condititons of their historical cores that preceded the disturbing effects of the new economic situation.

The enlightened absolute reign of the Emperor Joseph II (1780–1790) was a historical landmark, the beginning of the end of the feudal epoch and of its urban development and architecture. This era of reforms, beginning with the proclamation of imperial patents and ending with the revolutionary year of 1848, was a transitory period, agitated by a new mentality and a changing pattern of life.

Yet, throughout all those years, the hegemony of the nobility prevailed in the Czech lands, as pioneers in the field of factory mass-production and in the application of intensive methods of cultivation on their estates. It was also the great period of national revival, of the resurrection of the Czech language and literature and the beginning of Czech science.

The majority of new economic reforms affected, first of all, not the Royal Towns, but the estates and manors of the nobility, the newly founded spas, the fortified towns, and the countryside. The Classical Revival witnessed not only the decline of the old tradition of town planning, architecture, and handicrafts, but also the advent of new town-planning ideas and the early development of industrialization, railway building, river regulations, and a reconstruction of the road network.

After the Thirty Years' War, the Royal Towns, having been centers of handicraft and trade, assumed in the course of the 18th century the character of conservative, economically and socially stagnating communities, with restricted political rights, production, and trade activities. In the last quarter of the 18th century the difference between royal and feudal towns had more or less disappeared. Prague, no longer the capital of the monarchy, stagnated within its medieval boundaries (with the exception of the new town of Karlín) and maintained a ground plan dating from the time of Charles IV. It preserved the appearance of its Gothic-Baroque past until the middle of the 19th century.

Provincial and regional organs of the Estates of the land were raised to the national level, and customs frontiers between the Czech lands and Austria were abolished. Simultaneously, the monarchy furthered trade of the products made in the manufactories of the nobility. A centralized state administration with a strict hierarchy, ranging from regional and provincial offices to the Viennese Imperial and Royal Court, was formed. One of its components was the building administration, laying the foundations for modern building codes and regulations in the field of town planning and architecture.

Since the time of the Empress Maria Theresa, the State, represented by its bureaucratic machinery, grew ever more important as builder, designer, and supervisor of the numerous building regulations pertaining to law, fire, and health as well as the approval of plans for all buildings. This centralized hierarchy, governed by the spirit of rigorous rationalism, exerted an almost total influence not only on building activities in the towns and the countryside, but particularly on the reconstruction of the majority of remaining feudal towns.

The introduction of the Fire Regulations of 1785 resulted in very important changes in the traditional appearance of old towns. Thousands of Gothic roofs, with their gables turned to the street, disappeared and were replaced by roofs turning their gutters to the street and divided by fire walls.

Another consequence of the rationalism of the period was the demolition of a number of Catholic churches and monasteries by turning them over to the army to be used as storehouses or workshops.

After the Thirty Years' War, destroyed or damaged town fortifications were, in many cases, neither renewed nor repaired. On a military map of the end of the 18th century, only seven cities are indicated as fortress towns in Bohemia and Moravia: Prague, Cheb, Hradec Králové, Terezín, Josefov, Brno, and Olomouc. The walls which had formed the material and legal boundaries of feudal towns lost their function and, in the case of fortress towns, ceased to be their property.

At the same time, however, the first municipal parks were laid out on the site of dismantled fortifications and bastions. The most famous English park, the Chotek Gardens, was founded in 1733 on the Hradčany bastions in Prague. Simultaneously with the layout of new parks, the older parks, gardens, and estates of the secular and ecclesiastical nobility were opened to the public: the Lužánky Monastery Park in Brno, in 1786; the royal preserve and garden of Count Canal in Prague, in 1804; and the upper part of Petřín Hill in Prague, in 1836.

The new idea of beautifying towns through the introduction of verdure was an acknowledged principle of the majority of town planning schemes during the period of Classicist Revival. Vineyards, parks, gardens, and tree-lined avenues surrounded scores of towns at the beginning of the 19th century. Old farmsteads were rebuilt into summer and holiday residences of the upper classes.

The first embankments along rivers were built in the form of promenades, offering panoramic views, often of great beauty. The first embankment built in Prague was designed in 1836, in preparation for the construction of the second bridge of František I. For the first time, it opened up a view of the Hradčany; it was designed as a lookout terrace over parks, not as a public highway.

The large scale formerly limited only to the building activities of sovereigns, the Church, and the nobility began to manifest itself in the reconstruction of towns. Of particular significance, in this respect, were the roads connecting important municipalities. Old winding streets within the towns were rebuilt and, where they entered historical towns, the main roads of new suburbs were marked out. These main roads, designed for the army and the mail services, formed together with the so-called trade routes the basic network of the present road system in Czechoslovakia.

Special mention should be made of the construction of roads by the State and of river regulations during the years Count J. R. Chotek held the office of supreme burgrave of the Kingdom of Bohemia (1826–1843). At that time, roads were built connecting the Small Town with the Letná Terrace in Prague, known today as Chotek Road; the so-called Panorámka above Karlovy Vary (Karlsbad); and the winding roads near Loket, all on the Prague-Cheb route. Simultaneously the course of the river Elbe was regulated.

Together with the planning of roads for horse-drawn vehicles, iron bridges of English construction began to be built on the main highways and municipal thoroughfares: at Žatec in 1826, at Loket in 1835, and at Prague in 1841. The new bridge in Prague opened up the area of the former moats between the medieval Old Town and the New Town, where in the 19th century the most important public buildings were concentrated, such as financial institutions, cultural and social buildings, and the National Theatre.

Of particular importance to the towns were the buildings for public offices and the army, including training centers. Barracks were erected on the fortified territories belonging to the State. This explains, for instance, the location of the barracks on the western periphery of the historical core of the town of Plzeň and on the southern side of Hradec Králové. The sites of military training grounds formed highly valuable reserves for later building activities, such as the Letná Plain and the area known as Invalidovna, in Prague.

One of the most fundamental transformations initiated in the Classicist period was the appearance of rented accommodations, that is, of apartment houses. The oldest of such buildings in Prague, dating from the end of the 18th century, has not been preserved. It was designed by the architect Palliardi and retained the plan of a Baroque palace. After the abolition of serfdom in 1781, the interior of medieval dwelling plots was built over, increasing the building density of the urban area. This form of building activity, together with the spontaneous growth of old suburbs and neighboring villages and the laying out of new quarters along the main roads, prevailed to the end of the 1860s, in contrast to the systematically planned new residential districts.

The only new town founded during the Classicist Period was *Karlín*. It was built in 1817 by the provincial government, in order to make use of the flat territory between the Poříč Gate of the New Town and the Invalidovna in Prague for the construction of residential buildings according to a systematic plan. This plan conformed to the Building Regulations of 1815 for the capital city of Prague, its suburbs and environs, with special provisions for the form and method of the construction of Karlín. These regulations stipulated a regular and symmetric arrangement: the buildings not to have more than three floors, the uniform width of the main streets and the transverse ones to be 70.85 feet, the dimensions of the square with the church to be 472.32 feet by 472.32 feet, and an inn on the corner of every block. Noisy and obnoxious handicrafts were to be practiced only on the banks of the river Vltava. Since the building of Karlín dragged on to the end of the 19th century, these regulations were not fully adhered to. Like other towns built in the second half of the 19th century within the Prague territory, Karlín was founded as an independent community having no connection with the capital city. Thus, the advantage of integration of the historical industrial town in the structure of the royal capital of Prague that should have resulted from the decree of Emperor Joseph II, in 1784, was once again lost.

119. View of the former town of Karlín founded in 1817 to the east of the walls of Prague, as its first suburb. Its gridiron layout and the majority of its buildings in the style of the Classical Revival have been preserved to the present day. Near the square is the church of St. Constantinus and Methodius, built in 1854–1863, after a design by K. Rössner, adapted by I. Ullmann. Line drawing by J. Rybička, 1870.

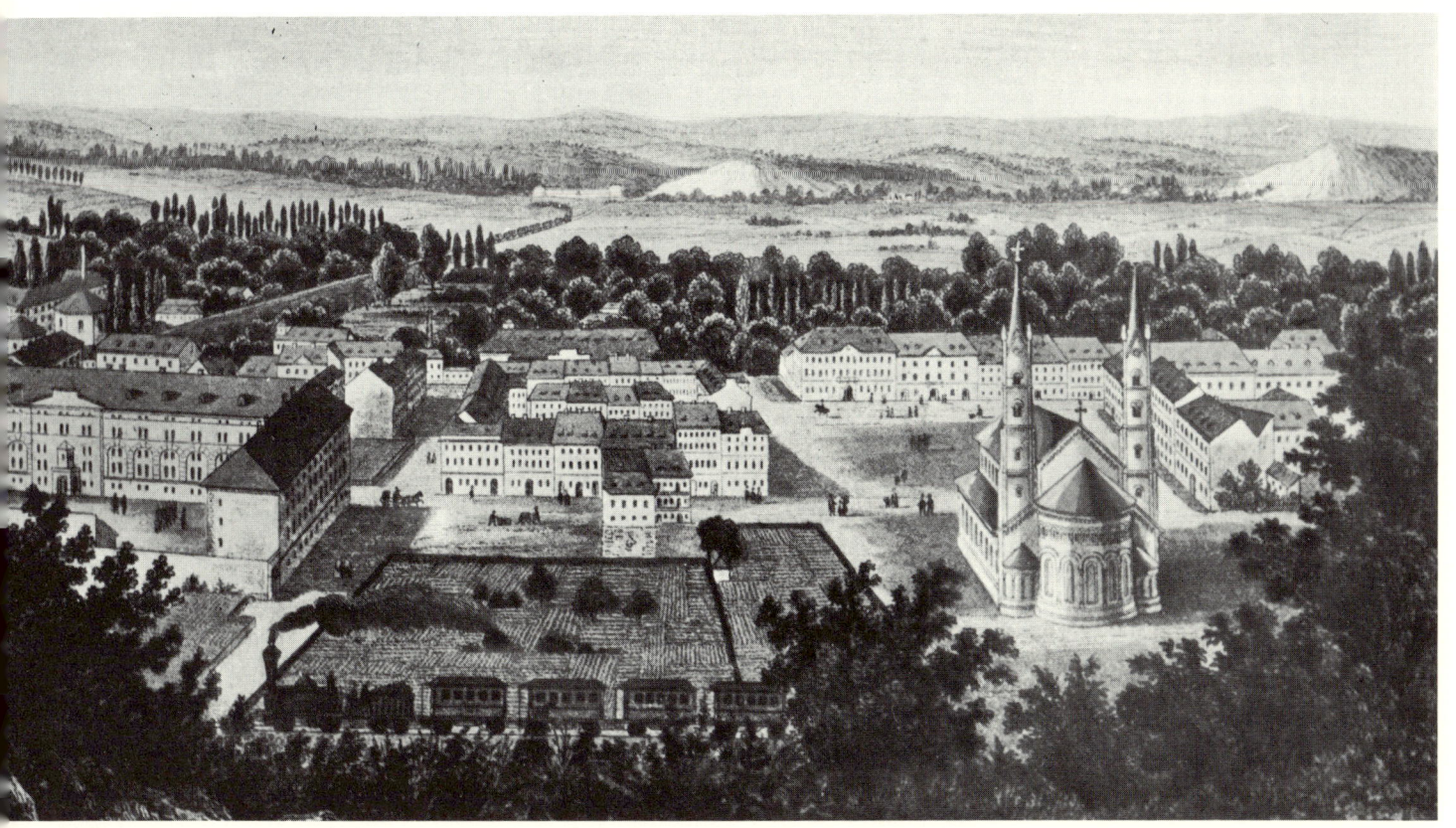

A special chapter in the history of the Classicist construction of towns was the founding of the spas of *Františkovy Lázně* and *Mariánské Lázně*, of *Teplice* and *Karlovy Vary*. Here it is possible to trace the whole of the town-planning activity of that period, in its most complex and most developed form. The connection of the residential districts with the natural environment, the abolition of restricting fortifications, and the application of experiences gained from the construction of the residences of the nobility had such successful results that these spas became models for the best towns, built on a larger scale, after World War II.

The turn of the 19th century was the final period for the building of country mansions and country villas in extensive parks, in the open landscape, or on the sites of older abandoned gardens. The reshaping of the landscape begun during the Baroque era continued in the second half of the 18th century, during the first stages of the Classical Revival. The character of the natural landscape was more and more preserved, the architectural element being represented merely by the unifying pattern of radial vistas, glades, and rondels.

The influence of the English park, asserting itself on the Continent in the last third of the 18th century, was first reflected in the Bohemian lands in romantic and sentimental decorations inspired by antique and exotic architecture, such as Greek and Egyptian pavilions, Tahitian temples, minarets, and the like. Typical of this mood were the parks in *Slezské Rudoltice, Vlašim, Terezino údolí* (Theresian Valley) near Nové Hrady, *Kroměříž*, and *Lednice*. Parks of a more mature design and di-

120. Airview of the oldest part of the West Bohemian spa of Františkovy Lázně (Franzensbad), built according to a Classicist design of 1791. The regular rectangle of the original layout is divided by two north-south streets, one leading to the František Spring in the south and the other to the church in the north, dating from 1812.

verse provenance were laid out even before the end of the century, in *Krásný Dvůr, Červený Hrádek,* and *Veltrusy* and, at the beginning of the 19th century, at *Kačina* (1802–1822) and *Lednice* (1808). The park of Lednice was gradually extended over the whole estate of Lednice and Valtice. Thus, a complex cultural landscape was shaped in the valley of the river Dyje, enlivened in the most significant places by Classicist pavilions, hunting lodges, and other buildings such as triumphal arches, elaborately arranged farmsteads, and artificial ruins of Gothic castles.

In the second quarter of the 19th century the Romantic conception of landscape design reached its culminating point in the gardens adjoining the castle of Kroměříž and in neo-Gothic architecture, as exemplified in the rebuilding of Lednice castle in 1845–1858.

The period of Classical Revival in Slovakia falls into the first half of the 19th century, although the early sporadic examples of Classicist architecture can be traced to the last few years of the 18th century. However, the development of Classicist architecture reflected the economic development of the Hungarian State, which led to the strengthening of the so-called Low Country (the present Hungary) and, consequently, to a considerable depopulation of the Upper Country, the present Slovakia. The great number of people who left Slovakia at that time included not only the aristocracy but also numerous architects and builders. Urban building activities were therefore sporadic, consisting of the construction of individual residential buildings such as palaces or functional structures such as hospitals, orphanages, old peoples' homes, cultural and entertainment centers, or structures for railway transport and industrial production, most of which were situated in gaps between the existing houses or in cleared parts of the towns. New streets were laid out with no regard for the previous street network.

Bratislava was the only exception. It was laid out on a gridiron plan, thus continuing the existing street system. The volume of construction was greater than in the previous periods, as a result of the influx of the population to the towns from the countryside. The first major examples of the Classical Revival can be observed in Bratislava, at this time still the capital of Hungary. Older buildings were reconstructed and new buildings erected after the designs of numerous architects, among which those by I. Feigler (1791–1847) were prominent. Gardens around palaces were laid out (the Mountain Park and the park at Petržalka), expressive symbols of the end of the town's confinement by medieval walls.

Apart from a marked concentration of building activities in Bratislava, Classicist architecture can be found all over Slovakia, often influencing folk architecture in a simplified form. This process considerably increased the number of builders who transferred their major interest to the countryside. While construction in the towns was mostly concentrated on the erection of tenement houses, in the country the gentry took to building residences, imitating as closely as possible the luxurious style of living of the high aristocracy. Thus, there originated dozens of minor single or two-storied mansions, often with Doric and Ionic colonnades at the front and garden façades. In the larger towns, theaters and hotels were built, while the so-called "reduta" buildings in smaller towns combined several functions of a social character, as at Kežmarok, Rimavská Sobota, and Jelšava.

CHAPTER 22

The Historic Towns in Modern Times

GRADUALLY, IMPORTANT changes came about in the whole structure of urban communities. A number of towns went through a period of economic stagnation, while others greatly increased in size. Large suburbs were constructed for the workers who flocked from the countryside to the rapidly growing factories. Whole industrial regions sprang up, coal mining developed, and railway companies built colonies for their workers.

At the beginning of the 19th century, the first railway tracks and factories were built; in 1835, there already were 88 cotton spinning mills and 102 textile works. In 1839, the town of Brno built its own railway station on the route to Vienna. Six years later Prague was connected by rail with Olomouc. Bratislava, with the important port of the Danube Steam Navigation Company, could also boast of a railway.

Apart from Prague, with its population of 100,000, the Bohemian towns in the feudal period had from 5,000 to 10,000 inhabitants. In 1830, no town in Bohemia had more than 20,000 inhabitants, except Prague with a population of 140,000. The limit of 10,000 was slightly exceeded in that year by only four towns: Liberec with 13,000 inhabitants, Cheb with 11,000, and Karlín and Plzeň with 10,000. However, the census of 1890 showed that the population of Plzeň exceeded 50,000, while the Prague conurbation already had 397,268 inhabitants.

In 1830, due to the rapid development of the textile industry, Liberec was the largest town after Prague. In 1890 Plzeň held second place as the center of the engineering industry. At that time, the suburbs of Prague grew in size, contributing considerably to the overall number of the inhabitants of the capital.

However, the development of towns and the process of settlement as a whole showed a considerable disproportion. In 1910 Prague and its suburbs had more than 500,000 inhabitants, Brno more than 120,000, Plzeň 78,000, Bratislava 73,000, České Budějovice 42,000, Košice 40,000, Ústí nad Labem 39,000, Moravská Ostrava 36,000, and Liberec 34,000. In 1930 the population of Prague numbered almost 1,000,000.

In general, only a few large towns increased in size and population, while the majority remained on the level of medium-sized or small towns. Fortifications were dismantled and, in many cases, replaced with parks or new streets. In conformity with Classicist principles, the most important example of such activities was the creation of a green belt around the historical core of Brno. In Prague this opportunity had been missed, and the gardens surrounding the New Town were irretrievably lost. The moat between the Old Town and the New Town was replaced by a street. At the same time, the Smetana Embankment—even today the most beautiful in Prague—was built. In 1804 the Royal Park was opened to the public and, in 1833, the Chotek Parks were laid out, linking up with Chotek Road.

Serious harm was inflicted on the historic cores of towns as walls and old gates were demolished, and "regulation" measures impaired the appearance of old streets and squares. The inner space of the blocks was built over with workshops and storehouses. Historic centers lost their residential value when the bourgeoisie moved to the new suburbs and historic buildings were occupied by the poor.

Only in exceptional cases was the construction of new buildings connected with more comprehensive town planning schemes. The structures of newly built town centers were rarely based on historical principles. Certain changes in urban centers were brought about by the increased number of administrative buildings and shops, the regulation of important thoroughfares, the rebuilding of town squares, the construction of embankments, and by the general shift of focal points toward the new railway stations. Most of the residential districts at the periphery of the towns, whose wealthy character was closely linked with the social class for whom they were intended, were laid out according to schematic plans. Here, the aim was usually to reserve the largest possible amount of space for apartment houses, while the basic functional, hygienic, and aesthetic requirements were generally overlooked in the process.

As a reaction to these disastrous changes, attempts were made to insure the protection of historical monuments by official and private organizations. On the whole, however, these efforts represented a none too successful fight against profit-seekers and speculators. At the most, only individual buildings of high value were saved.

At the turn of the 19th century, for instance, the historic Jewish quarter of Prague, one of the oldest parts of the medieval town, was demolished. No consideration was given to historical research, and only a few of the most valuable buildings were saved. The rest were pulled down, and high apartment houses were erected on land parceled out schematically, without regard for the historic structure of the street pattern.

The restoration of the independence of Czechoslovakia after World War I did not give rise to any important changes. It is true that Czechoslovakian architects came to the front in the movement toward a new functional architecture and rational town planning. However, their great efforts were restricted to the design and construction of individual buildings. Large-scale plans were drawn up for the bigger towns, and the first attempts at regional planning were made. But under the prevailing economic system these efforts met with limited success.

At this time, complex town-planning schemes were worked out for new communities by the footwear manufacturing firm of Baťa. The most important of these was *Zlín*, which at the beginning of the 20th century grew from a small mountain town into a contemporary industrial center.

As far as the preservation of the historic town centers was concerned, a change for the better was apparent, due to the fact that, in a number of towns, the focal point of new construction shifted beyond the historic cores of the towns. The actual restoration of historical monuments was limited, almost exclusively, to individual buildings like churches and castles. Old palaces were reconstructed to meet the needs of ministerial and other offices, particularly in Prague. Of considerable importance were the modifications of the Prague Castle, the Hradčany, as the seat of the President of the Republic, a work supervised by such outstanding architects as J. Plečník and P. Janák.

Today, Czechoslovakia can rightly be regarded as one of the European countries in which a wealth of historical buildings from all periods are preserved. The historic towns of Czechoslovakia are particularly interesting when considered from a typological aspect. The ground plans and spatial arrangements of such towns as Prague, Olomouc, Znojmo, Bratislava, and Brno illustrate the town-planning principles of the early feudal period. The plans of other towns reflect the complicated efforts required to apply the regular designs of the Middle Ages to the older historic cores of former walled-in settlements, castles, monasteries, and market villages. Finally, quite a number of towns bear witness to the purity and refinement of their extraordinarily developed and regular medieval plans, features only rarely encountered anywhere else.

The whole of this complex development was further enriched by the influence of natural conditions and, particularly, by the character of the terrain and the rivers. Towns were built on important headlands and hills, as well as in river valleys and on plains. Their plans were adapted to the configuration of the terrain, and often to the location of old trade routes leading to old market places or to important fords over rivers and streams.

Not even during the period of industrialization were the basic features of the historic towns destroyed. Even this period—with some exceptions—appreciated the outstanding values of the past. Thus, it is true to say that Czechoslovakian towns are, indeed, a legacy of historical architecture, where great industrial cities like Prague and Bratislava have preserved their historic cores, in all their extent and glory.

CHAPTER 23

CITY SURVEY/ CZECHOSLOVAKIA

Prague. The territory of Prague and its nearest surroundings belong to the oldest settled areas in Bohemia. Its geographical position in the center of the Bohemian basin, bordered by the mountain chains of Šumava (Bohemian Forest), Krušné Hory (Erz Mountains), Krkonoše (Riesengebirge) and Českomoravská vrchovina (Bohemian-Moravian Highlands), favored early settlement. The location of the capital of Bohemia was determined by the meander of the Vltava River, the widening of the river valley, and the lateral valleys of the tributary streams. All these factors were advantageous for settlement when sheltered sites in river valleys and elevated positions on hills and peninsulas were preferred. Archeological finds reveal that the Prague area has been occupied since 3000 B.C. and that in the Neolithic Age an agglomeration of agricultural villages existed on, or near, the site which was, at this time, an important meeting point of long-distance roads.

In the Bronze Age (about 1500 B.C.) the so-called Únětice Culture flourished in this region, although the population was not so numerous as in the preceding period.

Around 1200 B.C. a significant change took place. The Lusation people brought with them a new culture (Knovízská kultura), which prospered in the Prague territory. According to archeological finds of the ninth to the seventh centuries B.C., a dense net of settlements, almost resembling a conurbation, had developed. In the last pre-Christian centuries, the major part of Bohemia was occupied by Celts who had their main political and military center close to the site of Prague.

Toward the end of the age of the Great Migrations in the fifth to the sixth centuries A.D., the Prague area was densely populated. Walled-in settlements guarded the historic town nucleus in an almost complete circle.

The development of the settlements on both river banks was furthered by the important ford which, from the ninth century onward, was protected by the castle of Prague. It was also in this period that the northern and southern boundaries of the actual urban area were firmly established by the position of the Prague and the Vyšehrad castles, respectively. The new places growing up around the castles continued on the lines of the earlier settlements which had developed along the roads leading to the river crossings. In addition, new communities came into being between the two feudal centers, as either market or trading centers. The character of all these settlements can be described as urban because of their extent and differentiation of functions. As early as the 10th century a wooden bridge connected the banks of the Vltava River. An interesting account of Prague as an important center of the great Bohemian state of the 10th century has been left by Ibrahim Ibn Jacob, the Arab-Jewish merchant and traveler who visited it in A.D. 965. According to his report, Prague was built of stone and lime and was a rich trading community.

About the thirties of the 10th century the church of St. Vitus was erected within the area of the Prague Castle. The early development of the castle of Prague culminated in the construction of the palace and powerful stone fortifications, reinforced with bastions and prismatic towers.

In the third quarter of the 12th century the wooden bridge across the Vltava was replaced by a stone bridge. On its left bank, two ecclesiastical centers formed a bridgehead: the seat of the Order of the Knights of Malta (Hospitalers) and the palace of the Bishop of Prague.

The settlement on the right river bank passed through a different kind of development, with the exception of Vyšehrad Castle, whose rich architecture, now lost, must have competed with that of the castle of Prague.

The main features of the plan of the Old Town—partly ruined during the improvements at the turn of the 19th century—were the roads leading toward the river crossing and the radial streets converging on the central square, the present Old Town Square. In its neighborhood existed a walled-in area with a customhouse that was later to be a center of international trade.

Within the area of the Old Town, Romanesque town houses dating from the early feudal period have been preserved. They are built either around an inner courtyard or along the streets, grouped in a sequence of regularly arranged allotments. The ecclesiastical organization of early feudalism, that is, the institution of privately owned churches, gave rise to a number of minor churches dispersed among many secular Romanesque buildings on either bank of the river.

By the end of the 12th and the beginning

of the 13th centuries, the Prague territory had extended considerably. The overall length of the right bank settlement, from Vyšehrad to St. Peter's quarter, was about 3.1 miles. Romanesque Prague's numerous population was employed in royal and ecclesiastical services or engaged in trade and commerce, all characteristic of an urban community.

One of the most significant periods in the development of the Bohemian capital was the second half of the 13th century. Its gradual transformation to a regularly built city with legal privileges began on the right river bank, with the laying out of the Old Town in about 1230 and the erection of stone walls. To the southeast of the Old Town, and with a less dense population, the New Town grew up around St. Gall's Church, *nova civitas circa sanctum Gallum,* with a large square.

In the forties of the 13th century, the Gothic style appeared in Prague and, in the course of the following centuries, gave the city a new appearance, partly preserved to the present day. An example of the nascent art of Gothic town planning was Menši Město Pražské, the so-called Small Town of Prague, situated on the right river bank, below the Prague Castle. It was laid out as a town by King Přemysl Otakar II in the year 1257. In spite of adverse topographical conditions and the existence of an older settlement, the plan of the Small Town was regular, with a longitudinal square in the center. This plan may have been the first example of Gothic town planning within the territory of Prague.

The 14th century left a remarkable imprint on the historical and artistic monuments of the city. About the year 1320, another municipality was joined with the earlier town: the Hradčany quarter, in close proximity to the royal castle. Prague was elevated to an archbishopric in 1344. This event stimulated the erection of a new St. Vitus' Church. Its master architects were Matthew of Arras, until 1352, and Peter Parler.

In 1348, King Charles IV founded the New Town, thus enlarging the urban area by 701.48 acres, that is, to an overall size of 1,318.9 acres, with 40,000 to 50,000 inhabitants. The town planning program of the king was far-reaching, comprising, within the town walls, the entire area which extended from Vyšehrad to St. Peter's quarter on the right river bank, and the addition of large tracts of land in the south and east. The layout of the earlier town quarters remained almost intact. However, the open spaces or less densely built-up areas were replanned on a grand scale. A system of three large squares interconnected by a main line of communication was laid out. The southern square, the Cattle Market, was chosen as the principal center of the New Town. It was a long rectangle of 492 by 1,804 feet, covering almost 17.29 acres. Houses in the squares and the main streets were mostly three-storied. Many of them have been preserved to the present day, testifying to the vigorous architectural activities in the days of Charles IV and Wenceslas IV.

During the reign of Charles IV cultural and economic activities flourished in the Kingdom of Bohemia and its capital. In 1348 the University of Prague was founded; it is the oldest university in Central Europe. The old stone Romanesque bridge, which had been destroyed by floods, was replaced by a bridge of Gothic design, connecting the banks of the Vltava. Until the middle of the 19th century it remained the only bridge in the city.

After a short period of stagnation due to the saturation of the building market of the pre-Hussite era, architectural activities received a new stimulus, reaching their culmination in the 15th century. The chief architect was Benedict Rejt. The castle of Prague received a new festival hall, called after the ruling king, the Wladislav Hall. As early as 1493 Renaissance motifs were applied to the window ornaments of the new hall. Their use became more frequent toward the close of the first quarter of the 16th century. In 1538 the erection of a royal summer palace, the Belvedere, was begun in the vicinity of the castle. It is one of the purest and loveliest pieces of Renaissance architecture north of the Alps.

However, the main stimulus to a wide application of Renaissance building techniques and forms was a disastrous fire which visited the Small Town and the Hradčany quarter in 1541. The large-scale construction, during which a great number of new town houses were built, was carried out in the style of the Renaissance. Palaces of the nobility were erected, the area of the Small Town was extended, and a number of houses were built on new allotments. The characteristic skyline of the castle was altered, the

121. View of Prague in 1563.

122. General view of the Small Town of Prague and the Hradčany across the Vltava River, with the Charles Bridge in the foreground.

cathedral tower received a new helmet, the premises of the castle were considerably enlarged, and the royal gardens were laid out.

In the course of the second half of the 16th century and during the first two decades of the 17th century, the appearance of the city changed greatly. The streets were enlivened by a variety of façades decorated with graffiti and mural paintings and by the contrasting outlines of numerous gables. The interiors of several courts were adorned with arcaded balconies.

As early as the beginning of the 17th century, the first signs of the approach of the Italian Baroque appeared in the architecture of the Small Town and the Prague Castle. However, the rich and promising development of the late Renaissance was violently interrupted by the Revolt of the Bohemian Estates in 1618 and by the ensuing Thirty Years' War. This meant not only a fatal interruption in the historical development of the city, but also a fundamental change in its art and architecture.

After the defeat of the uprising in 1620, the political and economic conditions of Prague were radically altered. The new building enterprises were almost exclusively sponsored by the nobility and the clergy and no longer, to the same degree as previously, by the tradesmen and merchants. The new edifices built by the lords temporal and spiritual were out of harmony with the existing town organism. On the sites of demolished houses or blocks of houses, monumental early Baroque architectural complexes rose, differing in scale and proportion from older Prague buildings. The decision of Generalissimo Albrecht von Wallenstein to erect a magnificent palace with a loggia and an extensive garden in the Small Town of Prague may serve as a characteristic example. The building was begun in 1630, after twenty-eight houses and four gardens that had occupied the site had been demolished. Another example is the large number of existing houses that had to be pulled down to make room for the erection of the three huge building complexes of the Jesuit College.

The artists of the early Baroque period in Prague were almost exclusively Italians. During the second half of the 17th century the city underwent a significant change. Shortly after the end of the Thirty Years' War, new fortifications were built, enclosing in a continuous line the entire city.

In the last quarter of the 17th century the monopoly of Italian architects was no longer supreme. The leading personality of the time, the French artist Jean Baptiste Mathey, introduced the sober yet monumental cadenced design of Roman Baroque architecture to the Prague scene. Soon, however, the art of the High Baroque introduced a sudden change. It reached a high point as early as the first decade of the 18th century. Its main representatives were Giovanni Santini, Kilian Ignac Dientzenhofer, and František Maxmilián Kaňka. Their style was in no way a continuation of the preceding architectural

123. The Small Town Square in Prague, with the monumental Jesuit College (second half of the 17th century) and the adjoining Church of St. Nicholas (1704–1755). The presbytery with the cupola is the work of Kilian I. Dientzenhofer.

stages, but an entirely new and original means of expression, of composition and contrasting arrangements, of volumes and movements, and of artistic details. The streets and squares of Prague were adorned with works of art, sponsored mostly by the nobility and the Church. Numerous churches, palaces, and convent buildings were erected in the agitated forms of the High Baroque, while the town houses showed a more moderate use of Baroque design. Once again Prague became the leading artistic center of the whole Bohemian State.

This period paid much attention to the integration of larger town-planning schemes. The problems of axial and other kinds of perspective views were taken up, and the siting of new edifices was planned according to more sophisticated theories. The situation of St. Nicholas' Church in the Small Town of Prague, located by Dientzenhofer in a natural basin enclosed by the hills of Petřín and Hradčany, may serve as an example. The aesthetic appeal of the city was heightened by sculptures, a unique set of which remains a characteristic feature of the Charles Bridge. Private gardens of elaborate design were laid out as part of the aristocratic palaces. the most beautiful occupying the slopes of the Prague Castle and Petřín Hill. This period

124. View from Melantrich Street of the Gothic tower of the Old Town Hall in Prague.

125. *Below:* View from Hradčany through Úvoz Street toward the Small Town of Prague, with buildings from the Renaissance and Baroque periods.

126. *Above:* Plan of the city of Prague in 1848, showing the extent of the town prior to the origin of new suburbs in the course of the 19th century.

was interrupted by the outbreak of the Silesian and the Seven Years' Wars in the middle of the 18th century. The artistic activities of the second half of the 18th century resembled a stream with a wide but shallow river bed. Baroque forms appeared on many buildings, which were gradually simplified and more and more interspersed with new elements heralding the advent of Classicism.

A significant landmark in the development of Prague was the building of its first suburb, Karlín, on the southern river bank, at the eastern side of the city walls, in 1817. Since then Prague has spread in all directions, while for almost five centuries its area had been confined to the territory within the city walls.

The first half of the 19th century had a positive bearing on the development of the historic town nucleus. A broad new avenue, lined partly with imposing buildings and continuing for a short distance behind the new suspension bridge on the river bank of the Small Town, was laid out on the terrain of the former moats. In connection with the construction of a bridge, the first embankment was built, inaugurating radical changes in the orientation of the city toward the river.

The streets of Karlín, crossing each other at right angles, were lined by new Classicist houses. It was not till the middle of the 19th century that a fundamental change took place. Until the seventies, Prague remained enclosed by walls, beyond which new standardized suburbs began to spread. In the eighties, the historic nucleus was threatened by the demands of private developers requiring its reconstruction. Formless, clumsy tenement houses of the Austrian type were to be erected in the newly laid-out streets, and Prague was in danger of losing its individual character.

New suburbs grew up as independent towns or boroughs, with their own administrative centers, squares, and town halls. As early as 1784 the four main historical town quarters of Prague, the Old and the New Town, the Small Town and the Hradčany quarter, were merged into a single whole. Yet, it was not before 1920 that the historical town nucleus was joined by 37 towns, boroughs, and villages. By then the overall area of Greater Prague had more than three quarters of a million inhabitants.

127. A panoramic view of the Small Town of Prague, the Old Town, the New Town, and Vyšehrad.

Banská Štiavnica, Central Slovakia. Deposits of rare metal ores in the region of Central Slovakia attracted people as early as the 11th century A.D. By the beginning of the 13th century, several mining settlements had developed. It is probable that Banská Štiavnica, one of these settlements, showed signs of urban characteristics long before the Tartar invasion of Hungary (1241).

Following the invasion, a new mining center came into being, ensuring the town of Banská Štiavnica a first-rank position among the other mining towns.

The relationship of the original settlement to the new center concentrated in its vicinity has not yet been sufficiently clarified. However, the existence of a church and a Dominican monastery at the beginning of the 13th century proves that new quarters were developed around these two buildings. It is also probable that both parts of the settlement, the old and the new, grew equally for some time, but that the more recent one gradually gained in importance while the older one slowly lost its significance until it fell into decay at the beginning of the 15th century.

The new settlement was restricted in its extension by the relatively narrow valley, which served as a route leading from the south to the ore-bearing regions farther north. Because of the increase in population, in trade, and in mining activities, a new square was required. Due to the lack of a suitable central area, a site was chosen away from the main road on the slopes of the valley.

In view of its remote position a continuous fortification was not deemed essential. Merely the main roads leading into the town were closed with gates. The church, dating from the first half of the 13th century, was rebuilt into a fortified castle. Together with a Romanesque chapel, it was surrounded by a wall (1546–1559), thus giving rise to a defensive complex of buildings. The supervision of the building of these defenses is usually attributed to Pietro Ferrabosco. The fortifications of the town were later

128. Plan of the center of Banská Štiavnica, after a cadastral map of the second half of the 19th century.

strengthened by the so-called New Castle (1564–1571), with a watch tower and four turrets at the corners.

Regular rows of houses were erected, even where the configuration of the terrain was difficult, while minor buildings were scattered about the outskirts of the town. Gradually the medieval town changed when it was reconstructed in the 16th and 18th centuries. The square and the main streets were almost entirely rebuilt.

The existence of a well-preserved urban core and numerous historic buildings, including Gothic, Renaissance, and Baroque secular and ecclesiastical edifices, was the reason for declaring Banská Štiavnica a historical monument, enhancing the cultural importance of the town.

129. Square at Banská Štiavnica with the parish church of the 15th century, the tower of the Town Hall of the 17th century (right), and the New Castle of the 16th century (background).

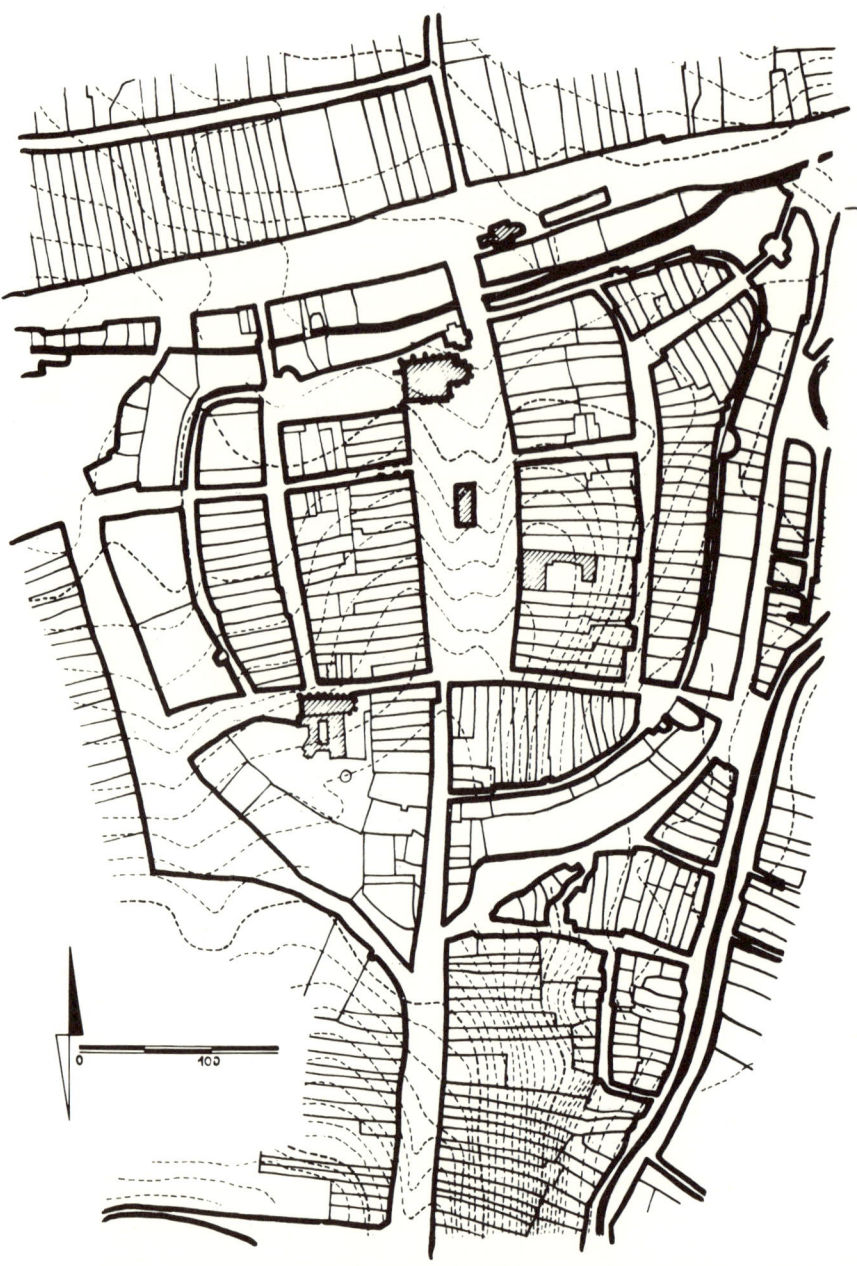

130. Plan of the historical center of Bardejov, after a cadastral map of the second half of the 19th century.

Bardejov, Eastern Slovakia. The town of Bardejov is one of the best preserved examples of medieval city planning in Slovakia, due mainly to its situation in the northeastern region of Slovakia outside the sphere of the initial impact of industrialization of the country.

The actual origin of the town has not yet been ascertained. We know, however, that as early as the first decades of the 13th century it was related in some way to the nearby Cistercian monastery. At the beginning of the 14th century, the settlement ceased to be dependent on the monastery. The population received privileges, permitting it to have its own municipal administration (1320). In 1376 Bardejov was raised to the status of a Royal Town.

The center of the town was occupied by a rectangular square, intersected by a trunk road that connected the town with other commercial centers of Eastern Slovakia participating in foreign trade. Along both sides of the square, stretching from north to south, two residential blocks originated, interrupted by transverse streets. The northern side of the square was closed by a church dating from the 14th century.

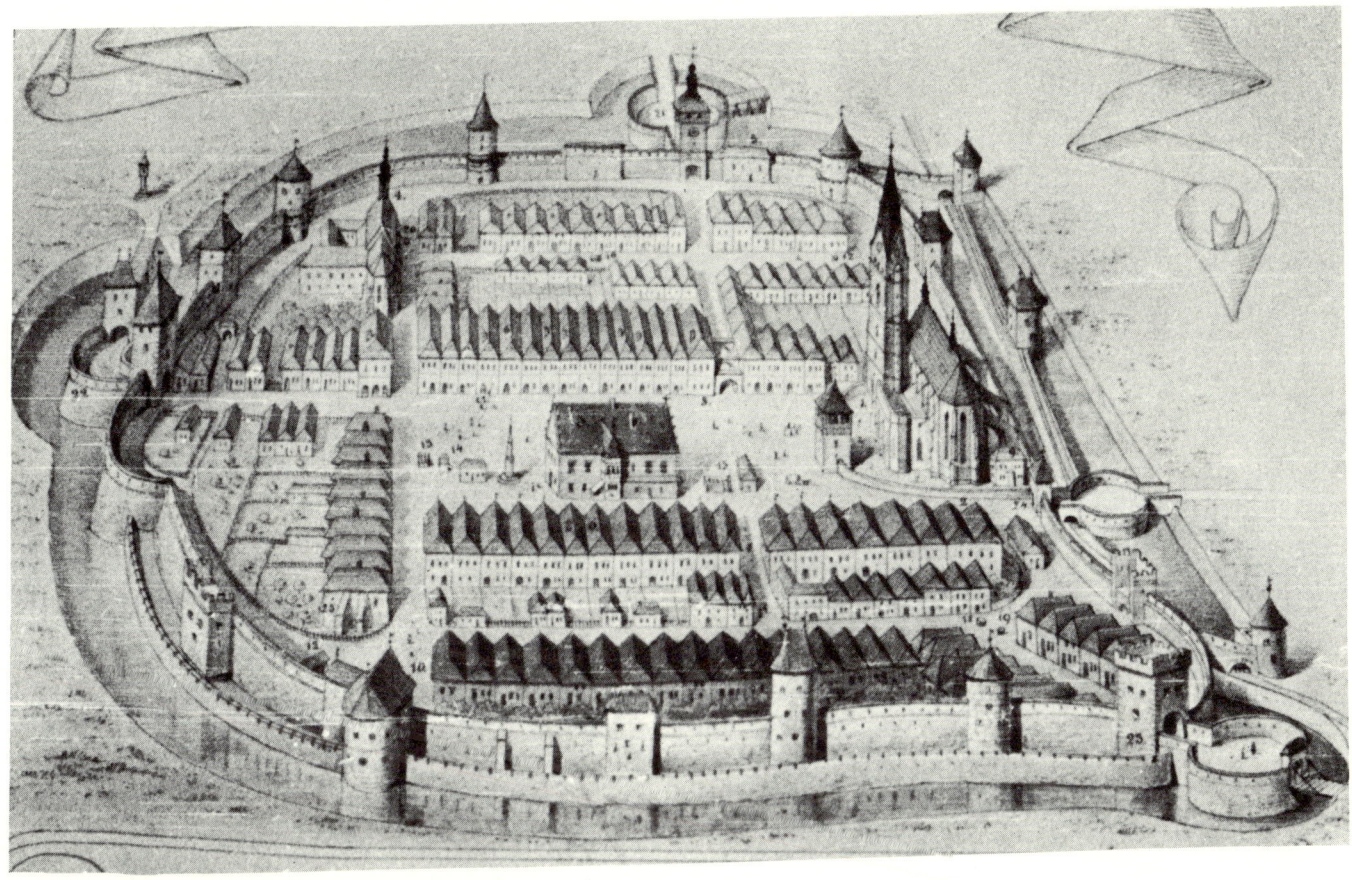

131. Reconstruction of the Gothic town of Bardejov. Drawing by A. Miszkovský, of the 19th century.

At the beginning of the 16th century (1505–1508), a town hall was erected in the square by the master builders, Alexander and Alexei. The ground floor is Gothic, while the upper floor shows Renaissance features. With its high gables and pitched roof, its Renaissance portals and window frames, this building is one of the first and most important architectural monuments of its type.

Situated near the frontier of Hungary, the need for defense resulted in the construction of a strong, double fortifications system (1325). Its walls, 26.2 feet to 32.8 feet high, were strengthened by bastions and gates with barbicans.

At the time of the construction of the walls the town was already surrounded by suburbs inhabited by people who did not share the civic privileges of the town population. In the 16th century the town played an important role in the history of Hungary as a center of Protestantism, which was reflected in the construction of cultural and educational buildings such as a grammar school and printing works.

After a great fire in 1534 the town was reconstructed, losing its Gothic character by the rebuilding of the façades of many houses in the Renaissance style.

Beginning with the last decades of the 16th century, a marked economic stagnation set in due to the foreign policy of the Hungarian rulers, the general unrest, and last, but not least, the frequent fires.

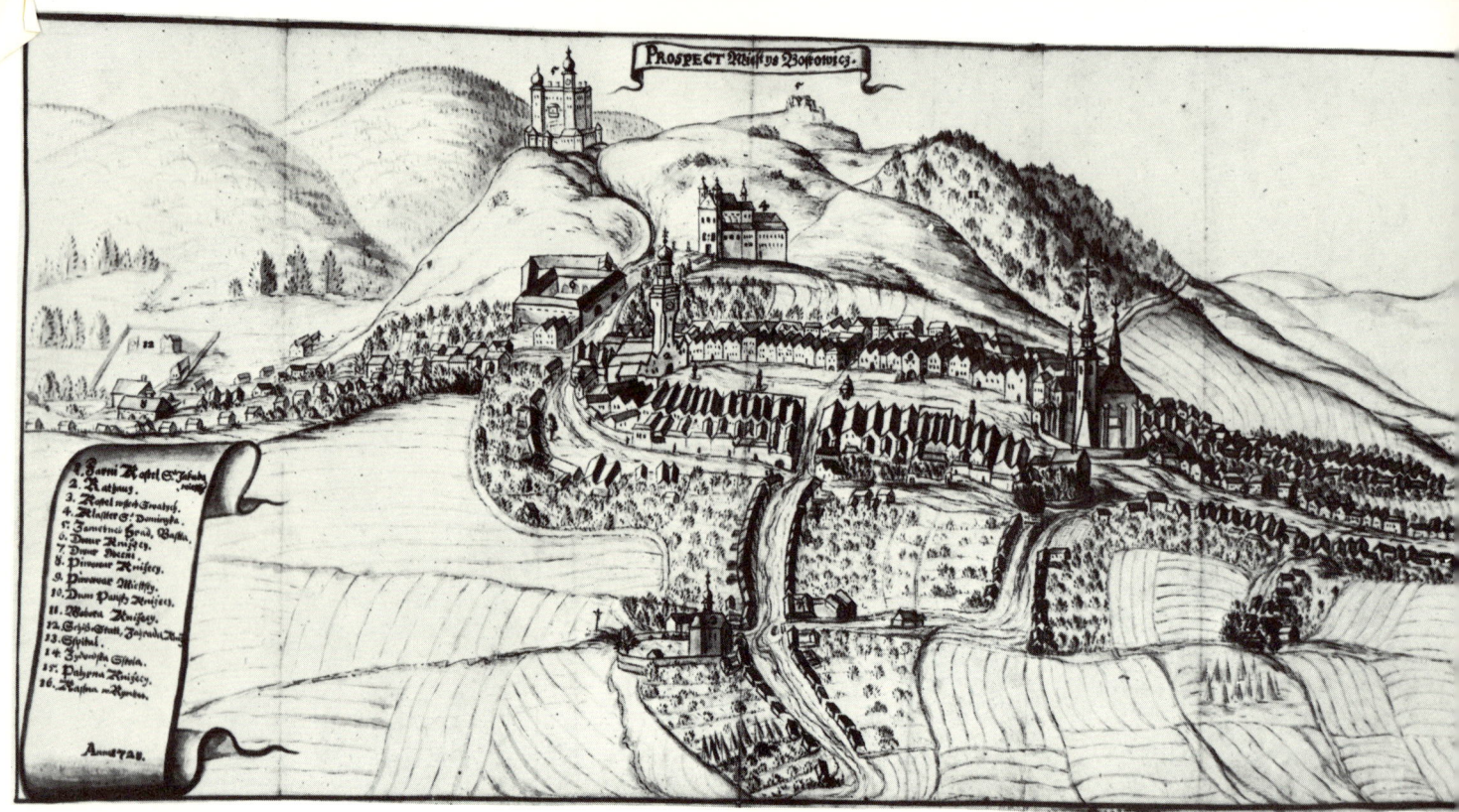

132. Old view of Boskovice from the collection of Dismas von Hoffer, 1723–1728.

Boskovice, Northern Moravia. The town of Boskovice, situated in the northwest of Moravia, was founded in the 13th century, probably on the site of an early feudal settlement at the foot of a castle.

The town is elliptical in shape, with an elongated square sloping down from the Renaissance town hall to the lower end with the church of St. James. The town was encircled by walls, with an inner ring road.

At the foot of the castle hill, a Classicist palace was built in the first quarter of the 19th century, on the site of a demolished Baroque convent. Between the palace and the southwestern corner of the town a walled-in ghetto, with its own gates and three synagogues, had been located since the 14th century. Built on an irregular plan, with several small squares, it was one of the largest ghettos in Moravia, with two thousand inhabitants in 1857.

Bratislava, Western Slovakia. The stronghold, subsequently the castle of Bratislava, has always been of great importance among the settlements situated on the right bank of the Danube, at the foot of the spurs of the Carpathian Mountains which, at this point, cut across the Danube lowland.

Recent archeological research has revealed the existence of fortifications and a settlement on the castle hill, dating from Celtic and Roman times. At the end of the ninth century, the castle was a stronghold of the Great Moravian Empire and, later, a Hungarian frontier fortress.

In the 12th century, a settlement existed at the foot of the castle. Its center was situated at the intersection of two trade routes, one from Olomouc in Moravia, the other from Nitra in Slovakia. Both routes were part of important intercontinental communications, using the ford below the castle to cross the Danube. The extent of the settlement below the castle was limited by the castle hill, the buildings being concentrated in the area of the present Kapitulská Street. The settlement thus extended into the present town, adjoining the village of Vydrica on the southwest. At the south end of Kapitulská Street stood the predecessor to the present cathedral, a small church consecrated to the Savior.

The existence of other settlements in the area of today's Obchodná ulica, Commercial Street (Széplak), in the village of foresters and fishermen, called Vydrica (situated on the territory of the present Karlova Ves, in an easterly direction), and in the vicinity of a road leading to the castle of Devín have all been identified.

In the 13th century, the settlement at the foot of the castle suffered from the Tartar invasion. As a result, a new settlement was founded on the site in the second half of the 13th century, between the area of the present Obchodná ulica, Commercial Street, and the old settlement below the castle. In 1291, King Andrew granted special privileges to this settlement, thus laying the foundations of a new town.

The new place became a Royal Free Town, while the older settlement below the castle remained subject to the administrator of Bratislava Castle. It did not merge with the town until the 14th century.

The extent of the original town was restricted by several natural factors: in the

133. Plan of the center of Bratislava.

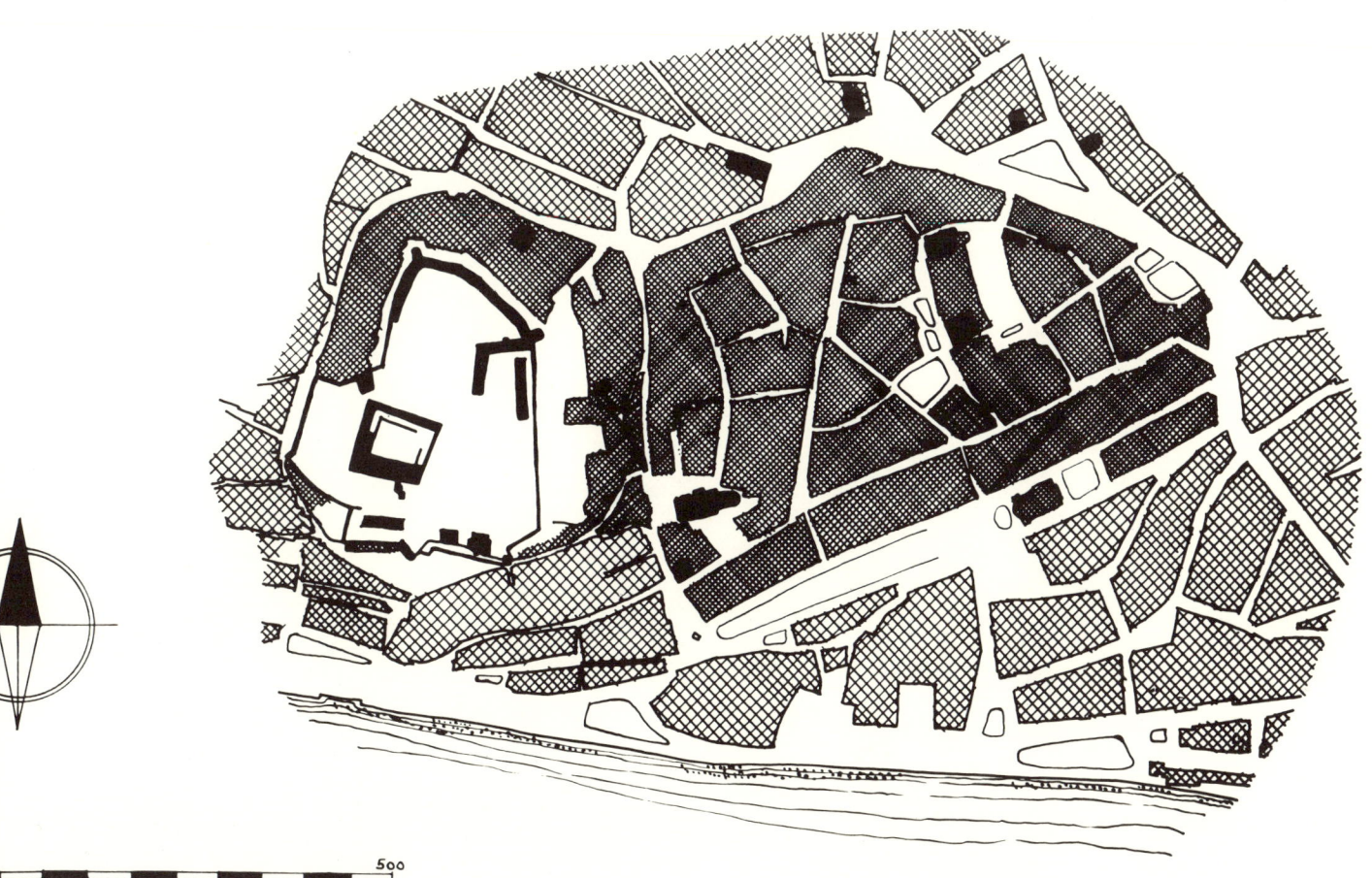

south, by branches of the Danube, with threats of floods; in the west, by the castle hill; and in the north and northeast, by a natural terrace raised several feet above the actual site of the town. A new town square was laid out in the vicinity of the Franciscan church and monastery, thus enlarging the relatively small existing square by an area in front of the church. The principal streets were fixed as early as the end of the 13th century. Later, this early street system was further developed by lanes subdividing some of the bigger blocks. Building activities at the end of the 13th century were concentrated mainly on the reconstruction of the Franciscan monastery (1279), the rebuilding of the parish church of St. Martin, and the construction of the town walls.

Originally there were three gates: The Michael Gate in the north; the Laurin Gate in the east, at the end of today's Leningrad Street, near the Hviezdoslav Theater; and the Vydrica Gate at the end of Captain Nálepka Street, formerly Dlhá ulica, Long Street, near the present Rybné námestie, Fish Square. A fourth gate was built later to connect the fishermen's settlement with the town. Known as Rybná brána, Fish Gate, it is situated at the end of the street of the same name.

In the course of the 14th century the economic importance of Bratislava grew rapidly. Together with the construction of the town walls, which continued throughout the 14th century, extensive building activities took place within the walls of the town, below the castle, in the suburbs, and in the castle itself.

The streets of the town were lined with new rows of houses. The house of Jakub, the mayor, was converted into a town hall. The square was improved, and other works were set on foot. Intensive building activities were also going on outside the town walls.

In the territory of the former village of Széplak, the new suburb of Schöndorf grew up. And outside all four gates, four new suburbs were built: the so-called Hospital Quarter originated in the vicinity of the Laurin Gate around the Church of St. Lawrence, and included the municipal hospitals of St. Elizabeth and St. Ladislav; to the southwest of this quarter, in the direction of today's Danube Street, the Danube suburb; and on the southern side of the town, toward the Danube, a fishermen's district adjoining the Rybná brána, Fish Gate. The biggest suburb came into existence around the Church of St. Michael. The extent of these suburbs was indicated by the line of palisades built by the municipality to protect the suburbs and improve the defenses of the town.

In the course of the 15th century a number of important constructions begun in the preceding century were terminated, such as the completion of St. Martin's and building in the area of the castle and in the castle itself. The Town Hall was completed in

134. Main square in Bratislava, with the Town Hall (16th century) and the Renaissance Jesuit church, on the left.

135. View of Bratislava in the 18th century. From the collection in the Municipal Gallery in Bratislava.

the first half of the 15th century, as the last structure of the Gothic period. In the second half of the century, traces of a new architectural style could be discerned, foreshadowing the architectural changes of the following centuries.

From the beginning of the 16th century on, the defenses of the town were strengthened. Walls were repaired and improved, and buildings in the suburbs were torn down (the churches of St. Lawrence, St. Michael, and St. Nicholas, below the castle). On the whole, however, the 16th century did not enrich the town with any outstanding architectural works. On the other hand, the importance of the town was increased by the transfer of the administration of the Hungarian State from Buda to Bratislava, when it became the capital of Hungary until 1848.

Because of the danger of Turkish attacks from the south not many architectural changes were initiated during the 17th century. Following improvements to the castle, it was also intended to rebuild the walls and fortifications in accordance with a project of the well-known military engineer, J. Priami. His plan did not materialize. It was a more or less theoretical design requiring further detailing, while the defeat of the Turks made its implementation unnecessary.

In the 18th century, building activity was dictated chiefly by the importance of the town as the capital of Hungary and one of the main seats of the Counter Reformation. This work resulted in the construction of a number of isolated buildings which imprinted a Baroque character on the town for many years. Of particular importance were the construction of churches and Capuchin and Trinitarian monasteries, the church of the Elizabethan nuns, and the completion of the monastery of the Brethren of Charity. All these ecclesiastical buildings, together with the subsequent Baroque reconstruction of the tower of the Michael Gate and the erection of sculptures and fountains, contributed to the rather haphazard Baroque appearance of the town.

In the second half of the 18th century, a number of so-called summer palaces were built outside the core area, such as the former Aspremont Palace and Grassalkovich Palace, all surrounded by extensive parks. This was the beginning of the incorporation of verdure in the organism of the town and of the effort to obtain access to the countryside for the townspeople. Horský Park (the Mountain Park), today's Janko Kráľ Park at Petržalka, Železná Studnička, and others were laid out at this time.

Although the plan of the town designed by Hillebrandt in 1765 has not been preserved, it can be assumed that the majority of changes in the layout of the town were based on his ideas, for example, the reconstruction of the square in front of the new Archbishop's Palace, the reconstruction of the present Hviezdoslav Square, Rudnay Square, and the planning of new blocks in today's Jesenský Street. The walls were dismantled about 1775, and the land gained by filling in the moat was turned over to new constructions.

Brno, Southern Moravia. The plain of the Danubian Basin penetrates deep into the territory of Moravia, in a northwest direction. This region, at the foot of the hills of the Bohemian-Moravian and Drahaňská Highlands, has been inhabited since prehistoric times. Its southern part is rich agricultural land, with the valleys of the rivers Dyje and Svratka bordered by enchanting forests that extend far into the Brno region. Here, many places have preserved their old original character. The western and northern sides of the town of Brno are surrounded by forests, penetrating into the built-up area of the town. This mixed urban and rural landscape would be perfect, if later architectural and industrial development, particularly mining activities, had not wrought excessive changes.

The beginning and the development of the occupation of the site of Brno, in the period of early feudalism, have not yet been clarified. Even before the origin of Great Moravia, there existed the stronghold of Staré Zámky to the east of Brno. Another important place in Great Moravia was the stronghold at Rajhrad, situated to the south of Brno, on a crossing over the river Svratka. Here, a Benedictine monastery was founded in the 11th century. Both strongholds can be considered predecessors of the town of Brno. Within the territory of the town, below Špilberk, there existed a settlement known as Staré Brno, or Old Brno, near a crossing over the river Svratka, on a north-south trade route.

However, as early as the first half of the 11th century, the focal point of the settlement shifted to the eastern side of Špilberk. On the nearby territory, at the confluence of the rivers Svitava and Svratka, Petrov Hill formed the natural *acropolis* of a settlement which developed as its *suburbium*. As early as 1048 Brno Castle existed on Petrov Hill, at the southwest border of the later Gothic town. The original market square of this *suburbium* was situated on the site of the present Vegetable Market, below Petrov Hill. Adjoining it on the eastern side was a Jewish quarter and a Bohemian community, both dating from the early feudal period.

Before the origin of the actual town, a second settlement had come into being to the north of the stream flowing through the later Big Square (known today as Freedom Square). Trade routes, passing through this area, led to the market buildings around the Vegetable Market. A traders' settlement inhabited by foreigners lay at the fork of these routes.

From these settlements the Gothic town of Brno originated, with its regular oval ground plan. The fortifications lent the town a new and homogeneous appearance. Of historical importance to the town of Brno is a document of King Václav I dating from the year 1243, proclaiming Brno a Royal Town.

The architectural development of the Gothic town proceeded rapidly, in accordance with its economic growth. At the end of the 13th and the beginning of the 14th century, Brno displayed a uniform appearance. Its network of streets, with a number of early feudal elements, was completed to the extent in which it was basically preserved to the end of the 18th century. The natural dominant of the town, Petrov Hill, was surrounded by fortifications. The skyline of Brno was considerably enlivened by a strong royal castle built on Špilberk Hill during the reign of King Přemysl Otakar II, in the third quarter of the 13th century.

With the exception of church buildings, the Gothic town consisted originally of wooden or timber-framed houses, stone buildings being mentioned as a rarity in contemporary documents. The town hall, the churches, and the monasteries, all reconstructed at a later date, were of a high artistic standard. Important remnants of the Gothic period are the core of Špilberk Castle, preserved in its entirety; part of the church of St. Peter; the Calvary; the Church of St. James; and numerous other buildings. Immediately outside the fortifications, on the southern side of the town, an Augustine monastery was founded in 1350.

Outside the walls lay Staré Brno, Old Brno, with the buildings of a Cistercian monastery erected in 1323 and several other communities dating from the same period. In the Gothic period industrial and trading suburbs grew up, known as the Brewers' Quarter, Ropemaker Street, Tanner Street, Thorny Street, Baker Street, and others.

More Renaissance than Gothic remains of buildings have been preserved, for example, the mansions of the Barons of Lípa on Náměstí svobody, Freedom Square, and of the Barons of Kunštát; part of the episcopal court below Petrov Hill; and certain monasteries. At that time a water supply was installed. The banks of the river flowing

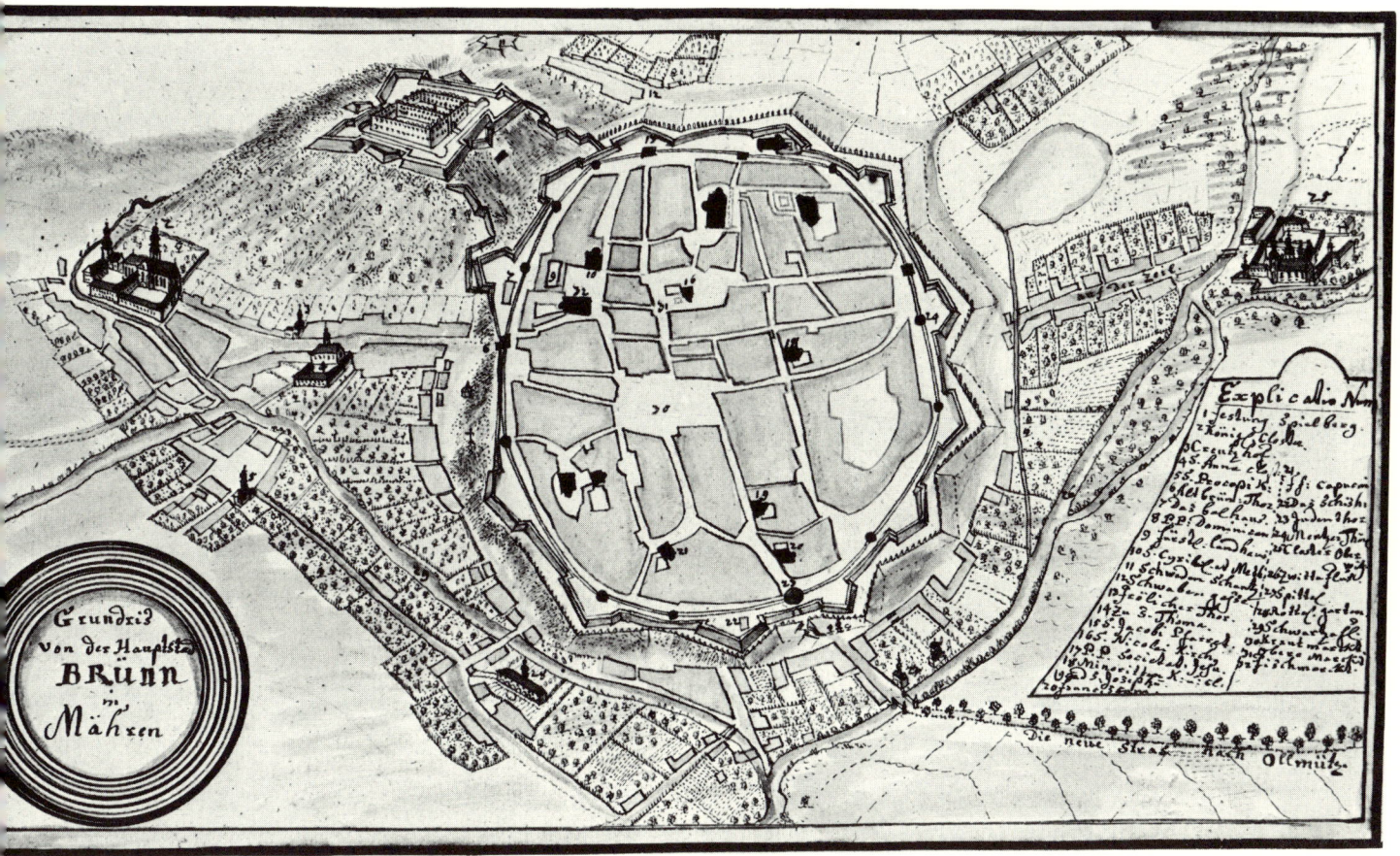

136. Plan of Brno by Friedrich Bernhard Werner, middle of the 18th century. The town and the Špilberk Castle are still surrounded by walls.

through the town were strengthened, and a number of cemeteries removed. Apart from the growth of workshops in the historical core of the town, the developing industry led to the expansion of handicraft villages as well as to the origin of new villages. During the Thirty Years' War the fortifications of the town and of Špilberk Castle were strengthened.

The Baroque period witnessed a further transformation of the town. The street system remained more or less the same, although considerable changes were carried out in the town's architecture. For the building of palaces, and the extension or new construction of monasteries and churches, a number of building sites were joined to form larger sites by the demolition of Gothic buildings. Thus, Dietrichstein Palace dominated the space of the Vegetable Market before the Thirty Years' War; the Minorites used a whole block which formerly included a garden for their convent; and the Augustinian Monastery of St. Thomas formed an entirely new complex of buildings outside the town walls, though its fortifications linked up with those of the town. A large part of the gardens of the Jesuit monastery was also built up. In addition, the monumental complex of utility buildings on Dominican Square grew considerably, incorporating a monastery of the preceding period. Finally, a number of military structures were erected within the historical core of the town.

The new system of fortifications, protecting Brno and Špilberk Castle, greatly transformed the periphery of the historical core. After the Thirty Years' War, when Brno resisted the siege of the Swedes, the town was gradually developed into a huge stronghold according to a plan by a French engineer, de Rochepine, which was not completed until the second third of the 18th century.

The first impact of the modern age on the economic and, later, the physical structure of the town made itself felt as early as the sixties of the 18th century. State-built factories for the processing of tobacco and the production of textiles in Nová ulice, New Street, proved so stimulating to private enterprise that when Joseph II succeeded to the throne Brno had already twenty textile plants.

217

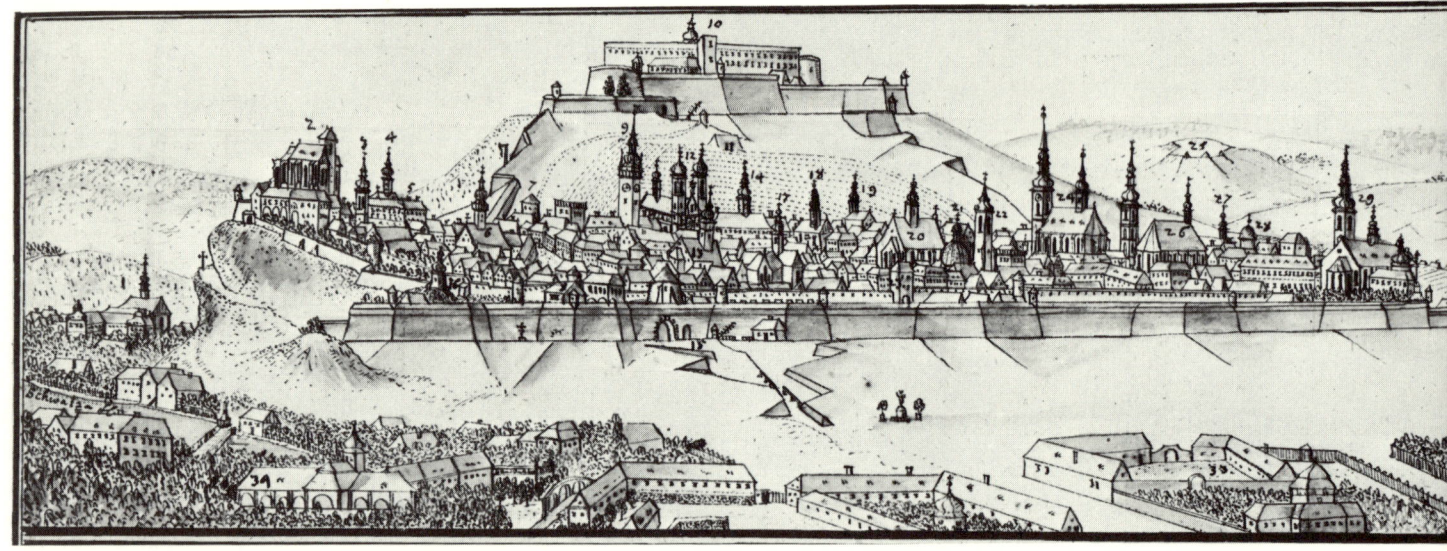

137. Brno from the southeast. Drawing by Friedrich Bernhard Werner, middle of the 18th century.

Leather and engineering works were established a short time later. At Oslavany and Rosice, near Brno, coal mining started. The Brno and also partly the Blansko Iron Works were directly responsible for the further industrial development of the town and its wider hinterland.

Historical Brno still remained confined within its walls, while industrial districts rapidly developed around it. By the end of the 18th century, Brno and its suburbs had about 20,000 inhabitants. The growth of urban industry attracted many country people to the town. Several quarters in the historical center and the older communities in the southeastern part of the town were overpopulated to such a degree by the influx of industrial workers that the pressure of population necessitated a radical solution. Before 1790, the first workers' colony was built on former Austrian territory, known as Šmálka, which existed until recent times. This was near the textile works in Nová ulice, New Street. Scores of large tenement houses were built for the workers near the factories.

A map of 1825 shows Brno still enclosed by walls. However, the fortifications of Špilberk Castle were demolished by order of Napoleon in 1809, and the areas thus gained were laid out as public parks.

After the demolition of the first parts of the fortifications, almost fifty years elapsed before the historic town was freed of its walls. The need of sites suitable for offices and cultural buildings in the town center led, in 1845, to extensive town planning studies. The terrain of the former fortifications was proposed to be built up, and the plan for the present inner circle appeared for the first time. However, it was the plan of 1862 which outlined in detail the formation of a circular road on the site of the dismantled fortifications. This road links up with the railway lines to Vienna and Prague, built several years earlier. In 1850, the historical center of Brno merged with the suburbs to form a single administrative community. By 1880, the town had 83,000 inhabitants.

138. *Opposite page:* **Tower of the early Gothic town hall at Brno (middle of the 13th century), with a Renaissance cupola of 1577 (foreground). In the background the early Baroque Church of St. Michael, completed in 1679.**

Cheb, Western Bohemia. The region of Cheb, encircled by mountains and forests and inhabited by Slavonic people in the eastern part, was united with the Bohemian State in the 10th century during the time of tribal centralization. The center of the whole region was the large Slavonic walled-in settlement of Cheb, the area now occupied by the medieval town nucleus. Its complex development was determined by historical changes resulting from the exposed situation of the town in the Bohemian borderland.

About the middle of the 11th century, the territory of Cheb was incorporated in the German Empire. By the middle of the 12th century, the town had passed into the hands of the Hohenstaufen dynasty. The Emperor Frederick Barbarossa, recognizing the strategic importance of the place, built a strongly fortified castle on the site of the former Slavonic settlement.

The strategic significance of the town as a borderland fortress and a communication and trade center at the junction of long-distance routes soon created conditions propitious for the further growth of the settlement. The town nucleus shows distinct traces of the original street pattern which preceded the regular layout of the town, particularly in regard to the orientation of the main communications artery leading toward the center of Bohemia.

At the beginning of the 13th century, the town was laid out on a regular ground plan, and was further developed after a devastating fire in 1270. The older district of the traders and merchants under the castle walls, with its narrow streets and small squares, differed in a marked way from the large-scale character of the eastern and southeastern parts of the nucleus, with a sloping square as its center. The building blocks adjoining the square, particularly along its southwestern side, were regularly arranged.

In the year 1265, during the reign of King Přemysl Otakar II, the territory of Cheb was returned to the Bohemian State. Many changes in the urban pattern, especially after the great fire of 1270, were due to direct orders by the King. It is probable that at this time Kamenná ulice, Stone Street, was laid out, connecting the square with the new bridge across the river Ohře (Eger). In its neighborhood the hospital of the Prague Order of the Knights of the Cross was established by the King.

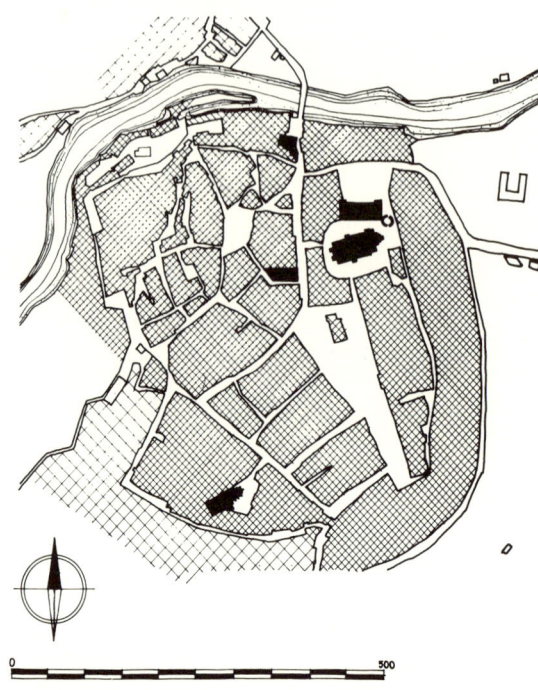

139. Plan of the historic nucleus of Cheb, after a cadastral map of 1841.

About the second half of the 14th century, many wooden or half-timbered houses were replaced by stone buildings.

The Renaissance did not assert itself with much vigor in the architectural scenery of the town. The exterior of the town houses of Cheb differed from that of other medieval Bohemian towns. Since the gutters ran parallel to the street, the rising and falling rhythm of the gables was missing. During this period the building standards for most houses remained rather low.

During the Thirty Years' War, the construction of a Baroque fortification system was begun, and the castle was changed into a citadel. The work took about a century to be completed.

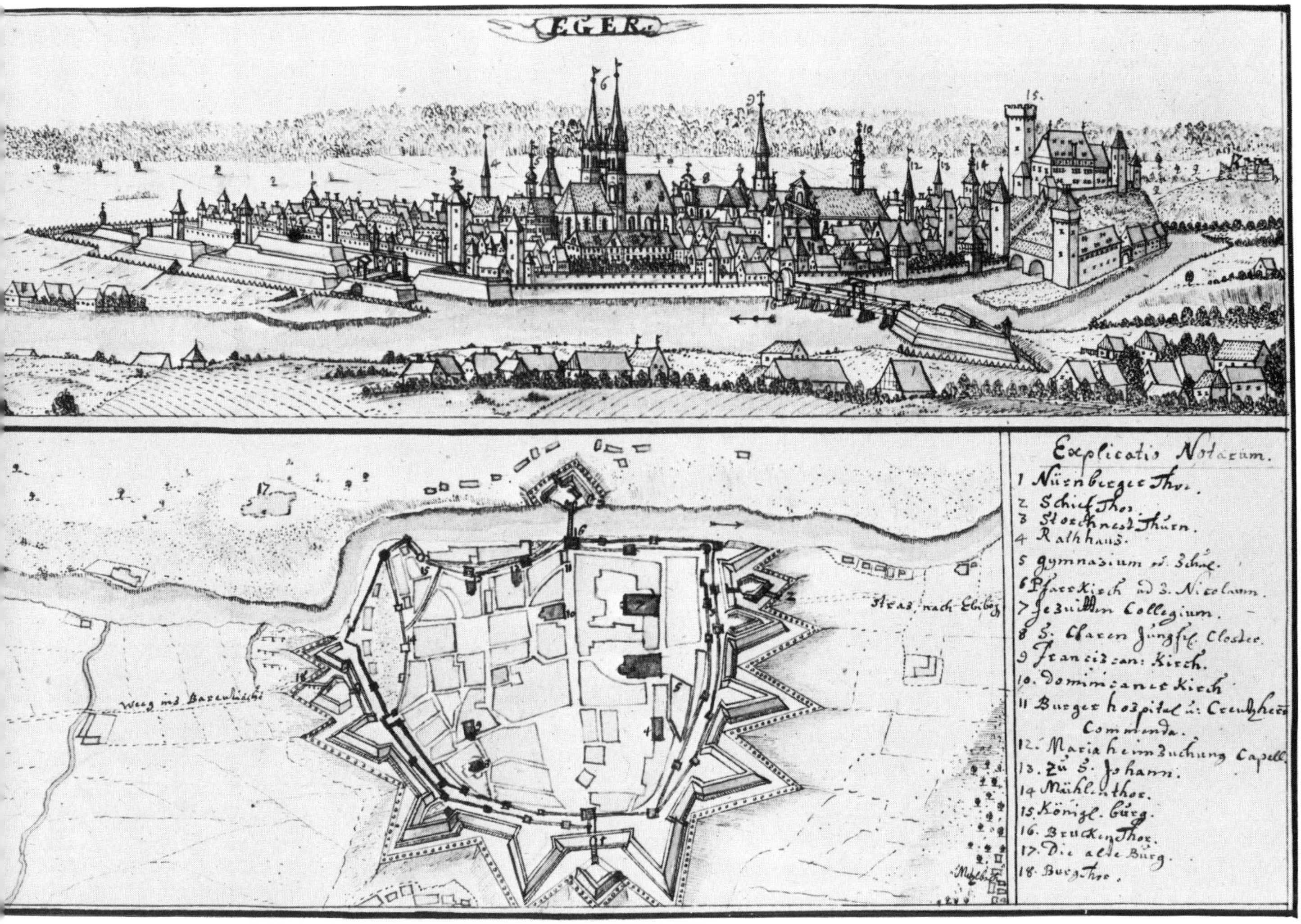

140. Plan and view of Cheb by Friedrich Bernhard Werner, middle of the 18th century.

141. Burgher's house at Cheb, built in the Middle Ages, with a Rococo façade, on the eastern side of the main square.

142. View of Cheb from the northwest. In the center, the Church of St. Nicholas (13th to 15th century), behind it the Gothic Minorite Church; on the right, the ruins of the Imperial Castle with the Black Tower.

During the earlier periods, the physical appearance of Cheb was only sporadically influenced by the architecture of the rest of Bohemia. It was not until the Baroque era that the town reflected the general tendencies of Bohemian art.

The Classicist period failed to enrich the appearance of Cheb. Nor did the great fires of 1792 and 1809 lead to more intensive building activities. This situation continued until the middle of the 19th century, when the suburbs began to expand and the historic nucleus lost its former significance as a town center.

Chomutov, Northern Bohemia. The town of Chomutov is an important center in the densely populated area at the foot of the Erz Mountains, Krušné Hory, in North Bohemia. In early feudal times, a village was founded at the ford over the Chomutovka brook. This village gradually changed into a borough, an *oppidum*, probably as early as the first half of the 13th century. In 1252, the feudal lord donated the borough of Chomutov to the Knights of the Teutonic Order, who erected there a stronghold. Not long afterward a walled town was founded on the site.

The center of the town is occupied by an oblong square. It widens at its northwestern corner to an irregularly shaped area dominated by the two main architectural symbols of the city, the parish church and the castle.

143. Square at Chomutov. On the right, the early Baroque Jesuit church (second half of the 17th century).

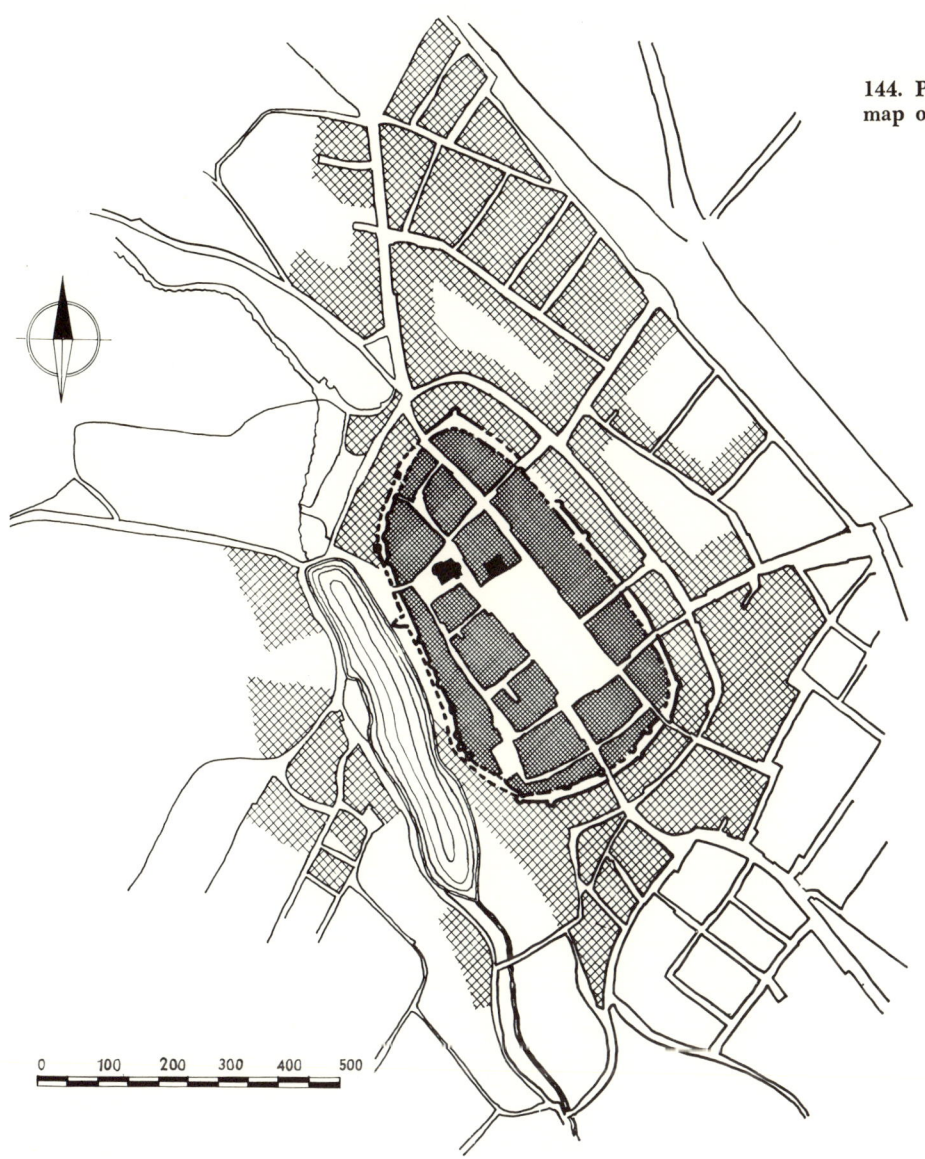

144. Plan of Čáslav, after a cadastral map of the middle of the 19th century.

Čáslav, Eastern Bohemia. Since the early feudal period, the stronghold of Čáslav has been the center of a large administrative district in East Bohemia, giving its name to the whole region. The oldest settlement existed at a place called *Hrádek,* that is, stronghold, which was separated from the present town by a shallow ravine. The site was later occupied by the castle of the barons of Chlum and the Church of the Virgin Mary. The settlement which rose in the vicinity of the ancient stronghold and castle occupied the site of the present parish church.

About 1260, Přemysl Otakar II, King of Bohemia, ordered his *locator,* Konrád Špitálský, to found a Royal Town on this favorable and traditional site, demanding that the town should have "three gates with towers, rounded towers, walls of the same width and height as in Kolín, and a water gate." These stipulations, including the water gate, were characteristic of the contemporary type of city walls. However, the document is even more valuable for its reference to the previously founded town of Kolín.

The experienced *locator* founded a magnificently designed town of an oval layout, with a rectangular square of about 820 by 328 feet. The town had double walls along its whole circumference, except along the southeastern

225

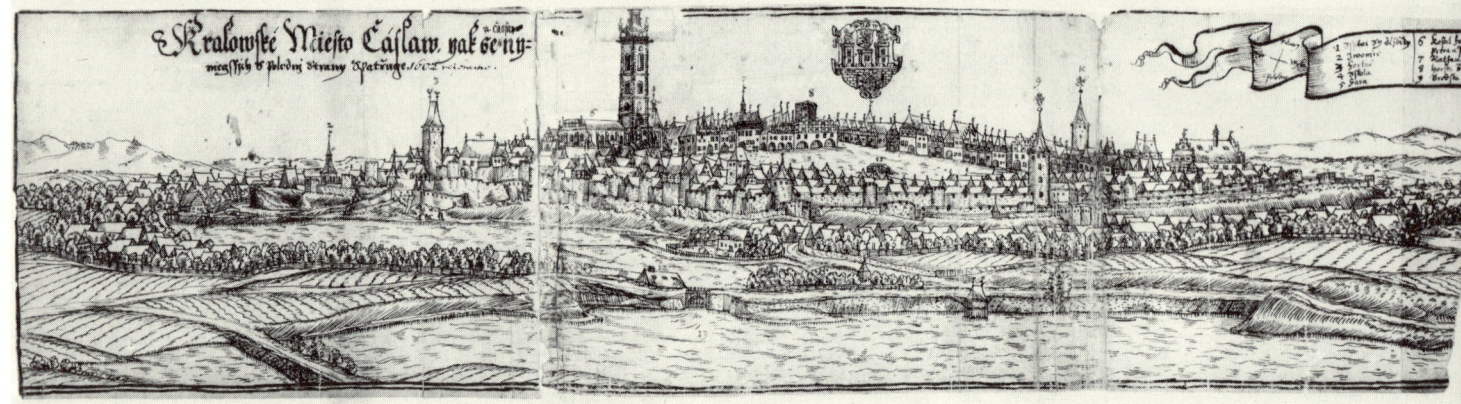

145. Drawing of the town of Čáslav by Johann Willenberg, 1602.

side. Here it was protected by a large artificial pond filled with waters from the Brlanka stream, eliminating the need for double walls along this side.

The two centuries from 1420 to 1620 were most prosperous for the town. It played an important part in the Hussite Movement when the Hussite Diet convened in Čáslav in June, 1421.

Punishment inflicted on the town for its participation in the rebellion against King Ferdinand in 1547 marked the beginning of its decline, ending in almost complete destruction during the Thirty Years' War. For a long time the town could not recover from these calamities. The only event of importance was the construction of a late Baroque town hall in 1765, which replaced the original Gothic building.

The town has retained its historic layout and the large rectangular square with a number of historic houses, the oldest dating from the second half of the 13th century. Its most important building, dominating its surroundings, is the church.

České Budějovice, Southern Bohemia. The situation of the town of České Budějovice, just below the confluence of the rivers Vltava and Malše on a flat strip of land sloping down toward the west and east, was particularly favorable for settlement. In the early feudal period, a small place with a church consecrated to St. Procopius originated on the east river bank. The advantage of this situation, in the center of the South Bohemian basin, was recognized by King Přemysl Otakar II, who founded in 1265 a fortified Royal Town about one mile south of the original settlement, at the confluence of both rivers and a stream. This new place formed an important link in the ingenious strategic system of Royal Towns situated at a certain distance from the frontiers of the country.

České Budějovice is one of the best examples of medieval town planning during the period of Přemysl Otakar II. The oval layout, somewhat deformed in its southern half, was partly dictated by the direction of the rivers, which afforded natural protection from the southwest and west as well as an ample water supply.

The effort to lay out a rectangular street system was highly successful. The center of the town was occupied by a large oblong square, with the streets entering it at the corners. The rectangular blocks around the square were more or less identical. The streets, crossing each other at right angles, formed a checkerboard pattern. The parish church was situated on a regular oblong block, connected with the northeastern corner of the main square. The historic center of the town measured approximately 2,290 by 1,500 feet.

Immediately after the foundation of the town, the construction of the walls and the church of St. Nicholas was begun. The main wall was strengthened by semicircular bastions and later, in the second half of the 14th century, by rectangular towers. An outer wall with bastions, no longer existing, was added in the later Middle Ages.

Several hundred old houses, partially dating from the 15th century, have been preserved in the historic center of České Budějovice. In the late Gothic period, the houses on the square were provided with arcades. However, the main period of reconstruction was the third quarter of the 16th century. Within a short time, České Budějovice changed into a beautiful Renaissance town with two-storied stone houses. The arcades were not limited to the square but extended gradually to the majority of the streets, giving a very specific and homogeneous character to the town.

České Budějovice retained its strategic importance during the Thirty Years' War. After 1639, it was surrounded with simple late-Renaissance fortifications with triangular bastions.

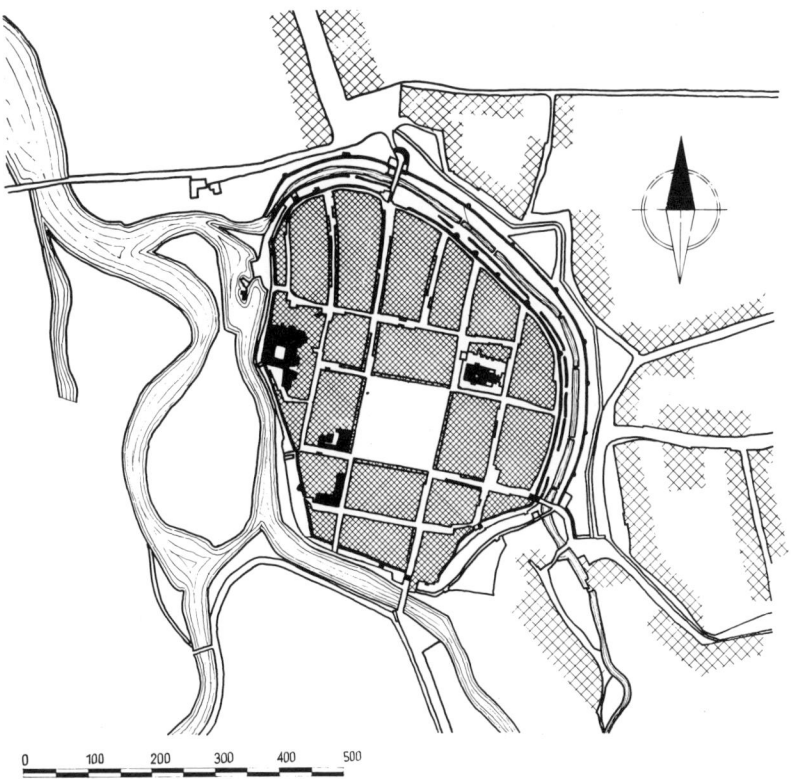

146. Plan of the historic core of České Budějovice, after a cadastral map of 1827.

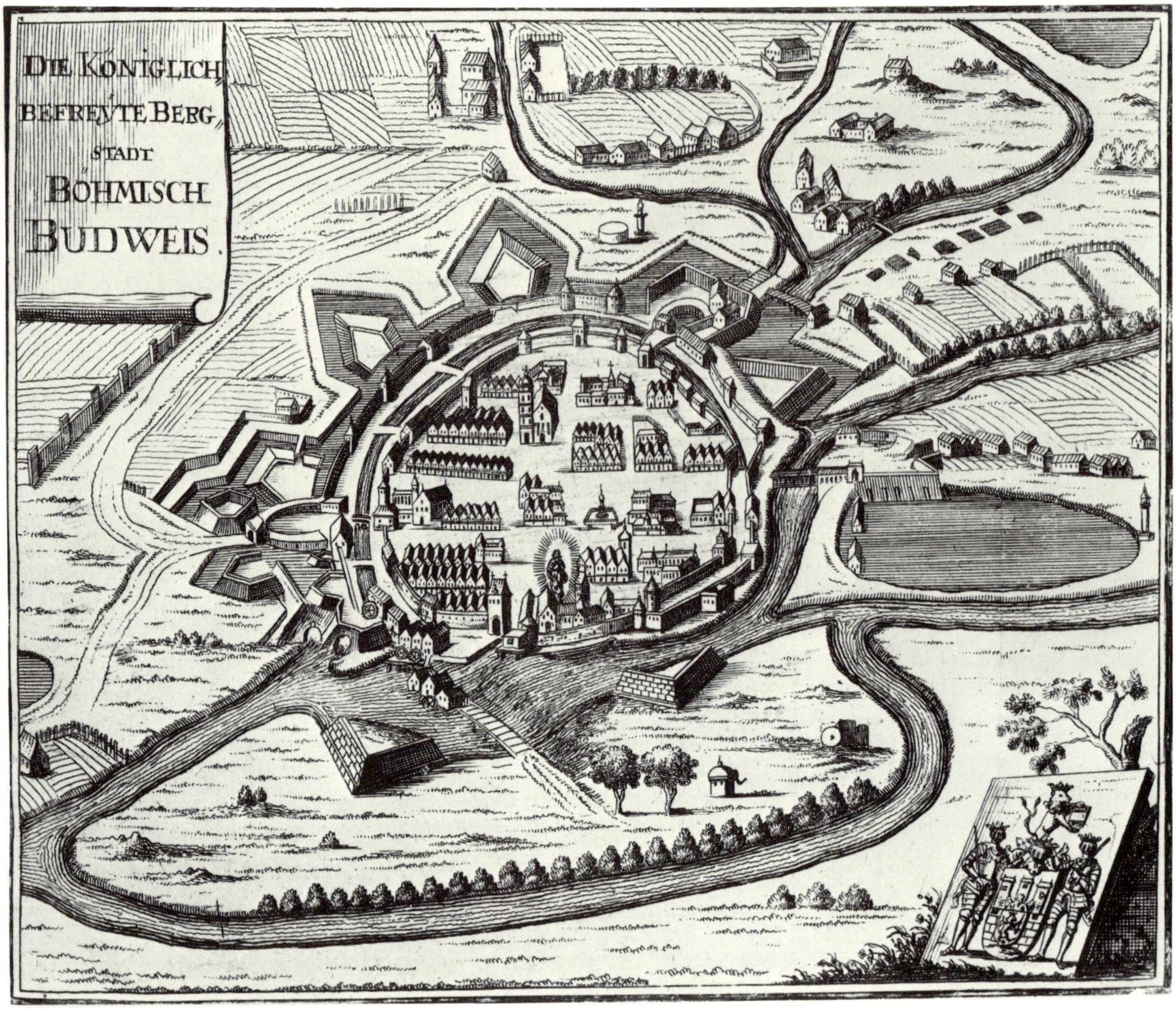

147. *Above:* View of České Budějovice in 1666.

148. General view of the square at České Budějovice, with typical arcades. In the corner, the Renaissance town hall, rebuilt in the Baroque style in 1730.

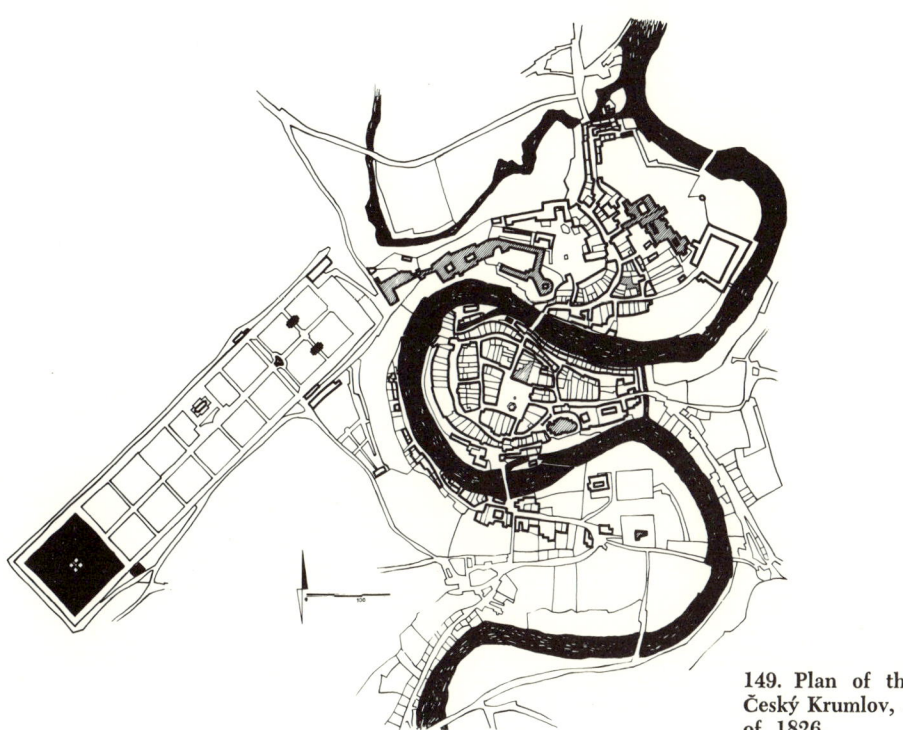

149. Plan of the historical core of Český Krumlov, after a cadastral map of 1826.

Český Krumlov, Southern Bohemia. Český Krumlov, on the meandering Vltava, presents a combination of dramatic landscape and monumental architecture. Its origin must have been inconspicuous since the town is situated at a distance from the main roads. The castle of Krumlov, seat of the feudal family of Vítkovec, was first mentioned in 1253. The existence of the castle was the reason for the founding of the town.

Český Krumlov was laid out in the second half of the 13th century on a pear-shaped headland above the river Vltava, opposite the castle, and connected with the neighboring territory by a narrow neck of land. The plan of the town nucleus was determined by the uneven ground and the size and shape of the area, so that the rectangular system could be applied only with considerable limitation.

The main city walls date from the beginning of the 14th century. In 1347, the town on the headland was merged with the community of Latrán into a single legal whole. Owing to its privileges, Český Krumlov equaled a Royal Town.

During the reigns of King Charles IV and Wenceslas IV, the prosperity of the town increased. About the middle of the 14th century a Minorite convent was founded outside the walls of Latrán, which was followed by the Convent of St. Clare and, at the end of the century, by a *beguinage*. The houses of the so-called New Town rose under the protection of the convent buildings.

150. Drawing of Český Krumlov by Friedrich Bernhard Werner, middle of the 18th century.

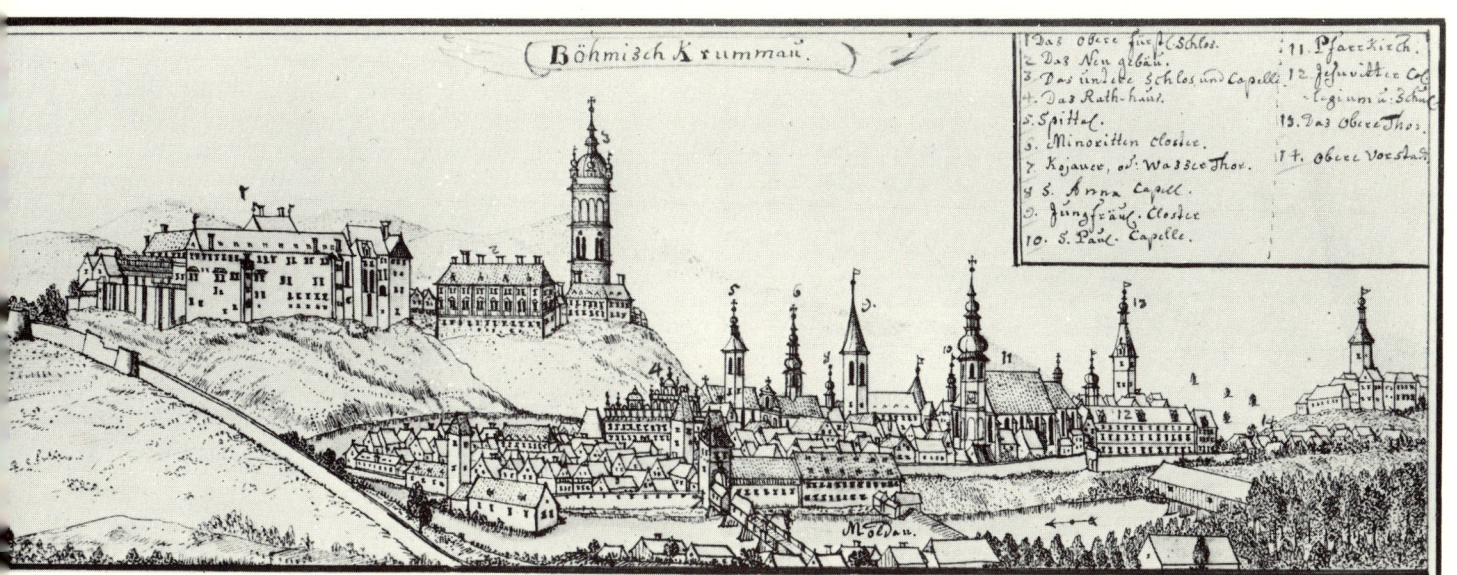

151. Partial view of Český Krumlov on both banks of the Vltava River. On the left, the Latrán, the old suburb below the castle; on the right, the town with the Gothic church built by Master Jan, nephew of Master Staněk (1407–1439).

Thanks to the firm rule of the feudal lords of Southern Bohemia, the Rožmberk family (known also as Lords of the Rose, after a five-petal rose in their coat of arms), who were foremost opponents of the Hussite movement, the town was saved from the disastrous effects of the war.

The Renaissance left a notable imprint on the architectural appearance of the town. Houses received new vaulted interiors, and façades were adorned with graffito decorations. Street fronts on either river bank were enriched by picturesque gables and attics. The motif of projecting stories supported by corbels was introduced into the architecture of the town.

The building activities of the Renaissance were not limited to the walled town and the Krumlov Castle. The suburbs were greatly extended, spreading far into the surrounding country. At the beginning of the Thirty Years' War, the town of Český Krumlov was one of the most imposing and solidly built towns of the Bohemian State.

Dolní Bojanovice, Southern Moravia. An ethnographical region, known as Moravian Slovakia, with an individual type of folk architecture, developed in the flat countryside of Southeastern Moravia. This fertile region was inhabited since the beginning of the Slavonic occupation of the country. Here, a number of villages developed, with rows of single-story buildings. The characteristic feature of these villages is their wide village green, which usually originated as the result of the location of farmsteads on both sides of a stream. The core of the village green of Dolní Bojanovice, mentioned for the first time in 1196, began in this way. The historic center of the village is dominated by the parish church. It is situated on a gentle slope, on the edge of the northern row of farmsteads, and is surrounded by a churchyard. It acquired its present appearance when it was reconstructed in 1734. The village was later extended by streets lined with two rows of farmsteads. At the end of this part of the village, a group of small cottages grew up. Toward the close of the 18th century small houses rose along subsidiary roads and, finally, on the original space of the village green itself.

The characteristic feature of the local architecture was a farmstead whose longer side extended along the village green or the road. The single-story house was adjoined by a farmyard, a barn being situated at the outer edge of the site. In Moravian Slovakia the houses were built mostly of clay. The soft surface of the buildings, which were covered with thatched roofs, led to the application of painted ornaments and the intensive use of color in the interiors of the houses, for which its architecture became famous. The entrances to the houses are protected by a kind of porch, called a *žudro*, which resembles an arcade moulded from clay. The façades of the houses, as well as the front parts of their porches and windows, were decorated with gaily colored vegetable motives.

In addition to its agriculture, this region is also known for its viticulture. A characteristic feature of the villages are the large wine cellars, forming separate architectural units next to the dwellings.

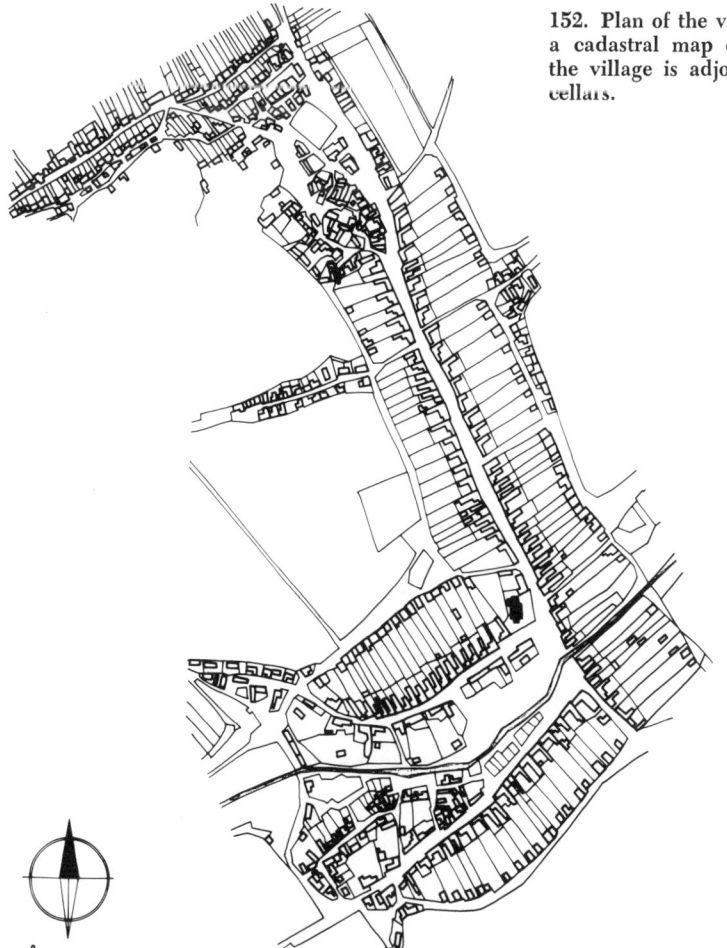

152. Plan of the village of Dolní Bojanovice, after a cadastral map of 1827. The northern side of the village is adjoined by a large group of wine cellars.

Domažlice, Western Bohemia. In the early feudal era, a frontier customhouse and a castle of the Přemyslides stood near a pass, on the old trade route leading from Bohemia to Regensburg. The community growing up around the castle developed along this trade route.

About the year 1260, Přemysl Otakar II built a fortified Royal Town in a good strategic position, to the west of the original settlement, and made it the administrative center of the border region.

The layout of the town was obviously influenced by the route of an old path, which was used as the axis of the large, longitudinal main part of the square, whose length was about 1,140 feet.

Domažlice ranks among the important historic towns of Czechoslovakia. In spite of numerous fires and dangerous frontier conflicts, it has retained its layout and a large number of architectural monuments.

The houses at the square, with arcades and Baroque or Classicist gardens, date mostly from the 16th century, the period in which the original wooden constructions were replaced with stone buildings.

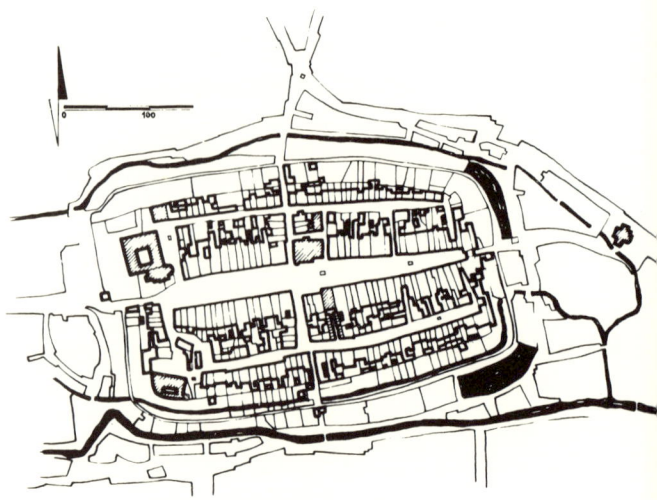

153. Plan of the historic core of Domažlice, after a cadastral map of 1838.

154. The "Lower" Gate of the last quarter of the 13th century at Domažlice.

232

Františkovy Lázně, Western Bohemia. The founding of Františkovy Lázně, Franzensbad, at the foot of the Erz Mountains, was in many ways similar to the origin of the later spa of Mariánské Lázně. The curative springs, in the shallow hollow of a swampy peatbog on territory belonging to the town of Cheb, were known since the later part of the Middle Ages. Empirical therapy was practiced at the end of the 16th century and, as early as 1707, the first building of the spa for guests was erected near the Franz Spring.

In 1781, apparently on the suggestion of Dr. Bernhard Adler of Cheb, the regional government decided that plans for a spa with the necessary institutions—a colonnade, parks, pathways, avenues, and individual buildings—should be worked out under the supervision of Father Tobias Gruber.

In the Czech lands, this project represents a unique example of the combination of rational Classicist town planning principles and those of the conventional fortifications system of a feudal town. The oblong plan of 705.20 by 738 feet, with a gridiron system of streets, resembles the layout of the fortified towns of Terezín and Josefov, founded in 1780 and 1781, respectively, though without fortifications. Františkovy Lázně has no town square. Instead, geometrically laid-out parks have been added in the north and south to the oblong urban center. The town itself is divided by two streets running north into three series of blocks that are interconnected by small streets. The third street, running north to south and dividing the eastern section, was built only gradually. The *point de vue* of both streets lies in the adjoining parks,

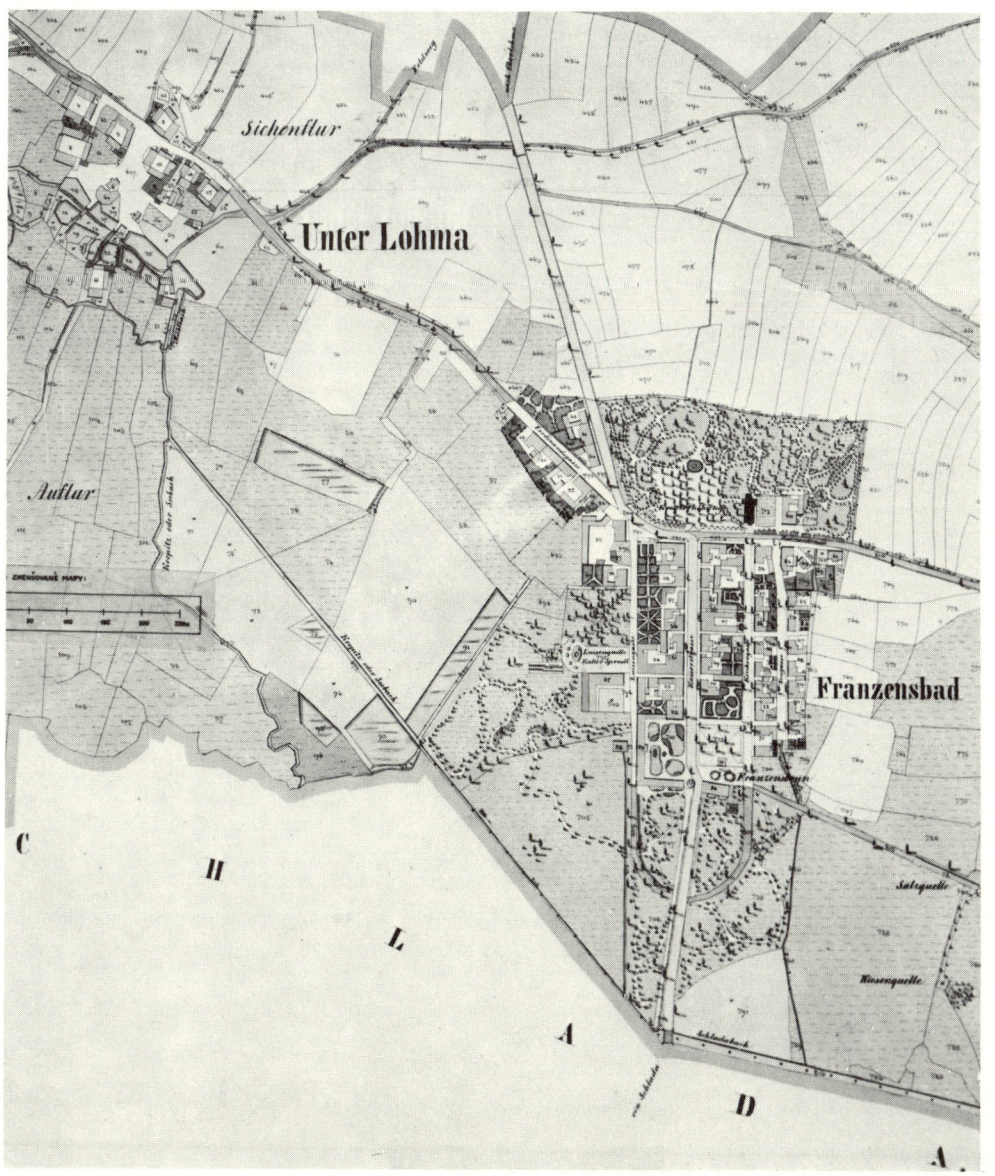

155. Reproduction of a cadastral map of Františkovy Lázně (1841), showing that parks had already been laid out on the northern, southern, and western sides of the town and that the swampy stream had been regulated.

233

while that of the main western axis, the Emperor Street, is the pavilion with the Franz Spring at the southern end and the rondel in the axis of the avenue on the northern side. The view from Church Street, completed in 1812, is a church built at the request of Emperor Franz I, according to a design by the Building Office of the Court.

The construction of the spa progressed rapidly, from the year 1792 to the Napoleonic Wars. In 1795, the construction of the Assembly Hall, with a ballroom and a restaurant on the southern side, was completed, together with a U-shaped colonnade housing the Franz Spring. Apart from these buildings, a road and a bridge leading to Cheb were built. The surrounding swamps were drained, and the area thus gained turned into parks with avenues of trees. During the Napoleonic Wars construction slowed down but, despite the conflict, the church was built, as well as a riding school.

After the war, the discovery of three new springs instigated further development of the spa. In 1827, the first public baths were built near the Louise Spring on the western side of the oblong sections of the town, and the first mud baths were opened. By the middle of the century the timber buildings of the colonnade and the pavilions were rebuilt in stone, together with a school, a theater, and residential buildings. In 1852, when the community became independent, the whole of Františkovy Lázně had 47 buildings.

By the middle of the 19th century, further construction was carried out by private entrepeneurs. In 1853, the regional government decreed mandatory maintenance of the individual character, architecture, and color scheme of every single building. The draining of the bogs and the establishment of parks surrounding the Classicist oblong core of the spa resulted in the creation of a greenbelt only partly interspersed by buildings. After 1865, the street system was further extended, with access roads leading to the station on the northern side of the central area. At the beginning of World War I, the architectural development of the spa had practically come to an end. The Classicist core of the town, with its single and two-storied buildings, sober façades, avenues of trees and surrounding parks, has been preserved to the present.

Frýdlant, Northern Bohemia. Frýdlant Castle was built in the middle of the 13th century by the feudal family of Ronovici as one of the four strategic strongpoints of their domain, on a steep basalt rock at the confluence of the little river Smědá and the brook Řásnice, in the northern part of the mountain chain of Jizerské hory. To the southeast of the castle, a small town of very regular pattern was laid out, with an almost circular outline. To the west, an earlier village of fishermen was located, probably older than the castle. At first the town flourished, due to its situation on new trade routes leading from Prague to Zhořelec (Görlitz) and from Žitava (Zittau) to the territory of Kladsko (Glatz). Later, however, the development of the town was impaired by the long struggle between the two wealthy trading centers of Zhořelec and Žitava over the use of these trade routes, resulting in the closing down of both roads.

Brick town walls, reinforced with square bastions and the towers of three gateways (now demolished), encircled nine blocks of dwelling houses that surrounded the central square. The town hall was located in the center of the square. The skyline of the town, including the castle and the palace, is dominated by the tower of the parish church.

In the second half of the 15th century and during the whole of the 16th century, the town prospered. The castle of Frýdlant was then rebuilt and changed into a palace. After the loss of the territory of Lusatia, Lužnice, only the Frýdlant region of the former territory of Žitava remained part of the Bohemian Kingdom. The town of Frýdlant has maintained the tradition of its textile industry from the 14th century, when Frýdlant had trade connections with the whole of Western Europe.

156. Plan of Frýdlant, after a cadastral map of 1841.

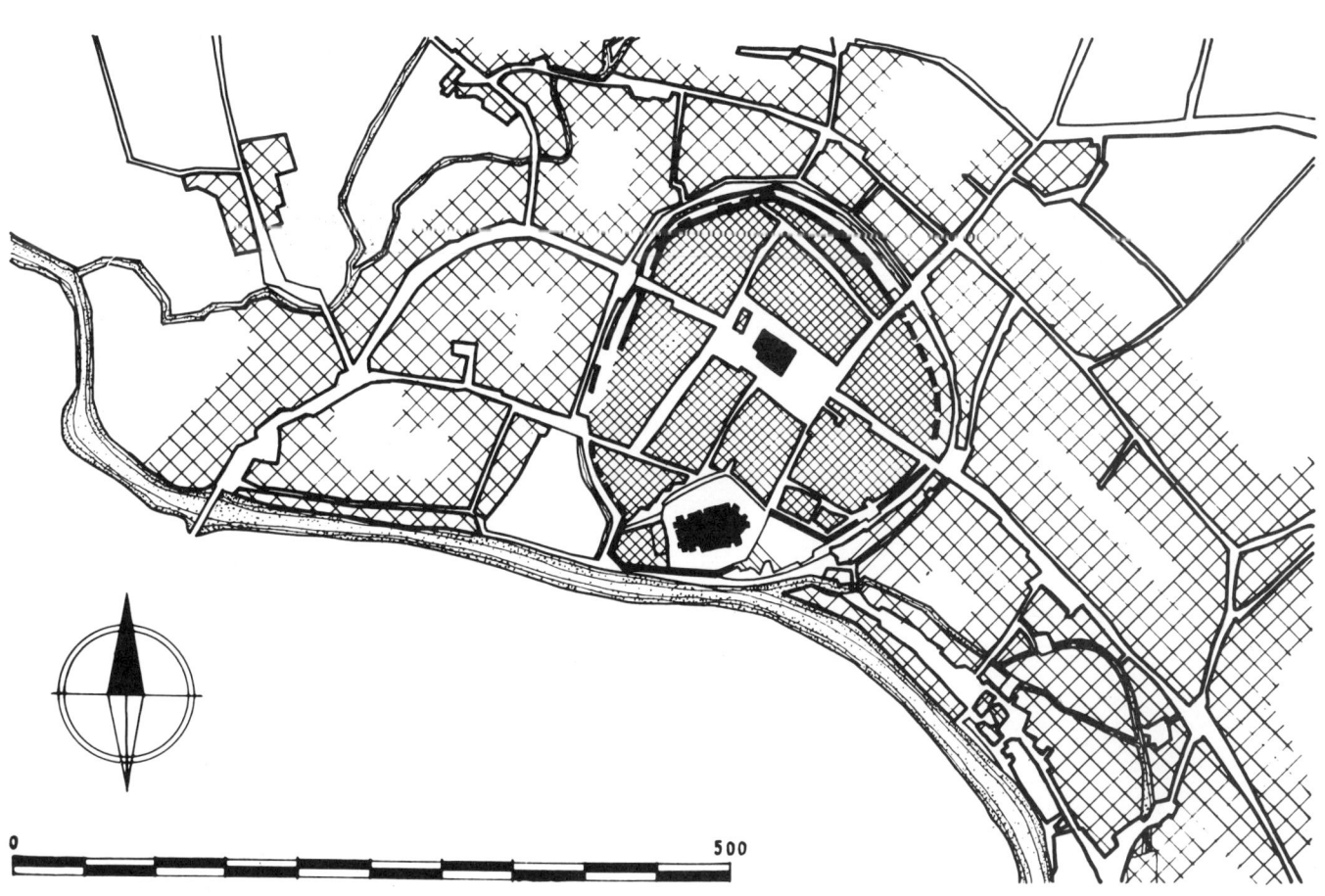

Fulnek, Northern Moravia. The history of the town of Fulnek has often been marred by tragic events. Yet despite all disasters—the last one a fire at the end of the war in 1945—it has retained its artistic legacy, mainly from the Baroque period.

The early origin of the town is unknown. It is possible that the town stands on the site of an older settlement, at the trade route connecting the center of Moravia with Silesia and Poland. It was situated near the Moravian-Silesian border and was protected by a strong fortified castle, a link in the system of frontier strongholds. By the year 1293, Fulnek was known as a town. Its gridiron plan followed the principles of all the early colonial settlements. The center was occupied by a square, now lined on three sides with rows of houses and dominated by the tall Renaissance tower of the town hall.

During the Renaissance the economic and cultural significance of the town increased. When Fulnek became the center of the Bohemian Reformation Movement, the edifice of the religious community of the Moravian Brethren was erected. In the following period, until the end of the 17th century, the Counter Reformation contributed greatly to the intensive building activities, stimulating the economic development of the place.

To this period, especially to the years from 1748 to 1760, belong the parish church and the adjoining rebuilt Augustinian Convent founded in 1389. The influence of the Counter Reformation led to the founding of another convent in 1674 by the Capuchine Order. At this time, the square and the neighborhood of the churches were adorned with Baroque sculptures. The Baroque rebuilding of the town was completed by the reconstruction of the castle, located on the summit of a steep hill and rising as a dramatic dominant over the town square.

157. Old view of Fulnek.

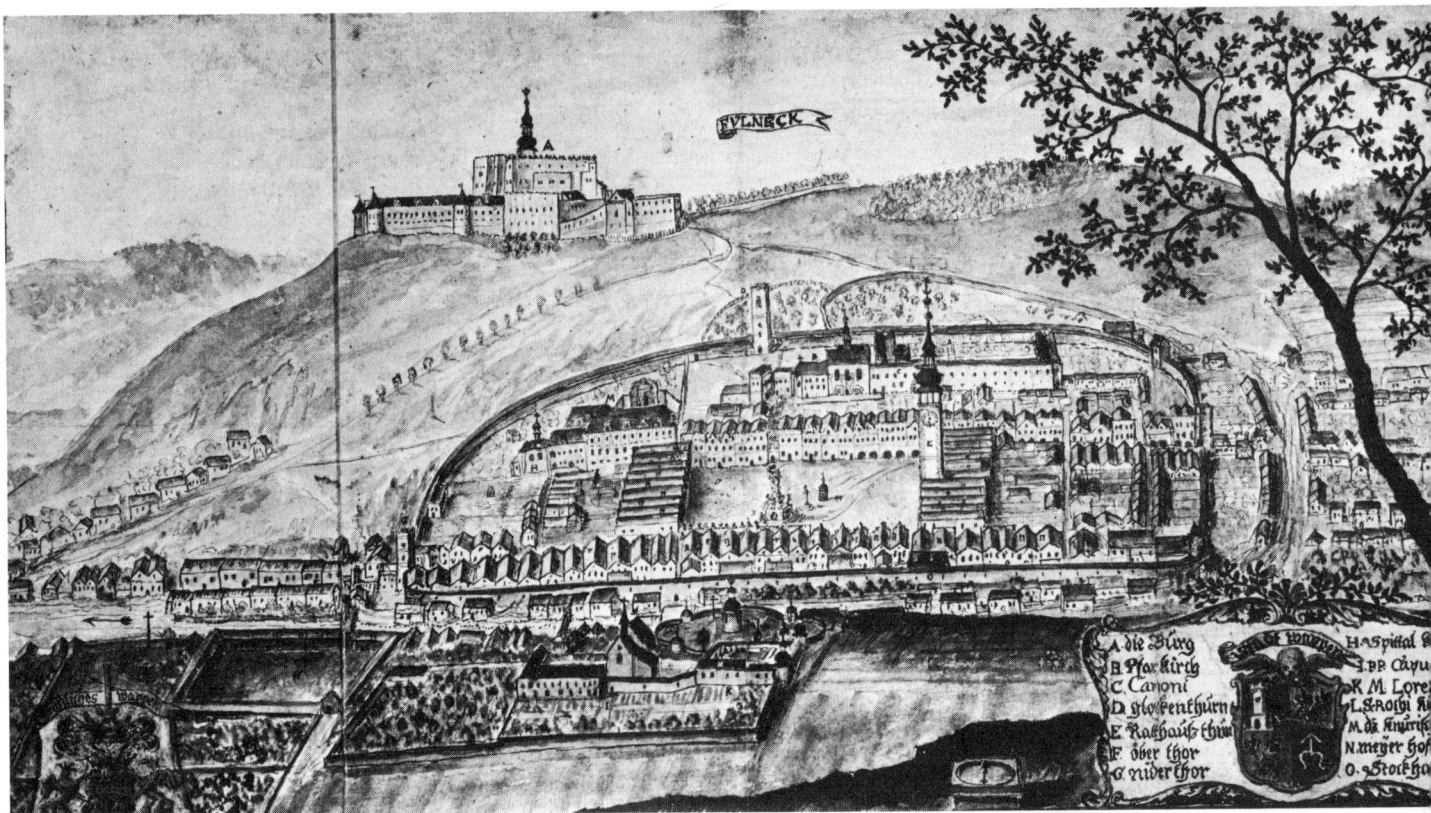

Hradec Králové, Eastern Bohemia. The triangular elevation above the confluence of the rivers Labe (Elbe) and Orlice, sloping steeply down in all directions and traversed by a ravine, was always considered a particularly suitable site for settlement. Even before the formation of the Bohemian State, a walled-in Slavonic settlement was located within the boundaries of the historical nucleus of the later town of Hradec. This settlement was the political center of Eastern Bohemia during the early feudal period, whose significance did not decline even after the centralization of the country under the Přemyslide dynasty. The town, called *Castrum Gradec,* became also the seat of an archdeaconship in 1073.

It may be assumed that the early center of the town occupied the site of the later royal castle, near the northern end of the walled-in settlement.

The importance of this center of Eastern Bohemia was the chief reason for raising Hradec to a Royal Town during the reign of King Přemysl Otakar I, probably in 1225. It is the earliest example of a regular town mentioned in written documents.

The new town occupied the entire area of the early walled-in settlement, on either side of the ravine. The shape of the headland and the incorporated early feudal centers did not permit the full development of a rectangular layout. The triangular shape of the Great Square very probably indicates traces of an earlier arrangement.

In the neighborhood of the castle a Minorite convent was founded. It disappeared at a later date, leaving no traces of its former existence. The limited size of the historical nucleus was the reason why, in the early days of the town, the newly founded Dominican monastery was located on an island in the river Elbe and, several decades later, a convent of Dominican nuns was erected in the suburbs.

The Hussite wars had a strong effect upon the architectural appearance of the town. The royal castle was destroyed, along with all the convents and several of the churches in the suburbs. These losses, however, were more than counterbalanced by the outstanding ideological and political position of the town attained in the course of the Hussite Revolution, when Hradec was one of the revolutionary centers. The body of the greatest military leader of the Hussite "Warriors of God," Jan Žižka of Trocnov, who died in 1424, lies interred under the pavement of the Church of the Holy Ghost.

It took a considerable time for the town to recover from the damages inflicted by the wars. One of the significant enterprises following the Hussite wars was the strengthening of the city walls. A conspicuous change in the aspect of the town itself did not take place till the end of the Gothic and the beginning of the Renaissance periods. In the few decades following the second half of the 16th century, many town houses were built, mostly with elaborate gables.

On the eve of the Thirty Years' War, Hradec Králové belonged to the most important towns of Bohemia, possessing more than seven hundred houses. During the war, its suburbs suffered the greatest damage. In the difficult years of the war's aftermath, building initiative was limited almost exclusively to the Church, the main stimulus being the founding of the Hradec bishopric. The first and greatest enterprise of the postwar period was sponsored by the Jesuit Order. In 1654 the building of the Church of our Lady was begun with twin church towers, later joined by the monumental edifice of the college. The church and college occupied the former site of eleven demolished houses that had been part of a block at the southern side of the Great Square.

The following periods brought about striking changes in the architectural appearance of the town nucleus. During the first decades of the 18th century, the Church of St. John of Nepomuk was built on the site of the former

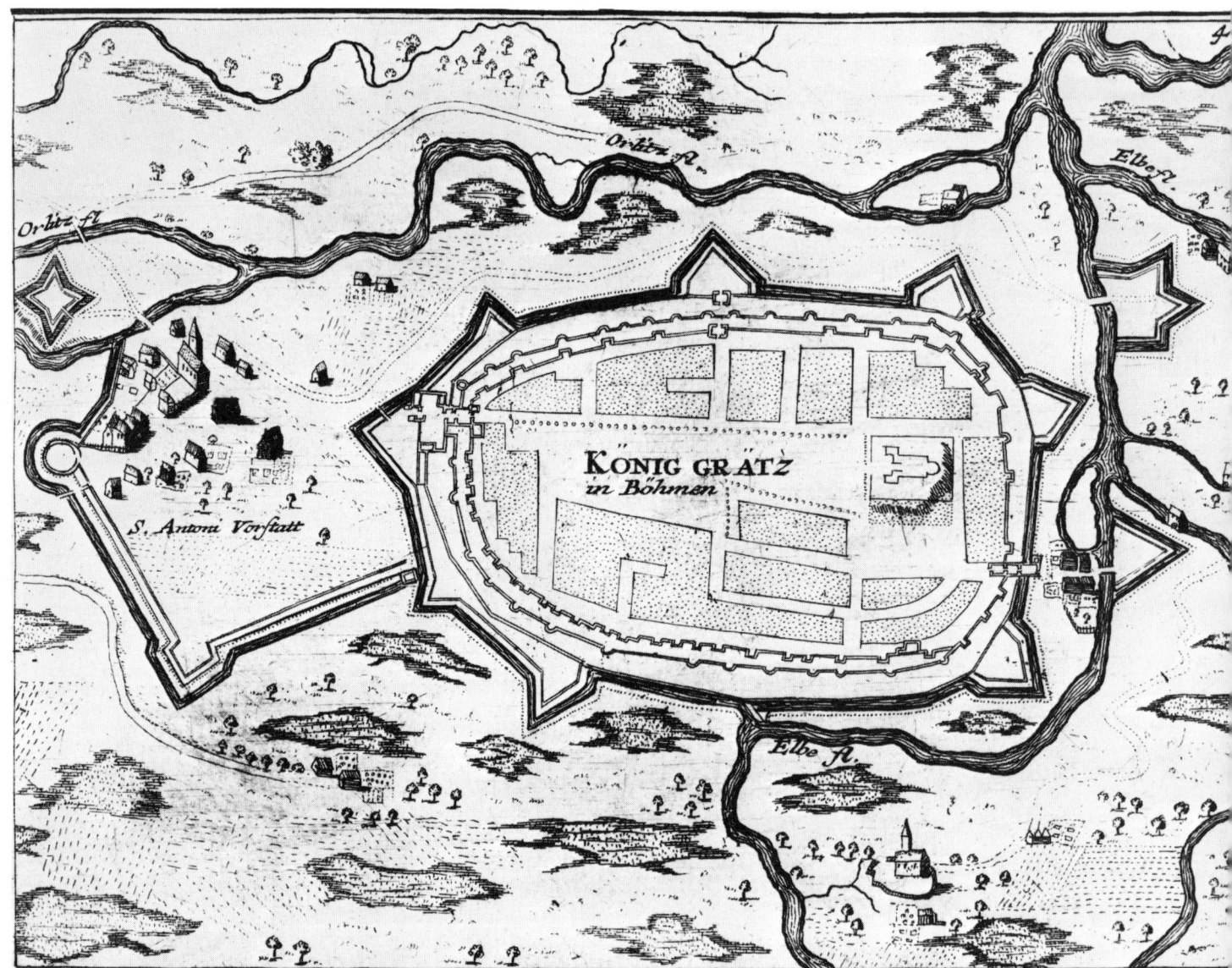

158. Plan of Hradec Králové. Engraving by Matthaeus Merian from *Topographia Bohemiae, Moraviae et Silesiae*, Frankfurt, 1650.

castle; and St. Clement's Church, several canons' houses, and the Episcopal residence were restored. At the western side of the Great Square a new town hall was erected in 1742, with twin towers added in the eighties of the 18th century. In the year 1748, the total number of houses amounted to four hundred and nine. After the great fire of 1762, Hradec never quite recovered its earlier prosperity.

The strategic significance of the town was particularly evident during the Silesian Wars. The fortifications of Hradec Králové were reinforced in 1745, a work for which sixty houses had to be pulled down in the Prague suburb close to the Prague Gate. After the Seven Years' War, Hradec was still regarded as of great military importance, a consideration which eventually led to the decision to make it a strong fortress. Construction began in 1766. All the suburbs were demolished, together with some churches built only a short time before. The town nucleus was enclosed with a complex system of contemporary fortifications, a work not completed until 1789.

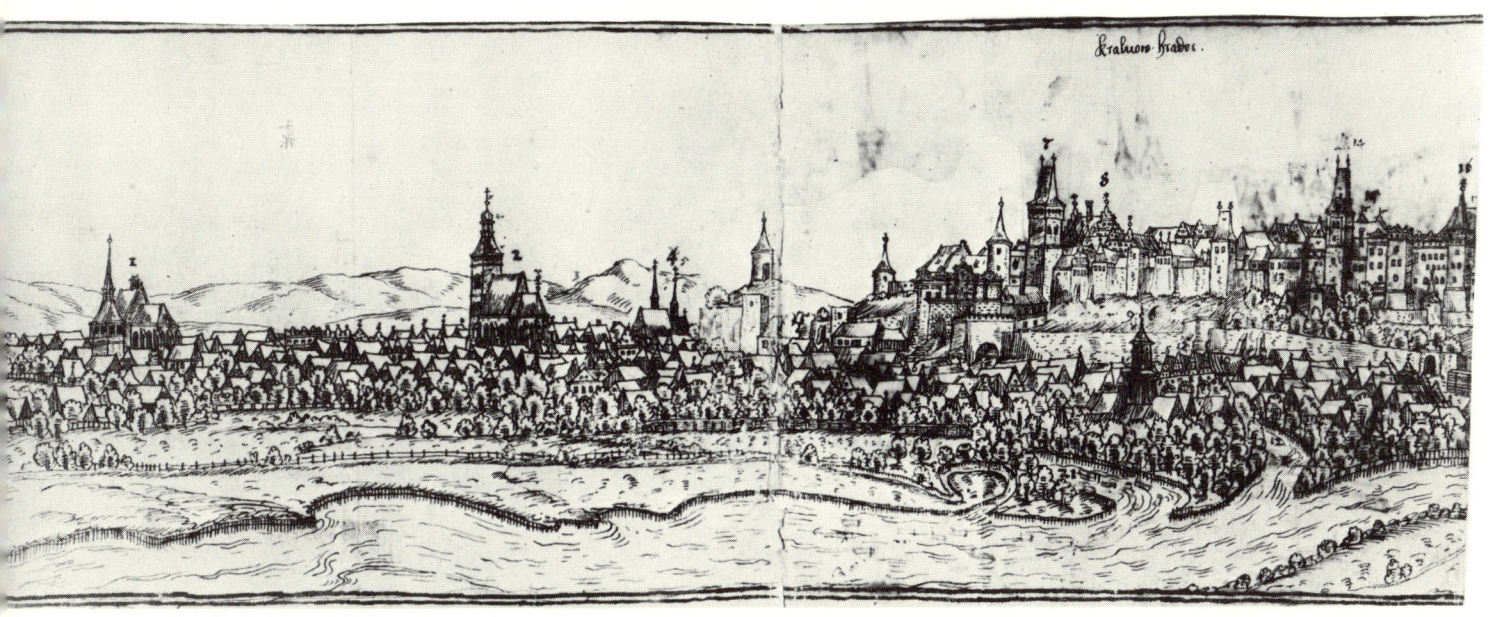

159. View of the western part of Hradec Králové with the suburb of Prague. Drawing by J. Willenberg from the turn of the 16th century.

160. Plan of the citadel of Hradec Králové before its construction in 1766.

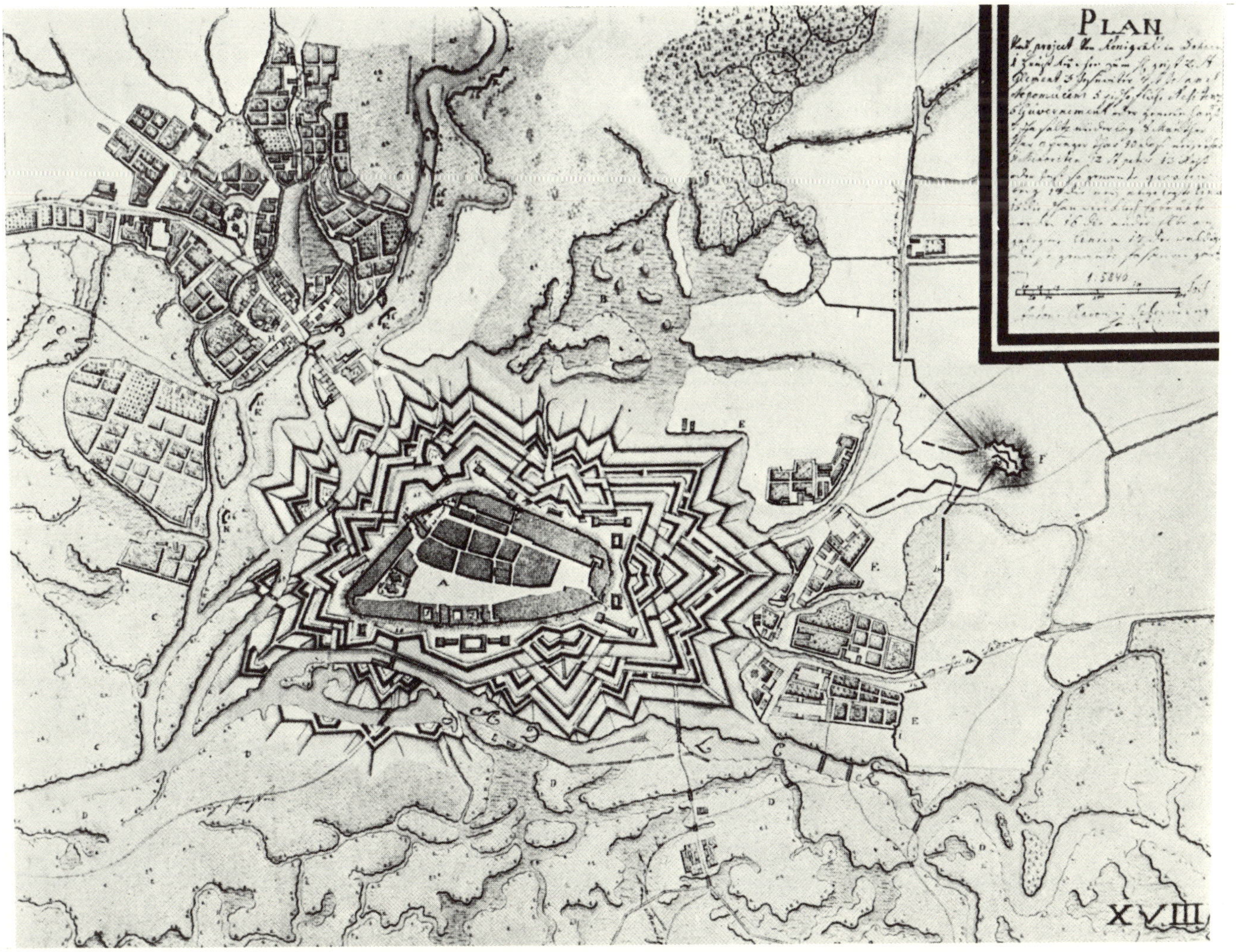

161. Plan of the village of Hruštín, after a cadastral map of 1874.

Hruštín, Central Slovakia. The village of Hruštín is situated in the Orava region, in the northern part of Central Slovakia, District of Námestovo, at a height of 2,286 feet above sea level. It was founded about 1580, in the last period of colonization of the Orava region, on the basis of the Vallachian law, *ius valachale*, in a wooded, unfertile area.

Like other Slovak villages of the time developing along one or both sides of adjoining secondary communications, Hruštín grew along a road connecting Oravský Podzámok and Námestovo.

The individual farms are now enclosed on all sides. The front of every plot is occupied by the farmhouse, adjoined by wooden outbuildings. With the exception of the stables, built of stone, all buildings are of timber and roofed with wooden shingles. A characteristic feature of the houses at Hruštín are their gables, whose peculiar shape is probably due to a chamber originally situated in the attic.

The population of the more than forty Vallachian villages in the Orava region was occupied mainly with cattle breeding and lumbering. In some periods, their duties have included the defense of the frontiers.

162. A row of farm houses at Hruštín from the 19th and 20th centuries.

Jaroměř and Josefov, Eastern Bohemia. The confluence of the rivers Elbe (Labe) and Úpa, particularly the place where the Elbe was crossed by a route leading to the region of Kladsko (Glatz), has since time immemorial been a favorable site for settlement. An early Slavonic stronghold on the west bank of the river was succeeded by the castle of Jaroměř, founded most probably by Prince Jaromír (1004–1012) on a headland east of the Elbe. This castle, like many others, became the nucleus of a Royal Town of moderate size, probably during the reign of King Přemysl Otakar II.

The center of the town is an elongated square, faced by two parallel rows of houses. The street leading to the eastern gate was narrowed by the austere parish and monastery church, built at the beginning of the 15th century. The church was incorporated in the city wall, its bell tower still shutting off the street in the manner of a gateway. The original nucleus was probably augmented to the east of the church by a fortified forefield, with only one street leading to the outer gate in the suburb.

The town of Jaroměř still possesses a number of historic town houses, mostly of Renaissance origin, with partly preserved arcades in the square. During the reconstruction of the town following the fire in 1680, some of the houses were embellished with Baroque gables. The characteristic atmosphere of the historical area of the square has not been impeded by the rather extensive building activities of this century.

In 1821, a suspension bridge was built in Jaroměř by the Czech engineer, Schirch. It was the first bridge of this kind on the European Continent.

163. Plan of Jaroměř, after a cadastral map of 1840.

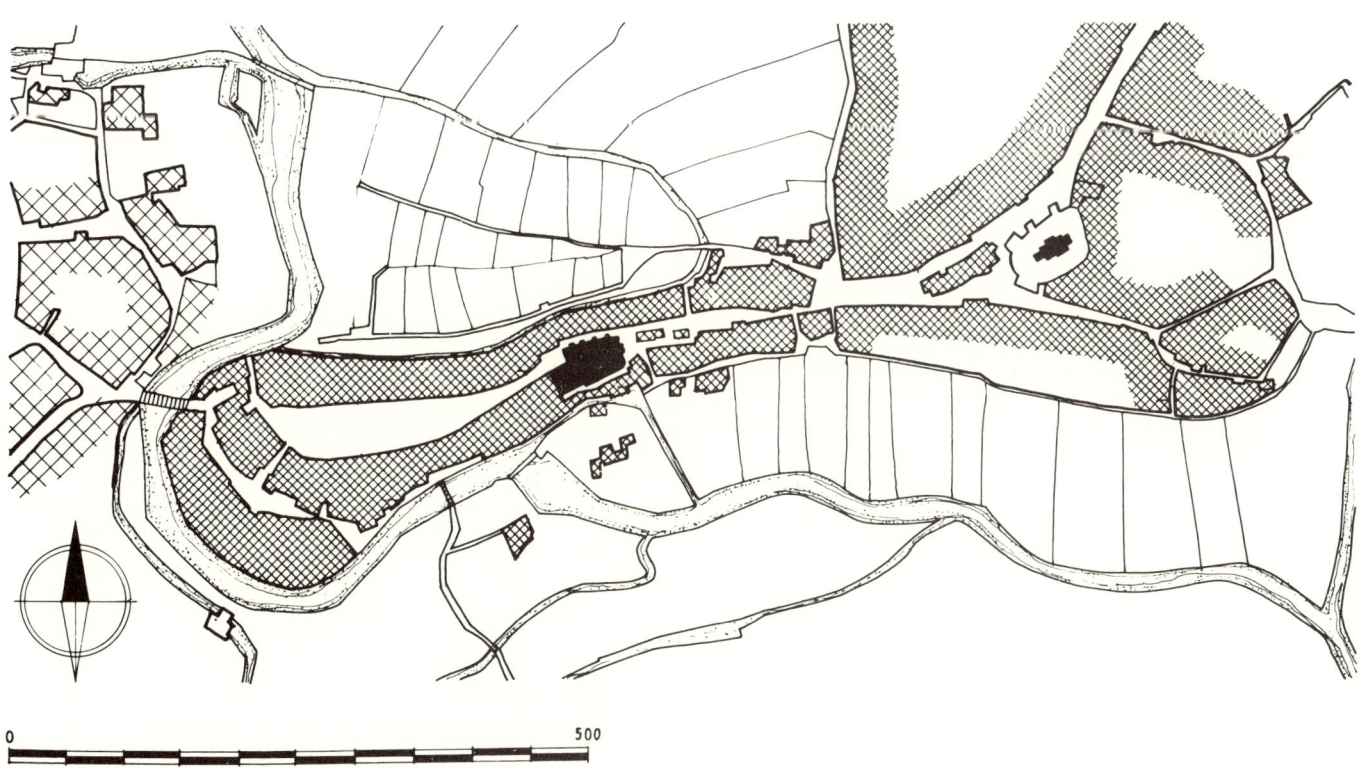

Today, the town of *Josefov* is an administrative part of Jaroměř. Its fortress, from the 18th century, superseded the fortifications of Jaroměř of the early feudal period. After Silesia had been joined to the Bohemian Kingdom during the first half of the 14th century, the territory at the confluence of the rivers Elbe, Úpa, and Metuje lost its strategic importance. It regained its significance when the military power of Prussia increased and Prussia annexed Silesia in the year 1763. In 1781 the building of a new fortress was begun near the confluence of the rivers Elbe and Metuje, after the plans by Louis Querlonde du Hamel, a general of French origin. It was roughly finished by the year 1787, when it received its name after its founder, the Emperor Joseph II.

The fortification system of Josefov was one of the most important examples of military engineering of the 18th century. It included all the basic improvements devised by Vauban and applied here by the military engineer Carmontaigne, as well as those of the so-called school of Mézières. The town and the fortifications were separated by a continuous belt of single and double barracks. In front of the barracks, the high brick walls of the bastions and curtains rose from the bottom of the trench and were protected by caponiers and ravelins at the more sheltered northern side of the fortress. In the remaining sections, with easier access, the fortifications were reinforced by antibastions, tenailles, and ravelins which were protected, in their turn, by special lunettes which formed a retrenchment.

The town within the walls was laid out on a rectangular plan with building blocks of unequal size, their variety dictated by the need for larger sites for military buildings. Public buildings were erected during the construction of the fortress, while town houses were put up from the year 1790 to the middle of the 19th century.

164. Plan of the citadel of Josefov after its completion (1780–1787).

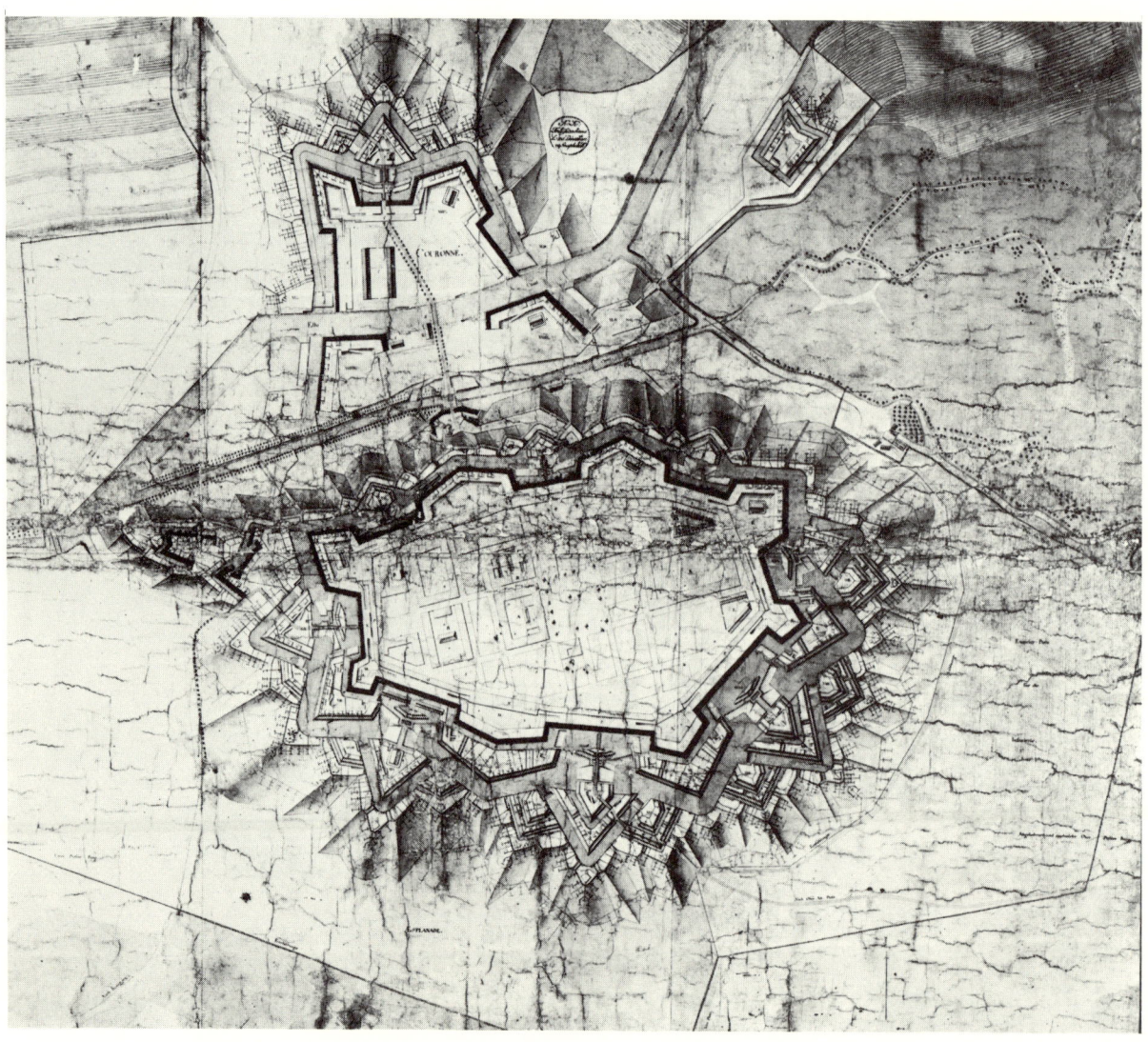

Jaroměřice nad Rokytnou, Southern Moravia.
The town is situated on the Moravian side of the Bohemian-Moravian Highland. It developed from a medieval agricultural riverside settlement. At the end of the 16th century, the barons of Lomnice converted the stronghold of Jaroměřice into a Renaissance castle consisting of a three-winged single-story building on an irregular ground plan.

Between 1700 and 1737 Jan Adam of Questenberk, the builder of the new castle, erected one of the most sumptuous Baroque palaces in Moravia. An ideal design, attributed to the architect Johann Lucas von Hildebrandt, who lived about 1700, shows a bird's-eye view of the whole ensemble of castle buildings, the cupola of the Church of St. Marguerite built over an oval plan, and a Baroque garden with rich French decorative parterres and canals. The major part of this design was executed, although a comparison of Hildebrandt's plan with the preserved Baroque version shows a more simplified construction.

165. View of the town and castle of Jaroměřice nad Rokytnou before the reconstruction of the castle at the end of the 17th century. Detail of a picture in the castle gallery of Jaroměřice.

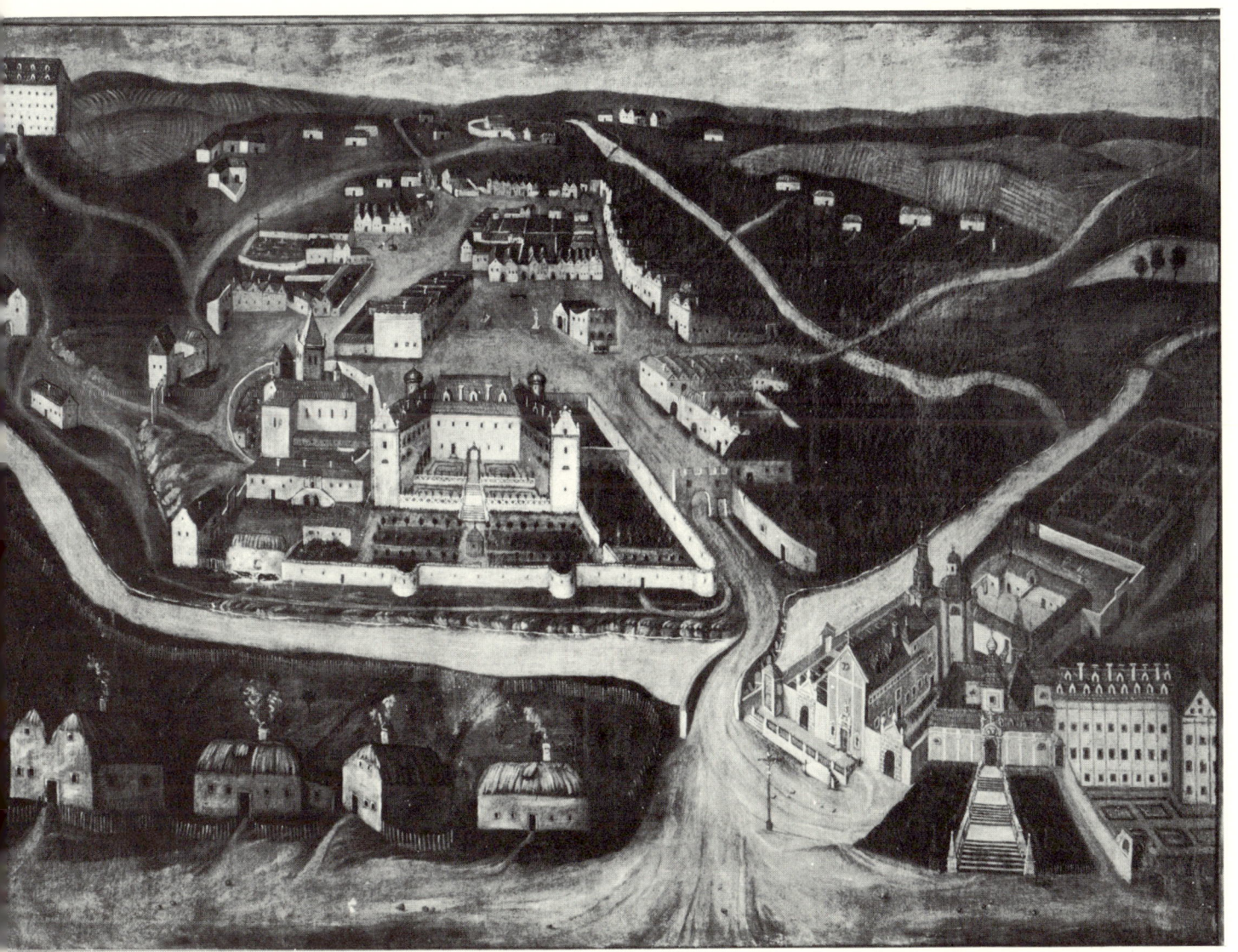

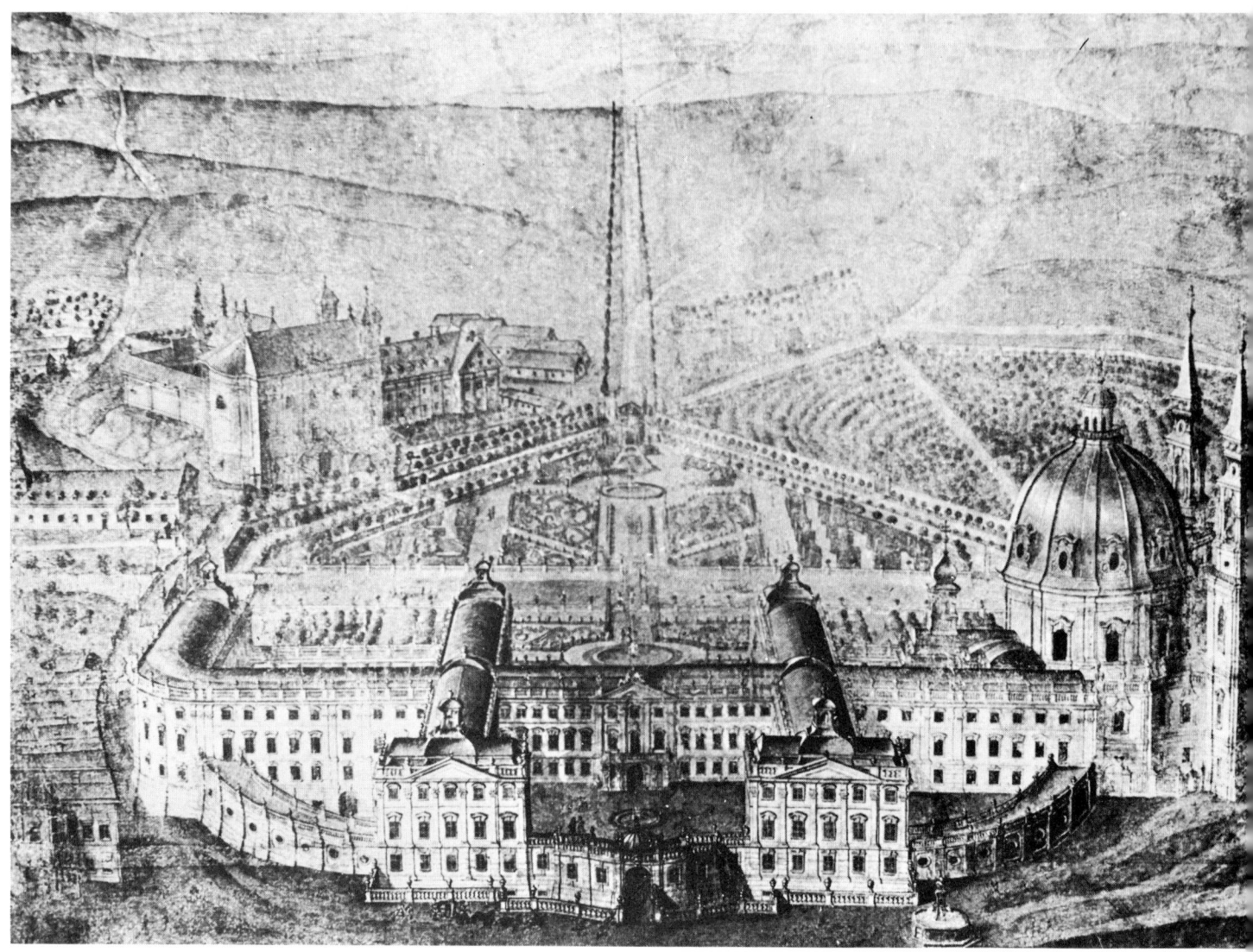

166. An ideal design of the reconstruction of the castle complex, with the Church of St. Margaret and the convent at Jaroměřice nad Rokytnou. Drawing from the beginning of the 18th century by Johann Lucas von Hildebrandt (?) in the collection of Jaroměřice Castle.

The approximately H-shaped castle is enclosed on the northern side by a courtyard. This court of honor, separated from the town by a moat of decorative rather than defensive character, creates, together with the adjoining square, an impressive space enhanced by the statue of the Holy Trinity. The southern courtyard of the rebuilt Renaissance part of the castle is designed as a garden terrace adjoining the lower garden. Perpendicularly to the axis of the garden flows the Rokytná stream, turned into an artificial canal bypassing a pentagonal island at the end of the garden. The canals were bordered by balustrades and sculptures, several of which have been preserved.

Beyond the garden, the main axis of the ensemble continued as a wide avenue leading far into the country. The western bank of the island was adjoined by an orchard, developed as a park at the beginning of the 19th century.

Jičín, Eastern Bohemia. Situated at the foot of the rock formation, Prachovské skály, on the upper course of the river Cidlina in the northeast of Bohemia, the region of Jičín was settled at a very early date. The town of Jičín, however, was not founded till the end of the 13th century, during the reign of King Wenceslas II, most probably on the site of an early feudal settlement. The form of the newly laid-out town was that of a regular oval, slightly compressed along its eastern boundary. The rectangular plan is therefore somewhat out of harmony with the outline of the town as a whole. The spacious square occupies a slightly eccentric position, with streets entering it at the corners and in the middle of its northern and southern sides.

During the late Gothic period the town of Jičín was enclosed with stone walls. The intensive building activity following the devastation of the town by two great fires in the second half of the 16th century resulted in the erection of a number of Renaissance town houses. The arcades of the square, dating partly from the late Gothic period, were completed in the second half of the 16th and first quarter of the 17th century. Since 1622 the estate of Jičín belonged to the domain of Albrecht von Wallenstein, Generalissimo of the Emperor's armies, who made Jičín his residence. Wallenstein's choice had a marked effect on the development of the town in regard to architecture and town planning.

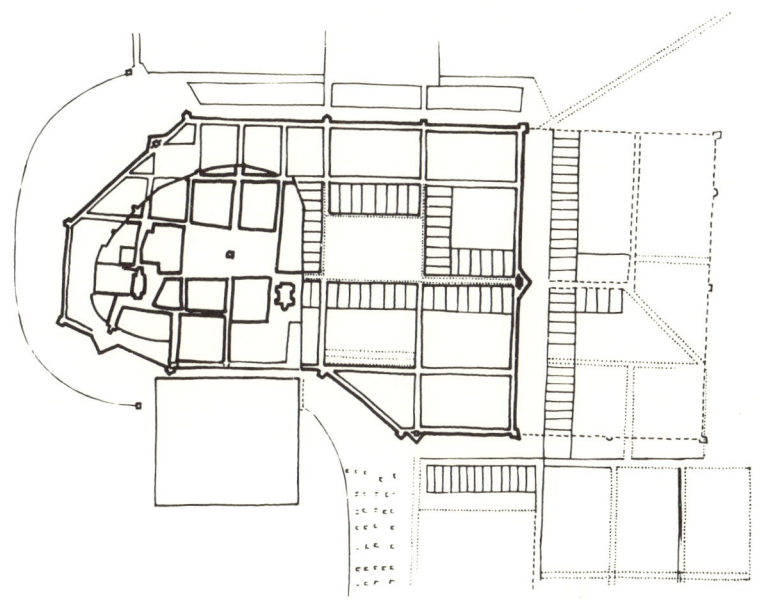

167. Copy of a plan by N. Sebregondi for the reconstruction of Jičín, in 1633.

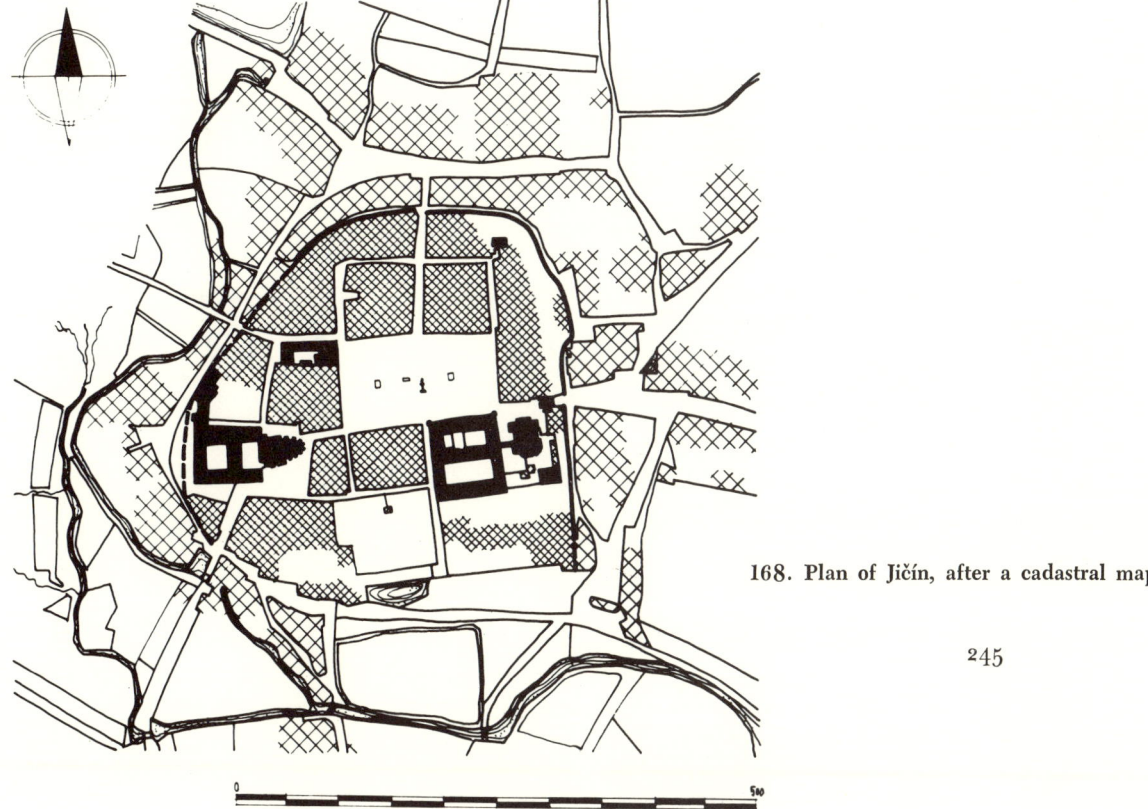

168. Plan of Jičín, after a cadastral map of 1842.

While the majority of Bohemian towns stagnated during the Thirty Years' War, Jičín underwent great changes in its appearance in a single decade. Wallenstein's building program was not limited to ecclesiastical or secular edifices only, but included the erection of town houses as well. Originally it was intended to build two hundred new houses, a number greatly exceeded later. The restyling of the castle was planned on a large scale. It was followed a few years later by the construction of the Jesuit college.

The initiative of the General was in no way limited to the area of the walled-in town, but extended also to the suburbs of Jičín. The plans included the layout of the New Town with an almost rectangular square south of the river Cidlina and, to the north of the town, the Carthusian Monastery. Halfway between Valdice and Jičín, a country seat with extensive gardens was built and connected with the town by a "colonnade" of lime trees. The plans prepared for the town by Wallenstein's architect, Nicolas Sebregondi, were not completed until 1633. The realization of these projects, however, was cut short by Wallenstein's assassination, in 1634. They provided for an extension of the urban area along its northern and eastern sides by the addition of rectangular building blocks to the medieval nucleus and for a square lined with arcades. To the east, outside the enlarged area, a new suburb with gardens had been proposed.

169. The square at Jičín with arcaded buildings, mostly from the 16th to 17th centuries. The southern part of the square is mainly occupied by the castle of Albrecht von Wallenstein.

Jihlava, Southern Bohemia. During the height of feudalism, the yield of silver mines was one of the main sources of the economic and political power of the Bohemian State. Before the middle of the 13th century, the principal mining center was Jihlava, situated on the border between Bohemia and Moravia. However, toward the end of the century it was overshadowed by Kutná Hora. Jihlava originated from a small community situated about half a mile north of the historical core of the town, at a point where the river Jihlava was crossed by a trade route from Bohemia to South Moravia. The development of the silver mines attracted a flood of settlers for whom suitable accommodations did not exist in Stará Jihlava. Consequently, after 1240, the settlement began to expand on the nearby headland.

Though its streets were laid out according to a regular plan, it is presumed that the original settlement grew in an uncontrolled manner. It was only during the reign of Přemysl Otakar II that conditions were stabilized and a regular network of streets was established. However, traces of an older system can still be found.

The center of the town is occupied by an extraordinarily large rectangular sloping square, one of the largest in Czechoslovakia. In the northwestern part was a group of merchants' houses with shops. The historical core of the town covers an area of about 2,600 by 1,900 feet.

Privileges granted the town by King Wenceslas I formed the basis of the well-known mining rights of Jihlava, making it the center of arbitration for a number of mining towns in Central Europe even at a time when the economic importance of mines had declined.

From the very beginning, the development of mining was accompanied by an intensive building activity. The prosperous town was protected by strong fortifications built at the end of the 13th and during the first decade of the 14th century. Large parts of the main walls, with semicircular towers, have been preserved. Its position on a headland and its fortifications made Jihlava an impregnable medieval stronghold which successfully resisted several sieges.

The majority of the buildings of Jihlava date from the Gothic period. However, the town acquired its predominant appearance following reconstructions after the fires in 1523 and 1551. Large buildings were erected which preserved late Gothic and early Renaissance details. Often their ground floors had two-aisled halls with pillars, which in several cases extended through their whole depth. A specialty of Jihlava were high, directly lighted halls in the center of the second floor.

In the last third of the 18th century and the first decade of the 19th, a new economic and architectural prosperity set in. Third stories were added to buildings, particularly to those on the square.

The emergence of factory production in the 19th century meant the end of Jihlava's spinning industry, famous since the Middle Ages.

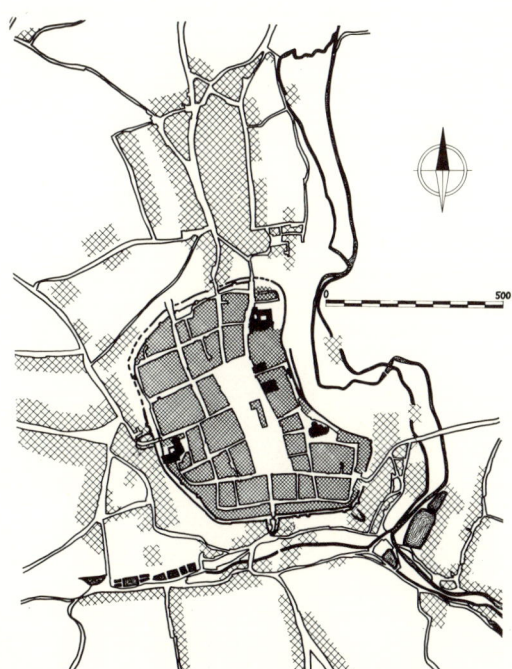

170. Plan of the historic nucleus of Jihlava, after a cadastral map of 1835.

171. Model of Jihlava at the beginning of the 15th century. Municipal Museum of Jihlava.

172. General view of Jihlava. Painting of the 18th century in the Municipal Museum of Jihlava.

Jindřichův Hradec, Southern Bohemia. A stronghold with a market community whose center was a small Romanesque church stood on the border between Bohemia and Moravia, on a headland near a passage over the river Nežárka. Due to its favorable position, protected by the configuration of the terrain, the river, and the lake—known later as Vajgar Pond—the settlement became one of the properties of the powerful South Bohemian family of Vítkovec.

Jindřich Vítkovec built a castle on the site of the old stronghold and gave the town its name, as a result of the reconstruction of the old market community.

In records of 1220, mention is made of Jindřichův hrad and *Novum Castrum,* and of the town as a *civitas* in 1293. The plan of the town, especially the part surrounding the square, indicates efforts to reconstruct the older community on a regular plan in the middle of the 13th century.

The presence of the wealthy noble family and of important trade routes leading from Bohemia through the town to Austria made Jindřichův Hradec one of the most significant centers of South Bohemia.

About 1470 the fortified "Great" or "Prague" suburb was renamed Nové Mešto, New Town. In the town and in its large suburbs a number of important buildings were erected which included two monasteries and, at the turn of the 17th century, a Jesuit College. The Renaissance period saw the peak of the architectural development of the town which thereafter, in the 17th century, declined through destruction and war. Not even the postal route established between Prague and Vienna or the development of its textile industry could restore its former prosperity.

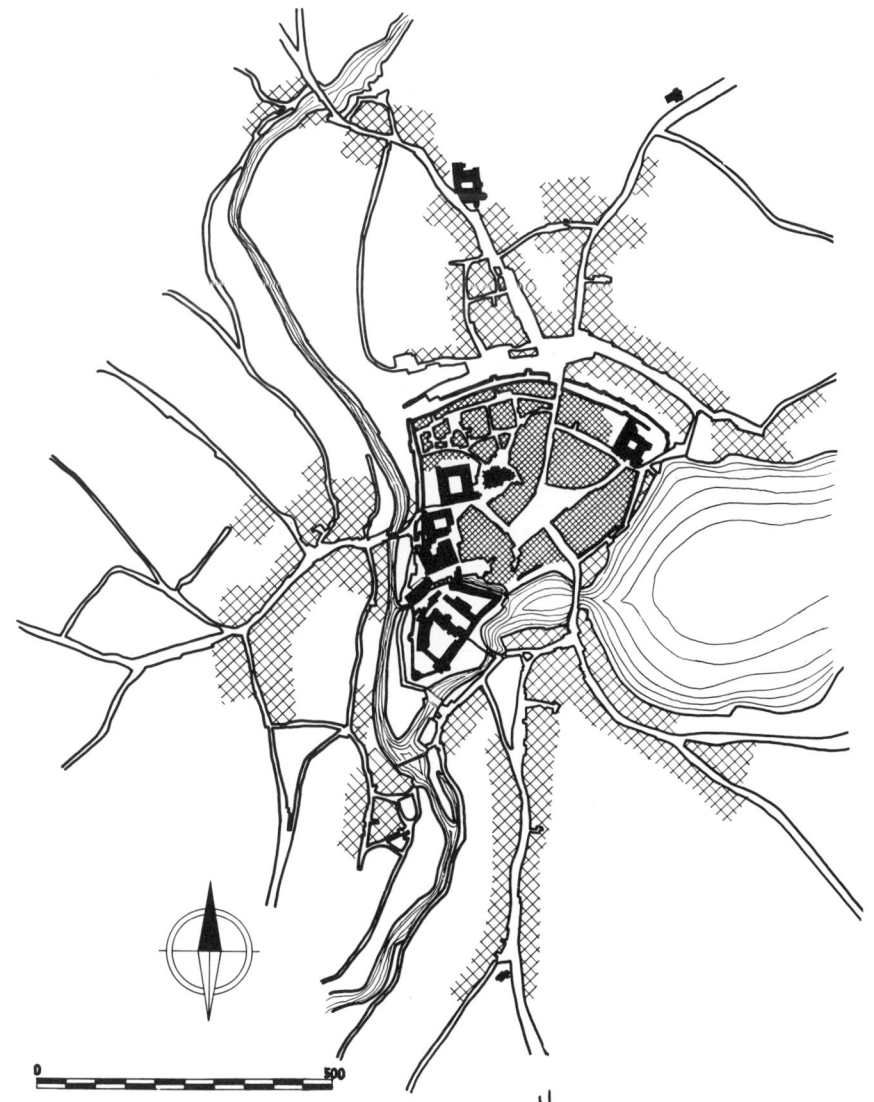

173. Plan of Jindřichův Hradec, after a cadastral map of 1828.

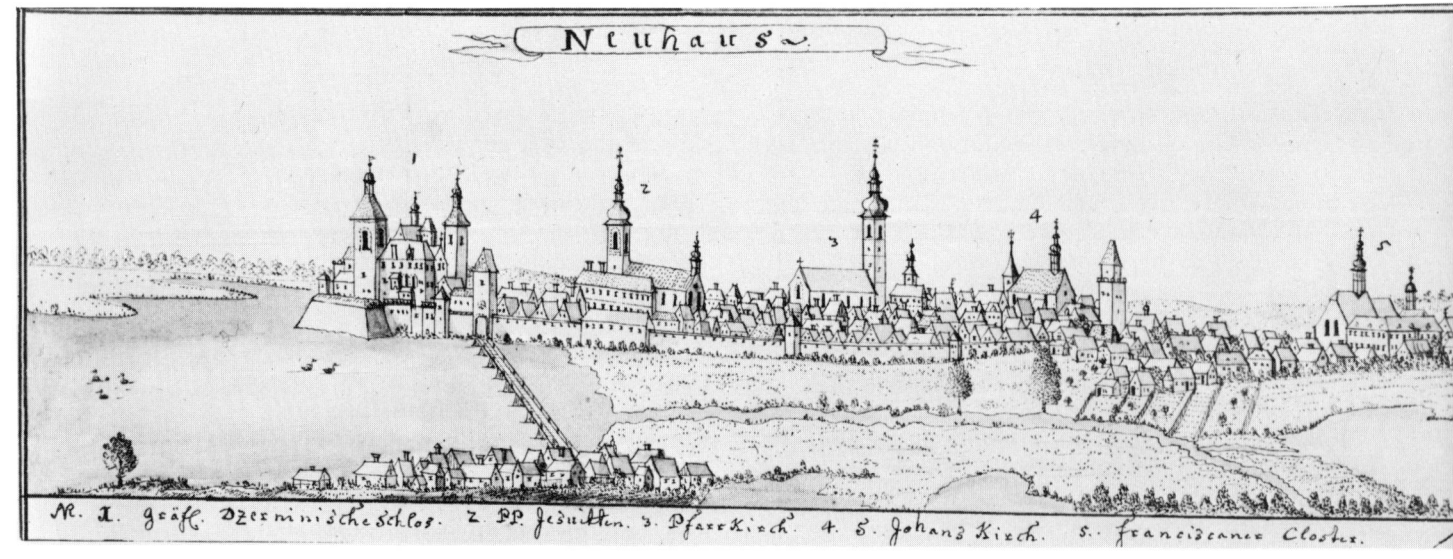

174. Drawing of Jindřichův Hradec by Friedrich Bernhard Werner, middle of the 18th century. On the left, across the bridge over the Vajgar Pond, the castle.

175. Square at Jindřichův Hradec, with the Baroque Pest Column of 1764–68.

Karlovy Vary (Karlsbad), Western Bohemia. The wide valley traversed by the Ohře river between the borders of the Erz Mountains in the north and the Slavkov Forest and the Doupava Hills in the south was the main center of settlement in this part of Bohemia. The valley forms the secondary axis of the main part of settlement in the western half of the region, below the Erz Mountains. At the south of the little river Teplá, whose crooked and deep course defines the border between the Slavkov Forest and the Doupava Hills, a settlement grew up whose importance was guaranteed by its numerous mineral springs.

This spa, the oldest in Bohemia, was named after the Roman Emperor and Bohemian King, Charles IV, the greatest town-planning entrepreneur of the feudal period in Central Europe. In the year 1370, he raised the small settlement, with a hunting lodge dating from 1358, to the level of a Royal Town.

Charles' son, King Wenceslas IV, bestowed upon the town the right to grant asylum to persons sought for criminal, political, and religious reasons and to fugitive serfs, but he stipulated that the town was not to be involved in war or to possess fortifications.

Thus, there arose the rare phenomenon of an unfortified open town with the right to grant asylum and with curative baths.

The town, which fortunately survived the Thirty Years' War, became a world-famous spa as early as the 18th century. In that period, the group of statues of the Holy Trinity (1716) in the marketplace and the monumental Baroque parish church of Mary Magdalena were erected by one of the great representatives of the Czech Baroque, Kilian Ignac Dientzenhofer. Many of the buildings of the town were destroyed by fire in 1759. Despite the fact that the reconstruction of the town was carried out on old Gothic sites, it gave the town a new Classicist appearance due, particularly, to the characteristic spa buildings, such as the Pump-room (1774), the Old Theater (1787), the New Mill Spa and colonnade (1798), the excursion place of

176. General view of Karlovy Vary. Engraving by Matthaeus Merian from *Topographia Bohemiae, Moraviae et Silesiae*, Frankfurt, 1650.

177. Center of Karlovy Vary, with the main spring and the church.

Poštovní dvůr, Stagecoach Yards of the Royal Mail (1791), the Czech Hall, and the Saxon Hall. The Classicist reconstruction of the town also brought about a radical change in the relation of the spa to the river Teplá. Embankments and promenades, carriageways, shops, and wooden bridges were built.

In the 19th century, the international popularity of the spa increased considerably, leading to a wave of construction, particularly in the second half of the century. Eight new springs on the left bank or in the bed of the river Teplá were discovered and exploited between 1827 and 1871. Consequently, residential buildings, sanatoria, and spa institutes had to be built behind Castle Hill and among the hills on the right bank, between the river Teplá and the new road to Prague.

Kežmarok, Northern Slovakia. Kežmarok received a charter in 1269. However, as early as 1251 a church with a settlement was mentioned in historical documents. The layout of Kežmarok underwent several changes. Its main axis consisted of a road passing through the Spiš region in the direction of Poland. It bifurcated in the vicinity of the town but was still included in its layout. The core of the town developed around the church, where an irregular square originated. After the principal communication had been shifted to the eastern edge of the urban area, a new space was gained which soon became the main square. A town hall was built at the crossing of the two roads. At the beginning of the 15th century, the town was enclosed by walls. Subsequent reconstructions were directed toward adjustments inside the walls.

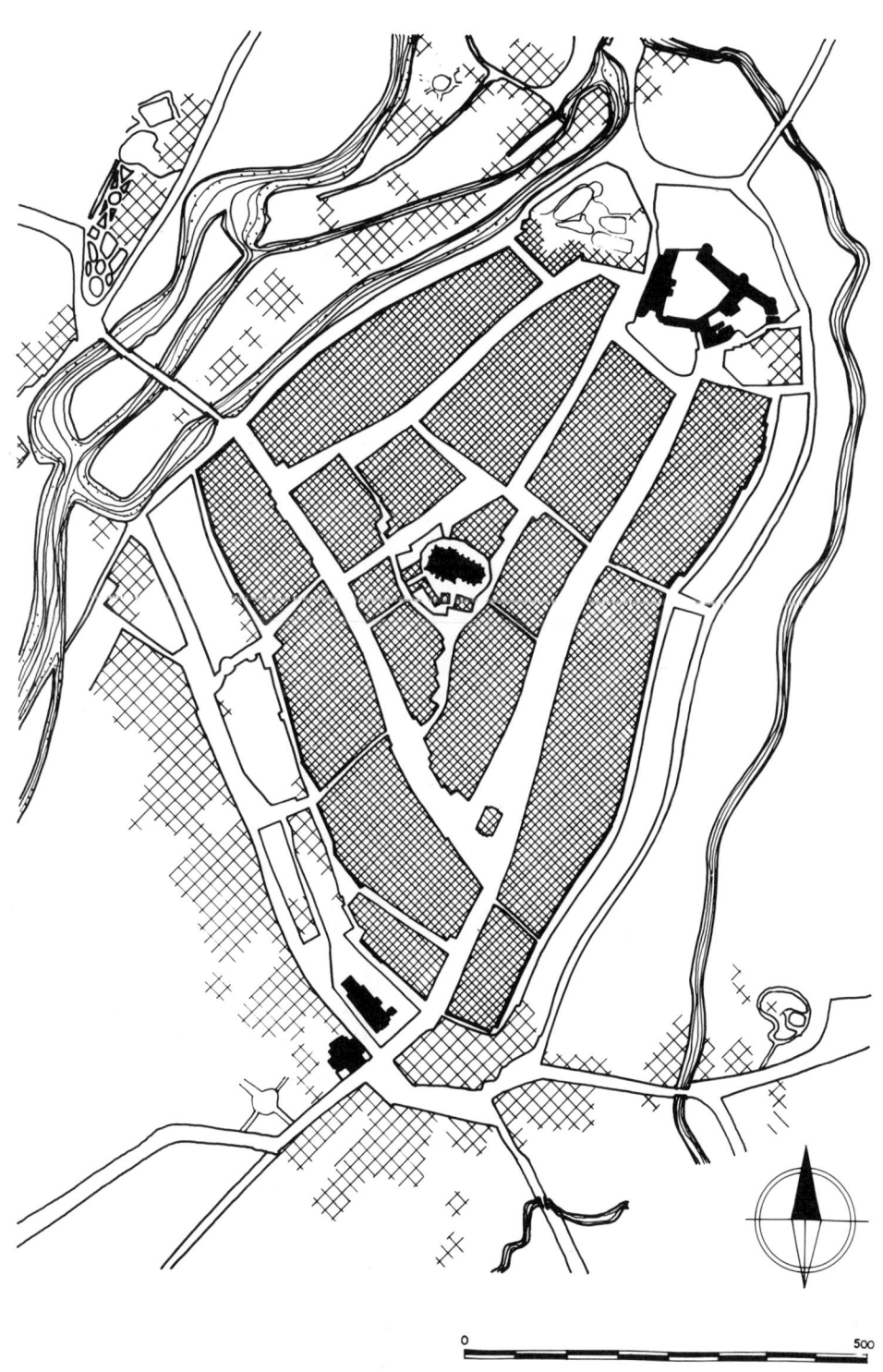

178. Plan of Kežmarok, after a cadastral map of 1870.

Klatovy, Western Bohemia. The site now occupied by the town of Klatovy was once a densely wooded area, with a village called "Klatov." The village had two Romanesque churches and was owned by the Squires Drslavici. About the year 1260, this place, on the important route connecting Bohemia and Bavaria, passed into the possession of King Přemysl Otakar II, who founded a Royal Town called Klatovy above the river, close to the earlier village.

The layout of this town, with its checkerboard plan within a slightly deformed ellipse, is of particular interest. It shows the typical composition of square blocks subdivided into long Gothic building plots. The center is occupied by a square, each of its sides being 328 feet long.

The town was an important Hussite fortress and, according to chiliastic belief, one of the five Bohemian towns predestined to be saved from destruction on the advent of Antichrist.

After the year 1600, Klatovy recovered from a series of devastating fires in the last quarter of the 16th century. During the Counter Reformation, the Jesuit Order settled in the town (1636), gradually taking over whole blocks of buildings in spite of the protests of the community. The houses in the square next to the town hall were pulled down and, in 1636, the construction of a large Baroque church with twin towers was begun. After a fire at the end of the 17th century, the Dominicans also built a new church.

The town prospered in the 18th century and became the administrative center of the region. Its citizens rebuilt or altered their Gothic houses according to the demands of the new style. The earlier façades disappeared under Baroque ornaments and, later, under the stucco decorations of the Empire Period.

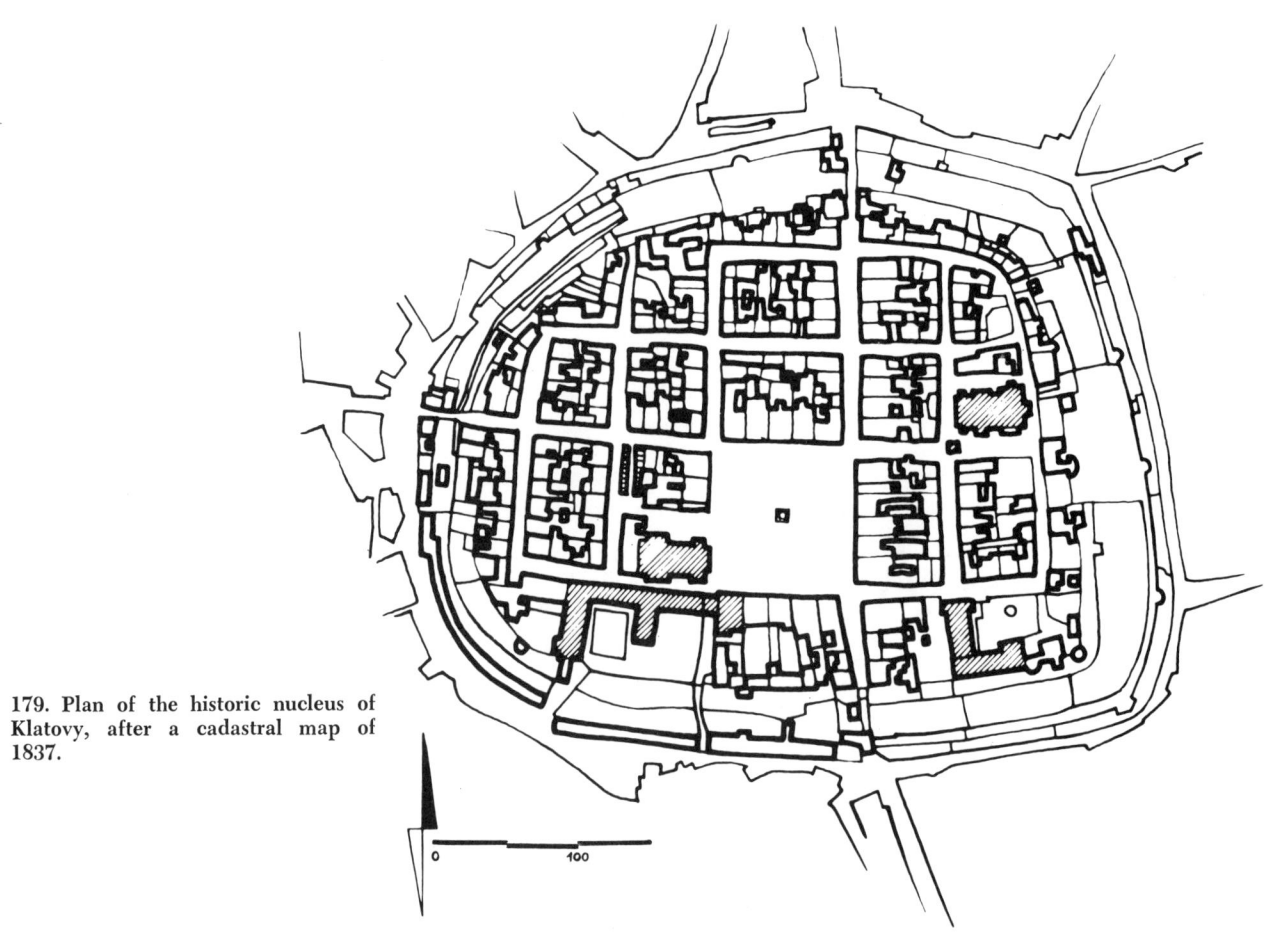

179. Plan of the historic nucleus of Klatovy, after a cadastral map of 1837.

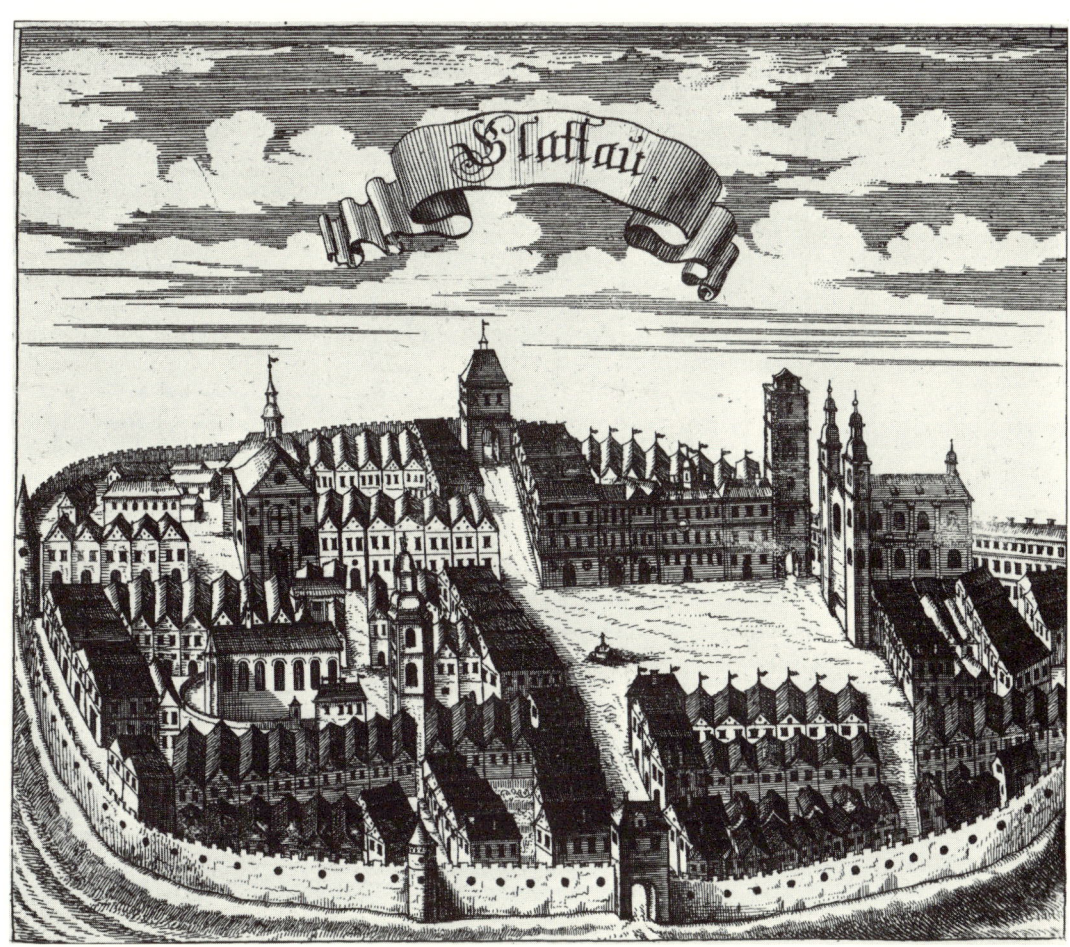

180. Drawing of the town of Klatovy from the second half of the 17th century.

181. Square at Klatovy. On the left, the Town Hall with the Black Tower (middle of the 16th century); on the right, the Jesuit church (middle of the 17th century).

Kolín, Central Bohemia. Attracted by the presence of silver mines, a group of early medieval towns grew up close to each other at the edge of the fertile and densely populated lowland of the river Labe (Elbe), between the massif of the Iron Mountains and the foothills of the Bohemian-Moravian Highland. Kolín is the westernmost community of these towns.

The central course of the river Labe, flowing with its numerous branches through swampy meadows intermingled with forests, represented many centuries ago a serious communications obstacle with but a few fords. One of them was probably near the village of Kolín, the present Starý Kolín (Old Kolín), about five miles to the east of the present town. The importance of this ford, probably increased by mining activities, induced Přemysl Otakar II, King of Bohemia, to found a new town near the former village. However, since this site was subjected to floods, the new town founded before 1261 was extended to the east of the village on a headland overlooking the river.

Since the new town was intended as the center of the nearby silver mines, the king took a personal interest in its development. The historic nucleus has an almost rectangular shape, with a slightly oblong square in its center. An interesting feature is a wide street leading from the Kouřim Gate to the center of the southern side of the square. The parish church of St. Bartholomew is situated at the highest point of the urban center, near the town walls. The layout of the historical core of Kolín is probably one of the oldest examples of a regular plan in Bohemia.

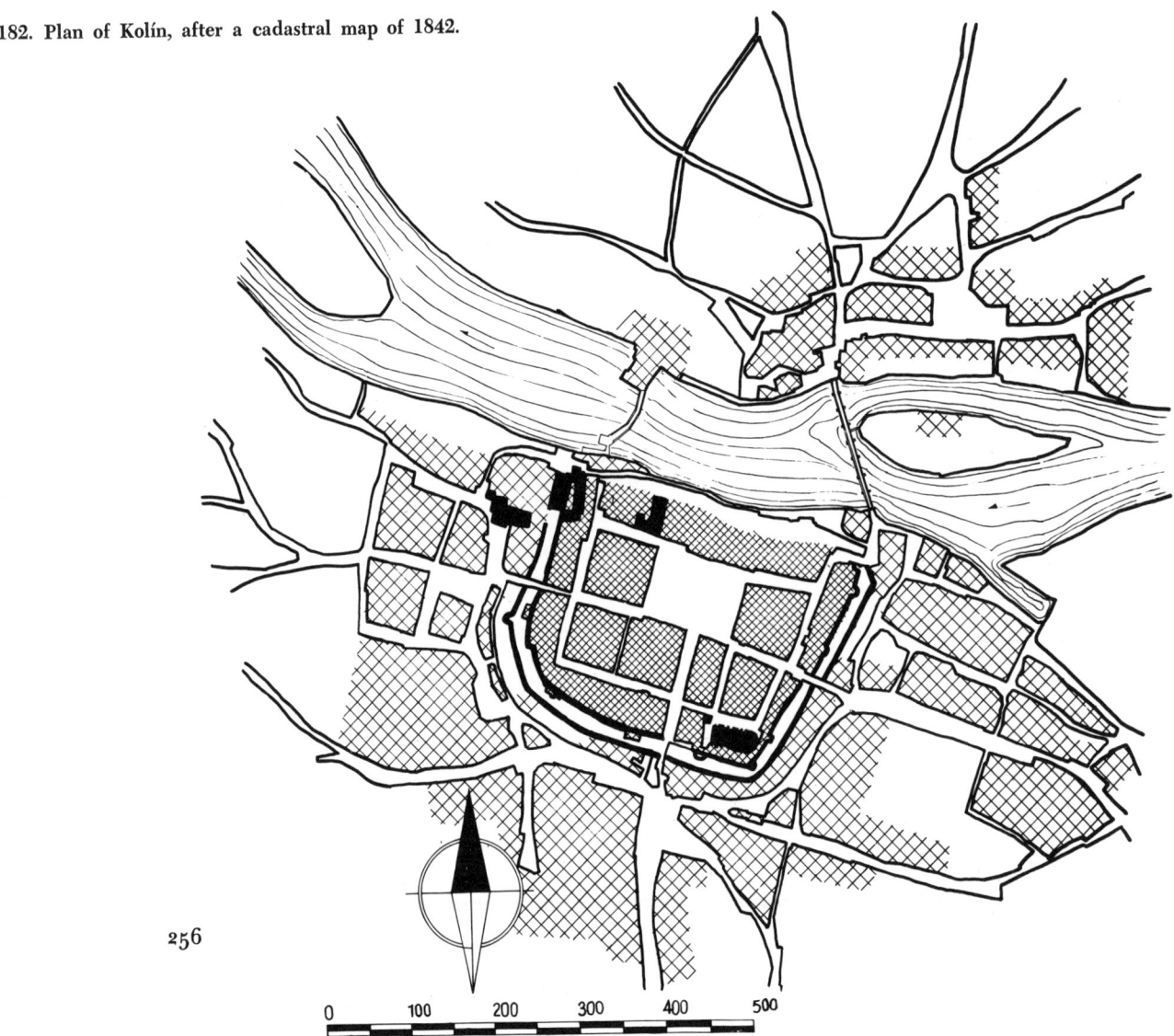

182. Plan of Kolín, after a cadastral map of 1842.

Košice, Eastern Slovakia. The date of origin of settlement on the site of the present town of Košice has hitherto been based on a report of 1249, the year in which the Hungarian King Béla IV conferred on Košice the privileges of a town. At the time of this event there were two settlements on the territory of the present Košice: Lower Košice and Upper Košice. In the last decades of the 13th century Košice was mentioned alternately as a settlement and as a town.

The medieval place was preceded by a Slavonic settlement, situated on the site of the former Slovenská (now Kováčská) Street, which, after the arrival of new immigrants in the middle of the 13th century, was considerably extended by adding several blocks of dwelling houses and the principal square. In the course of the 14th and 15th centuries, the original timber buildings were gradually replaced by stone houses.

As early as the 13th century the area of the main square included a simple church which, after a fire in 1378, was replaced by the Cathedral of St. Elizabeth. The Chapel of St. Michael rose on the southern side of

183. Plan of the town of Košice, and the fortress, in the 18th century.

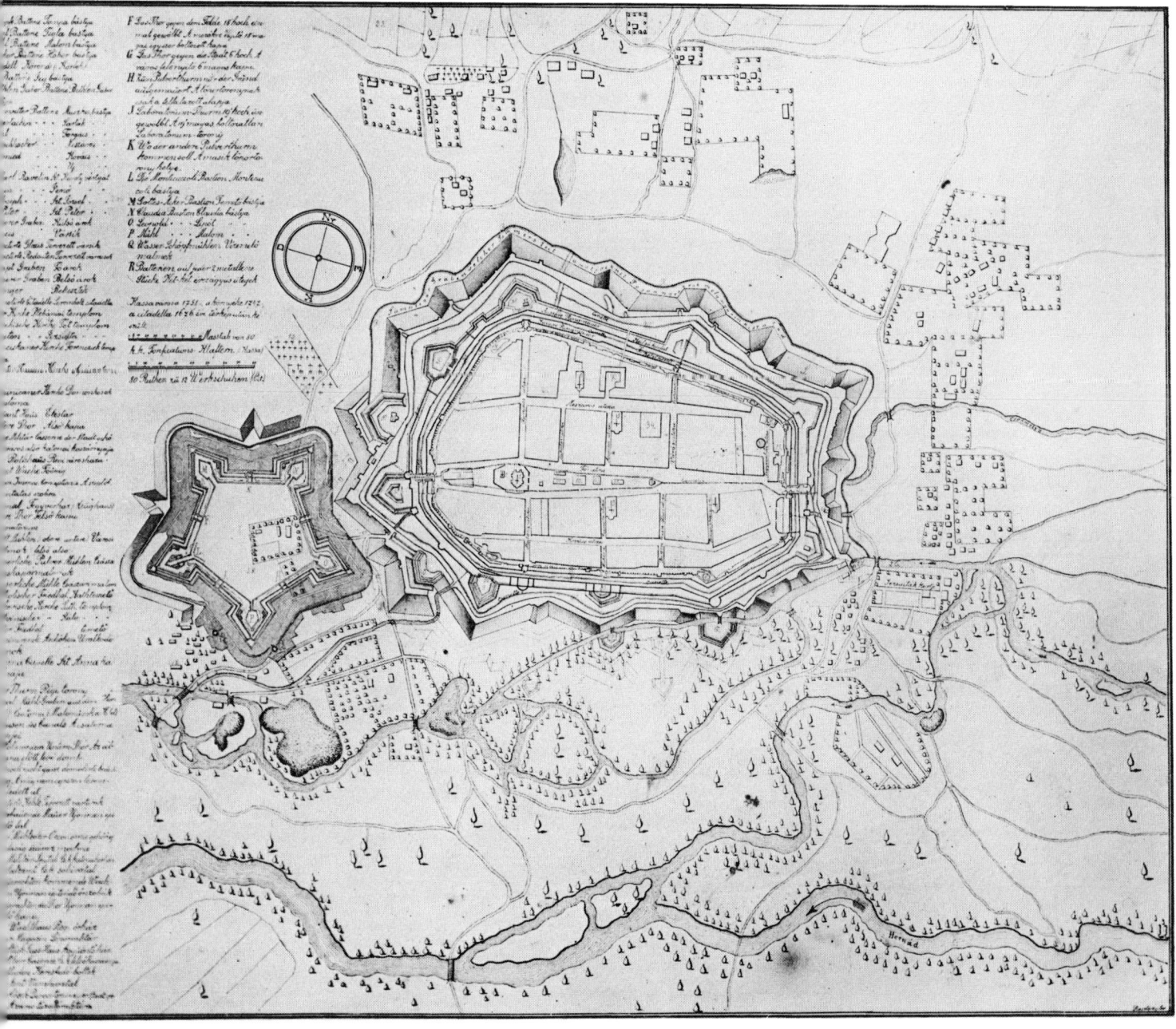

the square while the northern side was occupied by the Gothic town hall and other public buildings.

The medieval layout of Košice consisted of long, narrow lots formed by a network of longitudinal and transverse streets. During the course of development, additional secondary streets were laid out, connecting the square with the town's suburbs.

In 1628, a Renaissance belfry was erected on the main square to the north of the Cathedral. Later, after the demolition of the town hall (1754), a market hall, and other structures, the building up and filling in of the urban area proceeded steadily. Thus the medieval character of the town changed as Gothic buildings were reconstructed and Renaissance, Baroque, and Classicist palaces transformed the appearance of the main square. Among these buildings were the Governor's Residence (1779), the new town hall (1782), and the Forgách Palace.

Between the years 1671–1677, under the leadership of the Imperial Commander, General Montecuccoli, the fortifications were strengthened by a fort incorporating the more modern defense requirements.

The building activities of the 18th and 19th centuries were chiefly concentrated on the construction of houses in secondary streets. After the dismantling of the fortifications, a circular road was laid out following the course of the former town walls, while the remainder of the newly won terrain formed green open spaces around the town and provided new building sites for future use on the western and southern outskirts of Košice.

184. View of Košice in 1617 by Joris Hoefnagel.

Kouřim, Central Bohemia. More than a thousand years ago, Kouřim was an important center and a rival of Prague. At that time, its focal point was the so-called Stará Kouřim, a powerful stronghold to the east of the historical core.

By the 10th century, Stará Kouřim had disappeared. New community life developed on the smaller headland, around the churches of St. Kliment, St. Vojtěch, and St. George. However, it is highly probable that, even at that time, the nucleus of the third Kouřim existed within the area of the historical center, near the Church of St. Stephen.

The early importance of Kouřim as a feudal town was the decisive factor for its elevation to a Royal Town at the beginning of the reign of Přemysl II, an event mentioned in 1261. The outline of this fortified place has the shape of the letter D, with the fortifications following the configuration of the terrain and the main square set in the center.

An interesting feature of the town was the so-called Nové Město, New Town, a wide street leading from the north to the south along the western fortifications, at whose northern end the priory of the Sedlec Cistercian Monastery was situated.

The fortifications are still standing, more or less in their original extent, and represent perhaps the most remarkable defense system in the Czech lands. They consist of the main walls, with several bastions open to the interior, and of outer walls strengthened with numerous semicircular bastions and other safeguards. The fortifications were completed at the beginning of the 16th century.

The days of the economic importance of Kouřim were numbered. It stagnated, and never fully recovered from the Thirty Years' War. There are no important Baroque or Classicist buildings. Only the spacious square, the early Gothic Church of St. Stephen, and the monumental fortifications are witnesses to the former industrious life of the community.

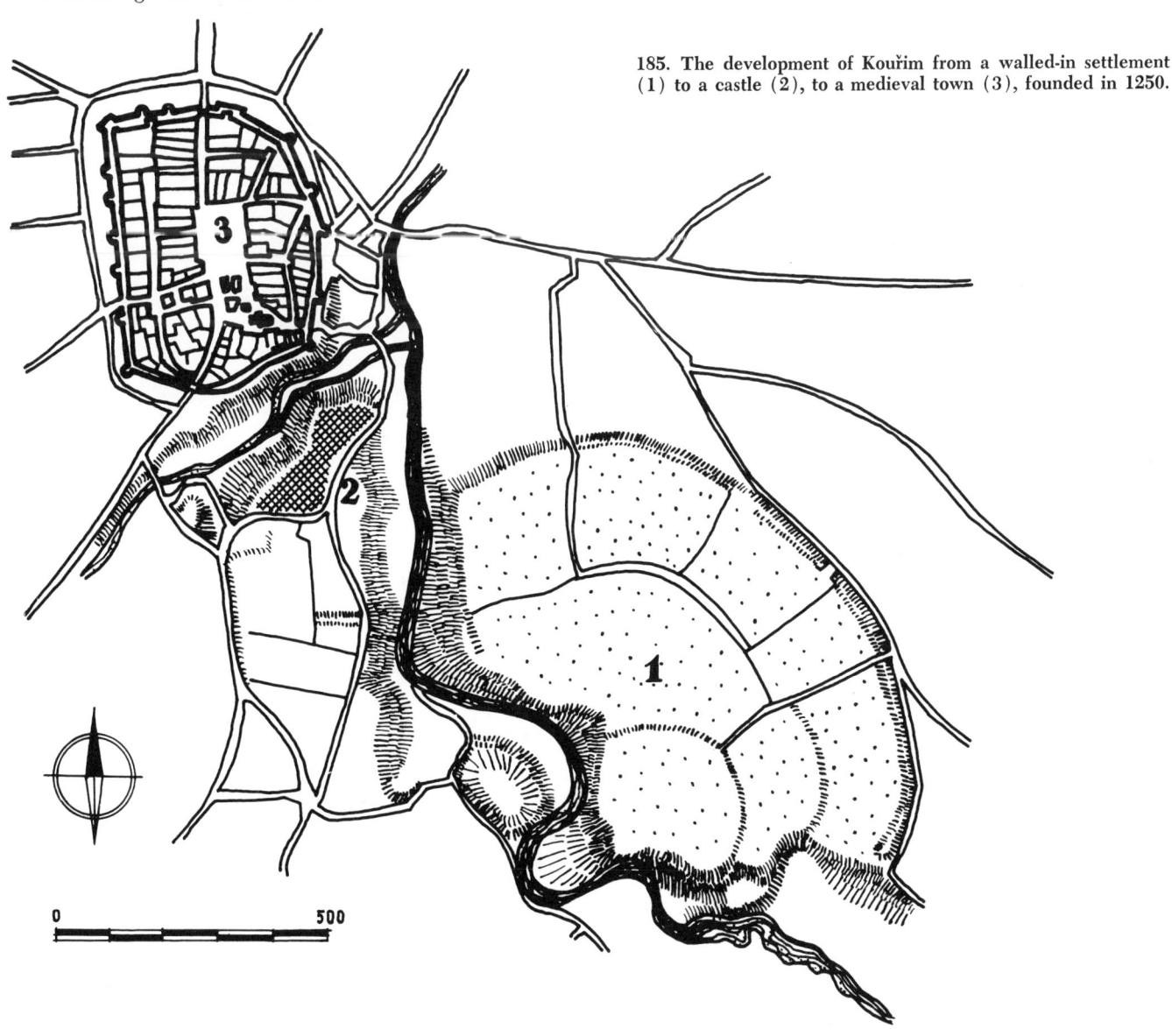

185. The development of Kouřim from a walled-in settlement (1) to a castle (2), to a medieval town (3), founded in 1250.

187. View of the center of Kremnica, with the castle and the castle church.

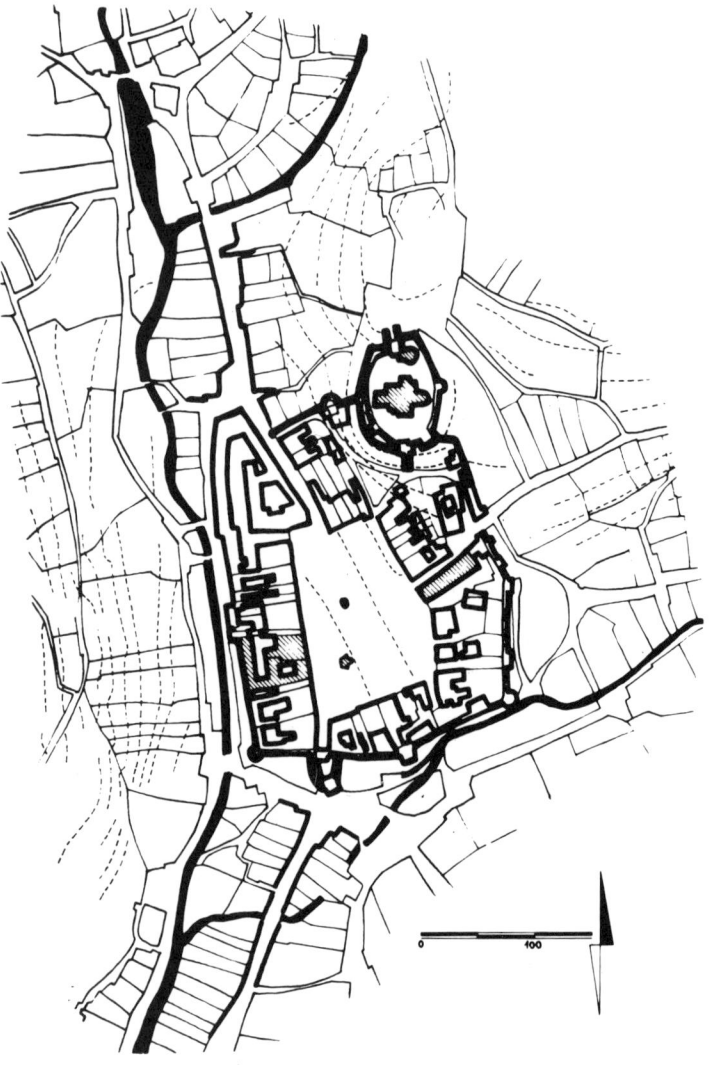

186. Plan of the present historic center of Kremnica.

Kremnica, Central Slovakia. Kremnica is one of the three most important mining towns in Central Slovakia. Its *raison d'être* was vast deposits of rare metals, which also determined its later development. When it received a charter in 1328, immigrants came from a neighboring settlement known as early as the 13th century. As a result of the growing importance of local mining activities, the town was chosen as the seat of the Royal Mining Chamber and the Hungarian mint.

There are only fragmentary reports on the original settlement, whose dispersed layout was dictated by the diverse features of

the landscape and the distribution of the natural deposits. The settlement on the site of the present town was of relatively recent origin. By the middle of the 14th century, all houses surrounding the large sloping square had been finished.

The defense of the town consisted originally only of the fortified castle at the edge of the urban area. At first, the castle comprised a complex of buildings of the 14th and 15th centuries, a two-storied circular chapel, and a two-aisled church. The construction of a double wall around the church, with a gate, a clock tower, and bastions—the first being built in the first half of the 15th century—gave the town a new defense system that fulfilled its function throughout the following century. However, the ever-growing importance of the town called for the strengthening of its defenses. This was realized by the construction of walls which encompassed not only the area around the square but also the fortified castle.

In the 16th century, the development of the town was retarded by the decline of the mining industry. Building activity was limited to a few reconstructions, thus preserving a great number of the original Gothic characteristics.

Kroměříž, Southern Moravia. The town of Kroměříž developed from a market village at a ford over the central course of the river Morava. The layout of the oldest part of the town is approximately crescent-shaped, slightly tapered toward the river, and still discernible in the southeastern part of the historic core of the town. In its center stands the parish church of Our Lady.

From the 13th century onward, the development of the town was closely linked with the episcopal residence, the principal seat of the bishops of Olomouc. In the sixties of the 13th century, Bishop Bruno built a castle and founded a new district of the town, with a marketplace in the center, adjoining the old market village. He surrounded the elliptical town with walls incorporating the old southwestern section. There were three gates: the Smith Gate, also called Upper Gate; the Water Gate, also known as Lower Gate; and the third gate, of more recent origin (about 1685), called Mill Gate and used only by the episcopal court.

The northwest corner of the main square, bordered with arcades, opens toward the episcopal residence built in the second half of the 17th century by Bishop Lichtenštejn according to a design by Filippo Luchese and Giovanni Pietro Tencalla, on the site of an older castle destroyed in the Thirty Years' War. In 1634, the whole town was levelled by the Swedes and remained in ruins for twenty years.

For a few months in the revolutionary year of 1848, the town became the capital of the Austrian-Hungarian Monarchy, when the government and the Congress, which were to give the Monarchy a new constitution, were moved to Kroměříž.

In the thirties of the 19th century, the Archbishop carried out the reconstruction of the episcopal gardens according to a design by Antonín Arche, based on Count Pückler's conception of landscape gardening which was then fashionable in Central Europe. The lower parterre was abolished and, beyond a branch of the river Morava, vast meadows

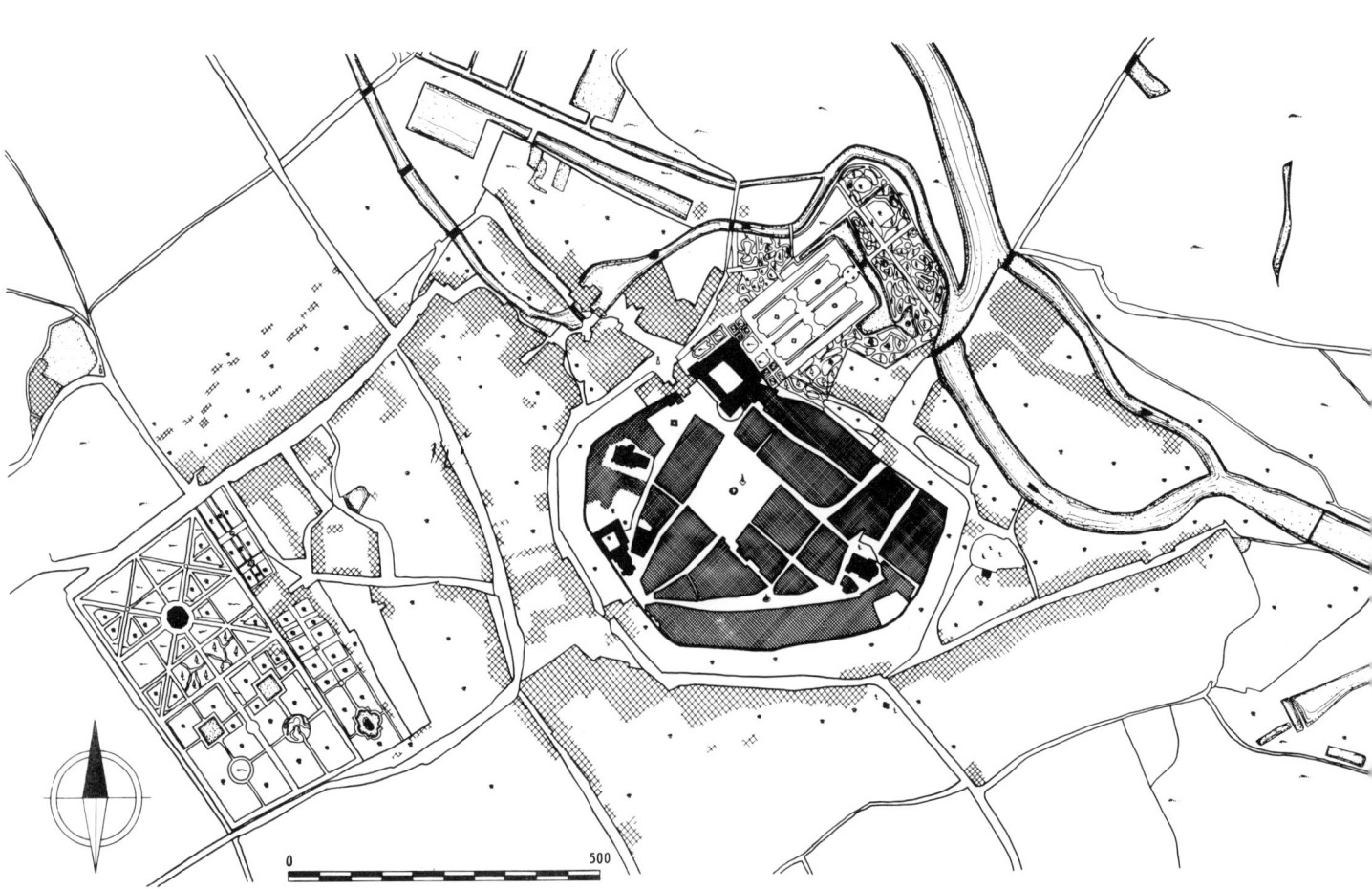

188. Plan of Kroměříž, after a cadastral map of 1830.

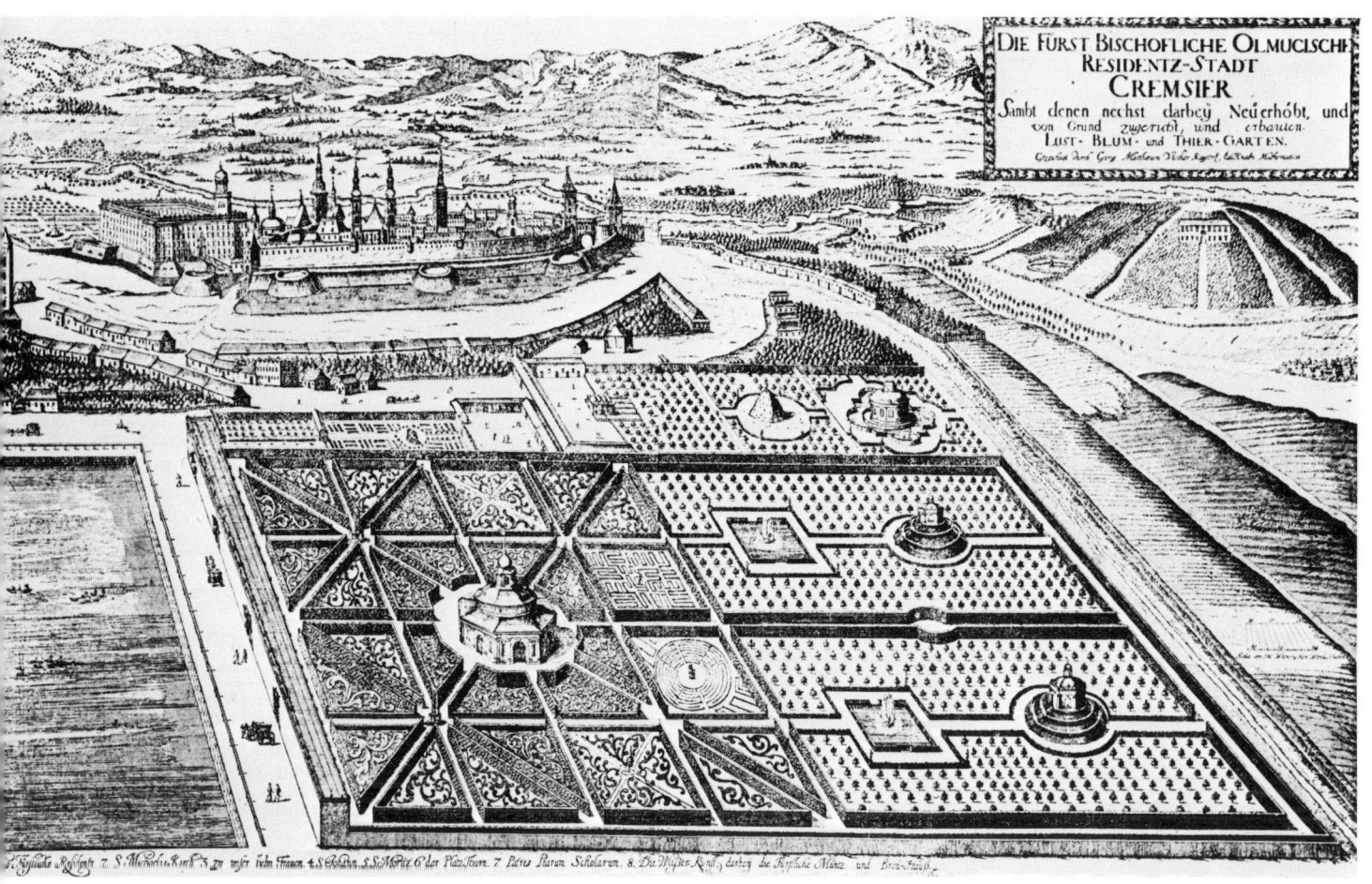

189. View of the Pleasure Garden at Kroměříž, laid out in 1666–1675, according to a design by F. Luchese and G. P. Tencalla, known as the Flower Garden since the 19th century. Engraving by J. van Nypoort after a drawing by G. M. Vischer of 1691.

were landscaped. Several valuable buildings designed in the style of the late classical revival by Antonín Arche, such as Maximilian's Farm, the Silver Bridge, and the Pompeian Colonnade, have been preserved.

The second garden, the so-called Květná or Flower Garden, was laid out as a pleasure ground outside the walls of the town on the site of the former Štěchovice Orchard, in the sixties of the 17th century. Its scale, buildings, and generally preserved original plan place it among the unique early European Baroque gardens. The layout was designed by the architect Filippo Luchese. The buildings were the work of Giovanni Pietro Tencalla, who supervised their construction after the death of the architect. The central area, divided radially by foot paths, was focused on a Summer House, with a system of water jets and other water devices. On both sides of the outer edge of the garden, placed symmetrically along its main axis, were pools and lookouts. The central part of the gardens was occupied by greenhouses, aviaries, a Dutch flower garden, hedges, and labyrinths.

Kuks, Eastern Bohemia. When the Bohemian Baroque approached its culmination, Kuks, a watering place and social center, rose near the valley of the Elbe in Eastern Bohemia. It was founded in 1694 by Count F. A. Špork, a practical and enterprising entrepreneur, who completed the whole scheme in a relatively short time.

The first buildings, a chapel above the mineral spring, called the Golden Vein, and the inn, were erected on the left river bank toward the end of the 17th century. Soon afterward, gardens were laid out along either side of the newly constructed bridge, and a temporary theater was established. With the growth of the social and cultural significance of Kuks and its renown as a watering place, local building activities increased. In 1710, Count Špork took up temporary residence in the town after a *chateau*, inns and guest rooms, a country mansion, the Philosophers' House, administrative buildings, and an adjoining village had been built, on the left bank of the river.

By 1710, building activities were in full swing, even on the right bank of the river. This year also witnessed the completion of the monumental main front of the hospital church, after the designs by Giovanni Battista Alliprandi.

While the left river bank has retained only fragments of the original architecture, the right river bank of Kuks, with its well-preserved church, hospital, and pleasure grounds, still remains a priceless example of Baroque art of the first decades of the 18th century.

190. View of Kuks, the spa of the aristocracy. On the right, the castle; on the left, the hospital. Engraving by M. Renz and J. D. Montalegri, 1723.

Kutná Hora, Central Bohemia. The region of Kutná Hora has been known since time immemorial because of the silver deposits found in the valley between the Iron Mountains, Železné hory, and the highlands of Central Bohemia. In the 10th century, a mint was located in the southeastern part of the present town of Kutná Hora, within the premises of the walled-in settlement of Malín. The latter was the property of the House of Slavník, the ruling family, who soon had to yield, however, to the growing power of the Přemyslide dynasty.

About the year 1142, the monastery of Sedlec was founded in the neighborhood of Malín, one of the oldest seats of the Cistercian Order in the Bohemian lands. In spite of repeated damages, the buildings of Sedlec are a living reminder of its Medieval and Baroque eras. Artistic activity was stimulated by the rich output of the silver mines which, for centuries, had a marked influence on the development of the nearby town of Kutná Hora, at one time the most important town of the Kingdom of Bohemia after the capital of Prague.

The discovery of exceptionally rich silver veins, at the close of the third quarter of the 13th century, was the occasion for the founding and rapid development of the town. The news of the silver mines of Kutná Hora soon spread all over Europe, calling forth a silver rush similar to the gold rush of California and Alaska. From far and near adventurers came to Kutná Hora, numbering about 100,000 people, according to contemporary—perhaps exaggerated—reports.

This period of bustling agitation did not leave time for thoughts on town planning and architecture. To this day, the plan of the historic nucleus of Kutná Hora testifies to the original growth of the town. Its design was largely determined by mining requirements, the location of the pits and access to the shafts. The partly preserved old communication system became the backbone of the street pattern. Since the community was located on the site of earlier settlements, densely popu-

191. Plan of the historic nucleus of Kutná Hora, after a cadastral map of 1839.

lated even in early feudal times, it can be taken for granted that the nucleus, or the neighborhood closest to it, was occupied by several villages, as indicated by the location of several small churches.

The town of Kutná Hora soon occupied an extensive territory with a partly radial ground plan. In the center of the town a number of regular blocks of houses grew up, and a complex system of market squares was laid out.

King Václav II (Wenceslas II), during whose reign the silver rush reached its high point, was fully aware of the economic and political importance of mining. He provided the mines of Kutná Hora with a firm legal basis in the form of the *ius regale montanorum,* a law that spread even to far-off countries.

Among the first buildings of architectural interest was the royal mint, the so-called Italian Court, Vlašský dvůr, where the output of the mines was gathered. Here, a great part of the economic power of the last Přemyslide kings, as well as those of the Luxemburg and Jagellon dynasties, had its origin.

In the 14th century, the whole town and its outskirts were transformed by an intensive building activity. The most important of the suburbs was located along the southern boundary of the original nucleus. The Gothic church, consecrated to the Holy Virgin, Panna Mária na Náměsti, has been preserved to the present day.

The Hussite Wars meant a break in the busy life of the growing town. After the defeat in 1421, it was set on fire by the retreat-

192. The Italian Court, originally the royal seat with a mint (13th to 14th centuries), at Kutná Hora.

193. The historic center of Kutná Hora, with one of the town's squares. In the background, on the left, the so-called Stone House, a Gothic building of the last quarter of the 15th century.

ing King Zikmund (Sigismund); it was rebuilt during the following decades of the 15th century. In the last quarter of this century the economic power of the town increased enough, thanks to the output of the silver mines, to support the construction of St. Barbara's Cathedral.

By the first half of the 16th century, mining was on the decline; by the 1540s, several big mines were no longer in operation. The town was thus deprived of its economic base. The period of the Renaissance may serve as an example of declining building activities. At that time, only a few individual buildings of architectural interest were erected, indicating that Kutná Hora could not keep pace with the majority of large Bohemian towns.

Kutná Hora suffered greatly during the Thirty Years' War when a number of houses were destroyed and never restored. However, the early Baroque era altered the architectural appearance of the town to a considerable degree, due to the influence of the Counter Reformation. In 1667, construction

194. In the foreground, the Gothic castle of Kutná Hora (15th century); behind the castle, the early Jesuit College (1626–1667); in the background, the Cathedral of St. Barbara (14th–16th centuries) built, among others, by Matouš Rejsk and Benedict Rejt.

of the Jesuit College was begun. Its huge but rather monotonous façade, originally adorned with three spires, is a Baroque counterpart of St. Barbara's Church.

The architectural and artistic efforts in the Baroque period gained even more ground at the beginning of the 18th century. The most sumptuous work was the unfinished Ursuline Convent designed by Kilian Ignac Dientzenhofer. Another renowned architect of the Baroque, František Maxmilián Kaňka, built the church consecrated to St. John of Nepomuk. Baroque decorations adorning the town houses became more frequent, even before the middle of the 18th century. Buildings received new façades and were embellished with rich gables.

The great fire of 1823 destroyed the southeastern part of the urban nucleus, which was later rebuilt in a rather nondescript Classicist manner. Since Kutná Hora had no industries and was situated away from the main routes of communication, its development lagged behind other towns in the 19th and the first half of the 20th century.

Kyjov, Southern Moravia. The town of Kyjov, situated at the border between the highland of Ždánský les and the lowland of Southern Moravia, was known as early as 1130 as a market village on the important route connecting Moravia with Hungary. This early settlement, with a church on the hill, became the suburb of a town founded to the west in the 13th century.

The plan of the town, enclosed by a double moat and simple fortifications with three gateways, was focused on a large square. The town hall, with a high Renaissance tower, was situated on the west side of the square, close to the walls where the old ghetto was located. Up to the 18th century, it had mostly two-storied timber houses, with arcades around the square.

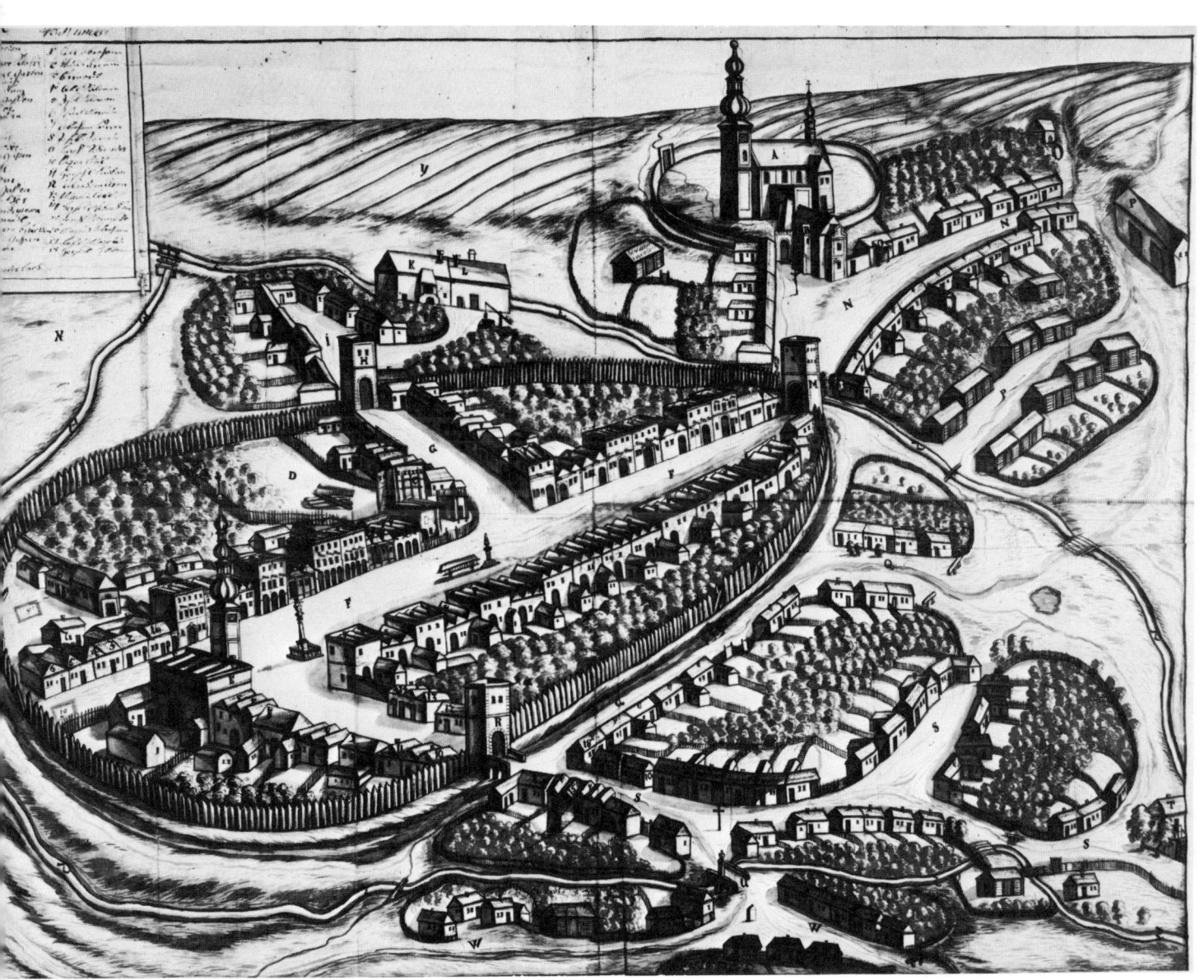

195. View of the town of Kyjov from the collection of Dismas von Hoffer (1723–1728).

Leopoldov, Western Slovakia. The development of the town was considerably impaired by the important Baroque fortress situated in the vicinity of the present settlement. It was constructed to replace the citadel of Nové Zámky, captured by the Turks in 1663. The main architect of the fort was Jan Melichar Arigsperger, who died shortly after the beginning of its construction (1665). His successor, Ján Unger, continued his work, adhering to the principles initiated by Arigsperger. The design of the fort, preserved to our day, was based on the experience of the military engineers of Italy and France. The hexagonal plan and the diagonal streets with a hexagonal square in the center represented a version of the Ideal Cities of Italy and France. In 1669 the fortress was completed, covering an area of 138.32 acres, including the walls and battlements. It lost its military function in 1854. The town, situated not far from the citadel, was reconstructed after the departure of the Turks in 1683.

196. Plan of the citadel of Leopoldov from the 17th century.

Levoča, Eastern Slovakia. Information concerning the existence of the original settlement, situated south of the present town, dates from the end of the 12th and the beginning of the 13th century.

The center of the town is a regular, rectangular square, extending from northeast to southwest and determining the main direction of the streets. Increasing trade favored the development of the town. Narrow lots, built up on one side only, were delimited by parallel main streets and a network of transverse streets and lanes. In the Middle Ages, Levoča's area exceeded that of other towns in the vicinity, making it one of the largest urban centers in Slovakia.

At the beginning of the 15th century, the town obtained the right to sell its goods in Hungary, but it soon felt the consequences of a general shift of trade to the West of Europe. The uncertain political situation in contemporary Hungary and the frequent outbreak of fires affected the town's growth unfavorably.

The defense system of Levoča utilized the natural conditions of the terrain as protection on three sides. However, toward the end of the 15th century, the town's fortifications were repeatedly modified in accordance with the contemporary requirements of new military techniques.

Most changes in the structure of the town originated in the 16th century when the square obtained its final appearance. The old town hall was replaced by a new building which, after 1599, was remodeled on Renaissance lines. All buildings characteristic of medieval commercial centers were concentrated, in the 16th century, around the square. Though the original plan of the square has

197. Plan of the historic center of Levoča, after a cadastral map of the second half of the 19th century.

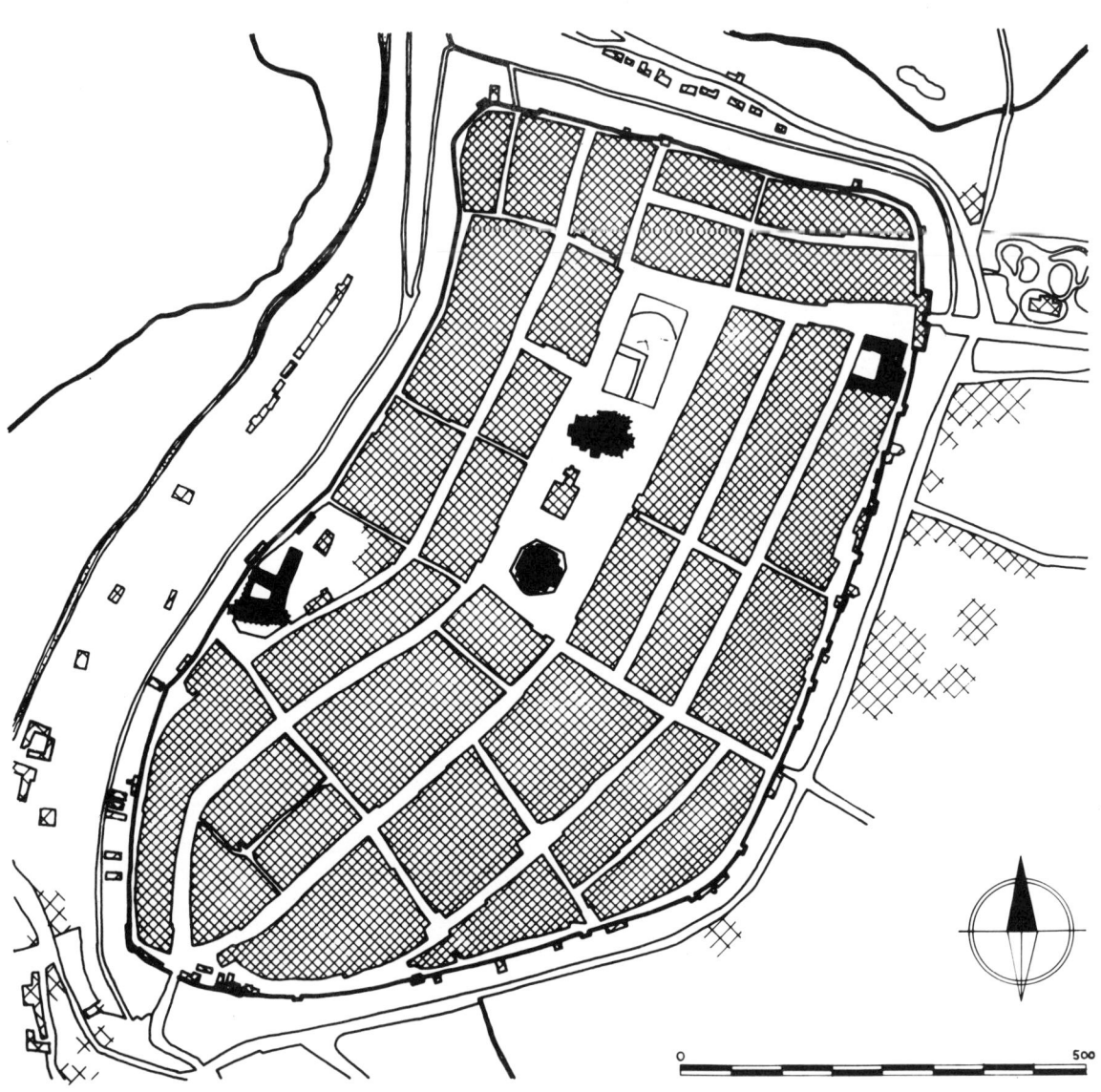

been preserved, the architectural appearance of its surrounding buildings underwent far-reaching changes. Some of these changes included the addition of arcades to the ground floors of houses and Renaissance and Baroque façades to the upper floors of the older buildings.

During the 17th and 18th centuries, the town lost its economic, political, and strategic importance. Furthermore, Levoča's remoteness from the main traffic routes not only interfered with the town's economic development but practically arrested all building activities. The resulting preservation of whole groups and blocks of Renaissance and Baroque burghers' houses as well as original timber buildings with Renaissance decorations is a unique legacy which today has turned Levoča into a national monument.

198. The Town Hall at Levoča (16th century), with the church founded in the 13th century.

Liptovská Teplička, Central Slovakia. The village of Liptovská Teplička is situated in the northern part of Central Slovakia in the District of Poprad, on the northern slopes of the Low Tatra Mountains at a height of 3,014 feet above sea level. It was founded in 1634 by Polish colonists; at present it is part of an agricultural mountain community, created by the clearing of the surrounding forest. It is inhabited by farmers and forest laborers.

The village is bisected by two streams, along which houses and communications developed. Its core is compactly built up. A characteristic feature of the village is the concentration of all barns in the southern part outside the village proper in the vicinity of the brooks. This measure was probably called forth as a precaution against fires.

The gables of the majority of the farmhouses face the public road. Behind every farmhouse, built with the typical tripartite plan of living room, hall, and chamber, are the stable and sheds enclosing the yard. The houses, mostly built of logs, are whitewashed or plastered and roofed with wood shingles. Window frames are usually painted in bright colors.

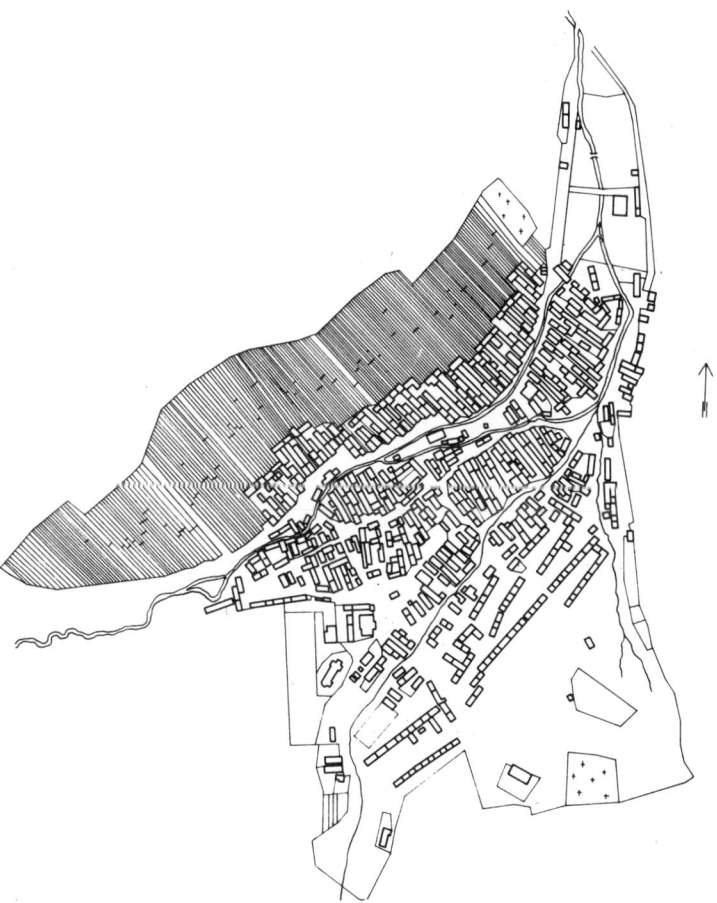

199. Plan of the village of Liptovská Teplička, after a cadastral map of 1866.

200. General view of the village of Liptovská Teplička.

Litava, Central Slovakia. This village is situated in the fertile Krupina Hills in the southern part of Central Slovakia in the District of Krupina, nestling in a shallow valley on the river Litavica, at a height of 1,509 feet above sea level. The village was first mentioned in 1035, and its church in 1168. Until the 19th century, Litava formed part of the property of the nearby Bzovík Abbey. To the southwest of the village was a castle of the same name, mentioned for the first time in 1307.

The most compact part of the village, with terrace houses, is situated on the western slope. The eastern and northern parts of the village are laid out very irregularly. The village has no pronounced center, the church being situated somewhat to the east.

The streets of the regular part of the village are characterized by an alternation of farmhouses and stables with large barns. The latter dominate the street picture with their high thatched roofs.

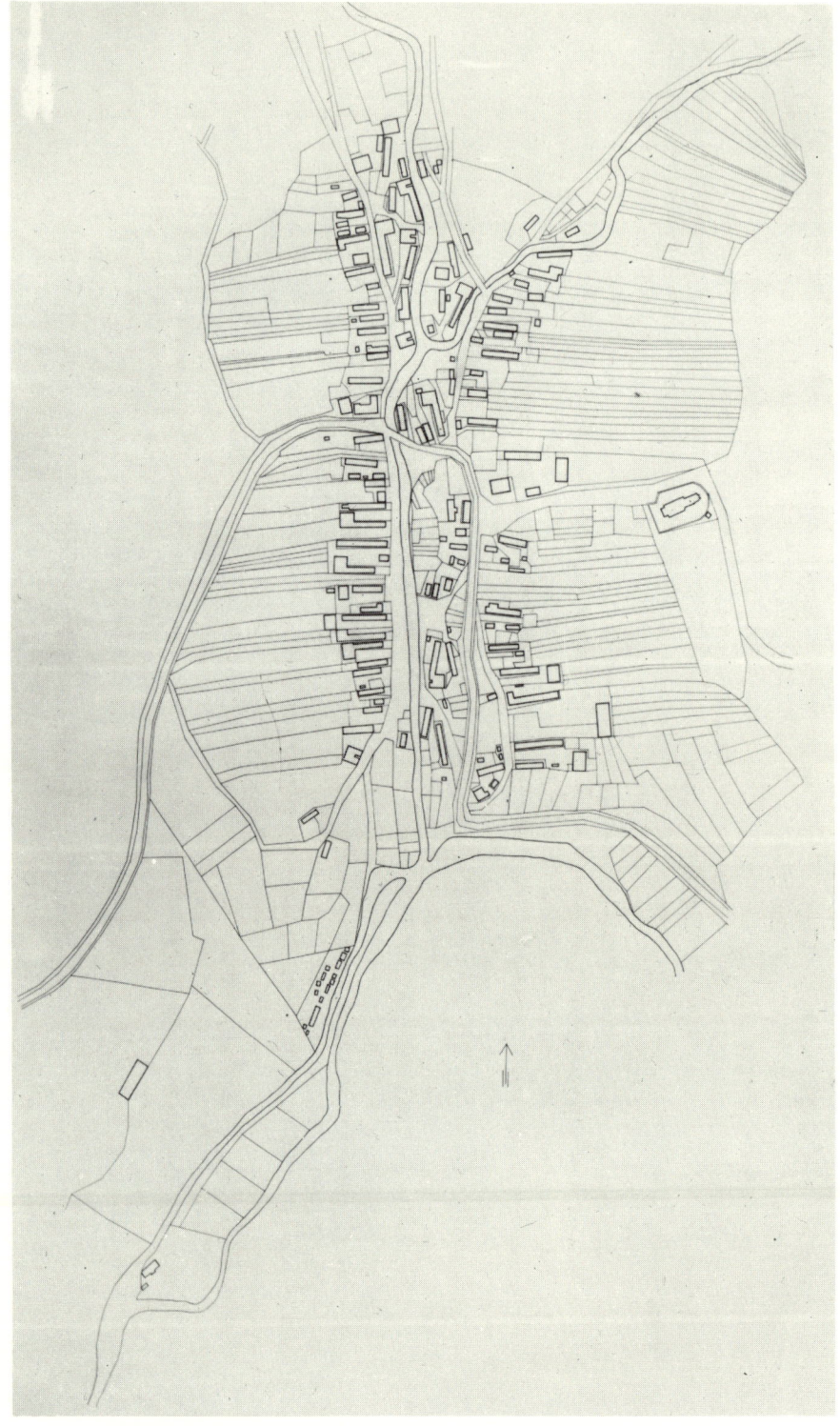

201. Plan of the village of Litava, after a cadastral map of 1935.

A characteristic feature of this region is the "double barn," whose U-shaped plan is probably due to the intention to cover the large barn area with a low and therefore wind-resistant roof.

Farmhouses are sometimes combined in pairs and adjoined by other farm buildings. They are built of stone, plastered, and covered with thatched roofs. Wherever the sloping ground affords favorable conditions, the houses are provided with cellars under their front parts.

202. A 19th-century farmstead in the village of Litava.

Litoměřice, Northern Bohemia. The name of the North Bohemian town is derived from an ancient independent tribe that settled on the headland of Litoměřice, at the point where the stream known as Pokratice flows into the river Elbe. The site of Litoměřice on a crossing over the Elbe was so favorable that the town retained its importance even after the formation of the Bohemian State, and the former tribal stronghold became a Royal Town.

Soon a *suburbium* and other settlements of an agricultural, handicraft, and mercantile character sprang up around the stronghold of Litoměřice. To its south, near the ford of the Elbe, the Fishermen's Quarter developed. It may be presumed that another settlement grew up at the eastern foot of the stronghold, where the Pokratice joins the Elbe River. North of Litoměřice, along the banks of the river, was the village of Zásada, and to the east of the town another village, called Újezd. Later, this group was apparently unified by a road from Litoměřice to Prague toward the east.

The development of Litoměřice in the Middle Ages differed from that of the majority of other Bohemian towns. Litoměřice became a Royal Town about 1227, thus ranking among the oldest of such towns in the country. Its original core was modest, incorporating the smaller part of the early feudal agglomeration. It probably included only the blocks of houses on the present square which, almost certainly, did not exist at that time. In the third quarter of the 14th century, under the reign of Charles IV, the town was expanded toward the east, and a large square was laid out. The building blocks are regularly spaced. The extended area was fortified, and the royal castle was built at the southwestern side of the walls.

The medieval fortifications of Litoměřice ranked among the strongest in the Czech lands. In spite of their repeated destruction, it can still be seen that they were part of the most remarkable defensive systems of the Middle Ages in this country.

Litoměřice suffered great damage in the course of the Thirty Years' War. However, the economic power of the town and the foundation of a bishopric in 1655 contributed to a rapid revival of building activities during the second half of the 17th century. In the first decade of the 18th century, a period of stagnation set in which lasted until the early 19th century. It was only in the 1840s that the town began to expand.

203. Plan of the historic center of Litoměřice. The dotted outline marks the location of the Slavonic walled settlement.

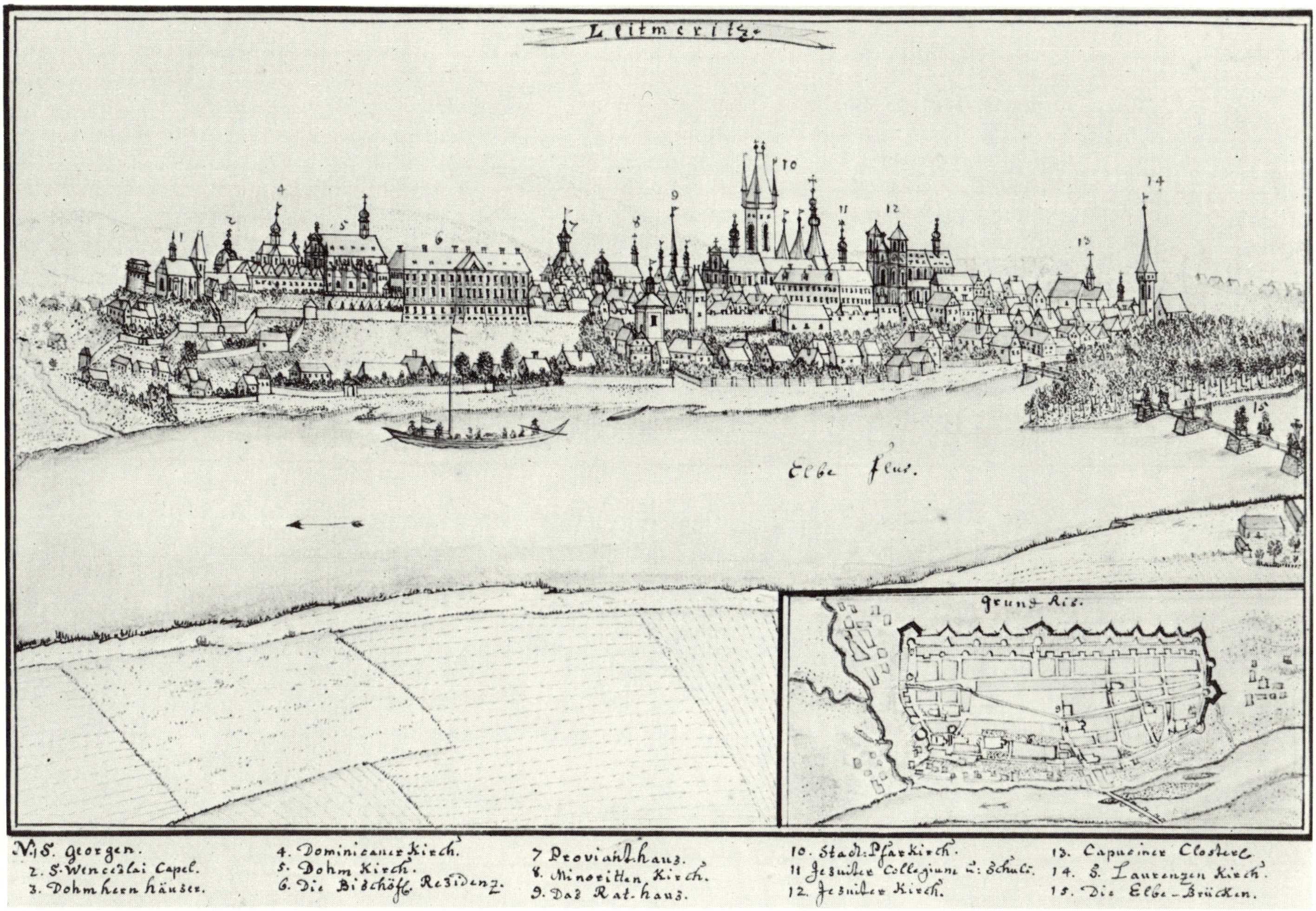

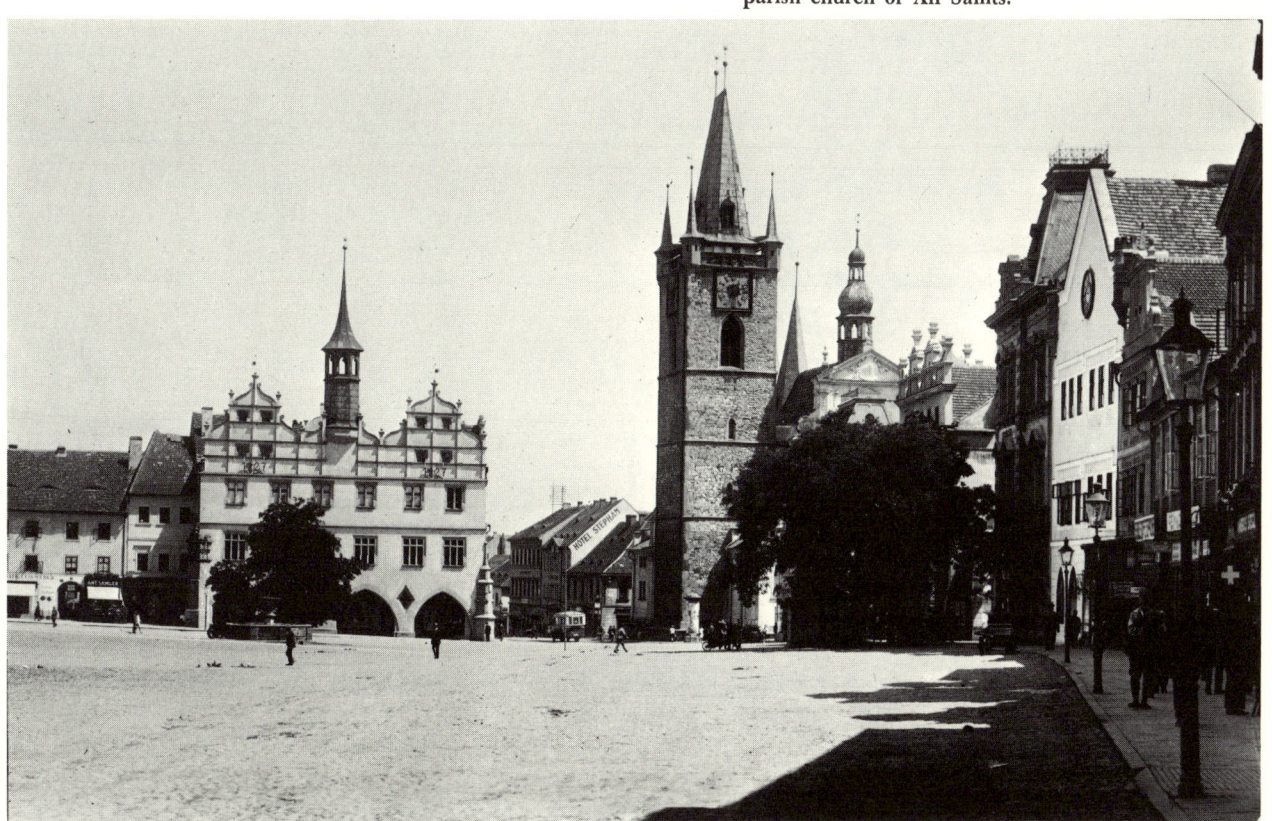

Litmeritz
Elbe flus.
Grund Ris.
N.1 S. georgen.
2. S. Wenceslai Capel.
3. Dohmhern häuser.
4. Dominicaner Kirch.
5. Dohm Kirch.
6. Die Bischöfl. Residenz.
7 Proviant haus.
8. Minoritten Kirch.
9. Das Rat-haus.
10. Stadt Pfar Kirch.
11 Jesuiter Collegium u: Schul.
12. Jesuiter Kirch.
13. Capuciner Closter.
14. S. Laurenzen Kirch.
15. Die Elbe-Brücken.

204. *Above:* General view of Litoměřice by Friedrich Bernhard Werner, middle of the 18th century.

205. *Below:* Southeast corner of the square at Litoměřice. On the left, the Gothic town hall built in 1537–1539; in the center, the Gothic tower of the parish church of All Saints.

Litomyšl, Eastern Bohemia. A castle on a trade route near the border of Moravia and Bohemia served in A.D. 981 as the administrative center of the region. In the settlement below the castle, a Benedictine monastery was built in 1098. In 1259, Přemysl II raised this market community to the status of a town; it became the seat of a bishopric in 1344. In 1356 an Augustinian monastery was erected.

In 1490 the so-called Horní Město (Upper or New Town) was established next to the castle. However, it never gained any importance and in no way overshadowed the significance of the old Dolní Město (Lower Town). At that time Litomyšl was one of the centers of the Unity of Brethren. Later it became the property of the wealthy Pernštejn family for whom, in the years 1568–1573, Giovanni Battista Avostalis built a magnificent Renaissance castle with arcades and graffiti on the site of the original stronghold. At the beginning of the 18th century, a num-

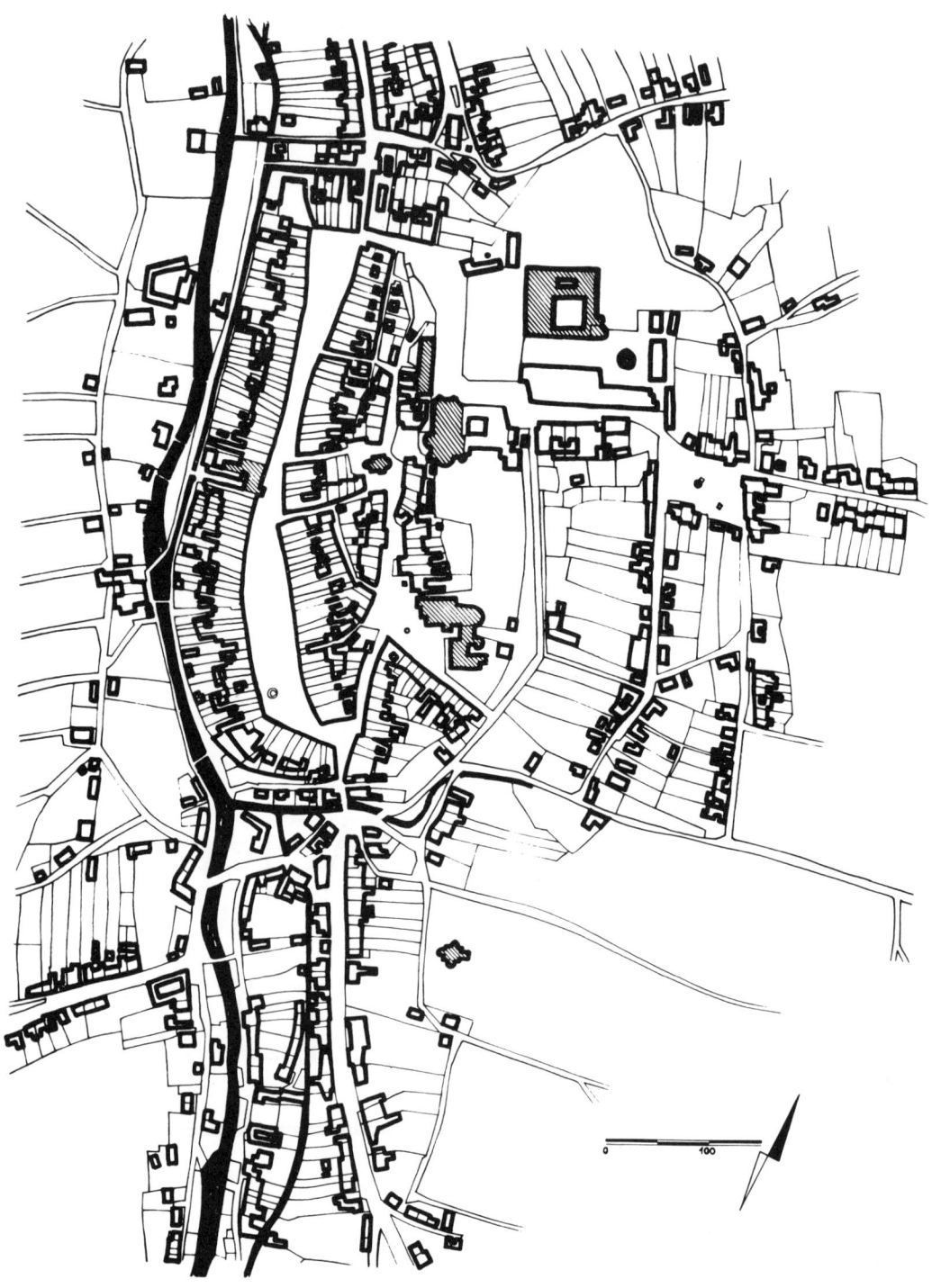

206. Plan of Litomyšl, after a cadastral map of 1839.

ber of important buildings were constructed in the town, including a Piarist college and church, a brewery, and stables.

Today Litomyšl ranks among the most charming and best preserved historical towns of Czechoslovakia. The elongated town square with the town hall is framed by historic buildings with arcades. The silhouette of the town is dominated by the mass of the castle and the towers of several churches.

207. Square at Litomyšl. On the left, the tower of the Town Hall from the 16th century.

Manětín, Western Bohemia. The small town of Manětín, rising on the former site of an early medieval settlement, was first mentioned in 1169 in a deed of the Bohemian King, Vladislav II. In its present form, Manětín represents one of the most characteristic Baroque complexes in the west of Bohemia. Its simple plan dates from the Middle Ages, when the original community was still a market village. Its main axis is an almost straight road running parallel to a brook, lined with houses on either side and adjoined by an irregular oblong square.

Manětín, which was raised to a town in 1382, underwent an interesting change during the Baroque era due to vigorous building activities, particularly after the great fire in 1712. The Gothic parish church was then rebuilt, and the original Renaissance castle was converted into a Baroque palace occupying the southern and lower side of the square. The rebuilding of the castle was soon followed by the restoration of the town hall and numerous two-storied houses lining the upper side of the square.

208. View of the square at Manětín. On the right, the Baroque castle, reconstructed in the second decade of the 18th century. The terrace below the castle is decorated with vases and Baroque sculpture. On the left, a row of modest Baroque houses from the first half of the 18th century.

Mariánské Lázně, Western Bohemia. Mariánské Lázně (Marienbad) is the youngest of the four world-famous Bohemian spas. In contrast to the other three, it was never a feudal town or village. It is situated on the border of a forest where the felling of trees and building were prohibited. At the beginning of the 19th century, a unique town-planning scheme was inaugurated in the deserted swampy valley, spreading from the south to the undulating plain on the southern flank of the Slavkov Forest. At the foot of the nearby Premonstratensian monastery of Teplá a settlement was founded whose layout resembled that of a medieval community. The nearby swamps were drained. At great cost, a spa was built which, thanks to its location, parks, and urban design, became one of the most beautiful resorts in Bohemia and, at the same time, a symbol of modern settlement of the second half of the 20th century.

The curative springs of the village of Úšovice, property of the Teplá Monastery since the 13th century, had been known for centuries to the local country population. However, it was only in the second half of the 18th century that interest arose in their exploitation for therapeutic purposes, with a plan for a spa to be supervised by medical research workers. The beginnings of a settlement in an inaccessible swampy forest inhabited by a few woodcutters began with the construction of timber and, later, stone buildings, near the individual springs. Except for a few interruptions—some lasting many years—construction continued from 1710 on. Nevertheless, Mariánské Lázně could boast no more than 13 buildings when the spa became an independent community in 1812.

An important decision on the status and construction of the spa was reached in 1813–1827: A decree of 1818, issued by the chief burgrave of the Czech lands, proclaimed that Mariánské Lázně was to be a public spa and that an English park should be laid out in its center, under the supervision of Václav Skalník, landscape gardener of the Lobkovic family. This decision determined the character and development of the spa. In the years 1818–1824 Václav Skalník created a central park, with the terrace of the main colonnade (between Cross Spring and the present Rudolph Spring) and a network of forest paths with lookout towers. This plan, with its smooth transition of parks into the natural landscape of the wooded hills and meadows on the southern side of the valley, became the basis for the further growth of the spa.

By the same decree, the working out of this plan was entrusted to Professor Jiří Fischer of the Prague Polytechnical School, also Inspector of the Czech Building Administration in Prague. In 1820 the plan was completed and printed. The construction of the spa continued on the basis of the plans of Václav Skalník and Jiří Fischer almost up to the time of World War I, when the available space was exhausted.

The basis of Václav Skalník's and Jiří Fischer's plans for the parks, streets, and the town itself was the valley surrounded by wooded hills. The old access road built in 1808 by the monastery from the south to the swampy valley has been preserved in the present plan of the town. It spans the Cross Spring and marks the border of the buildings around the promenade terraces, continuing southward to the central English Park.

Václav Skalník's park is the core of the whole composition. In the west, it is demarcated by the north-south road—the main structural axis of the whole plan—and in the north it leads to an asymmetrical oblong square. On the eastern side of the park, on the slopes of the hill, a row of buildings was constructed along three sides of a hexagon. The southern border of the central park is lined with the pavilions of the spa institutions.

The Empire buildings of the spa, and the pavilions over the springs—the Ferdinand Pavilion at Úšovice (1826–1827), the Cross Pavilion (1818), and the Rudolph Pavilion (1811), reconstructed in 1823—represent, together with a number of other spa structures, the oldest architectural monuments of the town. In 1889, the original Empire colonnade from 1826 was replaced by a construction of glass and cast iron. Most of the spa buildings —three churches, a theater, hotels, the casino, the cafes and restaurants—belong to the period of the greatest architectural development of the spa in the second half of the 19th century.

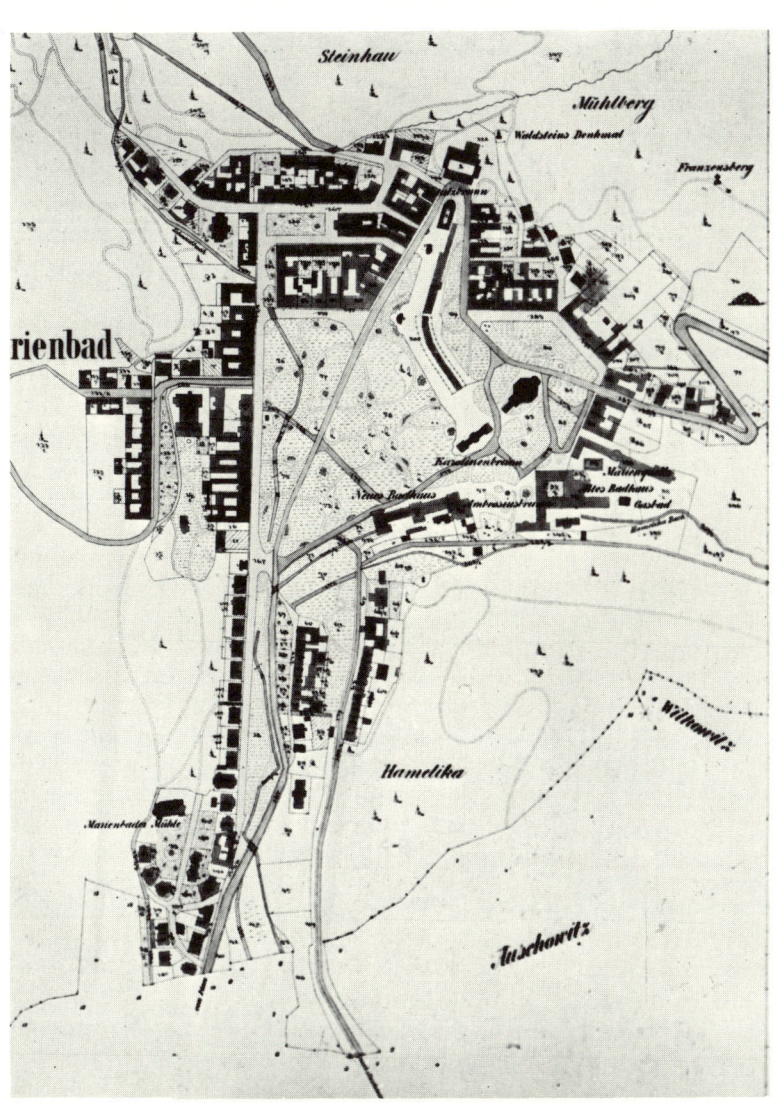

209. Reproduction of a cadastral plan of Mariánské Lázně, showing the almost completed development of the spa. The park, representing the main center with the arch of the colonnade, is bordered on the northern side by blocks of buildings and on the other sides by rows of buildings and pavilions. All the main axes are indicated on the plan as well as the oldest winding paths.

210. *Below:* View of the cast-iron colonnade and the Kříž Spring at Mariánské Lázně. In the background, the building of the management of the spa.

Mikulov, Southern Moravia. The formation of the Pavlovské vrchy, the Pavlov Hills, at the confluence of the rivers Jihlava, Svratka, and Dyje, has dominated the vast lowland in the south of Moravia since time immemorial. Since the prehistoric era it has attracted both settlements and important routes of communication. Archeological finds have revealed that the stalactite grottos of the Turold Hill, located inside the urban area of Mikulov, were inhabited in about 4000 B.C. and 2000 B.C.

In the vicinity of the village of Dolní Věstonice and other villages at the southern foot of the hills, archeological research discovered that an extensive settlement of mammoth hunters existed about 20,000 years before our era. Other finds and well-preserved earthworks show that the hill, particularly its highest peak, was crowned with a system of fortified settlements as early as the 10th century B.C. and that near the village of Mušov a *castellum* was founded by the Tenth Roman Legion in the second century A.D.

After the arrival of Slavonic tribes the whole area was extraordinarily densely settled. The urn burial ground with hundreds of grave mounds near the village of Přítluky dates from the fifth and eighth centuries of our era. The area around the hills contained a whole system of walled settlements, mentioned in the 9th to the 11th centuries. Archeological investigations carried out in recent times have disclosed fortified settlements of Great Moravia, particularly at Pohansko (pohan = pagan) in the vicinity of the town of Břeclav and in a place called Peter's Meadow, Petrova louka, near the village of Strachotín. The settlement of Pohansko, for instance, is a walled-in settlement with several outer baileys.

The territory of the early Slavonic settlements included the present area of the town of Mikulov, which was an important community at the foot of the hill. It was here that the route from the Baltic and from Poland branched off in two directions, to Vienna in the southwest and to Hungary via Břeclav in the southeast. Written records prove that a walled settlement grew up near this point, with a church consecrated to St. Wenceslas. Probably during the reign of King Přemysl Otakar II a castle was built on this place. About the thirties of the 14th century Mikulov was referred to as a town, and fortifications were constructed shortly afterward.

All phases of the town's gradual development are evident in the present plan, especially in the characteristic triangular form where the old route bifurcated.

Since the castle and the town were part of a feudal domain, their development was dependent on the resources and initiative of various noble families. Under Cardinal František Dietrichstein, during the end of the 16th and the beginning of the 17th century, a lively building activity occurred. The castle was rebuilt in accordance with the fashion of the time, and numerous secular and ecclesiastical buildings were erected under the supervision of Italian, Austrian, and native artists.

In the 19th century, economic stagnation set in, which was not relieved by the building of the railway between Mikulov and the towns of Břeclav and Znojmo.

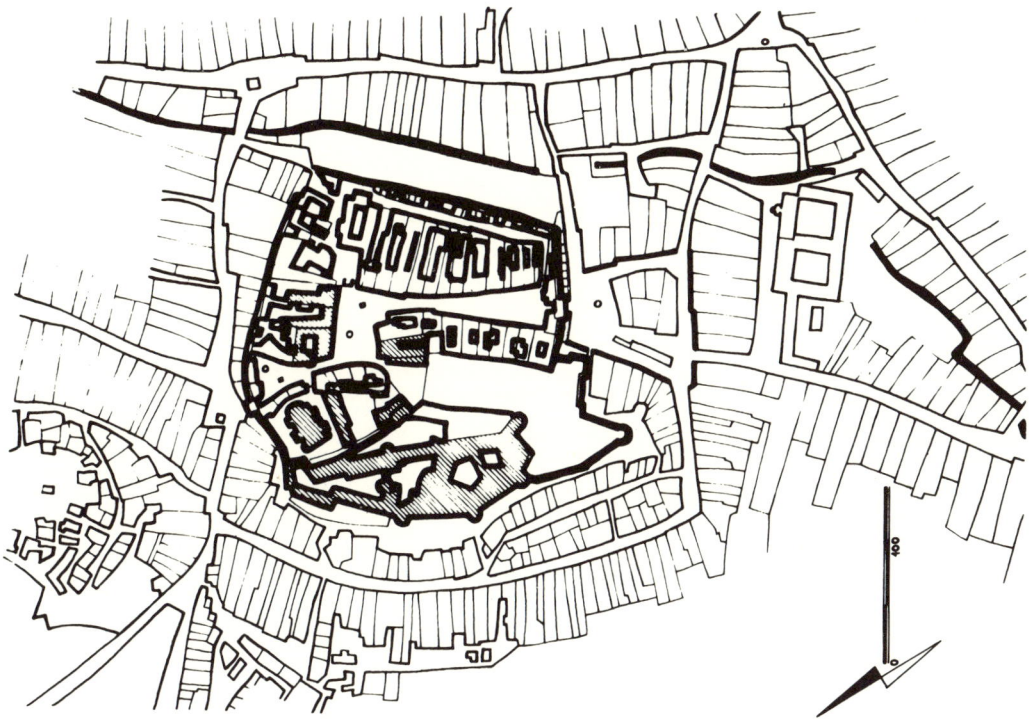

211. Plan of Mikulov, after a cadastral map of 1826.

212. Drawing of Mikulov from the Hoffer collection, 1723—1728.

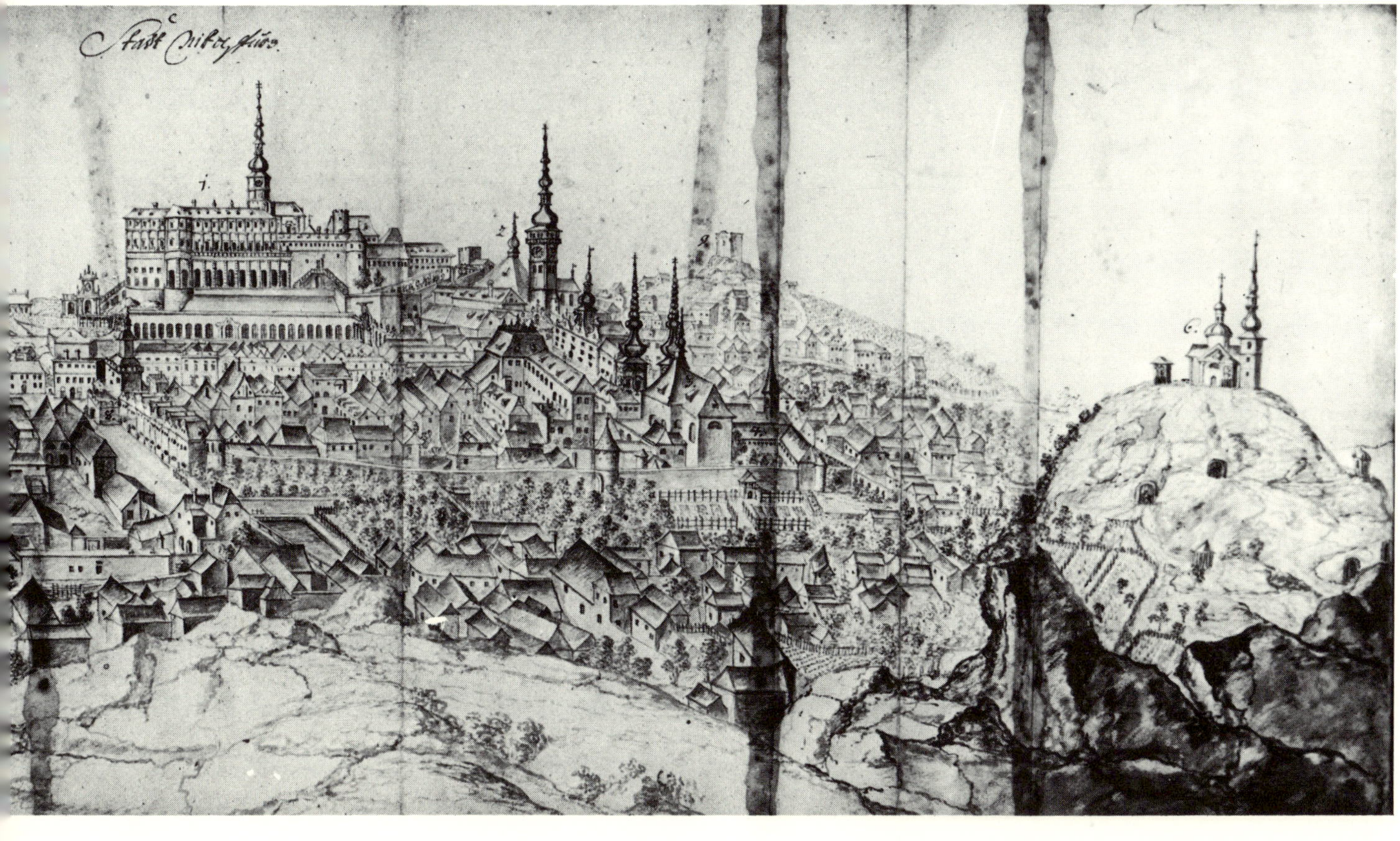

Mladá Boleslav, Central Bohemia. The headland overlooking the confluence of the rivers Klenice and Jizera, in a densely populated region, proved an ideal site for the building of a stronghold. Below this stronghold a community known as "Na podolci" soon sprang up. In the middle of the 13th century, it passed from the king to the Michalovic family, who rebuilt the castle and conferred the status of a small town on the market community.

On February 24, 1334, Ježek of Michalovic issued a document which stated: "For reasons of good will and on the advice of our friends we have transferred our town, which is called Mladá Boleslav, and located it on a small hill generally known as Hroby." The layout of the new town was determined by the headland on which it stood.

Mladá Boleslav played an important role during the Hussite Wars and resisted the Emperor Sigismund after the Battle at Lipany. Following the end of the Hussite Wars, it became a center of the religious sect of the Unity of Brethren. It was at this time that the town experienced its greatest economic development. In 1528, the former suburb known as Nové Město was included in its walls. In 1544, the Unity of Brethren began to build its headquarters, and in the years 1554–1559 they erected a town hall and, shortly afterward, a school. Mladá Boleslav's great wealth enabled the town to purchase its freedom from its feudal owner and, on July 3, 1600, the rights of a Royal Town from the Emperor Rudolf II.

The defeat of the uprising of the Estates in 1620 and the Thirty Years' War brought great changes to the town. Mladá Boleslav, known for its anti-Catholic attitude, was greatly affected by the levying of various contributions, and leading burghers and functionaries of the Unity of Brethren were exiled. It was not until the 18th and 19th centuries that the town began to recover from the additional calamities of several fires and the plague.

213. Plan of Mladá Boleslav, after a cadastral map of 1842.

Moravská Třebová, Western Moravia. In the third quarter of the 13th century, a member of the feudal family of Ryzmburk, who derived their name from a fortified castle in the Bohemian Erz Mountains, founded a town in a mountainous and wooded region of northwestern Moravia near a trade route leading from East Bohemia to Olomouc.

Moravská Třebová has the shape of a square with rounded corners. Its interior is divided by streets crossing each other at right angles and focused on a central square. The castle is situated in the southeastern area of the town.

After a fire in 1509, stone houses were erected and the fortifications were strengthened. A general reconstruction of the town in accordance with Renaissance principles took place after another fire in 1541, giving Moravská Třebová a more unified character. A new town hall with a slender octagonal tower was built on the southern side of the square.

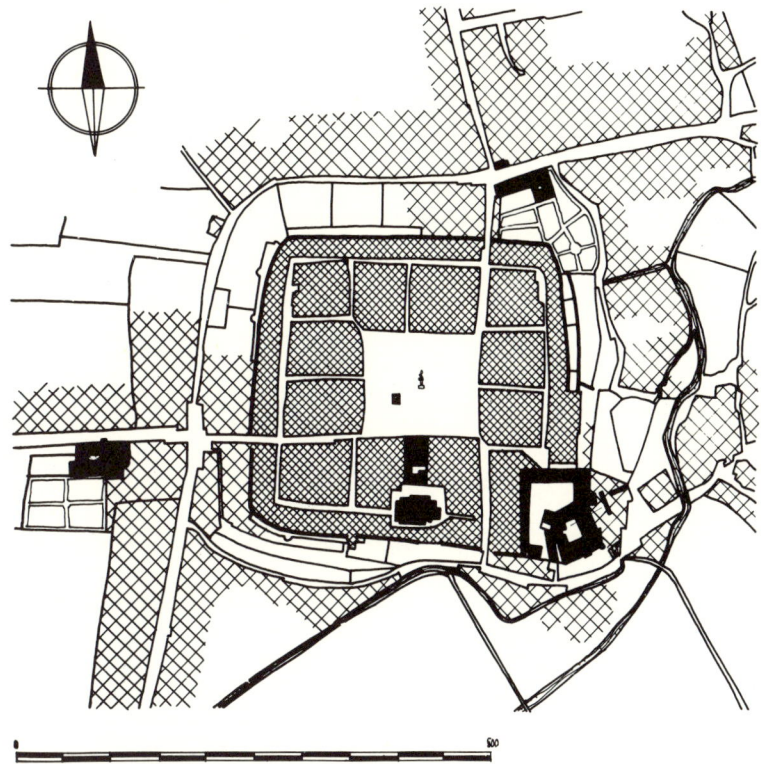

214. Plan of the historic nucleus of Moravská Třebová, after a cadastral map of 1835.

215. Airview from the northwest of the historic nucleus of Moravská Třebová. The town hall is located in the center of the southern front of the square, the parish church at the southern boundary, and the castle in the southeast corner of the town. Most buildings date from the 16th century.

Moravský Krumlov, Southern Moravia. The town of Moravský Krumlov is situated in hilly country bordering the Bohemian-Moravian Highlands. It succeeded an early Slavonic walled settlement, called Rokytná, on a nearby peninsula in the river of the same name. However, this settlement disappeared as early as 1146. The new community was founded in the 13th century, near the site of the older settlement on the peninsula.

Moravský Krumlov has a regular street system, with a rectangular square and a road following the slope of the peninsula. In the west, access to the town was protected by a castle. Near the eastern side of the nucleus, an Augustinian monastery was founded in the year 1355, while the northern side was occupied by the church.

The town was enclosed by a double wall, with one gateway in the south and another in the west. Further protection was provided by the river and the ponds around the headland. The area between the castle and the square was occupied by the ghetto, mentioned for the first time in 1402.

In the 16th century the castle was replaced by a magnificent arcaded palace. When its park was laid out, the fortifications facing the town were pulled down and the ditch separating the headland from the town was bridged over.

216. View of Moravský Krumlov, from the collection of Dismas von Hoffer, 1723–1728.

Most, Northern Bohemia. The name of the town, meaning bridge, recalls the crossing of a route connecting Prague and Meissen and passing the Lake of Komořany; this route existed in the Middle Ages in the basin between the mountain chains of Krušné hory and Středohoří, the Erz Mountains and Midland Hills. In early feudal times, a walled settlement grew up on Hnevín Hill, with a customhouse in the outer bailey, known as early as 1040 as "Hněvin most" or "Hňeva's Bridge."

The old settlement belonged to the family Hrabišici, but in 1257 it became the property of the Crown. King Wenceslas I built a royal castle on the hill, and about the middle of the 13th century King Přemysl Otakar II founded a Royal Town there, which was first mentioned in 1257.

Of considerable interest is the complex plan of the town, with three squares and extensive suburbs. The origin of this plan has been the subject of numerous discussions, particularly the situation of the original Slavonic settlement. The old nucleus of the medieval town with its three squares was the irregular triangle formerly called the Old Square, where the town hall was located. It may be assumed that two or three different communities existed in the area below the castle from which the earliest settlement originated. The remaining two regular squares were laid out in the Middle Ages. By the 14th century, all three squares had been enclosed within the walls.

The numerous privileges granted to the town and the fact that several monastic orders took up residence in Most testify to the importance of this fortified medieval place. Its economic prosperity was evident in imposing historic buildings, particularly in the church of the Blessed Virgin, rebuilt in 1515.

The town declined and was devastated by fires and visited by the plague in the Thirty Years' War. At the time of the Counter Reformation a number of buildings were reconstructed, but Most never regained its previous importance.

The 16th century witnessed the first attempts at coal mining in the vicinity of the town, and by the middle of the 18th century a number of small coal mines were opened. However, it was not until the end of the 19th century that the town became a main center of the North Bohemian lignite fields, with a developing industry and a greatly increased population.

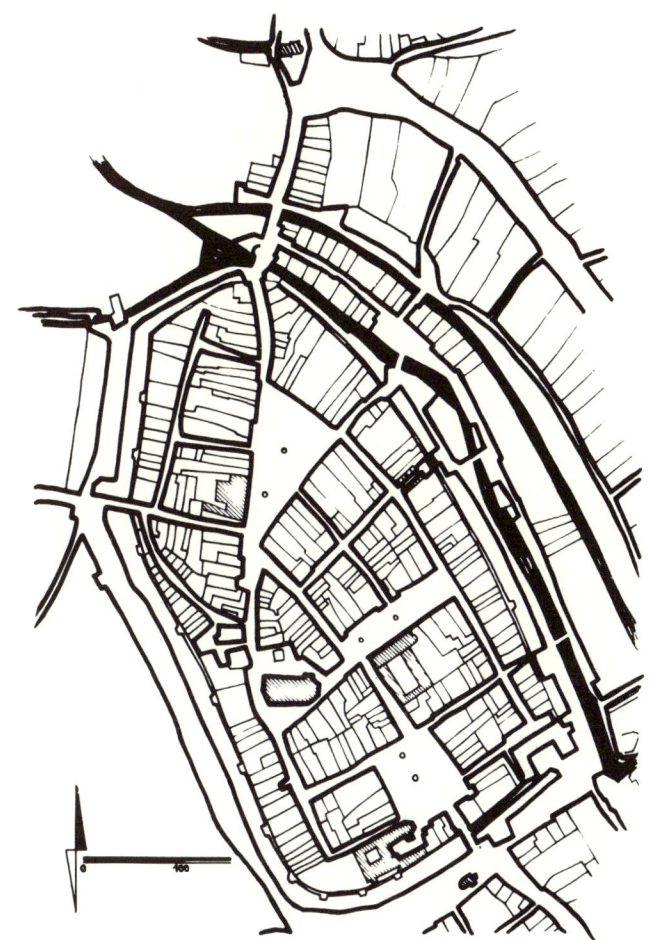

217. Plan of the historical town of Most, after a cadastral map of 1842.

218. The historic center of Most.

Netolice and Kratochvíle, Southern Bohemia.
The town of Netolice occupied the site of an early medieval village and castle mentioned by the chronicler Cosmas, in the 11th century, as a local center and strategic point on the route leading from Linz to Bohemia via the town of Vyšší Brod. The earlier settlement determined the layout of the town, which has maintained its original form to the present. A square, lined with a single row of houses in a later period, was located in the northwest of the urban area. Netolice is first mentioned as a town in the year 1263, when King Přemysl Otakar II donated it to the newly founded monastery of Zlatá Koruna.

To the west of Netolice, in a shallow valley, a village belonging to the town, called Petrův Dvůr or Peter's Farm, existed since the 14th century. In the years 1583 to 1589 the feudal lords of Rožmberk, Lords of the Rose, commissioned a country mansion in the valley, not far from the farm. It was built by the Italian architect, Balthazar Maio de Vonio. The palace of Kratochvíle (Pastime-Diversion-Sansouci) was laid out on a grand scale and surrounded with gardens subdivided by three brick walls, with two moats filled with water from a pond in the neighborhood. The main outer wall was reinforced with seven bastions. The two-storied entrance gate and the servants' quarters were located in the double front wall. In the southeastern corner near the wall stood the small Church of the Holy Virgin. The center of the whole building complex was the palace itself, a two-storied edifice constructed on piles in the marshy land, with a double mansard roof.

Netolice flourished in the 16th and 17th centuries. However, its development was impaired by its rather remote location from the main industrial centers. Thus Netolice has remained a typical agricultural town.

219. Plan of Netolice, after a cadastral map of 1837.

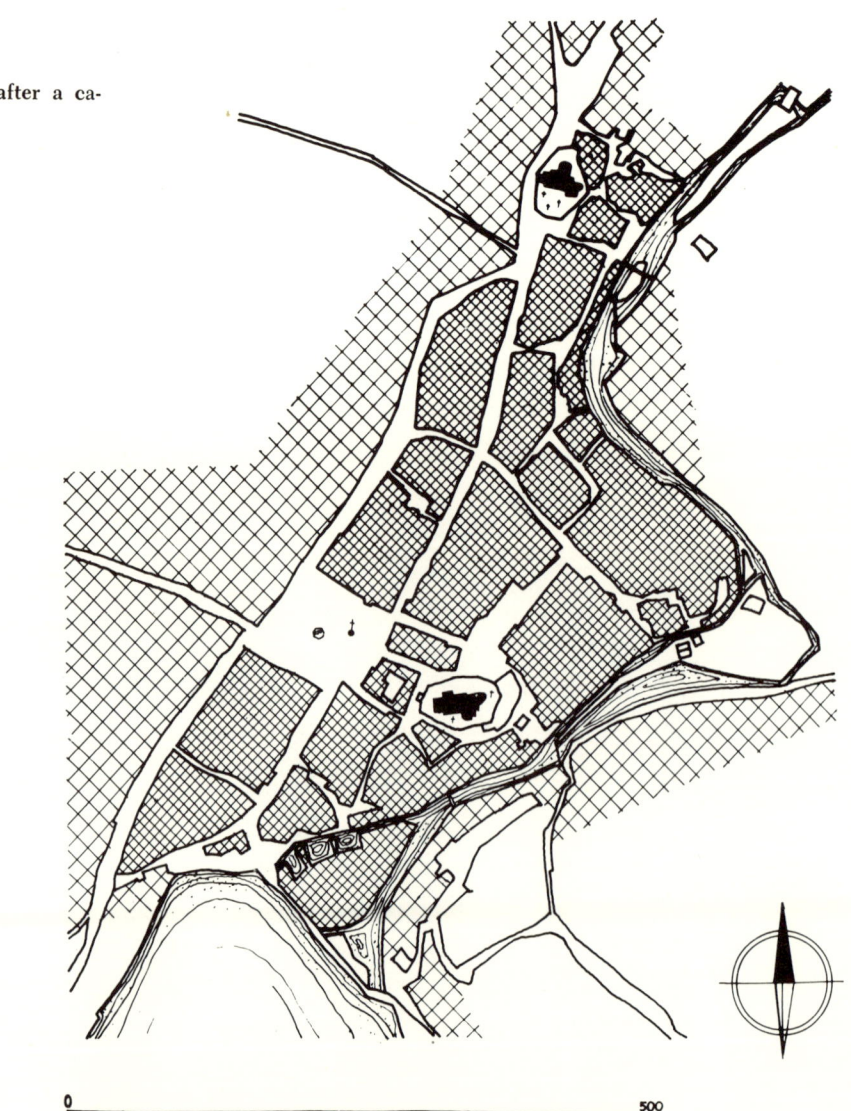

220. View of Netolice. Section of a painting by Jean de Verle, 1686.

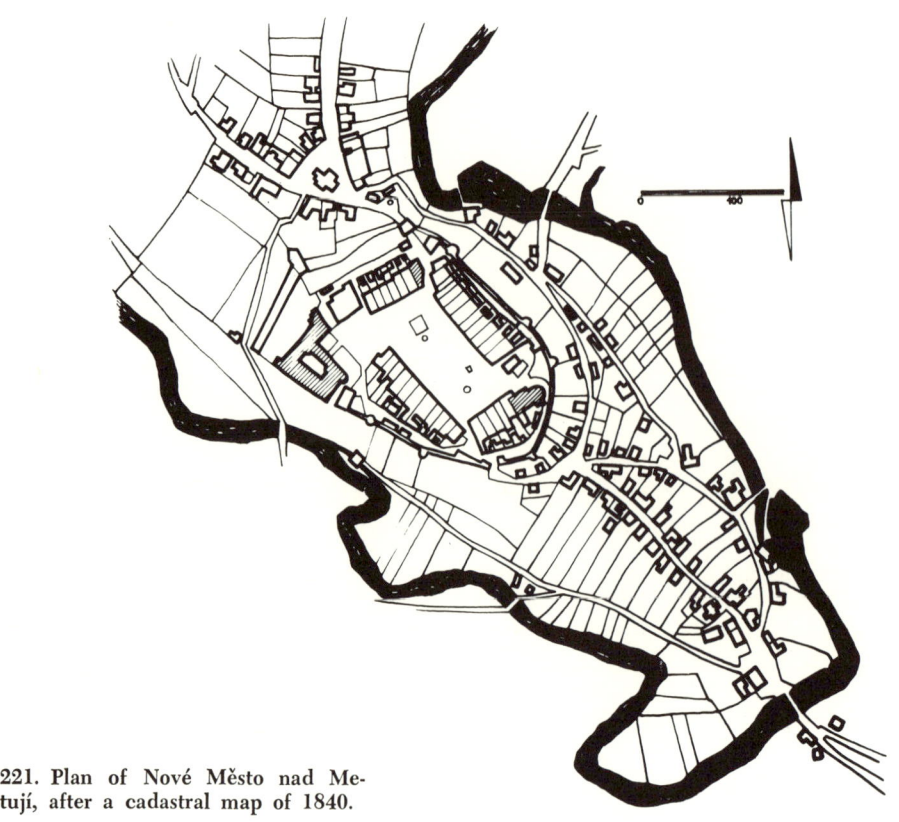

221. Plan of Nové Město nad Metují, after a cadastral map of 1840.

Nové Město nad Metují, Eastern Bohemia. In a deep forest in the northeastern part of Bohemia, at the ancient Czech-Polish frontier, a stronghold was erected on a headland over the river Metuje. When the stronghold ceased its function in the course of the 11th century, the focal point of settlement shifted to nearby Krčín on the river crossing, and the stronghold was deserted, after many centuries of use. In the last quarter of the 15th century, new life returned to the territory when a castle forming the core of the present Nové Město Castle was built on the site of the stronghold.

In 1501, Nové Město (New Town) was founded in the vicinity of this castle. The small area of the headland did not allow for the development of a more complex plan. The slightly rhomboid square is surrounded on all four sides by buildings whose backs abut the street known as Příbramská ulice along the inner side of the fortifications. The church was situated in the eastern corner of the square near the walls, and the northwest corner of the historic core was occupied by the castle.

The fortifications, built in the first quarter of the 16th century, consisted of single ramparts reinforced with high cylindrical towers and lower semicircular towers.

After a fire in 1526 in which the town was greatly damaged, the whole estate was purchased by the Pernštejn family, whose main activities were concentrated at Nové Město. An architect, whose name is unknown, was entrusted with the uniform design of all four sides of the square. Arcades and new façades with early Renaissance gables were built, although the arches of the arcades and the sequence of the gables did not always respect the division of the building sites. Nevertheless, the work was carried out in a uniform manner, including the application of prefabricated brick elements and the use of identical profiles of cornices and window casings. This activity, started in 1533, holds an important place in early Renaissance town planning in Central Europe. At about the same time, the defense system on the northern side of the town was strengthened by strong walls and a bastion. However, this scheme was never completely finished.

222. View of the square at Nové Město nad Metují, surrounded by buildings of the 16th century.

Toward the end of the 16th century Nové Město, with its fortifications and gables, ranked among the most picturesque and most attractive towns in Bohemia. The Thirty Years' War, however, ended all town-planning activities. After the town was burned in 1639, the restoration of the buildings was carried out unsystematically and without regard for the original unified composition.

In spite of repeated alterations, the Renaissance architecture of Nové Město, enclosed by medieval fortifications, has basically been preserved to the present day. Research has discovered a considerable part of the original Pernštejn façades and gables so that it was possible in 1953 to reconstruct the northern side of the square in its early Renaissance character of the thirties of the 16th century.

223. The northern section of the square at Nové Město nad Metují, with uniformly designed early Renaissance houses.

224. View through the early Renaissance arcades at the northeast side of the square at Nové Město nad Metují, dating from the second quarter of the 16th century.

Nové Zámky, Southern Slovakia. The layout of the present town in Southern Slovakia dates back to the Renaissance fort of the 16th century. The development of military engineering in Slovakia was closely connected with the protection of the territories against Turkish raids. Nové Zámky, built several years earlier than Palma Nova in Italy, is one of the few examples of an Ideal City.

The new fort of Nové Zámky was built on the site of a small strongpoint which no longer fulfilled its defensive purposes. Hence the Emperor Maximilian ordered a new fort to be built, according to a design by O. Baldigara. The construction of this fortified town began in 1573. Its regular hexagonal layout was enclosed in star-shaped walls with projecting bastions.

A square occupied the center of the town, on which the main streets converged, forming six building blocks. The area of the square was large enough for the erection of public and ecclesiastical buildings such as the church (1585).

The construction of the place was terminated seven years later. However, in the course of the following decades it was partially reconstructed. In 1685 it lost its strategic importance in the defense against Turkish invasions but was rebuilt for military purposes with the participation of French military engineers and was considered one of the important fortifications of Europe. When its walls were demolished in 1724, the town lost its function as a fortress.

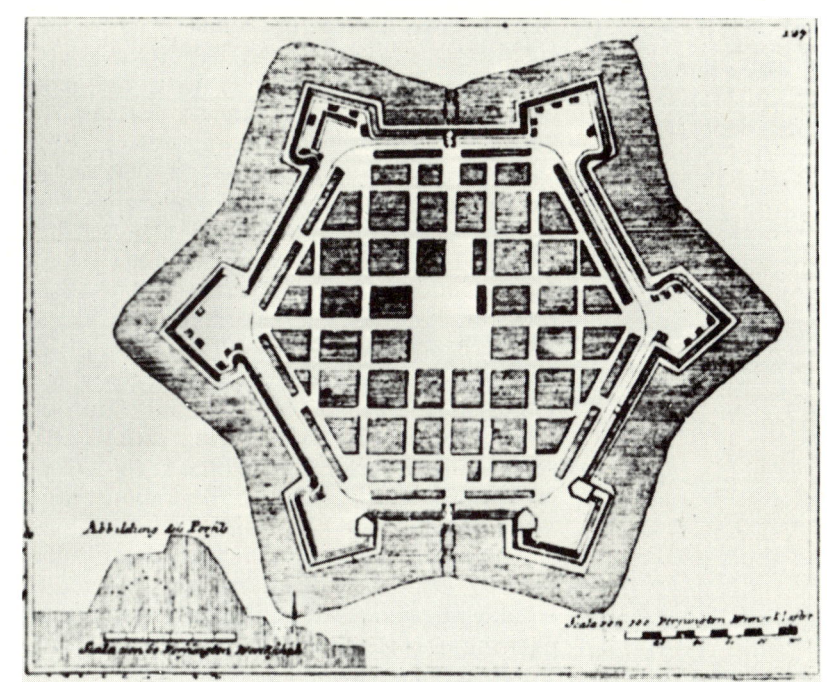

225. Plan of Nové Zámky in the 18th century.

226. Plan of the citadel of Nové Zámky in the 17th century. From the collection of the National Gallery in Bratislava.

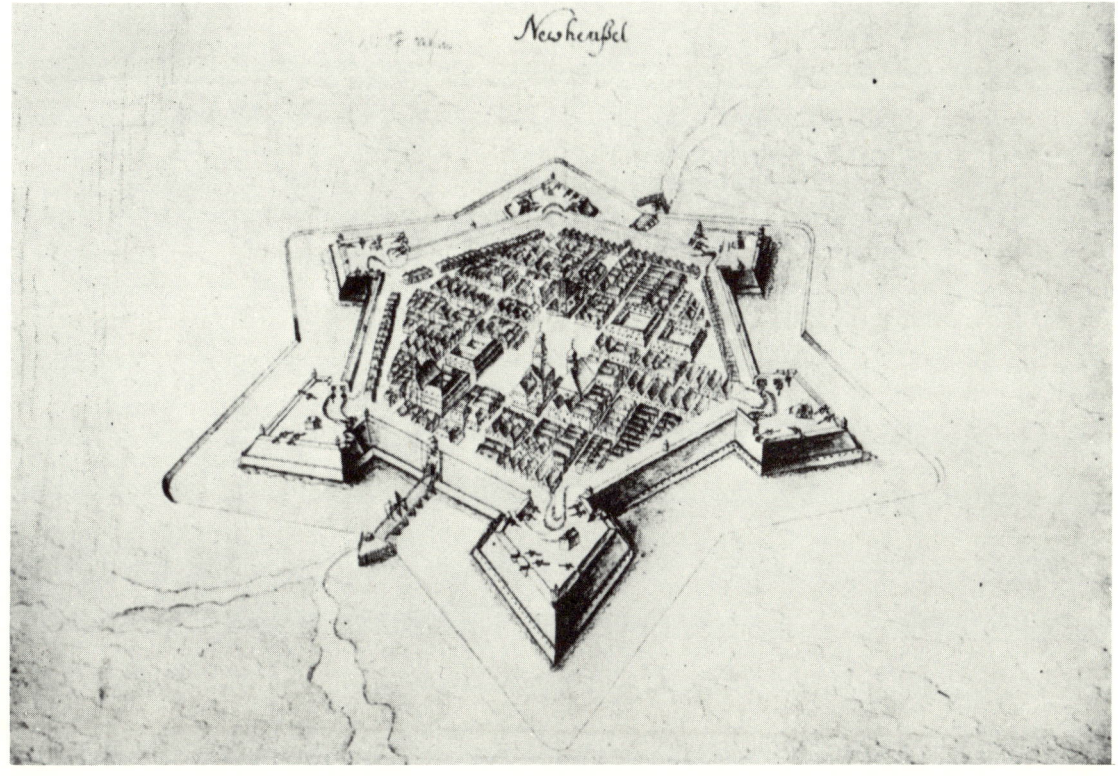

Nový Bydžov, Eastern Bohemia. The village of Bydžov, situated at the important route connecting Central Bohemia with the passages in the borderland forests leading to Silesia, was first mentioned in 1186. It had a radial ground plan. Later, it became a market town but lacked the conditions for a regular town layout. After 1300, King Václav II (Wenceslas II) founded a new town, Nový Bydžov, in a more advantageous position on the river Cidlina, about 1.9 miles southeast of the original settlement. Its plan, preserved to the present, reflects the highest standards of town planning in the countries of the Bohemian Crown during the Middle Ages, with the exception of the New Town of Prague, which was laid out about fifty years later.

The ideal scheme of the plan—not fully realized—was the square nucleus, with the equilateral square in its center and streets entering the square at the corners and in the center of its sides. The two central streets, running east-west, follow the main direction between the two town gates. Along the northern side, the square base is cut off by a rather irregular segment.

The original design can be deduced from the plan of the suburbs. The road, following the town boundary with blocks of houses grouped along its course, determines the square outline of the nucleus. However, the design is not limited to the periphery. The whole territory of Nový Bydžov, including the adjoining agricultural land, was evidently laid out according to uniform principles, a method not necessarily complying with the general notion of town planning in the 13th century. The town of Nový Bydžov represents a high point of the art of city planning during the Middle Ages, probably unparalleled in contemporary European practice.

The architecture of New Bydžov did not parallel the grand scale of the ground plan. With the exception of the Gothic parish church, built in the 14th century in the center of a quadrangular area south of the square, and the city walls, the medieval buildings were mostly timbered houses. Only during the Renaissance and Baroque periods were two-storied brick houses erected in the square, whose arcaded passages were abolished in the 19th century.

227. Plan of Nový Bydžov, after a cadastral map of 1841.

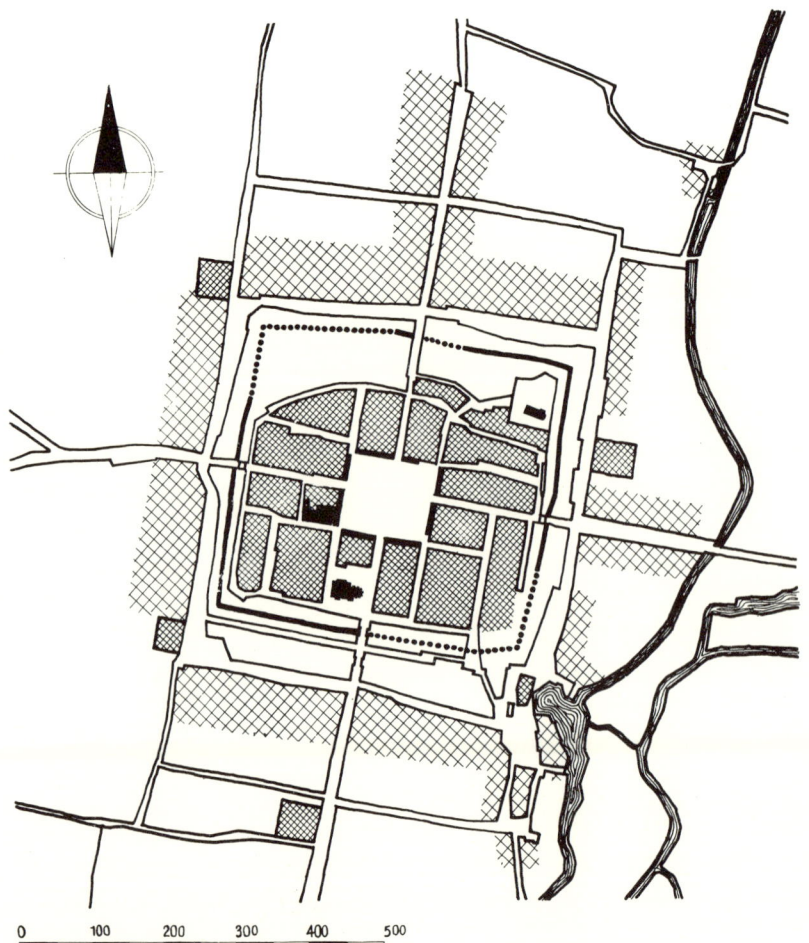

Nový Jičín, Northern Moravia. The village of Jičín grew up in the early Middle Ages at a stopping place on the trade route from Olomouc to Cracow in Poland. Toward the end of the 13th century, a castle was founded above the village that gradually changed into a strong medieval fortress. The community of Starý Jičín (Old Jičín) lacked the conditions necessary for the founding of a town. A town was therefore established on the brook Jičínka, about 1.86 miles from the village of Starý Jičín, in the second half of the 13th century.

The plan of Nový Jičín (New Jičín) is one of the purest examples of a regular design of a minor town. Square in outline, the town's design features a central public square and streets entering it at the corners. The blocks of houses grouped around the square are separated from those adjoining the walls by the main street, which leads to the church in the eastern part of the center and to the castle at the southern corner of the walls. The square and the streets entering it are lined by arcades. In the 16th century, the castle was converted into a palace and, toward the end of the century, a new town hall was erected in the square.

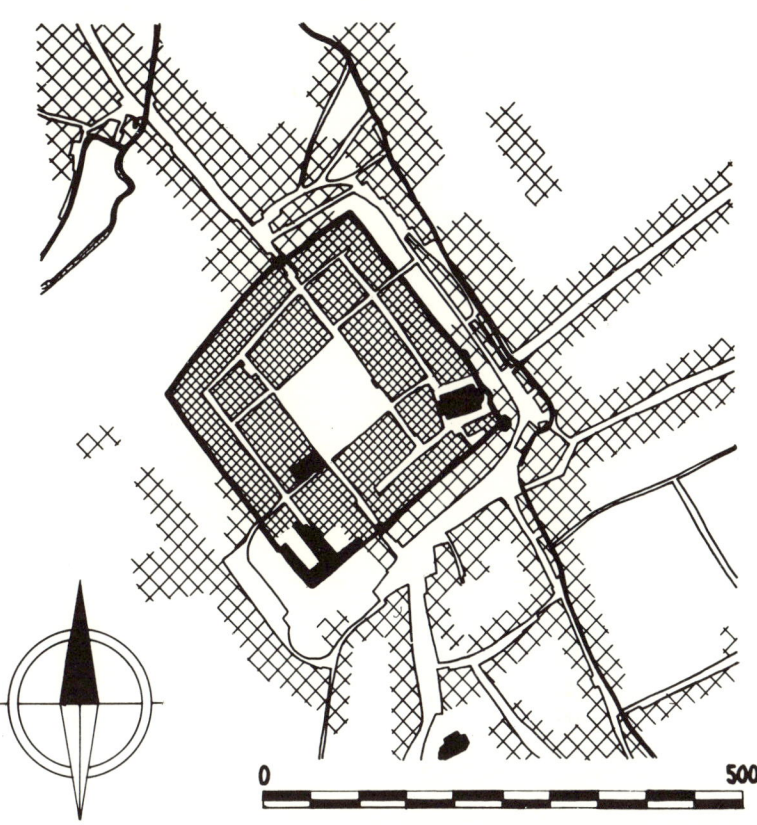

228. Plan of Nový Jičín, after a cadastral map of 1833.

229. Square at Nový Jičín lined by houses with Renaissance, Baroque, and Classicist façades, and a Renaissance belfry in the background.

Nymburk, Central Bohemia. The origin of a settlement on the site of the present town of Nymburk was a ford over the river Labe. This settlement was situated in the southeastern part of the fortified nucleus. The town was founded by King Přemysl Otakar II, in the third quarter of the 13th century.

The plan of the town had the usual oval shape, but the street system lacks the rectangular regularity characteristic of the second half of the 13th century. The layout consists of radial main streets following the early medieval lines of communication and transverse secondary streets following the oval circumference of the historic nucleus and old center of the original settlement. This combination of two street patterns gave rise to the trapezoidal shape of the square.

The Romanesque church built in the original settlement was replaced with a Gothic basilica. Medieval Nymburk was generally a brick-built town. Brick was used for the construction of the main city wall (first half of the 14th century), strengthened with slender rectangular bastions. Since the river afforded natural protection, a simple wall was sufficient to ensure the town's safety on this side. In front of the main gate was a barbican and an inner moat bordered on the outside by a rampart surmounted by a stone wall. This was followed by the outer moat, probably bordered by another rampart. The moats resembled Dutch *grachten*.

The square is still surrounded by numerous historic buildings with arcades, partly of Gothic origin. The most important building on the square is the Town Hall (1526), designed by the royal architect Benedikt Rejt.

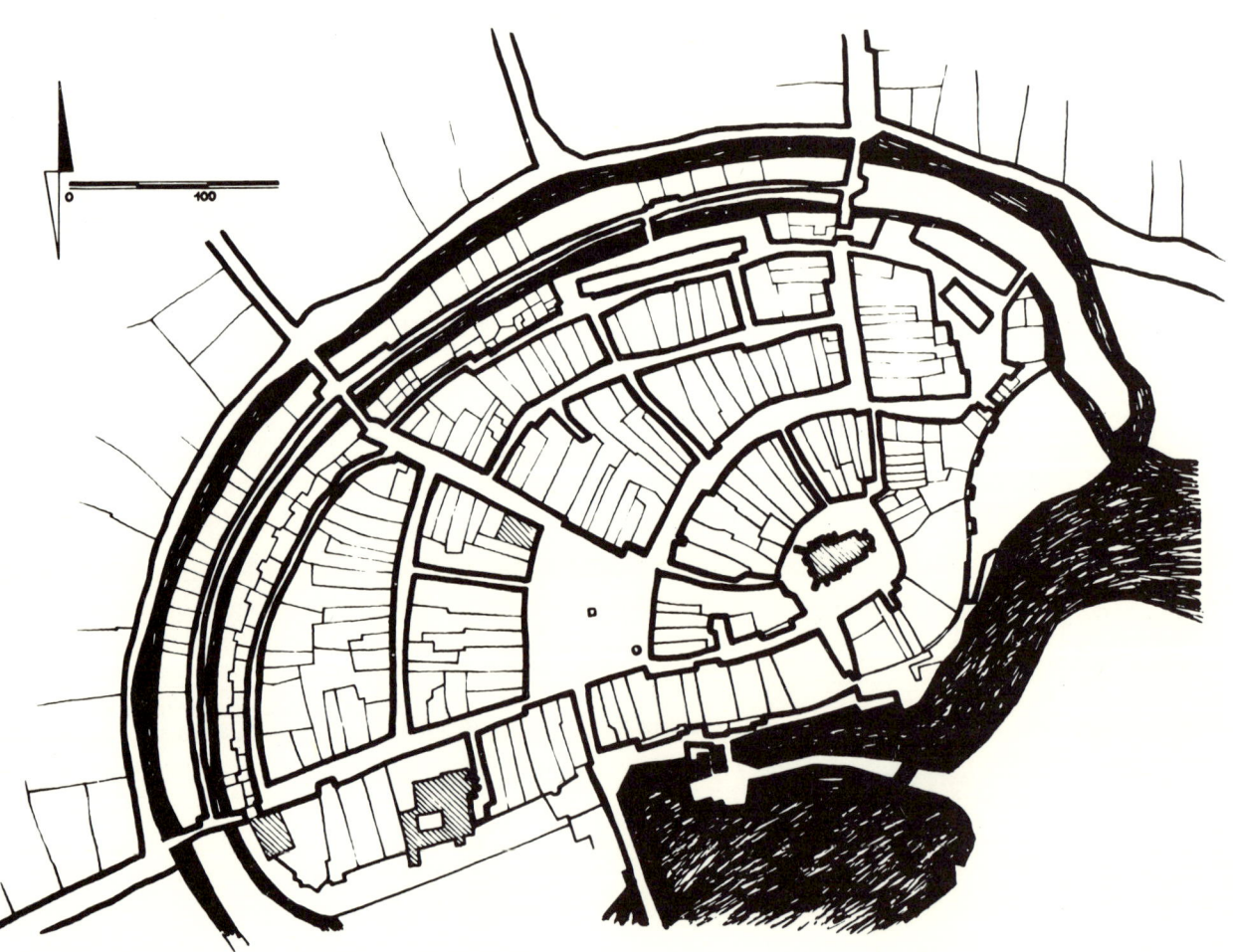

230. Plan of Nymburk, after a cadastral map of 1842.

Olomouc, Northern Moravia. The town of Olomouc developed at a ford near the confluence of the rivers Bystřice and Morava. The alluvial deposits of the Bystřice formed a bank in the river bed, and the nearby low hill called Olomoucký kopec (Olomouc Hill) acted as a natural dam in the flood plain. In former times the place was a crossing point of two trade routes, one of them being a branch of the Amber Road, which led from the town of Kroměříž to the region of Kladsko, Glatz, and farther north. The other, the so-called Polish route, connected the Elbe region with the cities of Cracow and Kiev.

The Olomouc Hill has probably been a sacred place of worship since time immemorial, but the prehistory of Olomouc still remains unexplored. Castles, as a form of settlement reflecting a more advanced social organization, may be expected in the late Bronze Age when Northern Moravia became the home of a people who buried their dead in urns. Some scholars refer to them as Protoslavs. The history of Olomouc after the ninth century, in the time of the Great Moravian Empire, is better known. During the reign of the Mojmír dynasty, in about A.D. 830, a Slavonic castle was built on the left bank of the river Morava, on a sandy hill in the flood plain opposite Olomouc Hill. The name of Olomouc is, no doubt, even older, dating from the sixth to the eighth century, and probably has a mythical meaning.

After the conquest of Moravia by the Bohemian Prince Oldřich (1017) his son, Prince Břetislav, gave the country a new administrative organization. The castle of Olomouc was built in the second quarter of the 11th century on Olomouc Hill, on the right river bank. As a seat of the Přemyslide dynasty, it was constructed in the same manner as the fortified Přemyslide seats in Bohemia of the end of the ninth century.

In the years following the death of Prince Břetislav, Moravia was divided into several parts (deals). Olomouc Castle remained the seat of the bishop when the city of Brno became the capital of Moravia, in 1646. The line of Moravian princes ruling over the deals ended about the year 1200. As a result, the inner part of Olomouc Castle was restored after a fire in 1204, as the center of the land administration, later called the New Castle (Nový Hrádek).

Since the 11th and 12th centuries, a Slavonic market village, *burgus sancti Blasii*, had been situated below the castle at the western side of the Olomouc Hill. It occupied the area of the present Square of the Red Army, formerly the Lower Square.

In 1248, King Wenceslas I exchanged a part of Olomouc—probably Czech Street with St. Maurice's church—with the bishop, purchasing the land for the founding of a Royal Town. The terrain was not particularly suitable for a settlement as swamps and marshes

231. Airview from the north, of the nucleus of Olomouc with two squares. In the center of the Upper Square, the Town Hall with tower and astronomical clock; to the right, the monumental statue of the Holy Trinity.

had been formed by deposits from the rivers. The area had to be drained by shifting the river bed to the western boundary of the future town, where it formed part of the fortifications. The town, endowed with city rights of the Magdeburg type, grew up around the original market village of St. Blase as its core. The shape of the town was triangular, touching with its apex the gate of the outer bailey on the headland.

Olomouc developed on the summit of Olomouc Hill, near the ford. Apart from the Upper Market Square, a new road was laid out. The Polish Route led directly to the bridge, passing through the outer bailey, and the other roads were adjusted to the new street pattern. From its earliest beginnings Olomouc had been enclosed by walls forming a self-contained whole, with two market squares in the center. After 1526, the territory of Bělidla, to the north, was included in the walls. At the same time, the town received new fortifications.

Toward the end of the Baroque period, in the years 1742–1757, the Empress Maria Theresa ordered the transformation of Olomouc into a large citadel, after the plans of the engineer P. F. Bechade de Rochepine. The fortifications of bastions with casemates and ravelins, small forts and redoubts, adopted the Vauban system and the principles developed by Dutch military engineers. During their construction, four suburbs and eleven villages were abolished, and the population was transferred to nine new settlements. The citadel itself was not dismantled until 1888.

232. Plan of the Baroque fortifications of Olomouc.

Ostrov near Karlovy Vary (Karlsbad), Western Bohemia. The mining town of Ostrov is situated on the river Bystřice, a tributary of the Ohře, in a valley between the hills of Doupovské vrchy and Krušné hory. It was founded in the 13th century and obtained the status of a town at the beginning of the 15th century. The historical center has an irregular oval shape, bordered on one side by the Bystřice and bisected by a streamlet flowing through the town. It has an oblong square, with a church at its western corner.

Ostrov is famous for the residence gardens of Julius Heinrich, Duke of Saxony, dating from the second quarter of the 17th century and reproduced in Merian's *Topographia Bohemiae, Moraviae et Silesiae* of 1650. The gardens, bordered by branches of the river Bystřice, are not focused on the castle or interrelated with each other. They represent a conservative type of the so-called pleasure gardens and recall the contemporary garden books of Vredeman de Vries and Salomon de Caus.

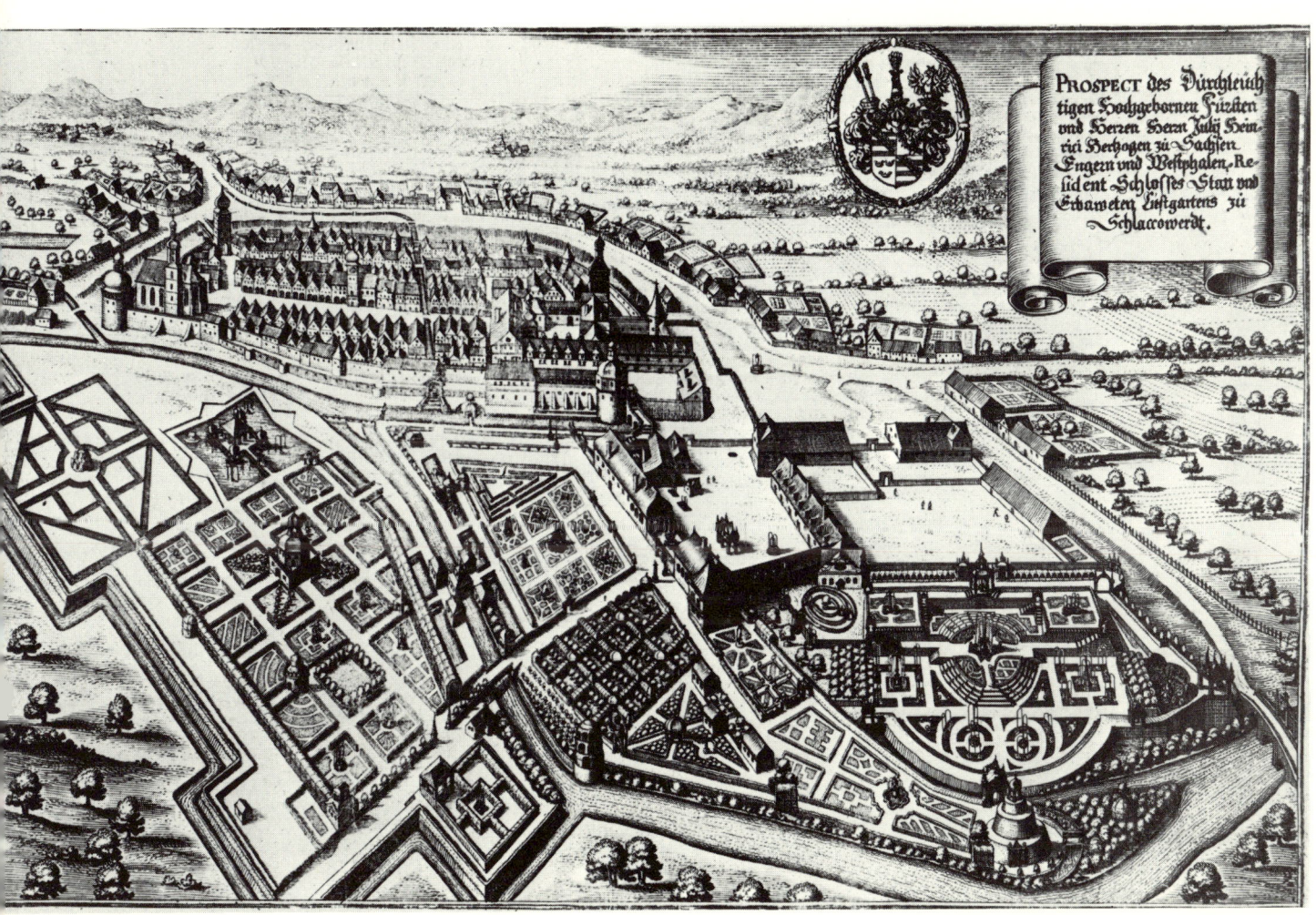

233. View of the town of Ostrov and the castle garden. Engraving by Matthaeus Merian from *Topographia Bohemiae, Moraviae et Silesiae*, Frankfurt, 1650.

Pardubice, Eastern Bohemia. The early beginning of this large industrial town of Eastern Bohemia was most inconspicuous. During the second half of the 13th century, a small town grew up near the confluence of the rivers Labe and Chrudimka, on the site of an early feudal settlement. Pardubice, situated near the river fords, was first mentioned in written documents of 1295. It was granted town privileges before 1340. After the middle of the 14th century, the parish church of Our Lady was founded, joining the older church of St. Bartholomew and the Monastery of the Cyriacensian Order. The town was ruled by the outstanding statesman of King Charles' court, the first Archbishop of Prague, Arnošt of Pardubice.

Hardly anything is known about the appearance of Pardubice in the 14th century. The nucleus, probably rectangular and of modest size, contained only the square and the building blocks facing it. In 1491, the Pardubice estate was bought by Sir William of Pernštejn, the richest and most powerful feudal lord in Bohemia. He chose the town of Pardubice and the nearby castle of Kunětická

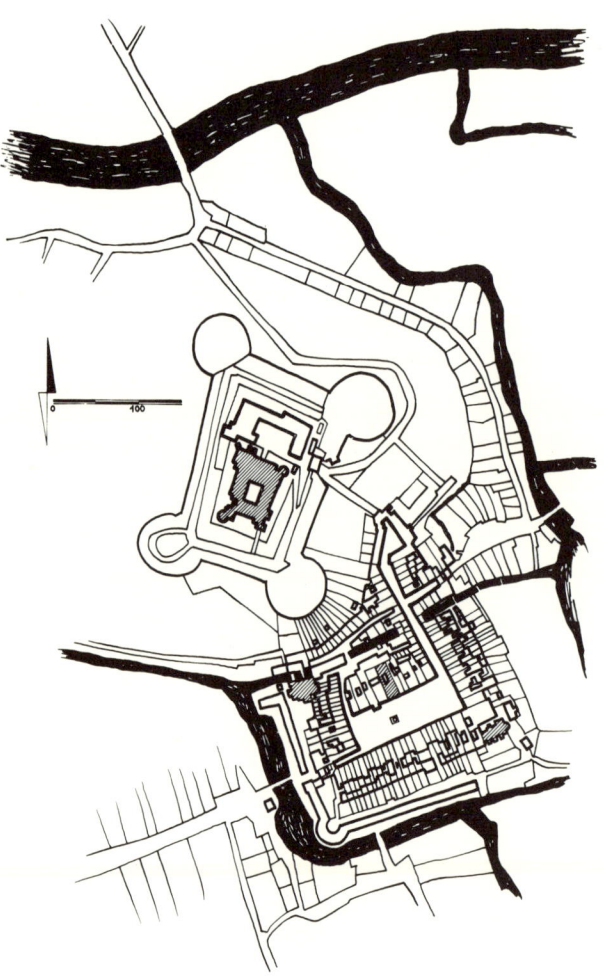

234. Plan of the historic nucleus of Pardubice, after a cadastral map of 1839.

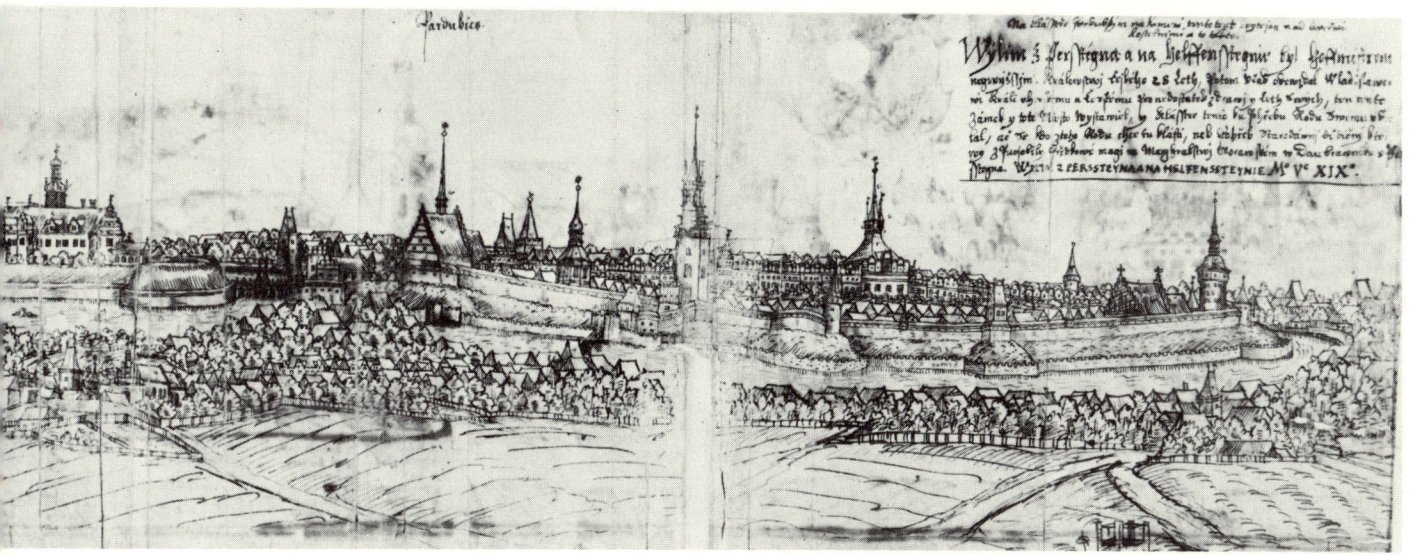

235. View of Pardubice from the southwest. Drawing by Johann Willenberg, 1602.

Hora as his residence. His building activities were chiefly centered on Pardubice Castle. The new fortifications consisted of massive earthworks with horseshoe-shaped rondels at the four corners of the walls. The fortifications included moats of exceptional width which gave the castle the appearance of an island. At the same time, the Gothic castle was rebuilt into an imposing *chateau,* with a richly furnished and decorated interior. The area occupied by the castle premises, including the fortifications, was larger than the town nucleus. A new borough, Příhrádek, was laid out along the northwestern side of the *chateau* on the territory of the town. A devastating fire in 1507 interrupted the extensive building activities of the town. During the following period of reconstruction the old plan of the town was practically erased as the ground was first leveled and then raised to a height of about 10 feet. On this new level, two-storied houses built of stone were erected on allotments situated along the improved and newly extended street system. It is probable that the area of the square was reduced by the addition of the northern building block.

The street connecting the square with the castle became the main traffic artery. The town center was protected on three sides by strong fortifications, including a wide moat similar to that of the castle. By 1515 the fortifications of both town and castle were completed.

Pardubice was again seriously damaged by a fire in 1538. The building activities following this disaster were not limited to the repair of damaged houses: A large-scale reconstruction took place under the leadership of George of Olomouc, who was appointed city architect by the feudal lord. The majority of the houses received an additional story, and their façades were adorned with gables. The building efforts were centered on the reconstruction of the square. Its four sides were unified by a continuous row of attics and gables, creating a uniformity also applied in adjoining streets. The reconstruction, following the fire in 1538 and introducing the Renaissance style to Pardubice, was completed after the middle of the 16th century.

The Thirty Years' War brought renewed suffering to the town, which took more than a century to recover. After a fire in 1751 a number of houses in the core area were reconstructed in accordance with late Baroque principles. However, the basic design of the buildings lining the square remained unchanged.

An important event in the development of the town was the construction of the railway line between the city of Olomouc and Prague in 1845. The following decades witnessed a considerable growth of the town, based on a rapidly developing industry. The original town nucleus with the castle became a mere fragment in the overall area of Pardubice. Today the town has 55,000 inhabitants.

236. Square at Pardubice, lined with late Gothic houses, rebuilt in the Renaissance in the first half of the 16th century. In front, the Column of the Virgin Mary (1680), completed in the second half of the 18th century. In the background, the Green Gate, built after the fire in 1538.

Pelhřimov, Southern Bohemia. The founding of Pelhřimov as a minor episcopal town in the Bohemian-Moravian borderlands was preceded by a complex development of the original settlement. About the middle of the 13th century, the market right was transferred from the settlement of Old Pelhřimov, founded in the 12th century and located about 1.24 miles west of the historic nucleus of the present town, to St. Guy's community. After the year 1289, the Bishop of Prague founded on the southern boundary of St. Guy's a walled town of elliptical shape, with a rectangular street net and a trapezoidal square.

The fortifications, dating from the second half of the 14th century, were considerably reinforced in the 15th century, influenced by the fortifications of the neighboring town of Tábor. The main rebuilding of the walled-in nucleus and the suburb took place in the second half of the 16th century, after the great fire in 1561. All four sides of the square were surrounded by Gothic and Renaissance arcaded buildings.

The late Baroque and Classicist epochs left remarkable traces on the façades of the town houses. In this respect, a group of gabled houses at the northern side of the square with Renaissance, Baroque, and Classicist gables and façades is of considerable interest.

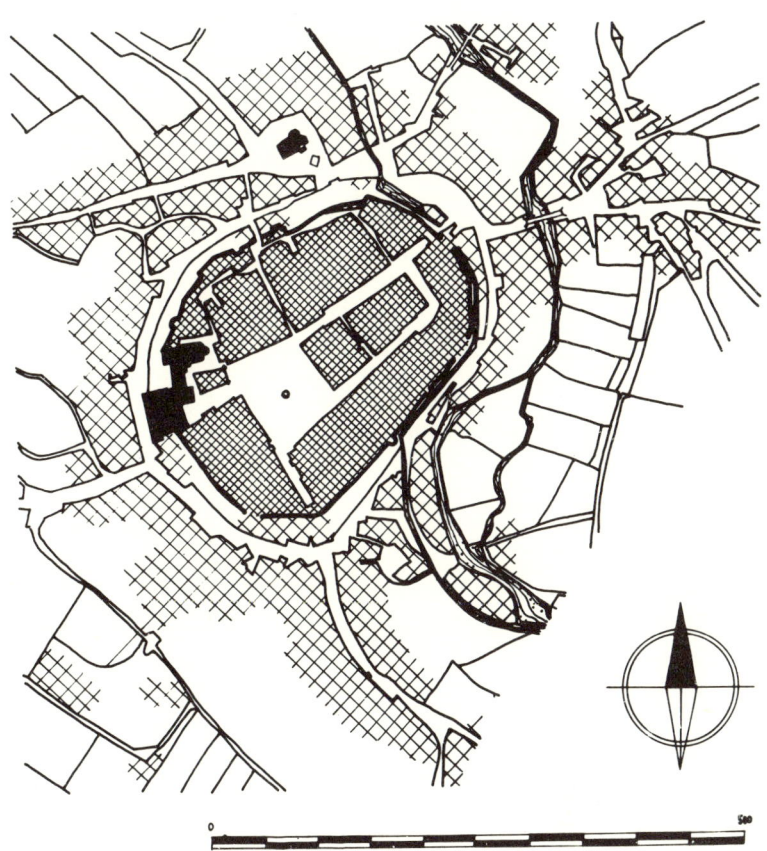

237. Plan of Pelhřimov, after a cadastral map of 1829.

238. View of gabled houses lining the northern side of the square at Pelhřimov. In the background, on the left, the parish church (14th to 16th centuries).

Písek, Southern Bohemia. In the early Middle Ages, a settlement situated on the northern bank of the Otava grew up at the ford where the former Golden Route leading from Prague to Bavaria crossed the river Otava. At this ford, King Přemysl Otakar II founded a Royal Town soon after his accession to the Bohemian throne, before 1254. The new Royal Town, situated half a mile east of the original settlement, ranks among the most interesting architectural and town-planning achievements of the Bohemian king. In the fifties of the 13th century, a royal castle was erected in the northwest corner of the walls, above the river, consisting of a four-winged palace whose inner courtyard was surrounded on the ground floor and the first floor by vaulted arcaded galleries.

The castle of Písek controlled the river crossing, spanned by the oldest stone bridge (13th century) still in use in Czechoslovakia. The 13th-century fortifications consisted of

239. Plan of the historic nucleus of Písek, after a cadastral map of 1837.

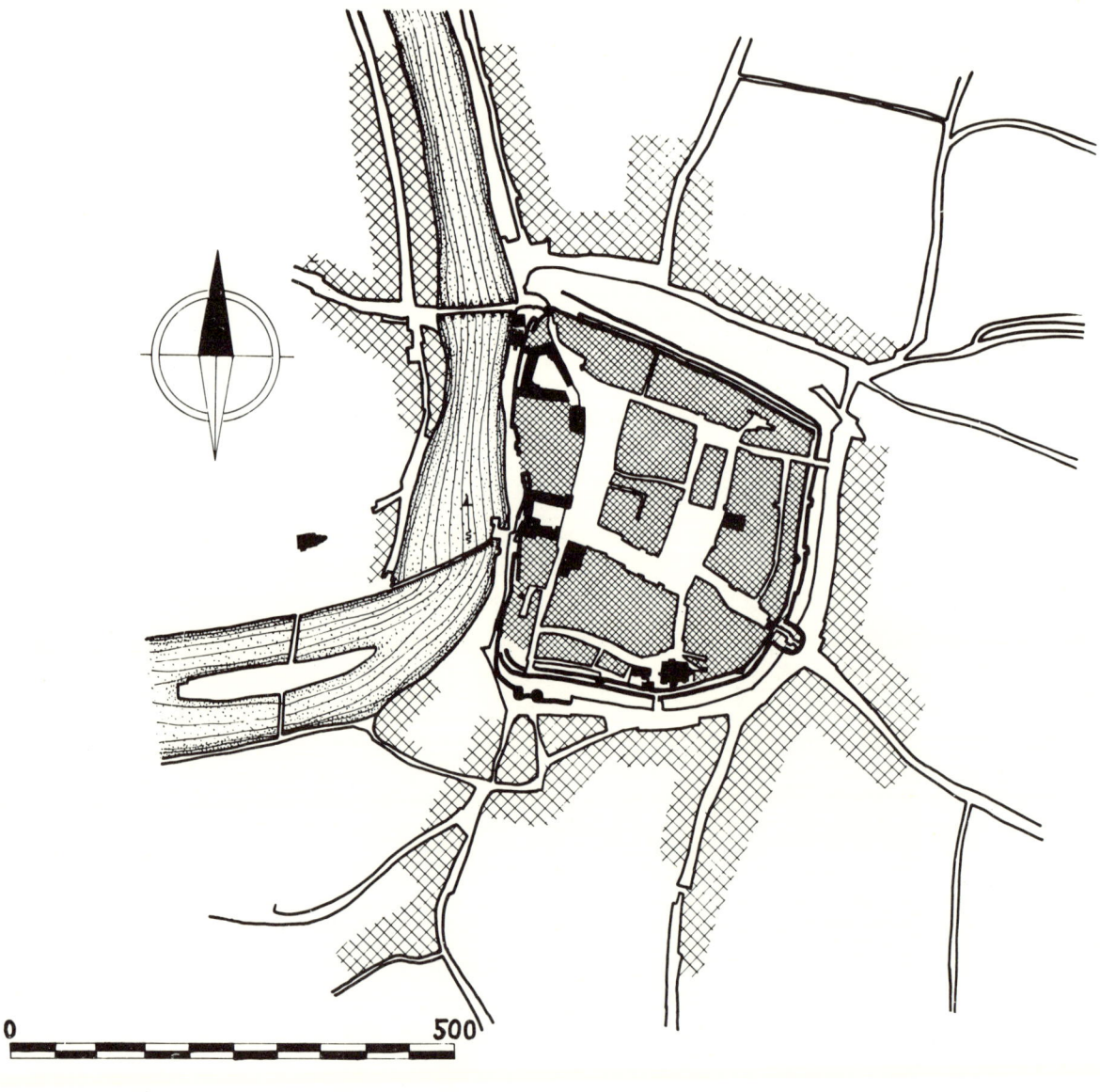

the main and secondary walls, a moat, and a rampart. Large sections of the original main wall, with several semi-circular bastions, have been preserved to this day. In the 16th century bastions were added to the rampart.

The layout of the old center, with two squares of different size and shape and connected by a wide road, suggests a rather complex development. Originally the center of the town was probably occupied by only one rectangular square, divided by a block of houses. This square shows traces of abolished arcades.

The parish church, dating from before 1260, is situated in the vicinity of the southern part of the walls. It is a massive three-aisled basilica with a pentagonal presbytery, originally with two towers—a typical feature of the early Gothic Cistercian-Burgundian architecture.

240. The historic nucleus of Písek. A group of burghers' houses was erected in the center of the original square during the Middle Ages.

Plástovice, Southern Bohemia. The village of Plástovice is one of a group of South Bohemian villages in the Hluboká Marshes. As late as the 19th century, their architecture reflected strong influences of the Baroque period. Plástovice is set in the picturesque frame of the South Bohemian countryside, dotted with ponds and streams, between the important towns of České Budějovice and Vodňany, in the vicinity of Hluboká Castle. The unique character of these South Bohemian villages is due to intensive building activities in the middle of the 19th century. The architectural values originating at that time remained more or less untouched by later developments. This is particularly true of Plástovice which presents, with its open spaces and individual buildings, the style of Bohemian folk architecture, the so-called "peasant Baroque."

The plan of Plástovice originated in the Middle Ages, long before the community was first mentioned in records. Its main characteristic is the large T-shaped village green, partly open on its southern side and sloping down to a stream, where verdure provides a natural frame for the farmsteads on the other sides of the main square. These farmsteads, with richly decorated gables, form the silhouette of the village green. The gables of the houses and cornlofts, bearing dates ranging from 1831 to 1868, are squat in shape, most of them being joined by shallow cornices and featuring gently curved contours. The village is separated from the fields beyond the houses by the walls of the barns at the end of the individual farmsteads.

The appearance of the individual farmsteads and the interior of the village influenced the plan of the community. On the northern side of the village, smaller farmsteads were built, rich in style, interesting in architecture, and unusual in this part of the country.

A picturesque supplement of the village is the typical South Bohemian forge with an arched vault in front, built in 1854, on the road leading from the village.

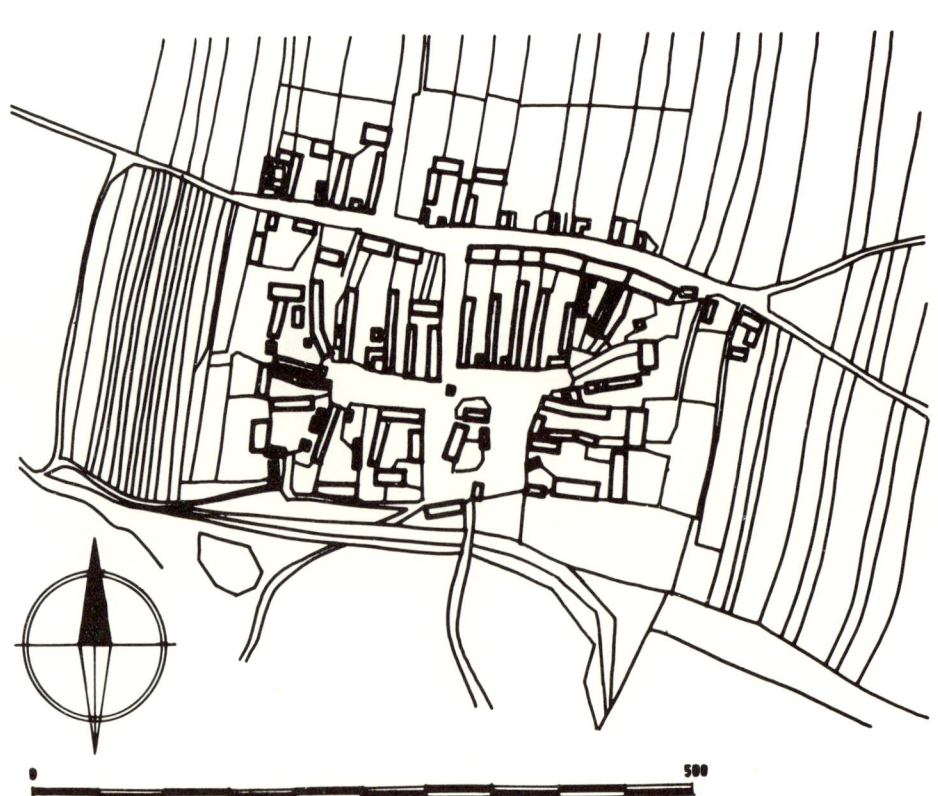

241. Plan of the village of Plástovice, after a cadastral map of 1827.

242. Farmstead (about the middle of the 19th century) on the northern side of the village green and a small chapel (1840), at Plástovice.

Prachatice, Southern Bohemia. Trade routes represent an important factor in the origin and development of towns. In the early Middle Ages, the village of Prachatice originated on a salt route called "Golden" because of the financial prosperity it brought. First mentioned in 1088, the village was situated not far from the place where the route from Bohemia to Bavaria led through a border forest. However, the original site of the village was unfavorable for development. Consequently, in the first third of the 14th century, a new fortified town was built about 1.24 miles to the south, taking over the function and rights of the old settlement, which reverted to its village status. Located at the foot of the hilly terrain leading to the Šumava Mountains (the Forest of Bohemia), Prachatice ranks among the best-preserved towns in Czechoslovakia, featuring historic buildings in a remarkable natural setting.

In spite of the considerable trading importance of the town in the 16th century—1,200 to 1,300 horses passed through it every week carrying salt and corn—its historic core is small in size. The hilly terrain and the course of the long trade routes gave a certain irregularity to the layout.

The outstanding characteristic of the plan of Prachatice is the circular street following the line of the fortifications. Situated in the street, joining the square with the Lower Gate in the eastern part of the town, was a church dating from the second half of the 14th century.

At the end of the 15th century, the wooden buildings were gradually replaced with stone structures, a precaution dictated by a devastating fire in 1507.

In the third quarter of the 16th century, Prachatice had become a Renaissance town. The façades of the buildings, newly covered with gaily colored graffiti, ended in variously shaped attics. In 1571, a town hall was constructed in the square. On the threshold of the Thirty Years' War, Prachatice was one of the most attractive small towns in Bohemia, but the war affected the town from the very beginning. Even before the Battle on the White Mountain in 1620, it was conquered and plundered. After the war a sharp decline in the salt trade set in until, at the beginning of the 18th century, it ceased altogether. This adverse development resulted in the impoverishment of the town and the suspension of all building activities during the Baroque period.

244. Prachatice seen from the southwest. Drawing by J. Willenberg, beginning of the 17th century.

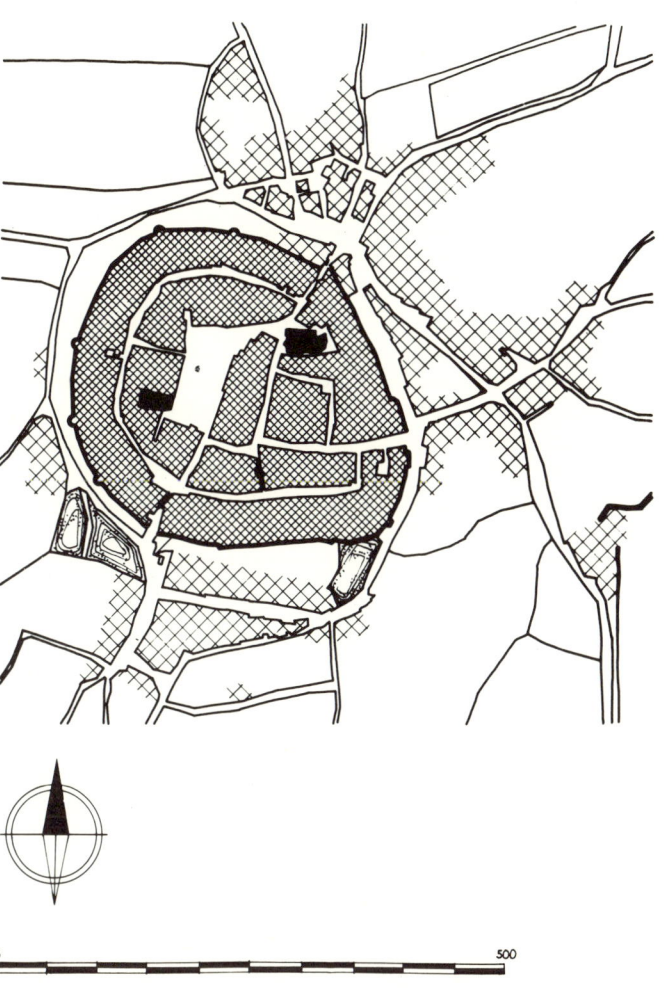

243. Plan of the historic nucleus of Prachatice, after a cadastral map of 1837.

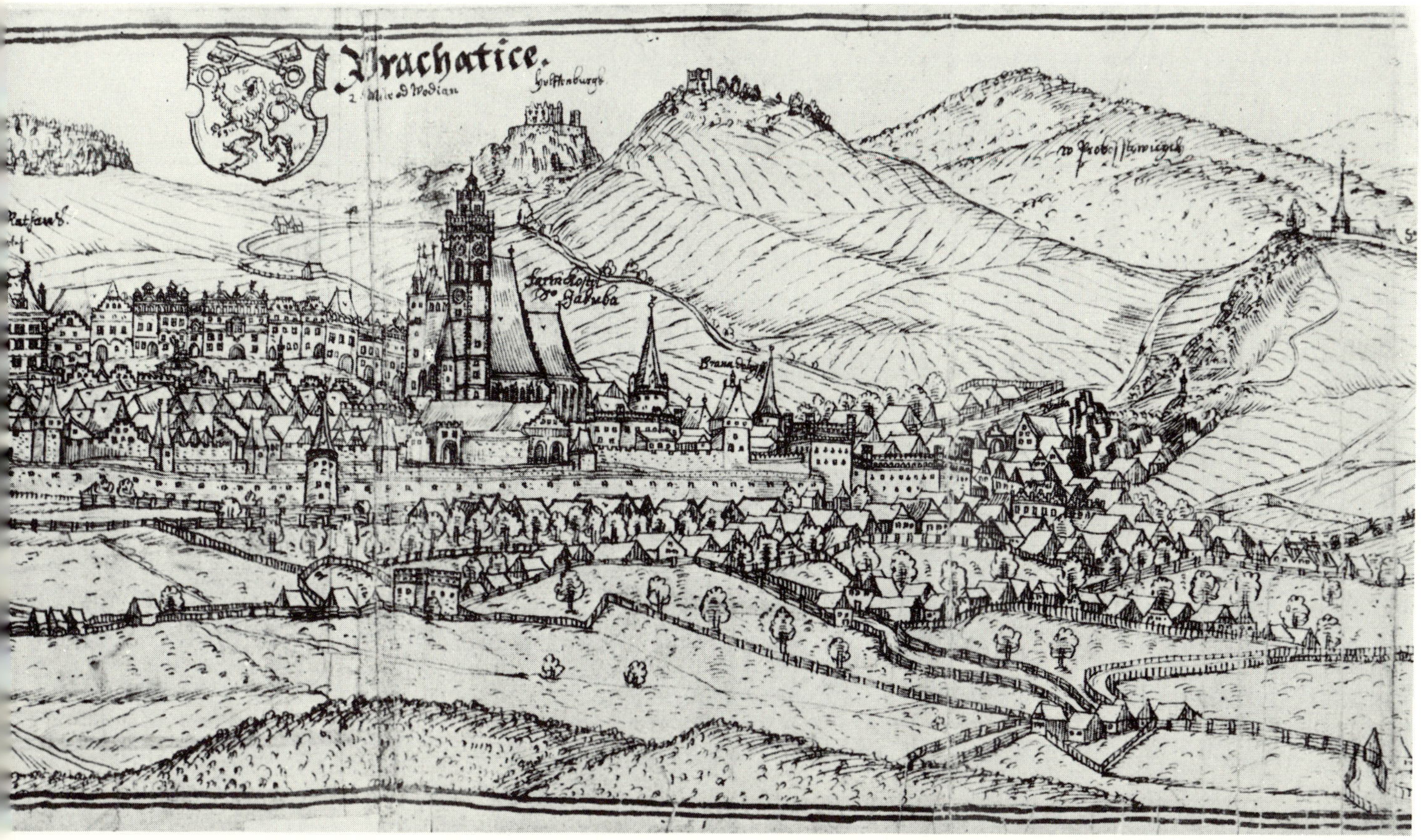

Prešov, Eastern Slovakia. As early as the 13th century the town of Prešov occupied a place of importance in the network of trade routes and commercial towns of Eastern Slovakia. In 1324 the inhabitants of the town obtained some privileges, and less than 50 years later Prešov became a Royal Free Town. The increasing importance of trade and the growing population necessitated the construction of new houses and the extension of the existing boundaries of the town. An elongated square grew up between the houses adjoining the rear part of the original settlement and those forming the new concave front. The rapid development of the town led to intensive building activities. In the course of the 15th century, the territory of the town was extended toward the west and the south. The town consisted of two blocks of buildings, one on each side of the square, intersected by several transverse connections. The area of the square was divided by a church in its center.

Between the 14th and 15th centuries the town was enclosed by walls. This layout was preserved until the end of the 16th century. During the following century, suburbs grew up and were included in the territory of the town after the demolition of the walls in 1673. The prosperity of the town led to some far-reaching reconstruction of houses in the vicinity of the square. The original Gothic buildings were gradually replaced by sumptuous burghers' houses with Renaissance mouldings, giving the square a new architectural appearance.

In the 19th century, existing suburbs were extended, using the areas gained by the demolition of the walls. However, a systematic town-planning procedure was lacking, a failure also applying to the beginning of the present century.

245. Plan of the historic center of Prešov, after a cadastral map of the second half of the 19th century.

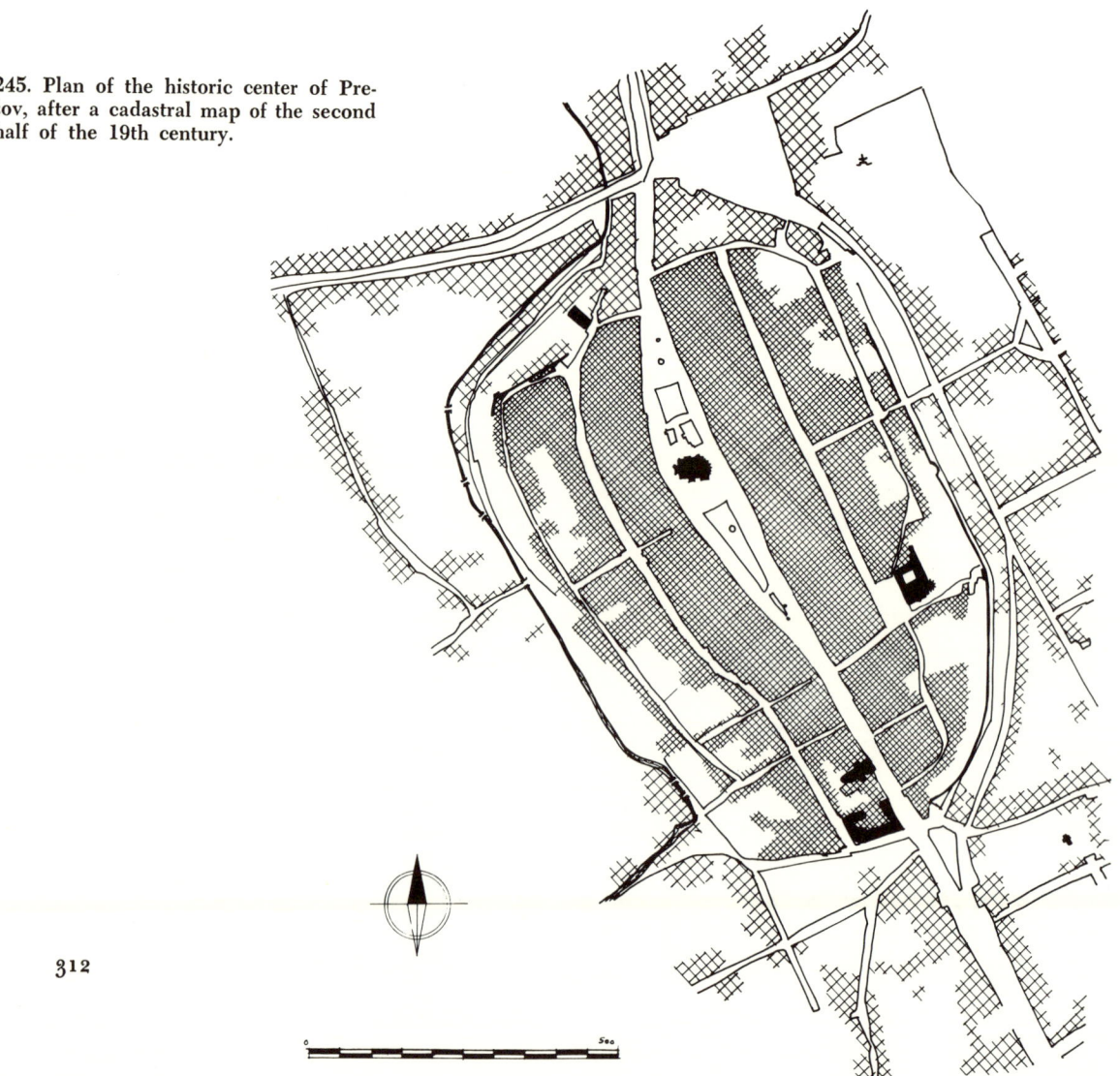

Ružindol, Western Slovakia. The village of Ružindol is situated in the western part of Slovakia, in the District of Trnava, 557.6 feet above sea level. It was mentioned for the first time in a document dating from 1300 as the property of the town of Trnava. In the 16th century, the village was inhabited by Croatians. In the first half of the 19th century, it became the property of the Brunschwick family of Dolná Krupá.

The village lies in a fertile agricultural region. Its terrace houses are built parallel to the main road. The individual plots of land are regular, their front parts being occupied by the farmhouse, with a covered passage adjoining the next house and creating a continuous street front. The barns are situated at the end of the plots. The main road bypasses the village, skirting the barns. The farmhouses are built of clay or brick and are plastered and painted. Some of the houses have retained their characteristic doorways.

246. Plan of the village of Ružindol, after a cadastral map of 1895.

247. Square at Sobotka, with a Classicist town hall.

248. Timbered town house (1754) at Sobotka.

Sobotka, Eastern Bohemia. The development of the town of Sobotka, in northeastern Bohemia, was closely connected with the history of the nearby castle of Kost, founded toward the end of the 14th century. The original village was first mentioned in 1287. Markets held there as early as the first half of the 14th century indicate that the large, almost rectangular marketplace, the later town square, was laid out toward the end of the 13th century in connection with the intensive colonization undertaken in those days by the population.

In 1498 Sobotka was raised to the status of a town, subject to the Lords of Kost. It was granted certain privileges, especially those concerning the erection of walls and gates.

Timbered houses, mostly from the second half of the 18th century, form part of the remarkable historical legacy of the town. In the center of Sobotka are elaborately designed two-storied houses, while groups of one-story, timbered cottages are located in the former suburb.

Stará Boleslav—Brandýs nad Labem, Central Bohemia. At certain times the crossing over the Elbe (Labe) by the trade route connecting Prague with Northern Bohemia became impassable. This fact may account for the founding of settlements on either bank of the river, from which the towns of Brandýs and Stará Boleslav developed.

Located on the southwestern bank of the river, Brandýs was of lesser importance than the opposite community of Stará Boleslav, a situation which reversed itself in modern times. At the turn of the 14th century, Brandýs was founded in the neighborhood of two earlier villages, protected by small strongholds. A castle, built on a steep rock, guarded the bridge across the river. In the 16th century, it was reconstructed as a Renaissance palace and has remained the dominating feature of the town to this day.

The town of Stará Boleslav, situated on the southeastern bank of the Elbe, passed through a different development. Probably not before the beginning of the 10th century, a castle was founded on a headland encircled by the river and protected by swamps. It was enclosed with walls at a later date.

At the northeast side of the castle a community grew up in the outer bailey, during the early feudal epoch. In 1351, the castle was surrounded with new fortifications. Parts of these fortifications and the eastern gateway have been preserved.

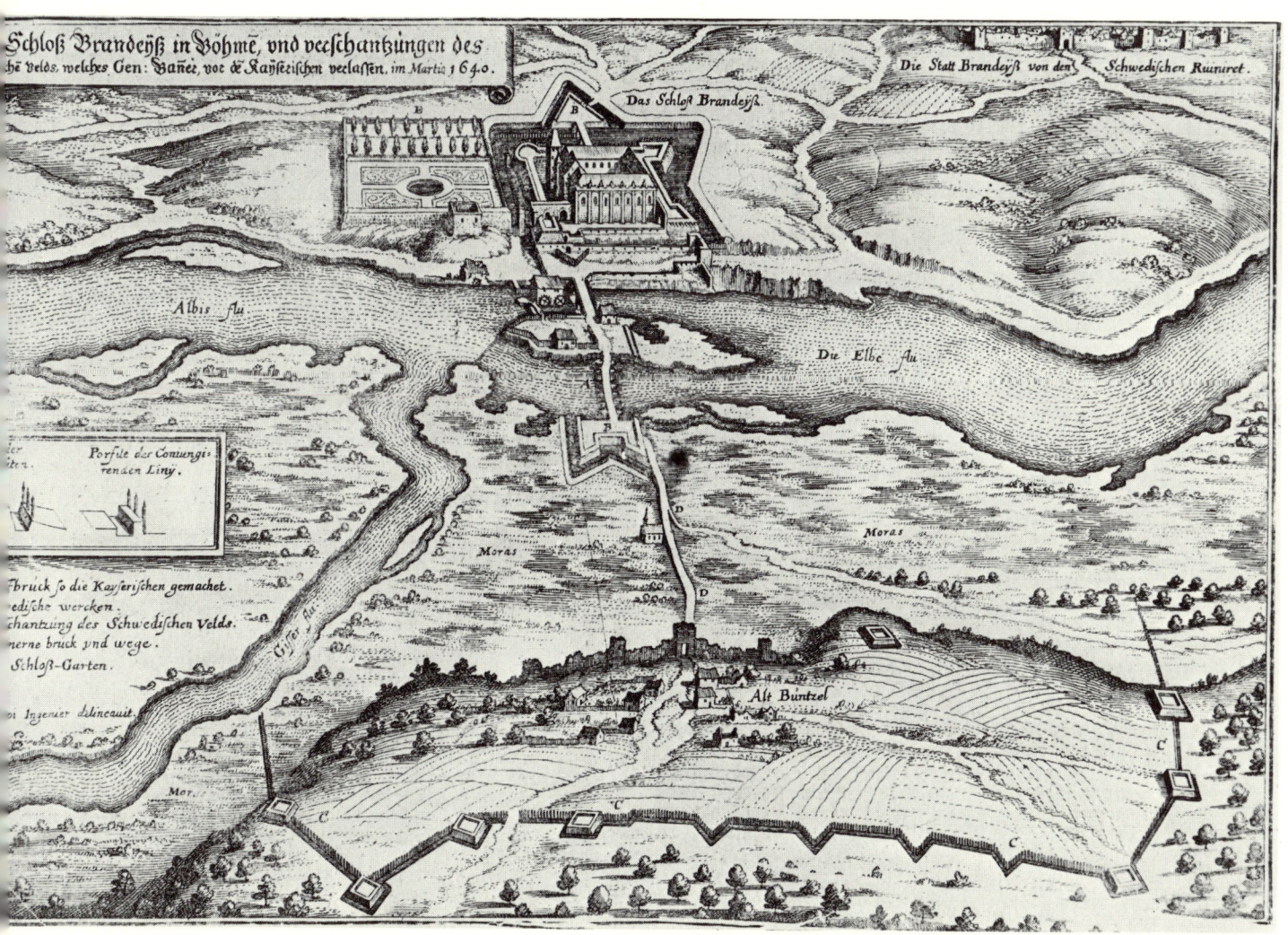

249. Plan of Stará Boleslav and Brandýs nad Labem, showing the relation of the two towns and the site of the Renaissance castle in 1640. Engraving by Matthaeus Merian from *Topographia Bohemiae, Moraviae et Silesiae*.

During the early period of the Counter Reformation, the town of Stará Boleslav gained in importance. In 1617 to 1623, a pilgrimage church was erected in the outer bailey of the castle on the site of the former small Romanesque place of worship.

Tracts of forest in the neighborhood of the town are a reminder of the former borderland forests that separated the territories of two tribes before the establishment of a sovereign Bohemian State in the 10th century.

The towns of Brandýs and Stará Boleslav are typical examples of twin towns located at river crossings.

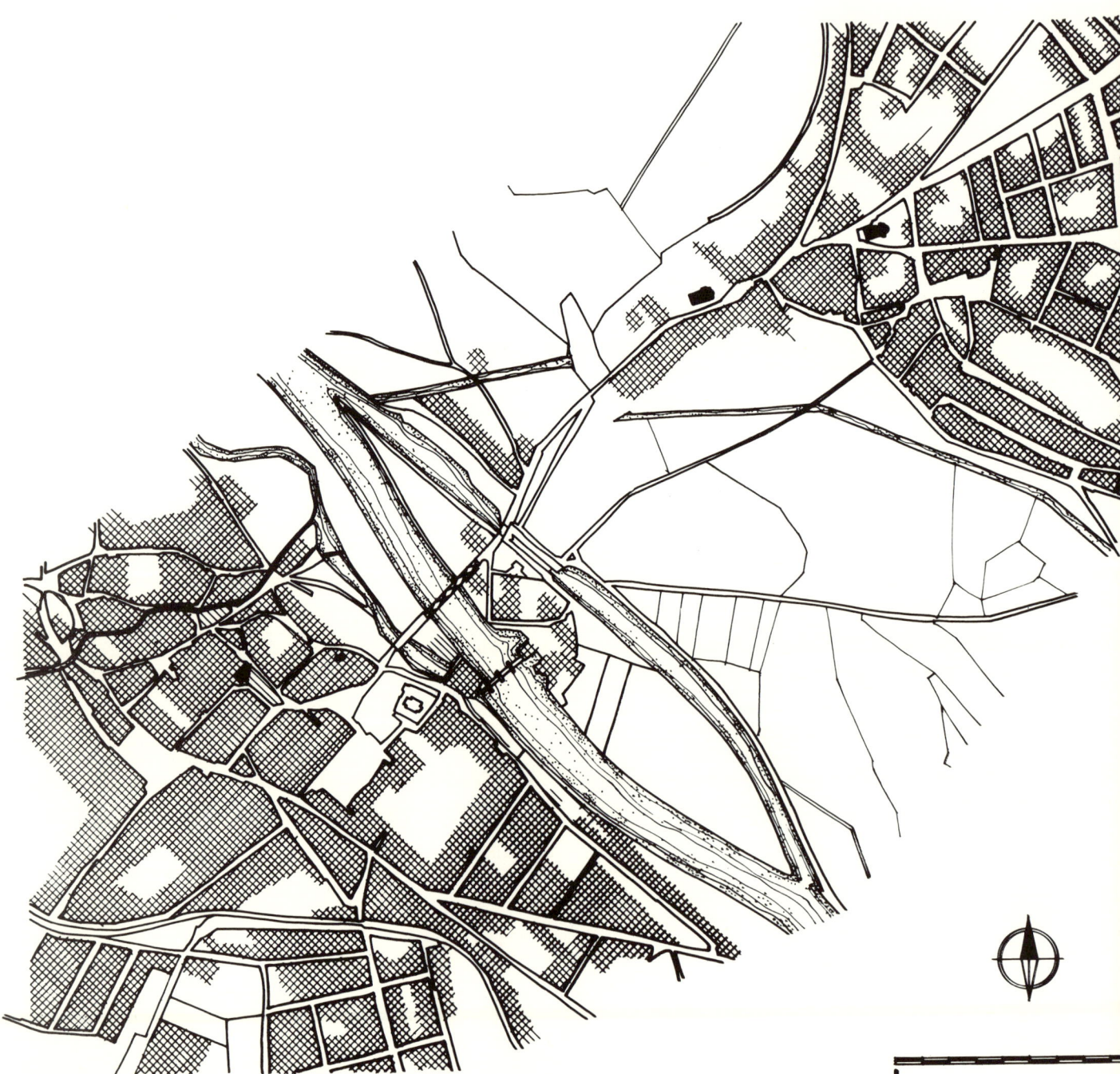

250. Plan of the twin towns of Stará Boleslav and Brandýs nad Labem.

Tábor, Southern Bohemia. The city of Tábor, the center of the Hussite Movement, was founded by the Hussites in the year 1420, on a steep peninsula in the bend of the river Lužnice in the south of Bohemia. According to earlier records, the site had been previously occupied by a walled settlement and, in the 13th century, by a castle with an outer bailey.

During the first revolutionary period, newcomers to the town had to put all their property into a common pool, in accordance with the words of the old chronicles that "in Tábor nothing is mine or thine, but it belongs to all in equal degree.... Private property is mortal sin. All people shall be brethren and there shall be no rulers and no dominion...." And so they took the name of "Brethren."

These principles were expected to help toward a better organization of society. For the first time in the history of mankind they became the basis for the founding of a new town. In their revolutionary character they surpassed even the views of the later Utopians.

After the defeat of the revolutionary Hussite Movement, Tábor changed to an ordinary town and reverted to the usual forms of social and economic organization. For the inhabitants of Bohemia, however, it always remained associated with the memories of its revolutionary community.

It is generally assumed that the irregular street pattern around the spacious central square had its origin in the wagon encampment of the first newcomers, encircling the

251. Plan of the historic nucleus of Tábor, after a cadastral map of 1830.

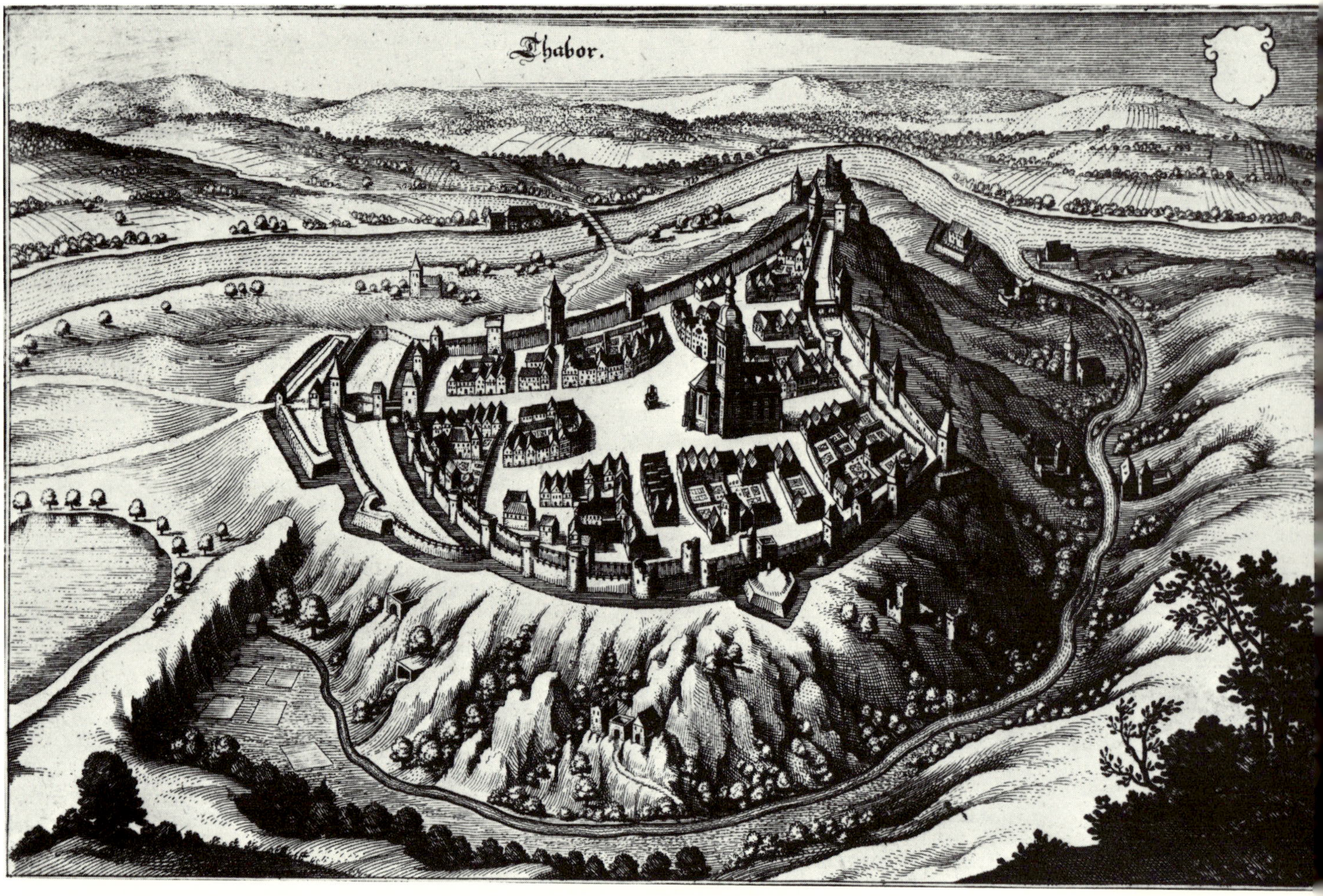

252. *Above:* The town of Tábor above the river Lužnice. The regular street pattern in this simplified view does not correspond to the actual layout of the town. Engraving by Matthaeus Merian from *Topographia Bohemiae, Moraviae et Silesiae*, Frankfurt, 1650.

253. *Below:* Square at Tábor with the Town Hall, built in 1440–1515.

254. Part of the medieval fortifications of Tábor, with the gateway and the round Kotnov Tower of the original castle, from the middle of the 14th century.

common meeting place of the people of Tábor. It has also been suggested that the irregular street system was dictated by defense considerations, enabling the people to fight in the streets and prevent the enemy from penetrating into the town center after the city walls had been stormed.

The fortifications, built immediately after the founding of the town and partly preserved, were outstanding examples of a medieval defensive system. The main wall was strengthened with battlements and numerous semicircular or polygonal towers and bastions. A remarkable innovation of the Tábor defense works, dating from the 15th century, were elongated semicircular or polygonal bastions of the outer wall, with covered passages for the defenders. The whole substructure of the town is traversed by an intricate system of underground passages of medieval origin.[1]

1. See pp. 158–160.

Terezín, Northern Bohemia. In the eighties of the 18th century, two fortified towns came into existence in Northern Bohemia, Terezín and Josefov, whose function it was to protect the northern border of the monarchy during the difficult period of the Austro-Prussian disputes. The first to be built, near the confluence of the rivers Ohře and Labe, was the fortress of Terezín (1780). It received its name from its founder, Joseph II, in honor of Empress Maria Theresa.

The construction of Terezín, supervised by Charles Nicholas von Steinmetz, proceeded at a remarkable rate and was completed in 1784. Terezín was proclaimed a Royal Free Town in 1782. Its fortifications were based on the Vauban system, improved by that of the so-called Mézières School. The main fortress on the western bank of the river Ohře has fortifications similar to those of the town of Josefov. Brick curtain walls protected by ravelins connected the bastions. The area between the Nová (New) and the Stará (Old) Ohře was enclosed by two parallel lines of bastions without ravelins. Linking up with those on the eastern side of the Stará Ohře was the so-called Small Fortress. An extensive irrigation system was built to ensure an adequate water supply for the fields in front of the fortress. The centrally situated oblong square is dominated at its eastern side by a church dating from the years 1805–1810. Most of the civil buildings in Terezín, which in 1830 could already boast 110 single-story houses, featured the sober characteristics of the Classicist period.

In 1882, the fortress was dismantled. In World War II, Terezín was one of the places where the German Nazis imprisoned and tortured many innocent victims. Today the Small Fortress is a national monument.

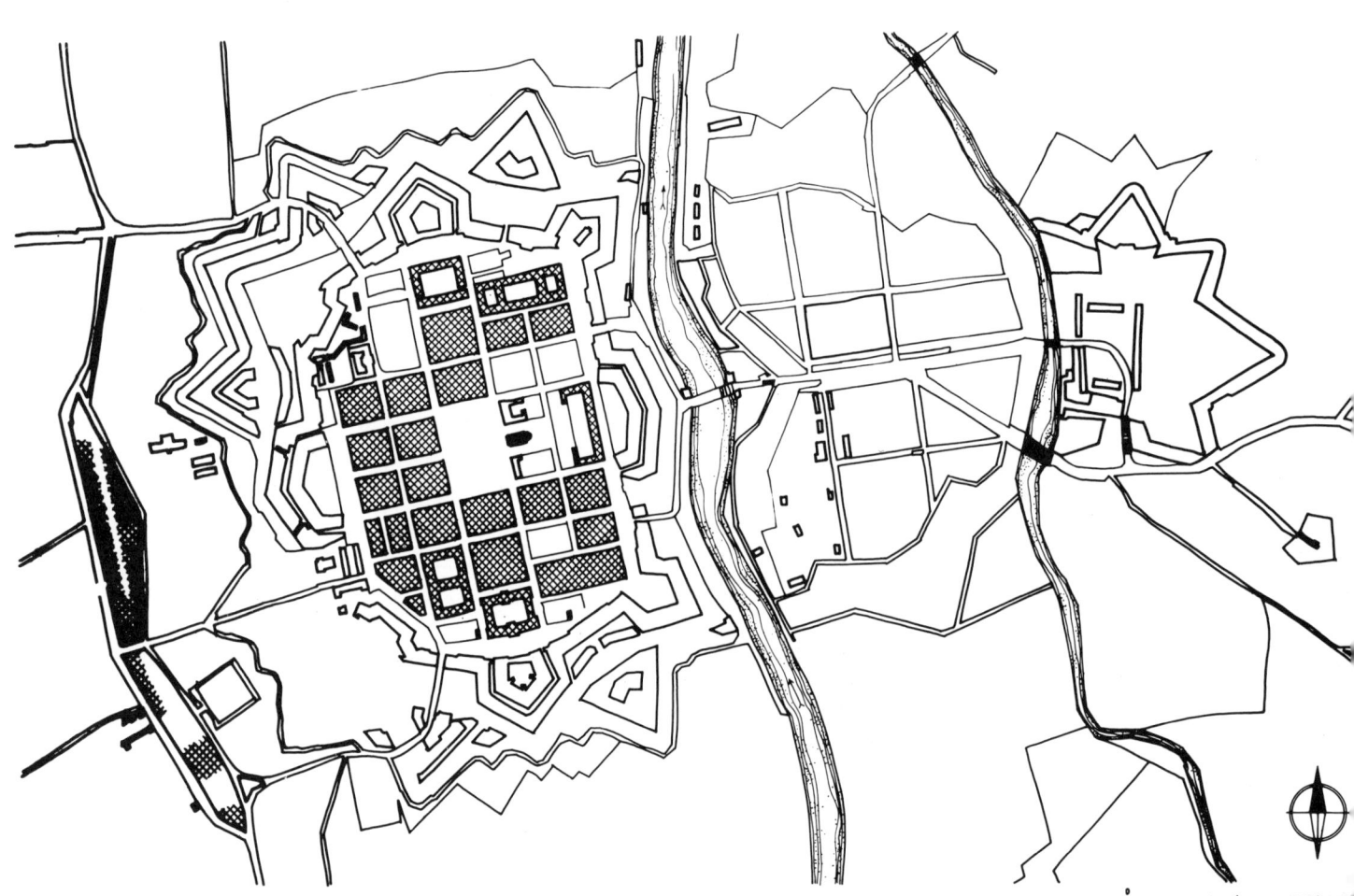

255. Plan of the citadel of Terezín, with the protruding Small Fortress.

Trnava, Western Slovakia. The town of Trnava was the first settlement in Slovakia to obtain town privileges (1238). Situated on a gently sloping terrain, it originated near the so-called Bohemian Route from Galicia to Slovakia. A widening on this road gave rise to a simple market square with a church in its center.

The town developed favorably during the 13th and 14th centuries, despite setbacks due to disasters afflicting the town. Work was not limited to the original urban center but included the building of a new road to Bratislava. Along this road a new settlement grew up, with a regular square in its center, to the west of the original settlement. Economic activities were gradually concentrated in the new part of the town, while the original settlement attained the character of an ecclesiastical center.

Numerous monasteries and churches were erected in the town. At the beginning of the 13th century only a parish church, a monastery of the Order of St. Clara, and a Dominican monastery existed in the core area. In the first half of the 14th century, a municipal hospital with the church of St. Elizabeth was built and, in 1363, a Franciscan monastery originated on the site of the present St. James' Church.

In the 13th century, Trnava had only very simple fortifications. More permanent walls were built after the town attained a more advanced structural and economic stage. Gradually, the fortifications were improved under the direction of the Italian military engineers Pietro de Spazio, Francesco da Pozzo, Pietro Ferrabosco, and others. The reconstructed walls enclosed the town in an almost regular rectangular shape, with four main gates and two minor gates controlling the exits. During the 17th and the beginning of the 18th century, many old buildings were reconstructed. As the seat of an archbishop, Trnava quickly grew into a center of the Counter Reformation, as witnessed by the large number of Baroque buildings in the town. Among the numerous new churches and monasteries erected at that time, the buildings of the University (1635–1777) hold a special place of importance. After the abolition of the Jesuit Order, the transfer of the University to Buda, and the removal of the archiepiscopate, the building activities of the Church ceased, reverting to the secular population of the town in the first few decades of the 20th century. At that time, part of the walls were dismantled, so that only fragments in the eastern and western parts of the town are preserved today.

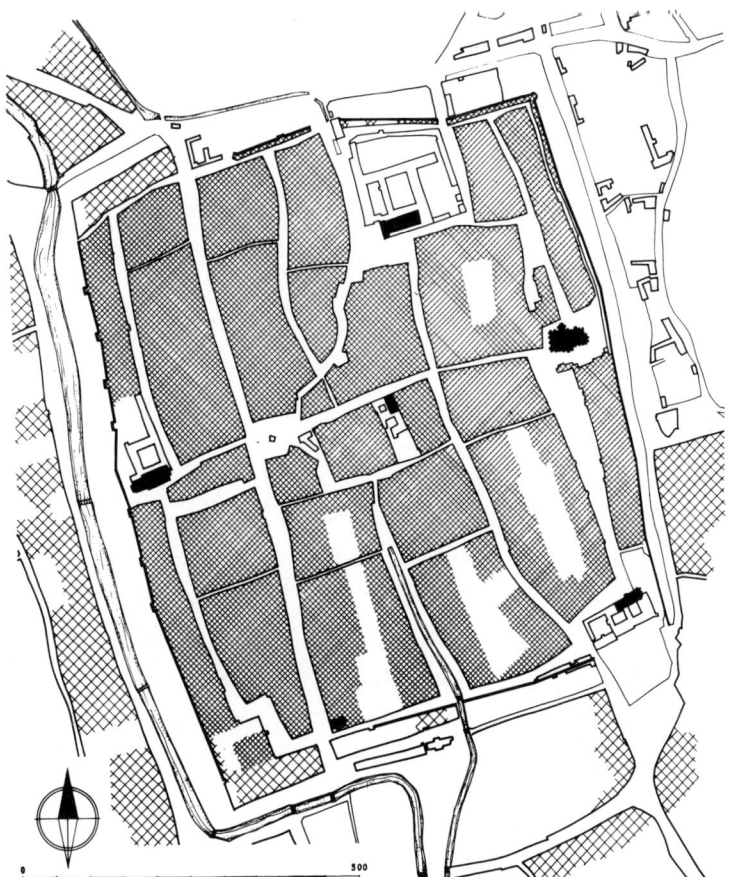

256. Plan of the historic center of Trnava.

257. View toward the parish church of St. Nicholas (end of the 14th and beginning of the 15th century) at Trnava.

Třeboň, Southern Bohemia. The early origin of the town of Třeboň was connected with the old route between Bohemia and Moravia. The settlement was located at the most convenient passage through the wooded marshy region between the arms of the river Lužnice. In the second half of the 13th century, Třeboň was laid out as a town by the feudal lords of Vítkovec. The town was enclosed with walls in the second half of the 14th century. All three gates have been preserved, though not in their original form.

In the forties of the 16th century, stone houses began to be erected in the town, a process which proceeded throughout the second half of the 16th century. At the same time, building activities spread to the immediate surroundings of the town, where reservoirs were laid out. The construction of one of the reservoirs, called Svět (The World), completed in 1573, considerably influenced the plan of the town since it required the abolition of part of the fortifications and two suburbs, one of which had been laid out only ten years previously.

258. View of Třeboň and its suburbs in 1693, by M. Stránský.

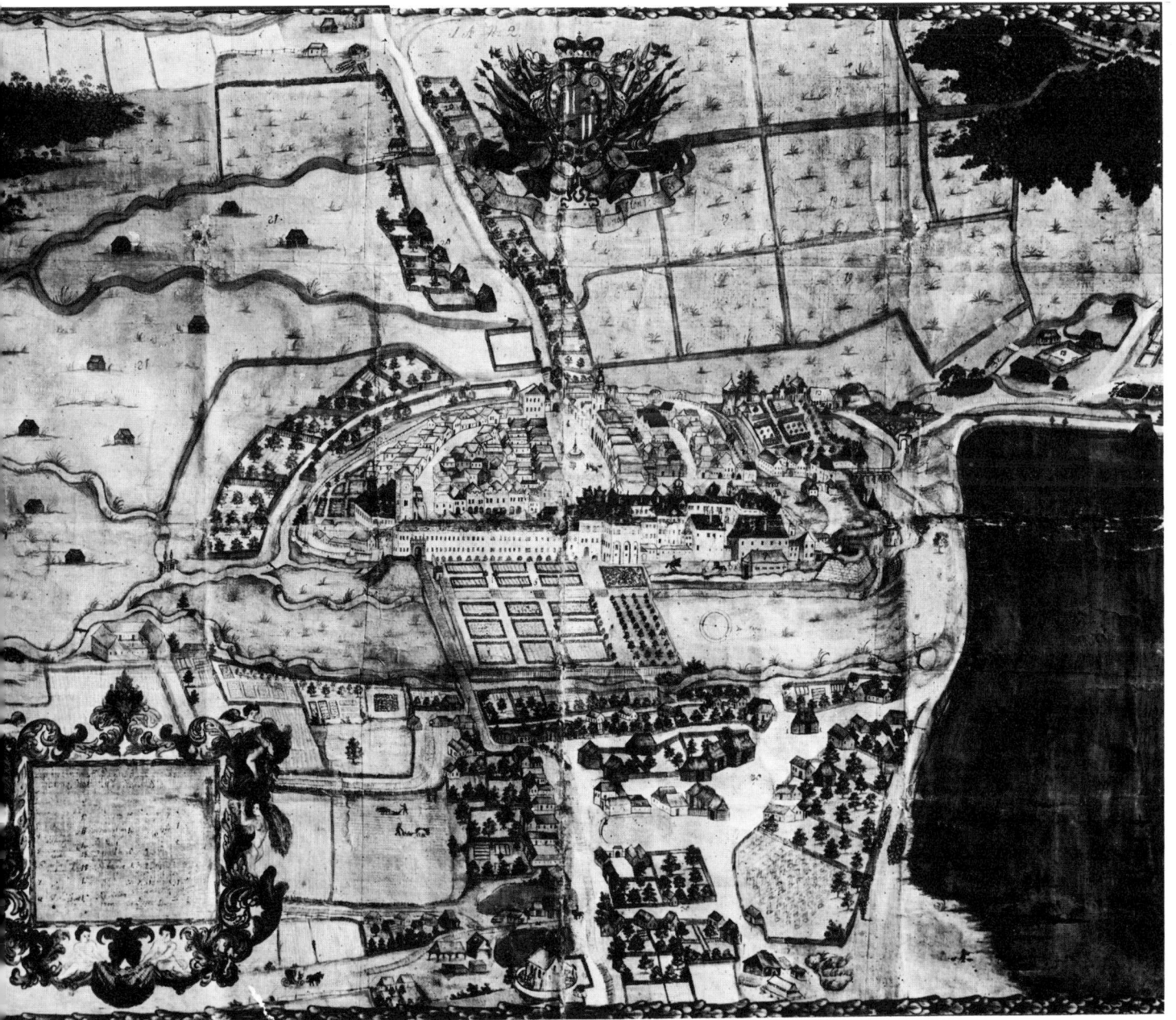

Uherské Hradiště, Southern Moravia. The town of Uherské Hradiště is situated in the fertile basin of Southern Moravia where the Morava River was once crossed by an important route from Hungary.

In the ninth century, the central area of the Great Moravian Empire was the region of the lower course of the Morava River. The basic units in the organization of this Slavonic state were the *civitates,* the *urbes,* or *hrady* (castles). Archeological investigations have established the existence of nine walled-in settlements of Great Moravia, mainly within the Southern Moravian territory, on the rivers Morava and Dyje. The area of the present Old Town (Staré město), near Uherské Hradiště, is the former site of one of these early settlements.

About the ninth century, this early settlement was protected by a ditch, 16.4 feet wide and 1,148 feet long. Toward the end of the first half of the ninth century the settlement was no longer spacious enough and was extended beyond the ditch. The new seat was fortified with a double trench which ran parallel to the old one for a length of about 4,500 feet. Toward the end of the ninth century, stockades were built behind the trenches and a new ditch, about 1.25 miles long, was added. The castle, covering an area of 617.5 acres, with its two outer baileys, was probably situated within the fortifications.

Foundations of two churches with burial grounds and a settlement with workshops and smelting furnaces of the jewelers have been discovered on the territory of the Old Town.

This settlement certainly was of greater significance than the neighboring communities of farmers and fishermen. Thus a large, town-like center existed on the territory of the Old Town about the middle of the ninth century. Being an important stronghold and an ecclesiastical, political, and administrative center, it stimulated the development of the densely populated area in the vicinity of the castle. This settlement around the castle, with its own fortifications, gave rise to an early urban agglomeration.

After the collapse of the Great Moravian Empire at the beginning of the 10th century, its urban centers were destroyed by Hungarian raiders. Only the Old Town survived from the earliest era. It had a marketplace as early as 1232, and a church consecrated to St. Michael.

Opposite the Old Town, an island in the river Morava lay directly on the so-called Hungarian Route, which crossed the flood plain of the river at its narrowest point, between the elevation called Sady on the left bank and the Old Town on the right river bank. A village of fishermen was located on the island. In 1257, King Přemysl Otakar II founded a new town on this island, "as a stronghold guarding the Hungarian frontier." The population of the town was recruited from the inhabitants of two neighboring villages and granted the right to hold two markets.

The town had a regular layout with two distinct areas, each with its own square. The southern square, trapezoidal with a funnel-

259. Plan of the historic nucleus of Uherské Hradiště, after a cadastral map of 1827.

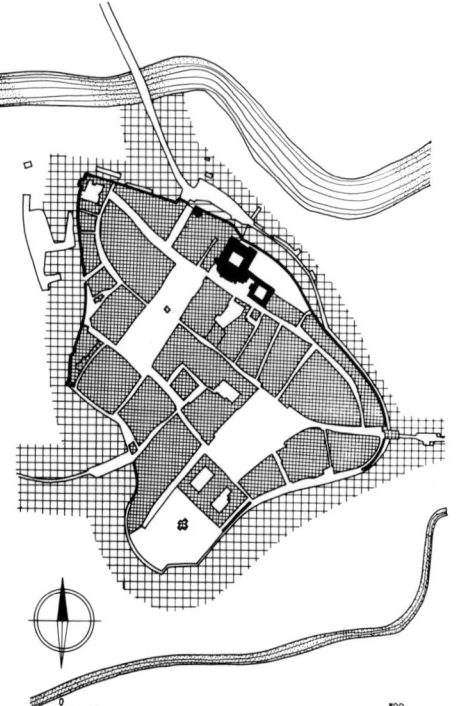

shaped widening, recalls the original layout. Up to the year 1785, its center was occupied by St. George's Church. The northern square is rectangular. The town quarters were separated by a brook, while the two marketplaces were connected by a narrow street. The town was encompassed by a circular street and protected by fortifications.

In the first half of the 14th century, stone walls with two gateways and a moat were constructed. In the third quarter of the 17th century, the town of Uherské Hradiště was changed into a citadel, guarded by curtains and bastions and an extensive inundation system. In 1491, a Franciscan monastery was built at the northern square, followed by a Jesuit college in the southern square in 1643.

After the citadel had been dismantled in 1782, the town and its new suburbs spread to the reclaimed area adjoining the river bank. Uherské Hradiště's favorable situation influenced the rapid development of the town. The original early settlements on both river banks were merged with the town on the island. Today it is an important communication center, with about 13,000 inhabitants.

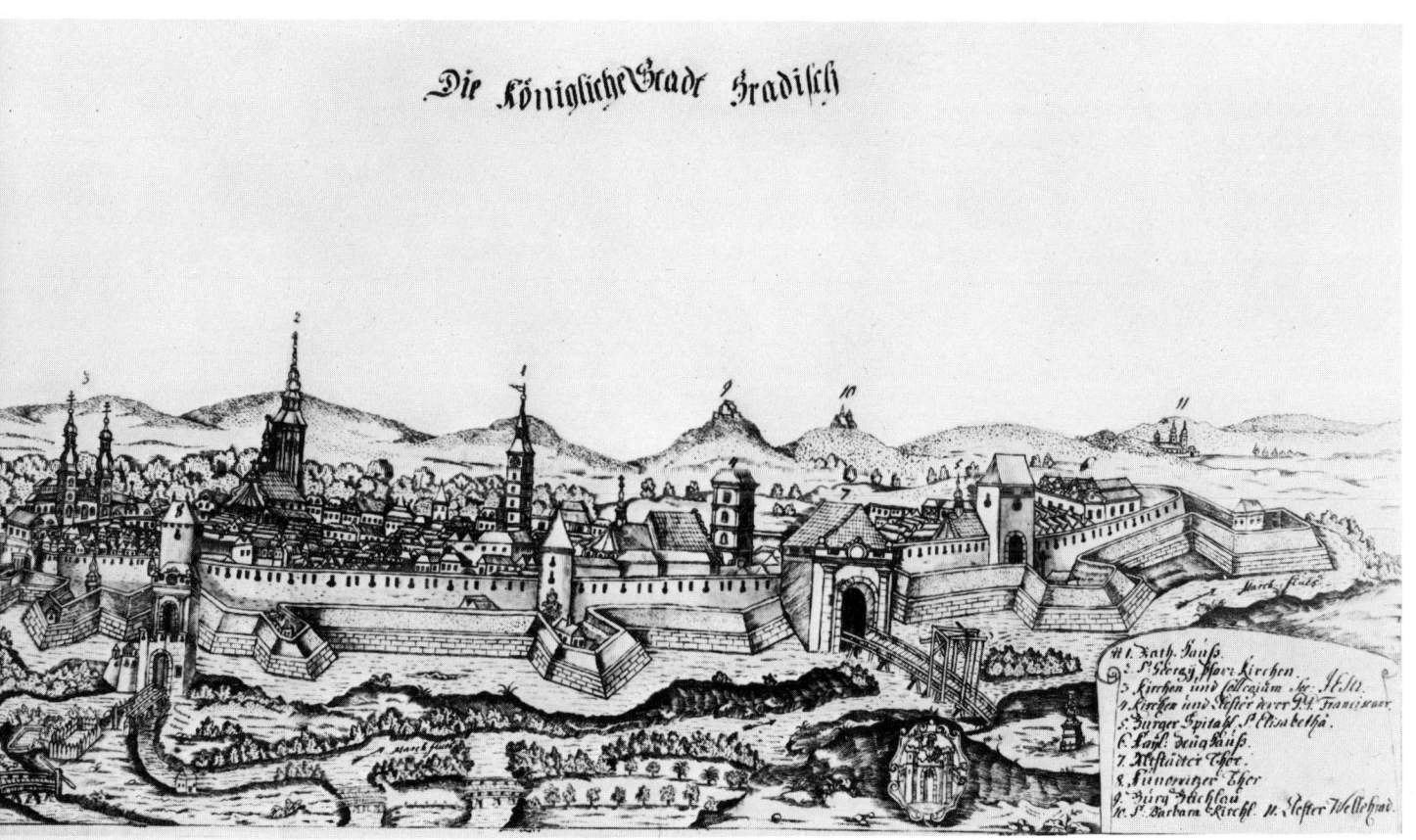

260. View of Uherské Hradiště. From the collection of Dismas von Hoffer, 1723–1728.

Uničov, Northern Moravia. The town of Uničov is situated on the river Oskava on the border of the fertile lowland of Haná, near a once important route connecting the city of Olomouc with the north of Moravia.

This position, the favorable conditions of defense in the marshy plain and, above all, the rich natural resources of precious metals and gold-bearing waters were the *raison d'être* for founding a rural settlement and, later, in 1224, the town and fortress. King Přemysl Otakar II confirmed its rights and privileges in the year 1234. Thus the town became the center of an extensive gold, silver, and iron mining region in the north of Moravia. The significance of Uničov lies not only in its early foundation as one of the first towns of the Bohemian Crown but also in the almost circular plan of the castle, preserved to the present day.

The town was founded in 1327 and called *Nova Civitas*. It was laid out on a circular ground plan with a square in the center. The streets lead from the corners of the square to the four gates placed at regular intervals in the walls.

The fortifications were built in several stages. They consisted of the high main wall with bastions and a lower wall with a covered passage for the defenders. The town was completely encircled by a moat. In 1643, during the war with Sweden, the medieval fortifications were reinforced with ravelins, redoubts, and earthworks outside the moat.

Uničov suffered heavily during the Thirty Years' War. Its importance as a mining center declined but, starting in 1768, the textile industry began to develop in the town.

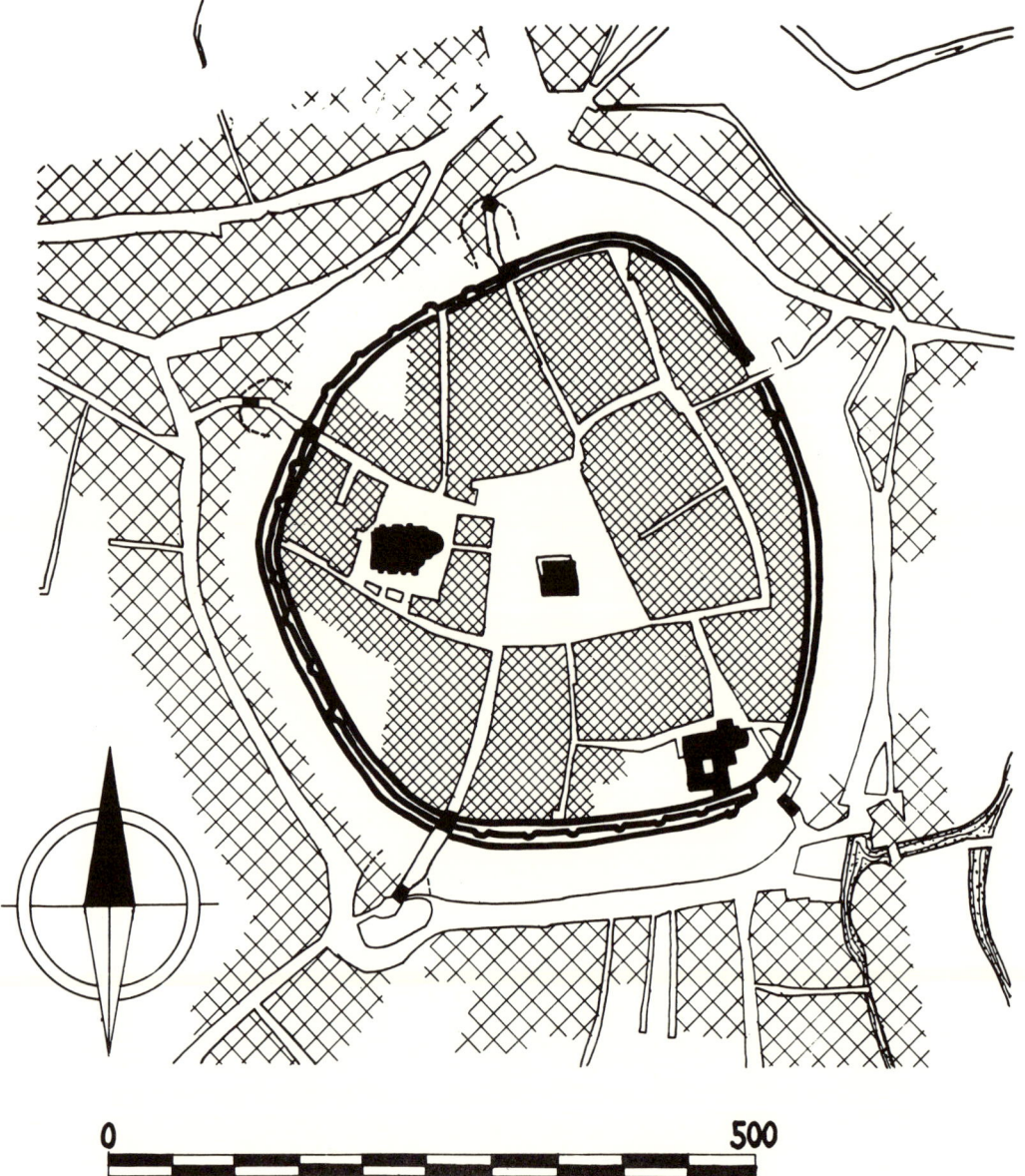

261. Plan of Uničov, after a cadastral map of 1833.

Žatec, Northern Bohemia. Žatec, on the River Ohře, was apparently the main seat of the powerful Lučan tribe of northwest Bohemia. The unceasing attacks of the Lučans against the north Bohemian estate of the Přemyslides finally brought about the fall of the former. Situated on a steep headland, Žatec became an important stronghold of the newly established Bohemian State. In the 11th century, the southern entrance to the castle was reconstructed into a big oblong marketplace with a Romanesque church situated in its center.

The early feudal settlement at Žatec was not restricted to the area of the former stronghold but spread to the territory of the medieval suburbs. Apart from Prague and Litoměřice, Žatec ranks as one of the most important early medieval Bohemian settlements. Under the reign of King Přcmysl II, Žatec was elevated to a Royal Town, probably in 1266. The fortified center occupied the territory of the former stronghold. The original early medieval marketplace in the neighborhood of the castle, with a church in its center, became too small in the 13th century. A new oblong square in the southern half of the nucleus, slightly widening toward the south, was laid out. A short street in the center of its southern side led to the former Prague Gate. The plan of the town was fairly regular, although the stronghold and the former early medieval layout prevented the application of a gridiron plan. The construction of the for-

262. Plan of the historic nucleus of Žatec, after a cadastral map of 1843.

263. The square of Žatec with arcaded houses of Gothic origin. In the center, the Column of the Virgin Mary (1712); in the background, the Town Hall.

tifications was completed at the end of the 13th and the beginning of the 14th centuries. The Golden Age of Žatec was probably the second half of the 14th century, when the old timber houses were replaced by single-story stone buildings. In 1386 the Town Council of Žatec requested the royal vice-chamberlain for permission to built arcades. The request was granted, with precise instructions as to the dimensions of the arcades. In 1380, the foundations were laid for the belfry on the southern side of the church. It is one of the oldest free-standing church towers in Bohemia.

In 1421, the fortifications of Žatec withstood the powerful attacks of the Crusaders who tried to conquer the town, which was one of the main centers of the Hussite Movement in Bohemia. However, in 1463, the fortifications were reconstructed, adopting and improving the latest features of the Hussite fortifications at Tábor.

The Renaissance did not assert itself to any great extent in the architecture of the town, nor did the following period of political and economic decline produce any outstanding changes. In the 18th century, however, a number of fires gave rise to considerable building activities that imprinted some late Baroque and early Classicist features on the town.

In the 19th century, Žatec became a center of the world trade in hops. Thanks to its situation on a headland, the historic nucleus has retained its dominating character to the present day.

Znojmo, Southern Moravia. The oldest Bohemian chronicler, Cosmas, a canon of the St. Vitus' Chapter in Prague (about 1045 to 1125), wrote that the boundaries of the Bohemian State were protected everywhere by deep forests and mountains, with the exception of South Moravia where they were guarded by the river Dyje. Cosmas' text is obviously an expression of the chronicler's sorrow over the loss of the South Moravian territory between the rivers Dyje and the Danube, after the war of 1041. The origin and increasing importance of Znojmo as an important frontier town was directly connected with the just-mentioned change of the Bohemian frontiers.

The town was preceded by a Great-Moravian stronghold above the confluence of the river Dyje with a brook and separated from the historical core of the town by a deep ravine.

The establishment of a new frontier in the second half of the 11th century increased the strategic importance of the Znojmo territory and the river crossing, which led to the construction of a castle.

About the second half of the 11th century, several settlements developed at the foot of the castle, on the territory of the feudal town. Not far from Znojmo a Premonstratensian monastery, known as Louka, was founded on the east bank of the river.

In a document of 1226, Znojmo was mentioned as covering the same area as the present historical core of the town. Its rather intricate shape was due to the configuration of the terrain. The town spread eastward on a narrow headland, occupied since the 11th century by the royal castle. The overall dimensions of the urban center were 2,132 by 3,116 feet.

A regular plan could only be applied in the eastern part of the town. The layout was influenced by the trunk roads, which formed an almost regular cross and determined the position of the four gates. The Upper Square originated at the crossing of these trunk roads, while the Lower Square was laid out in the southern part.

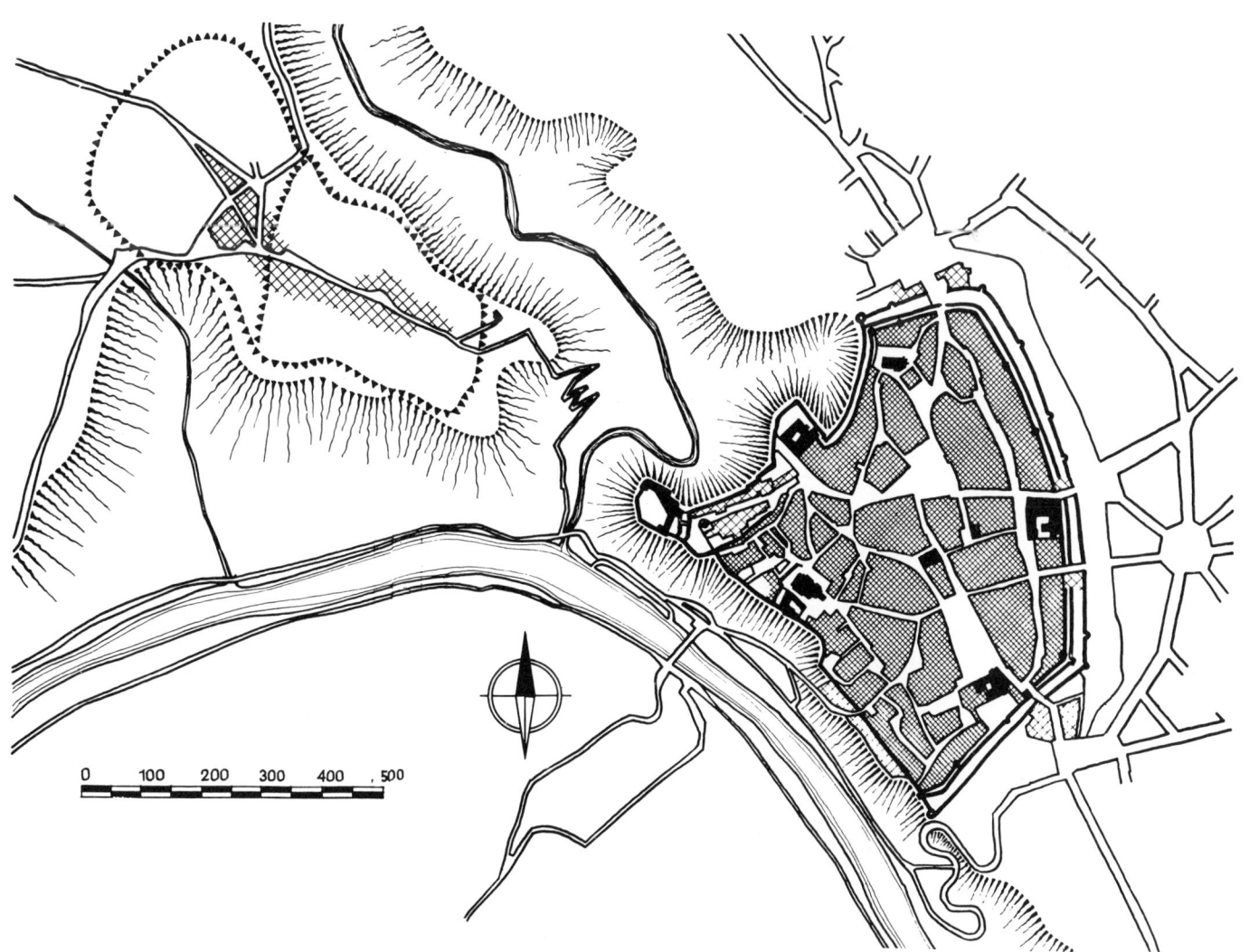

264. Plan of the historic nucleus of Znojmo. The dotted line (top left) indicates the location of the walled-in settlement of St. Hippolyte of the Great Moravian era.

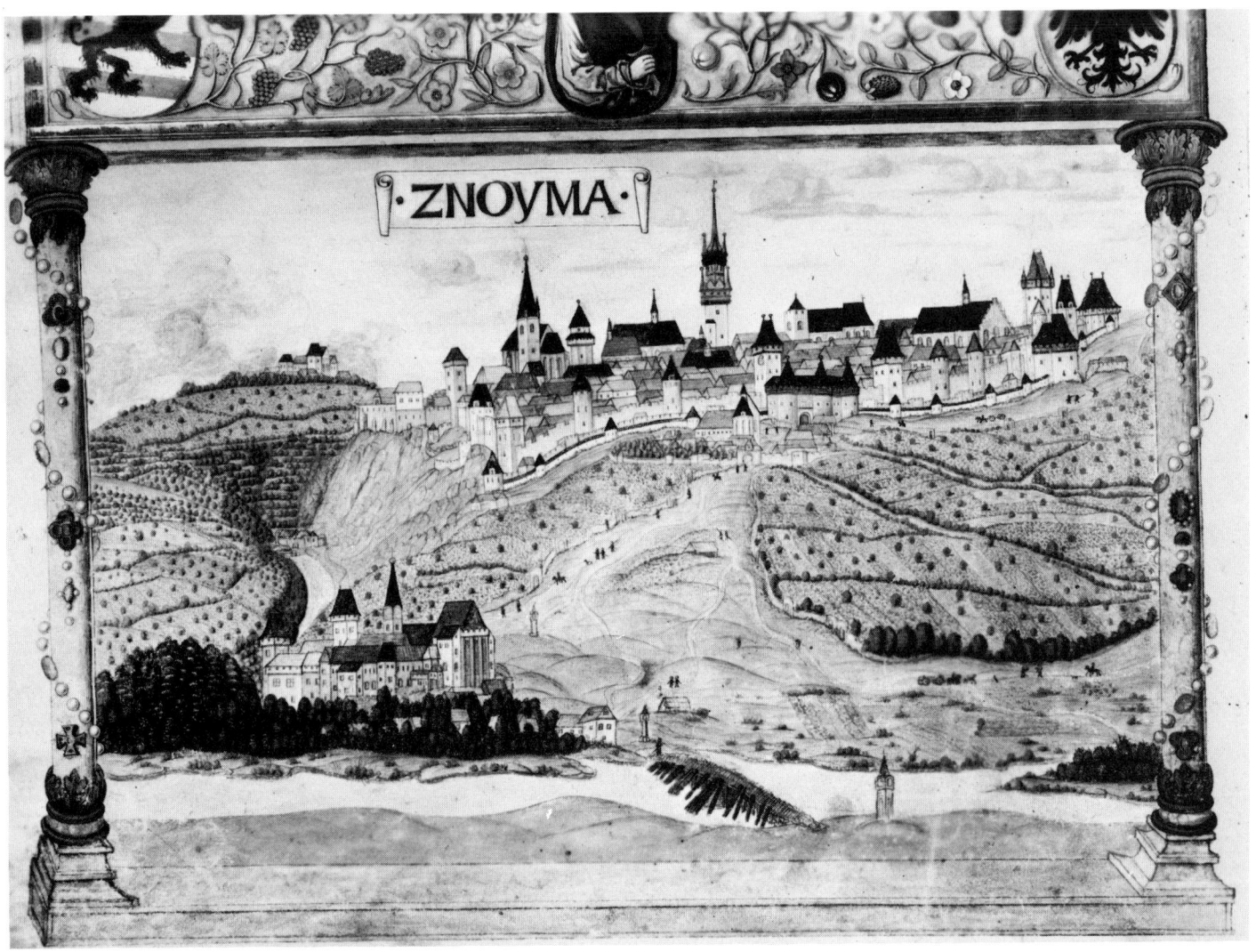

265. View of Znojmo from the southeast. Illustration of 1523.

One of the aims of King Přemysl Otakar II was to strengthen the defenses of the country. Like the majority of Bohemian and Moravian towns, Znojmo was influenced by this policy, although the town did not receive its fortifications until the end of the 13th century, under King Wenceslas II.

The Hussite Wars hardly affected the town of Znojmo. As early as the forties of the 15th century, the construction of public buildings began. Among the buildings erected at this time was the tower of the town hall (1445–1448), by Mikuláš of Sedlešovice.

The appearance of the town at the end of the Middle Ages is shown in a miniature painting dating from 1523 and incorporated in the book on town rights, by Štěpán of Vyškov. Not long after the painting had been made, a general reconstruction of the town began which was limited almost exclusively to dwelling houses. In a few decades the town changed considerably. Of decisive importance were the attics, which replaced the medieval gables.

By the beginning of the Thirty Years' War, Znojmo was one of the most beautiful towns in Bohemia. Sumptuous houses with long wings or arcaded courtyards surpassed in style many contemporary houses in Prague. The Thirty Years' War put a stop to this rich architectural development which did not revive until the 18th century.

266. General view of Znojmo. From the collection of Dismas von Hoffer, 1724.

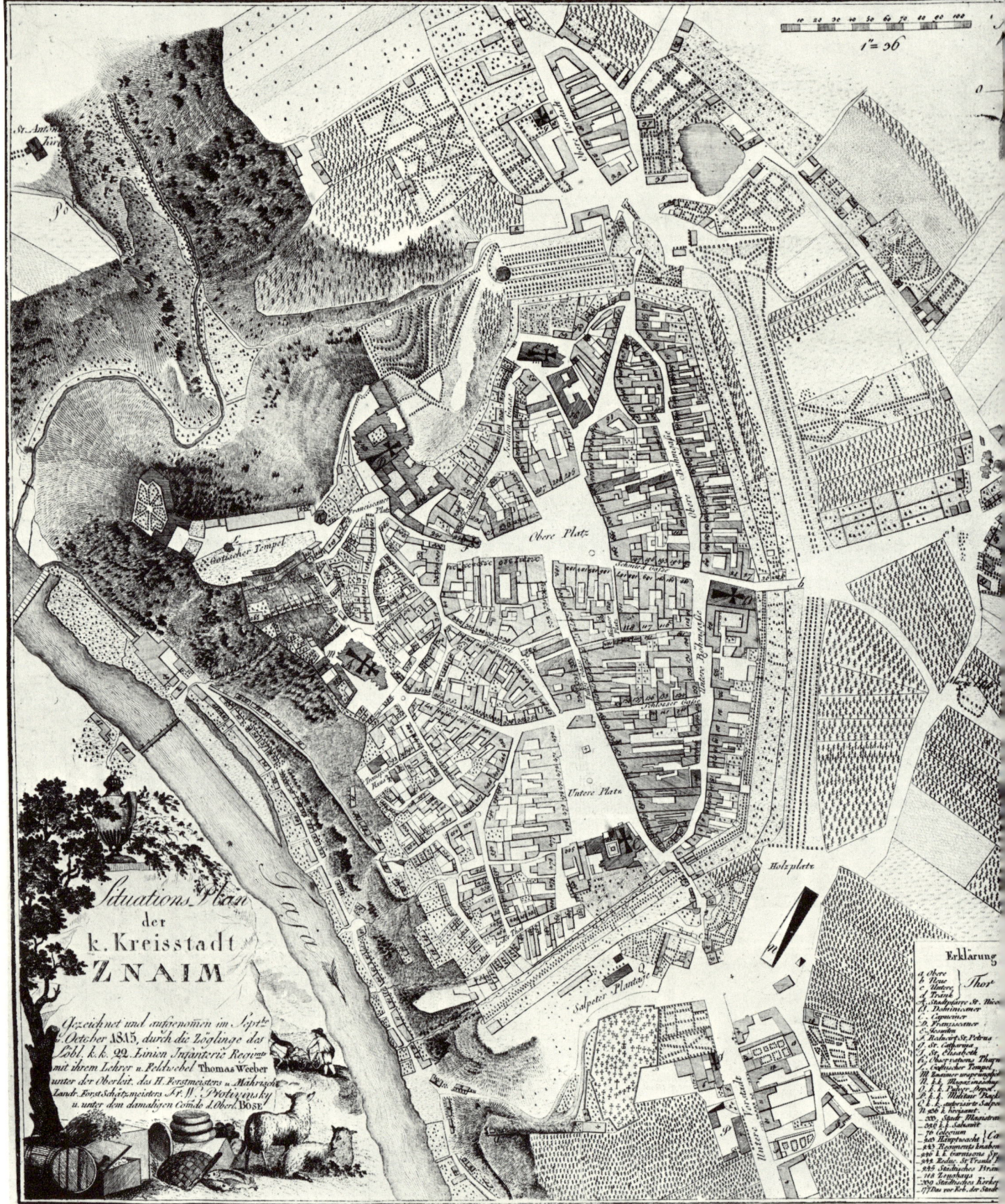

267. Plan of Znojmo in 1815.

Zvolen, Central Slovakia. In the 12th century, the colonization of Central Slovakia was centered on the area around the castle of Zvolen, situated on a trade route connecting Hungary and Poland. At the beginning of the 13th century a settlement originated not far from the castle which obtained the rights of a town in 1244. However, it was not until the second half of the 14th century that the town developed more vigorously.

The original houses were probably concentrated around a Romanesque church situated on the site of the royal castle. Due to a number of subsequent changes, the present layout of the square does not correspond to its original state. The first radical reconstruction of the square probably took place in the middle of the 14th century. It coincided with the construction of a royal castle as the dominant feature of the square, towering with its large mass over the small Gothic houses. Of the medieval public buildings in the square only the church has been preserved.

The construction of the walls, begun in

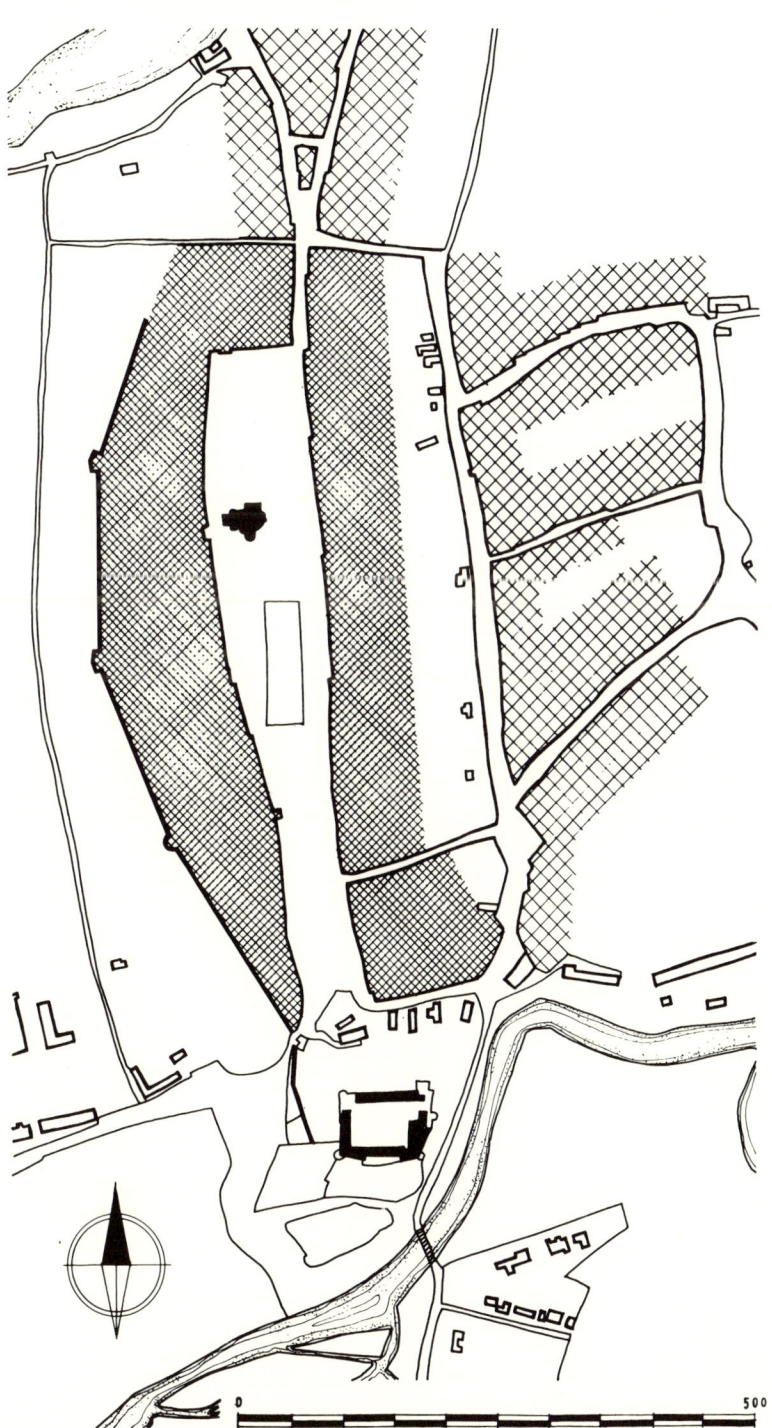

268. Plan of the historic core of Zvolen.

1541 and directed since 1590 by the Italian military engineer Giulio Ferrari, was not completed until 1635–1667. In their final shape the fortifications, consisting of a high wall with two bastions at the northern side and two circular towers on the two longer sides of the fort, determined the layout of the town which included the castle.

The town remained practically unchanged within its walls until the 19th century. In the course of the 19th century, Zvolen expanded, particularly toward the east and along the whole circumference of the old town core. These tendencies were also noticeable in the first half of the present century when another partial reconstruction of the square took place.

The important position of the town of Zvolen in the transportation system of the country, the great expansion of its industry, and the establishment of a university enhanced the importance of the town and promoted its expansion, as did the increase of its population, which today exceeds 21,000.

269. View of Zvolen in 1599, by Johann Willenberg.

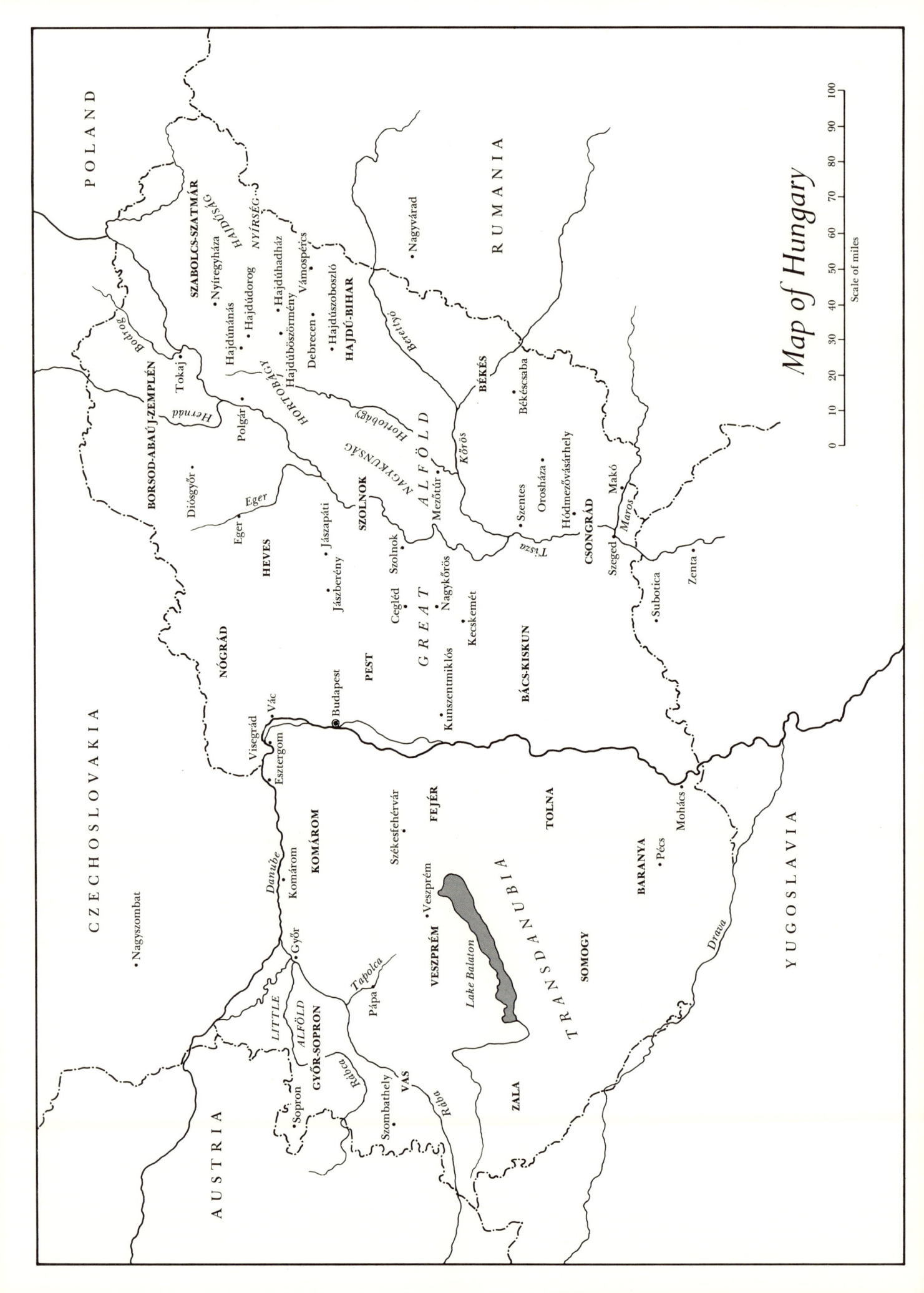

HUNGARY

Introduction
by E. A. Gutkind

CHAPTER 24

HUNGARY MAY BE divided into four main regions: the Kisalföld or Little Alföld (the Small Plain), the Nagyalföld or Great Alföld (the Great Plain), Transdanubia, and a chain of low mountains, the Bakony-Mátra-Bükk hills. The Danube separates the Little and Great Alföld geographically; each section has manifested a different social and political character throughout their historical development. The western part, the Little Alföld, was the Roman province of Pannonia from A.D. 10. It remained an outpost of the Roman Empire for several centuries, protected against the barbarian tribes of the Quadi and Marcomanni by a large number of troops and by fortresses along the banks of the Danube. In the first decade of the second century A.D., the province was organized as *Pannonia superior* and *Pannonia inferior*, the western and eastern portions, respectively; under Diocletian, a further administrative subdivision into four districts was made. *Sabaria* or *Savaria* (Steinamanger, Szombathely), *Arrabona* (Raab, Győr), *Sirmium* (near Sremska Mitrovica, Yugoslavia), and *Sopianae* (Fűnfkirchen, Pécs) may be mentioned as towns founded by the Romans. More open to Western influences and less exposed to the impact of the Turkish conquest, this part of Hungary adopted more social and political institutions from Austria than did the rest of the country. Most of this region is low-lying land, but it is traversed by the Hungarian *Mittelgebirge,* a chain of hills extending for 235 miles from Lake Balaton south of the Bakony Forest to the borders of Czechoslovakia in the northeastern Comitat of Borsod-Abaúj-Zemplén. These ranges separate the Little Alföld from Transdanubia, the plain of the Drava-Danube angle. Dunántúl, the Hungarian name of Transdanubia for the lands west of the Danube, is a reminder of the eastern origin of the Magyars, to whom this part of the country was "beyond the Danube."

The Little Alföld is drained by the Rába (and its tributaries), which winds its course through a flat valley until it reaches the Danube. Toward the southeast, the Kisalföld rises slowly toward the Bakony and Vértes mountains; in the west the rise is less gradual. In the north, the plain extends to the Danube and beyond into southwestern Slovakia. The loess-covered alluvium of the Little Alföld supports crop cultivation, whereas the damper areas provide pastures.

Transdanubia, the southeastern part of ancient Pannonia, has been efficiently cultivated for many centuries. Most of the towns in this area and in the Kisalföld were founded by German settlers, for instance, Sopron (Ödenburg), Pécs (Fűnfkirchen), Esztergom (Gran), and Székesfehérvár (Stuhlweissenburg), the oldest capital of Hungary. These towns are relatively small. The majority of the population live in villages of 3,000 to 5,000 inhabitants; on the plains, these villages have generally the form of a *Haufendorf,* a nucleated village, or a *Runddorf,* a ringfence village, and, along the valleys of the higher parts, of a *Strassendorf,* a roadside village.

The Danube separates Transdanubia and the Kisalföld from the Great Alföld, which stretches east of the river to the Carpathians. This vast, flat expanse, comprising about half of the total area of Hungary, is traversed by the Tisza River. During the Ice Age, the Danube and the Tisza deposited sand from the Alps and the Carpathians on the

The Land, History, and Settlement

339

Great Plain, covering much of the land between the two rivers with rough sand which the winds piled up into elongated dunes. The marshy area along the Tisza stopped the drifting sand from reaching the Tiszántúl, the region beyond the river. The valley of the Danube constitutes the most westerly section of the Great Alföld. The width of the river's flood plain ranges from approximately 4 miles to over 20 miles. Of the small number of settlements in this area, very few stand along the Danube. Except for the sand dunes, the region between the Danube and the Tisza is almost level. In the past, grass kept the sands from drifting. Now, vine and fruit trees seem to thrive on the warm, sandy soil. Viticulture is widespread on the sands around Kecskemét. However, sand drifts have partly covered the loess soils and have interfered with the natural drainage, leaving shallow lakes between the dunes. The high alkali content of the subsoil has made the land south of Kecskemét almost useless for agriculture. Nevertheless, there are large villages the size of towns in this sandy region, the Kiskunság. Kecskemét, with approximately 67,000 inhabitants, is the center of this district. The flood plain of the Tisza is even more extensive than that of the Danube, restricting east-west traffic to those points where the flood plain narrows and terraces stretch along both banks of the river. Several towns like Tokaj, Szolnok, and Szeged have grown up at such crossings. Tiszántúl, the East-Tisza region, is the largest part of the Great Alföld. Within the northern bend of the Tisza lies the Nyírség, an area of alluvial sand similar to the Kiskunság. The Nyírség is covered by extensive woodlands (*Nyír* meaning birch tree), and its sandy areas are used for grazing. The Nyírség is adjoined in the southwest by the Hajdúság, a sandy region partly covered by loess. Debrecen, the largest town of eastern Hungary, is situated in this area. Beyond the Tisza-Berettyó Canal extends one of the most uniquely "Hungarian" plains of the Great Alföld, the low-lying flat expanse of Hortobágy. Its grassy treeless steppe, a grazing ground for half-wild herds of cattle and horses, is drained by the slowly meandering Hortobágy. To the south of Hortobágy, between the Tisza and the Kőrös rivers, lies the Nagykunság, a loess-covered plain, most of which is under cultivation. Farms, shielded by a few locust or poplar trees, are dispersed over this region. Here and there the long arms of wells interrupt the low skyline typical of the Alföld. The Lower Tisza Plain, still another part of the Great Alföld, extends from the Kőrös River to the Romanian border. Here regular planned villages were established under Maria Theresa. Szeged, Hódmezővásárhely, and Békéscsaba are some of the towns in this part of Hungary.

The Great Alföld is the region of the large village-towns of Hungary where the population took refuge from the Turkish invasions, abandoning ravaged villages and desolate fields. The population of these huge agglomerations has been mainly engaged in agriculture, only slowly acquiring some features of urban communities. Around the town centers, which contain some larger buildings, stretch miles of uniform nondescript streets lined with rows of uniform one-storied white houses. Distances of 30 miles or more between the towns are not unusual. This concentration of the population in large compact settlements for reasons of protection and defense was only slightly modified when security was restored and the people began to build primitive shelters, the so-called *tanyák*,[1] where the men spent the summer working the land or tending the cattle, returning only in the winter to the towns and their families. The great distance from the towns to the fields made a daily journey to work impossible. It was not until more recent times that the temporary *tanyák* were turned into permanent isolated farms or groups of farms. Hence there are no villages in this region, but only a relatively small number of village-towns, with *tanyák* dispersed between them, almost completely isolated in spring and autumn, when the roads are virtually impassable.

It would be wrong to assume that the Great Plain of Hungary has always been a natural steppe in which the Magyars, possibly driven westward from the steppes of Central Asia by other nomadic tribes, settled at the end of the ninth century A.D. because they found it a congenial habitat, akin to their old homeland. This traditional view is hardly tenable in the light of our present knowledge and serious research, although definite evidence on the early condition of the land is almost completely lacking.[2] Professor Pounds quotes in this connection Otto of Freising, the biographer of Emperor Frederick Barbarossa, who in his *Gesta Friderici I. imperatoris,* written about the middle of the 12th century, described the plain as "rich in its arable fields" and "like the paradise of God or the fair land of Egypt."[3] How was it possible that this apparently fertile and well-wooded land was described by travelers of the 17th and 18th centuries as *puszta,* meaning "waste," or as "barren heaths"? Or by Dr. Richard Bright, in 1818, as "a dry sandy common, sometimes totally without vegetation, frequently with scarcely enough to bind the sand together. . . . In some places it was drifted by the wind into hillocks; in others it bore the rippled appearance observed on the sandy banks of rivers"?[4] The reasons for this transformation from a wooded and fertile plain to a grassy and sandy steppe are manifold. Part of the deforestation was certainly due to the devastation of the Turkish wars, though its extent should not be overestimated. Another source was the felling of trees for building and fuel, and still another was over-grazing. In general, it was malpractice and neglect which caused deterioration of the cover of vegetation and the subsequent loosening and erosion of the soil. Apart from these factors, the reports of the various travelers who described the plain as a desolate sandy steppe may have generalized from local conditions, assuming that what they had seen in one district was the same over the entire region. Scrutiny of historical records on the geographical characteristics of countries should have made us reluctant to accept their descriptions at face value; too often they are superficial and inaccurate.

---

1. *Tanya,* originally a Slavic word for fishermen's abodes—a fishing settlement—has, since the early 18th century, been used to denote a single farm or a group of farms, administratively and economically part of the parent settlement, that is, the large village or village-town.
2. N. J. G. Pounds. "Land Use on the Hungarian Plain." In: *Geographical Essays on Eastern Europe.* Indiana University Publications. Russian and East European Series. Vol. 24. 1961. Pp. 54–74.
3. In: *Monumenta Germaniae historica.* Lib. I. 32. Vol. XX. 1868.
4. R. Bright. *Travels from Vienna through Lower Hungary.* 1818. P. 197.

However, the fact remains that the land was badly neglected and that, in the 19th century, serious reclamation efforts were made involving reforestation, the extension of cultivated areas, and a change of the settlement pattern as the *tanya* system became permanent, creating focal points around which intensive cultivation and horticulture developed.

What factors formed and influenced the development of towns in Hungary? Is it possible to speak of specifically Hungarian towns, different in structure and appearance from those of other European countries? As far as function and morphology are concerned we have to distinguish between two distinct types of urban agglomerations: one based on Western traditions, the other on historical factors peculiar to the demands and conditions of nomadic pastoralism in the East. Towns of Westeuropean character like Esztergom, Buda, Győr, and Székesfehérvár grew up as seats of royal and ecclesiastical rulers and administrations, as strongpoints in strategically favorable locations, or as commercial centers at or near important trade routes and river crossings. Some were established on Roman ruins or later settlements. In general, their development followed the Western pattern.

The towns of the Great Alföld, on the other hand, differ in size, function, and origin. When Magyar tribes from the steppes in Russia settled on the Great Plain in the ninth century, they brought with them nomadic pastoralism. During the winter they established their camps on the Great Plain, during the summer in the mountains. This transhumance began to decrease around the 11th century as nomadic pastoralists were slowly replaced by agriculturists. Some scholars maintain that the towns of the Great Alföld originated in the camp system of nomadic tribes where the winter camp was more or less permanent, a "fixed" settlement, while the summer camp changed its location when the tribes and their herds moved their grazing grounds. However, the evidence for this hypothesis is too scanty for confirmation; the few agrarian towns that may have developed from such camps changed their character during the centuries following the Magyar and Cuman invasions.

What does seem certain is that pastoral activities necessitated a dispersed structure of settlement because large areas of unoccupied land were required for grazing. Village layouts reflect the function a settlement is meant to serve. As far as the Hungarian agglomerations of the Great Alföld are concerned, pastoralism influenced the structure of villages, that is, a group of houses was surrounded by fenced-in cattle enclosures, beyond which extended the open grazing lands, most of which were held in common. A similar pattern prevailed after the expulsion of the Turkish invaders. However, insecurity during the following periods drove more and more people to seek safety in those villages that had survived the turbulent years of war and devastation. Thus emerged the huge settlements, or village-towns, of the Great Alföld, whose areas were urban in size but whose functional life remained anchored in agriculture and its ancillary industries. Even today, they are less industrialized than the towns of northern and western Hungary.

Unlike other agrarian settlements whose development was furthered by intensive cultivation on restricted terrains, the village-towns of the Great Alföld have retained an economic base spread over vast regions. People inhabit the core area but work—or live and work during the summer—in the outer peripheral zone of production and in the *tanyák*. The municipal area comprises not only the compact urban center but also the surrounding gardens, vineyards, pastures, fields, and scattered settlements. The layout of these vast agglomerations is unsystematic and rural in character except for the center, a relatively small part of the urban area, which has a market or square, a church, shops, and some public buildings. Beyond this nucleus, one-storied buildings spread village-like to the outer areas. Radial streets, cutting through twisting lanes and increasing in width toward the periphery to accommodate the growing number of animals collected from the inner urban area to be taken to grazing in the outlying zone, lead quickly, like "cattle paths," from the center to the pastures. Some of the streets are wide and unpaved. A traveler who visited Hungary around the middle of the 19th century remarked: "In most cases the town is distinguished from the village only insofar as, in the latter, the herdsman drives a large and, in the former, a very large herd of cattle to the fields."[5] This may be an oversimplification, though based on a correct assessment of the structure of settlement where even the so-called towns were fundamentally agricultural communities.

Around the year A.D. 1000 the population began to be sedentary, to acquire some traits of Western civilization, and to engage in cultivation of the soil, though agriculture was not yet fully stationary. The land was divided according to tribes and clans and was worked collectively. The fields were of little value. At this early period, man was the greatest asset. How different this was to be in the 16th century, when a whole settlement of *adscripti glebae* was equivalent to the price of a mare, or a foal, one ox, or two cows, or four sheep, and when animals determined the value of human beings, not vice versa. As late as 1809 the Hungarian statistician Martin von Schwartner spoke of 1,305 *puszták*.[6] Throughout the centuries the meaning of the word *puszta* changed, from the original name for a steppe to the designation of pastures and, finally, to an isolated farmstead, representing in its variations three consecutive stages of rural civilization. The statistician further remarked that: "The sheep is shorn only for its master but the thousand people who live on every *puszta* have also to render services and pay taxes to the king and the Comitat and demand more food from the *puszta* than the sheep."

The early agrarian structure was molded by the founders of the Hungarian state, who brought with them from their homeland between the Don and the Dnieper the tribal and family customs that determined the distribution of land in their new home. The royal domain comprised all the territory not occupied by the Hungarian newcomers and represented, even in the 11th century, the major part of the country,

---

5. H. Ditz. *Die ungarische Landwirtschaft*. Volkswirthschaftlicher Bericht an das königl. Bayerische Staatsministerium des Handels und der öffentlichen Arbeiten. 1867.
6. *Statistik des Königreichs Ungern*. Vol. I. 1809. P. 114.

including the frontier districts where the population was organized on a military basis.[7]

The organization of this frontier population is of particular interest as an example of the first line of defense of a country in primitive conditions.[8] Since early times Hungary was surrounded by a wide girdle of enormous forests, with the exception of parts of the western and southern regions where marshes and the Danube formed a natural frontier. The permanent protection of these border zones was one of the most important tasks of the rulers and the inhabitants. The penetration of the forests by hostile invaders had to be prevented or, at least, be made as difficult as possible. Consequently, at all more open spaces obstacles were erected and maintained which consisted, according to the locally available material, of ditches or fences, earthen mounds, or barricades of stones or trees. These obstacles were called *indagines* or, in Hungarian, *gyepű*, forming uninterrupted chains only here and there traversed by roads. The intersections were known as "gates," *portae regni*, Gates of the Kingdom, and were often named after the nearest settlement or the neighboring country, for instance, Czech Gate, Polish Gate, Russian or German Gate. As the most exposed points of the defense system, these gates had to be especially carefully protected. The construction and maintenance of these *gyepű* was entrusted to the garrisons of the fortified castles of the royal comitat in which these gates were situated or to the servants of the lay and clerical feudal lords, whereas their actual protection was the duty of free men, of the *speculatores* or *exploratores*, of the *őrök*, the guards.

But the main obstacle to invaders was the existence of large tracts of no-man's-land that separated the country from its neighbors. Thus there were two frontier districts, the inner frontier enclosing the occupied land and the outer frontier zone, an empty wilderness or deliberately devastated land. These uninhabited separating spaces, stretching out beyond the *gyepű*, were called *gyepűelve*, that is, beyond the *gyepű*. It was only natural that these unoccupied regions, without clearly demarcated frontiers, gave rise to frequent disputes and even wars.

The kings of the Árpád dynasty realized that purely military measures could not guarantee the protection and possession of the frontier zones and that more constructive plans had to be put into operation. Consequently, they began to further the settlement of these territories; during the next centuries these areas were to constitute one of the main sources of royal power and wealth, especially when a certain scarcity of land of the royal domain—due to frequent and large grants to feudal lords—made itself felt. The new land grants in the frontier zones created a class of landed aristocracy. Here, they could expect to receive larger estates than within the interior of the country. This grant process was accompanied by extensive clearing of the woodlands and intensive settlement and, later, by the erection of fortified castles from which

---

7. J. Rutkowski. "Medieval Agrarian Society in its Prime." In: *The Cambridge Economic History*. Vol. I. 1942. P. 401.

8. K. Tagányi. "Alte Grenzschutz-Vorrichtungen und Grenz-Ödland: *gyepű* and *gyepűelve*," *Ungarische Jahrbücher*, Vol. I, 1921, pp. 105-21 *passim*.

the royal officials administered the country. Whereas at the beginning of the Árpád period only one or two estates were enfeoffed, we hear of later grants, in the 13th century, that included domains with ten, twenty, or even more villages. The result of this policy was an advance beyond the protecting lines of defense of the *gyepű* and a need for a new defense system. However, the large-scale organization of frontier protection could be efficiently maintained only as long as it was in the hands of the kings, who alone could supply the necessary number of guards. Gradually, especially from the 13th century onward, the magnates gained the upper hand, and the maintenance of the *gyepű* began to lapse. Fortified castles provided more efficient protection of the territory, and the economic exploitation of the forests proved to be a lucrative business. In the course of this development numerous forest villages were laid out, the so-called *scultetiae*. Here the frontier guards, who were gradually losing their jobs, could better escape the oppression of the feudal lords by living in compact communities rather than in isolated groups of peasant-soldiers.

The more the grants of large estates increased, the more emphatic became the distinction between the wealthier lords, the *barones* or magnates, and the lesser nobility, the gentry, until the former had definitely established themselves as the leading privileged class. The evolving manorial organization was based on slaves (in the Roman sense), on *adscripti glebae,* a class which disappeared during the 14th century, and on peasants who, though personally free and owning movable property, had to perform certain services regulated by the statutes of 1298 and 1351.[9] Gradually, the size of the farm unit allotted to a family became the main criterion of social status among the rural population, whose most numerous group were the *iobaggiones*. The unit of land called *sessio iobaggionalis* comprised, on an average, from 15 to 20 acres. Below this class were the *inquilini,* owning cottages and in some cases small plots, and the *sub-inquilini,* living and working on farms belonging to other people.

The medieval social structure distinguished between *coloni liberi,* consisting of indigenous as well as immigrant peasants, and the *coloni servi* who had to cultivate the fields of the conquerors. As in the West, settlement of the country was organized by the feudal lords and the Church as owners of the land. Of conditions in the 14th century we read:

Decline of bondage and of the founding of new urban communities, frequent, though small, land grants by the kings, and the increase of the number of noble families resulted in the distribution of cultivable landed property among more and more owners, whereby agriculture attracted, in general, a multitude of hitherto unemployed persons. The most important work was performed by the wealthy abbeys of the Benedictines, Cistercians and Premonstratensians, reclaiming the waste land and laying out new villages for industrious peasants in exchange for moderate services . . . and [for example] exemption from all taxes and dues for seventeen years. The agricultural initiative of the monks demonstrated to the secular lords the means whereby they could establish their prosperity without fighting each

---

9. J. Rutkowski, *op. cit.,* pp. 406 and 410.

other and without robbery, but with less danger and greater advantage. Many used this opportunity, thus furthering the striving for landed property and increasing the value and price of the land.[10]

As in the West, a system of military services and political privileges connected with land grants came into being. This system included the *urbarium* comprised of the totality of all compulsory services and dues and the hereditary rule of the *Avitizität*,[11] that is, the organization of landed property in ancient Hungary according to which family or clan estates called *Avitiz* estates—in many respects liable to restrictions—were distinguished from estates whose owners had unrestricted freedom of disposal.[12] Thus, after the introduction of private property by St. Stephen (997–1038), as the owner of the whole conquered land, and the dissolution of the clans with their strong consanguineous bonds there came into being above the powerless and propertyless classes a nobility that grew steadily stronger and wealthier. Their large estates were administered from fortified castles or favorably situated places, while the conditions of the peasantry deteriorated. This suppression finally led to a peasants' revolt in 1514. It failed, and the remaining privileges were abolished.

In the 15th century, the Hungarian plain was a fertile region with numerous villages which today can hardly be identified and have left practically no trace behind. The actual villages were small, but the village areas, the *hotters*, including fields, pastures, and forests, were large, corresponding to the needs of an extensive agriculture. The fields were close to the villages and surrounded by the *puszta*. Boundary markers, mostly earth mounds, indicated more how far away a proprietor had the right to keep his neighbor than how far the land was cultivated.

The rule of the Turks, from the middle of the 16th century, and the wars of liberation—Buda was recaptured in 1686—drove the population from the open villages, concentrated them in a reduced number of larger places, or led to their removal to less accessible sites, often on hilltops where nature provided protection and shelter. To this period belong the origins of the great village-towns, such as Szeged, Kecskemét, and Debrecen. This particularly interesting and best-known stage of the changing structure of settlement in Hungary was preceded by a slowly spreading extension of the inhabited area, to which reference has already been made. However, a short summary may be appropriate. During the early period settlement proceeded along the major rivers, especially in western Hungary. There followed, in the middle of the 12th century, the establishment of Hungarian frontier guards on strategically important lines in the no-man's-land surrounding the country. In the period of fortified castles and increasing colonization, from about

---

10. I. A. Fessler. *Die Geschichten der Ungern und ihrer Landsassen*. Vol. III. 1848. Pp. 1043–45 *passim*.

11. *Aviticitas* in Latin and *ősiség* in Hungarian, that is, the ancestral (*ősi*) property (*aviticum*) which could not be sold, in contrast to the *acquisitum*, the purchased land, which was free from this restriction.

12. D. von Sebess. "Die Agrarreform in Ungarn," *Ungarische Jahrbücher*, Vol. I, 1921, pp. 87–88.

1150 to 1300, numerous German settlers arrived, joining the Hungarian garrisons of the castles. In the following epoch of territorial separatism, the individual domains of feudal lords were more and more consolidated. Hungarian influence declined, especially in the west, and a steadily growing number of German knights and settlers established themselves in this part of the country. Then followed the period of Turkish occupation, accompanied by a large immigration of Croats, which resulted in a concentration of settlement and a deterioration of the soil. Swamps spread over considerable portions of the Hungarian plain; and a desultory extensive agriculture, made worse by the scarcity of labor, characterized these centuries. About 1720, the population of the whole country was hardly more than two and a half million.

External pressure from political events was only one factor contributing to the concentration of the population in large village-towns. It coincided with the internal policy of the lords of the estates, who welcomed it as a means for a more efficient control of the peasants and for the better arrondissement of their land. In this process, villages were broken up and their inhabitants transferred to other villages selected as nuclei for a new concentration of settlement. In their new locations they received houses and land, but they maintained their claims to their land in the deserted villages.

An example may illustrate this procedure. The village of Csaba, in the Comitat of Békés, was founded in 1715 on an ancient deserted site with a few Hungarian families. After two years it had grown to twenty-two families. At about the same time, a nobleman acquired almost the whole Comitat for 140,000 guilders and invited Slovaks as new settlers. Csaba grew so fast that the original *Mark* was soon insufficient, and more land had to be added from another neighboring estate. By 1800, the population had increased to 20,000, and by 1857 to 27,000. For a long time Csaba was regarded as the largest village in Europe. Numerous other villages developed on similar lines. The long distances to the fields did not work against this concentration of settlement, since the journey to the cultivated area was made only relatively rarely; long and severe winters with their long interruption of outdoor work, bad roads, and, last but not least, home industry tended to promote such concentration.[13]

The *Neoacquistica Commissio* of 1690 furthered the same trends. Its purpose was to allocate land to persons for genuine or alleged merits, the sole obligation being to settle it. This procedure was particularly common in the central part of the Alföld. The colonists were not equally distributed over the territory but were settled in already existing places or at especially favorable nodal points. This action explains, at least to a certain degree, why within the triangle of Subotica (Maria-Theresiopel, Yugoslavia), Debrecen, and Kunszentmiklós only relatively few small communities came into existence, whereas large village-towns grew up, far distant from each other, with enormous communal areas of 300,000 to 450,000 *Morgen*. On the other hand, for instance, in Translyvania (Siebenbűrgen, Romania), where free peasants settled

---

13. E. D. Beynon. "Migrations of Hungarian Peasants," *The Geographical Review*, Vol. 37, No. 2, 1937, pp. 214–28.

who were spared the direct pressure of feudal lords, the villages were smaller and closer together.[14]

The so-called liberation of the peasants under Maria Theresa's rule was but a feeble attempt at ameliorating their conditions and was thoroughly compatible with the strong authoritarian tendencies of the period. Servitude was only later transformed into a somewhat mitigated dependence on the landed proprietors when, in 1791, the formal principle of the feudal era, binding the peasant to the soil as *adscripti glebae*, was abolished.[15] The peasants' position did not change much, and may be compared with their lot immediately after the occupation of the Bucovina, as described in the *Bericht der oesterreichischen Behörden aus dem Jahr 1775*:

> The peasant owns no personal property. In the whole of the Bucovina the peasant has not a hand's breadth of terrain that belongs to him. He builds his house on alien soil which the landowner ... is entitled to take away at his pleasure.... [He has the right] to cut out *in concreto* from the [communal] land a field in which he may do what he likes so that one encounters everywhere fields and meadows mixed up in all directions ... [involving] a change of cultivation almost every year.[16]

Only the plot on which his house stood was an individual's property. The land was collectively used, involving certain restrictions for the individual peasant. Cultivation was still partly shifting from one place to another because the degree of exhaustion of the soil differed from field to field.

A certain trend toward individual land ownership developed but did not lead to a more equitable distribution of the land. For example, in the central region of the Alföld, in contrast to the mass of propertyless laborers, a class of landed proprietors emerged from the relatively small number of former bondsmen. The communal land was distributed among the peasants on the basis of their existing property, so that those who already owned most received most, a principle hardly dictated by social justice. These large estates could no longer be cultivated from the village-towns since the fields were often from 15 to 25 miles distant, as in Kecskemét or Szeged, respectively. To counteract this disadvantage, farm buildings and a house for the manager were erected on the outlying parts of the estates, the so-called *tanyák*. This first stage would perhaps be followed by the removal of the son of the owner to the *tanya* for the whole summer. This human transhumance was not

---

14. I. Takács. "Die wirtschaftlichen und sozialen Folgen der Wiederbesiedlung der ungarischen Tiefebene im 18. Jahrhundert. Tanyasiedlung," *Ungarische Jahrbücher*, Vol. 13, 1933.

15. E. Kún. "Sozialhistorische Beiträge zur Landarbeiterfrage in Ungarn," *Sammlung nationaleconomischer und statistischer Abhandlungen des Staatswissenschaftlichen Seminars zu Halle*, Vol. 37, 1903, pp. 87–89.

16. Quoted after K. Grünberg. *Studien zur Österreichischen Agrargeschichte*. 1901. Pp. 47–48 *passim*.

270. Airview of the *tanya* of Csorvás near Orosháza, in the Comitat of Békés. The farm, enclosed by fruit trees, is situated in the middle of wheatland. On the right are the barns and the living quarters; on the left, the farmyard with stables and storage places for tools, fodder for the animals, and other farming commodities.

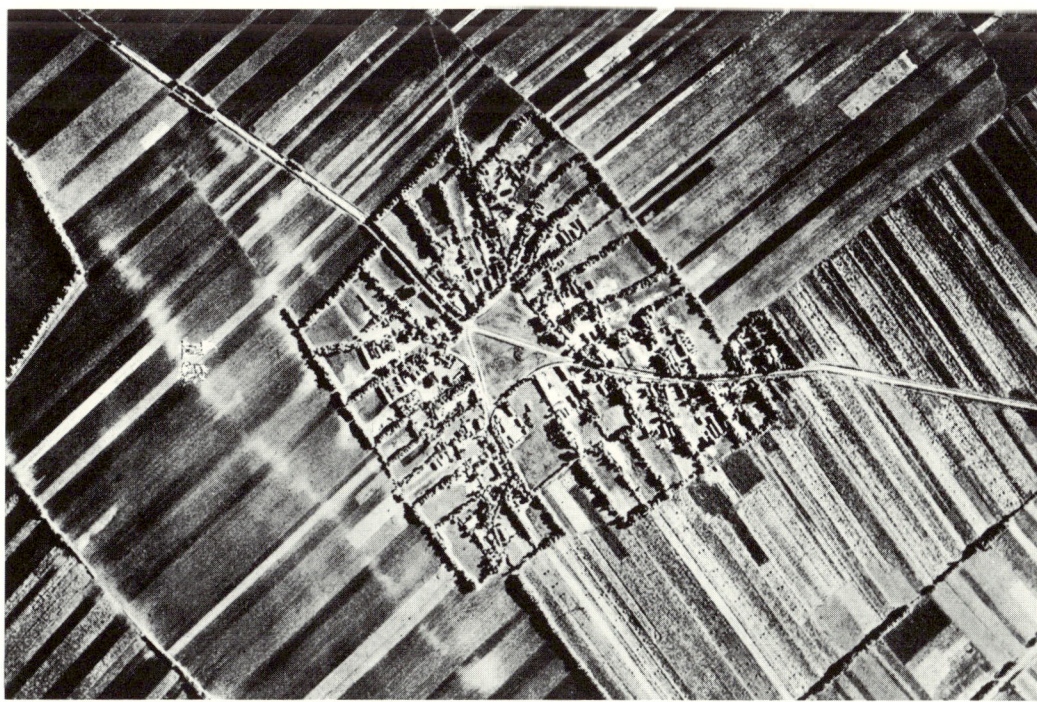

271. A cluster of farms around Nyíregyháza, east of the Tisza River, in the Comitat of Szabolcs-Szatmár. Groupings of single *tanyák*, called *bokor*, exist in different parts of the Alföld. Administratively, they are still an integral part of the parent settlement because they lack all communal institutions. The airview shows single farms on their own plots of land, fenced-in by bushes at or near either side of a road.

unusual. We know something similar from the large villages of Italy or from China where, in the first and second pre-Christian millennia, the population lived in groups on the fields during the summer.

After the consolidation of the fields, the *tanya* principle was often applied even to small communities. This furthered decentralization without directly influencing the village proper. Toward the end of the 18th century, 1,308 persons lived on *tanyák* around Kecskemét and about 21,000 in the country itself. By the middle of the 19th century there were 4,900 houses in this village-town and 300 in the countryside. In the course of this evolution two types of settlement developed: one consisting of unsystematically distributed single farms and the other of groups of farms around a center, indicating the contrast between the Hungarian and the Slavonic styles of living, possibly as a result of the stronger individualism of the Hungarian peasant and the stronger collectivism of the Slavonic peasants. The *tanya* system was, of course, inapplicable where the land of a peasant was intermingled with the shares of other peasants in *Gemengelage* and *Flurzwang* and community-regulated work existed, that is, as long as the fields of the individual peasants were distributed in so-called *Calculaturen* and the fallow fields served as common pastures. These practices varied independently of the continuation of servile labor, even in a modified form. As late as 1832 reforms were initiated to transform servile labor into hired labor and to settle the land with a property-owning population. Whole *puszták* were farmed out *en bloc* to communities to stimulate this process and to invite foreigners to settle on the land. In the same year Hungary had a population of about ten million, corresponding to an overall population density of 2.391 per geographical square mile, whereas the density of settlement was very low due to the great concentration of the population in village-towns. There were 10,350 villages and one town for every 400 villages, that is, for every 70 square miles. In 1805, there were 1.4 million peasant families out of a total rural population of 7 million. By the middle of the 19th century, the average size of a plot on the plain was 2.3 to 3 *Joch,* and a peasant owned on an average 20.2 to 21.9 *Joch.*[17] In the mountainous districts subdivision into lots was greater, ranging from 0.97 to 1.76 *Joch,* and the share of a peasant ranged from 16.3 to 26.0 *Joch*. This extreme dispersion of the landed property counteracted the decentralization of the large villages. In 1848, the land was freed from all restrictions, and the peasants were released from all services to the landed proprietors. By the middle of the 19th century the ten wealthiest families owned about one-sixth of the whole of the Hungarian land. The Esterházy family, the most famous representatives of this class, owned 29 domains with 60 small market towns, 414 villages, and 207 so-called *praedia* equal to 720,000 *Joch* of allodial land. These enormous estates were acquired in the course of centuries through enfeoffment, through more or less enforced consolidation, and through purchase. As late as 1736, for example, two estates in the Székesfehérvár (Stuhlweissenburg) Comitat, of 5,000 to 6,000 *Joch,* were let for 90 guilders per annum, that is, about one krone per *Joch*.

17. 1 Joch = 2 *Morgen*. A *Morgen* is a land measure of varying value in different countries. The Dutch *Morgen* equals 2.116 acres.

In general, industrial activities developed only in connection with agriculture. Until recent times craftsmen were rare in the villages, except for smiths, who were mostly gypsies. The townsmen were part-time farmers, and the home industry of the peasants produced what was needed in the rural households. Lack of capital and low population density worked against industrialization. Home industry, in addition to agricultural activities, began in consequence of the insufficient sustenance basis and first developed through the use of raw materials from the land or the communal forests. Production grew more varied only gradually, partly through the purchase of other raw materials. By the end of the 19th century, 71 groups of rural home industries were identified; pottery, earthenware, weaving, spinning, wicker-work, and carving were the leading occupations. The development of home industry proceeded in inverse ratio to the density of population and traffic: The larger the agglomerations and the better the connections, the less important and less varied the home industries.[18]

The structural characteristics of a village in the year 1857 provide a good example of the result of an imbalance in the distribution of settlement. In that year, the large village of Hódmezővásárhely had over 42,000 inhabitants, of whom about 4,000 were landowners, with 16,000 temporary workers and 2,500 laborers hired for days. There were 1,200 traders and craftsmen, all working almost exclusively for the needs of agriculture. There were 90 mills, 50 windmills, 9 watermills, and 15 oil mills. In 1852, the land belonging to the village, the *Mark,* covered 106,000 *Joch,* that is, about 11 square miles, of which about 58,000 *Joch* were under the plow, 13,000 *Joch* were meadows and gardens, 2,000 *Joch* were vineyards, 26,000 *Joch* were pastures, 163 *Joch* forests, and 1,000 *Joch* marshes, as well as 6,000 *Joch* of unproductive land. The village had 4,700 houses and 2,500 *tanyák.*

In general, certain geographical forms of settlement can be distinguished.

1. In the west, the settlement density is rather high, with 50 to 90 villages for every 1,000 square kilometers.

2. In northern Hungary, a zone of small villages extends into the mountainous regions, with 15 to 25 and 40 to 80 villages, respectively.

3. Farther south toward the interior, follows the zone of medium-sized villages, with 25 to 40 villages for every 1,000 square kilometers.

4. Southern Hungary forms a mixed settlement area, with 20 to 70 villages for every 1,000 square kilometers. This zone includes medium-sized villages as well as small settlements and *tanyák.* The relief of the terrain varies as do the field systems. In some instances, valley bottoms are used as meadows, terraces and hills for the cultivation of fields, gentle slopes for vineyards, and ridges of hills for forests.

5. In the zone of the large villages, each covering from 50 to 70 square

18. A. Braun and E. R. J. Krejcsi. *Der Hausfleiss in Ungarn im Jahre 1884. Ein Beitrag zur Lehre von den gewerblichen Betriebssystemen.* 1886.

kilometers, the number of villages decreases to 15 to 20 villages for every 1,000 square kilometers.

6. Finally, the zone of large village-towns averages only 6 to 7 settlements for every 1,000 square kilometers.[19]

Most travelers visiting Hungary in the first half of the 19th century remarked on the uniformity of all villages. Thus John Paget wrote in 1839:

The Puszta villages are large; they sometimes contain several thousand inhabitants. Nothing can be more simple or uniform than the plan on which they are built. One long, straight, and most preposterously wide street generally forms the whole village; or it may be that this street is traversed at right angles by another equally long, straight, and wide. Smaller streets are rare; but, when they do occur, it is pretty certain they are all parallel or at right angles with each other. All the cottages are built on the same plan; a gable-end with two small windows, shaded by acacias or walnuts, faces the street.[20]

And another traveler remarked in 1818:

In all their habitations is observed a perfect uniformity of design. A wide muddy road separates two rows of cottages which constitute a village. From amongst them there is no possibility of selecting the best or the worst; they are absolutely uniform. In some villages the cottages present their ends; in others, their sides to the road; but there is seldom this variety in the same village.[21]

These observations are superficial generalizations and, moreover, apply to only small parts of the country. There is, as a matter of fact, a considerable diversity of village types, dependent on the structure and quality of the soil, on the hydrographic conditions, or on ethnographical factors.

In the Alföld two principal types of villages or village-towns can be distinguished: villages that developed along radial streets and with the increase of population grew more compact in the interior, and villages that expanded outward in a ramifying net of streets like the veins of a leaf.[22]

The radial-nucleated village is, in many respects, similar to the towns of the Turkestan plain. The main characteristic of this type is that the roads converge on the central market square from the circular circumference, without interruption. The sectors between them are subdivided by a chaotic web of streets. A good example of this layout is the village of Jászapáti. Its circular shape and the outer circular roads follow the line of the protecting wall. The six main streets lead to the center, which today is still the focal point of the settlement, not simply

---

19. O. A. Isbert. "Probleme der Siedlungskunde in Ungarn," *Ungarische Jahrbücher*, Vol. 12, 1932, pp. 281–84. Despite the development of industrialization and transportation during the last 40 years, these figures still reflect some of the basic characteristics of the Hungarian settlement structure.

20. J. Paget. *Hungary and Transylvania*. Vol. I. 1850. P. 289.

21. R. Bright, *op. cit.*, p. 99.

22. G. Prinz. "Die Siedlungsformen Ungarns," *Ungarische Jahrbücher*, Vol. IV, No. 2, pp. 127–42, Nos. 3–4, pp. 335–52, 1924, *passim*.

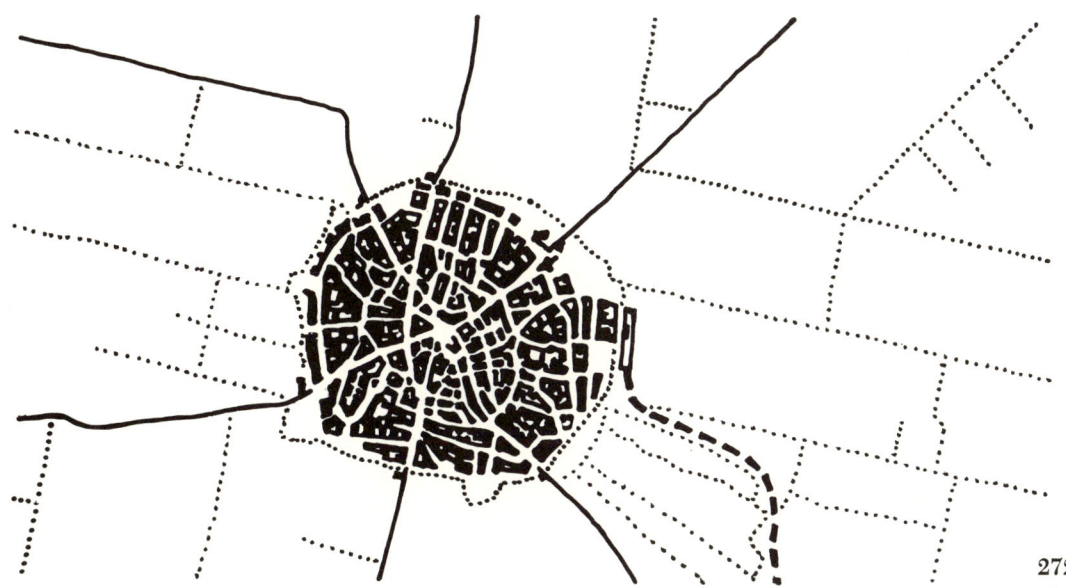

272. Plan of the village of Jászapáti in the north of the Great Alföld.

an intersection, but the center of attraction. That the layout was well planned and organized is obvious. The inner and the outer circular roads around the older and the newer parts, respectively, are indications of the growth of the village, and the numerous lanes and blind alleys testify to the increasing congestion of the interior. The whole is a combination of systematic planning and spontaneous growth.

An almost perfectly circular outline as at Hajdúböszörmény is rare. Its concentric ring roads are intersected by overland routes traversing the settlement and by radial streets that often divide before reaching the center. The division of radial streets is by no means characteristic of the walled-in, compact villages alone. For instance, at Hajdúhadház, twelve streets divide at the point where they enter the village from the surrounding territory.

273. Plan of Hajdúböszörmény in the Comitat of Hajdú-Bihar.

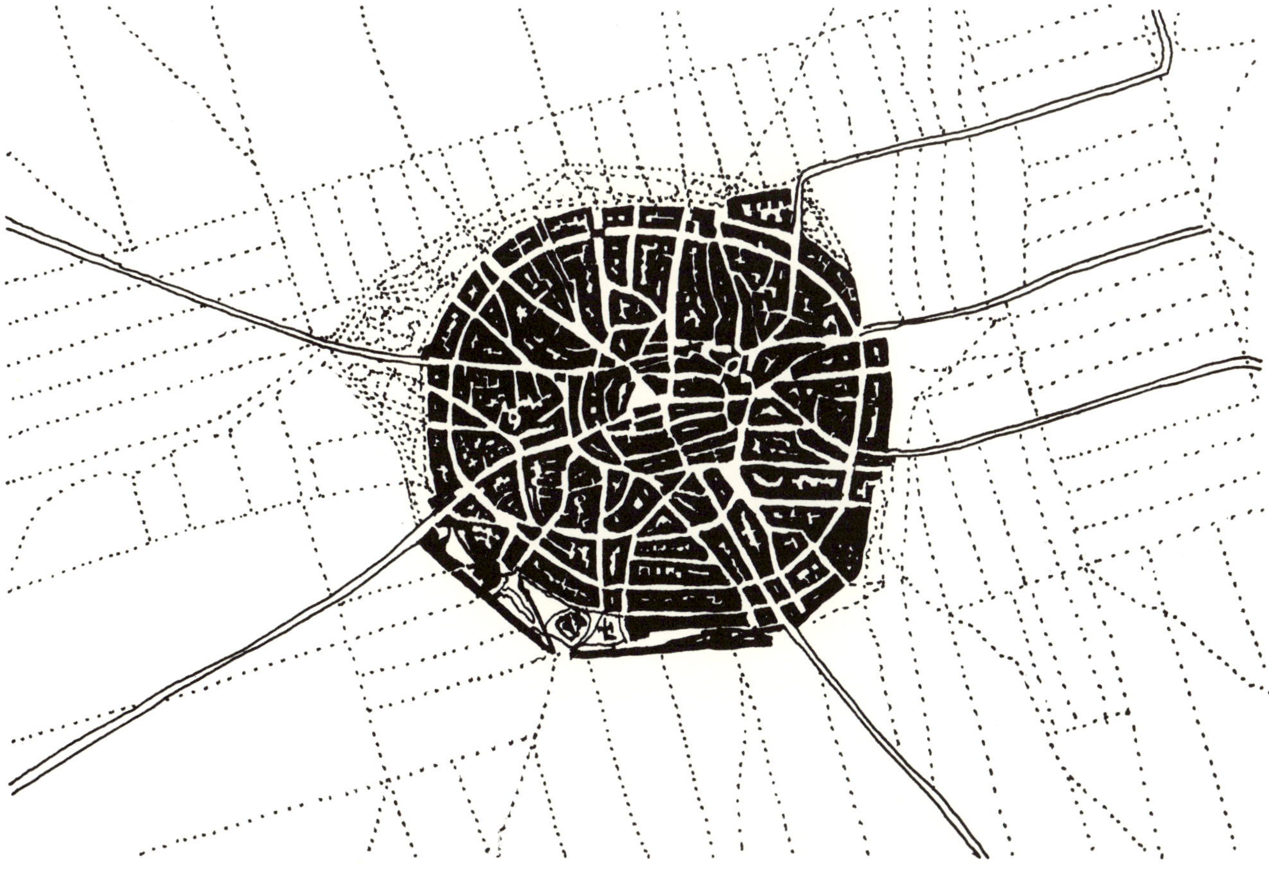

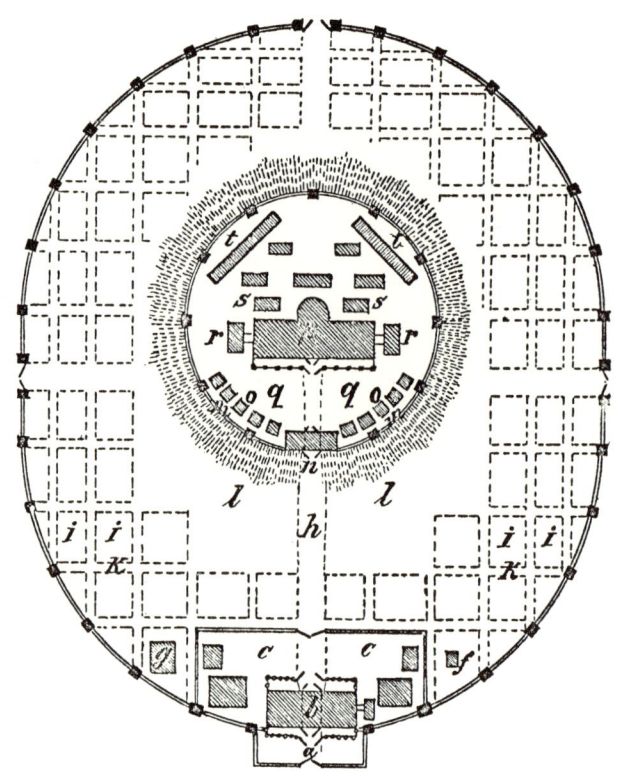

274. Attila's camp, based on Priscus' description in the *Fragmenta Historicorum Graecorum*. The camp area, surrounded by a wooden fence, has one main road (h) leading from the entrance gate (a) to the inner enclosure of Attila's palace. The main or entrance gate, several stories high, served as residence (b) for Onegesius, Attila's favorite and commandant of the camp. Onegesius' compound is surrounded by palisades (cc), with a bath (f) and an inn (g) outside the enclosure. The road (h) crosses an open area (11) which was probably used for military exercises. Small lanes (kk) further subdivided the camp area, giving access to the tents and huts of the warriors. The circular inner area is Attila's enclosure, surrounded by palisades with towers. The gate (n) leads into the compound. To the left and right of the gate are the buildings of Attila's wife and her retinue. (r) and (s) indicate the kitchen, cellar, and other household buildings; (q) the *Thing*, the *locus judicii*.

In this connection, the layout of the camp of Attila in the fifth century has often been compared to the village-towns of Hungary. In fact, such comparisons are without any foundation whatsoever. We know next to nothing of the details of this camp. Descriptions like the one given by Lavedan are mere conjectures.[23] Following his preoccupation in reducing the layout of cities to either a radial-concentric or a gridiron plan with corresponding variations, he concludes that Attila's camp *"était entouré d'une clôture en bois, de forme circulaire, destinée non à la défense, mais à l'ornement."* He goes on to postulate that the tents and huts of the soldiers *"formaient des cercles concentriques autour de la colline où s'élevait le palais royal,"* though he admits that *"nous ne savons rien"* on this point.

What we do know is based on the evidence of Priscus Panites, who visited the camp in A.D. 448. According to Thompson, he merely said that "Attila's headquarters consisted of a village—one of the largest he had seen during his travels in Scythia—and we must conclude therefore that the camp—if this is the right word—was neither circular nor rectangular but merely a shapeless conglomeration of dwellings like most other villages."[24] This conclusion is entirely plausible. The laby-

---

23. P. Lavedan. *Histoire de l'Urbanisme.* Vol. I. 1926. Pp. 270–71.
24. E. A. Thompson. "The Camp of Attila," *The Journal of Hellenistic Studies,* Vol. 65, 1945, pp. 112–15, *passim*.

rinthian agglomeration was the most common system—if a system it can be called—in the large settlements of Central Asia and was, most probably, introduced to Hungary under the Árpád rulers. The confusion seems to have been caused by Priscus' remark that there was a *peribolus,* an enclosure, around Attila's palace, and another one around the house of Onegesius, the most powerful personality after Attila. Priscus reported that the enclosure of Attila's residence was a wooden structure not intended for defense; concerning Onegesius' palisades, not adorned with towers as Attila's, we may conclude "that it was even less intended for military purposes." Thompson correctly draws attention to the fact that the

Hun camp was constructed at the cost of great trouble in the middle of a wide treeless plain [in the region of the Tisza], and every stone and every piece of timber used to build it had to be transported from a great distance to this site. The reason was military. The Huns wished their headquarters to lie on ground where their cavalry could manoeuvre freely and where there was no chance of a surprise. A palisade, surrounding the entire camp, would imply that the defenders were prepared to stand a siege, and a siege was entirely alien to the Huns' method of fighting.

These are very sensible observations, from which we may conclude that the camp was an open village with, probably, haphazardly arranged buildings, of which only the dwellings of the ruler and his first lieutenant were surrounded by enclosures. In this respect, the camp deserves a place in the discussion of the large Hungarian villages of the Alföld, with their often chaotic layout and one or a few nodal points within the inhabited area.

In general, the radial-nucleated villages are symmetrical and compact, though considerable variations occur. The market has the shape either of an irregular circle or, more rarely, of a square or rectangle. The compactness of the settlements in the valley of the Tisza can be explained as a precaution against flooding. The settlements outside the area subject to flooding are more loosened up. The circular form of the village may have been conditioned by considerations of defense: A more or less uninterrupted circular enclosure is more easily defensible than one with corners always more vulnerable and liable to attack. Especially for settlements in a flat and open steppe, the shortest circumference provides the greatest security. The sectors between the main radial streets are reservoirs for the increasing population; and only when these spaces are completely filled up does extension outward begin, preserving as far as possible the original plan and the system of sectors and circular roads.

Another type of village shows a more amorphous, tree-like plan. The central square is more an intersection of streets than a clearly delimited space, the streets mostly branching off at right angles and ramifying toward the periphery. If there is only one way out of the village, the street pattern converges on this one road. The basic shape of these villages approximates a square, and their layout is generally more systematic. These settlements grow outward from the beginning, which explains their tree-like growth. In Zenta, for instance, three to four straight principal streets emanate from the square situated not

275. *Above:* Plan of Zenta (now Yugoslavia), on the right bank of the Tisza River.

276. *Below:* Plan of Békéscsaba in the southeast of the Great Alföld.

centrally but peripherally; and, in Békéscsaba, the streets form a rectangular pattern, with square blocks subdivided by short secondary streets and lanes.

Different in plan are the villages of Transylvania, formerly belonging, in part, to Hungary. Like all *Haufendörfer*, they are irregular clusters of houses without any apparent system, covering a roundish compact area. These villages are located at one or several rivulets because the settlers did not dig wells. They tend to develop not so much parallel along the rivulets as at right angles to the streams, and they extend, as often as possible, to the next water source. Thus Magyarszákos, about 1.24 miles wide and 1.8 miles long, is situated on four rivulets. This village is an exception among the settlements of the Banat which were regularly laid out in the 18th century, whether on a more or less circular ground plan with the church in the center, or as street villages lined on both sides by houses, or as squares or rectangles with wide streets crossing each other at right angles. It is not unusual that more than half an hour is needed to drive in a horse-drawn carriage through these places.

277. Plan of the Transylvanian village of Magyarszákos.

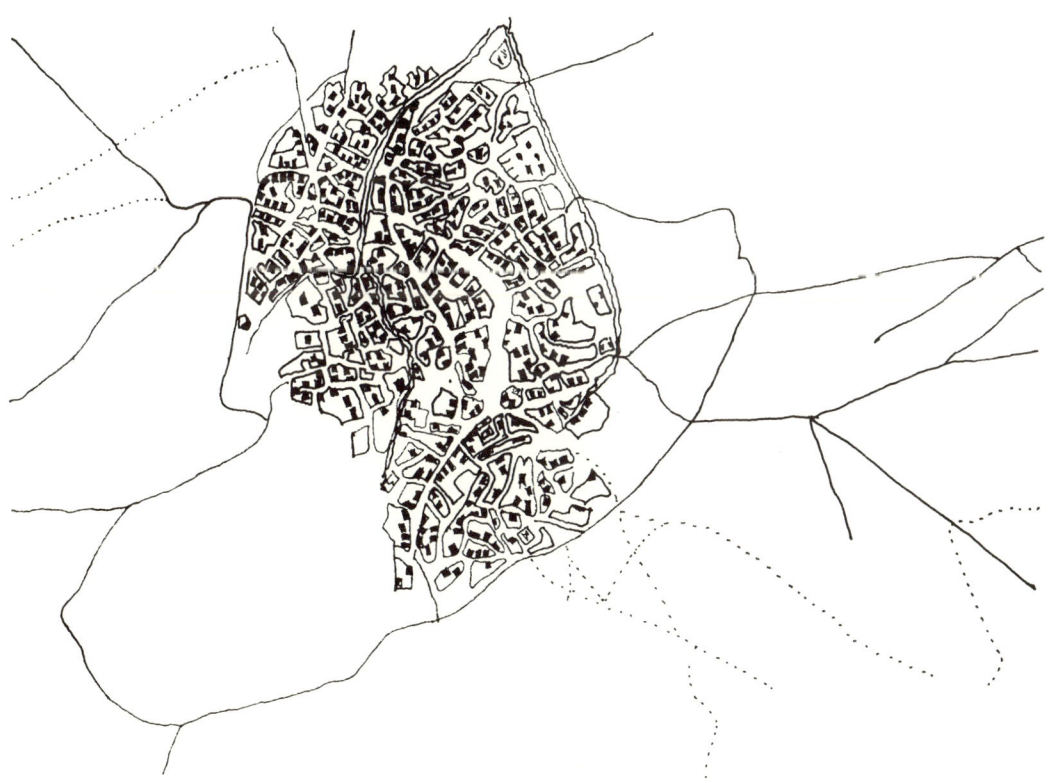

Different again are the villages in the former Hungarian Comitat Arad (now Romania), a transitional zone of settlement, with single farms surrounding street villages. The land and fields belonging to these villages are situated in the valley, while the villages are dispersed

278. Plans of the villages of Kurtakér (top) and Tornova (bottom), in the former Comitat of Arad (now Romania).

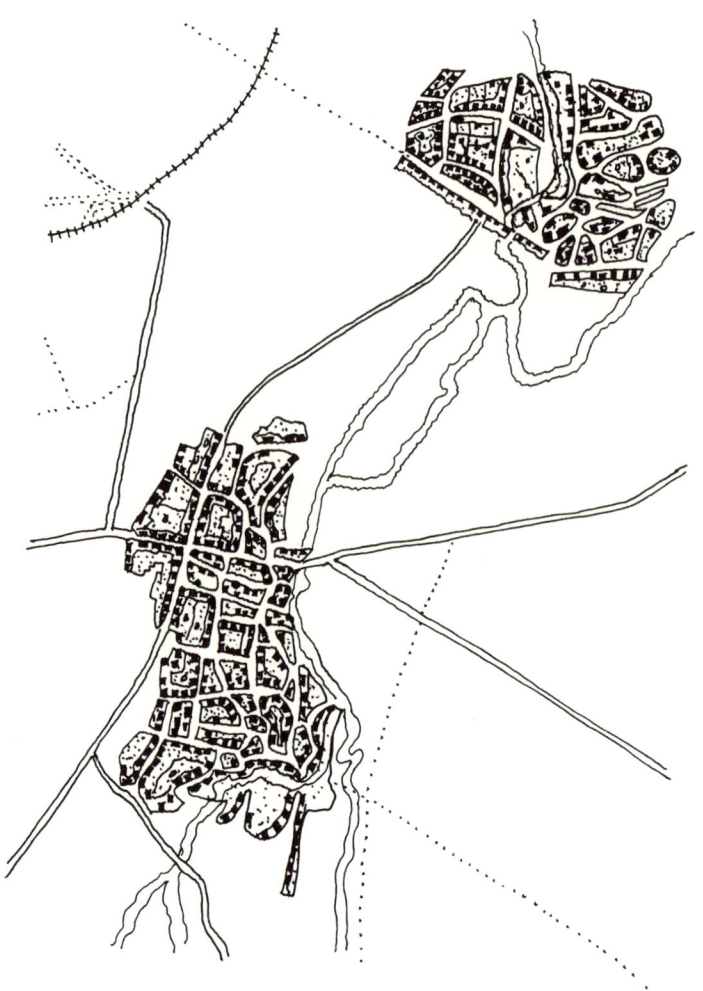

on the slopes of the surrounding hills. The field pattern of these places originated in the Walachian tribal settlements. The houses are grouped in loose clusters. The street system is not rationally adapted to the configuration of the terrain but developed from the footpaths running between the boundaries of the holdings.

The Serbian clustered villages laid out on Hungarian territory in the course of the settlement policy following the depopulation of the Alföld in the 18th century resemble those of Transylvania, although their houses are arranged in rows along ridges and rims of hills whenever possible, more rarely in the valleys. Slavonic influences most probably explain the greater proximity of close groupings. Until relatively recent times some villages had no streets, only field paths.

In the region of the Drava, flowing along a section of the Hungarian-Yugoslav frontier, the villages occupy the ridges of the hills, and the valleys remain empty. When the space on the hills grows too crowded for the expanding population, the villages spread to the other side of the hills or, if the hilltops widen into a plateau, extend near the edges in long rows. The swampy and frequently flooded valleys are unsuitable for settlement, though excellent for pastures.

In western Hungary, in the region of Sopron (Ödenburg), street villages preponderate. The houses are lined up along the main streets and, in some cases, along a few parallel streets; their lots adjoin them at the back. Farming and viticulture exist side by side.

The following essay by Professor I. Perényi on urban development in Hungary had to be slightly shortened and edited to avoid overlapping with the general text. This editing has not diminished the scope of the contribution nor changed, in any way, the substance of his work. As for all other countries covered in this work, the period under discussion terminates around the middle of the 19th century.[25]

---

25. It had been the author's intention to discuss the modern phase of urbanization in the countries represented in the *International History of City Development* in a final and concluding volume of the series. Ed.

Historical Development of Hungarian Cities
by Professor Imre Perényi

DEPARTMENT OF CITY PLANNING
TECHNICAL UNIVERSITY OF BUDAPEST

CHAPTER 25

Urban Development in Hungary

Urban Development to the Time of the Turkish Occupation

TOWARD THE END of the ninth century the Magyars, having bypassed Kiev, entered their new country through the northeastern and southeastern passes of the Carpathians. They settled among the Slavonic people who had populated the country before them. In the beginning the Magyars maintained their nomadic tribal system and adapted their settlements to their way of life. By the middle of the 10th century the defeat of their armies and the growing resistance of the Holy Roman Empire ended their expansion toward the west, forcing them to settle in the newly conquered land and become sedentary tillers of the soil. This was the beginning of the Hungarian State.

During the reign of King Stephen I (997–1038), the country was organized on a territorial basis. The king was the biggest landowner. Lord lieutenants collected taxes at the county seats, the royal castles, in order to maintain and strengthen the king's power. At the same time, the organization of the Church was consolidated. These developments furthered the trends toward an improvement of agriculture and a feudal structure of society. In a relatively short time the clan communities were abolished and replaced with servile labor, binding the free peasants to the landowners for whom they had to perform certain duties and deliver part of their crops. The sites of the Roman settlements in the country were used as quarries for materials for new buildings within the confines of the ruins.

At this time, there existed about a dozen places that later formed the basis of the network of Hungarian towns: the two royal seats, Esztergom (Gran) and Székesfehérvár (Stuhlweissenburg); clerical centers such as Vác (Waitzen), Pécs (Fünfkirchen), Győr (Raab), and Veszprém; Pest (Budapest), the merchant town; Sopron (Ödenburg); and some other settlements that gradually were evolving an urban character. Their primitive and badly built houses were haphazardly arranged without any definite street system.

Esztergom, royal residence and seat of the archbishop, lies at the foot of the Pilis Mountain at the confluence of the Danube, the Little Danube, and the Garam. The steep Castle Hill jutting out close to the Danube, forests rich in game, hot springs, and limestone caves favored an early occupation of the site, dating back to the Stone and Bronze Ages. Later the location attracted Celtic settlers. In Roman times a fortress, *Salva Mansio,* was erected as an important station in the defense system of the Pannonian *limes.* After the fall of the Roman Empire the site was settled by the Avars and later by Slavonic tribes, who were followed by the Magyars at the end of the ninth century. Toward the turn of the 10th century, it became the seat of the dukes and, up to the reign of Béla IV, the seat of the Hungarian kings. Under their protection it grew into a wealthy industrial and commercial town. Esztergom consisted of two parts: the Castle Hill and the walled-in town proper to the south, on the level ground of the banks of the Little Danube. Within the walls there were three distinct quarters: the section housing the royal retainers, the cathedral precincts, and the free town. The two gates, one in the south at the road to Dorog and the other one in the north, were connected by the main street leading through the town. A number of small villages surrounded the community. The erection of the royal palace was begun by Béla III on Castle Hill, whose northern section was

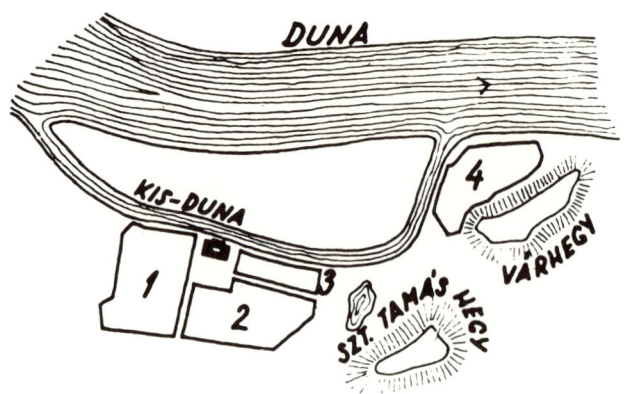

279. The medieval settlement of Esztergom at the Kis-Duna, the Little Danube. 1. *Vicus Latinorum*, the Latin quarter; 2. Settlement of the cathedral chapter; 3. Quarter of the royal retainers; 4. Northern town.

occupied by the seat of the archbishop and the cathedral chapter. The layout of the inner town at the foot of the hill on the banks of the Danube dates from the 13th century. Until the time of the Mongol invasion only the Castle Hill was fortified. Esztergom was easily taken by the Mongols, who burnt it to the ground in 1241. It was rebuilt and fortified with walls, bastions, and wide moats by Béla IV. When the royal residence was transferred to Buda, the archbishops became the sole residents on Castle Hill.

The Mongol invasions, lasting more than a year, resulted in a widespread devastation of the country in which the gains of two and a half centuries were lost. The ravaged country presented a disheartening sight with many towns and villages burnt to the ground. However, the invasions convinced the authorities, especially Béla IV who directed the reconstruction and the centralization of his kingdom begun by Stephen I, that a people cannot exist in an undefended country and without strongly fortified towns. Béla IV replaced the former frontier organization by ordering the construction of a chain of castles to which nobles and prelates, encouraged by land grants, made ample contributions. The majority of the castles were built on hills or mountains where the natural configuration of the terrain required little additional strengthening by brickwork or terracing.

The old strongholds were handed over to new settlers who moved to the castles, joining the former inhabitants, mostly serfs. In some cases, this movement was the beginning of the Hungarian middle class. In others, the regrouping led to the founding of new towns, especially mining communities, or to the construction of fortresses in the vicinity of older unfortified places, and to the removal of the inhabitants to safer sites such as Pest. Lay and clerical landowners were the leading agents in this development. In order to make their territories as self-sufficient as possible they endeavored to attract some basic trades and a variety of handicrafts. Artisans and craftsmen settled at the foot of the fortresses or in the plain. When marketing rights were procured, many settlements developed urban characteristics, especially those surrounded by walls or situated in the vicinity of fortified castles which guaranteed security, thus stimulating the accumulation of material wealth. Settlements on trade routes were particularly favored by compulsory regulations directing all traffic to these towns and requiring all foreign merchants and traders to unload their goods in these places.

Anybody who wanted to settle in a town was welcome. To further this trend the towns sided with the serfs, supporting their right to move to the towns where they hoped to find work and enjoy the same freedom as the townspeople. This movement gained momentum from the 16th century onward. However, hopes and expectations were not always fulfilled. Many of the newcomers found only temporary work and swelled the already considerable number of paupers. The urban population was further increased by numerous noblemen who sold their lands and moved to the towns where they were granted civic rights; others acquired property in the towns while retaining their estates. Thus the urban area within the walls gradually filled up and suburbs developed, mostly inhabited by the poorer classes.

Despite the steadily increasing number of traders and craftsmen, the main occupation of the townspeople remained what it had been for centuries: agriculture, vine growing, husbandry, and fishing. The urban areas expanded by the acquisition of adjoining land through private arrangement, later confirmed by royal charters. This was part of the official policy of city planning as conducted by Béla IV, of which Nagyszombat (Trnava, Czechoslovakia) in 1238, Pest in 1244, and Komárom (Komárno, Czechoslovakia) in 1265 are good examples.

The reign of the Árpád kings was followed by years of civil war until Charles Robert ascended the Hungarian throne (1308–1342) with the help of the bankers of Florence and Venice. His son, Louis the Great (1342–1382), continued the policy of the Angevin dynasty initiated by his father, that is, to reorganize the feudal system, strengthen the power of the central authorities, improve the finances of the country and balance the budget, and establish commercial relations with the neighboring nations. Charles Robert directed the energies and the interests of the big landowners to mining, thus beginning the capitalist exploitation of the ore deposits. Trade and industry grew, and the influence of the guilds increased steadily. In 1376, for example, there were 24 different trades organized in 17 guilds in the Saxon towns of Transylvania. In general the guilds were dominated, as everywhere else, by wealthy masters, while apprentices, day laborers, and journeymen were kept in inferior positions as proletarians. Building activities in the towns intensified, the well-to-do citizens erecting mostly two-storied houses of timber or stone.

During the reign of Sigismund of Luxembourg (1387–1437), the royal estates covered only five percent of the country's area, whereas those of the magnates occupied fifty-six percent, a clear indication of their political and economic power. These great landowners disposed of considerable amounts of money derived primarily from their villeins, while the income of the Crown remained irregular and even decreased, so that Sigismund was forced to pledge large parts of his estates and to fall back on the economic strength of the towns. The urban communities which were in a position to lend money received charters in return. The more important frontier towns were granted the right to intercept imports from which they could receive remuneration as commissioned agents. The king supported the reform of the complicated system of weights and measures that was impeding the free development of trade and tried to improve the customs regulations. He assisted foreign artisans settling in Hungary and invited craftsmen from the West to take part in the growing building activity. The reign of Sigismund was the

Golden Age of Hungarian medieval architecture: All over the country work on towns and fortified castles proceeded vigorously, many of the latter on a monumental scale, such as the castle at Buda and the enlargement of the castles at Visegrád and Diósgyőr. The king attached great importance to the fortification of towns, as was shown by the *decretum minor* of 1405 which made the erection of strong walls compulsory. To facilitate this task through financial concessions, exemption from taxes payable to the Crown was granted; for instance, to Késmárk exemption for 12 years was allowed, on condition that half this sum was to be used for repairing the walls and moats of the town.

According to contemporary records, 461 castles, 16,000 communities, and 571 towns existed in the 15th century. However, of all these places only about two dozen were industrial and trading towns of any importance, with 2,000 to 5,000 inhabitants. The rest were open agrarian settlements, villages, and market centers. The towns of Hungary differed in many respects from those of Western Europe. Basically, they were less densely built up, a feature that can be traced back to their agricultural character and the original village layout. This more open structure was common to the settlements of the Alföld, in contrast to those of Transdanubia and the northern parts of the country, where greater compactness and higher buildings prevailed because of the influence of Slavonic and German settlers. The relatively loose form of numerous settlements was the result of their more intimate relationship with the surrounding country. The hills and mountains in the immediate neighborhood were included in the inner towns as at Pécs, Buda, and Esztergom, creating picturesque and dramatic effects of great beauty.

The houses of the nobility and wealthy citizens in the centers of the towns were mostly multi-storied with arcades on the ground floor, the second floor supported by stone buttresses often projecting over the streets. Churches and castles towered above the low houses of the burghers. In the 13th and 14th centuries numerous donjons were erected in Transdanubia, such as those in Sopron and Bratislava (Czechoslovakia). Due to the general open development the distinction between streets and squares was less marked than in Western countries. The streets widened almost imperceptibly into squares, and squares were relatively large, often merging into each other. The character and layout of medieval streets varied greatly. Short sections of 5 to 8 buildings were systematically laid out, while others were arranged without any apparent system. The principal streets of Hungarian medieval towns were generally wider than the average height of the buildings adjoining them. As a result, the houses on one side of the street could be fully and easily viewed from the other.

Sopron, whose site had been occupied since the Neolithic period and later by Celts, Illyrians, and Romans, actually arose on a Celtic foundation on the Bécsi Hill, surrounded by earthworks. The Roman town *Scarabantia* stood on what is today the center of the town, where the route from Italy branched off to *Vindobona* (Vienna) and *Carnuntum.* Villas were dotted over the hills, but only a few statues to gods and ruins of the amphitheater and aqueducts bear witness to Roman Sopron.

The royal castle was probably built at the beginning of the 11th century on the site of the present inner town. The importance of medieval Sopron was due to its situation near the frontier. Ladislaus IV (1272–1290) elevated the central part, with the village around the castle and the settlement for bowmen in the forest, to the status of a town. This nucleus consisted of the present inner town, protected by the castle walls and moats. Donjons attached to the residences of the leading families and built before the construction of the fortifications in 1340 rose in all parts of the town. As in Italy or Spain they were not only status symbols but also important strongpoints in the internal strife between rival

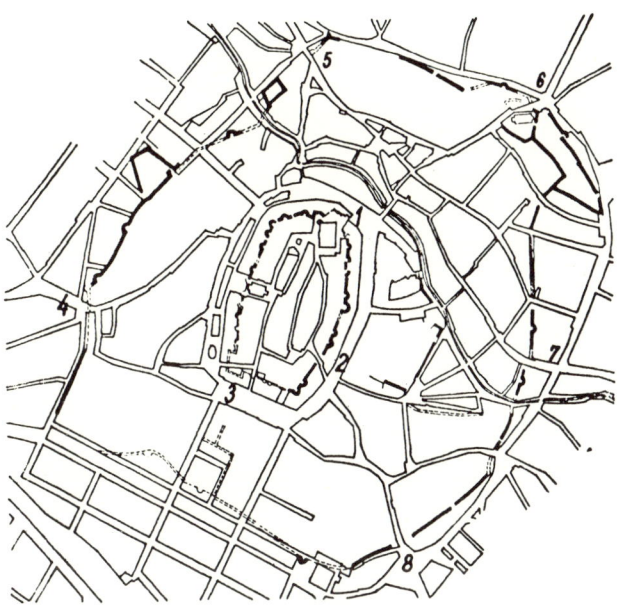

280. Plan of Sopron. The remains of the inner and outer walls of the castle are indicated with solid black lines, the ruins of walls with dotted lines. 1. Main Gate; 2. Rear Gate; 3. Italian Bastion; 4. Újtelek Gate; 5. Vienna Gate; 6. St. Michael's Gate; 7. Győr Gate.

noble families. In 1397, Sopron had about 2,100 inhabitants. By the end of the 15th century their number had increased so considerably that the inner town and the quarter around St. Michael's Church had become too small, and suburbs began to grow up. Sopron's importance increased steadily not only as a political center where coronations and diets took place but also as a place of learning. The Lutheran School, where Latin was taught, was founded in 1557 and was the first Hungarian secondary school.

Szeged, like Sopron one of the leading towns of medieval Hungary, is situated at the confluence of the Tisza and Maros rivers. Archeological finds have revealed that its site has been occupied for almost 3,000 years. Nine layers of successive cultures have been identified, all dating back to periods before the arrival of the Hungarians. In Roman times it was probably an entrepôt of some importance, since Roman roads reached this part of *Pannonia*. Subsequently it was settled by the Avars and, finally, by Hungarians who presumably established themselves on the island, where the fortress was later erected. The layout of this early settlement was based on the extended family: In the center stood the house of the head of the family; to its right and left, arranged in a semicircle on the banks of the river, were the homes of his sons and relatives.

281. Plan of Szeged after a map of 1713. 1. Castle; 2. The "Fence," the *palanka* (the palisaded camp).

This was the origin of the larger settlement of which Bertrandon de la Brocquière, traveling in this part of the world in 1433, wrote: "Szeged is a big open town, with one street about a mile long."

Szeged was first mentioned in records in 1138. At this time it had no fortifications. In 1241 the inhabitants had to flee before the approaching Mongol armies. After the end of the invasions, when fortresses were built all over the country, a strong royal castle was erected in Szeged, probably in the northern part of the island on which the first settlement had stood. This castle was a primitive structure with earthen walls that were replaced, after some time, by brick walls and towers. The king invited foreigners—mostly Bulgarians, Greeks, and Serbs—to settle around the castle. When the place was elevated to a Royal Town, the population increased rapidly, and the urban area was soon built up. Consequently, an open settlement was laid out at the foot of the castle, called "the Fence." Later it was surrounded by walls and moats. At this time, Szeged consisted of several more or less autonomous parts: the castle, "the Fence," and the lower and upper towns, each having its own council, jurisdiction, and other administrative institutions. It was not until the 15th century that these parts were united under one administration. The building density of the large district that had grown up on the plain varied considerably: Where the rivers obstructed expansion, the place was more loosely laid out, while along the roads the built-up area was more compact. The walled-in quarters were divided by streets running north-south and west-east. Here the building density was very high. After the completion of the fortifications the population increased through the influx of traders and artisans, reaching about 9,000 in 1522.

The most important settlements of this period were situated in the area of present day *Budapest*. With the political consolidation of Hungary, the development of Budapest began in Óbuda, and at the ford of Tabán, on both banks of the Danube. The Hungarian conquerors used the Roman amphitheater as their castle. Óbuda originated under the reign of Duke Géza, and during the reigns of Stephen III (1162–1172) and Béla III (1173–1196) it spread to the present Császár Bath. This poorly defended settlement was destroyed by the Mongols. For reasons of defense Béla IV moved his residence to Pestújhegy. After being declared the "Queen's Town," the place entered a period of prosperity. About this time, Óbuda consisted of three parts: the clerical and royal precincts and the civic section. The inhabitants were craftsmen, mostly millers; tradesmen, mostly foreigners; and employees and retainers of the court.

Even before the Mongol invasion Pest was an important trading center, first mentioned in 1148. Its inhabitants were a rather mixed lot of Hungarians, Ismaelites, Walloons, Flemings, Italians, and Germans. In this early period Pest's only protection was a wide moat. The church stood on the side of the Roman *castrum*, and two monasteries were situated a little farther from the center. During the reign of Béla IV, part of the population moved to Buda, and Pest became a suburb of Buda. As such it ceased to develop until its self-government was restored under Sigismund. At the time of Matthias I (1458–1490), better known as Matthias Corvinus, there were 22 different trades organized in nine guilds. Pest's uninterrupted growth as an important economic town

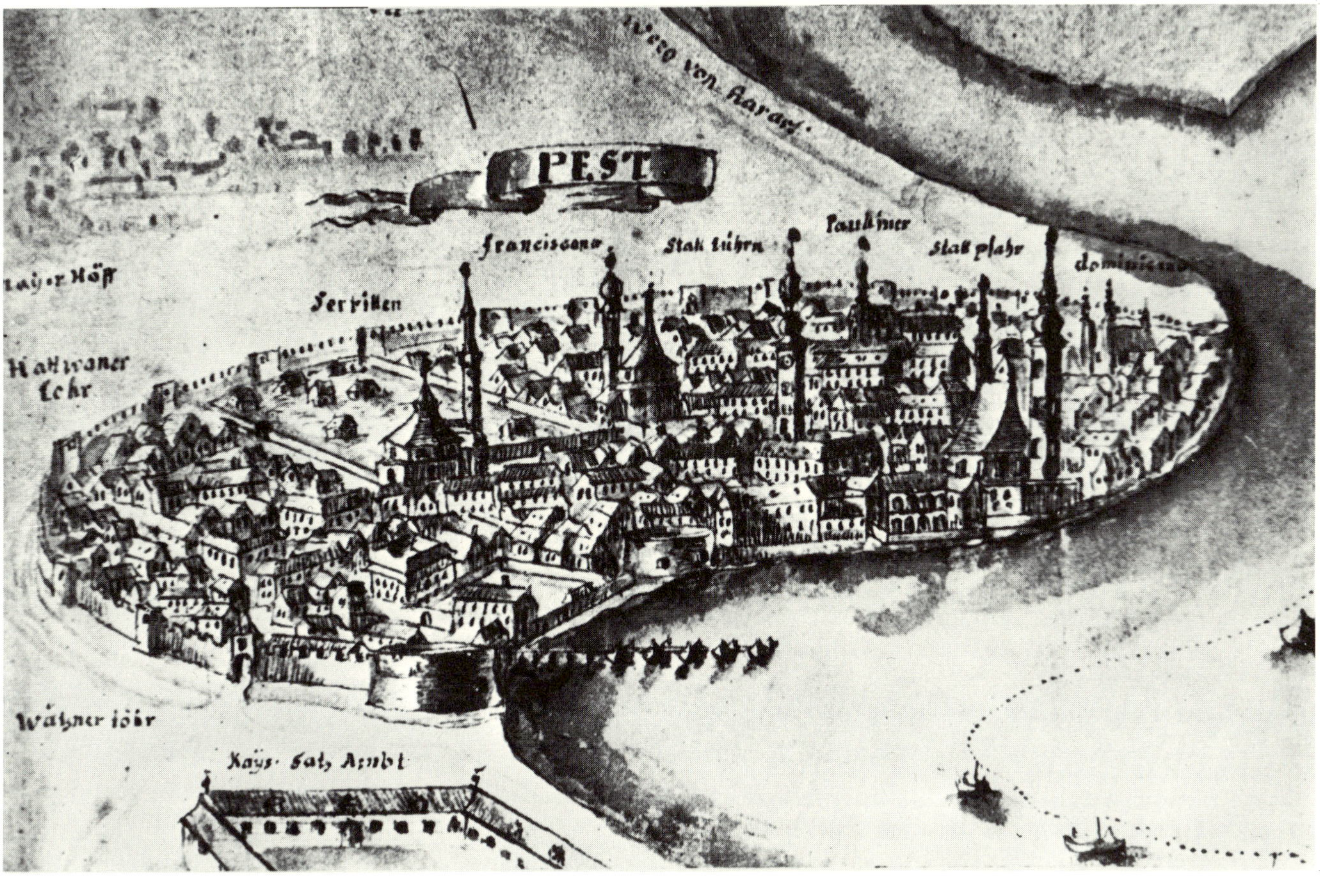

282. View of Pest in 1728.

dates from this period. Pest was fortified between 1440 and 1470 with strong walls, four gateways, and twelve massive, squat towers. It was surrounded by suburbs occupying an area larger than the walled-in town. Overland routes and ferry crossings determined the main structure of the street pattern. Traffic traversed the town from the north to the south along the two principal roads, which were crossed at right angles by other streets. Thus the most important streets of the present inner town originated during this period.

The port of Pest, called Kis-Pest and later Kelenföld, was developed on the other side of the Danube, where Tabán is situated today. The chief occupation of the population of this district, also of mixed ethnic elements, was agriculture and viticulture. In the center of this settlement stood the church, near the present Rudas Bath.

Béla IV fortified Buda and made it his residence. His palace stood on the strategically most advantageous site, called Pestújhegy, the present Castle Hill. Buda's population consisted mostly of Italians, Germans, and Flemings, who primarily engaged in agriculture and trading. There were but a few artisans and craftsmen. A monastery was built on Margaret Island, previously known as the Island of Our Lady. The town of Buda was situated at the foot of the castle, with market squares replac-

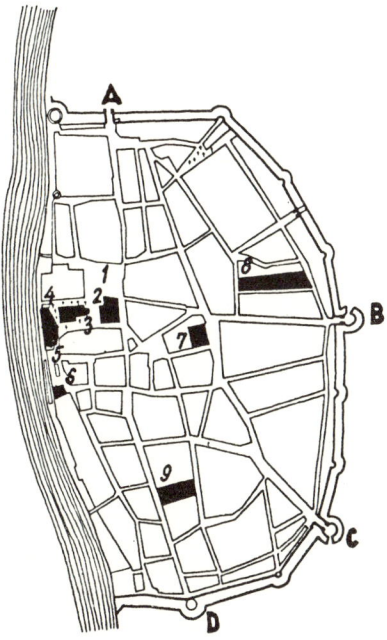

283. *Below:* Plan of Pest in the 18th century. 1. Main Square; 2. Town Hall; 3. Main church; 4. Rectory; 5. School; 6. Butchers' shops; 7. Warehouse; 8. County hall; A. Buda or Vác Gate; B. Hatvan Gate; C. Kecskemét Gate; D. Belgrade Gate.

284. General view of Buda, with the castle (left), the town (right), and the Danube in the foreground. Woodcut from Hartmann Schedel's *Liber chronicarum*, Nűrnberg, 1493.

ing the earlier market streets and churches distributed over the urban area. For reasons of defense, the streets near the gates were laid out not as straight and direct continuations of the gateways but at angles to the gates. Houses were grouped inside the town in front of the gates, to make the progress of invaders as difficult as possible. In 1437 Buda had 967 dwelling houses, a relatively large number due to the narrow, though deep, plots. Limestone was the most common building material. The suburb of St. Peter, including the source of the water supply, was also surrounded by walls.

After the death of Matthias the centralized organization of monarchical rule collapsed. The nobles, instead of fighting the Habsburgs and the Turks, struck blow after blow against the Hungarian State. By collecting taxes for themselves which should have gone to the exchequer, they undermined the financial solvency of the country and destroyed the national army, thus depriving the country of its most efficient protection. The lot of the peasant-serfs deteriorated considerably, their financial burdens growing more and more oppressive. Ever greater numbers were impoverished and thronged into the towns. In 1514 an open rebellion of the peasants broke out under the leadership of György Dózsa but was suppressed by the nobility, and the peasants were bound to the soil as serfs of their "natural" lords. The weakened military organization proved unable to withstand the onslaught of the Turkish army and was annihilated in 1526 in the battle of Mohács. Thus began 150 years of Turkish domination, and 400 years of Austrian rule.

285. Plan of Buda in the 17th century. 1. Parish church of Mary Magdalen; 2. St. Nicholas Church of the Dominican Order; 3. Church of Our Lady (Matthias); 4. Church of the Sigismund Chapter; A. Vienna Gate; B. Vizivaros Gate for pedestrians (Jesuit Stairs); C. Vízi Gate; D. Fehérvár Gate.

286. *Below:* The siege of Buda (right) in 1684. At the far end of the hill, the castle. Lower down, two mosques with minarets and, in the foreground still within the walls, the Christian church and a synagogue. The Turkish cemetery can be seen to the right of the castle hill. The lower town, like the upper town, has several mosques and minarets. In the foreground, shaded by trees, is the Turkish bath. Above the burnt bridge, on the other side of the Danube, is Pest. With its four mosques and minarets, its skyline presents an equally Turkish appearance. Engraving by Michael Wenig after a drawing by L. N. Hallart, chief adjutant to the Elector Maximilian Emanuel of Bavaria.

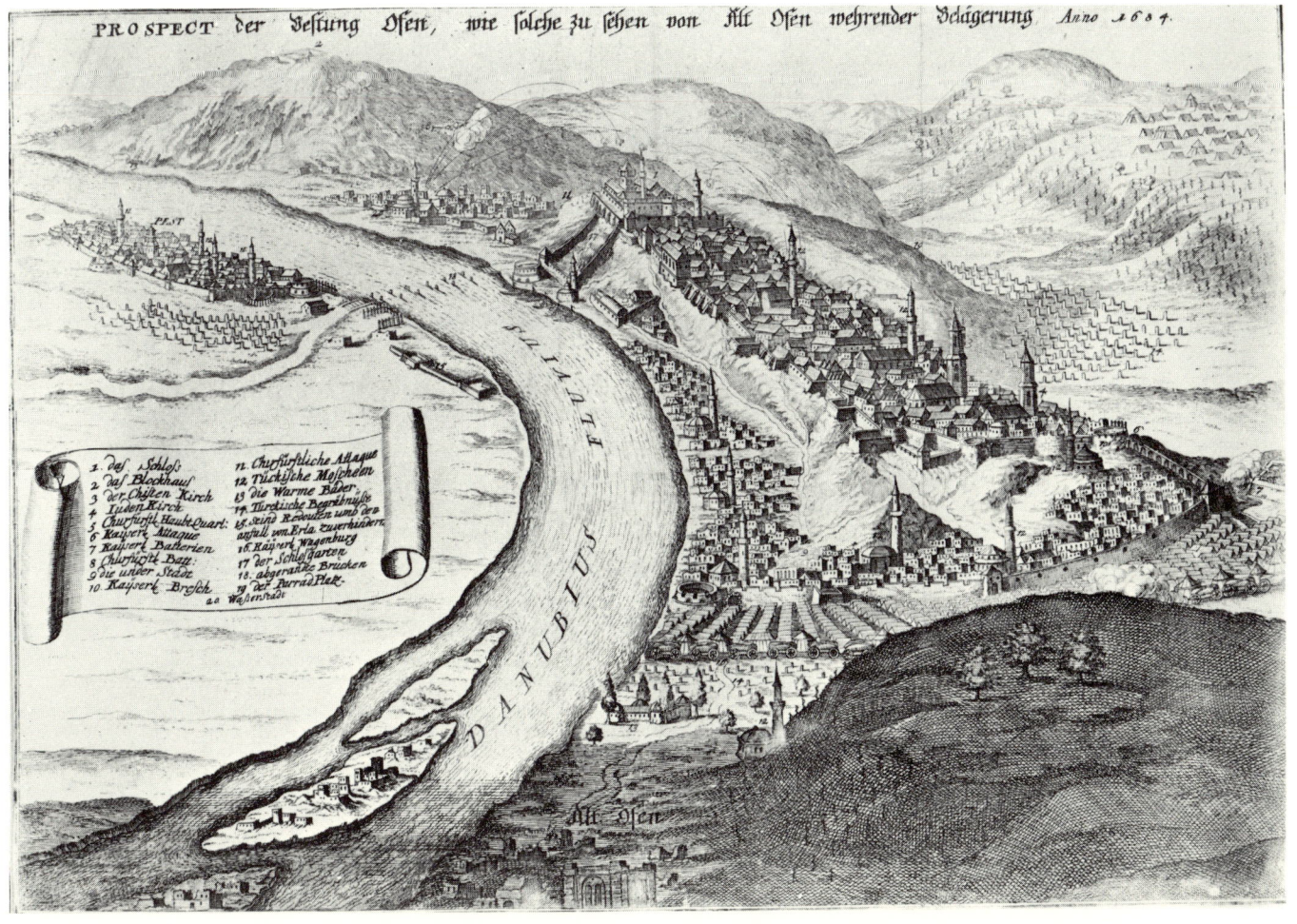

The Towns of Hungary under Turkish Rule

After the fall of Buda, in 1541, the country was divided into three parts. Most of the Alföld and a large region of Transdanubia south of Lake Balaton were annexed to the Turkish Empire for the next 150 years. The Habsburgs ruled over the western and northern counties, representing about one-third of the country, while Transylvania and some adjacent districts formed the independent state of Hungary.

There were no clearly fixed frontiers. The war spread from the subjugated territories to the region governed by Austria and to Transylvania. Castles were destroyed, and hundreds of devastated villages marked the routes of the Turkish armies. Settlements reconstructed on the ruins of communities overrun by the enemy were again razed to the ground, or decayed. The county of Bács, for instance, which in the reign of Matthias had five castles, 16 towns, and 213 villages, was completely deserted. In the county of Csanád 140 settlements were devastated; in Békés, 130; the same number in Csongrád; and 530 in Somogy. Even in the relatively well defended county of Veszprém about 30 villages were laid waste. The situation was the same in almost all parts of the country. Everywhere the regulation of the rivers was neglected; roads were impassable; forests were cut down; mines caved in; and overgrown ruins were characteristic features of the landscape. At this time the new structure of settlement and the enormous village-towns began to emerge.

The population of the declining villages moved to safer places ruled by the Turks where they enjoyed some sort of protection, provided they paid their taxes. Villages, with their surrounding land, were incorporated in the new settlements. The people crowded together within the relatively small inner sections, surrounded by gardens and orchards, by stables and outbuildings. Only a part of the land belonging to the new settlements was given over to cultivation. The chief occupation of the inhabitants was animal husbandry, and to a degree its needs determined the layout of the streets, that is, the street pattern was adapted to the route of the herds. There were no Turkish garrisons in these places and therefore no castles or fortifications. Fences gave some protection against marauders. Kecskemét, Cegléd, Nagykőrös, Halas, Jászberény, Mezőtúr, Makó and Hódmezővásárhely were islands accessible only with difficulty in the vast extent of the *puszta*.

Kecskemét was one of the typical village-towns. Situated on a sandy plain traversed by dunes, between the Danube and the Tisza, it was occupied by the Jazyges in the first century A.D. when they invaded the lands between the two rivers. Discoveries made in 1907 revealed that the Jazyges' settlement of *Partiscum* stood on the site of the present Kecskemét. During the reign of the Huns the Jazyges' settlements disappeared and, later, the whole area was occupied by the Avars. The conquering Hungarians settled in the inner part of the present town of Kecskemét, as substantiated by cemeteries discovered in 1896 at the market square. Soon the population began to increase. By the end of the 14th century Kecskemét, first mentioned as a town in 1415, was an important stopping place on the road from Pest to Szeged. The built-up urban area, shaped like an egg, was protected by fences, earthen mounds, and ditches and surrounded by fields and pastures. From the 15th century onward Kecskemét was the center of Cuman life.[1]

---

1. The Cumans were an ancient Turkish race. They settled, in the 13th century in the Alföld, between the Danube and the Tisza, the district known as Greater and Lesser Cumania. [Remark added by E. A. Gutkind.]

The Turkish army, on the way back from Buda after the battle of Mohács, looted Kecskemét and burned it to the ground. Its quick reconstruction and subsequent development was furthered by the Turks. When renewed warfare forced the abandonment of the neighboring villages in the Cumanian *puszta,* the inhabitants fled to the town. They leased the deserted or destroyed villages from the landowners and the Turks, paying rent to both. Agriculture remained the only occupation of the population.

After 1597, when the Turkish officials had left, the town formed a sort of alliance with Cegléd and Nagykőrös to manage its internal and external affairs. At this time Kecskemét was an important center for livestock marketing. Handicrafts were well developed, and artisans from places as far as Szeged moved to the town which, in this period, had about 530 houses. Turkish raids and ransoms demanded by the intruders, the plague of 1677–78, and a fire in 1678 inflicted great damage and much suffering on Kecskemét. The few public buildings were destroyed, among them the Franciscan monastery and several churches. Despite these calamities the town grew. By the end of the 17th century the number of houses had risen to 1,300. As the surrounding country was more and more deserted, the urban territory and population continued to increase. An enormous settlement came into being, including 37 villages and covering an area of 499,000 acres.

287. Plan of Kecskemét in the early 19th century. In the center of the haphazardly laid-out building blocks is the main square, with the Great Church, the Calvinist Church, the town hall, a Franciscan church and monastery, two schools, shops, and the big cellar of the market. The solid black line, beyond the built-up area, indicates shallow ditches. Horse-driven mills are widely distributed over the town. Several cemeteries are located outside the urban area.

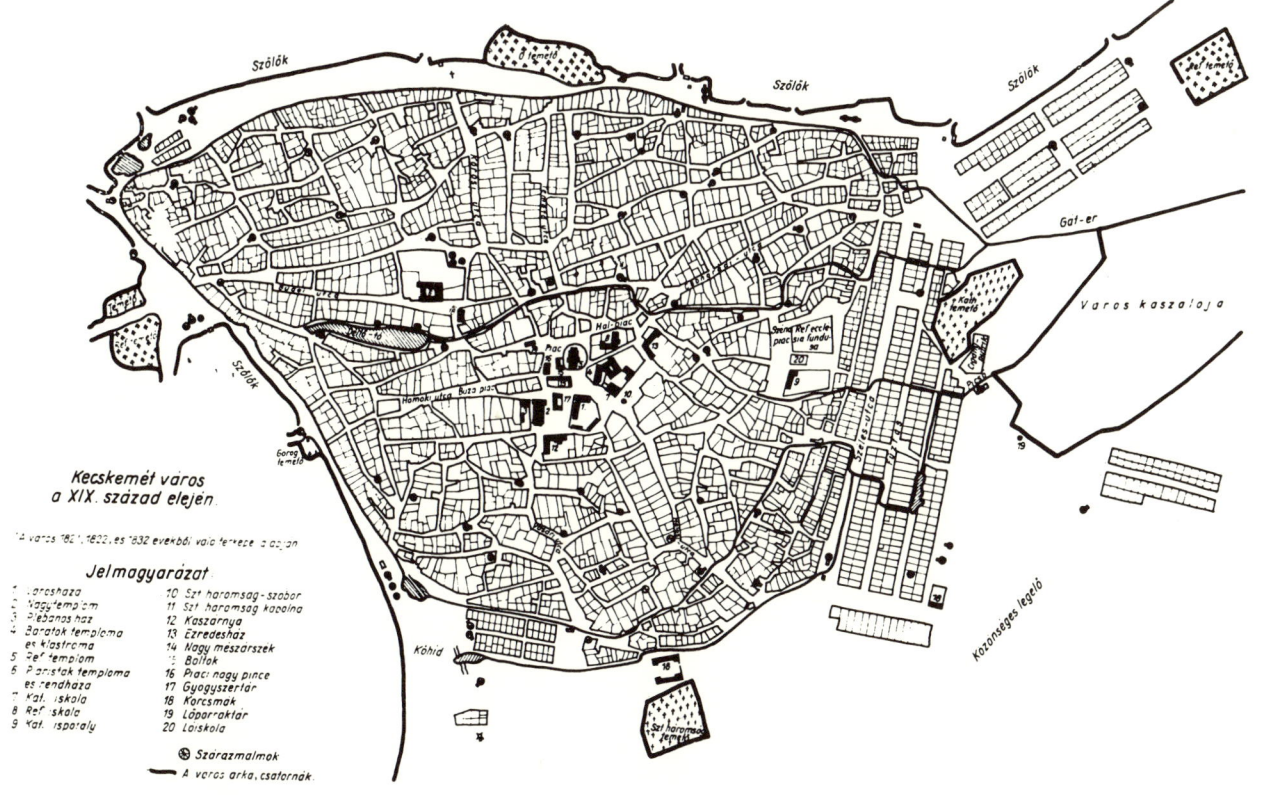

288. View of Kecskemét from the south, in the 19th century, from a charter of the guild of millers. Although local pride took precedence over topographical accuracy, the picture nevertheless gives a good idea of the main features of the town. Churches, a monastery, the Calvinist College, the town hall, and other public buildings rise above the low and simple houses of the inhabitants. The general appearance is rural, not urban, reflecting an agrarian rather than an industrial community. In 1826, Kecskemét had 17 windmills, some of which, appropriately for a millers' guild, are visible in the foreground. The frame bears the national emblem of Hungary (left), indicating Kecskemét's status of a Royal Free Town. In the center, the coat of arms of Kecskemét displaying a goat (*kecske*, meaning goat in Hungarian) and, on the right, the escutcheon of the Koháry family, the biggest landowners in the area. The grapevine of the decorative border symbolizes one of the town's chief economic activities, viticulture. Drawing by John Szokolay Hártó, engraved in 1829.

The centers of the Turkish military and civic administration differed from the village-towns of the indigenous population. Stationing considerable Turkish garrisons, they were fortified and engaged in trade and commerce. Because they were occupied by Turks these places were spared destruction. Barracks, *djamis* (Turkish places of worship), mosques and minarets, baths and bazaars erected during the long time of occupation lent them an oriental touch. Turkish and Christian inhabitants were strictly separated, the former living in the inner quarters of the towns, fortified by fences and walls. The presence of Turkish forces attracted an increasing number of people who crowded into the small space between the fence and the walls. Therefore, the houses had to be higher, with more stories, and suburbs grew up outside the gates. Supplying these garrison towns with food and maintaining them guaranteed a livelihood to the neighboring villagers.

Pécs was one of the towns that assumed a Turkish character during the occupation. After the Romans had left *Sopianae* (as Pécs was then known) it was occupied by Gepides, Goths, Lombards, and Avars. About A.D. 900 it passed to the Hungarians. In 1009 it became a bishopric, and from then on the town and the castle were the property of the bishops.

The town, with a small number of artisans, formed around the churches. However, its situation from a strategic point of view was unfavorable.

Following the Mongol invasions, which did not spare Pécs, it was fortified with walls and bastions that enclosed an approximately rectangular area. The fortifications were insignificant; the walls, relatively thin, were constructed of rubble. Yet, at the beginning of the 14th century Pécs ranked as one of the ten largest towns of Hungary. Its loosely built-up area covered 100 to 115 acres. The immediate vicinity of the bishop's castle remained free of buildings, and open spaces around the monasteries were used for cultivation. Suburbs, among them an artisans' settlement in the valley of the Tettye, surrounded the town.[2] The population of Pécs at this period has been estimated at 8,000 to 10,000 inhabitants. The founding of the university in 1367 was probably the most important event in the town's cultural life. In the 15th century, a water con-

2. The water of this stream was used for water mills, hence the name of the suburb, *vicus Malomszeg*, meaning suburb of the mills. The origin of this industrial suburb may date back to the early 12th century. [Remark added by E. A. Gutkind.]

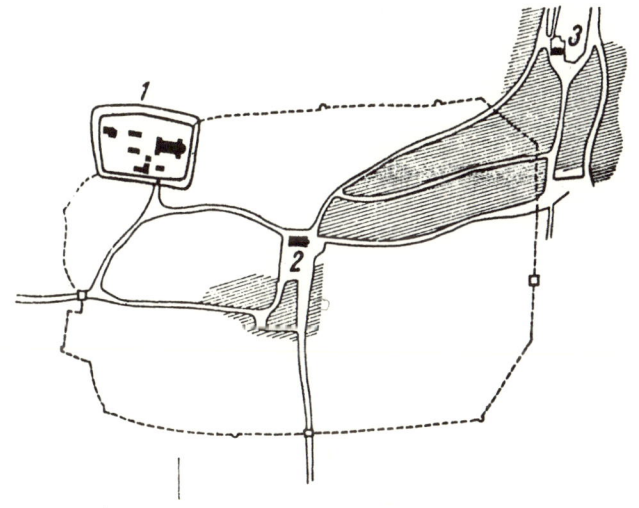

289. Plan of Pécs in the 12th century. 1. Episcopal castle; 2. Church of St. Bartholomew; 3. All Saints Church.

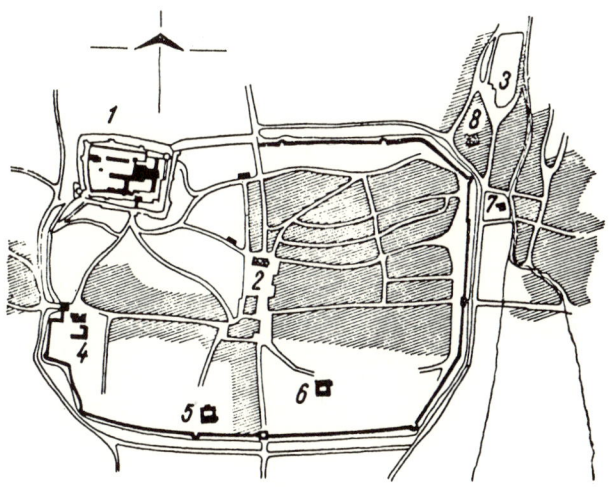

290. Plan of Pécs in the 15th century. 1. Episcopal castle; 4. Franciscan church and monastery; 5. Benedictine church and monastery; 6. Dominican monastery; 7. Augustinian monastery; 8. Convent or nunnery.

duit was installed, bringing the water of the Petrezselyem and Tettye springs to the town. Sidewalks within the urban area were paved.

After the battle of Mohács in 1526 the Turks set the town on fire but did not invade it. In 1541 it was besieged by Suleiman but successfully

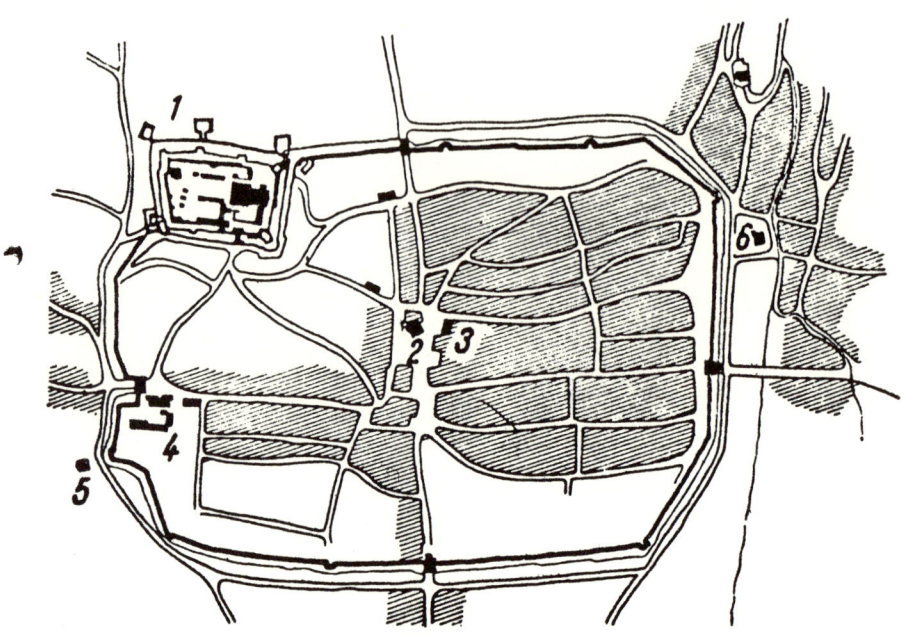

291. Plan of Pécs in the 17th century. 1. Castle; 2. *Djami* of Gazi Kaszim Pasha; 3. Bath; 4. School; 5. Mosque of Hassān Yakovali; 6. Mosque.

defended; however, it surrendered in 1543 after the garrison had deserted. In the 17th century the town was the center of the district of Pécs. During the 150 years of Turkish rule the racial and religious character of the population changed completely through the influx of Turks and Balkan Slavs. The Hungarian inhabitants were restricted to the suburbs. The inner town, reserved for the Turkish garrison, assumed a definite Turkish character. Although not much building was going on during the occupation (only erection of public buildings or alterations of existing ones), the Turks' activities changed the face of the town. There were 9 *djamis,* 10 mosques, 5 theological schools, 6 monasteries, 3 baths, and a great number of public wells; the streets were probably like those of all Islamic towns. With its colorful domed mosques and schools, graceful minarets, and flowers and plants, Pécs was a pleasant and picturesque town during the occupation. In 1554 the 2,500 to 3,000 inhabitants lived in 275 houses; by 1629 the population had increased to about 5,000 in 1,040 houses. The building density was low, with many gardens, orchards, and vineyards dispersed through the urban area. Almost every house had a garden and a water-tank.

At the beginning of the 17th century the undisguised lust for power of the Habsburgs, the savage looting by their mercenaries, and the violence of the Catholic reaction to the Reformation resulted in the forma-

292. View of Pécs in 1686. Several mosques and minarets are visible in this simplified view of the town. Engraving by Gian Giacoma de Rossi.

tion of an anti-Habsburg Independence Front. Its initiators were the free armies from the region of the Tisza, led by István Bocskay.[3] The peasantry sympathized with the rebels, and soon Transylvania and parts of Hungary were occupied. In 1605 Bocskay was elected Prince of Transylvania. After the campaign was over he settled his soldiers in so-called hajdú-towns (his soldiers were *hajdúk*).[4] The first hajdú-towns were founded at the beginning of the 17th century on the sites of deserted villages, as the first line of defense for the interior of the country. This purpose is obvious from the location of these military villages of 500 to 1,000 inhabitants between the river Hernád [a tributary of the Tisza] and the rivers Kőrös and Berettyó, such as Hajdúszoboszló, Hajdúböszörmény, Hajdúnánás, Hajdúhadház, Hajdúdorog, Polgár, and Vámospércs. These settlements, through the form of their layout, fulfilled a defensive function without violating the prohibition imposed by the Turks against building strongholds. A fortress-church with a watch tower and embrasures in its walls stood in the center of these towns. This

---

3. István Bocskay was a wealthy nobleman and, originally, an adherent of the emperor, who called the Turks to his aid against the Austrians. Ed.
4. *Hajdú* = Haiduk, the name of a special body of footsoldiers to whom the rank of nobility and a territory were given after 1605. Ed.

293. Airview of the inner area of Pécs. In the center, the domed parish church, formerly a mosque. In front of the church, in Széchenyi Square, a Holy Trinity Column. In the background (top left), the four-spired Romanesque cathedral dating from the 11th century and rebuilt in 1881–1891.

nucleus, surrounded by gardens with stables and outhouses for farming implements, was enclosed by fences. Thus something like the three zones of defense of the Hungarian castles was repeated in the hajdú-towns. The chief occupation of their inhabitants was animal husbandry.

A description of one of these settlements, Hajdúböszörmény, may be of interest. It was situated on the road from Nagyvárad [Oradea, Grosswardein, now Romania] to the northern counties through Debrecen. The first documentary evidence mentioning Hajdúböszörmény dates from 1300; some finds made on the site go back to an even earlier date. In the 14th century the settlement was granted market rights, and in the 15th century it had acquired a royal salt magazine and a salt hall.

At this time the small market town was owned by the family of the Hunyadis and housed 800 to 900 inhabitants. By the middle of the 16th century their number had declined to about 500, and toward the end of the century the site was completely deserted. In 1609, Gábor Báthori presented the area to the *hajdúk*. They did not settle on the site of the earlier town, but chose hitherto unoccupied land in the vicinity. The *hajdúk*, who were used to living as a group organized on military lines, formed their own distinctive administration. In 1676 the place was divided into 21 units, each with 15 to 25 families, and a lieutenant was placed at the head of the whole settlement. Its structure was as follows: The houses of the *hajdúk* were arranged along four streets which crossed the Debrecen-Tokaj highway at right angles; they stood on plots of about 40 to 50 square *öl* (*öl* meaning fathom, which equals 5 to 6 feet), fortified with fences and ditches. In the 17th century, because of the rapidly increasing population, the ditches had to be moved outward;

294. Airview of the village-town of Hajdúböszörmény, in the Comitat of Hajdú-Bihar of the Great Alföld. Up to the middle of the 18th century, the concentric streets of the built-up area covered only the present central part; stables and farmyards were situated in the outer zone, protected by a circular fence of thorny hedges, earthworks, and palisades. The inner town was divided into four quarters by streets radiating from the center. Blind alleys gave access to the houses along the main roads. The airview shows clearly the original street pattern.

two suburbs, one to the east and one to the west, grew up. The church and the town hall stood in the center of the town and were surrounded by fortifications consisting of bastions and brick walls with embrasures. The church tower, an isolated structure, served also as watch tower. (These fortifications were dismantled as late as the 19th century, making way for the main square.) The inner town was occupied by dwelling houses. Beyond the fences there were large, open sites of 800 to 900 square *öl*, the so-called yards for the cattle and fodder, which were separated from each other by hedgerows and ditches. This whole area was again enclosed by ditches and earthen mounds. Here stables, barns, and sheep pens were situated, and here slept the men who looked after the animals. In the 17th century, the inhabitants acquired the land of destroyed villages. The areas in the vicinity of the town were used for a self-supporting agriculture, while the more distant parts served as pastures. In 1702 the population numbered about 1,750; and, according to a census at the beginning of the 18th century, there was not a single artisan among them.

The towns in the western territory of Hungary suffered less during the wars than those in the more exposed districts, and they continued to grow. Two-storied houses, public buildings, monasteries, and churches were erected. One of these towns was *Sopron* (Ödenburg, near the Austrian border). In 1529 Turkish forces set fire to the unprotected suburbs, an event that led to the construction of new fortifications, involving the demolition of many buildings. In 1605 the suburbs were burnt again, this time by Bocskay's soldiers, the *hajdúk*. In the wake of this disaster the town was surrounded by walls and more compactly built up, with gardens attached to some of the houses. After the battle of Mohács, many wealthy people and artisans moved to Sopron from the territories under

295. *Opposite page:* Airview of Sopron, with the Beloiannisz Square and the former Benedictine or "Goat" Church (center left), built in the early 14th century and remodeled about 1480. In front of the church, the Baroque Holy Trinity Column erected in 1695–1701. Several streets enter the square at the corners without disrupting its spatial unity. The "Fire Tower," the *Stadtturm* and symbol of Sopron (left), has a cylindrical base dating from the Árpád period, a Renaissance gallery (1681), and a Baroque roof.

296. Előkapu (the Outer Gate), a street in Sopron. The name refers to one of the former town gates, part of the fortifications protecting Sopron. The houses adjacent to the gate followed the line of the fortifications. Hence the irregular, *en echelon* building line. In the background, the parish church of St. Michael.

297. Airview of a *Ringstrasse* in Sopron, following the course of the former fortifications. On the left, the Fire Tower.

298. The houses of the Two Moors in Mihály Street at Sopron are a fine example of peasant Baroque. Built about 1710, they are the work of anonymous artists. The gateway, supported by twisted columns and adorned with two Moors, connects the two houses. The gables are decorated with angels on each step of the outer edge, and niches for saints are above the windows.

Turkish rule. A period of prosperity set in, and industry and the arts developed. In 1676, a conflagration destroyed the inner town and two-thirds of the suburbs. Reconstruction began immediately. The appearance of the town changed: the Renaissance gave way to the Baroque; and the structure and form of the inner town, with its castle walls, assumed today's appearance. In 1678 the population numbered 8,500.

After Bocskay's death the fight against the Habsburgs was continued by Gábor Bethlen and, later, by György Rákóczi I, Prince of Transylvania. These rebellions, which often shook the Habsburg monarchy to its foundations, led to the formation of Transylvania and Eastern Hungary as an independent state. This independence, however, was short lived, mostly due to the misguided foreign and home policy of György Rákóczi II. The country again fell victim to Turkish invasions and was governed for a short time by Imre Thököly who, supported by the Turks, had turned successfully against Leopold of Halsburg, at the head of an army of exiled Protestants and dispossessed noblemen. Inspired by Thököly's success the Turkish army marched against Vienna where it was defeated and finally driven out of Hungary.

Urban Development in the 18th Century

The role of the conquering Turks was taken over by the colonizing Habsburgs, whose right to the succession to the Crown was recognized by the diet in 1687, a decision meaning, in reality, that Hungary was proclaimed a colony of Austria. The deserted territories recaptured from the Turks were populated by German settlers. But the peasantry and patriotic noblemen could not reconcile themselves to the fate of their country. In 1703, under the command of Ferenc Rákóczi II, the War of Independence began against Habsburg oppression. This enterprise was a failure because of the suppression of the interests of the peasant-serfs, the intrigues of the big landowners and the Church, and the unfavorable international situation. The Peace of Szatmár (1711) delivered Hungary again into the hands of the Habsburgs.

At the time of the census of 1715–1720, only 1,000 to 2,000 people lived in each of the remaining settlements of the Alföld such as Makó, Cegléd, Szentes, Mezőtúr, and Halas; and only a few settlements had 2,000 to 5,000 inhabitants, for instance, Hódmezővásárhely, Jászberény, and Nagykőrös. The population of Szeged was less than 5,000 including the military personnel, and that of Kecskemét only a little over 5,000. Debrecen, with its individual, Calvinist, and urban character, had perhaps 10,000 inhabitants at this time. At the beginning of the 18th century, only 47 settlements had the rank of town, with a total population of no more than 200,000.

The period to the end of the 18th century was marked by the progressive colonial penetration of the country. Productivity was restored and increased, in the interest of the Austrian feudal system and the growing Austrian bourgeoisie. Immigrants from foreign countries who were loyal to the Habsburgs received big land grants. At the same time, several thousand German peasants arrived; later, Serbian and Romanian peasants were settled in Hungary.

Although Austria was a state of feudal [so-called enlightened] despotism, her bourgeoisie had a certain influence on the government's policy, if for no other reason than their large contributions to the public finances. Consequently, the economic policy of the Court of Vienna tended to ruin Hungarian trade and industry. The more this Austrian class gained in importance, the more the development of Hungarian industry was restrained. The monopoly of Austrian industry in the Hungarian market was ensured by imposing heavy duties on imports from other countries (ten times higher than duties on Austrian goods) and by prohibiting the import of certain goods altogether. As a result, Hungary was reduced to supplier of foodstuffs and raw materials for the Austrian industry and remained an agrarian country with almost no industry and no merchant and tradesmen class worth mentioning. What remained of industrial activities had the character of handicrafts: In 1777 there were 14,000 independent master craftsmen among 34,000 workers. To make up for the low prices paid for Hungarian goods in the Austrian market, the landowners endeavored to increase agricultural production which, in its turn, required more forced labor on their farms. The peasantry became destitute as the serfs had to neglect their own fields to work on the land of their masters.

During the 18th century the expansion of towns could not keep pace with the increasing population. In 1780, fewer than 400,000 people lived in urban communities. Capital was scarce. Even at the end of the century Buda was still a small place and hardly to be distinguished from other small towns. In the Alföld no new towns developed, but in Transdanubia rural settlements began to form independent units with their neighboring villages. Prominent among Hungarian towns were some of the ecclesiastical residences, because of their sumptuous large-scale buildings, such as Vác, Pécs, Szombathely (Steinamanger), Veszprém, Esztergom, Székesfehérvár (Stuhlweissenburg), and Eger, and some of the towns on the Danube enjoying a certain prosperity from the river traffic, such as Pest, Komárom (Czechoslovakia), and Győr (Raab). Transdanubia and the Kisalföld had not suffered too much during the Turkish occupation and the wars of liberation. Since Vienna was the most important market and was relatively near, a lively trade in agricultural products ensued.

At this time the largest, most important town and commercial center was *Debrecen,* used for the storage of raw materials and produce from the eastern part of the country. Excavations have revealed that the site and vicinity of Debrecen have been occupied since the Stone Age. Hungarians settled in this area, probably not later than the 12th century. In the Middle Ages, settlements were built on the three higher ranges of dunes traversing the plain from northeast to southwest. In the 13th century nine villages existed in and around the Tocó Valley, four of them on the area of the present inner town: Debrecen, Szentlászlófalva, Szentmihály, and Torna or Boldogasszonyfalva. The terrain between the second and third villages was built up at the beginning of the 14th century on a more or less regular ground plan, with the castle of the feudal lords to the south, the market square of St. Andrew's not far from it, and the Dominican monastery to the north. The area south of the market was later also occupied by houses. By the end of the century the four

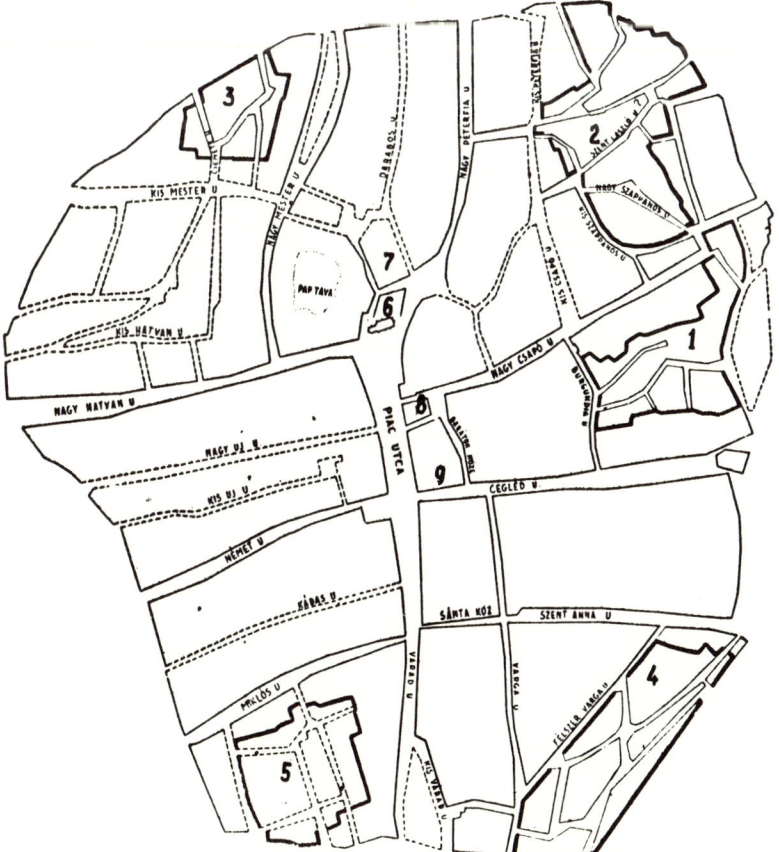

299. Development of the street pattern in the central area of Debrecen during the 14th and 15th centuries and the boundaries of the four original villages forming part of Debrecen's urban area, superimposed on the present site of the town. 1. Debrecen; 2. Szentlászlófalva; 3. Szentmihály; 4. Torna or Boldogasszonyfalva; 5. Area developed during the Fifteen Years War (1591–1606); 6. Church of St. Andrew; 7. Latin School, the later Kollegium; 8. Hospital; 9. Town hall.

▬▬ Boundaries of medieval villages

─── Streets during the 14th and 15th centuries

------ Streets and building blocks laid out during subsequent centuries villages had merged. In the 15th century the whole area of the present inner town had been given over to housing. At the time of János Hunyadi, who acquired the place in 1440 from the Serbian prince, Lázár Brankovics, and especially during Matthias' reign, Debrecen's economic and cultural importance grew. By the middle of the 16th century it was fortified by mounds and ditches, interrupted by four gates leading into the town. When the Turkish wars began, the inhabitants of the neighboring villages thronged to the town, an influx necessitating the division of the southern part of the urban area into lots for the newcomers. Toward the end of the 16th century, Debrecen had between 8,000 and 9,000 inhabitants. A further subdivision of the large blocks by new streets was therefore unavoidable. In the 16th and 17th centuries, Debrecen was the biggest town east of the Tisza River. Frequent fires, however, caused heavy damage, especially a conflagration of 1564 that destroyed half the town. Debrecen, which had passed relatively unscathed through the time of Turkish rule and liberation, lost most of its economic power during the 18th century. It was then that its social character changed to a typical middle-class and peasant town. While in 1714 the number of tradesmen and craftsmen amounted to 67 percent of the population, it had decreased to 46 percent in 1772. Trade and industry declined, and the town reverted in character and appearance to an enormous village. However, by the end of the century, the population had risen to about 30,000, making Debrecen the second largest town of the country after Pest. In the same century, 12 fires destroyed many of the thatched and badly built houses. More solid buildings were scarce because of the lack of more durable materials and skilled masons. (In 1775 the Masons' Guild consisted of only three masters, 15 assistants, and four apprentices.)

The 18th century was propitious for the unfolding of Hungarian town planning. Baroque architecture made its appearance first in the western and northern parts of the country; later it spread to all other regions. Mainly the work of Italian, German, and Austrian masters, it was usually limited to a small area and preserved the medieval structure of the town. In the center of these Baroque towns the buildings were mostly two-storied, while in the peripheral parts one-storied houses prevailed. Churches, monasteries, and palaces rose above the mass of the low houses of the citizens. The axial and symmetrical layout, typical of the European Baroque, remained alien to Hungary. The irregular town plan was preserved; and individual Baroque buildings, with their more modest and often asymmetrical façades, were fitted into the inherited medieval structure.

Among the many charming small towns of the Baroque period, one of the most characteristic and beautiful is *Eger*. For many centuries the history and development of many Hungarian towns in the mountainous regions were determined by their strategic value in relation to their geographical situation. Eger controlled and defended the busy road from the north to the Alföld. Surrounded by hills, it stands on the river Eger between the Mátra and Bükk mountains, in a valley opening to the Alföld. Before the arrival of the Hungarians the valley was inhabited by Slavs. King Stephen made Eger the center of a diocese. A castle was built in 1248 after the Mongol invasions. Its precincts included the cathedral and St. Stephen's Church, the bishop's residence, and the

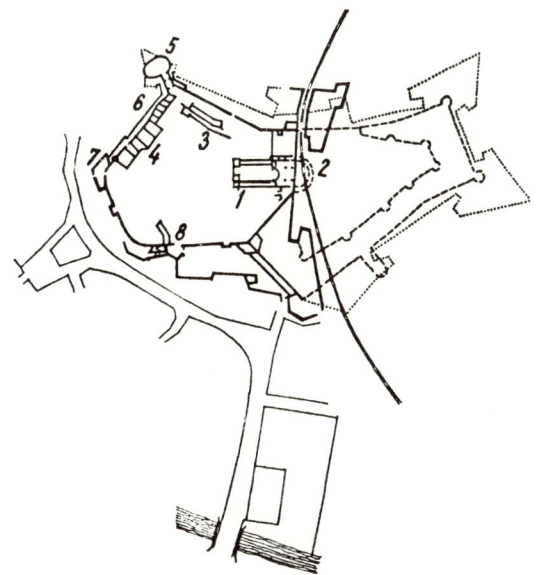

300. Plan of the citadel of Eger, one of the best examples of a pentagonal fortress with sharp-cornered bastions of the Italian type. 1. Basilica; 2. Szentély (Sanctuary) Bastion; 3. Episcopal Palace; 4. Chapter; 5. Föld (Earth) Bastion; 6. Tömlöc (Prison) Bastion; 7. Dobó Bastion; 8. Varkoch Gate.

houses of the canons, forming a small fortified town with its secular and religious buildings. At the beginning of the 16th century the inhabited area extended beyond the castle which, especially after its rebuilding by Italian military engineers in the 1550s, served an even more strategic function. After a brief siege it was captured by the Turks in 1596. The settlement that had grown up outside its walls was heavily damaged and had to be evacuated. Under Turkish rule, Eger shared the fate of many other towns. Many timber houses were erected, a building method continued even after the liberation.

The Austrians recaptured Eger in 1687. At this time it was apparently a well-kept town, surrounded by walls and bastions. Town life soon revived, above all because of Eger's situation on the trading route from Istanbul to Cracow. In 1699 it had about 3,900 inhabitants. The Emperor Leopold, fearing the rebellious populace might use it as a stronghold, ordered the castle destroyed in 1702—like many other Hungarian castles—and the blowing up of the "Beautiful Bastion." In 1783, the ruined castle was sold to Cardinal Esterházy; its underground prisons were filled in with debris, and the stones were used for new buildings. The first suburb of Eger was built in 1728, and the "New Town" was founded in 1758. Eger expanded by the addition of new quarters to the medieval core, whose irregular street pattern was gradually surrounded by a gridiron plan. The steets of the inner town were narrow and tortuous, more like alleys and passages. The plots were small and the building density was high. In 1764 a by-law required applications for building permits, enabling the authorities to make the necessary preparations. In 1787 the population numbered 16,852.

The development of the new center of Eger began in 1783. The construction of its clerical part was initiated with the erection of the Lyceum by Jakab Fellner. It was not finished until the beginning of the 19th century, as was József Hild's cathedral in the style of the classical revival. The rectangular square slopes down to the Lyceum, and the cathedral, standing on a site about 30 feet higher, with broad stairs

301. View of Eger in 1687, the year of its recapture by the Austrians. Minarets and mosques, erected by the invaders, add distinctive Turkish elements to the skyline. Engraving by Gian Giacomo de Rossi.

302. View of Eger from the castle hill, with the Servita Church in the center.

leading up to it, offers a monumental impression. The civic center, Kossuth Square, served as a market until 1790. In 1775, a church of the Minorites was erected on the longer side of this spacious oblong square. Next to it stood the Baroque town hall, preserved until 1898. The principal part of this urban renewal was executed in the short time of 50 years, apart from technical improvements such as the paving of the streets, begun in 1745, and the regulation of the river Eger by walls to prevent flooding.

By the end of the 18th century, new towns came into being in almost every region, though none was to rise in importance above the others in site and character. There was not yet a capital city that might be the political and cultural center of the country. Joseph II (1780–1790) attempted to suppress any semblance of Hungarian independence but the resistance of the Hungarian nobility and the influence of the French Revolution counteracted these renewed colonizing efforts. At the end of the century differences between the Austrian and Hungarian governing classes, between the landowners and the serfs, and other political and social differences within this country of many nations intensified. The 19th century inherited this internal strife and antagonism. The time for the battle for independence and social change was dawning.

Urban Development in the First Half of the 19th Century

The effects of the Industrial Revolution and the rising capitalist system were felt much later in Hungary than in the countries of Western Europe. In spite of this time lag, large-scale building activities took place all over the country, especially in Pest in the first half of the century.

The population of *Pest* rose from 29,870 in 1799 to 110,516 in 1848, while the number of inhabitants of Buda and Óbuda remained almost stationary at 40,500 during the same period. At the beginning of the 19th century the town began to expand rapidly. Pest had 1,146 houses in 1765, and 5,105 in 1840. During the same period Buda and Óbuda had about 4,000 and 750 houses, respectively, though of much smaller dimensions.

In 1801, the Palatine Joseph presented a memorandum to the Emperor, emphasizing the commercial importance of Pest and the need to introduce systematic town planning. He also instructed János Hild to prepare the first town planning scheme, to serve as the basis

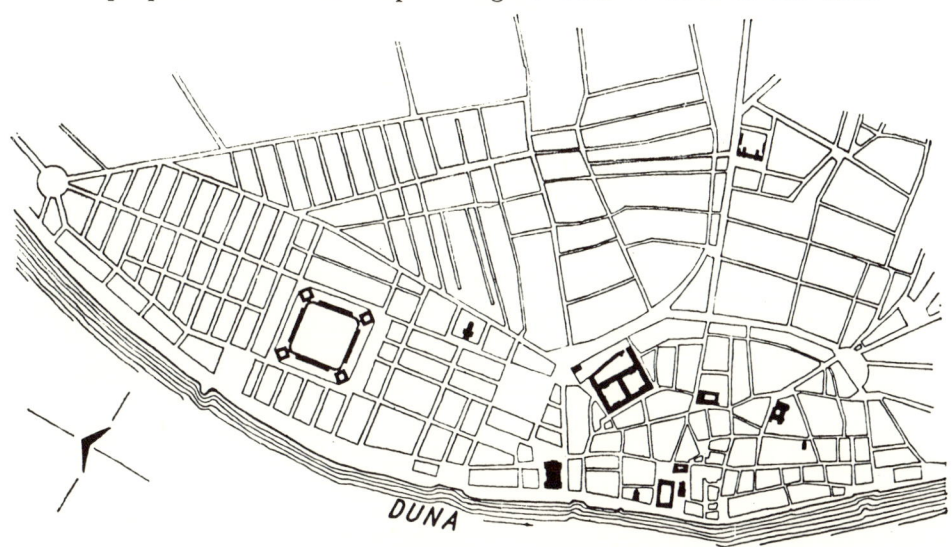

303. Plan of Pest by János Hild, 1805.

of the project submitted to the Emperor in 1805. Its outstanding feature was the large scale of the proposed extension for almost the whole northern sector, the southern and eastern urban areas, whereas only minor corrections and improvements were envisaged for the already built-up districts. The new quarters were to be laid out as a continuation of the existing structure, with a regular street pattern. In Hild's time only three streets led from the city walls northward to the present Engels Square: the Bálvány, Sas, and Nagykorona streets. The area toward the Danube was to be developed in relation to these streets, and several new squares were to be created. A broad promenade, with rows of trees, was suggested for the embankment. However, only parts of Hild's plan were carried out, although the uniform style of the buildings at the Danube and the width of the embankment reflect some of Hild's original ideas.

As a result of the Palatine Joseph's memorandum, a Planning Commission was set up in 1808. Under its guidance large-scale building activities started, especially in the Lipótváros District, where after a few years (in 1813) three squares, 13 streets, and 228 buildings were completed. The inner Erzsébetváros and Terézváros Districts were also rebuilt. Thus, through the activities of Mihály Pollack, József Hild (who alone designed more than 600 buildings), Mátyás Zitterbarth, and other architects, Classical Pest came into being. The new plans were monotonous and unimaginative, with a repetition of identical quadrangular blocks. In contrast to this lively activity in Pest, building in Buda during this period was only sporadic, consisting mainly of individual private and smaller houses. Other measures initiated by the Planning Commission included the construction of the Pest embankment along the Danube, the introduction of gas lighting in Pest and Buda, and the restoration of the city park. Yet the water supply, particularly in Pest, was still very primitive, supplied mainly from wells or direct from the Danube.

Two disasters befell the city during this period. In 1810, a great fire started in Buda, destroying hundreds of houses. No plan for rebuilding the affected districts was available. Reconstruction proceeded therefore along the existing old, narrow, and tortuous roads of the Middle Ages. The other disaster was the great flood of 1838. Of the more than 7,500 inundated houses in Pest, Buda, and Óbuda, 2,882 collapsed and others had to be demolished. Almost two-fifths of the destroyed houses were rebuilt, though with hardly any modification of the street system.

A plan to dig out the old, almost completely silted-up moat and transform it into a navigable canal like the Canal Grande in Venice, using its banks as building sites, never materialized because of the lack of enforceable building statutes (the first statute was not enacted until 1839) and, above all, the lack of purpose on the part of the municipal authorities.

The leading promoter of the development of Budapest as the capital of Hungary was the Hungarian statesman István Széchenyi (1791–1860). He was the first to suggest the union of Buda and Pest. As he wrote in 1828: "The name of our capital should be changed to Budapest, thus uniting the two towns which now dislike each other." On his initiative the Lánchid, the chain bridge, the first of the Danube bridges,

304. The Theater Square in Pest during the great flood in 1838.

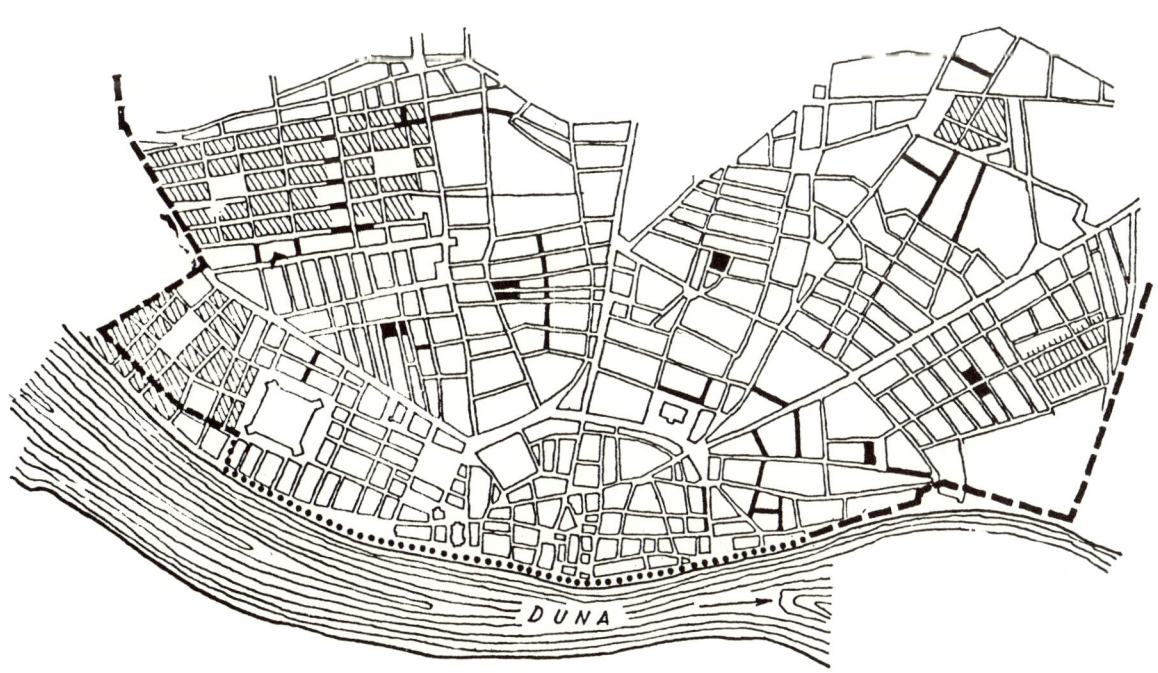

305. Plan of Pest after the flood of 1838. The solid black areas and lines indicate new streets and squares; hatching, the newly acquired building blocks; the broken line, the newly constructed embankments; and the dotted line, the projected but not constructed dikes along the Danube.

306. Plan of Pest (1839), based on official documents, showing the regulations undertaken after the great flood of 1838. This plan complements the diagrammatic scheme of Fig. 305.

was constructed in 1839, after a design by Adam Clark. The location of this bridge determined the site of the later bridges and, indirectly, the layout of the streets both in the city and the more distant quarters.

Széchenyi was also partly responsible for the construction of the road, railway, and waterway systems throughout the country. On his advice, four railway lines radiating from Budapest and four to six roads

308. *Opposite page:* Váci utca (Váci Street), one of the oldest streets in Pest, named after Vác, a town to the north of the city. The former Váci Gate was situated at the lower end of Váci Street. The drawing by Rudolf Alt shows the busiest section of the once elegant shopping street. Lithograph by Sandmann, 1845.

307. Airview of Budapest, showing the Széchenyi Lánchid, the Széchenyi chain bridge (foreground), and Margaret Island beyond the Parliament building on the left bank of the Danube.

309. The "Aldunasor," the Lower Danube Quay at Pest, with the Greek church in the foreground and the chain bridge in the background. Lacking adequate water works, Pest's supply from wells and the Danube was supplemented by water sold by the bucket from donkey carts (bottom left). Drawing by Ludwig Rohbock, engraved by Kolb in 1856.

from Budapest to the frontier were built. A winter harbor in a branch of the Danube was completed after a struggle of almost ten years. Many other eminently practical projects owed their realization to the farsightedness and energy of Széchenyi.

Classicism attained a high artistic level in Pest, though it hardly influenced the street pattern even where groups of new buildings had been erected. An exception was a row of houses on the embankment in Pest, of which only a few have survived. When rebuilding on this site began, the line of buildings was pushed back from the embankment at the present Roosevelt Square. Thus, one of the most beautiful ensembles of Europe, the so-called Kirakodó Square, was created. Palatial edifices, public buildings, apartment houses, hotels, restaurants, coffee houses, and parks enhanced the appearance of Pest, providing a splendid background to the busy life of the city in those days.

Not only in Pest, but in almost all Hungarian towns, Baroque architecture was more and more confronted by the symmetrical rigidity of the early 19th-century Classicism. A new harmony of these contrasting styles emerged, and a tendency to create unity in diversity of larger compositions was apparent in the erection of many, mostly two-storied houses. The country towns advanced at a much slower pace than the capital. Here the activity was mainly restricted to churches and public buildings, as in Baja, Nagykőrös, and Debrecen.

Up to the middle of the 19th century the agricultural and social character of *Debrecen* remained almost unchanged. The great demand for agricultural products during the Napoleonic Wars resulted in an even more one-sided development in the same direction. In 1802 a great fire destroyed one third of the town; 643 houses and 11 mills were reduced to ashes. This event was a blessing in disguise for the development of the town. It led to the preparation of the first town-planning statute and the beginning of a systematic renewal of the urban area, eliminating the narrow, tortuous lanes and streets and loosening up the congested quarters. Better and more fire-proof buildings of brick and tile were erected, and skilled labor was employed. In the local art school founded at the end of the 18th century, students were taught classical architecture under the guidance of Paul Beregszászi. Through their work a provincial variety of that style spread to all parts of the Debrecen region. The Reformed Church and the Kollegium, both the work of Mihály Péchy, and the Town Hall designed by Ferenc Povolny were built at this time. In 1811 another fire broke out, leading to the replacement of the labyrinthine street pattern by a more regular plan. Paving of streets, sewerage, and gas lighting were other improvements introduced during the 1840s and 1850s. Yet, despite these works, contemporary drawings show a village-like, disorganized mass of one-storied houses, with only churches and mills and a few two-storied buildings interrupting the unimpressive skyline.

310. View of Debrecen in 1860 from the charter of a guild.

In spite of the consolidation of absolute imperial power after the Revolution of 1848–49, the pre-revolutionary conditions could not be restored entirely. The old feudal ruling minority was compelled to share their influence with the rising middle class of Austria. The subsequent exploitation of Hungary by the Austrian bourgeoisie after the revolution strengthened the capitalist trends of Austrian industry,

Urban Development and the Growth of Capitalism

especially after the customs union of 1850. The more efficient Austrian industry gained unlimited control of the Hungarian market. However, slowly Hungarian capitalism began to develop, furthered by the emancipation of the serfs in 1848. The industrial activities of this early period involved the construction of railways and the establishment of agriculture-related and food-processing enterprises, the majority of which were controlled by Austrian capital and dependent on cheap Hungarian labor and raw materials.

In 1866, Austria lost the war with Prussia and was forced to make concessions and end colonial conditions in Hungary. The Austrian Empire was transformed into the Austro-Hungarian Dual Monarchy (1867), which led to a somewhat quicker pace of capitalist development and investment of foreign capital. After 1891, about 1,500 new factories were formed. By 1898, over 2,360 industrial establishments were in operation; those based on agriculture still remained in the lead.

In 1849, the Minister of the Interior of the Revolutionary Government issued a decree for the unification of the three towns of *Buda, Óbuda,* and *Pest*. This plan did not materialize: Only Buda and Óbuda were united, whereas the union of Pest and Buda had to wait until 1872. In the meantime the population had increased rapidly, nearly doubling in the 20 years from 1850 to 1870. The whole area added by the Hild plan (1801) had been built up, and houses had spread beyond the envisaged boundaries. A comprehensive development plan was still missing, and communication between the different districts remained difficult. The chain bridge could no longer cope with the increasing traffic. New industrial quarters, with workers' slums, began to grow up, but the construction of public utility works lagged behind.

The great reformer of this period, Mihály Táncsics, awakened the public conscience to the great natural beauties of Budapest, bestowed on the capital by its location on the Danube. His ideas were far-sighted, and many of his suggestions, such as the building of the Margit Bridge and a *forum* and the prohibition of basement living quarters, materialized.

Finally, in 1870, a Council for Public Utility Works was set up. One of its first tasks was the organization of a survey of the whole urban area as an indispensable preparation for a comprehensive town planning scheme. This survey was followed by an international competition for plans for a better and greater Budapest. The first prize was awarded to Lajos Lechner; the second to Frigyes Feszl; and the third to two English architects, Klein and Fraser. On the basis of the results of this competition, the Council drew up a new plan concentrating on the layout of two sites of major importance: Sugár Avenue, the present Népköztársaság Avenue, and the Outer Boulevard, the present Nagykörút. Drastic solutions were needed. The population increased rapidly; in 1850, Pest had 106,379 inhabitants and Buda and Óbuda together had 50,120 inhabitants—that is, the three towns had a total population of about 156,500. In 1900, the population had risen to 716,680 for the united city of Budapest.

The architecture of this period followed the general trend of romanticism and eclecticism that was common to all countries of Europe. In Budapest many public buildings, among them the Opera House, the

311. The Buildings of Parliament, on the Danube at Kossuth Square, Budapest, erected in 1883–1902 after designs by I. Steindl.

Academy of Sciences, the Royal Palace, the Parliament, and numerous apartment houses, were erected; and the city with its beautiful natural setting began to assume the appearance that made it famous.

Of other towns, *Szeged* may be mentioned. It had been liberated from the Turks in 1686, and the adjoining deserted countryside had gradually been repopulated by Serbian, German, and Dalmatian immigrants. Although the promising development of the town was gravely interrupted by the epidemic of 1710 and the floods of 1712, Szeged became the leading trading community of Southern Hungary in the 18th century. Beyond the fortifications, suburbs with long monotonous streets were laid out. The old inner town remained the commercial center. Lack of space made the combination of workshops, shops, and living quarters under the same roof unavoidable. In spite of this congestion, one-storied houses continued to predominate in the suburbs. The great extension of the cultivated area around the town made a daily journey to work impossible; the fields were sometimes 10 to 20 miles distant from the residential districts. Consequently, the farmers set up provi-

312. View of Szeged in 1686, at the time of the liberation from Turkish rule.

sional structures, *tanyák*, where they spent the whole summer, returning to the town for the winter season only. Later the younger members of the family lived permanently on the outlying farms; finally, the whole family moved out and came to town only for business. Steam boats plied the Tisza as early as 1848, and the first steam mills were built in 1854. This increased agricultural and industrial production did not manifest itself in commensurate building activities. By 1875 Szeged had 75,000 inhabitants and only a few larger buildings.

Due to its unfavorable geographical situation, Szeged had been visited by floods about 30 times in its history. However, not since the Turkish occupation had it experienced a calamity such as the great flood of 1879. The Tisza broke through the dikes about 12 miles north of the town and flooded almost the whole urban area. More than 5,460 houses collapsed, only 265 remained unaffected, and almost 60,000 inhabitants were driven from their homes. Reconstruction was directed by Lajos Lechner. His design was strongly influenced by Haussmann's plan for Paris, envisaging wide avenues and boulevards, large squares, and parks, as well as technical improvements such as water works, sewerage systems, and street lighting. In 1879–80, the town was surrounded by a dike 32.8 feet wide. The inner and the outer boulevards were raised 30 feet and 23 feet, respectively, as a further protection against floods. A plan to raise other areas of the town was abandoned because of financial difficulties.

Lechner's plan divided the urban area into three zones: The first zone was bordered by the inner boulevard and raised to its level. Here, higher brick buildings were permitted, forming continuous block fronts.

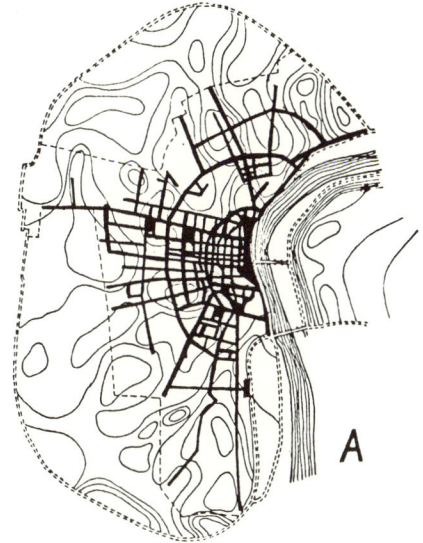

313. The plan of the "ideal level" for Szeged. The solid black lines and areas indicate the embanked streets and squares.

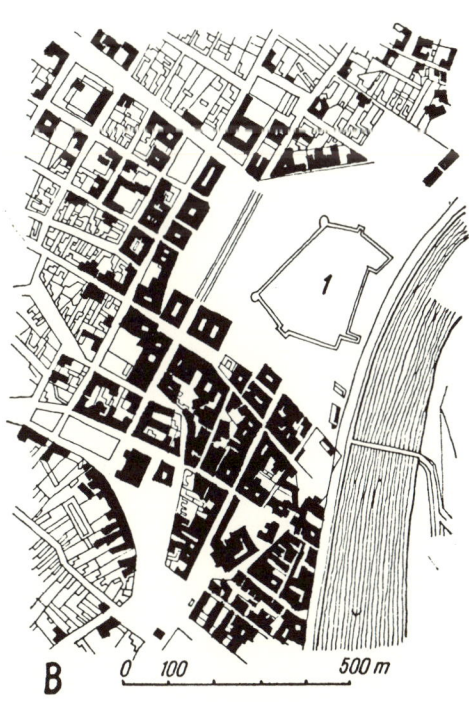

314. The solid black areas on this plan of Szeged show the undamaged buildings after the great flood.

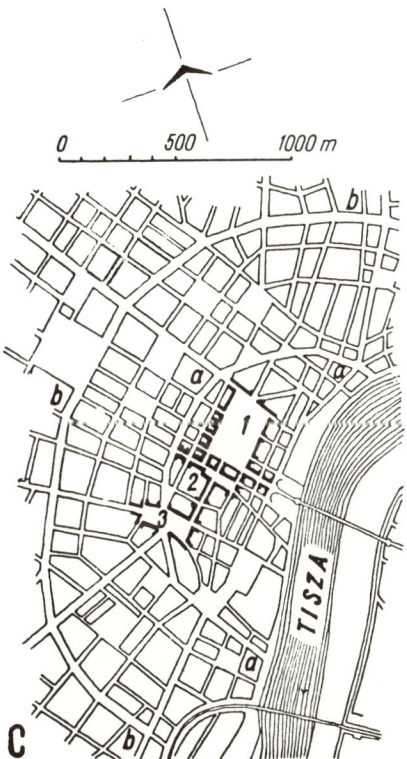

315. The rebuilt center of Szeged after the flood of 1879. 1. Széchenyi Square; 2. Klauzál Square; 3. Dugonics Square; a-a. Kiskörút or Small Boulevard (the inner boulevard); b-b. Nagykörút or Grand Boulevard (the outer boulevard).

399

The second zone, between the inner and outer boulevards, was to be occupied by houses of solid and mixed materials.[5] The third zone, a suburb beyond the outer boulevards, was reserved for simpler houses in a somewhat irregular development. The citizens received compensation of from 19 to 31 percent of their flood losses, part of it to be allocated in building materials. The authorities offered about 20 types of houses for the rebuilding of the town, from which the citizens could choose according to their financial means. Large areas were converted into parks; two boulevards, six avenues, and promenades were constructed; and numerous new public buildings were erected.

The progressive urbanization of the 19th century, especially during its second half, raised the towns of Hungary to the level of other towns of Europe, at least superficially. Budapest became a metropolis, and a dull uniformity spread over most of the urban communities. Land speculation and extortionate rents made sound town-planning policies impossible. The result was new congestion with all its attendant drawbacks and low-standard housing, particularly on the outskirts of industrial and mining towns.

---

5. Solid materials are brick, stone, and cement; mixed materials are sun-dried or sun-baked brick made of clay mixed with chaff, or such brick used with timber. In places like Szeged, houses are built of both solid and mixed materials, arranged in layers or otherwise alternating. Ed.

CHAPTER 26

Appendix
by E. A. Gutkind

The following notes are intended as a complementary survey to Professor Perényi's essay. They deal with a few additional aspects of some problems mentioned on the preceding pages.

Győr (Raab), Győr-Sopron. Győr is situated at the confluence of three rivers, the Rába (Raab), the Rábca (Rabnitz), and the Little Danube, the Moson branch of the Danube.[1] Several factors have favored the settlement of this site: a small elevation; an ancient route to Styria and Italy along the Rába Valley; and an open plain at the foot of the hills extending toward the east, that is, to the interior of the country. Recent excavations (1955) at the Káptalandomb (Hill of the Cathedral Chapter) have revealed that the site has been occupied for more than two thousand years. The Romans, who arrived in the first century A.D. in this part of Pannonia, founded an important *castrum* on the hill, outside whose walls a civilian settlement grew up about the time of Tiberius. It retained the Celtic name *Arrabona*, meaning Town at the Raab. This Roman town reached its greatest prosperity probably under Trajan and Hadrian. Opinions are divided as to the layout of *Arrabona:* was it a typical Roman checkerboard system or a gradually grown town? The answer is that it was probably both, that is, the Roman layout with *cardo* and *decumanus* was probably applied to the *castrum,* whereas the settlement outside grew spontaneously. The Roman garrison was withdrawn in A.D. 337, thus opening the territory at the confluence of the Rába and the Danube to the inrush of the Great Migrations. In 568 the Avars conquered the town and surrounded it with ring-fences. From this *hring* the Hungarian name Győr was derived, *gyűrű* meaning ring.

Toward the end of the ninth and at the beginning of the 10th century, the Hungarians settled in Győr. They apparently regarded it as a useful strongpoint, protected at the west by the Hanság marshes and connected with the heart of the country by the Danube and overland routes. At the turn of the millennium *Győr* was attached to the royal domain, and King Stephen made it the administrative and religious center of the western part of his kingdom. Because of its strategic location on an important waterway and trade routes, Győr developed favorably and soon became a lively market town. As such, Idrisi mentioned it in the 12th century. Hungarian records of the 13th century confirmed his observation, telling of visiting Italian and German merchants and of preferential tariffs granted to the inhabitants of Győr by several foreign towns.

At the foot of the hill, the later inner town developed with the cathedral chapter as feudal lord. Gradually several smaller settlements grew up around this nucleus. The increasing importance of the artisans and merchants in the export trade induced Stephen V, in 1271, to liberate the castle and the inhabitants of Királyföld—one of the settlements—from their subordination to the feudal lord. He elevated these areas to a Royal Free Town with self-government, granting to the inhabitants of the other settlements certain privileges such as the right to store goods, *ius stapulae,* the holding of an annual fair, and preferential duties.

This favorable development was slowed down in the middle of the 15th century by the Austrian occupation, which resulted in a loss of self-government, and by the Turkish invasion. However, in spite of these drawbacks Győr grew, its population increased, its wealth multiplied, and its appearance assumed a more urban character. Even the hill, the Káptalandomb, was built up more and more until the end of the 15th century. After the battle of Mohács (1526), the Austrian government made Győr a frontier fortress and the center of the defense system, extending from the Rába to Lake Balaton. The garrison was reinforced and billeted not only in the castle, which was too small, but also in the civilian town. In consequence of this influx, the town, which had consisted of hardly more than 100 houses around 1520, had more than 700 houses by 1567, of which 265 were occupied by soldiers and their families. The subdivision of the medieval agrarian plots increased the building density of the hill town so much that the garrison had almost no space to move in the narrow and tortuous lanes and alleys. This situation grew so bad that the district officer of Transdanubia, Egon Salm, was ordered in 1561 to rebuild the whole street system of the town. A fire of 1566 facilitated the reconstruction of the mass of streets and houses. The land register of 1567 reveals some interesting information on the rebuilding of the town. First of all, most houses were reconstructed in one to two years. Apparently the timber roofs had been burned down, and the majority of the houses built of stone or brick were easily repaired. Furthermore, the military engineers who conducted the work

---

1. V. Borbíró and I. Valló *Győr városépítéstörténete.* 1956. *Passim.*

preserved the core of the original layout. The regular checkerboard system characteristic of Győr even today was not the work of the military engineers but dates back, at least in its essential part, to the Middle Ages. The reconstruction of 1567 merely re-established the original form.

At the same time, the primitive medieval fortifications of the town were beginning to be replaced by contemporary defenses. The walls were reinforced and bastions added in accordance with the system devised by Italian military engineers. These works were constructed over a long period of time. In the 16th century, the citadel and the whole of the then-existing town were surrounded by strong walls with six redoubts, after plans by Pietro Ferrabosco. In the following century, the outer defenses with advanced bastions and ravelins were added under the direction of Francesco Wymes. The extramural settlements to the south of the citadel were repeatedly destroyed by Turkish attacks, and their inhabitants had to flee to the safety of the walled-in town. At this time the district of the present Nádorváros (the original Királyföld) received the name *civitas mortuorum*.

In 1594 Győr was captured by the Turks. Four years later it was retaken by the Austrians, an event celebrated all over Europe as tantamount to the liberation of the Continent and the Christian World from the threat of Turkish invasions. Reconstruction began, but slowly. However, by 1617, according to the land register of the same year, 600 houses had been rebuilt, with tiled roofs as a precaution against fire. This reconstruction was the basis of Baroque Győr. Numerous public buildings were erected, and others were re-

316. The recapture of Győr by the Austrians in 1598. Several town gates are clearly visible: the Vienna Gate (B) at the bridge over the Raab River, connecting the town with one of the suburbs; the Water Gate (C) at the bastion in the center of the wall facing the Danube, and the Weissenburg Gate (A) at the bridge in the foreground. The castle (D), with the church, is situated near the corner bastion at the Danube. A cemetery (V) is located outside the walls (bottom right). Important events like the recapture of Győr were printed as broadsheets, published as poems, or distributed as flyers. The print by John Siebmacher, illustrating the battle for Győr, served this purpose. From the *Ortelius Chronicle*, 1665.

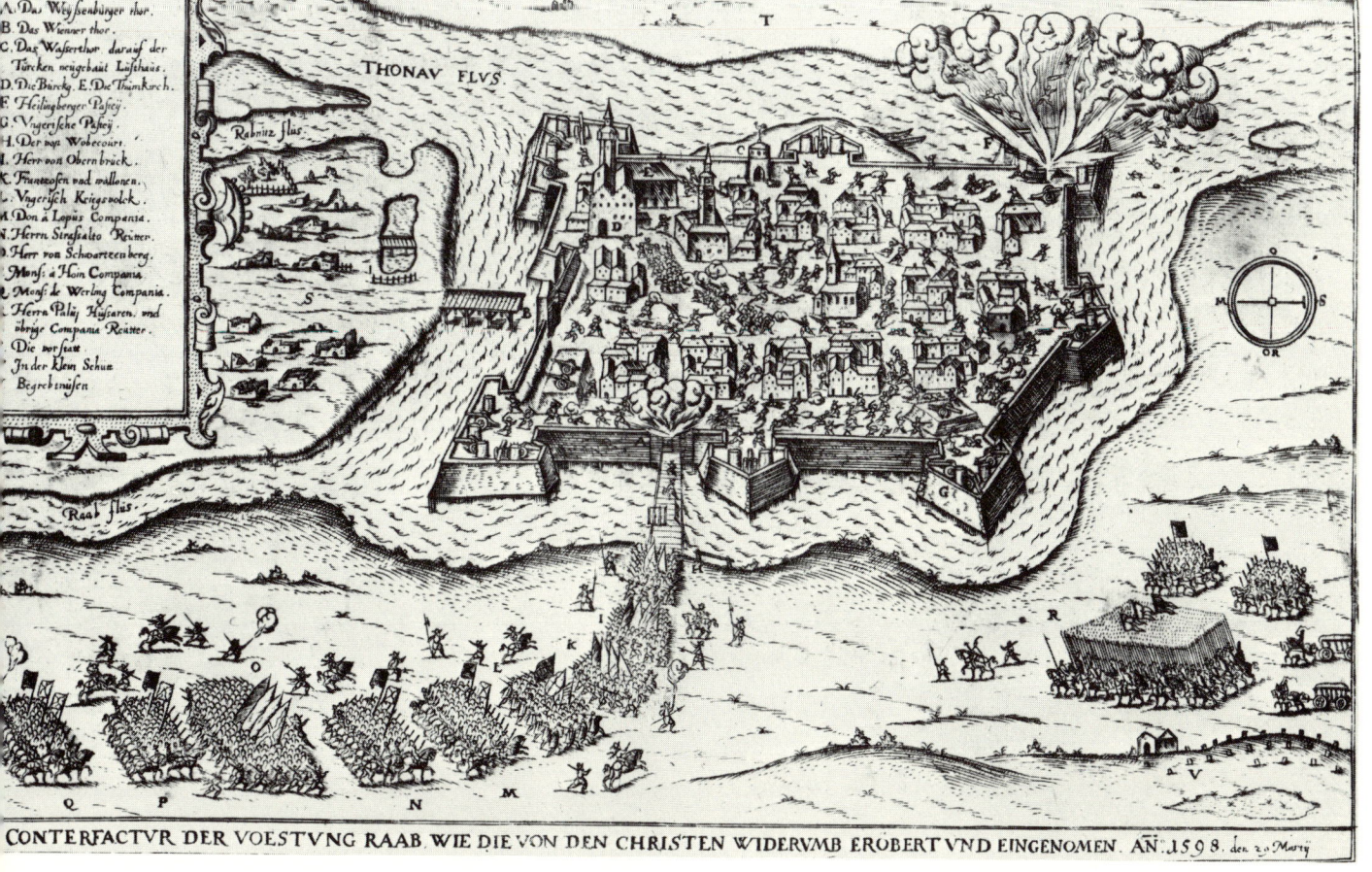

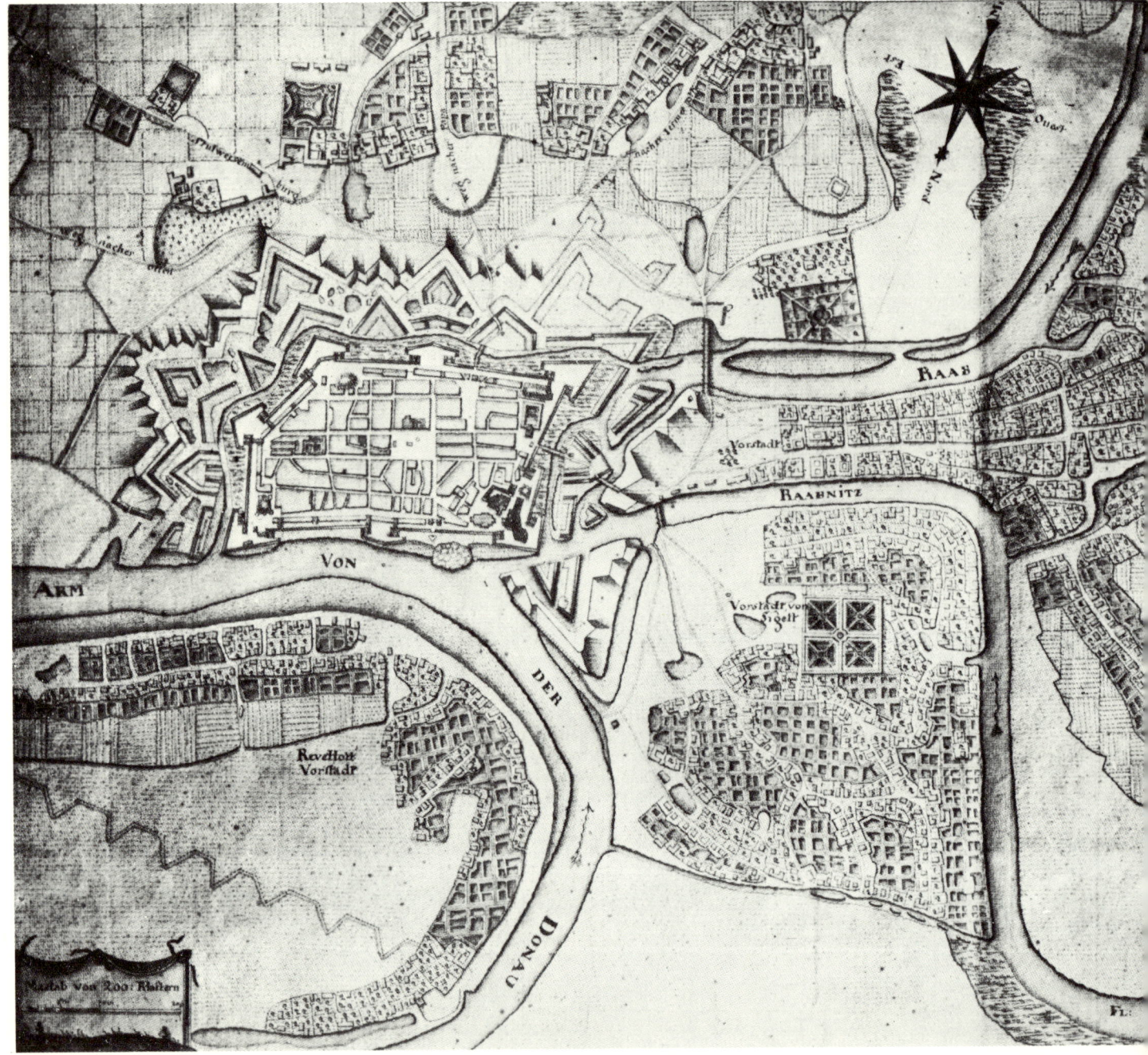

317. Map of Győr in 1740 showing the fortifications, the distribution of the building blocks, and the three rivers that separate the suburbs from the core area.

paired. In 1720 the town had 7,200 inhabitants, not counting the nobles; by 1780 Győr had from 11,000 to 12,000 citizens; of the wage-earners, artisans formed 12.5 percent, traders 2.5 percent, and occasional workers 16 percent.

Gradually, during the 18th century, the districts deserted in the Middle Ages were resettled. After the occupation of Győr by Napoleon in 1809, it was apparent that the fortifications of the 16th century were out of date. Their demolition, decided on in 1810, permitted the inner town and the suburbs to grow together. The new scheme, developed

318. Baroque houses, showing some of the stylistic features characteristic of Győr at this time: The Ott House (foreground), built in the middle of the 18th century, has pilasters from the second floor to the cornice; the corner house has an oriel, an architectural element also to be found on row houses.

319. An old street in Győr leading to the Chapter Hill, connecting the citadel with the former Danube Gate. The houses, some of them adorned with oriels, belonged to the Chapter of Győr. In front, in the center of a small square, the Arc of the Covenant (1731), one of the most beautiful Baroque monuments in Transdanubia.

320. Széchenyi Square, the main square at Győr, in 1845. On the right, the Benedictine Church erected by the Jesuits, with the Benedictine school. In the center, on the opposite side of the square, the palace of the Archabbot of Pannonhalma, the Benedictine abbey founded by St. Stephen, about 11 miles southeast of Győr. The chief abbot, holding the rank of a bishop, used this palace as his town residence. At the far end of the square, a Virgin Mary Column in front of the so-called Lloyd House, a modern building disrupting the unity of the Baroque appearance of the square. Colored drawing by Anton Fruhmann.

on a gridiron plan, was too large for the current demand; the districts to the west of the old town were therefore settled only very slowly, with one-storied or two-storied houses. While the housing density increased around the year 1800, the number of houses decreased from 1,490 to 1,327 between 1787 and 1828 because of an amalgamation of building plots, larger houses replacing several smaller ones, and the enlargement of existing dwellings.

In the second half of the 19th century, the corn trade dominated the economic life of Győr. The first factories were founded, and in 1850 the railway line from Vienna to Komárom, along the right bank of the Danube, was constructed, passing between the inner town of Győr and Nádorváros. With the modernization of communications the industrialization of Győr gained momentum. After 1900, large manufacturing enterprises had grown up to the east of the town, giving rise to a new industrial suburb.

Pápa, Veszprém. Pápa, a small town in Transdanubia, is situated at the border between the Bakony Forest and the plain, on the Tapolca River.[2] The town originated in two early settlements on a pond, the "broad water" formed by the river and used as early as the 13th century for the numerous mills in and near the town, giving rise to a lively home industry. In 1398 Pápa was already known as a *civitas*. Its central situation, the well-populated hinterland, and the relatively short distance to larger cities such as Győr and Veszprém furthered local industry and commerce so that Pápa enjoyed its first prosperity by the end of the 15th century. A castle was built inside the town, a market square was laid out in front of the castle gate, and a church was erected. The town, surrounded by a wooden fence, grew up around this nucleus. A few dairy farms remained outside the walls. In 1488 Pápa had about 2,900 inhabitants, a figure that decreased during the Turkish wars of the 16th century to 194 tax-paying hearths in 1531 and to 66 in 1566. As a precaution, the town was fortified with palisades and earthworks and garrisoned by 920 hussars as a strongpoint in the frontier defense against the Turks. Wars impoverished the place and slowed down its development in the 18th century. In 1734 there were 21 guilds paying taxes to the parish.

The second period of prosperity was connected with the rise of small industries in the 19th century. There were 70 furriers, 20 shoemakers, 120 fullers, 80 tanners, and 10 clockmakers, with hundreds of journeymen. However, since the railway was late in coming to Pápa, the small industries suffered a decline, causing an exodus of workers which the town tried to stem by establishing new factories. Nevertheless, Pápa was lagging behind the industrial development of other towns. In 1900, it had 17,000 inhabitants, which has risen to 25,000 today.

Although medieval Pápa was destroyed during the Turkish occupation, it retained its original structure. In the 18th century the town was rebuilt, introducing the simple forms of the Hungarian Baroque. The main square, one of the largest in Hungary, is dominated by the church and surrounded by one-storied houses, an arrangement similar to the layout of the main squares in Hungarian villages. In general, the wide streets and low buildings of Pápa create a horizontality characteristic of Hungarian towns.

2. L. Gerő. Baugeschichtliche Analyse einer Ungarischen Kleinstadt -Pápa," *Kwartalnik Architektury i Urbanistyki*, Vol. V, No. 3, Warsaw, 1960, pp. 309–20.

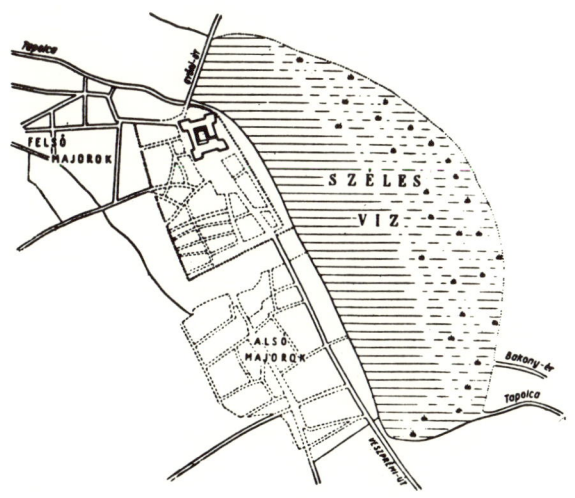

321. Pápa at the end of the 15th century. The castle of the Upper Town is surrounded by walls. The two settlements, the Upper and the Lower Town, belonging to the families of Garai and Pápai respectively and clearly separated during earlier periods, have grown together, forming the town of Pápa. To the right of the built-up area extends the "broad water."

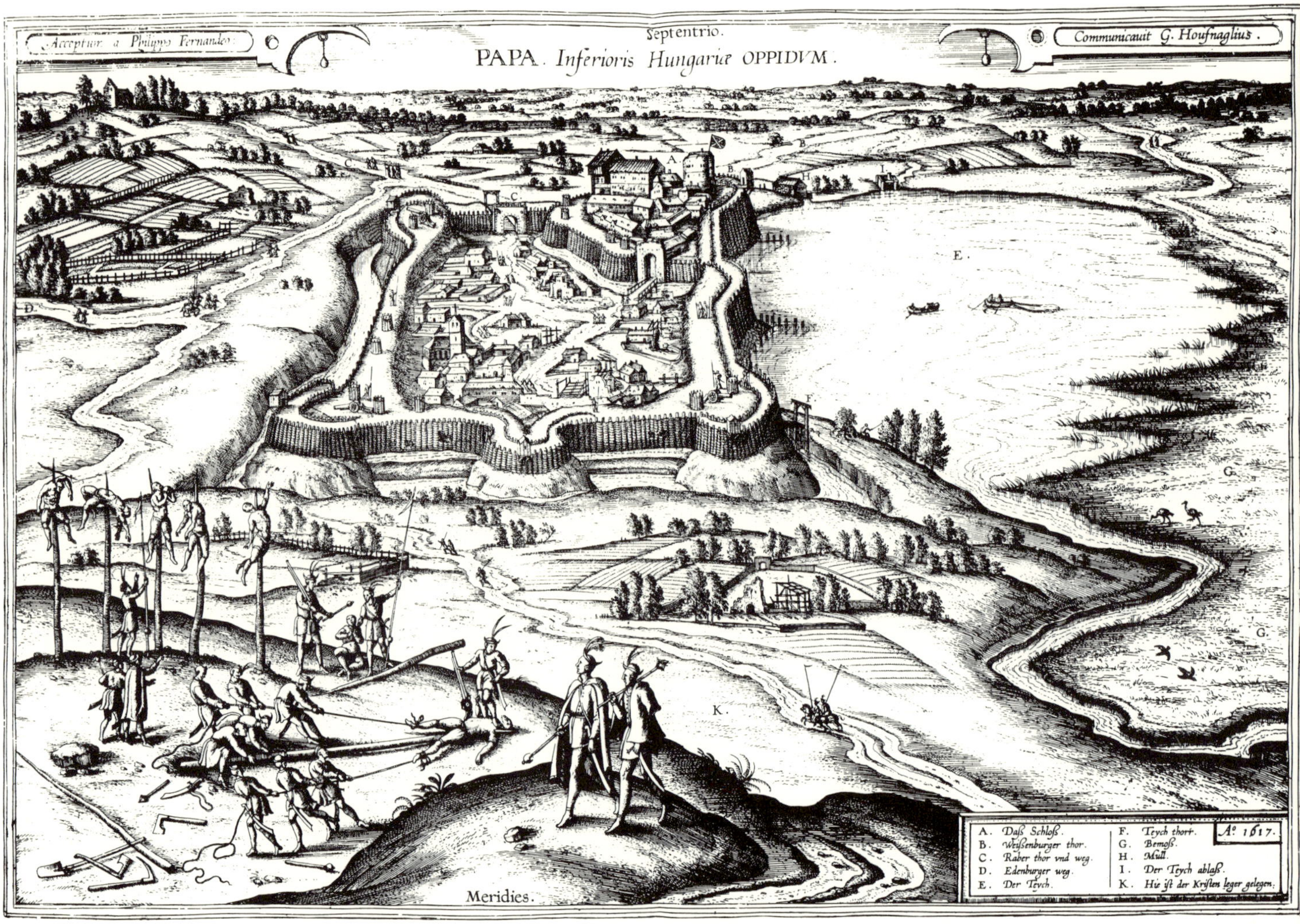

322. View of Pápa at the beginning of the 17th century. The castle (A) is situated in the Upper Town. The Raab or Győr Gate (C), leading to the road to Győr, can be seen in the rear wall of the Lower Town. On the right, extends the pond or "broad water." A mill (H) is visible at the far end of the pond near the wall and the Weissenburg Gate (B). Engraving from Georg Braun and Franz Hogenberg's *Civitates Orbis Terrarum*, 1618.

323. Painting of the Main Square at Pápa, with an idealized representation of the castle (left) at the end of the 18th century. The large square is dominated by the church and surrounded by low houses.

Szombathely (Steinamanger), Vas. As *colonia Claudia Sabaria*, the rank to which the former military station was elevated by the Emperor Claudius in A.D. 43, it was a flourishing center and the capital of Upper Pannonia for almost four centuries. In 1009, St. Stephen attached the town to the bishopric of Győr, and thereafter the small medieval settlement was subject to the lord bishops of that town. In records of the 13th century the place, strengthened with walls and strong towers, was mentioned as *Castrum Zombothel*. In 1407 the first privileges were granted to the town by the bishop of Győr; they resembled the rights enjoyed by the Royal Free Cities. A document of 1491, the peace treaty between the Emperor Maximilian I and the King of Hungary, contained, for the first time, the Latin and the German names of the town: *Castrum Sabaria vulgariter Stain am Anger*, whereto the author of the treaty added the rather fictitious explanation that when the knights of Charlemagne saw the Roman ruins, they exclaimed: "*Stein am Anger*"—stones at the *Anger* (village green). *Si non è vero, è ben trovato.*

It is unfortunate that no early representations of Szombathely have been preserved. The oldest illustration dates from 1749. Earlier records have been destroyed by fire, and those still extant refer only to the period after 1600, in a rather uninformative manner. We may conclude, however, that the bulk of the population was Hungarian and that only a few foreign artisans lived in the town in the 18th century. Industry and commerce were very modest since Szombathely was situated off the beaten track. After the plague of 1710 and 1711 had almost annihilated the population, killing about 2,000 people, an influx of German artisans and traders set in, leading in the last quarter of the century to tension between the German guilds and the Hungarian masters. A rise in the fortunes of the community followed the appointment of Bishop Johann Szily in 1777. At that time the population had grown to about 3,000. Soon after his arrival the bishop began the building of his residence (1778–1783) designed by Melchior Hefele, a pupil of the Würzburg school of architects. In 1791, the foundation stone of the cathedral was laid, and in 1793

324. Old view of Szombathely, about 1791. The episcopal residence (1), the cathedral (2), and the seminary, the Canonesses' House, (4) can be seen on the right; the county hall (6), the belfry (7), and the Franciscan monastery (8) are situated in the center.

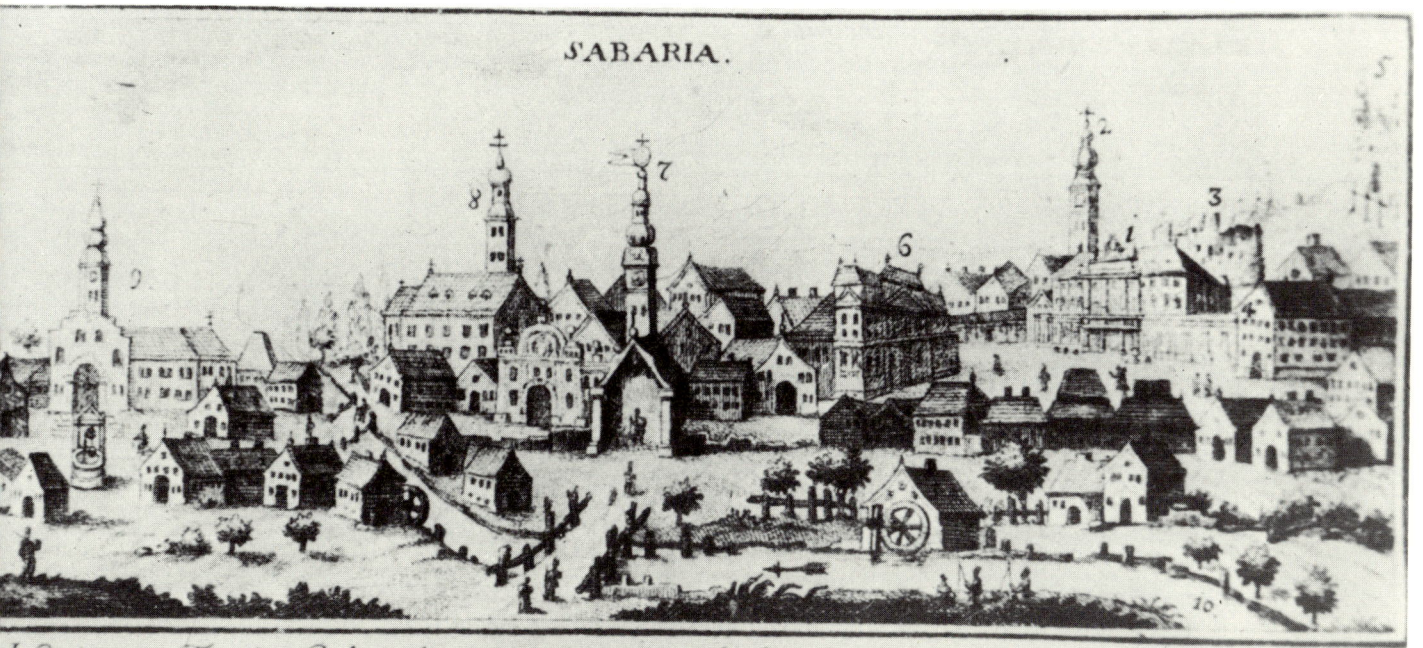

a seminary and a lyceum were erected; this construction was preceded by the establishment of printing works in 1788. At the same time, a number of private houses were built by Johann Georg Anreith. But, in general, the architectural character of Szombathely is unimpressive. It remained a small town, a late-comer, at the threshold of an era whose ideals and needs had hardly anything in common with the past.

The railway, opened in 1865, changed the economic picture. Industry and commerce revived. The population increased through a considerable immigration from 8,585 in 1857 to over 32,000 in 1910. Outlying communities were incorporated, and the built-up area expanded far beyond the original boundaries.

325. Airview of Szombathely with the cathedral in the foreground, the girls' college (lyceum) on the left, and the Episcopal Palace (1779–1783) on the right.

Esztergom (Gran), Komárom. Esztergom, situated on the right bank of the Danube, at the northern end of the Vörösvár Valley and the western spur of the Pilis Mountains, was the birthplace of St. Stephen and the residence of the Árpád kings and of the primate of the Catholic Church.[3] It was an important economic center until its destruction in the Mongol invasions. After the town was rebuilt by Béla IV (1235–1270), it recovered from the disaster and experienced a renewed prosperity.

It seems that the *Salva* of the Roman period was a Celtic tribal center. The Roman *castrum* was probably situated on the periphery of the present *Wasserstadt, Viziváros*, the archiepiscopal town. In A.D. 367 the fortifications were renewed, and a few years later a trading settlement, a *commercium*, was added. It would appear that Roman *Salva* consisted of a number of settlements, like the town of the Middle Ages. The Roman *castrum* may have existed until the first decades of the fifth century A.D. and perhaps for a short time afterward as a small Roman settlement. Before the arrival of the Hungarians, the site was occupied by a Slavonic people and called *Strigonium*. Its German name, Gran, was derived from the river Gran, *Garam*, which may have joined the Danube in this early period several miles more to the west than today.

The Árpád kings chose the Castle Hill as their principal residence. A suburb developed at its foot, probably at the beginning of the 11th century, whose inhabitants were artisan-bondsmen of the king and the Church and presumably also included members of the garrison of the castle. This suburb may have con-

---

3. K. Schünemann. *Die Entstehung des Städtewesens in Südosteuropa.* 1929. Pp. 40–140, *passim.* An extensive bibliography is contained in the footnotes.
D. Dercsényi and L. Zolnay. *Esztergom.* 1956. *Passim.* (In Hungarian).

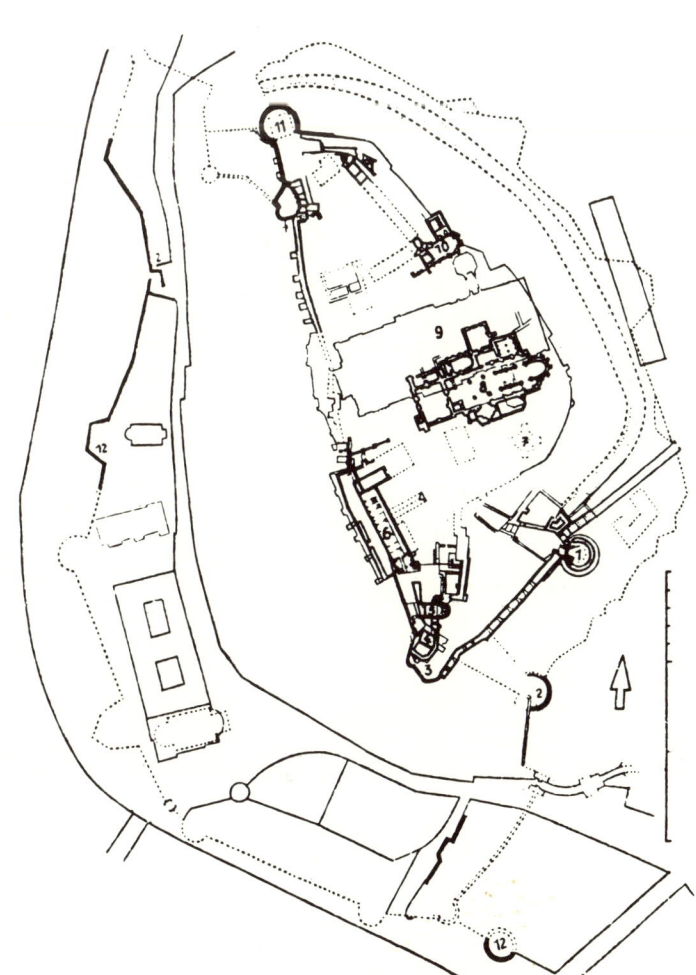

326. Plan of Esztergom, showing the citadel, the ground plans of some of its medieval buildings, and the course of the town walls. 1. Main Gate of the fortress with bulwark; 2. Post Gate with circular bastion; 3. Leopold Bastion; 4. Fortress tower, a residential tower or *Wohnturm*, and a castle from the Árpád period; 5. Fortress chapel; 6. Casemates; 7. The Roman *castrum*; 8. Medieval plan of the basilica of St. Adalbert; 9. Outline of the enlarged basilica; 10. Church of the martyr St. Stephen; 11. Danube Rondelle; 12. Town wall with bastions.

sisted of small groups of huts dispersed around the hill. This early place can hardly be described as a town; rather it was a royal enclave, a *Pfalz*, with the palace, the cathedral, and a few buildings belonging to it.

By the middle of the 12th century the character of the place had changed. Contemporary visitors speak of a trading center, a castle, and a town situated on the other bank of the Gran. Later, in 1189, Arnold of Lűbeck reports that the Emperor Frederick I, on his crusade, was received by the Hungarian king in Gran, the capital of Hungary, *Ungarorum metropolis*. The decisive factor in the development of an urban community was navigation on the Danube. All vessels using the waterway from Germany had to put in at Gran to pay the royal tribute, and this custom led gradually to the development of a staple-right from which the town derived considerable advantages.

The town of Gran was neither a systematic colonial foundation of the king nor the outgrowth of a rural settlement. The area within the town moat was not an organic unit. The land was owned by citizens and, to a large extent, by the cathedral chapter. The oldest elements of the settlement probably came into being in connection with a trade route from Southern Germany to Russia which followed the course of the Danube, crossing the river at Gran even before the Hungarian period. From the beginning of the 11th century, the place had a royal mint and probably a market. Soon merchants, presumably from Germany, began to settle on the territory of the market settlement. A church dedicated to St. Nicholas, the patron saint of sailors and merchants, was erected. To the north of this market place an even older village was situated, whose ownership was later claimed by the archbishop of Gran.

The actual formation of the town as an urban community can be traced back to the creation of the *vicus Latinorum*, the Latin quarter, in the second half of the 12th century. The official designation, still in use at the end of the 13th century, was *vicus Latinorum regalis civitatis Strigoniensis*, Strigonium being the Slavonic name of Gran before the the Hungarian occupation of the territory. In a topographical sense the *vicus* was

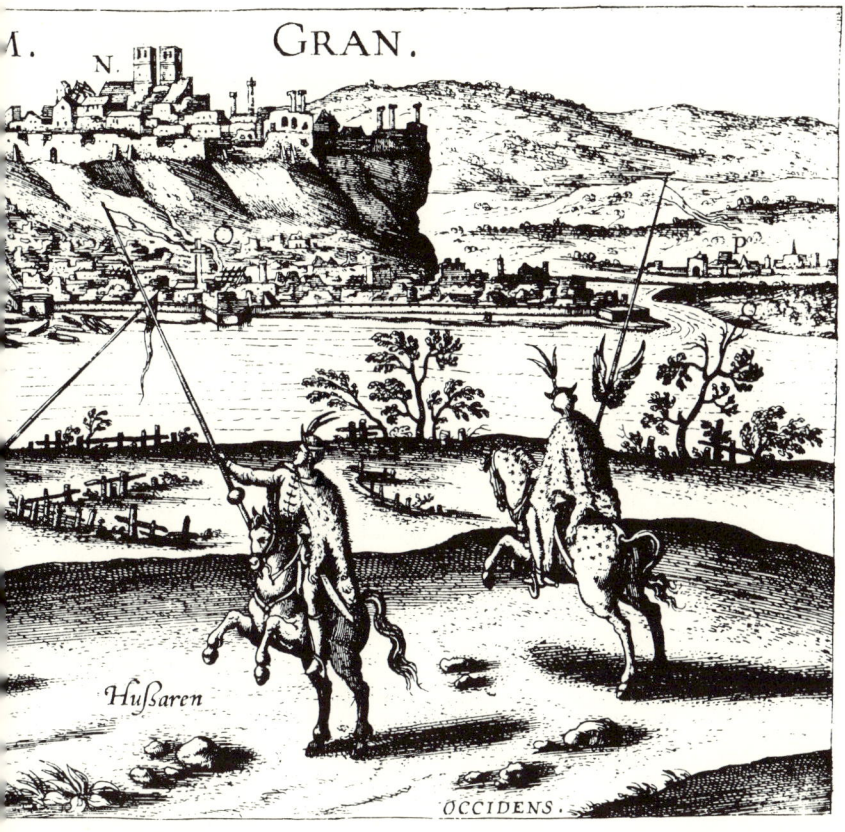

327. The castle of Esztergom on the castle hill, with the Vizivaros (Water Town), the archiepiscopal town below, in 1595. Confined on a small terrace between the castle hill, the Danube, and the Little Danube, the street system of the Vizivaros is oriented toward the river; two streets follow the course of the Danube, intersected by small lanes and side streets running toward the river. Engraving from Georg Braun and Franz Hogenberg's *Civitates Orbis Terrarum*, 1618.

one among several quarters of the town, but administratively it formed the town proper. Its town council represented the council of the whole town, just as the official abbreviated name *vicus Strigoniensis* referred to the whole Royal Town. The stone houses of the wealthy citizens were situated in the *vicus*, while the rest of the urban area, except for the banks of the Danube and the vicinity of the market, was occupied by simple timber houses. The inhabitants of the *vicus Latinorum*, the French-speaking citizens, were the leading social class not only politically but also economically. The few tradesmen, especially bakers and butchers, represented a minor group that could not compete with the merchants who invested their profits mostly in landed property, thus approaching the status of the nobility. The core of the *vicus Latinorum* was probably a market street running at a right angle to the river and parallel to the southern side of the market square. Its middle course was lined by storerooms, *camerae*, or *Kaufkammern*, which served for selling goods on the ground floor and storing them on the upper floor.

At the approach of the Turkish armies in 1543, almost the whole population left Gran, and the remaining garrison set the town on fire, thus ending the Royal Free Town of Gran. During the ten years of the Christian reconquest of this part of Hungary, from 1595 to 1605, the town remained deserted. An interesting account of Gran during the second phase of the Turkish occupation is contained in Ewliyā Čelebi's report of about 1665. He mentions a fortress near the former Royal Free Town, the Barutkhane-Palanka, that is, the powder-magazine palanka. According to Čelebi, it seems to have been square, with bastions at the four corners; however, a plan of 1767 shows a more rounded outline. Apparently it was just a small fort protecting the powder-magazine, with a circumference of about 600 paces. This interregnum is of interest insofar as it proves, in the words of Čelebi, that "at the time of the infidels a very large town called Érsekváros was said to have existed to the east of the fort, on the site now covered with vineyards."[4] In other words, the

4. Quoted after K. Schünemann, *op. cit.*, p. 43.

328. The Basilica or Cathedral of Esztergom (1822–1862) on the castle hill, 215 feet above the Danube. In the foreground, remnants of the old fortifications.

present Royal Town was a totally new foundation, dating from the time after the expulsion of the Turks.

Medieval Gran occupied the small area of about 123.5 acres. Since an extension was impossible because the whole surrounding territory outside the moat was owned by non-local people, the building density of Gran must have been relatively high. On the other hand, immigration of artisans and craftsmen in the 13th century was directed for the most part to the semi-urban settlements outside the moat, the majority of which were the property of the ecclesiastical authorities. The population of medieval Gran, around 1300, has been estimated at 12,000. This figure seems high for a place so restricted in its extension and should be taken with some reservation.[5]

5. *Ibid.*, p. 128.

Vác (Waitzen), Pest. Vác, on the left bank of the Danube where the river turns sharply south, is one of the oldest towns of Hungary.[6] The site has been occupied since Neolithic times, possibly by Celtic tribes followed by Romans, Slavs, Huns, Avars, and, finally, Hungarians. St. Stephen is said to have elevated the place to a bishopric. The first official record mentioning Vác is a charter of 1075. At that time and during the following centuries, municipal power was vested in the bishops; the inhabitants of the town, mostly traders and craftsmen, were subjects of the ecclesiastical lords. The center of Vác, with the cathedral and the episcopal residence, was surrounded by ramparts and a moat, while the buildings outside the walls were protected by hedges. This outer zone, including the church of St. Michael, developed after the Tartar invasion. South German immigrants at the time of Béla IV furthered industry, trade, and agriculture, thereby contributing greatly to the prosperity of the town. Hungarians and Germans lived in separate quarters; until the Turkish occupation the urban area was divided into a "Hungarian" and a "German" town.

6. I. Gál (ed.). *Ungarische Städtebilder.* 1944. Pp. 221–28.

Vác's dependence on the activities of the bishops made it an educational and cultural center. During the Middle Ages the bishops erected many public buildings, notably the cloisters, a hospital, and several churches, one of them outside the walls.

After the occupation of Buda by the Turks, Vác was ruled by Turkish authorities and turned into a frontier fortress for a century and a half. Mosques were erected, and the Koran was taught in Turkish schools. The Christian population withdrew to their own quarter, the Tabán, and engaged in viticulture. According to Ewliyā Čelebi's account, Vác had about 1,000 houses, 7 *djamis,* and 150 shops. Although these figures are somewhat inflated, Vác's situation on the Danube, one of the most important waterways in Europe, favored its economic development as a commercial center for the exchange of goods between Hungary and Turkey. The departure of the Turkish armies was followed by hard times, made even more oppressive by the policies of the Habsburgs. A few primitive huts and a few ruins were all that remained of the once flourishing town.

Although the Christian creeds were tolerated under Turkish rule, Catholics were always suspected of pro-Habsburg sympathies.

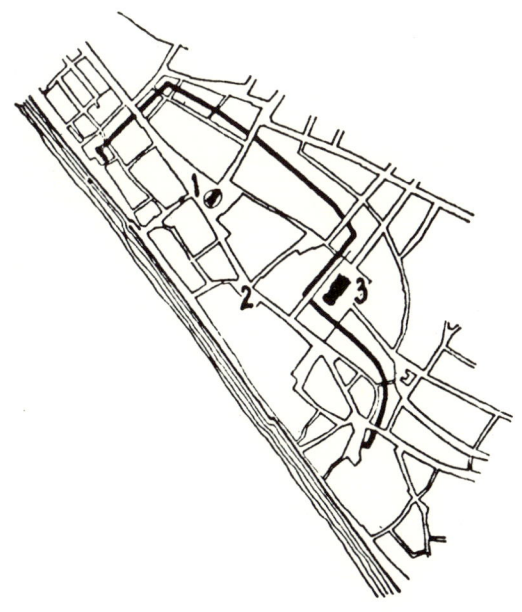

329. Plan of Vác at the beginning of the 18th century. 1. Fifteenth-of-March Square; 2. Holy Trinity Square; 3. Cathedral Square. The solid black line indicates the former walls of the castle.

Calvinists, on the other hand, were identified by the Austrians with Magyar nationalism. As the Reformation gained ground and a corrupt Church lost its hold over the people, Hungarian nobles, many of them Protestant, coveted the wealth of Catholic authorities, taking over their churches and other ecclesiastical buildings. With the expulsion of the Turks and the rise of the Counter Reformation, the situation changed. Extirpation of Protestantism became the objective. When the bishops returned to revive urban life, they demanded the restoration of all confiscated property. Protestants and their ministers were expelled from the town and were allowed to return only after a decree issued by Joseph II, in 1781; they settled in Little Vác, which is largely Protestant even today. The returned bishops initiated a lively building program. The cathedral begun by Károly Esterházy was

330. Vác in the 18th century. Engraving by János Fülöp Binder.

completed by Bishop Migazzi, who also erected the new episcopal palace, the town hall, a Piarist college, and a triumphal arch commemorating a visit of Maria Theresa to Vác. To further the regeneration of the town, the Austrian government, now mindful of its responsibility, sent Germans to Vác to repeople the place. They were settled in the lower town, while Hungarians occupied the upper town and Slovacs a district near the citadel. Under Maria Theresa the development of Vác continued. Farmers and wine-growers were installed, and several educational institutions were founded. This fruitful activity was cut short by the Emperor Joseph II, who discontinued all educational institutions and placed a garrison in the town, thus reducing it to the level of a village.

The proximity of the capital, improved river transportation, and the introduction of the railway in 1846 had the undesired effect of slowing down Vác's economic development. Commerce declined, since many of Vác's wealthier inhabitants preferred to travel to Budapest for their purchases. Though factories were erected along the route of the railway, Vác, at this time, displayed all the features characteristic of an episcopal see and a county town.

331. Airview of Vác. In the foreground, the episcopal cathedral built between 1761–1777.

Székesfehérvár (Stuhlweissenburg), Fejér. Székesfehérvár, one of the Hungarian towns which claim to be the oldest in the country,[7] stands in a marshy valley that connects the eastern plain with the Kisalföld in the west. It is unlikely that the site was settled by the Romans, though the marshes made it easily defensible. This advantage may have been a major factor in the decision of the Hungarian conquerors to establish their residence in this strategically favorable location. Privileges granted by St. Stephen in 1001 raised the place to the first Royal Free Town. These early privileges, together with later ones, became the basis of the municipal law, the *libertas Albanensis,* of many other Hungarian towns. The first written evidence of the town dates from 1002, in which the bishop of Veszprém referred to it as *Alba Regia.* The name Székesfehérvár indicates the importance of the town, *székes,* meaning the residence of the king, and *fehér,* white, something sublime, symbolizing the significance and nobility of the town. Hence, *Alba Regia,* the sublime Royal Town, which was to be the coronation and burial place of the kings from the 10th to the 16th century.

The site of the residence and the cathedral (begun about 1016), the so-called *castrum,* was enclosed by walls. In time—probably during the first half of the 12th century—this nucleus was surrounded by settlements on neighboring islands which rose above the marshes. The most important of these satellites was the *suburbium* of Buda, with several monasteries, the church of St. Nicholas, and a chapel of the cathedral chapter. Other suburbs were the "Island," the *insula,* the center of the Knights

7. J. Fitz. *Székesfehérvár.* 1957. (In Hungarian).

332. View of Székesfehérvár in 1601 which, though simplified, depicts the essential features of the place at this time. In the center, the actual town surrounded by walls, with the castle (C) in front. To the left and right of the urban area, the suburbs (D), (G), and (F). Bavarian and Austrian troops are encamped outside the palisades (bottom right), driving fleeing Turkish soldiers into the swamps that surround the town. A Turkish cemetery (R) can be seen in front of the Christian armies (right center). On the left (center), a road leads to Ofen (Buda). Engraving from the *Ortelius Chronicle,* published in 1665.

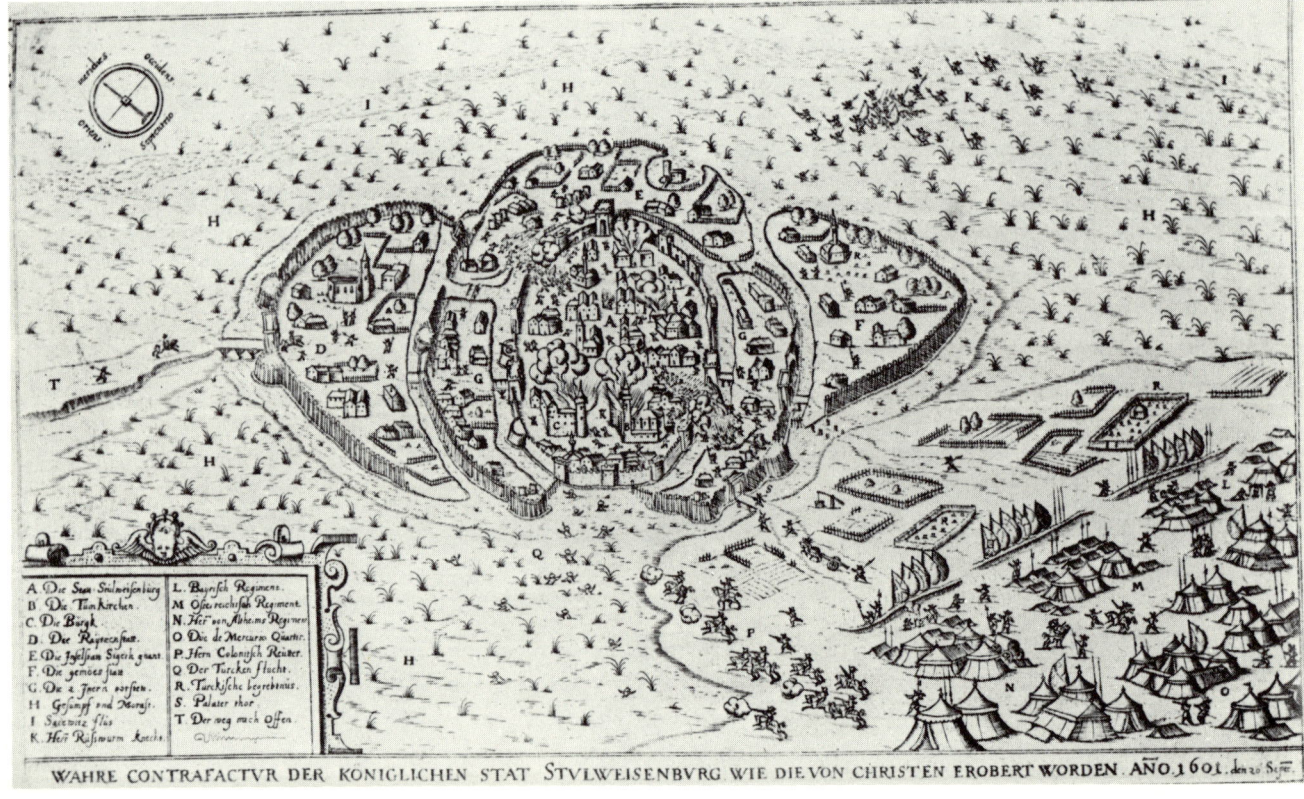

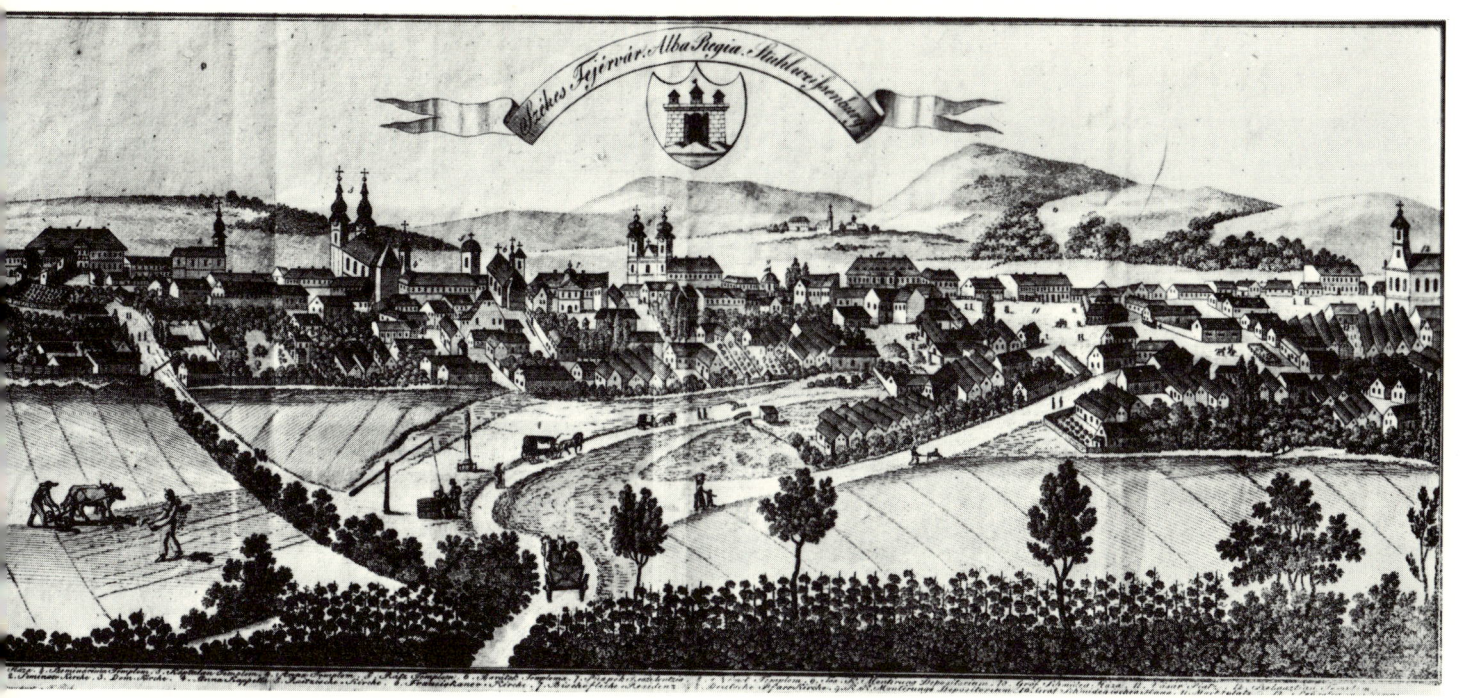

333. Székesfehérvár, about 1830. Engraving by Pick-Lenhardt.

Hospitallers of St. John (Johannite), and the *nova villa*, an agrarian settlement. Thus the structure of Székesfehérvár consisted of loosely integrated elements united by important roads from Győr, Esztergom, and Pest. The road from Pest joined the roads from Győr and Esztergom in the suburb of Buda, whence it continued in a westerly direction as a single street through the *castrum*, across the market square to the *insula*, where it branched off to the south and southwest and to the northwest toward Veszprém.

The inhabitants of the islands were at first the members of the royal court and bondsmen of the king; later, they were joined by other settlers, possibly servants of the royal household, and by the *latini*, immigrants of French origin who settled in the *suburbium*. After the Tartar invasion of 1241, the king strengthened his residence by settling the *latini* in the *castrum*.

Although urban jurisdiction was shared to some degree between the burghers and the heads of the main religious institutions, municipal power was firmly vested in the ecclesiastical authorities. The privileges granted by St. Stephen and later kings and the influx of the *latini* precluded the establishment of German municipal law which in some towns of Poland resulted in the displacement of the native population. As a Royal Free Town, and residence of the king, Székesfehérvár became a center of cultural life, of trade, and handicrafts. From 1001 to 1527 it was host to 29 diets.

The marshes, a protecting shield for the town in the early period, lost their importance in the 12th and 13th centuries. Székesfehérvár could not expand. Stagnation resulted, especially when the kings erected their palaces in Buda and visited the town less frequently. Toward the end of the Turkish occupation, that is, shortly before 1686, the *Regia Civitas*, including the palace, the basilica, other churches, and the fortifications, was ruined. All the royal tombs except one were destroyed and plundered. When the town was retaken in 1688, all that was left were 200 ruined houses, a few hundred inhabitants, 14 cows, and 13 horses.

Reconstruction had to begin with a repeopling of the town. Germans from Alsace-Lorraine and Austria and Slavs from the southern provinces of the Habsburg Empire were called in and settled among the greatly reduced Hungarian population. This second Székesfehérvár developed slowly as a Baroque town; numerous public and private buildings were erected in the following centuries.

The majority of the inhabitants of Székesfehérvár are descended from the settlers who arrived at the end of the 17th century. Old established families belong to the lower classes, which explains why there are no patricians in this ancient town.

334. Airview of the center of Székesfehérvár. On the right, the twin-towered cathedral. In the center, the Franciscan church and monastery. Behind it, the Episcopal Palace.

Veszprém, Veszprém. The origin of the upper fortified town of Veszprém dates back to the period of the Great Migrations, possibly to its foundation by the Avars. The Hungarians conquered it only after defeating a violent resistance by the occupants.[8]

The site was favorable for settlement, being situated between the Bakony Forest and Lake Balaton in a bend of the Séd, on a hill rising 120 feet above the river. On this hill the first settlement was formed in the eighth century. However, the area in the vicinity was inhabited since the Neolithic period, as numerous finds have revealed. A Roman station, *Balaca,* existed about 2.5 miles to the south of the present town.

The place received important privileges from St. Stephen and was made a bishopric in 1001. At the time of the Mongol invasions, numerous settlements had grown up in a semicircle around the nucleus on the hill. In 1313, Veszprém became the center of the Comitat, placed under the suzerainty of the bishop. The second half of the 15th century was an epoch of great prosperity for medieval Veszprém. During the Turkish wars the town changed hands ten times. When the invasions had ended, the once flourishing community was in ruins; only 38 houses in the lower town were still inhabited. Beszédkő, a small market settlement first mentioned in the 13th century, had developed outside the southern gate of the upper town. It was defended by a barbican with a strong tower.

With the 18th century, a peaceful period set in. The fortifications were dismantled. The damaged houses, churches, and other public buildings were repaired or replaced by new Baroque edifices. But when the bishop was appointed *comes* of the Comitat, Veszprém lost its character as a Royal Free Town. During the middle of the 18th century the double lordship of the bishop and the chapter began to be more oppressive, and the citizenry tried to regain their ancient rights and independence. However, their long-drawn-out struggle was not crowned with success until the second half of the 19th century.

Since the High Middle Ages, Veszprém had a large number of skilled artisans and traders, among them many millers, which made the town an important center of grain distribution during the Napoleonic Wars.

---

8. G. Korompay. *Veszprém.* 1957. (In Hungarian).

335. Airview of the center of Veszprém.

Debrecen, Hajdú-Bihar. Debrecen is situated on a sandy but fertile plain. Low wooded hills extend toward the east of the town while, in the west, the country slopes gently down to the Tisza.

The first official record referring to Debrecen as *villa Debrezun* dates from 1235.[9] Its subsequent rise in the 14th century was closely connected with the expansionist policies of the local feudal lord. As head of three Comitats, voivode of Siebenbűrgen, and palatine of Hungary, he controlled large domains, increasing his possessions, in part at least, through grants from the king. Thus, in the vicinity of Debrecen, seven villages and nine *puszták* came under the jurisdiction of the local manor. At this time, the place began to be built up and turned into a prosperous economic center for a large region. The local castle served also as court and seat for the Comitat meetings. Despite these developments Debrecen retained a rural character. It was not walled in and, therefore, lacked one of the prerequisites of medieval urban agglomerations.

The old layout is still discernible in the intricate network of narrow streets and alleys in the Upper Town. The roughly circular perimeter narrows toward the south. The street system is dominated by a north-south axis, crossed by the Hatvan[10] and the Csapó streets which divide the town into a northern and southern section. The slightly sloping terrain gave rise in the 15th century to an Upper and a Lower Town. The oldest part of Debrecen is situated in the Upper Town.

9. Karla Buse. *Stadt und Gemarkung Debrezin. Siedlungsraum von Bűrgern, Bauern und Hirten im ungarischen Tiefland.* Schriften des Geographischen Instituts der Universität Kiel. Vol. XI, No. 5. 1942.

10. The name means "Sixty," referring to 30 building plots on either side of the street. Ed.

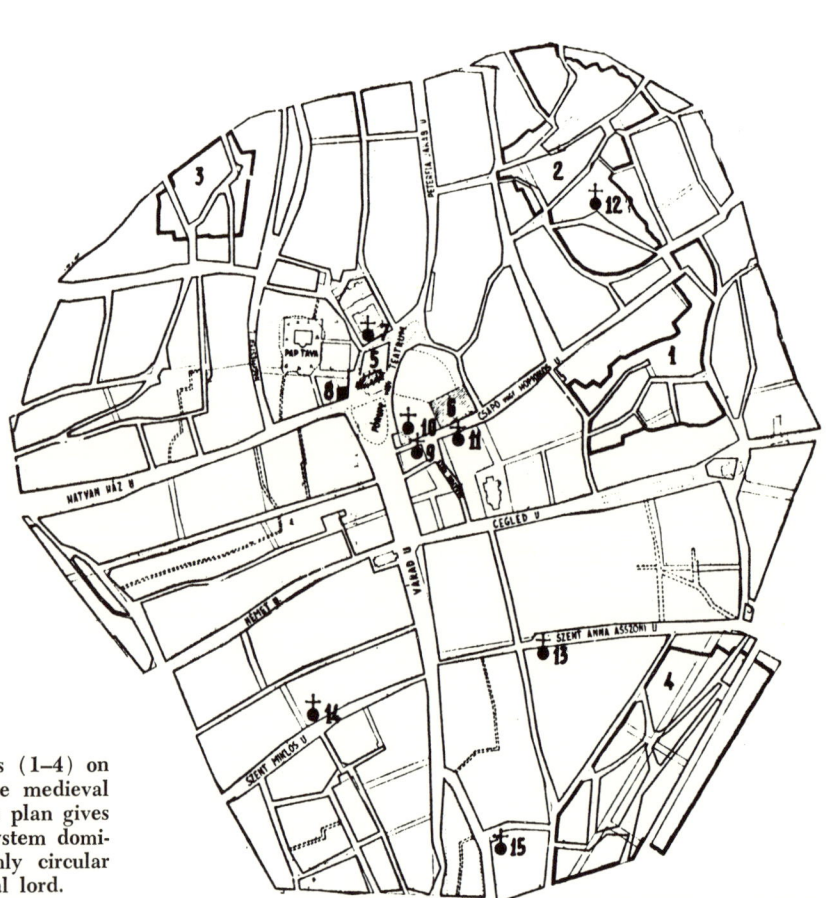

336. Plan of Debrecen, showing the early settlements (1–4) on the site of the present urban area, and some of the medieval buildings (6–15). Despite its diagrammatic form, the plan gives the basic elements of the urban structure: a street system dominated by a north-south axis contained within roughly circular boundaries. In the center, the castle (6) of the local lord.

The more open settlement structure is characteristic of the towns on the Alföld. Expansion of settlements on the Great Hungarian Plain was not impeded by natural obstacles. Moreover, absence of stones prevented the erection of confining walls, thus diminishing the contrast between urban area and open country. As a result, each inhabitant sought and acquired enough land for a house, sheds, primitive stables, and a garden. The plots were narrow and deep (about half an acre) and, extending behind the houses that lined a street, abutted the same kind of plots at the rear of the houses along the parallel street. These urban plots or gardens served chiefly as small orchards or vineyards, while each inhabitant—whether artisan, craftsman or trader—cultivated some land in the outlying regions and kept animals. Thus the population remained essentially peasant-burghers.

Eventually, around the middle of the 16th century, earthen ramparts with ditches and palisades were erected. In addition to four gates, small doors facilitated the daily pedestrian traffic to the fields. The urban core was surrounded by vineyards alternating with enclosures for cattle. Beyond this green belt extended the pastures, an area double the size of the actual settlement.

Animal husbandry was the main source of wealth. Cattle were exported to Augsburg and Nuremberg, pigs to Serbia and Bosnia, and horses to Siebenbűrgen and Galicia. Leather and woolen goods were sold, as well as honey and wine from the local vineyards. In the first half of the 14th century, artisans and craftsmen began to form guilds. There were tanners, furriers, fullers, carders, weavers, shoemakers, saddlers, and butchers, an array of trades based on animal husbandry.

Under Turkish rule, the influx of refugees from the surrounding areas caused a shift in the social structure. In the name of the Sultan, the Turkish invaders claimed the land they had conquered. The estates of the dispossessed feudal families were distributed to Turkish soldiers and officials, thus depriving the landowning patricians of their source of wealth. They left Debrecen for neighboring countries or, if they stayed, had to renounce their privileges and join the community as ordinary citizens. At the same time, refugees and former serfs settling in the town could, if able and ambitious, rise to the rank of burghers.

Although the Turkish wars interrupted Debrecen's development, it suffered less than other places. In fact, the town's thriving trade and relative wealth was a welcome source of income for the Turkish authorities. As early as the beginning of the 16th century, seven fairs were held annually. Thus, during the Turkish occupation, Debrecen turned into an important center for the exchange of goods between East and West, extending its economic ties far beyond the previous area.

The material progress was accompanied by a parallel rise in the intellectual sphere. The religious ferment of the time, reaching Debrecen through its east-west contacts, stimulated cultural activities. By the end of the 16th century, Calvinism had gained a firm foothold in the town. Its acceptance reflected the desire for independence in religious and political matters. The Kollegium, the college for students of law and theology founded by Franciscans in the early 16th century and taken over by Protestants in 1552, grew into a famous center of learning. Printing works were established at about the same time, providing eastern Hungary with Protestant and liberal literature. The "Rome of Calvinism," as Debrecen has been called, rose to a leading cultural position in the region of the Tisza.

However, the wars of the 17th century reduced the economic power of the town when Debrecen lost its position as a vital link in the trade between the Baltic and the Balkans. In addition, the restrictive policies of the Habsburgs suspended the town's trade with places outside the Austrian Empire. As a result, the majority of Debrecen's inhabitants reverted to agricultural activities.

With the extinction of the family of the only great landowner in 1618, Debrecen lost its last feudal inhabitant.[11] Because of this lack of feudal power in the 17th century, there are no great and ornate palaces and mansions. Moreover, the town's Calvinist population shunned the display of wealth and gave Debrecen an almost puritanical appearance. Or, as Robert Townson put it: "A deep Calvinist gloom pervades every thing."[12] Up to the 19th century, most houses had only one story, and even the town hall (1560) did not rise above the level of the surrounding buildings. In general, Debrecen's architecture remained that of a modest village-town whose livelihood was based on agriculture.

11. I. Balogh. *Debrecen.* 1958.
12. R. Townson. *Travels in Hungary with a Short Account of Vienna in the Year 1793.* 1797. P. 248.

337. Airview of Debrecen. In the center, the Piac utca runs into Kálvin-tér (Calvin Square), with the twin-towered Great Calvinist Church (1803–1818) or Nagytemplon. Behind the church, beyond the Emlék kert (Memorial Gardens) is the Kollegium.

338. The tree-lined Piac utca, with a double row of trees down its center, and the Great Calvinist Church at Debrecen. The generally low building line, even in the center of the town, is evident in this picture.

Dr. Richard Bright quotes a description of Debrecen given by Count Batthyány that may help to recapture the character and atmosphere of the town at the beginning of the 19th century.[13]

Singular as it may appear, scarcely any of the houses in this great city are above one story in height, and few are built on any regular plan. In summer you must wade through sand, and at other seasons through deep mud, even when you keep to the streets and public paths. The blank walls, the dark retail shops, the tobacco-pipe sellers, the smokers, and the dogs, the stillness which reigns in the midst of the daily business, and the earnestness which sits upon the countenance, all bring to mind a lively recollection of the dwellings of our Eastern neighbours. . . .

Dr. Bright then gives a list of trades and handicrafts carried on in Debrecen in 1807:

- 751 Hungarian shoemakers
- 12 German shoemakers
- 97 Hungarian slop tailors for supplying markets
- 50 Hungarian tailors
- 12 German tailors
- 104 Hungarian pelisse-makers or furriers
- 1 German do.
- 209 Cloakmakers
- 57 Great-coatmakers
- 25 Blanketmakers
- 6 Old clothes shops
- 12 German hatmakers
- 19 Hungarian hatmakers
- 37 Buttonmakers
- 6 Carriagemakers, Hungarians
- 186 Tanners
- 3 Snuffmakers
- 10 Curriers
- 4 Bead-ornament makers
- 58 Combmakers
- 1 Glover
- 2 Gold embroiderers
- 4 Beltmakers
- 41 Smiths, Hungarians
- 12 Cutlers
- 4 German smiths
- 1 Sword smith
- 1 Gunmaker
- 2 Knife-grinders
- 31 Locksmiths
- 1 Goldsmith
- 2 Coppersmiths
- 2 Tin-workers
- 4 Glaziers
- 2 Turners
- 2 German coachmakers
- 65 Hungarian wheelwrights
- 4 German wheelwrights
- 49 Saddlers
- 10 Weavers
- 1 Linen printer
- 5 Dyers
- 26 Master joiners
- 41 Master carpenters, Hungarian
- 5 Carpenters, Germans
- 6 Builders, Germans
- 1 Builder, Hungarian
- 40 Plasterers
- 15 Thatchers
- 1 Painter
- 15 Brick-burners
- 105 Potters
- 43 Turners of pipe ends
- 30 Coopers
- 24 Ropemakers
- 25 Oilmakers
- 78 Soap-boilers (besides mothers of families)
- 1 Piano-forte-maker
- 1 Sievemaker
- 1 Printer of books
- 10 Bookbinders
- 7 Barbers
- 4 Apothecaries
- 49 Butchers
- 19 Small butchers
- 84 Pork butchers
- 19 Dealers in honey
- 40 Millers
- 70 Bread bakers, women
- 16 Cake bakers, women
- 1 German baker
- 8 Kitchen gardeners
- 54 Bee-keepers
- 10 Dealers in hemp and tobacco
- 13 Ironmongers
- 3 German hucksters
- 2 Hungarian do.
- 90 Women selling fruit
- 40 Dealers in oxen and horses
- 76 Merchants and retail dealers
- 20 Cattle brokers

13. R. Bright. *Travels from Vienna through Lower Hungary.* 1818. Pp. 200 ff.

This list of trades is particularly revealing; it clearly shows that, with very few exceptions, all trades were intimately connected with the rural structure of this village-town.

For centuries Debrecen's boundaries remained almost unchanged while the building density of the urban area increased steadily. However, in the 1860s, when Debrecen's population had risen to 30,900, an extension in the northeast was finally carried out. Gradually, the size of the open spaces was reduced, not only in the center but also in the outlying areas, as new plots for additional buildings were required.

Nagykőrös, Pest. Nagykőrös is one of the towns of the Alföld which did not originate at road crossings or as market centers, but came into existence and maintained their initial character as settlements of cattle breeders, with a distinct social and economic organization.[14]

On the site of the present Nagykőrös, whose area comprises about 93,860 acres, several large camps were established in the 11th and 12th centuries. Nagykőrös was one of them, and its church was the religious center of five or six other camps. Because the territory was part of the royal domain, the inhabitants were not serfs of a feudal lord who owned the land and the settlements but were relatively independent, free to pursue their traditional pastoral activities and to preserve their social customs and the structure of their settlements within the wide framework of the royal estate.

Animal husbandry was the principal occupation of the settlers. Cultivation was of minor importance, to the extent that it hardly sufficed to supply their own needs. The camps consisted of loosely grouped round huts, with a baking oven in the center and corrals and stables between the huts. Excavations have shown that the culture of these people was still akin to the nomadic Hungarian traditions which they had brought with them from the East. The Mongol invasions (1241) destroyed the smaller camps, which were not restored after the end of the war. Their inhabitants concentrated in one larger and more compact camp around Nagykőrös. Consequently, the pastures were extended over the area of the abandoned camps, increasing the range of cattle-breeding. This did not change when the place was incorporated, in the 13th century, into the estate of a private landowner who, like his successors, was an absentee landlord and one of the wealthy magnates. The inhabitants continued their autonomy, paying merely taxes in money to the new feudal lord.

In records of the 15th century, Nagykőrös was mentioned as an *oppidum* and, always, as a community of cattle-breeders. At this time, the primitive huts of the early period had already been replaced by adobe houses, and the central oven by a tiled structure. The houses had retained their loose grouping, not lined

up along a street or around a square but irregularly arranged like tents in a camp. This inhabited area was surrounded by the girdle of corrals and stables. Implements for cultivation were still rare. However, the earlier affinity to the nomadic past was gradually disappearing. Nagykőrös had neither the character of a town, as we know it from the West, nor that of a settlement of serfs belonging to a feudal lord. It remained more or less an autonomous camp, deriving its livelihood from its traditional occupation of cattle-breeding on a vast territory.

In the Turkish wars many localities of the large hinterland were destroyed. Their inhabitants fled to Nagykőrös, and their fields and pastures were absorbed into its territory. As a result, Nagykőrös with about 5,000 citizens had, during the Turkish occupation, an area of 247,000 acres for its use. Far from decreasing, the importance of husbandry gained additional impetus through the war. Some people owned herds of several hundred heads of cattle. Cultivation was so insignificant that grain for the consumption of the population of Nagykőrös had to be imported from other districts. The Turkish authorities did not interfere with the autonomous position or the

---

14. I. Gál (ed.). *Ungarische Städtebilder.* 1944. Pp. 114–37.

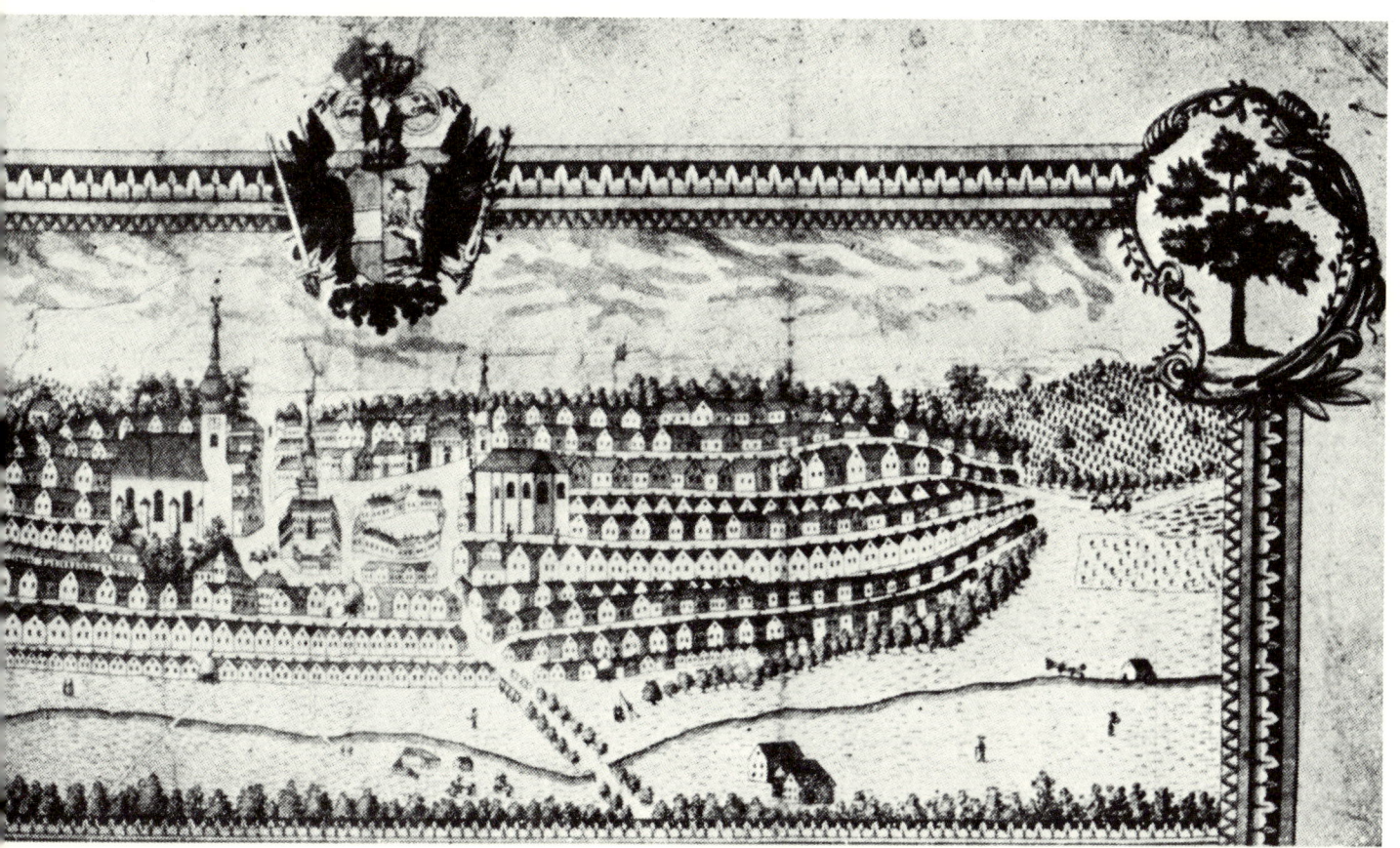

inner organization of the place but rather restricted their interests to levying considerable taxes.

Production methods and organization of labor were geared to animal husbandry, resulting in the so-called *kert*[15] system. It was based on the division of the inner settlement area into a zone of habitation—the closely grouped dwellings without outhouses between them—and the zone of the *kert*, that is, of the stables and other farm buildings serving the various activities of stockbreeding. This division dictated the whole economic order and mode of living. The center of life was the dwelling place, from which the other buildings were separated and located in accordance with their functional needs. The stables, where the implements were kept, fodder and fuel stored, and all the work needed for proper maintenance of the enterprise was carried out, were the hub of the working life. The fields belonging to the farmer were not concentrated in

339. View of Nagykőrös about 1800, from a guild charter. This stylized and simplified representation highlights some of the essential characteristics of a number of village-towns of the Great Alföld: horizontality and uniformity of low, simple buildings. The town rises like an island from the vast expanse of the plain. Single or row houses line a few long streets. Despite the size of its urban area, the town is rural in appearance. Only the center presents a zone with urban characteristics. Here, churches and public buildings rise above the one-story dwellings of the inhabitants, whose main income was based on agrarian activities and ancillary trades. An unusually large square, framed by churches, also serves as a marketplace.

---

15. The word *kert* is derived from *keríteni*, meaning to enclose. *Kerítés* is a fence or partition, something which encloses. Thus *kert* does not mean garden —as it sometimes has been mistakenly translated—but an area which surrounds or encloses the inner zone of habitation. Ed.

one piece but distributed over the whole cultivated area between the meadows and pastures. The area owned by one farmer, consisting of meadows, fields and pastures, was called *mezei kert,* field-garden, and may be regarded as the predecessor of the *tanya* system.

This system had nothing in common with the usual feudal structure of property rights. The right of the landed proprietor was merely a hypothetical ownership of the town, in recognition of which the inhabitants paid certain taxes. The social character of Nagykőrös may be defined as that of an agrarian organization based on the professional needs of a community of cattle-breeders. There were a few patrician families, but as a class, whether as a leading group or as an intellectual elite, they did not exert any influence during the Turkish occupation. However, toward the end of this era the social ascendancy of the nobility can be observed, and in the following period it was the nobility that played a decisive role.

After the end of Turkish rule, the Comitat resumed its operation, the landed proprietors renewed their claims, and the state tried to reintegrate the town in its organization. However, all these attempts did not fundamentally affect the autonomy of the community. Finally, Maria Theresa recognized the actual status of Nagykőrös and released the town from all its obligations. The noble families who resided in Nagykőrös aspired to have their property recognized as noblemen's estates and acquired additional land. As early as the beginning of the 18th century some of the old patrician families had become wealthy landowners, establishing themselves as the leading class of the local society and reducing the social status of the majority of the citizens to that of common peasants.

The rise of the middle class after 1848 and the resultant social changes put an end to the traditional organization of the community, while capitalism and economic development extinguished most remnants of the old way of life. Nagykőrös was absorbed into a widespread net of communications. The always insignificant trades, which had never developed a social order of their own, were superseded by industrial enterprises. By the middle of the 19th century the pastures had shrunk to about 29,640 acres and were divided among the citizens for cultivation. The *tanya* system was fully developed, and many *tanyák* became permanently inhabited farms. By the end of the 19th century winegrowing was carried on on a large scale. Despite these changes an urban middle class such as grew up in the cities and towns of the West did not form in Nagykőrös. The majority of the inhabitants were farmers with smaller and larger properties, and a minority were artisans and tradesmen. At the beginning of the 20th century, the town was surrounded by about 400 vegetable gardens, mostly owned by part-time vegetable gardners.

The outer areas, girdling the inner quarters of the town with its tortuous and narrow streets, were inhabited by two different classes of people. The district where the lower classes lived—the small shopkeepers, artisans, middlemen, and hawkers—was called Felszeg; the other district, the Alszeg, was the quieter residential quarter of farmers with large homesteads and *tanya* owners whose sons lived and worked on the *tanyák*. Their houses had only small yards, just sufficient to accommodate visitors from the *tanyák* with their vehicles and horses overnight.

The center of the town is occupied by an enormous square around which the churches are grouped, the public buildings, hotels and restaurants, a theater, and shops. There are no other churches either in the inner or outer zone of the *tanyák*. This "city" is encompassed by the residential quarters of the well-to-do population. All roads traversing the zone of the *tanyák* converge radially on the town, each arterial road receiving the smaller streets from the adjoining districts and, passing through the girdle of the vineyards, connecting the outlying *tanyák* with the large market square.

Acknowledgments for Illustrations

4. Photo: Archaeological Museum, Warsaw.
5. After W. Hołubowicz. *Opole w wiekach X-XIII.* Katowice. 1956.
7. After T. Wieczorkowski. *Z przeszłości Szczecina.* Wrocław-Warsaw-Cracow. 1964.
8, 28. After H. Münch. *Geneza rozplanowania miast wielkopolskich XIII i XIV wieku.* Cracow. 1946.
10. Photo: T. Hermańczyk.
11, 13, 19. After J. Pudełko. "Działka lokacyjna w strukturze przestrzennej średniowiecznych miast śląskich XIII wieku," *Kwartalnik Architektury i Urbanistyki,* No. 2, 1964.
12. After J. Pudełko. "Uwagi o niektórych zagadnieniach rozplanowania miast średniowiecznych w świetle studiów nad układem Środy Śląskiej," *Kwartalnik Architektury i Urbanistyki,* No. 1, 1962.
14. Photo: Plan und Karte, Műnster (Westf.).
15. After J. Pudełko. "Próba pomiarowej metody badania planów niektórych miast średniowiecznych w oparciu o zagadnienia działki," *Kwartalnik Architektury i Urbanistyki,* No. 1, 1964; and R. Stein. *Der Grosse Ring zu Breslau.* Breslau. 1935.
17. After W. Grabski. "Wybrane zagadnienia z urbanistyki średniowiecznego Krakowa," *Biuletyn Krakowski,* 1961.
18. After S. Żaryn. "Kamienica warszawska w XV i XVI wieku," *Kwartalnik Architektury i Urbanistyki,* No. 2, 1963.
24. After O. Kloeppel. *Das Stadtbild von Danzig in den drei Jahrhunderten seiner grossen Geschichte.* Danzig. 1937; and J. Stankiewicz. "Średniowieczne fortyfikacje Głownego Miasta w Gdańsku," *Studia i Materiały do Historii Wojskowości,* 1958.
25. After M. Rendschmidt. *Das alte Elbinger Bürgerhaus.* Elbing. 1933.
26. After E. J. Siedler. *Märkischer Städtebau im Mittelalter.* Berlin. 1914.
27. After W. Puget-Tomicka. "Kościół i klasztor panien bernardynek w Wieluniu," *Kwartalnik Architektury i Urbanistyki,* No. 1, 1963.
32. Photo: A. W. Birker.
34. After Z. Zieliński. "Rozwój terytorialny miasta oraz zabudowy Starego Rynku w Poznaniu," *Przegląd Zachodni,* Nos. 6-8, 1953.
36. After M. Benko. "Kilka uwag o zabytkowych domach podcieniowych w Stanisławowie i Latowiczu," *Ochrona Zabytków,* No. 4, 1955.
37. After F. Kotula. "Głowów, renesansowe miasteczko," *Biuletyn Historii Sztuki,* No. 1, 1954.
39, 43. After T. Zarębska. "O związkach urbanistyki węgierskiej i polskiej w drugiej połowie XVI wieku," *Kwartalnik Architektury i Urbanistyki,* No. 4, 1964.
40, 44, 45, 47. After W. Kalinowski. "Miasta polskie w XVI i pierwszej połowie XVII wieku," *Kwartalnik Architektury i Urbanistyki,* Nos. 3-4, 1963.
42. Photo: W. Kalinowski.
49. Photo: R. S. Watowski.
52. After J. Stankiewicz. *Strakowscy—fortyfikatorzy, architekci i budowniczowie gdańsey.* Gdańsk. 1955.
53. After G. Ciołek. *Ogrody polskie.* Warsaw. 1954.
58. After F. I. Tłoczek. *Rolnicze miasteczka w Wielkopolsce.* Warsaw. 1955.
59. After S. Zieleśkiewicz. "Rakoniewice—miasto rzemieślników," *Ochrona Zabytków,* No. 2, 1954.
60. After A. Liczbiński. "Góra Kalwaria," *Kwartalnik Architektury i Urbanistyki,* Nos. 3-4, 1957.
62, 70, 73-75. After T. P. Szafer. "Ze studiów nad planowaniem miast w Polsce XVIII i pocz. XIX w.," *Studia z historii budowy miast,* Warsaw, 1955.
63. After W. Trzebiński. *Działalność urbanistyczna magnatów i szlachty w Polsce XVIII w.* Warsaw. 1962.
64. After Z. Bieniecki. "Oś barokowa Warszawy," *Kwartalnik Architektury i Urbanistyki,* No. 4, 1960.
67. After L. Preibisz. *Zamek i klucz rydzyński.* Rydzyna. 1938.
68. After J. Glinka. "Plan Białegostoku w końcu XVIII stulecia," *Studia z historii budowy miast,* Warsaw, 1955.
76. After W. Kalinowski. "Rozbudowa Radomia w latach 1815-1830," *Studia z historii budowy miast,* Warsaw, 1955.
79. After O. Flatt. *Opis miasta Łodzi.* Warsaw. 1853.
83. After E. Szwankowski. "Kubickiego plan regulacji Pragi," *Biuletyn Historii Sztuki i Kultury,* No. 2, 1948.
88. After E. and J. Neustupný. *Czechoslovakia before the Slavs.* 1961. Published by Thames and Hudson Ltd., London, and Praeger Publishers Inc., U.S.A. Courtesy Thames and Hudson Ltd., London.
89, 90. After J. Filip. *Celtic Civilization and Its Heritage.* Prague. 1959.
91. After J. Poulík. *The Great Moravian Walled-in Settlement of Mikulčice.* Brno. 1962.
92. Courtesy of the Archives of the Prague Castle.

The following illustrations have been contributed by the Archives of the Státní ústav památkové péče a ochrany přírody, Prague: 93, 107, 112, 114, 115, 151, 166, 174, 180, 187, 190, 205, 207, 212, 218, 220, 229, 240, 252, 254.

94-97. Photo: E. Vasiliak.
99, 100. Photo: E. Vasiliak.
101. Photo: K. Plicka, Státní ústav památkové péče a ochrany přírody, Prague.
103, 105, 106. Photo: E. Vasiliak.
108. Photo: E. Vasiliak.
109. Photo: O. Hilmerová, Státní ústav památkové péče a ochrany přírody, Prague.
113, 117, 120. Photo: E. Vasiliak.
116. Photo: V. Uher, Státní ústav pro rekonstrukci památkových měst a objektů, Prague.
118. Photo: K. Vronský, Katedra teorie a vývoje architektury

Českého vysokého učení technického v Praze.
119. Photo: Archives of the Státní ústav pro rekonstrukci památkových měst a objektů, Prague.

The following photographs by V. Uher have been contributed by the Státní ústav pro rekonstrukci památkových měst a objektů, Prague: 122–124, 127, 141, 142, 165, 208, 222, 224.

125, 177. Photo: S. Voděra, Katedra teorie a vývoje architektury Českého vysokého učení technického v Praze.
129. Photo: Archives of the Výzkumný ústav teórie a dejín architektury Slovenskej vysokej školy technickej, Bratislava.
134. Photo: Archives of the Slovenský ústav pamiatkovej starostlivosti a ochrany prírody, Bratislava.

The following photographs by K. Vronský have been contributed by the Katedra teorie a vývoje architektury Českého vysokého učení technického v Praze: 138, 143, 154, 175, 198, 236, 238, 242, 247, 248, 253, 257, 263.

148, 192–194. Photo: V. Hyhlík, Státní ústav památkové péče a ochrany přírody, Prague.

162, 200, 202. Photo: J. Kanka, Výzkumný ústav teórie a dejín architektury Slovenskej vysokej školy technickej, Bratislava.
169, 223. Photo: Č. Šíla, Státní ústav památkové péče a ochrany přírody, Prague.
181. Photo: S. Divišová, Státní ústav památkové péče a ochrany přírody, Prague.
189. Photo: H. Hubáček, Výzkumný ústav pro výstavbu a architekturu, Prague.
215, 231. Photo: E. Vasiliak.

The following plans were reproduced by Vlasta Hoštová: 128, 130, 133, 139, 144, 146, 149, 152, 153, 156, 161, 163, 167, 168, 170, 178, 179, 182, 185, 186, 188, 191, 197, 199, 201, 203, 206, 211, 213, 214, 217, 219, 221, 227, 228, 230, 234, 237, 239, 241, 243, 245, 246, 250, 251, 255, 256, 259, 261, 262, 264, 268.

270, 271, 294. Courtesy Hungarian Embassy, London.
274. After K. G. Stephani. *Der älteste deutsche Wohnbau und seine Einrichtung.* Vol. I. 1902.
279. After A. Pleidell.

Courtesy Hungarian Academy of Sciences, Budapest: 282, 287, 288, 295, 301, 308, 309, 310, 318, 319, 320, 325, 326, 330, 333, 334, 337.

283. Reconstruction by F. Rómer.
285. After L. Gerő.
286. Courtesy Budapesti Történeti Múzeum.
289–291. After D. Dercsényi.

Courtesy Technical University of Budapest. Department of City Planning: 292, 312, 324, 331, 332, 335, 338.

Photo: R. Járai, Interfoto MTI, Budapest: 293, 296, 297, 298, 302, 311, 325, 328, 331.

323. Interfoto MTI, Budapest.
299, 336. After I. Balogh. *Debrecen.* 1958. Courtesy Képzőművészeti Alap Kiadóvállalata, Budapest.
300. After L. Gerő.
304, 306. Courtesy Bildarchiv der Österreichischen Nationalbibliothek, Vienna.
316. Courtesy New York Public Library, New York.
317. Courtesy Xántus János Múzeum, Győr.
321. After L. Gerő. "Baugeschichtliche Analyse einer ungarischen Kleinstadt — Pápa," *Kwartalnik Architektury i Urbanistyki,* Vol. V, No. 3, 1960. Courtesy Kwartalnik Architektury i Urbanistyki, Warsaw.
329. After D. Dercsényi.

Bibliography

POLAND

ABBREVIATIONS

BHS — *Biuletyn Historii Sztuki.* Warsaw.
BHSiK — *Biuletyn Historii Sztuki i Kultury.* Warsaw.
IUA — Instytut Urbanistyki i Architektury. Warsaw.
KAU — *Kwartalnik Architektury i Urbanistyki.* Warsaw.
PAN — Polska Akademia Nauk. Warsaw.
PAU — Polska Akademia Umiejętności. Cracow.
SHBM — *Studia z Historii Budowy Miast. Prace IUA.* Warsaw.
SHBMP — *Studia z Historii Budowy Miast Polskich. Prace IUA.* Warsaw.

CHAPTERS 2 AND 3

Aubin, H. "The Lands east of the Elbe and German Colonisation eastwards." In: *The Cambridge Economic History of Europe.* Vol. I. 1942.

Baedeker, K. *Nord-Ost-Deutschland.* 1889.

Bailly, Rosa. "Une vieille Cité Européenne. Esquisse de l'Évolution de Cracovie," *La Vie Urbaine,* 1932.

Baliński, M., and T. Lipiński, *Starożytna Polska pod względem historycznym, jeograficznym i statystycznym opisana* [Historical, Geographical and Statistical Description of Old Poland]. 2 vols. 1843–46.

Balzer, O. "Chronologia najstarszych kształtów wsi słowiańskiej i polskiej" [Chronology of the Oldest Types of Slavic and Polish Villages], *Kwartalnik Historyczny,* Vol. XXI, Nos. 3/4, 1910.

Bartolomäus, R. "Deutsche Einwanderung in Polen im Mittelalter," *Preussische Jahrbücher,* Vol. 86, 1896.

Brackmann, A. "Die Anfänge des polnischen Staates," *Sitzungsberichte der Preussischen Akademie der Wissenschaften,* Phil.-Hist. Class, No. XXIX, 1934.

Brandt, B. "Beobachtungen und Studien über die Siedlungen in Weissrussland," *Zeitschrift der Gesellschaft für Erdkunde,* 1918–19.

Bruce-Boswell, A. "Poland, 1050–1303." In: *The Cambridge Medieval History,* Vol. VI. 1929.

———. "Poland and Lithuania in the Fourteenth and Fifteenth Centuries." In: *The Cambridge Medieval History.* Vol. VIII. 1936 and 1959.

Buchwald, G. von. "Der Ursprung des Rundlings," *Globus,* Vol. 79, No. 19, 1901.

Buczek, K. *Ziemie polskie przed tysiącem lat* [Polish Lands a Thousand Years Ago]. 1960.

Bujak, F. "Studya nad osadnictwem Małopolski" [A Study of the Colonization of Little Poland], *Rozprawy Akademii Umiejętności,* Hist.-Phil. Class, Ser. 2, Vol. 47, 1905.

Burszta, J. *Od osady słowiańskiej do wsi współczesnej. O tworzeniu się krajobrazu osadniczego ziem polskich i rozplanowań wsi* [From the Slav Settlement to Today's Village. Formation of the Polish Settlement Landscape and of Village Forms]. 1958.

The Cambridge Economic History of Europe. Vol. I. 1966.

The Cambridge History of Poland. Ed. by W. F. Reddaway and others. 2 vols. 1941–50.

The Cambridge Medieval History. Vol. VII. 1958.

Codex diplomaticus maioris Poloniae. Vol. I. 1877.

Derzhavin, N. S. *Die Slaven im Altertum.* (German translation of the Russian *Slaviane v drevnosti*). 1946.

Dobrowolska, M. "The Morphogenesis of the Agrarian Landscape of Southern Poland," *Geografiska Annaler,* Vol. XLIII, Nos. 1–2, 1961.

Dziewoński, K. "Entwicklungsprobleme der frühmittelalterlichen Städte in Polen." In: *Städtebau. Geschichte und Gegenwart.* Ed. by G. Strauss, published by the Deutsche Bauakademie, Berlin. 1956.

———. "L'évolution des plans et de l'ordonnance des villes du Haute Moyen Âge en Pologne." In: P. Francastel (ed.). *Les Origines des Villes Polonaises.* 1960.

———. "The Plan of Cracow: Its Origin, Design and Evolution," *The Town Planning Review,* Vol. XIX, 1943–47.

Ehrenkreutz, S. *Beiträge zur sozialen Geschichte Polens im XIII Jahrhundert.* Warsaw. 1911.

Fisher, J. C. *City and Regional Planning in Poland.* 1966.

Francastel, P. (ed.). *Les Origines des Villes Polonaises.* 1960.

Friederichsen, M. *Landschaften und Städte Polens und Litauens.* 1918.

Friese, V. "Gründungsurkunde von Posen 1252. Ein Beitrag zur Geschichte des Magdeburgischen Rechts," *Zeitschrift der Savigny-Stiftung für Rechtsgeschichte,* Germ. Abt., Vol. 26, 1905.

Gąsiorowski, A. "Ze studiów nad szerzeniem się tzw. prawa niemieckiego we wsiach ziemi krakowskiej i sandomierskiej do r. 1333" [The Extension of Teutonic Law in the Villages of the Cracow and Sandomierz Lands until 1333], *Roczniki Historyczne,* Vol. XXVI, 1960.

Geppert, F. "Die Burgen und Städte bei Thietmar von Merseburg," *Thüringisch-Sächsische Zeitschrift für Geschichte und Kunst,* Vol. XVI, 1927.

Gieysztor, A. "Le origine delle città nella Polonia medievale," *Studi in onore di Armando Sapori.* 1957.

———. "Les origines de la ville slave." In: *Settimane di studio del Centro italiano di studi sull'alto Medioevo.* Vol. VI: *La città nell'alto Medioevo.* Spoleto. 1959.

———, and others (eds.). *History of Poland.* Warsaw. 1968.

Hager, K. *Die polnischen Städte. Grundlagen und Ergebnisse ihrer städtebaulichen Entwicklung.* Stuttgarter Geographische Studien. Reihe A, Heft 43. 1934.

Handbook for Travellers in Russia, Poland and Finland. London. 1865.

Hellmann, M. "Zur Geschichte des Städtewesens in Osteuropa," *Jahrbücher für Geschichte Osteuropas,* N.F., Vol. 4, No. 1, 1956.

Hensel, W. *Anfänge der Städte bei den Ost- und Westslawen.* 1967.

———. *Die Slawen im frühen Mittelalter.* 1965.

———. "En Pologne médiévale: l'Archéologie au Service de l'Histoire. 1. Villes et Campagnes," *Annales. Economies, Sociétés, Civilisations,* Vol. 17, No. 2, 1962.

———. "L'Étude des Villes du Haut Moyen Âge en Pologne au Moyen de la Méthode Archéologique," *Dacia,* N.S., Vol. V, 1961.

———. "Les origines des villes slaves occidentales et orientales," *Atti del VI Congresso Internazionale delle Scienze Preistoriche e Protostoriche,* Vol. I, 1963.

———. "Types de fortifications slaves du Haut Moyen-Âge," *Archaeologia Polona,* Vol. 2, 1959.

Institut d'Histoire de l'Académie Polonaise des Sciences. *L'Europe aux IXe-XIe Siècles. Aux origines des États nationaux. Actes du Colloque international sur les Origines des États européens aux IXe-XIe siècles.* Warsaw and Poznań, Sept. 7–13, 1965. 1968.

Instytut Urbanistyki i Architektury. *Studia z Historii Budowy Miast Polskich.* 1957.

Jablonowski, H. "Polens Hauptstädte. Ihr Wechsel im Lauf der Geschichte." In: *Das Hauptstadtproblem in der europäischen Geschichte.* (Jahrbuch für Geschichte des deutschen Ostens, Vol. I). 1952.

Jażdżewski, K. *Poland.* 1965.

Kaczmarczyk, K. "Ciężary ludności wiejskiej i miejskiej na prawie niemieckim w Polsce XIII i XIV w." [The Taxation of the Rural and Urban Population under German Law in 13th and 14th Century Poland], *Przegląd Historyczny,* Vol. XI, 1911.

Kaczmarczyk, Z. *Kolonizacja niemiecka na wschód od Odry* [German Colonization East of the Odra]. 1945.

Kasiske, K. *Die Siedlungstätigkeit des Deutschen Ordens im östlichen Preussen bis zum Jahre 1410.* Einzelschriften der Historischen Kommission für ost- und westpreussische Landesforschung, 5. 1934.

Kloeppel, O. "Die rechte Stadt Danzig, wie sie vor 500 Jahren aussah," *Der Städtebau,* Vol. 23, 1928.

Koebner, R. "Dans les terres de colonisation: marchés slaves et villes allemandes," *Annales d'Histoire Économique et Sociale,* Vol. 9, 1937.

———. "Locatio. Zur Begriffssprache und Geschichte der deutschen Kolonisation," *Zeitschrift des Vereins für Geschichte Schlesiens,* Vol. 63, 1929.

———. "The Settlement and Colonization of Europe." In: *The Cambridge Economic History of Europe.* Vol. I. 1942; 2nd ed. 1966.

Kötzschke, R. *Quellen zur Geschichte der ostdeutschen Kolonisation im 12. bis 14. Jahrhundert.* 2nd ed. 1931.

Konwiarz, R. "Alte Stadtbaukunst in Oberschlesien," *Der Städtebau,* Vol. 17, 1920.

Korn, G. *Breslauer Urkundenbuch.* Pt. I. 1870.

Kostrzewski, J. *Les Origines de la Civilisation Polonaise.* 1949.

Krallert, W., W. Kuhn, and E. Schwarz. *Atlas zur Geschichte der deutschen Ostsiedlung.* 1958.

Krebs, N. "Krakau und Warschau als Spiegelbilder polnischer Geschichte," *Zeitschrift der Gesellschaft für Erdkunde,* Nos. 1/2, 1940.

Krollmann, C. "Die Besiedlung Ostpreussens durch den Deutschen Orden," *Vierteljahrschrift für Sozial- und Wirtschaftsgeschichte,* Vol. 21, 1928.

Kuhn, W. *Geschichte der Deutschen Ostsiedlung in der Neuzeit.* Vol. II. 1957.

———. *Siedlungsgeschichte Oberschlesiens.* 1954.

Ładogórski, T. *Studia nad zaludnieniem Polski XIV wieku* [Studies on the Population of Poland in the 14th Century]. PAN, Instytut Historii. 1958.

Lekszycki, J. von (ed.). *Die ältesten grosspolnischen Grodbücher, 1386–1400.* Publicationen aus den K. Preussischen Staatsarchiven. Vol. 31, 38. 1887–89.

Łowmiański, H. *Podstawy gospodarcze formowania się państw słowiańskich* [Economic Foundations of the Genesis of the Slavic States]. 1953.

Ludat, H. "Die Bezeichnung für 'Stadt' im Slawischen." In: *Syntagma Friburgense.* 1956.

———. "Frühformen des Städtewesens in Osteuropa." In: *Studian zu den Anfängen des Europäischen Städtewesens.* Reichenau Vorträge 1955–1956. 1958.

———. *Vorstufen und Entstehung des Städtewesens in Osteuropa.* 1955.

———. "Zur Evolutionstheorie der slavischen Geschichtsforschung am Beispiel der osteuropäischen Stadt." In: *Aus Natur und Geschichte Mittel- und Osteuropas.* Giessener Abhandlungen zur Agrar- und Wirtschaftsforschung des europäischen Ostens. Vol. III. 1957.

Maas, W. "Erläuterungen zu zwei Siedlungen- und Nationalitätenkarten. Die Besiedlung Westpreussens 1466–1772," *Zeitschrift für Ostforschung,* Vol. VII, 1958.

———. "Mittelalterliche und spätere Siedlungsräume. Dargestellt am Schlochauer Land," *Zeitschrift für Ostforschung,* Vol. V, 1956.

———. *Zur Siedlungskunde Westpreussens. 1466–1772.* 1958.

Maleczyński, K. "Najstarsze targi w Polsce i stosunek ich do miast przed kolonizacją na prawie niemieckiem" [The Oldest Markets in Poland and the Towns before Colonization on the Basis of German Law], *Studya nad Historyą Prawa Polskiego,* Vol. 10, No. 1, 1926.

———. *Die ältesten Märkte in Polen und ihr Verhältnis zu den Städten vor der Kolonisierung nach dem deutschen Recht.* 1930.

———, M. Morelowski, and A. Ptaszycka. *Wrocław. Rozwój urbanistyczny* [Wrocław. Its Urban Development]. Warsaw. 1956.

Marschalleck, K. H. "Burgenprobleme zwischen Elbe und Oder." In: *Frühe Burgen und Städte. Beiträge zur Burgen- und Stadtkernforschung.* Deutsche Akademie der Wissenschaften. Schriften der Sektion für Vor- und Frühgeschichte. Vol. II. 1954.

Martiny, R. "Die Formen der ländlichen Siedlungen in der Provinz Posen," *Zeitschrift der Historischen Gesellschaft für die Provinz Posen,* Vol. 28, 1913.

Masłowski, J. "Kolonizacja wiejska na prawie niemieckim w województwach sieradzkim, łęczyckim, no Kujawach i w ziemi dobrzyńskiej do r. 1370" [Rural Colonization under German Law in the Voivodships of Sieradz and Łęczyca, in Kujawy and the Dobrzyn District up to 1370], *Roczniki Historyczne,* Vol. XIII, 1937.

Meitzen, A. "Urkunden Schlesischer Dörfer." In: *Codex Diplomaticus Silesiae.* Vol. IV. 1863.

Merian, Matthaeus. *Topographia Electorat Brandenburgici et Ducatus Pomeraniae.* 1652.

Mielke, R. "Die alt-slawische Siedlung," *Zeitschrift für Ethnologie,* Vol. 55, 1923.

Ohnesorge, W. "Ausbreitung und Ende der Slawen zwischen Nieder-Elbe und Oder," *Zeitschrift des Vereins für Lübeckische Geschichte und Altertumskunde,* Vol. XII, No. 2, Vol. XIII, No. 1, 1910–11.

Pounds, J. G. (ed.). *Geographical Essays on Eastern Europe.* Indiana University Publications. Russian and East European Series. Vol. 24. 1961.

Quirin, K. *Die deutsche Ostsiedlung im Mittelalter.* 1954.

Pommersches Urkundenbuch. Vol. II. Ed. by R. Klempin and R. Prümers. 1868.

Ptaśnik, J. *Miasta i mieszaństwo w dawnej Polsce* [Towns and Urbanism in the Old Poland]. 1949.

Rakowski, K. von. *Die Entstehung des Gross-*

grundbesitzes im XV und XVI Jahrhundert in Polen. 1899.

Rendschmidt, M. *Das alte Elbinger Bürgerhaus.* 1933.

Rhode, G. *Geschichte der Stadt Posen.* 1953.

———. *Die Ostgrenze Polens.* Vol. I: *Im Mittelalter bis zum Jahre 1401.* 1955.

Roepell, R. *Über die Verbreitung des Magdeburger Stadtrechts im Gebiete des alten polnischen Reichs ostwaerts der Weichsel.* 1857.

Rostworowski, A. J. F. C. von. *Die Entwicklung der bäuerlichen Verhältnisse im Königreich Polen im 19. Jahrhundert.* Sammlung nationalökonomischer und statistischer Abhandlungen des staatswissenschaftlichen Seminars zu Halle. 1896.

Rutkowski, J. *Histoire économique de la Pologne avant les partages.* 1927.

———. "Medieval Agrarian Society in its Prime. Poland, Lithuania and Hungary." In: *The Cambridge Economic History of Europe.* Vol. I. 1942.

Schlesinger, W. "Forum, villa fori, ius fori. Einige Bemerkungen zu Marktgründungsurkunden des 12. Jahrhundert aus Mitteldeutschland." In: *Aus Geschichte und Landeskunde. Forschungen und Darstellungen Franz Steinbach zum 65. Geburtstag gewidmet von seinen Freunden und Schülern.* 1960.

Schlüter, O. *Wald, Sumpf und Siedelungsland in Altpreussen vor der Ordenszeit.* 1921.

Schmid, H. F. "Die Burgbezirksverfassung bei den slavischen Völkern in ihrer Bedeutung für die Geschichte ihrer Siedlung und ihrer staatlichen Organisation," *Jahrbücher für Kultur und Geschichte der Slaven,* N. F., Vol. II, No. 2, 1926.

———. "Die sozialgeschichtliche Erforschung der mittelalterlichen deutschrechtlichen Siedlungen auf polnischem Boden," *Vierteljahrschrift für Sozial- und Wirtschaftsgeschichte,* Vol. XX, 1928.

Schmidt, E. "Städtegründung zur Zeit Kasimirs des Grossen," *Zeitschrift der historischen Gesellschaft für die Provinz Posen,* Vol. 13, 1898.

Schubart-Fikentscher, Gertrud. *Die Verbreitung der deutschen Stadtrechte in Osteuropa.* 1942.

Schuchhardt, K. *Die Burg im Wandel der Weltgeschichte.* 1931.

Schultz, F. "Die Stadt Kulm im Mittelalter," *Zeitschrift des Westpreussischen Geschichtsverein,* Heft XXIII, 1888.

Seidel, W. "Der Beginn der Deutschen Besiedlung Schlesiens," *Darstellungen und Quellen zur schlesischen Geschichte,* Vol. XVII, 1913.

Siedler, E. J. *Märkischer Städtebau im Mittelalter.* 1914.

Stumpe, F. *Der Gang der Besiedlung im Kreise Oppeln.* Schriftenreihe der Vereinigung für oberschlesische Heimatkunde, 1. 1932.

Thietmar, Bishop of Merseburg. *Kronika Thietmara.* Z tekstu łacińkiego przetłumaczył, wstępem poprzedził i komentarzem opatrzył Marian Zygmunt Jedlicki. Biblioteka Tekstów Historycznych. Vol. III. Poznań. 1953.

Tyc, T. *Die Anfänge der dörflichen Siedlung zu deutschem Recht in Grosspolen (1200-1333).* Translation from the Polish original. 1930.

Tzschoppe, G. A., and G. A. Stenzel. *Urkundensammlung zur Geschichte des Ursprungs der Städte und der Einführung und Verbreitung deutscher Kolonisten und Rechte in Schlesien und der Ober-Lausitz.* 1832.

Voellner, H. "Die Entstehung des Städtewesens im westpreussischen Weichselland," *Zeitschrift für Ostforschung,* Vol. IX, 1960.

Warnke, Cjarlotte. *Die Anfänge des Fernhandels in Polen.* 1964.

Wöhlke, W. "Das Land zwischen Masuren und dem Bug: Erschliessung, Bild, Probleme," *Abhandlungen der Akademie der Wissenschaften in Göttingen,* Math.-Phys. Class, Ser. 3, No. 27, 1966.

Zaborski, B. *Über Dorfformen in Polen und ihre Verbreitung.* 1930.

Zajchowska, Stanisława. "Die Entwicklung der Besiedlung in Polen," *Geografiska Annaler,* Vol. XLII, No. 4, 1960.

Ziółkowska, Hanna. "Ze studiów nad najstarszym targiem polskim" [Study of the most ancient markets in Poland], *Slavia Antiqua,* Vol. IV, 1953.

CHAPTERS 3 TO 8

GENERAL HISTORY, TOWN PLANNING
AND ARCHITECTURE

Arnold, S., and M. Żychowski. *Outline History of Poland.* Warsaw. 1963.

Bachmann, F. *Die alten Städtebilder.* Leipzig. 1939.

Ciołek, G. *Ogrody polskie.* Part I: *Przemiany treści i formy* [Polish Gardens. Part I:

Changes in Content and Form]. Warsaw. 1954.

Czarnecki, W. *Planowanie miast i osiedli.* Vol. I: *Wiadomości ogólne; Planowanie przestrzenne* [Town and Settlement Planning. Vol. I: General Information; Spatial Planning]. 2nd ed. Warsaw. 1965.

Dmochowski, Z. *The Architecture of Poland.* London. 1956.

Dobrowolski, T. (ed.). *Historia sztuki polskiej w zarysie. Od wczesnego średniowiecza do czasów ostatnich* [Outline of the History of Polish Art. From the Early Middle Ages to Recent Times]. 3 vols. 2nd ed. Cracow. 1965.

Egorov, I. *Gradostroitel'stvo Bielorussii* [Town Building in Byelorussia]. Moscow. 1954.

Górska-Gołaska, K. *Katalog planów miast i wsi wielkopolskich.* No. 1: *Powiaty (wg stanu z r. 1918): Poznań-Zachód, Poznań-Wschód, Grodzisk, Nowy Tomyśl, Obornike* [Catalogue of Town and Village Plans in Wielkopolska. No. 1: The Districts of Poznań-West, Poznań-East, Grodzisk, Nowy Tomyśl, Oborniki in 1918]. Poznań, 1961.

Ilustrowany katalog źródeł kartograficznych do historii budowy miast polskich [Illustrated Catalogue of Cartographic Sources for a History of Polish Town Building]. Nos. 1–7. Warsaw. 1951–62.

Kaczmarczyk, Z. *Kolonizacja niemiecka na wschód od Odry* [German Colonization to the East of the Odra]. Poznań. 1945.

Katalog zabytków sztuki w Polsce [Catalogue of Art Monuments in Poland]. Published in Volumes (voivodships) and Numbers (counties). Warsaw. 1951–

Keyser, E. *Verzeichniss der ost- und westpreussischen Stadtpläne.* Königsberg. 1929.

———. *Deutsches Städtebuch. Handbuch der städtischen Geschichte.* 4 vols. Stuttgart. 1941.

Kluźniak, S. *Urbanizm* [Town Planning]. Warsaw. 1937.

Krakowski, S. *Problematyka miejska w historiografii polskiej. Ze szczególnym uwzględnieniem okresu 1929–1949* [The Urban Problem in Polish Historiography. With Special Reference to the Period 1929–1949]. Łódź. 1950.

Król, A. *Budownictwo wojskowe* [Military Architecture]. Vol. I. Warsaw. 1935.

Kulejewska-Topolska, Z. *Nowe lokacje miejskie w Wielkopolsce od XVI do końca XVIII wieku. Studium historyczno-prawne* [New Urban Foundations in Wielkopolska from the 16th to the End of the 18th Century. A Historical and Juridical Study]. Poznań. 1964.

Kuncewicz, A. *Plany przeglądowe miast polskich* [Survey Maps of Polish Towns]. Warsaw. 1929.

Łodyński, M. *Centralny katalog zbiorów kartograficznych w Polsce* [Central Catalogue of Cartographic Collections in Poland]. Nos. 1–2. Warsaw. 1961–63.

Łoza, S. *Architekci i budowniczowie w Polsce* [Architects and Builders in Poland]. Warsaw. 1954.

Manteuffel, T. (ed.). *Historia Polski.* Vol. I: *Do roku 1764* [History of Poland. Vol. I: Until the Year 1764]. 3rd ed. Warsaw. 1960.

Miłobędzki, A. *Zarys dziejów architektury w Polsce* [Outline of the History of Architecture in Poland]. 2nd ed. Warsaw. 1966.

Ostrowski, W. *Materiały do historii budowy miast* [Material for a History of Town Building]. Warsaw. 1955.

———, T. P. Szafer, and W. Trzebinski. "W sprawie metody badań nad historią budowy miast" [Notes on Research Methods in Urban History], *KAU*, Vol. 2, Nos. 3–4, 1957.

Pazyra, S. *Geneza i rozwój miast mazowieckich* [Genesis and Development of Masovian Towns]. Warsaw. 1959.

———. (ed.). *Miasta polskie w Tysiącleciu* [Polish Towns in the Millennium]. 2 vols. Wrocław. 1965–67.

Ptaśnik, J. *Miasta i mieszczaństwo w dawnej Polsce* [Towns and Townspeople in Poland in Times Past]. 2nd ed. Warsaw. 1949.

Rutkowski, J. *Historia gospodarcza Polski (do 1864 r.)* [Economic History of Poland (up to the Year 1864)]. Warsaw. 1953.

Ryciny w "Topografii Śląska" F. B. Wernhera [Illustrations in "The Topography of Silesia" by F. B. Wernher]. Seria Prac Własnych, IUA, No. 12. Warsaw. 1953.

Samsonowicz, H. "Badania nad dziejami miast w Polsce" [Research on the History of Towns in Poland], *Kwartalnik Historyczny*, Vol. 72, No. 1, 1965.

Słownik geograficzny Królestwa Polskiego i innych krajów słowiańskich [Geographic Dictionary of the Polish Kingdom and other Slavic Countries]. 15 vols. Warsaw. 1880–1904.

Słownik geograficzny Państwa Polskiego [Geographic Dictionary of the Polish State]. Vol. I, No. 1. Warsaw. N.d.

Sosnowski, O. "O planach osiedli sprzężonych w Polsce" [Plans of Linked Settlements in Poland], *BHSiK*, Vol. 4, No. 2, 1935.

Studia z Historii Budowy Miast [Studies from the History of Town Building]. Prace IUA. Vol. V, No. 1 (14). Warsaw. 1955.

Studia z Historii Budowy Miast Polskich [Studies from the History of Polish Town Building]. Prace IUA. Vol. VI, No. 2 (17). Warsaw. 1956–57.

Tołwiński, T. *Urbanistyka*. Vol. I: *Budowa miasta w przeszłości* [Town Planning. Vol. I: Town Building in the Past]. 3rd ed. Warsaw. 1947.

Topolski, J. *Badania nad dziejami miast w Polsce* [Research on the History of Towns in Poland]. Studia i Materiały do Dziejów Wielkopolski i Pomorza. Vol. VI, No. 2. Poznań. 1960.

Trawkowski, S. *Katalog planów miast w Zbiorach Archivum Państwowego w Radomiu* [A Catalogue of Town Plans in the State Archives of Radom]. Warsaw. 1957.

Trzebiński, W., and T. P. Szafer. *Katalog planów miast polskich w zbiorach Niemieckiej Biblioteki Państwowej w Berlinie* [A Catalogue of Town Plans in the Collection of the German State Library in Berlin]. Part 1. Warsaw. 1957.

Wejchert, K. *Miasteczka polskie jako zagadnienie urbanistyczne* [Small Polish Towns. A Problem in Town Planning]. Warsaw. 1947.

Widoki architektoniczne w malarstwie polskim 1780–1880. Katalog [Architectural Scenery in Polish Painting, 1780–1880. Catalogue]. Warsaw. 1964.

Wróblewska, G. "Ukształtowanie przestrzenne nowożytnych miast Wielkopolski od roku 1500 do rozbiorów" [The Structure of New Towns in Wielkopolska from the Year 1500 to the Time of the Partitions], *KAU*, Vol. 10, No. 2, 1965.

Wuttke, H. *Städtebuch des Landes Posen*. Codex diplomaticus. Allgemeine Geschichte der Städte im Lande Posen. Geschichtliche Nachrichten von 149 einzelnen Städten. Leipzig. 1864.

Zabytki sztuki w Polsce. Inwentarz topograficzny [Art Monuments in Poland. Topographical Inventory]. 4 vols. Warsaw. 1938–50.

CHAPTER 4

"L'artisanat et la vie urbaine en Pologne médiévale," *Ergon*, Vol. 3, Warsaw, 1962.

Buczek, K. *Targi i miasta na prawie polskim. Okres wczesnośredniowieczny* [Towns and Fairs under Polish Law. The Period of the Early Middle Ages]. Wrocław. 1964.

Dziewoński, K. "Zagadnienie rozwoju miast wczesnośredniowiecznych w Polsce" [The Problem of Town Expansion in Poland in the Early Middle Ages], *KAU*, Vol. 2, Nos. 3–4, 1957.

Francastel, P. (ed.). *Les Origines des Villes Polonaises*. Paris. 1960.

Gieysztor, A. "Les origines de la ville slave." In: *Settimane di studio del Centro italiano di studi sull'alto Medioevo*. Vol. VI: *La città nell'alto Medioevo*. Spoleto. 1959.

———. "From *forum* to *civitas*: Urban Changes in Poland in the Twelfth and Thirteenth Centuries." In: *La Pologne au XIIe Congrès International des Sciences Historiques à Vienne*. Warsaw. 1965.

———. "Villes et campagnes slaves du Xe au XIIIe siècle." In: *IIe Conférence Internationale d'Histoire Economique*. Paris. 1965.

Hensel, W. *Archeologia o początkach miast słowiańskich* [The Archeology of the Earliest Slavic Towns]. Wrocław. 1963.

Lalik, T. "Początki miast w Polsce" [The Origins of Towns in Poland], *Kwartalnik Historyczny*, Vol. 67, No. 1, 1960.

———. "Z sagadnień genezy miast w Polsce" [The Problems of the Origin of Towns in Poland], *Przegląd Historyczny*, Vol. 49, 1958.

Maleczyński, K. *Die ältesten Märkte in Polen und ihr Verhältnis zu den Städten vor der Kolonisierung nach dem deutschen Recht*. Osteuropa Institut, No. 4. Breslau. 1930.

Münch, H. *Geneza rozplanowania miast wielkopolskich XIII i XIV wieku* [The Genesis of Town Layouts in Wielkopolska in the 13th and 14th Centuries]. Cracow. 1946.

———. "Początki średniowiecznego układu miejskiego w Polsce ze szczególnym uwzględnieniem Śląska" [The Beginnings of Medieval Town Layouts in Poland with Special Reference to Silesia], *KAU*, Vol. 5, No. 3, 1960.

Świechowski, Z., and J. Zachwatowicz. *Dzieje budownictwa w Polsce według Oskara Sosnowskiego*. Vol. I: *Do połowy XIII wieku* [History of Architecture in Poland according to Oskar Sosnowski. Vol. I: To the Middle of the 13th Century]. Warsaw. 1964.

Tymieniecki, K. (ed.). *Początki Państwa Polskiego* [The Beginnings of the Polish State]. 2 vols. Poznań. 1962.

CHAPTER 5

Bimler, K. *Die schlesischen massiven Wehrbauten*. 4 vols. Breslau. 1940–42.

Fuhrmann, K. H. *Gründung und Grundriss der Stadt des deutschen Ritterordens in Preussen*. Berlin. N.d.

Kaczmarczyk, Z. *Monarchia Kazimierza Wielkiego* [The Monarchy of Kazimierz the Great]. 2 vols. Poznań. 1939–47.

———. *Polska czasów Kazimierza Wielkiego* [Poland during the Reign of Kazimierz the Great]. Cracow. 1964.

Kloeppel, O. *Siedlung und Stadtplanung im Osten*. Breslau. 1926.

Lange, O. *Lokacje miast Wielkopolski właściwej na prawie niemieckim w wiekach średnich* [The Founding of Towns in Wielkopolska in the Middle Ages under German Law]. Lwów. 1925.

Małowist, M. *Tezy do dyskusji nad budową miasta średniowiecznego* [Suggestions for a Discussion on the Building of a Medieval Town]. Prace IUA. Vol. I, No. 1. Warsaw. 1951.

Manteuffel, T. *Powstanie i organizacja miast średniowiecznych* [Origin and Organization of Medieval Towns]. Warsaw. 1930.

Münch, H. "Melioratio terrae nostrae. Szkice z dziejów miast Polski średniowiecznej" [Melioratio terrae nostrae. Sketches from the History of Towns in Medieval Poland], *KAU*, Vol. 10, No. 2, 1965.

Piekarczyk, S. *Studia z dziejów miast polskich w XIII i XIV w.* [Studies of the History of Polish Towns in the 13th and 14th Centuries]. Warsaw. 1955.

Pudełko, J. "Rynki w planach miast śląskich" [Market Squares in the Plans of Silesian Towns], *KAU*, Vol. 4, Nos. 3–4, 1959.

———. "Działka lokacyjna w strukturze przestrzennej średniowiecznych miast śląskich XIII w." [The Original Plots in the Spatial Structure of Medieval Silesian Towns in the 13th Century], *KAU*, Vol. 9, No. 2, 1964.

———. "Próba pomiarowej metody badania planów niektórych miast średniowiecznych w oparciu o zagadnienie działki" [The Survey of Plots as a Method of Analyzing the Plans of Some Medieval Towns]. *KAU*, Vol. 9, No. 1, 1964.

Siedler, E. J. *Märkischer Städtebau im Mittelalter*. Berlin. 1914.

Thiersch, U. "Ordensstädte im Reichsgau Danzig-Westpreussen," *Bauen, Siedeln, Wohnen*, No. 24, 1940.

Weymann, S. *Cła i drogi handlowe w Polsce Piastowskiej* [Tolls and Trade Roads in Poland during the Piast Period]. Poznań. 1938.

Zagrodzki, T. *Regularny plan miasta średniowiecznego a limitacja miernicza*. [A Regular Plan of a Medieval Town and Cadastral Limitations]. Wrocław. 1962.

CHAPTER 6

Alexandrowicz, A. "Miasteczka Białorusi i Litwy jako ośrodki handlu XVI i w I połowie XVII wieku" [Small Towns in Byelorussia and Lithuania as Centers of Commerce in the 16th and First Half of the 17th Century], *Rocznik Białostocki*, Vol. I, Białystok, 1961.

Czołowski, A. *Dawne zamki i twierdze na Rusi Halickiej* [Former Castles and Fortresses in the Halicz Region]. Lwów. 1892.

Eimer, G. *Die Stadtplanung im schwedischen Ostseereich 1600–1715*. Stockholm. 1961.

Herbst, S. *Miasta i mieszczaństwo Renesansu polskiego* [Towns and Townsmen of the Polish Renaissance]. Warsaw. 1954.

———. *Polska kultura mieszczańska przełomu XVI i XVII w.* [The Culture of the Polish Burgher at the Turn of the 16th and 17th Centuries]. Studia Renesansowe. Vol. I. Wrocław. 1956.

Kalinowski, W. "Miasta polskie w XVI i pierwszej połowie XVII wieku" [Polish Towns in the 16th and the First Half of the 17th Century], *KAU*, Vol. 8, Nos. 3–4, 1963.

Komornicki, S. S. "Kultura artystyczna w Polsce czasów Odrodzenia" [Cultural and Artistic Life in Poland during the Period of the Renaissance]. In: *Kultura Staropolska*. Cracow. 1932.

Naronowicz-Naroński, J. *Budownictwo wojenne* [Military Architecture]. Warsaw. 1957.

Trzebiński, W. "Polskie renesansowe założenia urbanistyczne. Stan i problematyka badań" [Polish Urban Foundations during the Renaissance. State and Problems of Research], *KAU*, Vol. 3, Nos. 3–4, 1958.

Zarębska, T. "O związkach urbanistyki węgierskiej i polskiej w drugiej połowie XVI w." [On Hungarian and Polish Town Planning during the Second Half of the XVI Century], *KAU*, Vol. 9, No. 4, 1964.

CHAPTER 7

Baranowski, I. *Komisje Porządkowe (1765–1788)* [Regulating Committees (1765–1788)]. Rozprawy Wydziału Historii-Filozoffi, PAU, Vol. XLIX. Cracow. 1907.

Bobrowski, Z. *Budynki użyteczności publicznej w Polsce wieku Oświecenia* [Public Buildings in Poland during the Period of the Enlightenment]. Studia i Materiały do Teorii i Historii Architektury i Urbanistyki, PAN. Sekcja Architektury i Urbanistyki, Vol. III. Warsaw. 1961.

Herbst, S. "Jurydyka." In: *Słownik historyczny sztuk plastycznych* [Urban Settlement. In: A Historical Dictionary of the Fine Arts]. Zeszyt wydany z okazji obrad Pierwszego Kongresu Nauki Polskiej. Warsaw. 1951.

Korzon, T. *Wewnętrzne dzieje Polski za Stanisława Augusta, 1764–1794* [The Domestic History of Poland at the Time of Stanisław August, 1764–1794]. 6 vols. 2nd ed. Cracow. 1897–1898.

Kula, W. *Szkice o manufakturach w Polsce XVIII wieku* [Sketches on Manufacture in Poland in the 18th Century]. 2 vols. Warsaw. 1956.

Lorentz, S. "Architektura wieku Oświecenia w świetle przemian w życiu gospodarczym i umysłowym" [Architecture in the Age of the Enlightenment in the Light of Changes in Economic and Intellectual Life], *BHS*, Vol. 13, No. 4, 1951.

Szafer, T. P. "Ze studiów nad planowaniem miast w Polsce XVIII i początku XIX w." [Studies on City Planning in Poland during the 18th and the Beginning of the 19th Century]. In: *SHBM*. Warsaw. 1955.

Trzebiński, W. "Ze studiów nad historią budowy miast prywatnych w Polsce wieku Oświecenia" [Historical Studies on the Building of Private Towns in Poland during the Period of the Enlightenment]. In: *SHBM*. Warsaw. 1955.

———. *Działalność urbanistyczna magnatów i szlachty w Polsce XVIII wieku* [The Planning and Building of Cities by Magnates and the Gentry in 18th-century Poland]. Warsaw. 1962.

CHAPTER 8

Breyer, A. *Deutsche Tuchmachereinwanderung in den ostmitteleuropäischen Raum von 1550 bis 1830*. Leipzig. 1941.

Czarnecki, W. *Zmiany układów przestrzennych miast wielkopolskich w XIX wieku* [Changes in the Layouts of Cities in Wielkopolska during the 19th Century]. Poznań. 1964.

Gąsiorowska, N. "Z dziejów przemysłu w Królestwie Polskim" [From the History of Commerce in the Polish Kingdom], *Ekonomista*, Vol. 22, Nos. 1–2, 1922.

———. *Górnictwo i hutnictwo w Królestwie Polskim, 1815–1830* [Mining and Metallurgy in the Polish Kingdom, 1815–1830]. Warsaw. N.d.

Helmigk, H. J. *Oberschlesische Landbaukunst um 1800*. Berlin. 1937.

Kaczmarek, R. "Źródła do historii miast łódzkiego okręgu przemysłowego w XIX w." In: *Materiały do historii miast, przemysłu i klasy robotniczej w okręgu łódzkim* [Sources for a History on the Towns of the Łódź Commercial District in the 19th Century. In: Materials for a History of Towns, Commerce, and the Laboring Class in the Łódź District]. Vol. II. Warsaw. 1958.

Kalinowski, W., and S. Trawkowski. *Uwagi o urbanistyce i architekturze miejskiej Królestwa Kongresowego w pierwszej połowie XIX wieku* [Comments on City Planning and Urban Architecture of the Congress Kingdom in the First Half of the 19th Century]. Studia i Materiały do Historii i Teorii Architektury i Urbanistyki, PAN. Komitet Architektury i Urbanistyki, Vol. I. Warsaw. 1956.

Kuhn, W. *Kleinsiedelungen aus Friderizianischer Zeit*. Stuttgart. 1918.

Kula, W. *Kształtowanie się kapitalizmu w Polsce* [The Formation of Capitalism in Poland]. Warsaw. 1955.

Lepucki, H. *Działalność kolonizacyjna Marii Teresy i Józefa II w Galicji 1772–1790* [The Colonization under Maria Theresa and Joseph II in Galicia, 1772–1790]. Badania z dziejów społecznych i gospodarczych. No. 29. Lwów. 1938.

Ostrowski, W. *Świetna karta z dziejów planowania w Polsce. 1815–1830* [A Brilliant Page in the History of Planning in Poland. 1815–1830]. Warsaw. 1949.

———. *Budownictwo przemysłowe Zagłębia Staropolskiego w okresie Królestwa Kongresowego* [Commercial Building in Zagłębie Staropolskie during the Congress Kingdom]. Prace IUA, Vol. I, No. 2. Warsaw. 1951.

Wąsicki, J. *Miasta zachodniego pogranicza Wielkopolski 1793–1815* [Cities of the Western Borderland of Wielkopolska, 1793–1815]. Poznań. 1960.

———. *Opisy miast polskich z lat 1793–1794* [Descriptions of Polish Cities from the Years 1793–1794]. 2 vols. Poznań. 1962.

———. *Pruskie opisy miast polskich z końca XVIII w.* [Prussian Descriptions of Polish Towns from the End of the 18th Century]. Departament Białostocki. Poznań. 1964.

DETAILED STUDIES OF INDIVIDUAL CITIES

Aleksandrów

Jażdżyńska, J. *Monografia miasta przemysłowego Aleksandrów w latach 1822–1870* [Monograph of the Commercial City of Aleksandrów in the Years 1822–1870]. Łódź. 1954.

Augustów

Szafer, T. P., and W. Trzebiński. *Projekty przebudowy Augustowa 1815–1830* [Projects for the Remodeling of Augustów, 1815–1830]. Prace IUA, Vol. II, No. 3. Warsaw. 1952.

Białystok

Glinka, J. "Plan Białegostoku w końcu XVIII stulecia" [Plan of Białystok at the End of the 18th Century]. In: *SHBM*. Warsaw. 1955.

Mościcki, H. *Białystok, zarys historyczny* [Białystok. A Historical Outline]. Białystok. 1933.

Biecz

Bujak, F. *Materiały do historii miasta Biecza (1361–1632)* [Material for a History of the City of Biecz (1361–1632)]. Cracow. 1914.

Kaleta, R. (ed.). *Biecz. Studia historyczne* [Biecz. Historical Studies]. Wrocław. 1963.

Bielsk Podlaski

Herbst, S. "Bielsk Podlaski." In: *SHBMP*. Warsaw. 1957.

Biskupin

Kostrzewski, J. (ed.). *Sprawozdanie z prac wykopaliskowych w grodzie kultury łużyckiej w Biskupinie w powiecie żnińskim, III, za lata 1938–1939 i 1946–1948* [Report on the Excavations of the Lusatian Culture Stronghold of Biskupin, in the District of Żnin, III, for the years 1938–1939 and 1946–1948]. Poznań. 1950.

Brody

Baracz, S. *Wolne miasto handlowe Brody* [The Free Commercial City of Brody]. Lwów. 1865.

Sosnowski, O. "Studium pierwotnego założenia (1586) i obwarowania (1630–1635) miasta Brodów" [A Study of the Foundation (1586) and Fortifications (1630–1635) of the City of Brody], *BHSiK*, Vol. 2, No. 4, 1934.

Brzeg

Dziewulski, W., and S. Golachowski. "Brzeg." In: *SHBMP*. Warsaw. 1957.

Zlat, M. *Brzeg*. Wrocław. 1960.

Brzeżany

Maciszewski, M. *Brzeżany w czasach Rzeczypospolitej Polskiej* [Brzeżany during the Polish Republic]. Brody. 1911.

Bydgoszcz

Posadzy, W. "Bydgoszcz." In: *SHBMP*. Warsaw. 1957.

Chełmno

Gąsiorowski, E. "Rynek i ratusz chełmiński" [The Market and Town Hall of Chełmno], *KAU*, Vol. 10, No. 1, 1965.

Ciechocinek

Raczyński, M. *Materiały do historii Ciechocinka* [Material for a History of Ciechocinek]. Warsaw. 1935.

Cracow

Banach, J. (ed.). *Przemiany dziejowe otoczenia Wawelu* [Historical Changes in the Environs of the Wawel]. Cracow. 1953.

Borowiejska-Birkenmajerowa, M., and J. Demel. *Działalność urbanistyczna i architektoniczna senatu Wolnego Miasta Krakowa w latach 1815–1830* [The Planning and Building Activities of the Senate of the Free City of Cracow in 1815–1830]. Studia i Materiały do Teorii i Historii Architektury i Urbanistyki. PAN. Sekcja Architektury i Urbanistyki, Vol. IV. Warsaw. 1963.

Czapska, A., and P. Gartkiewicz. *Rynek w Krakowie* [The Marketplace in Cracow]. Seria Prac Własnych, IUA, No. 17. Warsaw. 1954.

Dabrowski, J. (ed.). *Kraków. Studia nad rozwojem miasta* [Cracow. A Study of the Development of the City]. Cracow. 1957.

Dobrowolski, T. *Sztuka Krakowa* [The Art of Cracow]. 3rd ed. Cracow. 1964.

Grabski, W. "Wybrane zagadnienia z urbanistyki średniowiecznego Krakowa" [Some Problems in the Planning of Medieval Cracow], *Biuletyn Krakowski*, Vol. III, Cracow, 1961.

Jamka, R. *Kraków w pradziejach* [Cracow in Prehistory]. Vol. I. Wrocław. 1963.

Jamroz, J. "Układ przestrzenny miasta Krakowa sprzed lokacji 1257 r." [The Layout of the City of Cracow before its Refounding in 1257], *Biuletyn Krakowski*, Vol. II, Cracow, 1960.

Mitkowski, J. "Lokacja Krakowa i powstanie układu urbanistycznego miasta" [The Founding of Cracow and the Origin of the Layout of the City], *Ochrona Zabytków*, Vol. 8, No. 3 (30), 1955.

Münch, H. "Kraków do roku 1257 włącznie" [Cracow until 1257 Inclusive], *KAU*, Vol. 3, No. 1, 1958.

——. *Plan miasta Krakowa Ignacego Enderle z lat (1802–1805) 1807–1808 tak zwany Senacki* [The So-called Senate Plan for the City of Cracow by Ignacy Enderle from (1802–1805) 1807–1808]. Cracow. 1959.

Rederowa, D. "Studia nad wewnętrznymi dziejami Krakowa porozbiorowego 1796–1809." Part I: "Zagadnienia urbanistyczne" [Studies on the Internal History of Post-Partition Cracow, 1796–1809. Part I: Urban Problems], *Rocznik Krakowski*, Vol. XXXIV, No. 2, Wrocław, 1958.

Swiszczowski, S. "Założenie i rozwój miasta Kazimierza" [The Founding and Development of the City of Kazimierz], *Biuletyn Krakowski*, Vol. III, Cracow, 1961.

Częstochowa

Braun, J. *Częstochowa. Rozwój urbanistyczny i architektoniczny* [Częstochowa. Urban and Architectural Development]. Warsaw. 1959.

Krakowski, S. *Stara Częstochowa. Studia nad genezą, ustrojem i strukturą ludnościową i gospodarczą Częstochowy (1220–1655)* [Old Częstochowa. Studies on the Origin, Structure, Population, and Economic Organization of Częstochowa (1220–1655)]. Częstochowa. 1948.

Działdowo

Gause, F. *Geschichte des Amtes und der Stadt Soldau.* Wissenschaftliche Beiträge zur Geschichte und Landeskunde Ost-Mitteleuropas, No. 38. Marburg/Lahn. 1958.

Elbląg

Carstenn, E. *Geschichte der Hansestadt Elbing.* Elbing. 1937.

Hauke, K., and H. Stobbe. *Die Baugeschichte und die Baudenkmäler der Stadt Elbing.* Stuttgart. 1964.

Sierzputowski, W. "Układ przestrzenny Elbląga w świetle historii" [The Layout of Elbląg in the Light of History], *Ochrona Zabytków*, Vol. 8, No. 2 (29), 1955.

Gdańsk

Groth, P. "Cenniejsze zabytki kartograficzne w. XVI–XVIII znajdujące się w Wojewódzkim Archiwum Państwowym w Gdańsku" [The More Valuable Cartographic Records from the 16th–18th Centuries in the Provincial State Archives of Gdańsk], *Studia i Materiały do Dziejów Wielkopolski i Pomorza*, Vol. IV, No. 1, 1958.

Jażdżewski, K. *Gdańsk wczesnośredniowieczny w świetle wykopalisk* [Early Medieval Gdańsk in the Light of Excavations]. Gdynia. 1961.

Kamińska, J., L. J. Łuka, and A. Zbierski (eds.). *Gdańsk wczesnośredniowieczny* [Gdańsk in the Early Middle Ages]. 5 vols. Gdańsk. 1959–64.

Kloeppel, O. *Das Stadtbild von Danzig in den drei Jahrhunderten seiner Grossen Geschichte.* Danzig. 1937.

——. *Die Wiederherstellung des alten Stadtbildes von Danzig seit der nationalen Erhebung.* Danzig. 1935.

Simson, P. *Geschichte der Stadt Danzig.* 4 vols. Danzig. 1916–18.

Stankiewicz, J. *Strakowscy—fortyfikatorzy, architekci i budowniczowie gdańscy* [The Strakowski Family—Military Engineers, Architects, and Builders of Gdańsk]. Gdańsk. 1955.

——. "Nadmorska twierdza w Wisłoujściu" [The Coastal Fortress in Wisłoujście], *KAU*, Vol. 1, No. 2, 1956.

——. "Średniowieczne fortyfikacje Głównego Miasta w Gdańsku" [The Medieval Fortifications of the Center of the City of Gdańsk], *Studia i Materiały do Historii Wojskowości*, Vol. IV, 1958.

——, and B. Szermer. *Gdańsk. Rozwój urbanistyczny i architektoniczny oraz powstanie zespołu Gdańsk-Sopot-Gdynia* [Gdańsk. Its Urban and Architectural Development and the Origin of the Gdańsk-Sopot-Gdynia Complex]. Warsaw. 1959.

Giecz

Kostrzewski, B. *Giecz—pomnik historii kultury państwa polskiego* [Giecz—A Monument in the History of Culture of the Polish State]. Poznań. 1961.

———. *Z najdawniejszych dziejów Giecza* [From the Earliest History of Giecz]. Polskie Towarzystwo Archeologiczne. Popularnonaukowa Biblioteka Archeologiczna, No. 9. Wrocław. 1962.

Wędzki, A. "Rozwój i upadek grodu gieckiego" [The Development and Decline of the Castle Town of Giecz], *Studia i Materiały do Dziejów Wielkopolski i Pomorza*, Vol. IV, No. 2, 1958.

Głogów Małopolski

Herbst, S. "Uwagi nad renesansowym rozplanowaniem Głowowa" [Comments on the Renaissance Layout of Głowów], *BHS*, Vol. 16, No. 1, 1954.

Kotula, F. "Głowów—renesansowe miasteczko" [Głowów—A Renaissance City], *BHS*, Vol. 16, No. 1, 1954.

Gniezno

Topolski, J. (ed.). *Dzieje Gniezna* [The History of Gniezno]. Warsaw. 1965.

Żurowski, K. "Gniezno, stołeczny gród pierwszych Piastów w świetle źródeł archeologicznych." In: *Początki Państwa Polskiego. Księga tysiąclecia.* Vol. II: *Społeczeństwo i kultura* [Gniezno, the Capital City of the First Members of the Piast Dynasty in the Light of Archeological Sources. In: The Beginnings of the Polish State. Vol. II: Society and Culture]. Poznań. 1962.

Góra Kalwaria

Liczbiński, A. "Góra Kalwaria—lokacja i układ przestrzenny miasta (1670–1690)" [Góra Kalwaria—Foundation and Layout of the City (1670–1690)], *KAU*, Vol. 2, Nos. 3–4, 1957.

Grudziądz

Biskup, M. "Rozwój przestrzenny miasta Grudziądza" [The Spatial Development of the City of Grudziądz], *Rocznik Grudziądzki*, Vol. I, Grudziądz, 1960.

Frycz, J. "Układ urbanistyczny i architektura Grudziądza" [Layout and Architecture of Grudziądz], *Rocznik Grudziądzki*, Vol. I, Grudziądz, 1960.

Jarosław

Borowiejska-Birkenmajerowa, M. *Jarosław.* Seria Prac Własnych, IUA, No. 24. Warsaw. 1955.

Wondás, A. *Szkice do dziejów Jarosławia* [Historical Sketches of Jarosław]. 3 vols. Jarosław. 1934–36.

Kalisz

Osiemnaście wieków Kalisza [Eighteen Centuries of Kalisz]. 3 vols. Kalisz. 1960–62.

Kamień Pomorski

Kiersnowski, R. "Kamień i Wolin" [Kamień and Wolin], *Przegląd Zachodni*, Vol. 7, Nos. 9–10, 1951.

Leciejewicz, L. "O położeniu słowiańskiego grodu w Kamieniu" [The Location of the Slavic Castle in Kamień], *Studia i Materiały do Dziejów Wielkopolski i Pomorza*, Vol. 5, No. 1, 1959.

Kazimierz Dolny

Husarski, W. *Kazimierz Dolny.* Warsaw. 1953.

Rutkowski, H. *Kazimierz Dolny. Rozwój urbanistyczny i architektoniczny* [Kazimierz Dolny. Urban and Architectural Development]. Warsaw. 1966.

Kępno

Grot, Z., and M. Mika. "Kępno." In: *SHBMP*. Warsaw. 1957.

Koło

Burszta, J. (ed.). *Sześćset lat miasta Koła* [Six Hundred Years of the City of Koło]. Poznań. 1963.

Kołobrzeg

Laciejewski, K., W. Łosiński, and E. Tabaczyńska. *Kołobrzeg we wczesnym średniowieczu* [Kołobrzeg in the Early Middle Ages]. Wrocław. 1961.

Kowalenko, W. "Najdawniejszy Kołobrzeg (VIII–XIII w.)" [Ancient Kołobrzeg (VIII–XIII Centuries)], *Przegląd Zachodni*, Vol. 7, Nos. 7–8, 1951.

Koronowo

Posadzy, W. "Koronowo." In: *SHBMP*. Warsaw. 1957.

Kruszwica

Grześkowiak, J. (ed.). *Kruszwica. Zarys monograficzny* [Kruszwica. Monographic Outline]. Toruń. 1965.

Łęczyca

Lalik, T. "Stare miasto w Łęczycy. Przemiany w okresie poprzedzającym lokacje" [The Old Town in Łęczyca. Changes in the Period Preceding the Foundation], *Kwartalnik Historii Kultury Materialnej*, Vol. 4, No. 4, 1956.

Nadolski, A. "Łęczyca we wczesnym średniowieczu" [Łęczyca in the Early Middle Ages]. In: *Ziemia Łęczycka. Szkice o teraźniejszości i przeszłości*. Łódź. 1964.

Tomczak, A. "Zarys rozwoju przestrzennego Łęczycy od XIII do XIX w." [Outline of the Physical Development of Łęczyca from the 13th to the 19th Century]. In: *Ziemia Łęczycka. Szkice o teraźniejszości i przeszłości*. Łódź. 1964.

Legnica

Dziewulski, W. "Legnica." In: *SHBMP*. Warsaw. 1957.

Kazimierczyk, J., and J. Rozpędowski. "Palatium w Legnicy" [The Palatium in Legnica], *KAU*, Vol. 6, No. 3, 1961.

Lidzbark Warmiński

Biskup, M. "Rozwój przestrzenny Lidzbarka Warmińskiego" [The Spatial Development of Lidzbark in Warmia], *Komunikaty Mazursko-Warmińskie*, No. 4 (74), 1961.

Ogrodziński, W. *Lidzbark Warmiński* [Lidzbark in Warmia]. Warsaw. 1958.

Łódź

Kaczmarczyk, K. "Lokacja Łodzi na prawie niemieckim w r. 1387" [The Foundation of Łódź under German Law in the Year 1387], *Rocznik Łódzki*, Vol. 1, 1929.

Popławska, I. "Budownictwo domów rzemieślniczych w Łodzi w pierwszej połowie XIX w." [The Building of Housing for Workers in Łódź in the First Half of the 19th Century], *Łódzkie Studia Etnograficzne*, Vol. VII, 1965.

Rynkowska, A. *Działalność gospodarcza władz Królestwa Polskiego na terenie Łodzi przemysłowej w latach 1821–1831* [Economic Activities of the Government of the Polish Kingdom in the Area of Industrial Łódź in 1821–1831]. Łódź. 1951.

———. "Początki rozwoju kapitalistycznego miasta Łodzi. 1820–1864" [The Beginning of Capitalistic Development in the City of Łódź, 1820–1864]. In: *Materiały do historii miast, przemysłu i klasy robotniczej w okręgu łódzkim*. Vol. IV. Warsaw. 1960.

Lublin

Gawarecki, H., and C. Gawdzik. *Lublin. Krajobraz i architektura* [Lublin. Landscape and Architecture]. 2nd ed. Warsaw. 1964.

Gawdzik, C. "Rozwój urbanistyczny Starego Lublina" [Urban Development of the Old City of Lublin], *Ochrona Zabytków*, Vol. 7, No. 3 (36), 1954.

Kalinowski, W., and S. Trawkowski. "Przebudowa Lublina w Królestwie Kongresowym (w latach 1817–1820)" [The Remodeling of Lublin during the Congress Kingdom (1817–1820)], *Ochrona Zabytków*, Vol. 7, No. 3 (36), 1954.

Mazurkiewicz, J. *Jurydyki lubelskie* [Settlements of Lublin]. Wrocław. 1956.

Riabinin, J. *Materiały do historii miasta Lublina, 1317–1792* [Material for a History of the City of Lublin]. Lublin. 1938.

Lwów

Mańkowski, T. *Początki nowożytnego Lwowa* [The Beginnings of Modern Lwów]. Prace Sekcji Historii Sztuki i Kultury, Towarzystwo Naukowe we Lwowie. Vol. I. Lwów. 1929.

Papée, F. *Historia miasta Lwowa w zarysie* [An Outline of the History of Lwów]. 2nd ed. Lwów. 1924.

Tomkiewicz, W., and J. Witwicki. *Lwów—dzieje wojenne obwarowań miasta* [Lwów. The Military History of the City's Fortifications]. Warsaw. 1939.

Malbork

Górski, K. *Dzieje Malborka* [History of Malbork]. Gdynia. 1960.

Mińsk Mazowiecki

Benko, M. "Rozwój miasta Mińska Mazowieckiego" [The Development of the City of Mińsk in Masovia]. In: *Planowanie Miast*, IUA, Vol. V. Warsaw. 1951.

Lutostańska, A. "Mińsk Mazowiecki—Sandomierz" [Masovian Mińsk—Sandomierz]. In: *SHBMP*. Warsaw. 1957.

Nidzica

Gregorovius, J. *Die Ordensstadt Neidenburg in Ostpreussen*. Marienwerder. 1883.

Nieśwież

Taurogiński, B. *Z dziejów Nieświeża* [From the History of Nieśwież]. Warsaw. 1937.

Nysa

Dziewulski, W. "Nysa." In: *SHBMP*. Warsaw. 1957.

Schoenaich, G. *Die alte Bischofsstadt Neisse.* Oppeln. 1935.

Opole

Dziewulski, W. "Miasto lokacyjne w Opolu w XIII-XV w." [The Location City in Opole in the 13th–15th Centuries]. In: *Studia Śląskie*. Vol. I. Opole. 1958.

Pasłęk

Helwig, R. *Die Geschichte der Stadt Pr. Holland.* Wissenschaftliche Beiträge zur Geschichte und Landeskunde Ost-Mitteleuropas, No. 46. Marburg/Lahn. 1961.

Piotrków Trybunalski

Kalinowski, W., and H. Rutkowski. "Piotrków Trybunalski" [Tribunal Piotrków], *Ochrona Zabytków,* Vol. 7, No. 2 (25), 1954.

Płock

Nowowiejski, A. J. *Płock—monografia historyczna* [Płock. Historical Monograph]. Płock. N.d.

Staszewski, K. *Plany i pomiary miasta Płocka oraz gruntów podmiejskich od roku 1793 do lat ostatnich* [Plans and Surveys of the City of Płock and the Surrounding Country from 1793 to Recent Times]. Płock. 1938.

Szafrański, W. *Początki Płocka w świetle wykopalisk archeologicznych* [The Origin of Płock in the Light of Archeological Excavations]. Płock. 1964.

Poznań

Czarnecki, W. *Plany historyczne miasta Poznania* [Historical Plans of the City of Poznań]. Prace Komisji Budownictwa i Architektury, Poznańskie Towarzystwo Przyjaciół Nauk. Vol. 1, No. 1. Poznań. 1961.

Dziesięć wieków Poznania [Ten Centuries of Poznań]. 3 vols. Poznań. 1956.

Hensel, W. *Poznań we wczesnym średniowieczu* [Poznań in the Early Middle Ages]. 3 vols. Wrocław. 1959–61.

Ruszczyńska, T., and A Sławska. *Poznań.* Warsaw. 1953.

Warkoczewska, M. *Widoki Starego Poznania* [Views of the Old City of Poznań]. Poznań. 1960.

Zieliński, Z. "Rozwój miasta Poznania od końca X do XVIII w. [The Development of the City of Poznań from the End of the 10th Century to the 18th Century], *Kronika miasta Poznania,* Vol. 20, No. 4, 1949.

———. "Rozwój terytorialny miasta oraz zabudowy Starego Rynku w Poznaniu" [The Physical Development of the City and Old Marketplace in Poznań], *Przegląd Zachodni,* Vol. 9, Nos. 7–8, 1953.

Racibórz

Dziewulski, W., and S. Golachowski. "Racibórz." In: *SHBMP*. Warsaw. 1957.

Kutzner, M. *Racibórz*. Wrocław. 1965.

Radom

Jędrzejewicz, J. (ed.). *Radom. Szkice z dziejów miasta* [Radom. Historical Sketches of the Town]. Warsaw. 1961.

Kalinowski, W. "Rozbudowa Radomia w latach 1815–1830" [The Extension of Radom in the Years 1815–1830]. In: *SHBM*. Warsaw. 1955.

Luboński, J. *Monografia historyczna miasta Radomia* [Historical Monograph of the City of Radom]. Radom. 1907.

Rawa Mazowiecka

Kalinowski, W., and S. Trawkowski. "Przebudowa Rawy Mazowieckiej w okresie konstytucyjnym Królestwa Polskiego (1815–1830)" [The Rebuilding of Masovian Rawa during the Constitutional Period of the Polish Kingdom (1815–1830)]. In: *SHBM*. Warsaw. 1955.

Rawicz

Kazimierczak, J. *Rawicz, gród Przyjemskich. Historyczny rys powstania i rozwoju miasta (1638–1938)* [Rawicz, Castle of the Family of Przyjemski. A Historical Outline of the Origin and Development of the City (1638–1938)]. Warsaw. 1938.

Rydzyna

Preibisz, L. *Zamek i klucz rydzyński* [The Castle and Domain of Rydzyna]. Rydzyna. 1938.

Rzeszów

Błoński, F. (ed.). *Pięć wieków miasta Rzeszowa XIV-XVIII* [Five Centuries of the City of Rzeszów, XIV-XVIII]. Warsaw. 1958.

Pęckowski, J. *Dzieje miasta Rzeszowa do końca XVIII w.* [History of the City of Rzeszów until the End of the XVIII Century]. Rzeszów. 1913.

Sandomierz

Buliński, M. *Monografia miasta Sandomierza* [Monograph of the City of Sandomierz]. Warsaw. 1879.

Kalinowski, W., and others. *Sandomierz*. Warsaw. 1956.

Sejny

Herbst, S. "Analiza układu przestrzennego miasta Sejny" [An Analysis of the Layout of the City of Sejny]. In: *Materiały do dziejów ziemi sejneńskiej*. Prace Białostockiego Towarzystwa Naukowego, No. 1. Białystok. 1963.

Siemiatycze

Gilewski, I. K. *Siemiatycze. Zarys monografii od pradziejów do 1939 r.* [Siemiatycze. A Monographic Outline from Prehistoric Times Until 1939]. Siemiatycze. 1958.

Środa Śląska

Kindler, P. *Geschichte der Stadt Neumarkt*. Neumarkt. 1934.

Kozaczewski, T. "Z zagadnień urbanistycznych Środy Śląskiej" [Urban Problems of Silesian Środa], *KAU*, Vol. 7, No. 4, 1962.

Pudełko, J. "Niektóre zagadnienia rozplanowania miast średniowiecznych w świetle studiów nad układem Środy Śląskiej" [Some Problems Concerning the Layout of Medieval Cities in the Light of Investigations of the Plan of Silesian Środa], *KAU*, Vol. 7, No. 1, 1962.

——— . "W sprawie Środy Śląskiej" [Silesian Środa], *KAU*, Vol. 8, Nos. 3–4, 1963.

Świdnica

Dziewulski, W. "Świdnica." In: *SHBMP*. Warsaw. 1957.

Świebodzin

"Geneza miasta Świebodzina" [Genesis of the City of Świebodzin], *Przegląd Zachodni*, Vol. 7, Nos. 9–10, 1951.

Szczecin

Chłopocka, H. "Lokacja Szczecina na prawie niemieckim" [The Foundation of Szczecin under German Law], *Przegląd Zachodni*, Vol. 8, Nos. 3–4, 1952.

Dembińska, M. (ed.). *Z przeszłości Szczecina* [From the Past of Szczecin]. Wrocław. 1964.

Dzieje Szczecina [History of Szczecin]. 2 vols. Warsaw. 1963.

Orlińska, H. "Materiały kartograficzne Starego Szczecina" [Cartographic Materials of the Old City of Szczecin], *Szczecin*, Nos. 5–6, 1962.

Szczecin i Wolin we wczesnym średniowieczu [Szczecin and Wolin in the Early Middle Ages]. Wrocław. 1954.

Wachowiak, B. *Port średniowiecznego Szczecina* [The Medieval Port of Szczecin]. Gdańsk. 1955.

Wehrmann, M. *Geschichte der Stadt Stettin*. Stettin. 1911.

Zaremba, P., and H. Orlinska. *Urbanistyczny rozwój Szczecina* [Urban Development of Szczecin]. Poznań. 1965.

Szczuczyn

Karpowicz, M. "Architekci warszawscy w Szczuczynie na przełomie XVII i XVIII wieku" [Warsaw Architects in Szczuczyn at the Turn of the 17th and 18th Centuries], *BHS*, Vol. 19, No. 3, 1957.

Sztum

Biskup, M., and M. Zdzitowiecka. "Sztum." In: *SHBMP*. Warsaw. 1957.

Tarnów

Dutkiewicz, J. E. *Tarnów*. Warsaw. 1954.

Czapska, A., and Z. Dolatowski. *Rynek w Tarnowie* [The Market Square in Tarnów]. Seria Prac Własnych, IUA, No. 22. Warsaw. 1954.

Leniek, J., F. Ferzig, and F. Leśniak. *Dzieje miasta Tarnowa* [History of the City of Tarnów]. Tarnów. 1911.

Tomaszów Lubelski

Peter, J. *Szkice z przeszłości miasta kresowego* [Sketches from the Past of a Borderland City]. Zamość. 1947.

Toruń

Gąsiorowscy, M., and E. *Toruń*. Warsaw. 1963.

Kruszelnicki, Z. "Dawne widoki Torunia" [Early Views of Toruń], *Studia Pomorskie*, Vol. II. Wrocław. 1957.

Piskorska, H. *Zbiory kartograficzne archiwum miasta Torunia* [Cartographic Collections in the Archives of the City of Toruń]. Toruń. 1938.

Tymieniecki, K. (ed.). *Dzieje Torunia* [The History of Toruń]. Toruń. 1933.

Trzebnica

Broniewski, T. *Trzebnica*. Wrocław. 1959.

Dziewoński, K. "Geografia Trzebnicy i Ujazdu Trzebnickiego w okresie wczesnośredniowiecznym" [Geography of Trzebnica and the Ujazd Trzebnicki in the Early Middle Ages], *Studia Wczesnośredniowieczne*, Vol. I, Warsaw. 1952.

Tuchola

Wojtowicz, J. (ed.). *Tuchola. Zarys monograficzny* [Tuchola. A Monographic Outline]. Toruń. 1962.

Warsaw

Biegański, P. "Koncepcja Placu Teatralnego na tle twórczości Antoniego Corazziego" [The Plac Teatralny Project viewed in relation to Antoni Corazzi's general work], *BHSiK*, Vol. 5, Nos. 3–4, 1937.

Bieniecki, Z. "Oś barokowa Warszawy" [The Baroque Axis of Warsaw], *KAU*, Vol. 5, No. 4, 1960.

Dziewulski, S. *Warszawa*. Part I: *Dzieje miasta—topografia—statystyka* [Warsaw. History of the City—Topography—Statistics]. Warsaw. 1913.

Gieysztor, A. "Początki Warszawy i zamku warszawskiego" [The Beginnings of Warsaw and the Warsaw Castle], *Wiedza i Życie*, Nos. 6–7, 1950.

———, S. Herbst, and E. Szwankowski. "Kształty Warszawy" [The Morphology of Warsaw], *BHSiK*, Vol. 9, Nos. 1–2, 1947.

Herbst, S. *Ulica Marszałkowska* [Marszałkowska Street]. Warsaw. 1949.

Karczewski, A. J. M. "W sprawie regulacji Placu Krasińskich w Warszawie" [The Regulation of Krasiński Square in Warsaw], *BHSiK*, Vol. 6, No. 1, 1938.

———. "Z dziejów trasy Belweder—Zamek—Żoliborz" [History of the Route Belweder—Castle—Żoliborz]. In: *SHBM*. Warsaw. 1955.

Małcużynski, W. *Rozwój terytorialny miasta Warszawy* [The Physical Development of the City of Warsaw]. Warsaw. 1900.

Miłobędzki, A. "Nowo-odkryte Varsaviana w archiwum Tylmana z Gameren" [Newly Discovered Varsaviana in the Archives of Tylman of Gameren], *KAU*, Vol. 6, No. 1, 1961.

Smoleński, W. *Komisja Boni Ordinis Warszawska (1765–1789)* [The Boni Ordinis Commission of Warsaw (1765–1789)]. Warsaw. 1913.

Sosnowski, O. *Powstanie, układ i cechy sieci ulicznej na obszarze Wielkiej Warszawy* [The Origin, Layout, and Characteristics of the Street System of Great Warsaw]. Studia do Dziejów Sztuki w Polsce. Vol. II. 1930.

Szczypiorski, A. *Ćwierć wieku Warszawy (1806–1830)* [A Quarter Century of Warsaw (1806–1830)]. Wrocław. 1964.

Szkice Nowomiejskie [Sketches of the New City of Warsaw]. Warsaw. 1961.

Szkice Staromiejskie [Sketches of the Old City of Warsaw]. Warsaw. 1955.

Szwankowski, E. "Kubickiego plan regulacji Pragi" [Kubicki's Plan for the Prague District of Warsaw], *BHSiK*, Vol. 10, No. 2, 1948.

———. *Warszawa. Rozwój urbanistyczny i architektoniczny* [Warsaw. Urban and Architectural Development]. Warsaw. 1952.

Tatarkiewicz, W. *Łazienki Warszawskie* [The Warsaw Łazienki]. Warsaw. 1957.

Tomkiewicz, W. "Warszawa w XVII wieku" [Warsaw in the XVII Century], *Kwartalnik Historyczny*, Vol. 72, No. 3, 1965.

Varsaviana w zbiorach drezdeńskich. Katalog planów i widoków Warszawy oraz rysunków architektonicznych budowli warszawskich okresu saskiego [Varsaviana in the Dresden Collections. Catalogue of Plans and Views of Warsaw as well as Architectural Drawings of Warsaw's Buildings during the Saxon Period]. Warsaw. 1965.

Wardzińska, K. *Dawne widoki Warszawy* [Early Views of Warsaw]. Warsaw. 1958.

Zachwatowicz, J. "Regulacja Placu Bankowego w Warszawie według projektu Corazziego" [Regulation of the Plac Bankowy in Warsaw according to Corazzi's Plan], *BHSiK*, Vol. 2, No. 4, 1934.

Zagrodzki, T. "Analiza rozplanowania Starego Miasta w Warszawie" [An Analysis of the Layout of the Old City of Warsaw], *KAU*, Vol. 1, No. 3, 1956.

Żaryn, S. "Kamienica warszawska w XV i XVI wieku" [The Warsaw Tenement House in the XV and XVI Centuries], *KAU*, Vol. 8, No. 2, 1963.

Zarys najdawniejszych dziejów obszaru Wielkiej Warszawy [An Outline of the Earliest History of the Territory of Great Warsaw]. Warsaw. 1963.

Wilno

Łowmiańska, M. *Wilno przed najazdem moskiewskim 1655 r.* [Wilno Prior to the Muscovite Invasion of 1655]. Wilno. 1929.

Narębski, S. *Zarys urbanistycznego rozwoju Wilna i plan jego zabudowania z r. 1817*

[An Outline of the Urban Development of Wilno and its Layout from the Year 1817]. Prace i materiały sprawozdawcze Sekcji Historii Sztuki, Towarzystwo Przyjaciół Nauk w Wilnie. Vol. II. Wilno. 1935.

Remer, J. *Wilno.* Poznań. 1934.

Wilno i ziemia wileńska [Wilno and the Territory of Wilno]. 2 vols. Wilno. 1930.

Wiślica

Zagrodzki, T. "Wstępne studia nad planem Wiślicy" [Introductory Studies of the Plan of Wiślica]. In: *III Konferencja Naukowa w Warszawie 13 i 14 kwietnia 1962.* Warsaw. 1964.

Wizna

Kamiński, A. "Wizna na tle pogranicza polsko-rusko-jaćwieskiego" [Wizna against the Background of the Polish-Ruthenian-Jacwiezian Borderland], *Rocznik Białostocki,* Vol. I, Białystok, 1961.

Włocławek

Grześkowiak, J. *Włocławek przed tysiącem lat* [Włocławek One Thousand Years Ago]. Włocławek. 1960.

Morawski, M. *Monografia Włocławka (Włocławia)* [A Monograph of Włocławek (Włocław)]. Włocławek. 1937.

Wolin

Filipowiak, W. *Port wczesnośredniowiecznego Wolina* [The Early Medieval Port of Wolin]. Materiały Zachodnio-Pomorskie, Vol. II. Szczecin. 1956.

———. "Wolin—największe miasto Słowiańszczyzny zachodniej." In: *Szkice z dziejów Pomorza. 1. Pomorze średniowieczne* [Wolin—the Largest Town of the Western Slavs. In: Sketches of the History of Pomerania. 1. Medieval Pomerania]. Warsaw. 1958.

Szczecin i Wolin we wczesnym średniowieczu [Szczecin and Wolin in the Early Middle Ages]. Wrocław. 1954.

Wrocław

Burgemeister, L. (ed.). *Kunstdenkmäler der Stadt Breslau.* 4 vols. Breslau. 1930–34.

Długoborski, W., J. Gierowski, and K. Maleczyński. *Dzieje Wrocławia do roku 1807* [History of Wrocław Up To the Year 1807]. Warsaw. 1958.

Golachowski, S. "Głos w dyskusji nad genezą rozplanowania średniowiecznego Wrocławia" [Discussion of the Genesis of the Medieval Layout of Wrocław], *KAU,* Vol. I, No. 1, 1956.

Kozaczewski, T. "Początki i rozwój Wrocławia do roku 1263" [The Origin and Development of Wrocław until the Year 1263], *KAU,* Vol. 4, Nos. 3–4, 1959.

Maleczyński, K. *Dzieje Wrocławia.* Part I: *Do roku 1526* [The History of Wrocław. Part I: Until the Year 1526]. Katowice. 1948.

Morelowski, M. *Rozwój urbanistyki Wrocławia przed kolonizacją z lat 1241–1242* [The Development of Wrocław's Layout Before Its Colonization in the Years 1241–1242]. Sprawozdania Wrocławskiego Towarzystwa Naukowego. Vol. VI. Wrocław. 1954.

Müller, E. *Die Altstadt von Breslau. Citybildung und Physiognomie. Ein Beitrag zur Stadtgeographie Breslaus.* Breslau. 1931.

Schultz, A. "Topographie Breslaus im 14. und 15. Jahrhundert," *Zeitschrift des Vereins für Geschichte Schlesiens,* Vol. X, 1871.

Stein, R. "Die Siedlungsgeschichte Breslaus bis 1263 vom Stadtplan aus beurteilt." In: *Beiträge zur Geschichte der Stadt Breslau.* Book I. Breslau. 1934.

———. *Der Grosse Ring zu Breslau.* Breslau. 1935.

Trawkowski, S. "Ołbin Wrocławski w XII w." [The Wrocław Ołbin in the XII Century], *Roczniki Dziejów Społecznych i Gospodarczych,* Vol. XX, 1958.

Zamość

Herbst, S. *Zamość.* Warsaw. 1954.

———, and J. Zachwatowicz. *Twierdza Zamość* [The Zamość Fortress]. Warsaw. 1936.

Kalinowski, W. *Rynek w Zamościu* [The Market Square in Zamość]. Warsaw. 1954.

Miłobędzki, J. A. "Ze studiów nad urbanistyką Zamościa" [Studies on the Urban Planning of Zamość], *BHS,* Vol. 15, Nos. 3–4, 1953.

CZECHOSLOVAKIA

CHAPTER 9

Association of Czechoslovak Architects and the State Board for Construction. *Town Planning in Czechoslovakia.* 1958.

Atlas Československé socialistické republiky. 1966.

Atlas Republiky československé. 1935.

Bachmann, A. *Geschichte Böhmens.* 2 vols. 1899–1905.

Bőhm, J., B. Havránek, J. Kolejka, J. Poulík, and V. Vaněček. *The Great Moravian Empire. Thousand Years of Tradition of State and Culture*. Prague. 1963.

Bosl, K. *Das Grossmährische Reich in der politischen Welt des 9. Jahrhunderts*. Sitzungsberichte der Bayrischen Akademie der Wissenschaften. Phil.-Hist. Kl., Heft 7. 1966.

———. (ed.). *Handbuch der Geschichte der Bőhmischen Länder*. Collegium Carolinum. Vol. I. 1967.

Bretholz, B. *Geschichte Bőhmens und Mährens bis zum Aussterben der Přemysliden (1306)*. 1912.

Brosche, W. "Beiträge zur Vor- und Frűhgeschichte der Karlsbader Landschaft," *Bohemia, Jahrbuch des Collegium Carolinum*, Vol. VI, 1965.

The Cambridge Medieval History. Vols. VI-VIII. 1957-59.

Childe, V. G. *The Prehistory of European Society*. 1958.

"Die Chronik der Bőhmen des Cosmas von Prag." Ed. by B. Bretholz. In: *Monumenta Germaniae Historica. Scriptores Rerum Germanicarum*. N. S. Vol. II. 1955.

Chyský, J., M. Skalník, and V. Adamec. *Guide to Czechoslovakia*. 1965.

The Czechoslovak Academy of Sciences. *The Great Moravia Exhibition. 1100 Years of Tradition of State and Cultural Life*. 1964.

Derzhavin, N. S. *Die Slaven im Altertum*. (German translation of the Russian *Slaviane v drevnosti*). 1946.

Dobiáš, J. "Il limes romano nelle terre della repubblica Cecoslovacca." In: *Quaderni dell'Impero. Il limes romano*. Istituto di Studi Romani. VIII. Rome. 1938.

———. "Le strade romane nel territorio Cecoslovacco." In: *Quaderni dell'Impero. Le grandi strade del mondo romano*. Istituto di Studi Romani. V. 1937.

Ehrich, R. W. "Homolka: A Fortified Neolithic Viilage in Bohemia," *Archaeology*, Vol. 9, No. 4, 1956.

L'Europe à la Fin de l'Âge de la Pierre. Actes du Symposium consacré aux Problèmes du Néolithique Européen. Prague-Liblice-Brno, Oct. 5-12, 1959. 1961.

Fekete, S. "Siedlungsformenkarte der Slowakei," *Geographica Helvetica*, No. 1, 1948.

Filip, J. *Popelnicová pole a počátky železné doby v Čechách* [The Urn Fields and the Beginning of the Iron Age in Bohemia]. 1936-37.

Fredegarii Chronicorum Liber Quartus. Translated by J. M. Wallace-Hadrill. 1960.

Friedrich, W. "Die historische Geographie Bőhmens bis zum Beginn der deutschen Kolonisation," *Abhandlungen der K. K. Geographischen Gesellschaft in Wien*, Vol. IX, No. 3, 1912.

Fűgedi, E. "Kirchliche Topographie und Siedlungsverhältnisse im Mittelalter in der Slowakei," *Studia Slavica*, Vol. V, Nos. 3-4, 1959.

Geppert, F. "Die Burgen und Städte bei Thietmar von Merseburg," *Thüringisch-Sächsische Zeitschrift für Geschichte und Kunst*, Vol. XVI, 1927.

Das Grossmährische Reich. Tagung der wissenschaftlichen Konferenz des Archäologischen Instituts der Tschechoslowakischen Akademie der Wissenschaften, Brno-Nitra, Oct. 1-4, 1963. 1966.

Grunzel, J. "Über die deutschen Stadtrechte Böhmens und Mährens," *Mitteilungen des Vereines für Geschichte der Deutschen in Bőhmen*, Vol. 30, 1892 and Vol. 31, 1893.

Hensel, W. *Anfänge der Städte bei den Ost- und Westlawen*. 1967.

———. *Die Slawen im Frűhen Mittelalter*. 1965.

———. "Les origines des villes slaves occidentales et orientales," *Atti del VI Congresso Internazionale delle Scienze Preistoriche e Protostoriche*, Vol. I, 1963.

———. "Types de fortifications Slaves du Haut Moyen-Âge" *Archaeologia Polona*, Vol. II, 1959.

Hoenig, A. *Deutscher Städtebau in Bőhmen. Die mittelalterlichen Stadtgrundrisse Bőhmens mit besonderer Berücksichtigung der Hauptstadt Prag*. 1921.

Horák, B. *Geografický a ethnografický obraz českých zemí v době římského cisařství* [A Geographical and Ethnographical Picture of the Bohemian Lands at the Time of the Imperium Romanum]. Rozpravy Československé akademie věd. 1955.

Hrůza, J. *Česká města* [Bohemian Cities]. 1960.

Institut d'Histoire de l'Académie Polonaise des Sciences. *L'Europe aux IXᵉ-XIᵉ Siècles. Aux origines des États nationaux*. Actes du Colloque international sur les Origines des États européens aux IXe-XIe Siècles. Warsaw and Poznań, Sept. 7-13, 1965. 1968.

Kaminsky, H. *A History of the Hussite Revolution*. 1967.

Kavka, F. "Die Städte Böhmens und Mährens zur Zeit des Přemyslidenstaates." In: *Die Städte Mitteleuropas im 12. und 13. Jahrhundert*. Published by the Archiv der Stadt Linz. 1963.

Klimesch, J. M. "Die Ortsnamen im südlichen und südwestlichen Böhmen," *Mitteilungen des Vereines für Geschichte der Deutschen in Böhmen*, 1908, 1909, 1911.

Koebner, R. "Dans les terres de colonisation: marchés slaves et villes allemandes," *Annales d'Histoire Économique et Sociale*, Vol. 9, 1937.

Kőtzschke, R. *Quellen zur Geschichte der ostdeutschen Kolonistation im 12. bis 14. Jahrhundert*. 2nd ed. 1931.

Krallert, W., W. Kuhn, and E. Schwarz. *Atlas zur Geschichte der deutschen Ostsiedlung*. 1958.

Krofta, K. "Bohemia to the Extinction of the Přemyslids." In: *Cambridge Medieval History*. Vol. VI. 1929.

Líbal, D. "Rozwój miast Czeskich od XI wieku do rewolucji Husyckiej" [The Development of Czech Towns from the XI Century to the Hussite Revolution], *Kwartalnik Architektury i Urbanistyki*, Vol. III, Nos. 3–4, Warsaw, 1958.

Liczbiński, A. "Z wycieczki po miastach Czeskich" [A Tour of Czech Towns], *Kwartalnik Architektury i Urbanistyki*, Vol. III, Nos. 3–4, Warsaw, 1958.

Limes Romanus Konferenz, Nitra. Slowakische Akademie der Wissenschaften. Archäologisches Institut in Nitra. 1959.

Lippert, J. *Socialgeschichte Böhmens in Vorhussitischer Zeit*. 2 vols. 1896–98.

Malaschofsky, A. "Beiträge zur Siedlungsgeographie der Slowakei," *Südostforschungen*, Vol. VI, Nos. 1–2, 1941.

Merian, Matthaeus. *Topographia Bohemiae, Moraviae et Silesiae*. Frankfurt. 1650.

Mezník, J. "K otázce struktury českých měst v době předhusitské," [The Question of the Structure of Bohemian Cities in Pre-Hussite Times], *Sborník prací filosofické fakulty Brněnské university*, řada historická, C 12, 1965.

Motyková-Šneidrová, Karla. *Die Anfänge der römischen Kaiserzeit in Böhmen*. Fontes Archaeologici Pragenses. Vol. 6, 1963.

Neustupný, E. and J. *Czechoslovakia before the Slavs*. 1961.

Neustupný, J. "Fortifications appartenant à la Civilisation Danubienne Néolithique. Premières Bourgades en Europe Centrale," *Archiv Orientální*, Vol. XVIII, No. 4, 1950.

Die österreichisch-ungarische Monarchie in Wort und Bild. 24 vols. 1886–1902.

Palacký, F. *Geschichte von Böhmen*. 5 vols. 1864–65.

Poulík, J. "The latest Archeological Discoveries from the Period of the Great Moravian Empire," *Historica*, Vol. I, 1959.

———. "Die neuesten Entdeckungen aus Hauptburgen des Grossmährischen Reiches," *Jahrbuch für Fränkische Landesforschung*, Vol. 19, 1959.

Preidel, H. *Die Anfänge der slawischen Besiedlung Böhmens und Mährens*. 2 vols. 1954–57.

———. *Das Grossmährische Reich im Spiegel der Bodenfunde*. 1968.

———. "Handel und Verkehr in den Sudetenländern während der zweiten Hälfte des ersten Jahrtausends n. Chr.," *Südost-Forschungen*, Vol. V, Nos. 2–3, 1940.

———. *Slawische Altertumskunde des östlichen Mitteleuropas im 9. und 10. Jahrhundert*. Pt. I. 1961.

———. *Die vor- und frühgeschichtlichen Siedlungsräume in Böhmen und Mähren*. 1953.

Quirin, K. H. *Die deutsche Ostsiedlung im Mittelalter*. 1954.

Schaller, J. *Topographie des Königreichs Böhmen*. 7 vols. 1785–87.

Schmid, H. F. "Die Burgbezirksverfassung bei den slavischen Völkern in ihrer Bedeutung für die Geschichte ihrer Siedlung und ihrer staatlichen Organisation," *Jahrbücher für Kultur und Geschichte der Slaven*, N. F., Vol. II, No. 2, 1926.

Schránil, J. *Die Vorgeschichte Böhmens und Mährens*. 1928.

Schwarz, E. "Die Volkstumverhältnisse in den Städten Böhmens und Mährens vor den Hussitenkriegen," *Bohemia, Jahrbuch des Collegium Carolinum*, Vol. II, 1961.

Seton-Watson, R. W. *A History of the Czechs and Slovaks*. 1943.

Šimák, J. V. "Středověká kolonisace v zemích českých" [Medieval Colonization of Czech Lands], *České dějiny*, Vol. I, No. 5, 1938.

Simonyi, D. "Slawische Burgwälle," *Archivum Europae Centro-Orientalis*, Vol. VIII, 1942.

Städtebaugeschichte und Aufbau in historischen Städten. Exkursionskatalog und Report der Konferenz der Československá akademie věd, Deutsche Bauakademie, Polska Akademia Nauk, Slovenská akadémia vied auf Schloss Dobříš, Czechoslovakia, 1957.

"Stradonitz." In: *Reallexicon der Vorgeschichte*. Ed. by M. Ebert. Vol. XII. 1928.

Svoboda, B. *Čechy a římské imperium* [Bohemia and the Roman Empire]. 1948.

Tacitus. *De Germania*. Loeb Classical Library. 1963.

Trillmich, M. *Siedlung und Wirtschaft im Isergebirgsland bis an die Schwelle des Industriealters*. 1939.

Vogt, K. *Die Burg in Böhmen bis zum Ende des 12. Jahrhunderts*. 1938.

Wanklyn, Harriet. *Czechoslovakia*. 1954.

Weizsäcker, W. "Eindringen und Verbreitung der deutschen Stadtrechte in Böhmen und Mähren," *Deutsches Archiv für Landes- und Volksforschung*, Vol. I, No. 1, 1937.

———. *Quellenbuch zur Geschichte der Sudetenländer*. Veröffentlichungen des Collegium Carolinum. Vol. 7. 1960.

Werner, Friedrich Bernhard. *Delineatio & repraesentatio notabilissimorum prospectuum . . . Regiae bohemicae metropolis Pragae . . .* Augsburg. 1720 (?).

Wolny, G. *Die Markgrafschaft Mähren, topographisch, statistisch und historisch geschildert*. 6 vols. 1835–42.

Workman, H. B. *The Dawn of the Reformation*. Vol. II: *The Age of Hus*. 1902.

Zalčík, T. "W sprawie genezy miast Orawskich" [On the Origin of the Layout of Orawan Towns], *Kwartalnik Architektury i Urbanistyki*, Vol. II, Nos. 3–4, Warsaw, 1957.

Zatschek, H. "Die Witigonen und die Besiedlung Südböhmens," *Deutsches Archiv für Landes- und Volksforschung*, Vol. I. No. 1, 1937.

Zycha, A. "Über den Ursprung der Städte in Böhmen und die Städtepolitik der Přemysliden," *Mitteilungen des Vereines für Geschichte der Deutschen in Böhmen*, Vol. 52, 1914 and Vol. 53, 1915.

CHAPTERS 10 TO 23

Architektura v českém národním dědictví [The Czech National Architectural Heritage]. Ed. by Z. Wirth and A. Müllerová. Prague. 1961.

Bél, M. *Compendium Hungariae Geograficum ad exemplar Notitiae Hungariae Novae*. 1753.

———. *Notitia Hungariae Novae historico-geographica*. 1735–37.

Benešová, M. "Význam československých lázní ve vývoji 19. století" [The Importance of Czechoslovak Spas during the 19th Century]. In: *Yearbook of the Czech Technical University*. Prague. 1958.

Česká akademie věd a umění. *Soupis památek historických a uměleckých v Království českém od pravěku do počátku XIX. století* [A List of Historical and Artistic Monuments in the Czech Kingdom from Ancient Times to the Beginning of the 19th Century]. Prague. 1897–1930.

Československá společnost pro šíření politických a vědeckých znalostí. *Československá vlastiveda*. Vol. II: *Dejiny*. Svazek I [A History of Czechoslovakia. Vol. II: The History. Book I]. Prague. 1963.

Chaloupecký, V. *Staré Slovensko* [Ancient Slovakia]. Bratislava. 1923.

Dějepis výtvarného umění v Čechách [The History of Czech Fine Arts]. Ed. by Z. Wirth. Prague. 1931.

Dokoupil, Z., P. Nauman, D. Riedl, and I. Veselý. *Historické zahrady v Čechách a na Moravě* [Historical Gardens in Bohemia and Moravia]. Prague. 1957.

Dostál, O. "Architektura české vesnice na rozhraní 18. a 19. století" [The Architecture of the Czech Village at the End of the 18th and the Beginning of the 19th Centuries]. In: *Yearbook of the Czech Technical University*. Prague. 1958.

———. "Le village en Tchécoslovaquie et son développement." In: *Zemědělské stavby*. 1958.

Foltýn, L., A. Keviczký, and I Kulm. *Architektúra na Slovensku do polovice XIX. storočia* [Architecture in Slovakia until the Mid-nineteenth Century]. Bratislava. 1958.

Güntherová-Mayerová, A. "Barokové umenie na Slovensku" [Baroque Art in Slovakia], *Pamiatky a múzeá*, Vol. IV, No. 4, 1955.

———. *Dejiny a súpis výtvarných pamiatok Oravy* [A History and Inventory of Orava Art Monuments]. Martin. 1944.

———. "Renesančné umenie na Slovensku" [Renaissance Art in Slovakia], *Pamiatky a múzeá*, Vol. IV, No. 3, 1955.

———. "Románske umenie na Slovensku" [Romanesque Art in Slovakia], *Pamiatky a múzeá*, Vol. III, No. 2, 1954.

Hoffmann, J. *Staré umění na Slovensku* [Ancient Art in Slovakia]. Prague. 1930.

Hosák, L. *Historický místopis země moravskoslezské* [Historical Topography of the Moravian-Silesian Lands]. 9 Pts. Brno. 1933–38.

Hrady a zámky [Castles and Palaces]. Ed. by

J. Hilmera. Prague. 1958.

Hrůza, J. *Česká města* [Czech Towns]. Prague. 1960.

Janšák, Št. *Slovensko v dobe uhorského feudalizmu* [Slovakia during the Period of Hungarian Feudalism]. Bratislava. 1932.

———. *Staré osídlenie Slovenska* [Old Settlements in Slovakia]. N.d.

Koláček, F. *Pôdorys severoslovenských miest* [The Plans of North-Slovakian Towns]. Bratislava. 1933.

Korabinsky, J. M. *Atlas Regni Hungariae portatilis.* Pressburg. 1817.

———. *Geographisch-historisches und Produkten Lexikon von Ungarn.* Pressburg. 1786.

Križko, P. *Dejepisný nástin o zakladaní nových osád v XII. a XIV. storočí* [Historical Survey of the Founding of New Settlements in the 12th and 14th Centuries]. 1888.

Kuča, O. "Zámecké zahrady v Kroměříži, K analyse architektonické zahrady a přírodního parku v období 1790–1850" [The Castle Gardens of Kroměříž: An Analysis of the Formal Garden and the Natural Park, 1790–1850], *Umění*, Vol. IV, 1958.

Kutal, A., D. Líbal, and A. Matějček. *České umění gotické I.* [Czech Gothic Art I.]. Prague. 1949.

Láznička, Z. *Moravská města* [Moravian Cities]. Brno. 1948.

———. *Typy venkovského osídlení na Moravě* [Types of Rural Settlements in Moravia]. Brno. 1946.

Líbal, D. *Gotická architektura v Čechách a na Moravě* [Gothic Architecture in Bohemia and Moravia]. Prague. 1948.

———. "Die Methode der historisch-urbanistischen und architektonischen Forschung bei der Rekonstruktion historischer Städte." In: *Städtebau. Geschichte und Gegenwart.* Materialien der Konferenz Erfurt, 1956. Berlin. 195–

———. "Rozwój miast Czeskich od XI wieku do rewolucji Husyckiej" [The Development of Czech Towns from the XI Century to the Hussite Revolution], *Kwartalnik Architektury i Urbanistyki*, Vol. III, Nos. 3–4, Warsaw, 1958.

Mencl, V. *Středověká architektúra na Slovensku I.* [Medieval Architecture in Slovakia I.]. Prague-Prešov. 1937.

———. *Středověká města na Slovensku* [Medieval Towns in Slovakia]. Bratislava. 1938.

Menclová, D. "O středověkém opevnění našich měst" [On the Medieval Fortifications of our Cities], *Zprávy památkové péče*, Vol. X, 1950.

———. *Přehled vývoje architektury na Slovensku od XVII. do poloviny XIX. století* [A Survey of the Architectural Development in Slovakia from the 17th to the Middle of the 19th Century]. Bratislava. 1934.

Merian, Matthaeus. *Topographia Bohemiae, Moraviae et Silesiae . . .* Frankfurt. 1650.

Orth, J., and F. Sládek. *Topograficko-statistický slovník Čech* [Topographical-Statistical Dictionary of Bohemia]. Prague. 1870.

Palacký, F. *Popis Králowstwí Českého* [A Description of the Czech Kingdom]. Prague. 1848.

Pelikán, O. *Slovensko a rímske impérium* [Slovakia and the Roman Empire]. Bratislava. 1960.

Pinkava, V. *Vznik a rozvoj královských měst na Moravě* [Origin and Evolution of the Royal Free Towns in Moravia]. 1922.

Pohl, J. *Typy vesnických sídel v Čechách* [Types of Rural Settlements in Bohemia]. Prague. 1935.

Pražák, V. "K problematice základních půdorysních typů lidových staveb v Československu" [To the Problems of Some Characteristic Plans of Czechoslovak Folk Architecture], *Československá Ethnografie*, Vol. VI, No. 4, 1958.

Profous, A. *Místní jména v Čechách* [Town Names in Bohemia]. Prague. 1947–57.

Prokop, A. *Die Markgrafschaft Mähren in kunstgeschichtlicher Beziehung. Grundzüge einer Kunstgeschichte dieses Landes mit besonderer Berücksichtigung der Baukunst.* Vols. III-IV. Vienna. 1904.

Rejnuš, M. "K otázce rozmnožování královských měst za vlády Přemysla Otokar II" [To the Question of the Increase of Royal Towns at the Time of Přemysl Otokar II], *Časopis Matice moravské*, Vol. 76, 1957.

Riedl, D. *Vývoj měst v Čechách a na Moravě* [The Development of Towns in Bohemia and Moravia]. Research Institute of Building and Architecture, Prague. Vol. I. Brno. 1953.

Říkovský, F. *Základy k sídelnímu zeměpisu Československa* [The Foundations of Settlement Geography in Czechoslovakia]. Brno. 1939.

Schaller, J. *Topographie des Königreichs Böhmen.* Prague. 1785–90.

Sedláček, A. *Hrady, zámky a tvrze Království*

českého [Castles, Palaces, and Fortresses of the Czech Kingdom]. Vols. I-XII. Prague. 1882–1927.

———. *Místopisný slovník historický Království českého* [A Topographical-historical Dictionary of the Czech Kingdom]. Prague. 1895–1908.

Šimák, J. V. "Středověká kolonisace v zemích českých" [Medieval Colonization in Czech Territories], *České dějiny*, Vol. I, No. 5, 1938.

Sommer, J. G. *Das Königreich Böhmen, statistisch-topographisch dargestellt*. Vols. 1–16. Prague. 1833–49.

Starý, O. (ed.). *Československá architektura od nejstarší doby po součastnost* [Czechoslovak Architecture from Ancient Times to the Present]. Prague. 1962.

Topographisches Lexikon von Böhmen. Prague. 1852.

Ústav stavebných hmôt a konštrukcií. *Klasicistická architektúra na Slovensku; príspevok k jej dejinám* [Classicist Architecture in Slovakia. A Contribution to its History]. Bratislava. 1955.

Varsík, B. *Vznik a rozvoj miest na Slovensku v 13. a 14. storočí* [Origin and Development of Towns in Slovakia in the 13th and 14th Centuries]. 1958.

Vlastivěda moravská. Pt. 2: *Místopis Moravy* [The History of Moravia. Pt. 2: Topography of Moravia]. Brno. 1897–1929.

Vojtísek, V. *Česká města* [Czech Towns]. 1940.

Vydra, J. *Ľudová architektúra na Slovensku* [Folk Architecture in Slovakia]. Bratislava. 1958.

Wágner, V. *Dejiny výtvarného umenia na Slovensku* [History of Fine Arts in Slovakia]. Trnava. 1930.

———. *Veľká Morava a naša doba* [Great Moravia and Our Time]. Bratislava. 1963.

———. *Vývin výtvarného umenia na Slovensku* [The Development of Fine Arts in Slovakia]. Bratislava. 1948.

Wirth, Z. (ed.). *Umělecké památky Čech* [The Artistic Monuments of Bohemia]. Prague. 1957.

———, and J. Benda. *Státní hrady a zámky* [Castles and Palaces]. Prague. 1955.

———, and A. Matějček. *Česká architektura XIX. stol.* [Czech Architecture in the 19th Century]. Prague. 1922.

Banská Bystrica

Šášky, L. "Banská Bystrica," *Pamiatky a múzeá*, Vol. IV, No. 2, 1955.

Škultéty, J. *Banská Bystrica v minulosti* [Banská Bystrica in the Past]. N.d.

Banská Štiavnica

Jankovič, V. *Banská Štiavnica v XVI. storočí* [Banská Štiavnica in the 16th Century]. N.d.

Plicková, Ester. *Banská Štiavnica*. Martin. 1957.

Šášky, L. "Pamiatky Banskej Štiavnice" [Monuments of Banská Štiavnica], *Pamiatky a múzeá*, Vol. VI, No. 1, 1957.

Bardejov

Križanová, E. "Mesto Bardejov" [The City of Bardejov], *Pamiatky a múzeá*, Vol. V, No. 1, 1956.

Krpelec, B. *Bardejov a jeho okolie dávno a dnes* [Bardejov and Surroundings in the Past and Today]. Bardejov. 1935.

Bechyně

Menclová, D. *Bechyně, státní zámek a město* [Bechyně, Castle and Town]. Prague. 195–?.

Benešov nad Ploučnicí

Šamánková, E. *Benešov nad Ploučnicí*. Prague. 1963.

Blatná

Menclová, D. *Blatná. Státní hrad, město a okolí* [Blatná. Castle, Town, and Environs]. Prague. 1953.

Bratislava

Bokeš, F. *Vývin osídlenia mesta Bratislavy* [The Development of the Settlement of the City of Bratislava]. 1938–39.

Chaloupecký, V. *K nejstarším dějinám Bratislavy* [To the Oldest History of Bratislava]. Bratislava. 1922.

Lehotská, V., V. Mencl, and D. Menclová. *Bratislava; stavebný vývin a pamiatky mesta* [Bratislava. The Architectural Development and Monuments of the City]. Bratislava. 1961.

Mencl, V., and D. Menclová. *Bratislava, stavební obraz města* [Bratislava. An Architectural Picture of the City]. Prague. 1936.

Menclová, D. *Hrad Bratislava* [The Castle of Bratislava]. Prague. 1935.

Ratkoš, P., and others. *Bratislavský hrad* [The Bratislava Castle]. Bratislava. 1960.

Šášky, L. "Náčrt stavebného vývoja Bratislavského podhradia" [Architectural History of the Castle District in Bratislava], *Pamiatky a múzeá*, Vol. IV, No. 3, 1955.

Brezno

Hreblay, A. *Brezno a okolie* [Brezno and Environs]. Bratislava. 1954.

Šášky, L. "Brezno," *Vlastivědný časopis*, Vol. XI, No. 4, 1962.

Brno

Bretholz, B. *Geschichte der Stadt Brünn.* Vol. I. 1911.

Fuchs, B. *Vývoj komposice půdorysné osnovy na obrazu města Brna* [The Development of the Layout of Brno]. Brno. 1946.

———, and E. Hruška. *Studie k územnímu plánu brněnské oblasti* [A Study of the Ground Plan of the District of Brno]. Brno. 1949.

Hálová-Jahodová, C. *Brno; stavební a umělecký vývoj města* [Brno. The Architectural and Artistic Development of the City]. Prague. 1947.

———. *Das historische Geländeprofil der mittelalterlichen Stadt Brno.* Brno. 1964.

Buchlov and Buchlovice

Bartušek, A., K. Svoboda, and others. *Buchlov; státní hrad a okolí* [Buchlov. State Castle and Environs]. Prague. 1956.

Svoboda, K., and collaborators. *Buchlovice. Státní zámek a okolí* [Buchlovice. State Castle and Environs]. Prague. 1953.

Český Krumlov

Mencl, V. (ed.). *Český Krumlov.* Prague. 1948.

Šamánková, E., and J. Vondra. *Český Krumlov.* Prague. 1961.

Cheb

Wanie, P. "Der Stadt Eger geschichtlicher Entwicklungsgang bis zur Mitte des XVI. Jahrhunderts," *Mitteilungen des Vereines für Geschichte der Deutschen in Böhmen*, Vol. 51, No. 1, 1912, No. 3, 1913.

Dačice

Bartušek, A. *Dačice; státní zámek, město a památky v okolí* [Dačice. Castle, Town, and Monuments in the Vicinity]. Prague. 1960.

Křížek, F., and V. Černá. *Dačice.* Prague. 1943.

Dobruška

Hejna, A. *Opočno. Státní zámek a památky v okolí* [Opočno. The State Castle and the Monuments in the Vicinity]. Prague. 1962.

Dolní Bojanovice

Máčel, O., and J. Vajdiš. *Slovácko. Architektonický vývoj vesnice* [The Architectural Development of the Village in the Region of Slovácko]. Prague. 1958.

Frýdlant

Kotrba, V. *Frýdlant. Státní hrad a památky v okolí* [Frýdlant. The State Castle and Monuments in the Vicinity]. Prague. 1959.

Fulnek

Rokyta, H. *Fulnek.* Prague. 1955.

Hlohovec

Felcán, A. *Hlohovec. Kedysi, dnes a zajtra* [Hlohovec. Yesterday, Today, and Tomorrow]. N.d.

Hromadová, L. "Hlohovec," *Vlastivědný časopis*, Vol. XI, No. 1, 1962.

Holešov

Kuča, O. "K vývoji zámecké zahrady v Holešově" [To the Development of the Castle Garden at Holešov], *Umění*, Vol. V, No. 1, 1957.

Richter, V. "Filiberto Luchese na Moravě" [Filiberto Luchese in Moravia], *Ročenka Kruhu pro pěstovaní dejin umění za rok 1934*, Prague, 1935.

Horaźdovice

Birnbaumová, A. *Horaźdovice.* Prague. 1941.

Horšovský Týn

Dvořaková, V. *Horšovský Týn.* Prague. 1954.

Hradec Králové

Kubíček, A., and Z. Wirth. *Hradec Králové.* Prague. 1959.

Hybe

Klein and Tesnoskalský. *Oppidum Hybe.* 1942.

Jaroměřice nad Rokytnou

Bartušek, A., and T. Kubátová. *Jaroměřice nad Rokytnou. Státní zámek, město a okolí* [Jaroměřice nad Rokytnou. State Castle, Town, and Environs]. Prague. 1953.

Jičín

Morávek, J., and Z. Wirth. *Valdštejnův Jičín* [Valdštejn's Jičín]. Prague. 1946.

Jihlava

Bartušek, A. *Umělecké památky Jihlavy* [The Artistic Monuments of Jihlava]. Havlíčkův Brod. 1960.

Hoffman, F. *Jihlava v husitské revoluci* [Jihlava during the Hussite Revolution]. Havlíčkův Brod. 1961.

Šamánková, E. *Jihlava*. 1955.

Jindřichův Hradec

Hilmera, J. *Jindřichův Hradec; městská památková reservace a státní zámek* [Jindřichův Hradec. The Town's Historical Area and Castle]. Prague. 1957.

Teplý, F. *Dějiny města Jindřichova Hradce* [The History of the Town of Jindřichův Hradec]. 1927–34.

Kežmarok

Hýroš, Št. *Kežmarok; jeho páni a okolie* [Kežmarok. Its Lords and Surroundings]. N.d.

Komlóšová, M. "Mesto Kežmarok" [The City of Kežmarok], *Pamiatky a múzeá*, Vol. VI, No. 2, 1957.

Klatovy

Wágner, V. *Klatovy*. Prague. 1948.

Komárno

Filous, J. *Pevnosť Komárno* [The Fortress of Komárno]. Komárno. 1930.

Isakovičová, M. "Komárno," *Vlastivědný časopis*, Vol. XI, No. 1, 1962.

Košice

Jursa, A. "Stavebný vývoj Košíc" [Architectural Development of Košice], *Pamiatky a múzeá*, Vol. VI, No. 4, 1957.

Šášky, L. "Košice," *Pamiatky a múzeá*, Vol. IV, No. 1, 1955.

Varsík, B. *Osídlenie Košickej kotliny I* [The Settling of the Košice Basin I]. Bratislava. 1964.

———. *Slovenská ulica v Košiciach a vznik mesta* [Slovak Street in Košice and Origin of the City]. 1948.

Zalčík, T. "O niektorých urbanistických otázkach Košíc" [Some Urban Questions of Košice], *Pamiatky a múzeá*, Vol. VI, No. 4, 1957.

Kouřim

Líbal, D. *Kouřim*. Prague. 1943.

Kremnica

Bornemissa, J. *Kremnica, Nová Baňa a okolie* [Kremnica, Nová Baňa, and Their Surroundings]. Kremnica. 1939.

Lamoš, T. *Sídelný zemepis Kremnice* [The Geography of the Settlement of Kremnica]. Bratislava. 1948.

Matunák, M. *Z dejín slobodného a hlavného banského mesta Kremnice* [From the History of the Free and Chief Mining City of Kremnica]. Kremnica. 1928.

Šášky, L. "Kremnica," *Pamiatky a múzeá*, Vol. V, No. 2, 1956.

Kroměříž

Jůza, V., I. Krsek, J. Petrů, and V. Richter. *Kroměříž*. Prague. 1963.

Kuča, O. "Zámecké zahrady v Kroměříži, K analyse architektonické zahrady a přírodního parku v období 1790–1850" [The Castle Gardens of Kroměříž. An analysis of a Formal Garden and Natural Park, 1790–1850], *Umění*, Vol. IV, 1958.

Nypoort, Justus van der. *Album pohledů na Kroměříž* [A Book of Illustrations of Kroměříž]. 1961.

Peřinka, F. V. *Dějiny Kroměříže* [The History of Kroměříž]. 3 vols. Kroměříž. 1913–17.

Vacková, J., and collaborators. *Kroměříž. Městská památková reservace a státní zámek* [Kroměříž. The Town's Historical Area and the State Castle]. 1960.

Kuks

Blažíček, O. J. *Kuks. Hospitál a Betlém* [Kuks. Hospital and Betlém]. Prague. 1959.

Kutná Hora

Herout, J. "Středověký půdorys a opevnění Kutné Hory" [Medieval Layout and Fortifications of Kutná Hora], *Zprávy památkové péče*, 1949.

Matějková, E. *Kutná Hora*. Prague. 1962.

Wirth, Z. *Kutná Hora, město a jeho umění* [Kutná Hora. The Town and its Art]. Prague. 1930.

Lednice and Valtice

Charvátová, E., and B. Štorm. *Lednice; státní zámek* [The State Castle of Lednice]. Prague. 1955.

Witzany, M. *Die Marktgemeinde Eisrub*. Lednice. 1907.

Leopoldov

Sedlák, F. "Z dejín pevnosti Leopoldov" [From the History of the Fortress of Leopoldov], *Vlastivědný časopis*, Vol. XII, No. 4, 1963.

Levice

Dorotjak, D., and T. Zalčík. "K výstavbe Levíc" [To the Building of Levice], *Pamiatky a múzeá*, Vol. X, No. 2, 1961.

Levoča

Horváth, P. "Z minulosti stredovekej Levoče" [From the Past of Medieval Levoča], *Pamiatky a múzeá*, Vol. V, No. 3, 1956.

Liberec

Technik, S., and V. Ruda. *Liberec minulosti a budoucnosti* [Liberec in the Past and Future]. Liberec. 1961.

Lipník nad Bečvou

Menclová, D. *Helfštejn*. Prague. 1961.

Liptovská Teplička

Zalčík, T. "Vývin miest a mestečiek Liptova" [The Development of Cities and Towns in the Liptov Region], *Pamiatky a múzeá*, Vol. IX, No. 4, 1960.

Litoměřice

Votoček, O. *Litoměřice*. Prague. 1955.

Martin

Florek, P. *Turčiansky Sv. Martin v stredoveku; stredoveký vývin slovenského mesta* [Turčiansky Sv. Martin in the Middle Ages. The Medieval Development of a Slovak Town]. 1941.

Güntherová-Mayerová, A. "Pamiatky pozdnej gotiky v Turci" [Late Gothic Monuments in the Turiec Region], *Sborník MSS*, 1937.

Menclová, D. *Stredoveká architektúra v Turci* [Medieval Architecture in the Turiec Region]. 1936.

Mikulčice

Poulík, J. "Dvě velkomoravské rotundy v Mikulčicích" [Two Great Moravian Rotundas in Mikulčice]. In: *Monumenta Archeologica*. Vol. XII. Prague. 1963.

———. "The Latest Archeological Discoveries from the Period of the Great Moravian Empire." In: *Historica I*. Historical Sciences in Czechoslovakia. Prague. 1959.

———. *Staří Moravané budují svůj stát* [The Old Moravians Build Their State]. Gottwaldov. 1963.

———. "Výsledky výzkumu na velkomoravském hradišti 'Valy' u Mikulčic" [The Findings of Excavations in 'Valy', the Area of the Great Moravian Castle, near Mikulčice], *Památky archeologické*, Vol. XLVIII, No. 2, 1957.

Mikulov

Kostka, J. *Mikulov*. 1962.

Modra

Lehotská, D. *Dejiny Modry, 1158–1958* [History of Modra, 1158–1958]. Bratislava. 1961.

Moravská Třebová

Pechová, O. *Moravská Třebová*. Prague. 1957.

Netolice and Kratochvíle

Středa, F. D. *Zámek Kratochvíle* [The Castle of Kratochvíle]. Umělecké památky Čech. Prague. 1952.

Nitra

Boháč, J. *Dejiny staroslávnej Nitry* [The History of Old Glory Nitra]. Nitra. 1928.

Eisner, J., S. Fermánek, S. Janšák, V. Mencl, and V. Wágner. *Nitra, dejiny a umenie nitrianskeho zámku* [Nitra. The History and Art of Nitra Castle]. Trnava. 1933.

Horna, F. *Nitra*. 1964.

Wágner, V. *Nitra*. Nitra. 1964.

Nové Město nad Metují

Mannsbarth, J. *Nové Město nad Metují*. Prague. 1947.

Pavel, J. *Nové Město nad Metují; městská památková reservace, státní zámek a památky v okolí* [Nové Město nad Metují. The Town's Historical Area, State Castle, and the Monuments in its Vicinity]. Prague. 1962.

Nové Mesto nad Váhom

Kahounová, D. "Nové Mesto nad Váhom a jeho stavebný vývoj" [Nové Mesto nad Váhom and its Architectural Development], *Pamiatky a múzeá*, Vol. X, No. 2, 1961.

Opava

Láznička, Z. "Půdorysy slezských měst" [The Layouts of Silesian Towns], *Slezký sborník*, Vol. 43, 1945.

"Opava," *Sborník k 10. výročí osvobození města*, Opava, 1956.

Pardubice
Pavel, J. *Pardubice*. Prague. 1954.

Pelhřimov
Polesný, K., and Z. Wirth. *Pelhřimov*. Pelhřimov. 1911.

Plzeň
Mencl, V. *Plzeň*. Plzeň. 1961.

Polička
Líbal, D., and L. Rem. *Polička*. Prague. 1961.

Potštejn
Helfert, J. *Potštejn*. Klub turistů. 1948.

Prachatice
Hilmera, J. *Prachatice*. Prague. 1954.

Prague
Čarek, J. *Románská Praha* [Romanesque Prague]. Prague. 1947.
Chaloupecký, V., J. Květ, and V. Mencl. *Praha románská* [Romanesque Prague]. Prague 1948.
Filip, J. *Praha pravěká* [Prehistoric Prague]. Prague. 1949.
Fiala, Z. *Die Anfänge Prags. Eine Quellenanalyse zur Ortsterminologie bis zum Jahre 1235.* 1967.
Líbal, D. *Tisíc let pražské architektonické tvorby. Kniha o Praze* [A Thousand Years of Prague's Architectural Development. The Book of Prague]. Prague. 1962.
Poche, E., and J. Janáček. *Prahou krok za krokem* [Step by Step Through Prague]. Prague. 1963.
Tomek, V. V. *Dějepis města Prahy* [History of the City of Prague]. 8 vols. 1855–1910.
Wirth, Z. *Prague in Pictures of Five Centuries.* 1954.

Prešov
Dorotjak, D. "Pôdorys Prešova a jeho vývoj" [The Layout of Prešov and its Development], *Pamiatky a múzeá*, Vol. V, No. 4. 1956.
Križanová, E. "Prešov," *Pamiatsky a múzeá*, Vol. V, No. 4, 1956.
Sabol, Št. *Prešov v minulosti a dnes* [Prešov in the Past and Today]. Bratislava. 1943.

Prievidza and Bojnice
Hodal, F., and D. Menclová. *Hrad Bojnice* [The Castle of Bojnice]. Bratislava. 1956.

Novák, J. *Bojnice a okolie* [Bojnice and Its Environs]. Brno. 1922.

Příkazy
Kšír, J. "Lidové stavebnictví no Hané" [Folk Architecture in the Haná Region], *Československá Ethnografie*, Vol. IV, No. 4, 1956.

Prostějov
Janoušek, V. *Dějiny Prostějova* [The History of Prostějov]. Brno. 1938.
Mathon, J. *Prostějov*. Prostějov, 1924; Prague 1947.

Rokycany
Černá, V. *Rokycany*. Prague. 1946.

Ružomberok
Houdek, I. *600 rokov z minulosti bývalého výsadného mesta Ružomberku* [600 Years from the Past of the Former Free City of Ružomberok]. Ružomberok. 1943.

Rychnov nad Kněžnou
Pavel, J. *Rychnov nad Kněžnou*. Prague. 1963.

Sabinov
Wágner, V. *Sabinov*. Košice. 1962.

Skalica
Dúbravský, F. *Slobodné mesto so zriadeným magistrátom uhorským* [The Free City of Skalica, Seat of the Hungarian Magistrate]. Skalica. 1928.
Hýbl, R. *Počátky města Skalice* [The Beginnings of the City of Skalica]. N.d.
Kahoun, K. "Skalica," *Pamiatky a múzeá*, Vol. IX, No. 1, 1960.

Slaný
Wirth, Z. *Slaný*. 1938.

Slavkov u Brna
Kubátová, T. *Slavkov; státní zámek, město a okolí* [Slavkov. State Castle, Town, and Environs]. Prague. 1955.

Spišská Nová Ves
Vojtaš, M. *Spišská Nová Ves*. Spišská Nová Ves. 1957.
Zalčík, T. "Spišská Nová Ves," *Vlastivědný časopis*, Vol. XI, No. 3, 1962.

Spišská Sobota
Komlóšová, M. "Spišská Sobota," *Pamiatky a múzeá*, Vol. VI, No. 2, 1957.

Spišský Hrad

Horna, R. *Stručný náčrt dejín Spiša* [Brief Outline of the History of the Spiš Region]. Bratislava. 1957.

Menclová, D. *Spišský hrad* [Spiš Castle]. Bratislava. 1957.

Špirko, J. Umelecko-historické pamiatky na Spiši I [Art-Historical Monuments in the Spiš Region I]. Spišská Kapitula. 1933.

Šternberk

Hosák, L. *Středověká kolonisace v oblasti Jeseníků* [Medieval Colonization in the Jeseníky Region]. N.d.

Strakonice

Birnbaumová, A. *Město Strakonice* [The City of Strakonice]. Prague. 1947.

Sušice

Líbal, D. *Sušice. Minulosti západočeského kraje II.* [Sušice. The Past of the West Bohemian Region II.]. 1963.

Telč

Richter, V. *Telč*. Prague. 1953.

Teplice

Teplice Lázně v Čechách [The Spa of Teplice in Bohemia]. Teplice. 1957.

Třebíč

Bartušek, A. *Třebíč*. Prague. 1959.

Třeboň

Matouš, F. *Třeboň*. Prague. 1964.

Trenčín

Menclová, D. *Hrad Trenčín* [The Castle of Trenčín]. Bratislava. 1956.

Trnava

Dubnický, J. *Ranobarokový univerzitný kostol v Trnave* [The Early Baroque University Church in Trnava]. Bratislava. 1948.

Húščava, A. *Najstaršie výsady mesta Trnavy* [The Oldest Privileges of the City of Trnava]. Bratislava. 1939.

Jursa, A. "Trnava," *Pamiatky a múzeá*, Vol. VI, No. 3, 1957.

Varsík, B. *Vznik a počiatky mesta Trnavy* [The Origin and the Beginnings of the City of Trnava]. 1957.

Wágner, V. *Sborník 1238–1938–Trnava* [Collected Writings about Trnava, 1238–1938]. Trnava. 1938.

Uherské Hradiště

Böhm, J., and others. *Velká Morava; tisíciletá tradice státu a kultury* [Great Moravia. A Thousand-Year-Old Tradition of State and Culture]. Prague. 1963.

Jůzová, A., and V. Jůza. *Uherské Hradiště*. Gottwaldov. 1958.

Úštěk

Farka, M. "Město Úštěk a jeho stavební vývoj" [The City of Úštěk and its Architectural Development], *Zprávy památkové péče*, Vol. XXI, Nos. 1–2, 1961.

Veltrusy

Nauman, P. *Zámecký park ve Veltrusích* [The Castle Park in Veltrusy]. Prague. 1955.

Špecinger, O. *Chotkovské Veltrusy* [Chotek's Veltrusy]. Kralupy nad Vltavou, b.d., c. 1960.

Wenig, A. *Veltrusy, park a zámek* [Veltrusy. Park and Castle]. Prague. 1917.

Zálší

Dostál, O. "Příspěvek k poznání vývoje jihočeské lidové architektury" [A Contribution toward the Knowledge of the Development of South Bohemian Folk Architecture], *Památková péče*, Vol. 23, No. 1, 1963.

Žatec

Líbal, D. *Žatec*. Prague. 1958.

Žilina

Lombardini, A. *Stručný dějepis slobodného města Žiliny* [A Brief History of the Free City of Žilina]. Martin. 1874.

Zalčík, T. "K niektorým urbanistickým problémom Žiliny" [To Some Urban Problems of Žilina], *Vlastivědný časopis*, Vol. XI, No. 2, 1962.

Znojmo

Líbal, D., and L. Havlík. *Znojmo*. Prague. 1961.

Zvolen

Baník, J. *Slobodné a královské mesto Zvolen* [The Royal Free City of Zvolen]. Martin. 1891.

Menclová, D. *Hrad Zvolen* [The Castle of Zvolen]. Bratislava. 1954.

Wágner, V. *Zvolen v minulosti a dnes* [Zvolen in the Past and Present]. Bratislava. 1959.

HUNGARY

CHAPTER 24 AND APPENDIX

Alföldi, A. *Der Untergang der Römerherrschaft in Pannonien.* 2 vols. 1924–26.

———. "Zur Geschichte des Karpathenbeckens im 1. Jahrhundert v. Chr.," *Archivum Europae Centro-Orientalis,* Vol. VIII, 1942.

Altheim, F. *Geschichte der Hunnen.* Vol. I, 1959; Vol. IV and V, 1962.

Baedeker, K. *Austria-Hungary.* 1911.

Bálint, A. "Szeged," *Nouvelle Revue de Hongrie,* Vol. 58, No. 2, 1938.

Bálint, S. *Szeged városa* [The City of Szeged]. 1959.

Balogh, I. "Adatok az Alföld középkori régészetéhez" [Data on the Medieval Archeology of the Alföld], *Archaeológiai Értesítő,* Vol. 80, 1953.

Banner, J. "Szeged települése" [The Settlement of Szeged], *Föld és Ember,* Vol. V, 1925.

Bartha, A. "Hungarian Society in the Tenth Century and the Social Division of Labour," *Acta Historica,* Vol. IX, Nos. 3–4, 1963.

Bátky, S. von. "Das ungarische Bauernhaus," *Ungarische Jahrbücher,* Vol. 18, Nos. 2–4, 1938.

Bél, M. *Notitia Hungariae Novae historico-geographica.* 1735–37.

Beynon, E. D. "Migrations of Hungarian Peasants," *The Geographical Review,* Vol. 37, No. 2, 1937.

Bierbauer, V. "L'arcade hongroise," *Nouvelle Revue de Hongrie,* Vol. 60, No. 5, 1939.

———. "La forme urbaine de la plaine hongroise," *Nouvelle Revue de Hongrie,* Vol. 62, No. 6, 1940.

———. *Magyarország Repülőgépről* [Hungary from the Air]. 1937.

Bonomi, E. "Die Ansiedlungszeit des Ofener Berglandes," *Südost-Forschungen,* Vol. V, Nos. 2–3, 1940.

Braun, A., and E. R. J. Krejcsi. *Der Hausfleiss in Ungarn im Jahre 1884. Ein Beitrag zur Lehre von den gewerblichen Betriebssystemen.* 1886.

Braun, G., and F. Hogenberg. *Civitates Orbis Terrarum.* 1572–1618.

Bright, R. *Travels from Vienna through Lower Hungary.* 1818.

Brocquière, Bertrandon de la. *The Travels of Bertrandon de la Brocquière... to Palestine, and His Return from Jerusalem Overland to France, during the Years 1432 & 1433.* Translated by T. Johnes. 1807.

Burghardt, A. F. *Borderland. A Historical and Geographical Study of Burgenland, Austria.* 1962.

Bűnker, J. R. "Typen von Bauernhäusern aus der Gegend von Oedenburg," *Mitteilungen der Anthropologischen Gesellschaft in Wien,* Vol. 24, N.F., No. 4, 1894.

The Cambridge Medieval History. Vol. IV, Pt. 1, 1966; Vol. VI, 1957; Vol. VIII, 1959.

Csánki, D. *Magyarország történelmi földrajza a Hunyadiak korában* [Geography of Hungary during the Hunyadi Period]. 5 vols. 1890–1913.

Csaplovics, Johann von. *Topographisch-statistisches Archiv des Königreichs Ungern.* 2 vols. 1821.

Csatkai, E. *Sopron.* 1956.

Demian, M. *Tableau Géographique et Politique des Royaumes de Hongrie, d'Esclavonie, de Croatie, et de la Grande Principauté de Transilvanie.* 2 vols. 1809.

Den Hollander, A. N. J. "The Great Hungarian Plain: A European Frontier Area," *Comparative Studies in Society and History,* Vol. III, No. 1, 1960, and No. 2, 1961.

Ditz, H. *Die ungarische Landwirthschaft.* Volkswirthschaftlicher Bericht an das königl. Bayerische Staatsministerium des Handels und der öffentlichen Arbeiten. 1867.

Ember, Gy. *Zur Geschichte des Aussenhandels Ungarns im XVI Jahrhundert.* Studia Historica. Academiae Scientiarum Hungaricae. 44. 1960.

Entz, G., I. Genthon, and J. Szappanos. *Kecskemét.* 1961.

Enyedi, G. "Le village hongrois et la grande exploitation agricole," *Annales de Géographie,* Vol. 73, 1964.

Erdei, F. *Die ungarische Stadt.* Published by the Wissenschaftliche Ausschuss der Ungarisch-Deutschen Gesellschaft. No. 2. 1942.

Ewliyā Čelebi, Muḥammad Zillí ibn Derwīsh. *Evlia Cselebi török világutazó magyarországi utazásai....* [The Journey of Ewliyā Čelebi, Turkish Traveler in Hungary....]. According to the Commission of the Hungarian Academy of Sciences, translated and annotated by I. Karácson. Hungarian Academy of Sciences. 2 vols. 1904–08.

Fehér, G. "Bulgarish-ungarische Beziehungen in den V-XI Jahrhunderten," *Keleti Szemle,* Vol. 19, No. 2, 1921.

———. "Die landnehmenden Ungarn und ihr Verhältnis zu den Slawen des mittleren

Donaubeckens," *Studia Slavica*, Vol. III, Nos. 1-4, 1957.

Fessler, I. A. *Die Geschichten der Ungern und ihrer Landsassen*. 10 vols. 1823-49.

Finály, G. "A római birodalmi limes fölkutatásáról Pannoniában" [On the Discovery of the Roman Imperial limes in Pannonia], *Archaeológiai Értesitő*, 1905.

Fournier, A. "Handel und Verkehr in Ungarn und Polen um die Mitte des 18. Jahrhunderts," *Archiv für Oesterreichische Geschichte*, Vol. 69, 1887.

Frőhlich, R. "Acumincum vidéke és a régi pannoniai limes" [The District of Aquincum and the Pannonian limes], *Archaeológiai Értesitő*, 1892.

Fügedi, E. "Beiträge zur Siedlungsgeschichte der Slowaken im 18. Jh. auf dem Gebiet des heutigen Ungarn," *Studia Slavica*, Vol. XI, Nos. 3-4, 1965.

Gál, I. (ed.). *Ungarische Städtebilder*. Published for the Ungarische Städteverband. 1944.

Gerő, L. *Magyar Városképek* [Hungarian Townscapes]. 1953.

———. *Magyarországi várépítészet* [Military Architecture of Hungary]. 1955.

———. "Überreste mittelalterlicher Bauten und Stadtmauern in den ungarischen Städten," *Kwartalnik Architektury i Urbanistyki*, Vol. V, Nos. 1-2, Warsaw, 1960.

———. "Włoskie fortyfikacje bastionowe na węgrzech" [Italian Fortifications with Bastions in Hungary], *Kwartalnik Architektury i Urbanistyki*, Vol. IV, Nos. 1-2, Warsaw, 1959.

Gesztelyi Nagy, L. *Magyar Tanya* [The Hungarian Tanya]. 1928.

Glaser, L. "Dunántúl középkori úthálózata" [The Medieval Road System of Transdanubia], *Századok*, Vol. 63, 1929.

Graf, A. "Übersicht der antiken Geographie von Pannonien," *Dissertationes Pannonicae*, Musei Nationalis Hungarici, Ser. I, Fasc. 5, 1936.

Granasztói, P. "A magyar városépitészet sajátosságai" [Characteristics of Hungarian Urbanism], *Településtudományi Közlemények*, No. 8, 1956.

———. "Morphologische Probleme des ungarischen Städtebaues." In: *Städtebau. Geschichte und Gegenwart*. Ed. by G. Strauss, published by the Deutsche Bauakademie, Berlin. 1956.

———. "Zagadnienia współczesnej urbanistyki w miastach zabytkowych" [The Problems of Contemporary City Planning in Historical Towns], *Kwartalnik Architektury i Urbanistyki*, Vol. V, Nos. 1-2, Warsaw, 1960.

Grünberg, K. *Studien zur Österreichischen Agrargeschichte*. 1901.

Győrffy, Gy. *Einwohnerzahl und Bevölkerungsdichte in Ungarn bis zum Anfang des XIV Jahrhunderts*. Studia Historica. Academiae Scientiarum Hungaricae. 42. 1960.

Győrffy, I. "Hajdúböszörmény települése" [The Settlement of Hajdúböszörmény], *Föld és Ember*, Vol. VI, 1926.

———. "A Magyar tanya" [The Hungarian tanya], *Földrajzi Közlemények*, Vol. 65, Nos. 4-5, 1937.

———. "La 'tanya'," *Nouvelle Revue de Hongrie*, Vol. 48, No. 3, 1933.

Häckel, E. "Der Hausbesitz im alten Pest," *Südost Forschungen*, Vol. V, No. 4, 1940.

Hanusz, S. "Die Städte im Königreich Ungarn," *Ungarische Revue*, 1883.

Heimler, K. *Die Soproner Altstadt*. 1941.

Hóman, B. *Geschichte des Ungarischen Mittelalters*. 2 vols. 1940-43.

Iorga, N. *Geschichte des osmanischen Reiches*. 5 vols. 1908-13.

Isbert, O. A. "Probleme der Siedlungskunde in Ungarn," *Ungarische Jahrbücher*, Vol. 12, 1932.

Jeszenszky, A. "La ville hongroise et l'esprit nomade," *Nouvelle Revue de Hongrie*, Vol. 62, No. 4, 1940.

Kaán, K. *A Magyar Alföld* [The Great Hungarian Plain]. 1927.

Károlyi, A., I. Perényi, K. Tóth, and L. Vargha. *A Magyar Falu Épitészete* [Hungarian Village Architecture]. 1955.

Király, B. K. "Peasant Movements in Hungary in 1790," *Südostforschungen*, Vol. XXVI, 1967.

Kiss, I. "The Agrarian Towns of Hungary," *Hungarian Quarterly*, Vol. IV, No. 3, 1938.

Klocke, H. "Der gesellschaftliche Aufbau eines magyarischen Dorfes. Verpelét im Komitat Heves," *Ungarische Jahrbücher*, Vol. 14, 1934.

Kniezsa, I. "Pseudorumänen in Pannonien und in den Nordkarpathen," *Archivum Europae Centro-Orientalis*, Vol. I, 1935, Vol. II, 1936.

———. "Ungarns Völkerschaften im XI. Jahrundert," *Archivum Europae Centro-Orientalis*, Vol. IV, Nos. 1-4, 1938.

Kohl, J. G. *Austria. Vienna, Prague, Hungary, Bohemia and the Danube*. 1843.

———. *Hundert Tage auf Reisen in den österreichischen Staaten.* 5 vols. 1842.

Kollautz, A. "Die Awaren. Die Schichtung in einer Nomadenherrschaft," *Saeculum,* Vol. 5, No. 2, 1954.

Komoróczy, G. "La société hongroise au XVIe siècle," *Nouvelle Revue de Hongrie,* Vol. 60, No. 5, 1939.

Korabinsky, J. M. *Atlas Regni Hungariae portatilis.* Pressburg. 1817.

———. *Geographisch-historisches und Produkten Lexikon von Ungarn.* Pressburg. 1786.

Krallert, W., W. Kuhn, and E. Schwarz. *Atlas zur Geschichte der deutschen Ostsiedlung.* 1958.

Kún, E. "Sozialhistorische Beiträge zur Landarbeiterfrage in Ungarn," *Sammlung nationaleconomischer und statistischer Abhandlungen des Staatswissenschaftlichen Seminars zu Halle,* Vol. 37, 1903.

Laub, R. *Die Dorfstädte des Alfölds als siedlungsgeographische Erscheinung.* Dissertation. Munich. 1955.

Lavedan, P. *Histoire de l'Urbanisme.* Vol. I. 1926.

Léderer, E. "A legrégibb magyar iparososztály kialakulása" [The Evolution of the Oldest Hungarian Craftsmen Class], *Századok,* Vol. 62, 1928.

———. *La Structure de la Société hongroise du Début du Moyen-Âge.* Studia Historica. Academiae Scientiarum Hungaricae. 45. 1960.

Leixner, O. "Kolonisten Siedlungen des XVIII. Jahrhunderts in Südungarn," *Der Städtebau,* Vol. 18, 1921.

Lendl, E. "Siedlungsgeographische Probleme aus dem Donauschwäbischen Lebensraum," *Deutsches Archiv für Landes- und Volksforschung,* Vol. III, Nos. 3-4, 1939.

———. "Zur Geographie der ländlichen Siedlungen Ungarns," *Mitteilungen der Geographischen Gesellschaft in Wien,* Vol. 81, Nos. 1-2, 1938.

Leuschner, K. "Die Landwirtschaftlichen und socialen Verhältnisse im westlichen Ungarn." In: *Staatswissenschaftliche Studien.* Vol. II. 1888.

Lewicki, T. "Uwagi o niektórych wczesnośredniowiecznych węgierskich drogach handlowych" [Certain trade routes in Hungary in the High Middle Ages], *Slavia Antiqua,* Vol. XIV, 1967.

Lewis, W. S. "Some Aspects of Tanya Settlement in Hungary," *Scottish Geographical Magazine,* Vol. 54, No. 6, 1938.

Lukinich, E., A. Fekete-Nagy, and L. Makkai (eds.). *Documenta Historiam Valachorum in Hungaria Illustrantia usque ad Annum 1400 p. Christum.* Études sur l'Europe Centre-Orientale, No. 29. Budapest. 1941.

Macartney, C. A. *The Magyars in the Ninth Century.* 2nd ed. 1968.

Maggiorotti, L. A. *Architetti e Architetture Militari.* Vol. II: *Gli Architetti Militari Italiane in Ungheria.* 1936.

Mályusz, E. "Geschichte des Bürgertums in Ungarn," *Vierteljahrschrift für Sozial- und Wirtschaftsgeschichte,* Vol. XX, 1928.

———. "A magyarság és a városi élet a középkorban" [The Hungarians and Urban Life in the Middle Ages], *Századok,* Vol. 78, 1944.

Marczali, H. *Hungary in the Eighteenth Century.* 1910.

Mayer, R. "Die Alföldstädte," *Abhandlungen der Geographischen Gesellschaft Wien,* Vol. 14, No. 1, 1940.

McNeill, W. H. *Europe's Steppe Frontier, 1500–1800.* 1964.

Mendöl, T. "Berufliche Struktur und Stadtbild als Merkmale des städtischen Charakters in Ungarn," *Ungarische Jahrbücher,* Vol. 16, Nos. 2-3, 1936.

———. "Morphologie der Städte des Alföld," *Tisia,* Arbeiten der III. (Mathematisch-Naturwissenschaftlichen) Abteilung der Wissenschaftlichen S. Tisza Gesellschaft in Debrecen, Vol. I, No. 1, 1936.

———. "Néhány szó az alföldi város kérdéséhez" [Some Comments on the Problem of Towns in the Alföld], *Földrajzi Közlemények,* Vol. 67, 1939.

Michaelis, H. *Beiträge zur Kulturgeographie des Südbanats und Nordserbiens.* 1939.

Mócsy, A. *Die Bevölkerung von Pannonien bis zu den Markomannenkriegen.* 1959.

Mollay, K. *Das Ofner Stadtrecht.* 1959.

———. "Scarbantia, Ödenburg, Sopron. Siedlungsgeschichte und Ortsnamenkunde," *Archivum Europae Centro-Orientalis,* Vols. 9–10, 1943–44.

Moór, E. "Bemerkungen zur Siedlungskunde und Ortsnamenskunde Westungarns," *Ungarische Jahrbücher,* Vol. 18, No. 1, 1938.

———. "Ungarische Flussnamen," *Ungarische Jahrbücher,* Vol. VI, 1926.

———. *Westungarn im Mittelalter im Spiegel der Ortsnamen.* 1936.

Nagy, L. "Adalékok a Fejér megyei jobbágyság történetéhez (1543–1768)" [Data on the History of Serfs in the Comitat of Fejér (1543–1768)], *Alba Regia*, Vol. I, 1960.

———. "Le grandi strade romane in Ungheria." In: *Quaderni dell'Impero. Le grandi strade del mondo romano*. Istituto di Studi Romani. XI. 1938.

Neueste statistisch-geographische Beschreibung des Königreichs Ungarn, Croatien, Slavonien und der ungarischen Militär-Grenze. 1832.

Oertel, Hieronymus. *Ortelius redivivus et continuatus, oder, Der ungarischen Kriegs-Empörungen, Historische Beschreibung . . . von dem 1395. bisz in das 1607. Jahr . . .* Frankfurt am Main. 1665.

Die österreichisch-ungarische Monarchie in Wort und Bild. 24 vols. 1886–1902.

Otto of Freising. *The Deeds of Frederick Barbarossa.* Translated and annotated by C. C. Mierow. 1953.

———. "Gesta Friderici I. imperatoris." In: *Monumenta Germaniae historica.* Vol. XX. 1868.

Pach, Zs. P. "The Development of Feudal Rent in Hungary in the Fifteenth Century," *The Economic History Review*, Vol. XIX, No. 1, 1966.

———. *Das Entwicklungsniveau der feudalen Agrarverhältnisse in Ungarn in der zweiten Hälfte des XV Jahrhunderts.* Studia Historica. Academiae Scientiarum Hungaricae. 46. 1960.

Paget, J. *Hungary and Transylvania.* 2 vols. 1850.

Pardoe, Julia S. *City of the Magyars, or, Hungary and her Institutions in 1839–40.* 3 vols. 1840.

Pataki, V. "A XVI. századi várépítés Magyarországon" [The Building of Fortresses in Hungary in the 16th Century], *Jahrbuch des Wiener Ungarischen Historischen Instituts*, 1931.

Patterson, A. J. *The Magyars: Their Country and Institutions.* 2 vols. 1869.

Paulovics, C. "Il limes romano in Ungheria." In: *Quaderni dell'Impero. Il limes romano.* Istituto di Studi Romani. IV. 1938.

Pécsi, M., and B. Sárfalvi. *The Geography of Hungary.* 1964.

Peeters, Jacobus. *Civitates Hungariae Turcis ereptae.* 1684.

Perényi, I. "Trois villes Hongroises sous la domination Ottomane au XVIIe siècle." In: *Actes du Premier Congrès International des Études Balkaniques et Sud-Est Européennes.* Vol. III. 1969.

———. *A Városépítés Története* [History of Urban Development]. 1961.

Pleidell, A. "A magyar várostörténet első fejezete" [The First Chapter of Hungarian Urban History], *Századok*, Vol. 68, 1934.

———. *A nyugatra irányuló magyar külkereskedelem a középkorban* [Hungarian Exports to the West in the Middle Ages]. 1925.

Pounds, N. J. G. "Land Use on the Hungarian Plain." In: *Geographical Essays on Eastern Europe.* Indiana University Publications. Russian and East European Series. Vol. 24, 1961.

Prinz, G. "Die Siedlungsformen Ungarns," *Ungarische Jahrbücher*, Vol. IV, Nos. 2, 3–4, 1924.

———, J. Cholnoky, P. Teleki, and L. Bartucz. *Magyar Föld, Magyar Faj* [Hungarian Land, Hungarian Race]. 4 vols. 1938.

Priscus. *Fragmenta Historicorum Graecorum.* Ed. by K. and T. Mueller. Vol. IV. Paris. 1851.

Probszt, G. von. *Die niederungarischen Bergstädte. Ihre Entwicklung und wirtschaftliche Bedeutung bis zum Übergang an das Haus Habsburg (1546).* 1966.

Rohbock, L. *Ungarn und Siebenbürgen in malerischen Original-Ansichten ihrer interessantesten Gegenden, Städten . . .* 1857.

Rózsa, Gy. *Budapest Régi Látképei (1493–1800)* [Old Views of Budapest (1493–1800)]. 1963.

Rungaldier, R. "Kecskemét. Landschaft und Wirtschaft im Mittelpunkt der ungarischen Flugsandkultur," *Mitteilungen der Geographischen Gesellschaft in Wien*, Vol. 74, Nos. 4–6, 1931.

———. "Natur- und Kulturlandschaft zwischen Donau und Theiss," *Abhandlungen der Geographischen Gesellschaft in Wien*, Vol. XIV, 1943.

———. "Szegedin: Landeskundliche Skizze einer südungarischen Stadt," *Geographischer Anzeiger*, Vol. 32, No. 3, 1931.

Rutkowski, J. "Medieval Agrarian Society in its Prime. Poland, Lithuania and Hungary." In: *The Cambridge Economic History.* Vol. I. 1942.

Schedel, Hartmann. *Liber chronicarum.* Nürnberg. 1493.

Schilling, G. "Adalékok az Alföld földrajzához" [Data on the Geography of the Alföld], *Földrajzi Közlemények*, Vol. 59, 1931.

Schimscha, E. *Technik und Methoden der*

Theresianischen Besiedlung des Banats. 1939.

Schőnebaum, H. "Die Bedeutung der Siedlungsvorgänge für die Entstehung des Ungarischen Komitats." In: *Deutsche Siedlungsforschungen.* Rudolf Kőtzschke zum 60. Geburtstage dargebracht von Freunden, Fachgenossen und Schűlern. 1927.

Schűnemann, K. *Österreichs Bevölkerungspolitik unter Maria Theresia.* 1935.

Schwartner, M. von. *Statistik des Kőnigreichs Ungern.* 3 vols. 1809–11.

Sebess, D. von. "Die Agrarreform in Ungarn," *Ungarische Jahrbücher,* Vol. I, 1921.

Sebestyén, K. Cs. "Der Ursprung des ungarischen Bauernhauses," *Ungarische Jahrbücher,* Vol. 16, No. 1, 1936.

Simonyi, D. "Slawische Burgwälle," *Archivum Europae Centro-Orientalis,* Vol. VIII, 1942.

Soó, R. von. "Die Entstehung der ungarischen Puszta," *Ungarische Jahrbücher,* Vol. VI, 1926.

Die Stadt in Sűdosteuropa. Struktur und Geschichte. 8. Internationale Hochschulwoche der Sűdosteuropa-Gesellschaft gemeinsam veranstaltet mit dem Sűdost-Institut vom 25. bis 28. Oktober 1966 auf Burg Liebenzell. Sűdosteuropa-Jahrbuch. Vol. 8. 1968.

Stadtmüller, G. *Geschichte Sűdosteuropas.* 1950.

———. "Die Ungarische Grossmacht des Mittelalters," *Historisches Jahrbuch,* Vol. 70, 1951.

Stephani, K. G. *Der älteste deutsche Wohnbau und seine Einrichtung.* Vol. I. 1902.

Szabó, I. *La Répartition de la Population de Hongrie entre les Bougardes et les Villes dans les Années 1449–1526.* Studia Historica. Academiae Scientiarum Hungaricae. 49. 1960.

Székely, Gy. *Landwirtschaft und Gewerbe in der ungarischen ländlichen Gesellschaft um 1500.* Studia Historica. Academiae Scientiarum Hungaricae. 38. 1960.

———. "A pannóniai települések kontinuitásának kérdése és a hazai városfejlődés kezdetei" [The Question of Continuity of Pannonian Settlements and the Beginnings of Urban Development in Hungary]. In: *Tanulmányok Budapest Múltjából.* 1957

———. "Le rôle de l'élément magyar et slave dans la formation de l'État hongrois." In: *L'Europe aux IXe-XIe Siècles. Aux origines des États nationaux.* Actes du Colloque international sur les Origines des États européens aux IXe-XIe siècles. Warsaw and Poznań, Sept. 7–13, 1965. 1968.

Szilágyi, J. *Aquincum.* Published by the Hungarian Academy of Sciences. 1956.

Szűcs, J. *Városok és kézművesség a XV. századi Magyarországon* [Cities and Handicrafts in 15th-Century Hungary]. 1955.

Tagányi, K. "Alte Grenzschutz-Vorrichtungen und Grenz-Ödland: *gyepü* und *gyepüelve,*" *Ungarische Jahrbücher,* Vol. I, 1921.

———. "Geschichte der Feldgemeinschaft in Ungarn," *Ungarische Revue,* 1895.

Takács, I. "Die wirtschaftlichen und sozialen Folgen der Wiederbesiedlung der ungarischen Tiefebene im 18. Jahrhundert. Tanyasiedlung," *Ungarische Jahrbücher,* Vol. 13, 1933.

Tárnoky, I. "Ungarn vor Mohács," *Südostforschungen,* Vol. XX, 1961.

Thompson, E. A. "The Camp of Attila," *The Journal of Hellenistic Studies,* Vol. 65, 1945.

———. *A History of Attila and the Huns.* 1948.

Tomaschek, W. "Zur Kunde der Hämus-Halbinsel. II. Die Handelswege im 12. Jahrhundert nach den Erkundigungen des Arabers Idrisi," *Sitzungsberichte der Akademie der Wissenschaften in Wien,* Phil.-Hist. Class, Vol. 113, 1887.

Tompa, F. von. "25 Jahre Urgeschichtsforschung in Ungarn 1912–1936," *Bericht der Römisch-Germanischen Kommission,* 24/25, 1934–35, Deutsches Archäologisches Institut, 1937.

Townson, R. *Travels in Hungary with a Short Account of Vienna in the Year 1793.* 1797.

Treiber, K. "Wirtschaftsgeographie des ungarischen Grossen Alfölds," *Schriften des Geographischen Instituts der Universität Kiel,* Vol. II, No. 2, 1934.

Türkische und Ungarische Chronica. Nűrnberg. 1663.

Vámos, F. "Nomadenzelt und Magyaren," *Ungarische Jahrbücher,* Vol. 13, 1933.

Vernadsky, G., and M. de Ferdinandy. *Studien zur ungarischen Frühgeschichte.* Südosteuropäische Arbeiten, No. 47, 1957.

Weis, E. "Le village hongrois," *Nouvelle Revue de Hongrie,* Vol. 56, No. 4, 1937.

Zeiller, Martin. *Beschreibung des Kőnigreichs Ungarn und darzu gehőriger Landen, Städte, und vornehmster Oerther . . .* Ulm. 1664.

CHAPTER 25

Balogh, I. *Debrecen.* 1958.
Beynon, E. D. "Budapest: An Ecological Study," *Geographical Review,* Vol. 33, No. 2, 1943.
Borbíró, V., and I. Valló. *Győr városépítéstörténete* [Urban History of Győr]. 1956.
———. "A magyar városépitéstörténeti kutatás feladatai és módszertana" [Objectives and Methodology of Enquiries into the History of Hungarian City Planning], *Településtudományi Közlemények,* No. 3. 1953.
Borsos, B., A. Sódor, and M. Zádor. *Budapest. Épitészettörténete, városképei és műemlékei* [Architectural History, Townscape and Historical Monuments of Budapest]. 1959.
Csatkai, E. *Sopron.* 1954.
Csontos, J. *Városaink Mátyás korában* [Our Cities during the Reign of King Matthias]. 1893.
Dercsényi, D., and P. Granasztói. *Vác.* 1960.
———, F. Pogány, and Z. Szentkirályi. *Pécs.* 1956.
———. *Pécs városképei és műemlékei* [Townscape and Historical Monuments of Pécs]. 1966.
Dercsényi, D., and L. Zolnay. *Esztergom.* 1956.
Entz, G., I. Genthon, and J. Szappanos. *Kecskemét.* 1961.
Fitz, J. *Székesfehérvár.* 1957.
Gerő, L. *Eger.* 1954.
———. *Pápa.* 1959.
Granasztói, P. *Város és épitészet* [City and Architecture]. 1960.
Győrffy, I. *Az alföldi kertes városok* [Rural Towns on the Hungarian Plain]. 1926.
———. "Hajdúböszörmény települése" [The Settlement of Hajdúböszörmény], *Föld és Ember,* Vol. VI, 1926.
Heckenast, G., and others. *A Magyar nép története* [History of the Hungarian People]. 1953.
Héjj, M. *Visegrád.* 1957.
Hóman, B. *A magyar városok az Árpádok korában* [Hungarian Cities in the Age of the Árpáds]. 1908.
Horler, M. *Szentendre.* 1960.
Horváth Jr., B., L. Marjalaki Kiss, and K. Valentiny. *Miskolc.* 1962.
Károlyi, A., and T. Szentléleky. *Szombathely városképei műemlékei* [The City and Monuments of Szombathely]. 1967.
Kelényi, O. "La grande inondation de Pest vue par les contemporains," *Nouvelle Revue de Hongrie,* Vol. 59, No. 4, 1938.

Koppány, T., P. Péczely, and K. Sági. *Keszthely.* 1962.
Korompay, Gy. *A városi főterek kialakulása* [The Development of City Squares]. 1940
———. *Veszprém.* 1956.
Lettrich, E. *Kecskemét és tanyavilága* [Kecskemét and its System of Farmsteads]. 1968.
Major, J. "A kőzépkori magyar városkép problémájához" [An Approach to the Problem of the Medieval Hungarian Townscape], *Településtudományi Közlemények,* No. 7, 1955.
———. "A magyar városhálózatról" [The Network of Hungarian Cities], *Településtudományi Közlemények,* No. 16, 1964.
———. "A magyar városok és városhálózat kialakulásának kezdetei" [The Beginning of the Formation of Towns and Town Networks in Hungary], *Településtudományi Közlemények,* No. 18, 1966.
Major, M. *Épitészettörténet* [History of Architecture]. 1957–60.
Makkai, L. *Erdélyi városok* [Cities in Transylvania]. 1940.
Mályusz, E. "A magyarság és a városi élet a középkorban" [The Hungarians and Urban Life in the Middle Ages], *Századok,* Vol. 78, 1944.
Mendöl, T. *Általános településföldrajz* [General Settlement Geography]. 1963.
Nagy, Z., and I. Papp. *Szeged.* 1960.
Ormos, I. *Kerttervezés története és gyakorlata* [History and Practice of Landscape Architecture]. 1967.
Pasteiner, Gy. *Középkori épitészetünk topográfiája* [The Topography of our Medieval Architecture]. 1908.
Perényi, I. "Budapest fejlesztésének időszerű kérdéseiről" [Contemporary Problems of Urban Development in Budapest], *Településtudományi Közlemények,* No. 10, 1958.
———. *A városépités története* [History of Urban Development]. 1961.
Pleidell, A. "A magyar várostörténet első fejezete" [The First Chapter of Hungarian Urban History], *Századok,* Vol. 68, 1934.
Pogány, F. *Terek és utcák művészete: történeti áttekintés* [The Art of Squares and Streets: Historical Survey]. 1954.
Preisich, G. *Budapest városépitésének története* [History of City Planning in Budapest]. 1960.
Rados, J. *Tata.* 1964.
Salamon, F. *Buda-Pest Története* [History of Buda-Pest]. 3 vols. 1878–85.

Szalay, J. *Városaink a XIII. században* [Our Cities in the 13th Century]. 1878.
Vámos, F. "Budapest városképének alakulása József nádor korától napjainkig" [The Development of Budapest's Townscape from the Age of the Palatine Joseph until Today], *Magyar Mérnök és Építész Egylet közlönye*, Nos. 9–12, 1926.
Zádor, M. *Kaposvár.* 1964.
Zakariás, G. S. *A Budai Batthyáni tér* [The Batthyáni Square in Budapest]. 1958.

APPENDIX

Debrecen

Balogh, I. *A cívisek társadalma* [The Society of the Burghers]. 1946.
———. *Debrecen.* 1958.
Bierbauer, V. "Urbanisme dans la plaine hongroise. L'exemple de Debrecen," *Nouvelle Revue de Hongrie*, Vol. 64, No. 3, 1941.
Buse, Karla. *Stadt und Gemarkung Debrezin. Siedlungsraum von Bürgern, Bauern und Hirten im ungarischen Tiefland.* Schriften des Geographischen Instituts der Universität Kiel. Vol. XI, No. 5, 1942.
Győrffy, I. "Nyíregyháza és Debrecen településformája" [The Structure of Settlement of Nyíregyháza and Debrecen], *Föld és Ember*, Vol. IX, 1929.
Passuth, L. "Sexcentenary of Debrecen," *The New Hungarian Quarterly*, Vol. III, No. 5, 1962.
Szabó, I. "A debreceni tanyarendszer kialakulása" [The Development of the Tanya System of Debrecen], *Föld és Ember*, Vol. IX, 1929.
Szűcs, I. *Szabad királyi Debrecen város történelme* [History of the Royal Free Town of Debrecen]. 3 vols. 1870–71.
Zoltai, L. *Települések. Egyházas es egyháztalan falvak Debrecen város mai határa és külső birtokai területén a 11.-14. századokban* [Villages with and without Churches on the Territories of the Present City of Debrecen and its Outlying Possessions in the 11th-14th Centuries]. 1925.

Esztergom

Balogh, A. "Esztergom középkori helyrajzáról" [On the Topography of Medieval Esztergom], *Esztergom Évlapjai*, 1930.
Csillag, Mária. *Esztergom története a tizenötéves török háboru alatt* [A History of Esztergom during the Fifteen-Years Turkish War]. 1916.
Dercsényi, D., and L. Zolnay. *Esztergom.* 1956.
Schünemann, K. *Die Entstehung des Städtewesens in Südosteuropa.* 1929.
———. "Esztergom. Der ungarische Name der Stadt Gran," *Ungarische Jahrbücher*, Vol. VII, 1927.

Győr

Borbíró, V., and I. Valló. *Győr városépítéstörténete* [Urban History of Győr]. 1956.
Borovszky, S. (ed.). *Magyarország vármegyéi és városai.* Pt. 8: *Győr vármegye* [Counties and Cities of Hungary. Pt. 8: Győr County]. 1908(?).
Csizmadia, A. "Győr küzdelme a szabad királyi városi rangért" [Győr's Struggle to Achieve the Rank of a Royal Free Town], *Győri Szemle*, 1943.
———. "Győr városjoga as Árpádok alatt" [Győr s Urban Rights under the Árpáds], *Győri Szemle*, Vol. XI, 1940.
Fehér, I. *Győr megye és város egyetemes leirása* [A General Description of the Town and County of Győr]. 1874.
Hammer, Gy. *Győr, városföldrajzi tanulmány* [Győr. An Urban Geographical Study]. 1936.
Kalmár, G. "Győr megye történeti földrajza a középkorban" [Historical Geography of Győr County in the Middle Ages], *Föld és Ember*, 1924.
Lovas, E. "Győr város kialakulásának vázlata" [Outline of Győr's Urban Development], *Győri Kalendárium*, 1940.
Maggiorotti, L. A., and F. Banfi. *La fortezza di Giavarino in Ungheria ed i suoi architetti militari italiani, specialmente Pietro Ferabosco.* Atti dello Istituto di Architettura Militare. 1932.
Szabady, B. "Győr város fejlődésének rövid története" [A Short Outline of the Urban Development of Győr], *Magyar Építőművészet*, 1943.
———. "Győr város kialakulása" [Urban Evolution of Győr], *Győri Szemle*, 1942.
Villányi, Sz. *Győr vár és város helyrajza, erődítése, háztelek és lakossági viszonyai a 16. és 17. században* [Ground Plan, Fortifications, Housing, and Population of the Fortress and City of Győr in the 16th and 17th Centuries]. 1882.

Pápa

Gerő, L. "Baugeschichtliche Analyse einer ungarischen Kleinstadt—Pápa," *Kwartalnik*

Architektury i Urbanistyki, Vol. V, No. 3, Warsaw. 1960.

———. *Pápa*. 1959.

Székesfehérvár

Dercsényi, D. "Székesfehérvár, St. Stephen's City," *Hungarian Quarterly*, Vol. IV, No. 1, 1938.

Fitz, J. *Székesfehérvár*. 1957.

Fügedi, E. "Székesfehérvár középkori alaprajza és a polgárság kezdetei Magyarországon" [The Medieval groundplan of Székesfehérvár and the Formation of the Bourgeoisie in Hungary], *Településtudományi Közlemények*, No. 20, 1967.

Szombathely

Alföldi, A. "Adalék Szombathely Római településtörténetéhez. Zur Entstehung der Colonia Claudia Savaria" [Data on the History of the Settlement of Szombathely. Zur Entstehung der Colonia Claudia Savaria], *Archaeologiai Értesítő*, Ser. III, Vol. IV, Nos. 1–2, 1943.

Fettich, N. *Colonia Claudia Savaria. Szombathely a római uralom alatt* [Colonia Claudia Savaria. Szombathely under Roman Rule]. 1939.

Kádár, Z., and L. Balla. *Savaria*. 1958.

Károlyi, A., and T. Szentléleky. *Szombathely városképei, műemlékei* [The City and Monuments of Szombathely]. 1967.

Vác

Dercsényi, D., and P. Granasztói. *Vác*. 1960.

Veszprém

Békefi, R. "Veszprém a középkorban." In: K. Hornig. *Veszprém multja és jelene* [Veszprém in the Middle Ages. In: K. Hornig. The Past and Present of Veszprém]. 1912.

Erdélyi, G. *Veszprém város története a török idők alatt* [A History of the City of Veszprém during the Turkish Period]. 1913.

Korompay, G. *Veszprém*. 1957.

Index

A

Adscripti glebae: see Serfdom
Aigner, P. C.: *see* Congress Kingdom
Alba Regia: see Székesfehérvár (Stuhlweissenburg)
Aleksandrów, 100
Alliprandi, Giovanni Battista, 180, 264
Alwernia, 86
Amber Route, 18, 299
Andrew III (Ondřej), 155, 213
Animal husbandry, 423, 426
Anjou (Angevin) dynasty, 155-156; Charles Robert, 155-156, 156-157, 365; Louis the Great, 365
Annopol, 57
Arcades, 227, 293, 328
Archbishop Jacob of Gniezno, 4-5
Arche, Antonín: *see* Kroměříž
Arigsperger, Jan Melichar: *see* Leopoldov
Aristocracy (nobility): *see* Classes, social and professional
Arnošt of Pardubice: *see* Pardubice
Árpád dynasty, 344-345; Béla III, 363, 368; Béla IV, 154, 257, 364, 365, 368, 411; King Stephen (Saint), 346, 363, 386, 402, 409, 411, 415, 418, 421; Ladislaus IV, 367; Ondřej (Andrew) III, 155, 213; Stephen III, 368; Stephen V, 402
Arrabona: see Győr
Artisans and craftsmen: *see* Classes, social and professional
Attila, camp of, 354-355; Onegesius, 355; Priscus Panites, 354-355
Augustów, 55, 107
Augustus II, the Strong, Elector of Saxony, 78-80, 82
Augustus III, 80
Austrian: eighteenth-century colonization of Hungary, 384; planning activities in Poland, 89; *see also* Habsburg, House of
Avitizität, 346
Avostalis, Giovanni Battista: *see* Litomyšl

B

Babiak, 100
Baldigara, O., 170, 295
Bannmeile: see Urban
Bánovce nad Bebravou, 157
Banská Bystrica, 155, 168, 169
Banská Štiavnica, 155, 168, 184-185, 208-209
Baranów, 69
Barca, 112
Bardejov, 156, 168, 210-211; town hall, 211
Baroque: Broggio, Octavio, 177; Deybel, Johann Siegmund, 80; Dientzenhofer, Christopher, 177, 177-178; Dientzenhofer, Kilian Ignac, 177, 177-178, 203, 251, 268; fortress, 270, 300; gardens, 175, 181-182, 263, 301; in Czechoslovakia, 171-186; in Hungary, 386-389; in Poland, 78-86; in Slovakia, 184-185; Jauch, Joachim Daniel, 80; Kaňka, František Maxmilián, 177, 179, 203-204, 268; landscape architecture, 182; Naumann, Johann Christoph, 78; peasant Baroque, 308; Pőppelmann, Karl Friedrich, 80; Pőppelmann, Matthäus Daniel, 78, 80; Prague, 203-207; residences and palaces, 78-81, 82-84, 172, 174, 243-244; Santini, Giovanni, 177, 179-180, 180, 182, 203-204; towns, 171-176, 177-182, 184-185, 185-186; *see also* Rydzyna, Łazienka Królewska, calvaries
Battle of Mohács, 370
Battle of the White Mountain, 171
Bechyně, 132, 146
Będzin, 42, 43
Békéscsaba, 340, 357
Béla III, 363, 368
Béla IV, 154, 257, 364, 365, 368, 411
Bělá pod Bezdězem, 145
Benedictines, 345
Bergemann, F.: *see* Congress Kingdom
Bernardine Friars, 48
Beroun, 145, 146
Bethlen, Gábor, 383
Biała Podlaska, 69, 84
Białaczów, 86
Białystok, 77, 83; Branicki residence, 83; Deybel, Johann Siegmund, 83
Bieliński, Franciszek: *see* Warsaw
Bielsk Podlaski, 48
Biłgoraj, 57
Bishop Hozjusz, 69
Bishop Stefan Wierzbołowski: *see* Góra Kalwaria
Biskupin, 17-18
Bochnia, 34
Bocskay, István, 377, 380
Bohemia, 129-130
Bohemian: rebellion of Estates, 171, 203, 286; Romanesque architecture, 133
Bohemian Brethren (Unity of Brethren), 62, 286
Bohemian Route, 135, 321
Boii, 113, 122
Bojanowo, 62
Boleslav I, 129
Bolesław the Brave, 13, 20
Boni Ordinis Commissions, 86
Boskovice, 163, 212; Lords of, 164
Brandýs nad Labem, 315-316
Bratislava, 135, 155, 167, 168, 169, 184-185, 195, 196, 198, 213-215; Aspremont Palace, 184, 215; Feigler, I., 195; Grassalkovich Palace, 184, 215; Hillebrandt, Franz Anton, 184, 185, 215; population in 1910, 196; Theresianeum, 184
Braun, Matthias, 179, 182
Brezno, 157
Bridges, 192, 241; Széchenyi Lánchid, 390-392

Brno, 131, 137, 175, 177, 191, 198, 216-219; Lužánky Monastery Park, 191; population, 196, 218; Rochepine, P. F. Bechade de, 217; Staré Brno, 216
Brocquière, Bertrandon de la: *see* Szeged
Brody, 57, 60; Żółkiewski, Stanisław, 60
Broggio, Octavio, 177
Broumov, 140
Brudzew, 62
Bruntál, 136, 137
Brzeg (Brieg), 31
Brzeżany, 54
Bučovice, 164-165; Ferrabosco, Pietro, 164-165
Buczacki, 54
Buda, 342, 366, 368, 369-370, 385, 389, 390; *see also* Budapest
Budapest, 368-370, 390-392, 396-397; Buda, 342, 366, 368, 369-370, 385, 389, 390; Council for Public Utility Works, 396; Lechner, Lajos, 396; Óbuda, 368, 389; Pest, 363, 365, 368-369, 385, 389-394; Pestújhegy, 368, 369; Széchenyi, István, 390-394; Táncsics, Mihály, 396
Budzanów, 54
Buildings: apartments, 192; barracks, 192; burghers' houses, 165-166, 181; ecclesiastical, 135, 166, 173-174, 174-175, 184, 237-238; Gothic residential in Bohemia and Moravia, 149-151; siting of, 133; town halls, 149, 166, 180, 211
Burghers: *see* Classes, social and professional
Bydgoszcz (Bromberg), 42; population in the 16th century, 64
Bylany, 111, 121
Bylaws: *see* Fire regulations
Bytča, 169

C

Calvaries, 74-75, 81-82; Góra Kalwaria, 74-75
Calvinism: *see* Debrecen
Carmontaigne: *see* Josefov
Casimir the Great: *see* Kazimierz the Great
Čáslav, 139, 144, 225-226; Land Diet (Hussite Diet), 160, 226; Špitálský, Konrád, 225
Castle: *see* Fortified, castles
Cegléd, 372, 384
Česká Lípa, 140, 175
České Budějovice (Budweis), 140, 140-141, 172, 180, 227-228; arcades, 227; fortifications, 227; Martinelli, Anton E., 180; population in 1910, 196
Český Krumlov, 140, 163, 172, 229-230; Latrán, 229
Charles IV, 148, 149-150, 201, 251; *Corona regni Bohemiae*, 148
Charles, Robert, 155-156, 156-157, 365
Charter, 28-29
Cheb (Eger), 175, 180, 191, 220-223; population in 1830, 196
Chełmno (Kulm), 36, 37, 40, 42; *ius culmense*, 37
Chełmno Law (*ius culmense*), 37
Chodzież, 74
Chomutov, 145, 174, 224
Chotěboř, 140
Chotek, Count J. R., 192
Chrudim, 132, 139, 180
Chýňava, 148
Ciechocinek, 101; Marconi, H., 101
Cistercians, 130, 265, 345
Cities: founded by Polish magnates, 54; Ideal, 295; medieval Polish, 26-51; number of Polish, 52; of the Teutonic Order, 37-40; Polish, during first half of the 19th century, 88-108; population in Congress Kingdom, 93-94; Renaissance Polish, 52-69; Royal foundations in Poland, 48; seventeenth and eighteenth-century Polish, 70-87; *see also* towns
City: councils, medieval Polish, 44-45; plots, 28-29; proto-city in Poland, 22; rights, 28-29
City planning: by Austrian authorities in Poland, 89; by Prussian authorities in Poland, 88-89; by Russian authorities in Poland, 89; by Swedish authorities in Poland, 70-73; *see also* Town planning
Civitates forenses: see Settlements
Classes, social and professional: *adscripti glebae*, 343, 345, 348; aristocracy (nobility), 162-165, 173, 183, 190, 370, 428; artisans and craftsmen, 185, 423; Bohemian Estates, 171; *coloni liberi*, 345; *coloni servi*, 345; *inquilini*, 345; *iobaggiones*, 345; magnates, 345, 365; merchants, 145; peasants, 348, 370
Classical (Classicist) Revival: in Hungary, 394-395; in Slovakia, 195; in Warsaw, 101-106; parks and gardens in Czechoslovakia, 194-195, 196; planning, building, and construction in Czechoslovakia, 191-194; *see also* Františkovy Lázně
Coloni liberi: see Classes, social and professional
Coloni servi: see Classes, social and professional
Colonization: "Dutch colonization" in Great Poland, 73; eighteenth-century Austrian of Hungary, 384; German in Poland, 4-5; of mountainous and sub-mountainous regions in Czechoslovakia, 183-184; under German law, 5
Comenius, Jan Amos, 171
Congress Kingdom, 16; Aigner, P. C., 92, 105; Bergemann, F., 92; economic, planning, and building activities, 92-107; General Council for Buildings, Surveying, Roads, and Navigation, 93; Groffe, A., 92, 93, 106; Municipal Commission, 93; population of cities, 93-94; Trausolt, F. J., 92; Zawadski, S., 92
Corazzi, Antoni: *see* Warsaw
Corona regni Bohemiae, 148
Cosmas, 290, 329
Count Batthyány: *see* Debrecen
Counter Reformation, 74-75, 171, 172, 215, 236, 267-268, 321, 416
Cracow, 16, 19, 22, 32-34, 42, 89, 107-108; Okól, 33; population in the 13th century, 42; population in the 14th to 15th centuries, 45; population in the 16th century, 64; university, 45; Wawel, 20; *see also* Kazimierz
Cracow Republic, 107-108
Csaba, 347
Cumans, 372, 372 n.
Czechoslovakian: agricultural settlements, 182-183; Baroque, 171-186; Baroque fortresses, 270, 300; Baroque gardens, 175, 181-182, 263, 301; Baroque residences, 172, 174, 243-244; Celtic settlements, 122-123; Classicist parks and gardens, 194-195, 196; Classicist planning, building, and construction, 191-194; Early Bronze Age settlements, 112; early feudal settlements, 130-133; early feudal towns, 130-133; early feudal villages, 132-133; early settlement, 111-116, 121-124; feudal towns, 136-144; fortress towns, 170, 186, 191, 242, 270, 320; gardens, 164-165, 175, 181-182, 262-263, 301; Gothic residential buildings, 149-151; hill-forts, 115; hilltop settlements 112; industrialization, 190, 196, 217-218;

466

location towns, 130, 130 n.; manufactories, 177, 185, 190; manufacturing towns, 197; medieval towns, 145-157; mining towns, 145, 155, 156-157, 166-167, 208-209, 247-248, 260-261, 265-268, 326; Neolithic settlements, 111; *oppida,* 113; origin of towns, 129-132; palaces, gardens, and parks, 164-165, 194-195, 262-263, 290; peasant Baroque, 308; pre-location towns, 130 n., 132; Renaissance, 162-170; Renaissance fortifications, 169-170; Renaissance gardens, 164-165; Renaissance towns, 166-170; Residence Towns, 163-164, 170; rural settlement, 187-189; settlement by the Romans, 123-124; Stone Age settlements, 121; town halls, 149, 166, 180, 211; towns and the Hussite Movement, 158-160; towns during the Baroque period, 171-176, 177-182, 184-185, 185-186; towns in the 19th and 20th centuries, 196-198; twin-towns, 315-316; urban population, 196; village architecture, 231; villages in the 18th century, 182-184, 185, 187-189; *see also* Royal Towns (Royal Free Towns), Spas

Czerwonogród, 48
Częstochowa, 98
Czortków, 54

D

Dąbie, 71, 88
Dąbrowa, 86
Dačice, 180
Debrecen, 340, 346, 384, 385-386, 395, 422-425; Boldogasszonyfalva, 385; Calvinism, 423; Count Batthyány, 425; János Hunyadi, 386; Kollegium, 395, 423; layout, 422; nineteenth-century trades and crafts, 425; Szentmihály, 385; Szentlászlófalva, 385; Torna, 385; trades based on animal husbandry, 423; under Turkish rule, 423
Decretum minor: see Fortifications
Defense, of Hungarian frontiers, 344-345
Deybel, Johann Siegmund, 80, 83
Dientzenhofer, Christopher, 177, 177-178
Dientzenhofer, Kilian Ignac, 177, 177-178, 203, 251, 268
Dobšiná, 157
Dolní Bojanovice, 231
Dolní Věstonice, 121
Domažlice, 132, 140, 142, 160, 232
Donjons: *see* Fortifications
Dózsa, György, 370
Drohiczyn, 48
Duchy of Warsaw, 16, 89
Dunántúl: *see* Transdanubia
Dvůr: *see* Králové Dvůr

E

Ebertowski, Ignacy: *see* Radom
Eger, 385, 386-389; Cardinal Esterházy, 387; Fellner, Jakab, 387; Hild, József, 387
Elbląg (Elbing), 39, 40, 71-73; population in the 16th century, 64; Thomé, Heinrich, 73
Emperor Leopold I, 387
Emperor Maximilian, 295
Emperor Rudolph II, 175, 286
Esterházy, 350; Cardinal Esterházy, 387
Esztergom (Gran), 339, 342, 363-364, 366, 385, 411-414; Barutkhane-Palanka, 413; Castle Hill, 363-364, 411-412; Ewliyā Čelebi, 413; *Salva (Salva Mansio),* 363, 411; *Strigonium,* 411; *vicus Latinorum,* 412-413; Viziváros *(Wasserstadt),* 411
Ewliyā Čelebi, 413

F

Feigler, I.: *see* Bratislava
Fellner, Jakab, 387
Ferdinand I, 161
Ferrabosco, Pietro, 164-165, 169, 208, 321, 403
Ferrari, Giulio, 169, 170, 334
Ferrari, Pompeo: *see* Rydzyna
Filipów, 55
Fire regulations, 191
Fischer, Jiří: *see* Mariánské Lázně
Fontana, J. K.: *see* Kozienice
Fortifications, 51, 65-68, 144, 149, 169-170, 172, 191, 238, 242, 259, 300, 319, 320, 403; built by Swedes in Poland, 70-73; *decretum minor,* 366; donjons, 366, 367; *gyepű,* 344; ponds as elements of, 165, 226; *portae regni,* 344
Fortified: camps, 3, 73; castles, 8, 43-44, 134, 169, 364; *grody,* 8, 18 n., 18-21; hill-forts, 115; hilltop settlements, 112; *oppida,* 113, 122
Forum: see Settlements
Frampol, 77-78
Františkovy Lázně (Franzensbad), 194, 233-234
Frederick II, 88
Frederick Barbarossa, 220
Frýdlant, 235
Fugger, 161, 168
Fulnek, 236

G

Gąbin, 97
Gardens: Baroque, 175, 181-182, 301; in Kroměříž, 262-263; Renaissance, 164-165; *see also* Łazienka Królewska
Gdańsk (Danzig), 14, 19, 36, 39, 40, 42, 45; population in the 14th to 15th centuries, 45; population in the 16th century, 64
General Council for Buildings, Surveying, Roads, and Navigation: *see* Congress Kingdom
George of Olomouc: *see* Pardubice
George of Poděbrad, 160
German law *(ius teutonicum),* 5, 28; *see also* Magdeburg Law, Lübeck Law
Ghettos, 175, 197, 212
Gilly, David: *see* Prussian
Głogów (Glogau), 42; *see also* Głogów Małopolski
Głogów Małopolski, 53-54; *see also* Głogów (Glogau)
Gniew, 39, 40
Gniezno (Gnesen), 8, 19
Golden Route, 306, 310
Góra Kalwaria, 74-75; Bishop Stefan Wierzbołowski, 74; King Michał Korybut Wiśniowiecki, 74
Gothic: Cistercian-Burgundian style, 144; Jagellonian, 161; residential buildings in Bohemia and Moravia, 149-151; town planning in Prague, 201
Graff, I.: *see* Rydzyna
Great Alföld (Nagyalföld), 339, 339-342; Hajdúság, 340; Hortobágy, 340; Kiskunság, 340; Lower Tisza Plain, 340; Nagykunság, 340; Nyírség, 340; settlement structure, 423; *tanya (tanyák),* 341, 341 n., 348-350, 397-398, 428; Tiszántúl, 340; towns (vil-

lage-towns), 340-341, 342-343, 384, 385-386, 422-428; villages, 352-357
Great Moravian Empire, 115, 126, 299, 324; Mojmír dynasty, 299
Great Poland (Wielkopolska): "Dutch colonization," 73; Renaissance cities, 60-62; seventeenth and eighteenth-century cities, 73-74
Grocholice, 97
Grody: see Fortified
Grodzisk Wielkopolski, 62
Groffe, A.: *see* Congress Kingdom
Grudziądz (Graudenz), 39, 89
Grzymułtowski, Krzysztof: *see* Rakoniewice
Guilds, 44, 162, 365
Gyepű: see Fortifications
Gyepűelve, 344
Győr (Raab), 339, 342, 363, 385, 402-406; *Arrabona*, 339, 402; Ferrabosco, Pietro, 403; fortifications, 403; population, 404; Wymes, Francesco, 403

H

Habsburg, House of, 161, 171, 184, 376-377, 383, 384; Ferdinand I, 161; Emperor Leopold I, 387; Emperor Maximilian, 295; Emperor Rudolph II, 175, 286; Joseph II, 89, 188-189, 190, 193, 242, 320, 389, 416; Maria Theresa, 89, 185, 188, 300, 320, 340, 348, 416, 428
Hajdúböszörmény, 353, 377, 378-380
Hajdúdorog, 377
Hajdúhadház, 353, 377
Hajdúk, 377, 377 n., 379, 380
Hajdúnánás, 377
Hajdúság: *see* Great Alföld
Hajdúszoboszló, 377
Halas, 372, 384
Hamel, Louis Querlonde du: *see* Josefov
Havlíčkův Brod, 140
Hel, 40
Henry the Bearded, 30, 30-31
Herculesco, 169
Hild, János, 389-390
Hild, József, 387, 390
Hildebrandt, Johann Lucas von, 180, 243
Hillebrandt, Franz Anton, 184, 185, 215
Hlubčice, 136
Hluboké Mašůvky, 111
Hódmezővásárhely, 340, 351, 372, 384
Horní Litvínov, 177
Horšovský Týn, 145
Hortobágy: *see* Great Alföld
Hospites, 26
Hostinné, 140, 140-142
Hotters: see Villages
Houses: burghers', 165-166, 181; farm, 231, 273; Romanesque, 200
Hradčany: *see* Prague
Hradec Králové, 132, 136, 137, 171, 177, 180, 186, 191, 237-239; fortifications, 238; Hussite Movement, 237
Hradiště, 122
Hruštín, 240
Hudlice, 148
Hungarian: Baroque, 386-389; frontier defense, 344-345; hajdú-towns, 377-380; land grants, 344-345; landownership, 350; occupation of Slovakia, 133-135; population, 347, 350; settlement density, 350, 351-352; social structure and medieval landownership, 345-346; spread and changing structure of settlement, 346-348; *tanya* system, 341, 341 n., 348-350, 397-398, 428; towns, 342-343, 366-370, 372-383, 384-395, 396-400, 402-428; urban development, 363-400; village-towns, 340-341, 343, 372-373, 384, 385-386, 426-428; villages, 339, 346, 351-359
Husiatyn, 54
Huss, John, 149, 158
Hussite Movement, 158-160, 167, 226, 237, 317, 328; and towns, 158-160, 254; George of Poděbrad, 160; Huss, John, 149, 158; Land Diet (Hussite Diet), 160, 226; "towns of the sun," 158; Žižka, Jan, 158, 237; *see also* Tábor

I

Ibrahim Ibn Jacob, 129, 200
Industrialization: in Czechoslovakia, 190, 196, 217-218; in eighteenth-century Poland, 86; in Hungary, 351, 395-396; *see also* Industry
Industry: home industries, 351; iron, 6-7, 101; mining, 166, 168, 185, 265-267, 289; salt, 101; textile, 96-98, 100-101, 190, 217; *see also* Manufactories
Inowłódz, 43
Inquilini: see Classes, social and professional
Iobaggiones: see Classes, social and professional
Irrigation, and regulation systems, 165
Ivanovce, 112

J

Jablonné, 138, 180
Jáchymov, 166-167
Jáchymov (Moravia), 187
Jagellon dynasty, 160-161, 266; King Vladislav, 160
Janów, 57
Janów Lubelski, 57, 59-60
Jaroměř, 132, 140, 241-242; suspension bridge, 241
Jaroměřice nad Rokytnou (Jaroměřice), 180, 182, 243-244; Hildebrandt, Johann Lucas von, 243
Jasov, 154, 184
Jastrów, 62
Jászapáti, 352-353
Jászberény, 372, 384
Jauch, Joachim Daniel, 80
Jazyges: *see* Kecskemét
Jeleniowo, 86
Jelitkowo: *see* Tomaszów Lubelski
Jesuits, 69, 172, 174, 184, 237, 254; Clementinum (Prague), 174, 203; churches and colleges of, 69, 174, 203, 237, 254, 268
Jevíčko, 142
Jičín, 145, 172, 175, 245-246; New Town, 246; Sebregondi, Nicolas, 172, 246; Wallenstein, Albrecht von, 172, 245-246
Jihlava, 137, 138, 166, 180, 247-248
Jindřichův Hradec, 140, 163, 249-250
Joendl, J. F., 187
Josefov, 186, 191, 242; Carmontaigne, 242; Hamel, Louis Querlonde du, 242; Joseph II, 242
Joseph II, 89, 188-189, 190, 193, 242, 320, 389, 416
Józefów, 77; Potocki, Andrzej, 77
Józefów Ordynacki, 77; Zamoyski, Tomasz, 77
Julius Henrich, Duke of Saxony: *see* Ostrov
Jurydyka: see Settlements

K

Kadaň, 140
Kalinowski, 54
Kalisz (Kalisch), 8, 18, 42, 44, 88-89, 101, 106-107; Marconi, H., 106; Reinstein, F., 106; Szpilowski, S., 106; Tournelle, F., 106
Kalwaria Zebrzydowska, 74
Kamień, 40
Kaňka, František Maxmilián, 177, 179, 203-204, 268
Kargowa, 73; Unruh, 73
Karlín: *see* Prague
Karlovy Vary (Karlsbad), 194, 251-252
Kazimierz, 42, 45, 108
Kazimierz the Great, 14, 42, 45
Kecskemét, 340, 346, 350, 372-373, 384; Cumans, 372, 372 n.; Jazyges, 372; *Partiscum,* 372
Kert system: *see* Nagykőrös
Kežmarok, 155, 168, 253
King John, 145-146
King Michał Korybut Wiśniowiecki: *see* Góra Kalwaria
King Sigismund (Zikmund), 160, 286, 365-366
King Stephen (Saint), 346, 363, 386, 402, 409, 411, 415, 418, 421
King Vladislav, 160
Kis-Pest: *see* Pest
Kisalföld: *see* Little Alföld
Kiskunság: *see* Great Alföld
Kitajgród, 57
Kladruby, 138
Kladsko (Glatz), 136
Klatovy, 140, 140-141, 160, 174, 254-255
Kock, 86
Kolín, 139, 140-141, 144, 225, 256
Kolno, 48
Koło, 42
Koloman reform, 135
Komárno, 154, 169-170, 365; *see also* Komárom
Komárom (Komárno), 365, 385
Koniecpolski, 54
Konrad of Mazovia, Prince, 36
Konstantynów, 97, 100
Korycin, 77
Košice, 154, 168, 169, 185, 257-258; population in 1910, 196
Kounic, Count D. C.: *see* Slavkov
Kouřim, 127-128, 139, 140, 259
Kozienice, 85; Fontana, J. K., 85
Králové Dvůr, 140
Krásna Hôrka, 169
Krasnopol, 86
Krasnosielsk, 100
Krásný Dvůr, 164, 195
Kratochvíle, 164, 290; Rožmberk, 290; Vonio, Balthazar Maio de, 290; *see also* Netolice
Kremnica, 156-157, 168, 185, 260-261
Krnov (Jägerndorf), 136, 136-137
Kroměříž, 145, 164, 175, 177, 194, 195, 262-263; Arche, Antonín, 262; gardens, 262-263; Lichtenštejn-Kastelkorn, Count Charles, 175, 262; Luchese, Filippo, 175, 262, 263; Tencalla, Giovanni Pietro, 175, 262, 263
Krupina, 155, 169, 170
Krynki, 55
Krzemionki Opatowskie, 17
Kuks, 182, 264; Alliprandi, Giovanni Battista, 264; Bethlehem, 182; Špork, Count F. A., 182, 264

Kunsztów, 86
Kutná Hora, 145, 166, 181, 265-268; *ius regale montanorum,* 266; Sedlec, 265
Kyjov, 269
Kysucké Nové Mesto, 156

L

Ladislaus IV, 367
Łańcut, 69
Land: grants, 344-345; ownership, 5-6, 348, 350; Raabization process, 187; tenure, 28-30, 345-346; *urbarium,* 346
Layout: calvary, 74-75; eighteenth-century Czechoslovak village, 187-188; fourteenth-century urban Polish, 42-44; medieval Bohemian, 296; medieval urban Polish, 30; of cities of the Teutonic Order, 39-40
Łazienka Królewska, 85
Lębork (Lauenburg), 39, 40
Lechner, Lajos, 396, 398-400
Łęczyca (Lentschiza), 8, 24, 30, 42, 89, 107
Lednica, 8
Lednice, 194-195
Legnica (Liegnitz), 31
Leopoldov, 170, 270; Arigsperger, Jan Melichar, 270; Unger, Ján, 270
Lesná, 187
Leuthner, Abraham: *see* Loket
Levice, 169
Levoča, 154-155, 168, 271-272
Liberec, 172; population, 196; Wallenstein, Albrecht von, 172
Lichtenštejn-Kastelkorn, Count Charles: *see* Kroměříž
Lipnice, 148
Lipno, 88
Liptovská Teplička, 273
Liptovský Hrádok, 185
Litava, 274-275
Lithuania, Grand Duchy of: towns and villages, 55-56
Litoměřice, 131, 149, 171, 177, 276-277
Litomyšl, 132, 140, 142, 278-279; Avostalis, Giovanni Battista, 278; Pernštejn, 278
Litovel, 140
Little Alföld (Kisalföld), 339, 384-385; Pannonia, 339; *Pannonia inferior,* 339; *Pannonia superior,* 339
Locator, 4, 5, 225
Locus forensis: *see* Settlements
Łódź, 97, 98, 101
Loket, 140, 144, 180, 192; Leuthner, Abraham, 180
Łomża, 48
Louis the Great, 365
Louny, 140
Lower Tisza Plain: *see* Great Alföld
Łowicz, 35, 69
Lublin, 106-107; Groffe, A., 106; population in the 16th century, 64; Stompf, J., 107
Lubniewice, 74
Lubochňa, 185
Luchese, Filippo: *see* Kroměříž
Ludwinów, 89
Lübeck Law, 39-40
Lusetian Culture: Biskupin settlement, 17-18
Luxemburg dynasty, 145-146, 266; Charles IV, 148, 149-150, 201, 251; King John, 145-146; Sigismund (Zikmund), 160, 286, 365-366; Wenceslas IV, 149, 149-150, 251

Lvov Lemberg), 42, 89
Lwówek, 31

M

Magdeburg Law, 28, 37, 48, 300
Magnates: *see* Classes, social and professional
Magnuszew, 86
Magyars, 363
Magyarszákos, 357
Makó, 372, 384
Malbork, 39, 40
Manětín, 180, 181, 280; Santini, Giovanni, 180
Manufactories: eighteenth-century Bohemian and Slovakian, 190; eighteenth-century Polish, 86; seventeenth and eighteenth-century Bohemian, 177, 185, 190; Tyzenhaus, Antoni, 86
Marconi, H.: *see* Ciechocinek, Warsaw, Kalisz
Margonin, 74
Maria Theresa, Empress, 89, 185, 188, 300, 320, 340, 348, 416, 428
Mariánské Lázně (Marienbad), 194, 282-283; Fischer, Jiří, 282; Skalník, Václav, 282
Markets, 21-22; *novum forum*, 26
Marschhufendörfer: *see* Villages
Martin, 156
Martinelli, Anton E.: *see* České Budějovice
Mathey, Jean Baptiste: *see* Prague
Matthew of Arras: *see* Prague
Matthias Corvinus (Matthias Hunyady-Corvinus), 164, 167
Matthias Hunyady-Corvinus: *see* Matthias Corvinus
Mazovia, 34-35
Mělník, 132, 140
Menší Město Pražské: *see* Prague, Small or Lesser Town
Merchants: *see* Classes, social and professional
Mezőtúr, 372, 384
Michalovic, Ježek: *see* Mladá Boleslav
Międzychód, 74
Mieszko I, 3, 13, 20
Mikulčice, 126-127; Na Valech, 127
Mikulov, 180, 284-285
Military engineers: Arigsperger, Jan Melichar, 270; Baldigara, O., 170, 295; Carmontaigne, 242; Ferrari, Giulio, 169, 170, 334; Ferrabosco, Pietro, 164-165, 169, 208, 321, 403; Hamel, Louis Querlonde du, 242; Herculesco, 169; Pozzo, Francesco da, 169, 321; Priami, J., 215; Rochepine, P. F. Bechade de, 218, 300; Sebregondi, Nicolas, 172, 246; Spazio, Francesco de, 169; Spazio, Pietro de, 169, 321; Spozzo, Martin, 169; Testo, 160; Unger, Ján, 270; Vedano, Alessandro da, 169; Wymes, Francesco, 403
Mining towns, 145, 155, 156-157, 166-167; *see also* Banská Štiavnica, Jihlava, Kremnica, Kutná Hora, Uničov
Mladá Boleslav, 146, 166, 286; Michalovic, Ježek, 286
Modra, 157, 168
Monastic orders: Benedictines, 345; Bernardine Friars, 48; Cistercians, 130, 265, 345; Jesuits, 69, 172, 174, 184, 237, 254; Premonstratensians, 130, 345
Mongol invasions, 364
Monuments: protection of, 197; statues, 181, 182; Trinity (Virgin Mary) colums, 184-185
Morando, Bernardo: *see* Zamość
Moravian Brethren, 166, 236

Moravská Třebová, 140, 163, 164, 287
Moravský Krumlov, 288
Most, 140, 288-289
Municipal: law, 418; medieval Polish government, 44-45; parks, 191; privileges, 28-29, 166, 418; *see also* Chełmno Law, German Law, Lübeck Law, Magdeburg Law
Municipal Commission: *see* Congress Kingdom

N

Nagyalföld: *see* Great Alföld
Nagykőrös, 372, 384, 395, 426-428; animal husbandry, 426; *kert* system, 427-428, 427 n.; *tanya*, 428; under Turkish rule, 426-428
Nagykunság: *see* Great Alföld
Nagyszombat (Trnava), 365
Narol, 57
Naumann, Johann Christoph, 78
Neoacquistica Commissio, 347
Netolice, 290; *see also* Kratochvíle
Nicolas I, 107
Nidzica (Neidenburg), 39
Nieśwież, 69
Nitra, 135, 154, 169, 185
Nová Baňa, 157
Nová Ves, 187
Nové Kestřany, 187
Nové Kopisy, 187
Nové Město nad Metují, 163-164, 293-294; Pernštejn, 293; Renaissance town planning and architecture, 293-294
Nové Mesto nad Váhom, 154
Nové Město pod Smrkem, 166
Nové Zámky, 170, 270, 295; Baldigara, O., 170, 295; Emperor Maximilian, 295
Novum forum: *see* Markets
Nový Bydžov, 145, 296; medieval plan, 296; Václav (Wenceslas) II, 296
Nový Jičín, 140, 297
Nowe Miasto Lubawskie, 39
Nowe Miasto Wielkopolski, 74
Nowogród, 48
Nowy Dwór, 86
Nowy Koniecpol, 57
Nowy Sącz (Neu Sandec), 34
Nowy Targ (Neumarkt), 42
Nowy Tomyśl, 86
Nyírség: *see* Great Alföld
Nymburk, 132, 140, 146, 298; fortifications, 298; Rejt, Benedikt, 298
Nysa, 31, 42

O

Obrzycko, 62
Óbuda, 368, 389; *see also* Budapest
Okól: *see* Cracow
Okopy Świętej Trójcy, 76
Olomouc, 131, 137-138, 166, 174-175, 175, 177, 186, 191, 198, 299-300; fortifications, 300; Maria Theresa, 300; Rochepine, P. F. Bechade de, 300
Ondřej III: *see* Andrew III
Onegesius: *see* Attila, camp of

Opatówek, 101
Opava, 131, 136, 137
Opole, 19
Oppida: see Settlements
Osek, 190
Ostrov (Ostrov nad Ohři), 140, 142, 175, 301; Julius Heinrich, Duke of Saxony, 175, 301; Residence gardens, 175, 301
Ostrów Wielkopolski, 74
Otto of Freising, 341
Ozorków, 100

P

Pabianice, 97
Paccassi, Nikolaus: *see* Prague
Pakość, 74
Palaces, gardens, and parks, 78-81, 82-84, 85, 164-165, 194-195, 262-263, 290; *see also* Jaroměřice nad Rokytnou
Palliardi: *see* Prague
Pannonia, 339; *Pannonia inferior*, 339; *Pannonia superior*, 339
Pannonia inferior: see Pannonia
Pannonia superior: see Pannonia
Pápa, 407-408
Pardubice, 163, 165, 302-304; Arnošt of Pardubice, 302; George of Olomouc, 303; Pernštejn, Sir William, 302-303
Parks: during the Classical Revival, 194-195; municipal, 191; palace, 79-81, 85, 164-165, 290
Parler, Peter: *see* Prague
Partition of Poland, 16; tripartite planning activities, 88-89
Partizánská Lupča, 155
Peasants: *see* Classes, social and professional
Pécs (Fünfkirchen), 339, 363, 366, 374-376, 385; *Sopianae*, 339, 375; under Turkish rule, 376
Pelhřimov, 145, 305
Pernštejn, Lords of, 163, 165, 278, 293, 302-303
Pest, 363, 365, 368-369, 385, 389-394; Hild, János, 389-390; Hild, József, 390; Kis-Pest (Kelenföld), 369; Palatine Joseph, memorandum of, 389, 390; Planning Commission, 390; Pollack, Mihály, 390; Zitterbarth, Mátyás, 390; *see also* Budapest
Pestújhegy: *see* Budapest
Petruzzi, V.: *see* Slavkov
Piast dynasty, 3, 13-14; Bolesław the Brave, 13, 20; Kazimierz (Casimir) the Great, 14, 42, 45; Mieszko I, 3, 13, 20; Władysław Łokietek (the Short), 14
Pierroni, G., 172
Piotrków, 42
Písek, 140, 144, 160, 180, 306-307
Plástovice, 308-309; peasant Baroque, 308
Płock, 35, 42, 44, 88-89, 107
Plzeň (Pilsen), 145, 166; population, 196
Podbiel, 185
Poddębice, 100
Podhajce, 54
Podolinec, 154
Pöppelmann, Karl Friedrich, 80
Pöppelmann, Matthäus Daniel, 78, 80
Polanians, 3, 18, 20
Polgár, 377
Polička, 139, 180
Polish: artisans' villages, 96-99; Baroque residences, 78-81, 82-84; Bronze Age settlements, 17-18; calvary layout, 74-75, 81-82; cities founded by magnates, 54; cities of the 17th and 18th centuries, 70-87; cities of the first half of the 19th century, 88-108; cities of the Teutonic Order, 37-40; city plots, 28-29; city rights, 28-29; clothiers' villages, 88; early urban settlement, 17-24; fortified camps, 3; fortified castles, 8, 43-44; *grody*, 8, 18 n., 18-21; manufactories in the 18th century, 86; medieval cities, 26-51; medieval city councils, 44-45; medieval suburbs, 48; medieval urban layout, 30; medieval urban population, 45; Neolithic settlements, 17; number of cities, 52; population in the 10th and 11th centuries, 3; proto-city, 22; Renaissance cities, 52-69; Royal cities, 48; spread of settlement, 3-7; suburbs in the 16th and 17th centuries, 68; textile towns, 100-101; urban layout in the 14th century, 42-44; urban population and cities in the Congress Kingdom, 93-94; villages, 4, 6, 7
Pollack, Mihály, 390
Ponds, canals, and reservoirs, 165, 323; Svět, 323
Population: in Hungary, 347, 350; medieval urban Polish, 45; of Alföld settlements, 384; tenth and eleventh-century Polish, 3; urban in Czechoslovakia, 196
Portae regni: see Fortifications
Potocki, 54
Potocki, Andrzej: *see* Stanisławów, Józefów
Poznań (Posen), 8, 19, 22-23, 28, 32, 88-89; population in the 16th century, 64
Pozzo, Francesco da, 169, 321
Prachatice, 146, 160, 166, 310-311
Prague, 129, 130, 137, 173-174, 175, 177-179, 191, 192, 196, 197, 198, 200-207; Baroque, 203-207; Castle, 186, 201; Cathedral of St. Vitus, 146, 201; Charles Bridge, 181, 204; Chotek Gardens, 191; Clementinum (Jesuit College), 174, 203; Czernin Palace, 174; Dientzenhofer, Christopher, 179; Dientzenhofer, Kilian, 179, 203; ghetto, 197; Hradčany, 146, 201; Kaňka, František Maxmilián, 203; Karlín, 193, 196, 207; Mathey, Jean Baptiste, 203; Matthew of Arras, 201; New Town, 148, 149, 201; Old Town, 137, 200, 201; Paccassi, Nikolaus, 186; Palliardi, 192; Parler, Peter, 201; population, 196, 207; Rejt, Benedict, 201; Renaissance, 201-203; Romanesque houses, 200; Royal Gardens, 164, 196; Santini, Giovanni, 203; Small or Lesser Town (Menší Město Pražské), 139, 172, 177-179, 201; university, 148, 201; Vrtba Garden, 179
Prague League, 160
Předmostí, 121
Přehýšov, 148
Premonstratensians, 130, 345
Přemysl, 129
Přemysl Otakar I (Přemysl I), 136, 138, 143, 237
Přemysl Otakar II (Přemysl II), 139-140, 144, 145, 201, 220, 225, 232, 254, 256, 259, 278, 288, 290, 298, 306, 324, 326, 327
Přemyslide dynasty, 129, 145, 265, 266, 299; Přemysl Otakar I (Přemysl I), 136, 138, 143, 237; Přemysl Otakar II (Přemysl II), 139-140, 144, 145, 201, 220, 225, 232, 254, 256, 259, 278, 288, 290, 298, 306, 324, 326, 327; Přemysl the Ploughman, 129; Prince Břetislav, 299; Wenceslas I, 138, 143, 216, 247, 288, 299; Wenceslas II, 145, 266, 296; Wenceslas III, 145
Přerov, 140
Prešov, 155, 185, 312

Priami, J., 215
Prievidza, 157, 184
Prince Břetislav, 299
Prince Oldřich, 299
Princess Anna Jabłonowska, 86; Kock, 86; Siemiatycze, 86
Priscus Panites: see Attila, camp of
Production: metal, 168, 185
Prostějov, 149
Protestantism, 211; see also Debrecen, Calvinism
Prussian: builders and architects in Poland, 92; Gilly, David, 89; planning activities in Poland, 88-89
Przemyśl, 21
Ptolemy, 123
Puck, 40
Pukanec, 169-170
Pułtusk, 35, 88
Puszta (puszták), 341, 343
Pyrzyce, 40

R

Raabization process, 187
Raczki, 77
Radom, 24, 42, 44, 95-96, 97; Ebertowski, Ignacy, 95; Sadkowski, Józef, 95
Rákóczi I, György, 383
Rákóczi II, Ferenc, 384
Rákóczi II, György, 383
Rakoniewice, 73-74, 97; Grzymułtowski, Krzysztof, 73
Rakovník, 145
Rawa Mazowiecka, 30, 97, 107
Rawicz, 61, 97
Reihendörfer: see Villages
Reinstein, F.: see Kalisz
Rejt, Benedict, 201, 298
Renaissance: Czechoslovak towns, 166-170; fortifications, 169-170; gardens, 164-165; in Czechoslovakia, 162-170; in Slovakia, 167-170; Polish cities, 52-69; town planning and architecture, 293-294; towns in Slovakia, 167-168, 168-169
Reservoirs: see Ponds, canals, and reservoirs
Rimavská Sobota, 156
Ring-fence village: see Villages
Roads: nineteenth-century Czechoslovak, 192
Rochepine, P. F. Bechade de, 217, 300
Rogoźno, 74
Roman: *Arrabona*, 339, 402; *colonia Claudia Sabaria*, 339, 409; province of Pannonia, 339; *Salva (Salva Mansio)*, 363, 411; *Scarabantia*, 366; settlement in Czechoslovakia, 123-124
Romanesque: architecture in Bohemia, 133
Royal Towns (Royal Free Towns), 136, 139-140, 149, 190-191, 402; see also Bardejov, Bratislava, Brno, České Budějovice, Domažlice, Esztergom, Győr, Hradec Králové, Jaroměř, Karlovy Vary (Karlsbad), Klatovy, Kouřim, Litoměřice, Mladá Boleslav, Most, Olomouc, Písek, Prešov, Szeged, Székesfehérvár, Terezín, Uničov, Žatec
Rožmberk, 165, 230, 290; Rožmberk Pond, 165
Rožňava, 157
Russian: planning activities in Poland, 89
Ružindol, 313
Ružomberok, 157, 184
Rychnov nad Kněžnou, 179-180, 181
Ryczywół, 91; Sadkowski, J., 91
Rydzyna, 82-83; Ferrari, Pompeo, 82; Graff, I., 83
Rzeszów, 42, 69

S

Sabaria (Savaria): see Szombathely (Steinamanger)
Sadkowski, Józef, 91, 95
Salva (Salva Mansio): see Esztergom
Samo, 114-115, 125
Sandomierz, 19, 24, 34, 42
Santini, Giovanni, 177, 179-180, 180, 182, 203-204
Šaštín, 190
Saxon Axis: see Warsaw
Scarabantia: see Sopron (Ödenburg)
Schwartner, Martin von, 343
Scultetiae, 345
Sebregondi, Nicolas, 172, 246
Sedlec: see Kutná Hora
Sedlo, 122
Serfdom: abolition of, 189, 396; *adscripti glebae*, 343, 345, 348; liberation of peasants, 348
Settlement: and servile labor in Hungary, 350; density in Hungary, 350, 351-352; early Czechoslovak, 111-116, 121-124; early feudal structure in Slovakia, 133-134; early Polish urban, 17-24; Hungarian rural, 351-359; of Hungarian frontier territories, 344-345; Roman in Czechoslovakia, 123-124; rural in Czechoslovakia, 187-189; Slavonic in Czechoslovakia, 125-128; spread and changing structure of Hungarian, 346-348; spread of Polish, 3-7; structure of towns on the Alföld, 423; *tanya* system, 341, 341 n., 348-350, 398, 428; types of, 21, 350; under German Law, 5
Settlements: agricultural, 182-183, 342-343; Celtic in Czechoslovakia, 122-123; *civitates forenses*, 22; Early Bronze Age in Czechoslovakia, 112; early feudal in Czechoslovakia, 130-133; Eneolithic in Czechoslovakia, 112; fortified hilltop, 112; *forum*, 8; *jurydyka*, 68; *locus forensis*, 8; market centers, 8-9; Neolithic in Czechoslovakia, 111; *oppida*, 113, 122; Polish Bronze Age, 17-18; Polish Neolithic, 17; Stone Age in Czechoslovakia, 121; *villa forensis*, 8, 22
Siemiatycze, 86
Sieniawski, 54
Sieradz, 24, 101
Skalice, 157, 168
Skalník, Václav: see Mariánské Lázně (Marienbad)
Slaný, 145
Slavkov (Austerlitz), 177; Kounic, Count D. C., 177; Petruzzi, V., 177
Slavník, 129, 265
Slovakia, 133-135; Baroque in, 184-185; Baroque towns, 184-185; Classical (Classicist) Revival in, 195; fortifications, 169-170; Hungarian occupation of, 133-135; medieval towns, 154-157; Renaissance in, 167-170; Renaissance towns, 167-168, 168-169; Residence and fortress towns, 170; Turkish invasion of, 168
Slovenská Lupča, 157
Smolník, 157
Sobotka, 314
Sochaczew, 24
Sokul, 54
Sopianae: see Pécs
Sopron (Ödenburg), 339, 363, 366-367, 380-383; *Scarabantia*, 366

Spas, 101, 182, 194; Ciechocinek, 101; Františkovy Lázně (Franzensbad), 194, 233-234; Karlovy Vary (Karlsbad), 194, 251-252; Kuks, 182, 264; Mariánské Lázně (Marienbad), 194, 282-283; Teplice, 194
Spazio, Francesco de, 169
Spazio, Pietro de, 169, 321
Spazzo, Antonio: *see* Trnava
Spezza, O., 172
Spišská Nová Ves, 157, 185
Špitálský, Konrád: *see* Čáslav
Špork, Count F. A., 182, 264
Spozzo, Martin, 169
Squares: Bankowy Square, 101; eighteenth-century in Czechoslovakia, 180-181; elongated in Czechoslovakia, 142; market, 49-50; medieval in Czechoslovakia, 143; Teatralny Square, 105; Trzy Krzyże Square, 105
Środa Śląska, 31
Stanislaus Augustus: *see* Stanisław August Poniatowski
Stanislaus Axis: *see* Warsaw
Stanisław August Poniatowski (Stanislaus Augustus), 84-86, 92
Stanisławów, 76; Potocki, Andrzej, 76
Stará Boleslav, 315-316
Stará Lubovňa, 156
Stary Sącz (Alt Sandec), 34
Statues: *see* Monuments
Stephen III, 368
Stephen V, 402
Štítník, 157
Stompf, J.: *see* Lublin
Strakonice, 185
Stříbro, 138
Strongholds, fortified Renaissance residences, 68-69
Stryków, 91; Sadkowski, J., 91
Strzegom (Striegau), 31
Suburbium, 8, 20, 21; *see also* Suburbs
Suburbs, 214; artisans', 375, 375 n., medieval Polish, 48; sixteenth and seventeenth-century Polish, 68; *see also Suburbium*, Karlín
Suchowola, 86
Šumperk, 140
Suraż, 48
Sušice, 140, 146, 160
Suwałki, 77, 107
Svitavy, 140, 142
Swarzędz, 62
Świdnica (Schweidnitz), 31
Świecie (Schwetz), 39
Szamocin, 74
Szarogród, 57
Szczebra, 86
Szczecin (Stettin), 8, 19, 40, 42, 70-71; Traytorens, Frans de, 71
Szczuczyn, 77
Széchenyi, István, 390-394
Szeged, 340, 346, 367-368, 384, 397-400; Brocquière, Bertrandon de la, 368; Lechner, Lajos, 398-400; reconstruction plan after the great flood, 398-400
Székesfehérvár (Stuhlweissenburg), 339, 342, 363, 385, 418-420; *Alba Regia*, 418
Szentes, 384
Szlichtyngowa, 62
Szolnok, 340
Szombathely (Steinamanger), 339, 385, 409-410; Bishop Johann Szily, 409-410; *Sabaria (Savaria; colonia Claudia Sabaria)*, 339, 409

Szpilowski, S.: *see* Kalisz
Szydłów, 42

T

Tábor, 158-160, 165, 171, 317-319; and the Hussite Movement, 317; fortifications, 159, 319; Jordan Pond, 165
Tachov, 140, 146
Tacitus, 113-114
Táncsics, Mihály: *see* Budapest
Tanya (tanyák), 341, 341 n., 348-350, 397-398, 428
Tarnopol, 54
Telč, 149, 165, 172, 174
Tencalla, Giovanni Pietro: *see* Kroměříž
Teplice, 194
Terezín, 186, 191, 320; Charles Nicholas von Steinmetz, 320; fortifications, 320
Testo, 169
Teutonic: Order (Knights), 14, 36-40, 224; tribes, 113-114
Thirty Years' War, effect on towns and settlement, 171-172, 176, 183, 203, 289
Thököly, Imre, 383
Thomé, Heinrich: *see* Elbląg
Thurzo, 168
Tisovec, 185
Tiszántúl: *see* Great Alföld
Tokaj, 340
Tomaszów Lubelski, 56-57, 59; Jelitkowo, 56
Tomaszów Mazowiecki, 100
Tomaszpol, 57
Topoľčany, 156
Toruń (Thorn), 37, 40, 42; population in the 16th century, 64
Tournelle, F.: *see* Kalisz
Tovačov, 163
Town halls: *see* Buildings
Town leagues, 160
Town planning: and the Hussite Movement, 158-159; gardens as elements of, 164-165; in the Classical Revival period, 191-194; instrument of state policy, 139; medieval Bohemian, 296; scheme for Pest, 389-390; scheme for Szeged, 398-400; *see also* City planning
Towns: and the Hussite Movement, 158-160, 254; artisans', 73-74, 86; Czechoslovak in the 19th and 20th centuries, 196-198; during the Baroque period, 171-176, 177-182, 184-185, 185-186; early feudal, 130-133; eighteenth-century Hungarian, 384, 385-389; feudal Bohemian and Moravian, 136-144; fortress, 170, 186, 191, 242, 270, 320; founded by Polish magnates, 54; hajdú-towns, 377-380; Hungarian village-towns, 340-341, 343, 372-373, 384, 385-386, 426-428; in Hungary, 342-343, 366-370; location towns, 130, 130 n.; manufacturing, 197; medieval Bohemian and Moravian, 145-151; medieval Polish, 26-51; medieval Slovakian, 154-157; mining, 145, 155, 156-157, 166-167, 208-209, 247-248, 260-261, 265-268, 326; nineteenth-century Hungarian, 389-395, 396-400; origin of Czechoslovak, 129-132; Polish, 9; Polish, during first half of the 19th century, 88-108; pre-location towns, 130 n., 132; Renaissance Czechoslovak, 166-170; Renaissance Polish, 52-69; Renaissance Slovakian, 167-168, 168-169; Residence, 163-164, 170; Royal, 136, 139-140, 149, 190-191, 402; royal foundations in

473

Poland, 48; seventeenth and eighteenth-century Polish, 70-87; textile, 100-101; "towns of the sun," 158; Turkish administrative centers in Hungary, 374-376; twin-, 315-316; under Turkish rule in Hungary, 372-383; *see also* Cities, Royal Towns (Royal Free Towns), Spas

Trade: routes, 18, 135, 299, 310; *see also* Amber Route, Bohemian Route, Golden Route

Trades and crafts, 21, 407, 423, 425

Transdanubia (Dunántúl), 339, 385

Trausolt, F. J.: *see* Congress Kingdom

Trávčice, 187

Traytorens, Frans de: *see* Szczecin (Stettin)

Třebíč, 142

Třeboň, 323; Svět, 323; Vítkovec, 323

Trenčín, 156, 185

Trinity (Virgin Mary) columns: *see* Monuments

Trnava, 154, 168, 169, 184, 321-322; Ferrabosco, Pietro, 321; Pozzo, Francesco da, 321; Spazio, Pietro de, 321; Spazzo, Antonio, 184; *see also* Nagyszombat (Trnava)

Trutnov, 140

Trzciel, 74

Trzebnica, 26

Turek, 98

Turkish: administrative centers in Hungary, 374-376; invasion of Slovakia, 168; occupation of Hungary, 372-383

Turnov, 185

Týnec nad Labem, 132

Tyzenhaus, Antoni, 86; Dąbrowa, 86; Jeleniowo, 86; Krasnopol, 86; Kunsztów, 86; Suchowola, 86; Szczebra, 86

U

Uherské Hradiště, 174, 175, 324-325; Přemysl Otakar II, 324

Ujazd, 31

Ujazdów, 74

Ulanów, 57

Unger, Ján: *see* Leopoldov

Uničov, 136, 137, 172, 326

Unity of Brethren: *see* Bohemian Brethren

Unruh: *see* Kargowa

Urban: *Bannmeile*, 5; early Polish settlement, 17-24; jurisdiction, 5; law, 5, 28, 39-40, 48, 300; medieval Polish population, 45; population in Congress Kingdom, 93-94; population in Czechoslovakia, 196; privileges, 28-29, 166, 418; *Weichbild*, 5

Urbanization: of Great Poland, 60-62, 73-74; of Podolia and the Ukraine, 76-77

Urbarium, 346

Ústí nad Labem, 140; population in 1910, 196

V

Vác (Waitzen), 363, 385, 415-417; Counter Reformation, 416; Joseph II, 416; Maria Theresa, 416

Václav I: *see* Wenceslas I

Václav II: *see* Wenceslas II

Valtice, 180

Vámospércs, 377

Vedano, Alessandro da, 169

Veszprém, 363, 385, 421

Villa forensis: *see* Settlements

Village-towns: *see* Towns

Villages: architecture in, 231; artisans', 96-99; Celtic in Czechoslovakia, 122; clothiers', 88; early feudal in Czechoslovakia, 132-133; eighteenth-century in Czechoslovakia, 182-184, 185, 187-189; *Haufendörfer*, 357; hotters, 346; in the Banat, 357; in Hungary, 339, 346, 351-359; in Poland, 4, 6, 7; in the Comitat Arad, 357-358; *Marschhufendörfer*, 7; medieval Bohemian, 146-148; radial-nucleated, 352-353, 355; *Reihendörfer*, 7; ring-fence, 7, 114, 132; *scultetiae*, 345; village-towns, 340-341, 343, 372-373, 384, 385-386, 426-428; *Waldhufendörfer*, 7; *see also* Csaba, Dolní Bojanovice, Hódmezővásárhely, Hruštín, Liptovská Teplička, Litava, Plástovice, Ružindol

Vilna, 74

Vítkovec, 229, 249, 323

Vladislav II, 130, 133, 280

Vodňany, 132, 146

Volyně, 166

Vonio, Balthazar Maio de: *see* Kratochvíle

Vredeman de Vries, 175

Výsluní, 166

Vysoké Mýto, 139, 140

W

Waldhufendörfer: *see* Villages

Wallenstein, Albrecht von, 172, 203, 245-246

Wallenstein, Count V. V., 177

Warsaw, 35, 78-82, 84-85, 89, 101-106; Bankowy Square, 101; Bieliński, Franciszek, 84; calvary, 81-82; Corazzi, Antoni, 101-105; Deybel, Johann Siegmund, 80; Jauch, Joachim Daniel, 80; Łazienka Królewska, 85; Marconi, H., 106; Marywil, 105; Naumann, Johann Christoph, 78; New Town, 45; Paving Commission, 84; Pöppelmann, Karl Friedrich, 80; Pöppelmann, Matthäus Daniel, 78, 80; Pole Marsowe, 106; population in the 16th century, 64; royal residence, 78-81; Saxon Axis, 79-81; Stanislaus Axis, 84-85; Teatralny Square, 105; Trzy Krzyże Square, 105; Warecki Square, 105-106; Zamkowy Square, 106; *see also* Ujazdów

Wasilków, 55

Wąsosz, 48

Wawel: *see* Cracow

Weichbild: *see* Urban

Wejherowo, 74

Wenceslas I (Václav I), 138, 143, 216, 247, 288, 299

Wenceslas II (Václav II), 145, 266, 296; *ius regale montanorum*, 266

Wenceslas III, 145

Wenceslas IV, 149, 149-150, 251

Wieleń, 74

Wielkopolska: *see* Great Poland

Wieluń, 42, 44

Witkowo, 74

Wizna, 88

Władysław Łokietek (the Short), 14

Władysławów, 74

Wolin, 19, 40

Wrocław (Breslau), 8, 19, 22, 30-31, 31, 45; population in the 13th century, 42; population in the 14th to 15th centuries, 45; population in the 16th century, 64

Wüstungen, 6

Wymes, Francesco, 403

Z

Zaborowo, 62
Załoźce, 54
Zambrów, 48
Zamość, 56, 57-59; Morando, Bernardo, 57, 59; Zamoyski, 59
Zamość Fee Tail: *see* Zamoyski, Jan
Zamoyski, 54
Zamoyski, Jan, 56-60; Zamość Fee Tail, 56, 57, 59
Zamoyski, Tomasz, 56-60, 77
Zaniemyśl, 74
Žatec, 131, 140, 181, 192, 327-328
Závist, *oppidum* at, 122
Zawadski, S.: *see* Congress Kingdom

Zduńska Wola, 100
Zenta, 355-357
Zgierz, 97
Žilina, 156, 185
Žitava, 140
Zitterbarth, Mátyás, 390
Žižka, Jan: *see* Hussite Movement
Zlín, 197
Złoczów, 54
Złotoryja, 30
Žlutice, 140
Znojmo, 131, 137, 198, 329-331
Żółkiew, 57
Żółkiewski, Stanisław: *see* Brody
Zvolen, 154, 169, 333-334